International Encyclopedia of

POLITICAL SCIENCE

VOLUME 4

Editorial Board

International Encyclopedia of POLITICAL SCIENCE

VOLUME 4

EDITORS

BERTRAND BADIE
Sciences Po, Paris, France

DIRK BERG-SCHLOSSER
Philipps-Universität Marburg, Germany

LEONARDO MORLINO
LUISS Guido Carli, Italy

SAGE reference
Los Angeles | London | New Delhi
Singapore | Washington DC

IPSA AISP
Developed in partnership with the
International Political Science Association

SAGE

Los Angeles | London | New Delhi
Singapore | Washington DC

FOR INFORMATION:

SAGE Publications, Inc.
2455 Teller Road
Thousand Oaks, California 91320
E-mail: order@sagepub.com

SAGE Publications Ltd.
1 Oliver's Yard
55 City Road
London EC1Y 1SP
United Kingdom

SAGE Publications India Pvt. Ltd.
B 1/I 1 Mohan Cooperative Industrial Area
Mathura Road, New Delhi 110 044
India

SAGE Publications Asia-Pacific Pte. Ltd.
33 Pekin Street #02-01
Far East Square
Singapore 048763

Publisher: Rolf A. Janke
Assistant to the Publisher: Michele Thompson
Developmental Editor: Diana E. Axelsen
Production Editor: Tracy Buyan
Reference Systems Manager: Leticia Gutierrez
Reference Systems Coordinator: Laura Notton
Copy Editor: QuADS Prepress (P) Ltd.
Typesetter: C&M Digitals (P) Ltd.
Proofreaders: Kristin Bergstad, Kate Peterson
Indexer: Mary Mortensen
Cover Designer: Janet Kiesel
Marketing Manager: Kristi Ward

Printed in the United States of America.

Library of Congress Cataloging-in-Publication Data

International encyclopedia of political science / edited by Bertrand Badie, Dirk Berg-Schlosser, Leonardo Morlino.

8 v. cm.
A SAGE Reference publication.
Includes bibliographical references and index.

ISBN 978-1-4129-5963-6 (cloth)

1. Political science—Encyclopedias. I. Badie, Bertrand. II. Berg-Schlosser, Dirk. III. Morlino, Leonardo

JA61.I58 2011
320.03—dc22 2011009801

11 12 13 14 15 10 9 8 7 6 5 4 3 2 1

Contents

4

List of Entries

Reader's Guide

Comparative Politics, Theory, and Methods

Case and Area Studies

Epistemological Foundations

Gender and Race/Ethnicity

International Relations

Political Science, International
Institutionalization
Postmodernism in International Relations
Psychological Explanations of International Politics
Realism in International Relations
Superpower

Peace, War, and Conflict Resolution

Alliances
Arms Race
Bilateralism
Bipolarity and Multipolarity
Civil War
Collective Security
Conflict Resolution
Conflicts
Détente
Diplomacy
Disarmament
Domestic Politics and International Relations
Empire
Foreign Policy Analysis
Genocide
Imperialism
Intervention
Intervention, Humanitarian
Judicial Decision Making
Judicialization of International Relations
Mediation in International Relations
Militias
Multilateralism
National Interest
Natural Resources
Neutrality
Pacifism
Participation, Contentious
Peace
Peacekeeping Positive Peace
Power and International Politics
Preemptive War
Psychological Explanations of International Politics
Sanctions
Secession
Security and Defense Policy
Security Cooperation
Security Dilemma
Sovereignty
Strategic (Security) Studies
Superpower
Territory
Terrorism, International
Transatlantic Relations
Unilateralism
United Nations
Violence
War and Peace
Warlords
Westphalian Ideal State
World Systems Theory

Political Economy

Capitalism
Central Banks
Class, Social
Cost–Benefit Analysis
Economic Policy
Economic Statecraft
Economic Theories of Politics
Foreign Aid and Development
Inequality, Economic
International Monetary Fund (IMF)
International Political Economy
Labor Movement
Market Economy
Market Failure
Monetary Relations
Multilateralism
Multinational Corporations (MNCs)
Nongovernmental Organizations (NGOs)
Policy, Employment
Political Economy
Privatization
Property
Protectionism
Public Budgeting
Public Employment
Public Goods
Redistribution
Social Stratification
Sustainable Development
Tax Policy
Trade Liberalization
Traditional Rule
Tragedy of the Commons
Transaction Costs
Transformation, Economic

Welfare Policies
Welfare State
World Bank
World Trade Organization (WTO)

Political Parties

Christian Democratic Parties
Cleavages, Social and Political
Communist Parties
Conservative Parties
Green Parties
Liberal Parties
One-Party Dominance
Parties
Party Finance
Party Identification
Party Linkage
Party Manifesto
Party Organization
Party System Fragmentation
Party Systems
Social Democracy
Socialist Parties

Political Philosophy/Theory

African Political Thought
Anarchism
Charisma
Communism
Communitarianism
Conservatism
Constitutionalism
Contract Theory
Democracy, Theories of
Discursive Institutionalism
Ethics
Fascism
Fundamentalism
Greek Philosophy
Idealism in International Relations
Liberalism
Liberalism in International Relations
Libertarianism
Liberty
Maoism
Marxism
Mercantilism
Nationalism
Neoliberal Institutionalism
Neoliberalism
Normative Political Theory
Normative Theory in International Relations
Pacifism
Pluralism
Political Class
Political Philosophy
Political Psychology
Political Theory
Postmodernism in International Relations
Realism in International Relations
Revisionism
Rights
Secularism
Socialism
Stalinism
Statism
Theocracy
Utilitarianism
Utopianism

Equality and Inequality

Cost–Benefit Analysis
Equality
Equality, Political
Justice
Marxism
Racism
Socialist Systems

Formal and Positive Theory

Bureaucracy, Rational Choice Models
Game Theory
Principal–Agent Theory
Prisoners' Dilemma
Rational Choice
Social Choice Theory
Veto Player

Theorists

Durkheim, Émile
Hegel, Georg Wilhelm Friedrich
Hobbes, Thomas
Kant, Immanuel
Locke, John
Machiavelli, Niccolò

Political Sociology

Public Policy and Public Administration

Public Policy

Policy Formulation
Policy Framing
Policy Instruments
Policy Learning
Policy Network
Policy Process, Models of
Prospect Theory
Reorganization
Risk and Public Policy
Self-Regulation
Soft Law
Stages Model of Policy Making
Think Tanks
Tragedy of the Commons
Transaction Costs

Public Administration

Administration
Administration Theory
Audit Society
Auditing
Autonomy, Administrative
Budgeting, Rational Models
Bureaucracy
Bureaucracy, Rational Choice Models
Bureaucracy, Street-Level
Civil Service
Corruption, Administrative
Effectiveness, Bureaucratic
Governance
Governance, Administration Policies
Governance, Informal
Governance, Multilevel
Governance, Urban
Governance Networks
Groupthink
Health Policy
Intelligence
Pay for Performance
Performance
Performance Management
Planning
Police
Politicization of Bureaucracy
Politicization of Civil Service
Public Budgeting
Public Employment
Public Goods
Public Office, Rewards
Regulation
Representative Bureaucracy
Responsiveness of Bureaucracy
Secret Services
Security Apparatus

Qualitative Methods

Analytic Narratives: Applications
Analytic Narratives: The Method
Configurational Comparative Methods
Data, Textual
Discourse Analysis
Ethnographic Methods
Evaluation Research
Fuzzy-Set Analysis
Grounded Theory
Hermeneutics
Interviewing
Interviews, Elite
Interviews, Expert
Mixed Methods
Network Analysis
Participant Observation
Process Tracing
Qualitative Comparative Analysis
Quantitative Versus Qualitative Methods
Thick Description
Triangulation

Quantitative Methods

Aggregate Data Analysis
Analysis of Variance
Boolean Algebra
Categorical Response Data
Censored and Truncated Data
Cohort Analysis
Correlation
Correspondence Analysis
Cross-National Surveys
Cross-Tabular Analysis
Data, Archival
Data, Missing
Data, Spatial
Data Analysis, Exploratory
Data Visualization
Event Counts
Event History Analysis
Experiments, Field

Religion

G

GAME THEORY

Game theory is the study of rational behavior in situations of interactive decision making—that is, situations in which two or more individuals make decisions that jointly determine an outcome about which the participants have differing preferences or information. As a theory, it aims to articulate the criteria and implications of such decision making, defining principles of idealized strategic choice. These principles can then be used to clarify explanatory and normative concepts of human interaction. An experimental branch examines the extent to which real decision makers in a laboratory setting realize those principles and identifies regular patterns of departure from them. As an empirical tool, game theoretic models of social phenomena yield empirical predictions suitable for testing with observational data. Originally applied to economics, game theory has found application across the social sciences, as well as in biology (where in effect the "selfish gene" and natural selection replace individual strategic decision making) and literary theory (where game theory principles have been used to explicate portrayals of conflict and cooperation, as well as the interaction between author and reader).

Following scattered preliminaries during the period from 1910 to 1927, game theory was essentially created by the mathematician John von Neumann in a paper published in 1928 defining strategic play in finite games of pure conflict with two players. In collaboration with the economist Oskar Morgenstern, von Neumann authored *Games and Economic Behavior* (published in 1944), further developing the theory and beginning its application to problems of economic interaction. Rapid theoretical development followed World War II, and the theory made its first scattered appearances in the political science journals in the 1950s. By the 1980s, game theory had become the primary model-building tool of rational choice political science, with applications in virtually all subfields. International relations saw some of the earliest use of game theory, which came to be especially common in the study of crisis bargaining and the inception of war. The scholars of U.S. politics were also early adopters, applying game theory extensively to legislative processes, electoral competition, and even school budget referendum politics. Many of the American politics applications were generalized to similar questions concerning legislative and electoral politics in comparative perspective, but game theoretic applications to coalition formation, class relations, and ethnic politics were pioneered in comparative politics. In political theory, game theoretic tools were proving useful for gaining new normative understanding in areas such as collective action and constitutionalism.

Game theory itself consists of two main branches: (1) noncooperative and (2) cooperative. Noncooperative game theory focuses on individual decisions, dwelling on problems of strategic moves and incentives, and attempting to explain not only conflict and competition but also the attainment of commitment, coordination, or cooperation in groups. This entry dwells mostly on the noncooperative branch, constructing in detail the two major formulations used there, namely, the *strategic* and *sequential* forms; the major theories of how each form of game is solved; and the correspondences between them. Cooperative game theory focuses on the abilities and actions of coalitions, often assuming that coordination and cooperation can be attained as needed and asking how they will be employed to realize and distribute gains or losses. Cooperative game theory may be taken to subsume not only coalition games but also the foundations of social choice theory and voting theory, although the latter have important overlaps with noncooperative theory as well. The final section summarizes the basic features of the fundamental cooperative game formulation, the *characteristic function* form.

Strategic Games

The strategic game formulation portrays two or more players choosing simultaneously and independently among (possibly different) sets of feasible strategies. Most simply, a *strategy* may represent a simple action: the casting of a vote, for example. More generally, however, each strategy may encompass a complex scheme of conditional actions, reactions, and randomizations, as if chosen entirely in advance and then automatically implemented. The techniques involved in solving strategic games play important roles in analyzing sequential games as well. Political scientists have applied strategic games to a wide variety of political interactions. In some, the choices are, for all intents and purposes, literally simultaneous—secret-ballot voting, for example. More often, the model is used to understand choices with an important simultaneous aspect, such as candidate or party electoral competition and international military confrontations. Strategic games have also proven highly useful in the conceptualization of problems important in political theory and political economy, such as commons problems, free rider problems, and the role of coordination in the formation and interpretation of constitutions.

General Formulation

Three elements specify an elementary strategic game:

1. a set of players, designated for convenience as N or $\{1, 2, \ldots, n\}$, with individual players labeled i, j, and so on;
2. a number of *strategy sets*, one for each player, with i's strategy set denoted S_i; and
3. for each player i, a real-valued *utility function* u_i defined on the set of all outcomes of the game.

For games of *perfect information*, all players are assumed to know the full description of the game: who the players are, what their strategic opportunities are, and what their utility functions are. The players are each to choose, simultaneously and independently, one strategy from their respective strategy sets. One thinks of the resulting *strategy profile* $s = (s_1, s_2, \ldots, s_n) \in S$ as identifying an *outcome*, and the utility function u_i on S represents the preferences of player i. Traditionally, the utility derived by player i when the players choose strategy profile s, $u_i(s)$, is called player i's *payoff* from s. (In many concrete applications, distinct strategy profiles may lead to identical substantive "outcomes," such as "Candidate A wins the election"). Finally, it is often convenient to write s_{-i} for $(s_1, s_2, \ldots, s_{i-1}, s_{i+1}, \ldots, s_n)$, the profile of all players other than i, and to let (s_i, s_{-i}) denote s as well. The utility function, by definition, is meant to capture completely the preferences of a player. This includes any considerations the player may give to attaining some sort of winning margin over other players, to avoiding or seeking risk, or to such considerations as altruism, revenge seeking, and the like. Game theory is not inherently a theory of selfish preferences or material preferences; however, its applications have traction only insofar as correct assumptions about player preferences are employed.

The analysis of some games involves the use of probabilities and expected utility, sources of which are examined below. In the absence of such features, only the players' preference *orderings* over outcomes matters in the analysis of strategic play. If probability is involved, however, then payoffs must be cardinal, in the sense of being von Neumann-Morgenstern utility functions based on preferences over "lotteries" of outcomes. Even so, applying any positive linear transformation of any player's utility function does not affect the analysis of strategic play. Usually, game theory avoids the comparison of payoff values across players for exactly the same reason that such interpersonal comparisons of utilities are eschewed in microeconomic theory: The absolute numbers are taken to have no objective meaning, apart from the ordinal preferences (whether over outcomes or lotteries) from which they are derived. When the number of players and the number of strategies are small, a strategic game can be conveniently described with a *payoff matrix*, which often also gives meaningful labels for the players and strategies in a particular model. For example, Prisoners' Dilemma is often represented as shown in Table 1 where, for example, if Player 1 chooses "Defect" and Player 2 chooses "Cooperate," the payoffs are indicated by the two numbers in the bottom-left cell: 5 for Player 1 and 0 for Player 2. The payoff result in a cell is often written as (5, 0).

Rational Play in Strategic Games

The main concern of game theory is to define what it means for players to choose rationally in such an environment of interactive decision making. A basic concept for defining rational choice is the *best response*: Given that the players other than i choose the strategies s_{-i}, a best response to s_{-i} is a strategy s_i in S_i that maximizes $u_i(s_i, s_{-i})$. If S_i is not finite (as is common in many games of bargaining and of electoral and legislative competition), additional assumptions are needed to ensure existence of a best response. Notice that there may be more than one best response, each giving the same utility. In that case, each best response is called a *weak* but not a *strict best response*. (Note, however, when authors speak of the *set* of player i's weak best responses to s_{-i}, they mean to include the strict best responses as well: that set is a singleton when there is only one best response to s_{-i}, a multiple-element set when there is more than one best response—and the empty set if there is no best response due to an infinite S_i.)

Table 1 A Typical Payoff Matrix: Prisoners' Dilemma

		Player 2	
		Cooperate	Defect
Player 1	Cooperate	3, 3	0, 5
	Defect	5, 0	1, 1

The standard formulation of rational strategic play is *Nash equilibrium*. A strategy profile s^* is a Nash equilibrium if and only if for each i, $s_i = s_i^*$ maximizes $u_i(s_i, s_{-i}^*)$ over S_i. In general, Nash equilibria can be identified by deriving the correspondence of best responses of each i to all possible s_{-i},

$$B_i(s_{-i}) = \{s_i \in S_i | s_i \text{ maximizes } u_i(s_i, s_{-i})\}$$

and then finding the intersection of those correspondences, that is,

$$\{(s_1, s_2, \ldots, s_n) | \text{for each } i, s_i \in B_i(s_{-i})\}.$$

This definition satisfies two criteria for strategic rationality. First, each player chooses a best response to the choices he or she anticipates the other players will make, while anticipating that the other players too are strategically rational. This criterion alone defines a weaker solution concept, a *rationalizable* strategy profile. As we will see, however, this may or may not result in outcomes in which each player has chosen a best response to the actual choices of all other players.

Second, Nash equilibrium satisfies a criterion of what one might call rational *experienced* play. This criterion is embodied in the assumption that each player's anticipation of the others' choices actually matches those choices. Suppose groups of n individuals in a population of much larger size are randomly combined from time to time to play a single iteration of the original game and that all have information about how the game is being played. Each individual has a contingent strategy plan—that is, a plan of which strategy to choose if placed in the role of Player 1, Player 2, . . . , or Player n. Suppose further that individuals revise their plans when they observe that an alternative strategy could have yielded a higher payoff to profiles recently played than did the player's previous intended choice and that those revisions tend to adopt higher payoff strategies against the observed actions of others. In this setting, any population strategy profile that does not induce a Nash equilibrium for every possible assignment of n individuals to the player roles in the game will be subject to such change by some player. That is, only Nash equilibria can be stable. (The literature on *learning in games* formalizes this intuition.)

Coalitionally Rational Play

The ideas of best response and hence of Nash equilibrium imagine, in effect, that every player considers only individual deviations from a profile. For equilibrium profiles in some games, however, it may be the case that two or more players could all have achieved higher payoffs had they all chosen differently. The analysis of possible coalitional action in a strategic game can sometimes be accomplished through a version of Nash equilibrium that inquires not only about individual departures from a strategy profile but also about simultaneous departures by several players. For any strategy profile s and any subset or *coalition* of players $C \subseteq N$, write s_C for the list of strategies chosen by players in C, s_{-C} for the list of strategies chosen by players not in C, and let (s_C, s_{-C}) also denote s. A strategy profile $s^* = (s^*_C, s^*_{-C})$ is a *strong Nash equilibrium* if for every coalition C and for every feasible alternative list of strategies s_C (where for each $i \in C$, $s_i \in S_i$), there is some member j of C for whom

$$u_j(s_C, s^*_{-C}) \leq u_j(s^*_C, s^*_{-C}).$$

That is, for no coalition is it possible to find an alternative profile for coalition members such that all would have been strictly better off had all chosen those alternative strategies, given the strategies of nonmembers. Note that a strong Nash equilibrium is a Nash equilibrium, since the coalitions in the definition must include single-element sets of players, $C = \{i\}$. However, not every Nash equilibrium is a strong Nash equilibrium. Moreover, no strongly inefficient strategy profile can be a strong Nash equilibrium, since the coalitions in the definition must include the universal coalition, $C = N$.

For example, in the Prisoners' Dilemma, (Defect, Defect) is a Nash equilibrium but not a strong Nash equilibrium, since all members of the universal coalition C = {Player 1, Player 2} could have achieved a higher payoff had they instead chosen (Cooperate, Cooperate). The latter profile, however, is not a strong Nash equilibrium either, since the singleton coalition C = {Player 1} could strictly improve its members' payoffs by instead choosing Defect. The Prisoners' Dilemma has no strong Nash equilibrium.

Mixed Strategies and Existence of Nash Equilibrium

A game may not have any Nash equilibria in such deterministic (or "pure") strategies. A classic example is the game usually called "Matching Pennies," shown in Table 2. More generally, this happens in games in which one player wants, in some sense, to match the other but not vice versa: Rock-Paper-Scissors and Soccer Penalty Kicks are also common examples. Such examples are not confined to games of pure conflict, however. In such situations, it behooves a player to be as unpredictable as possible to his or her opponent. Game theorists denote this through the device of a *mixed strategy*, in which player i randomizes over S_i. In an analysis allowing mixed strategies, a strategy is denoted by a probability distribution over S_i. (The set of all mixed strategies includes all the deterministic strategies as well, which are denoted by degenerate probability distributions placing all weight on one element of S_i.) And in that setting, players are assumed to choose strategies so as to maximize *expected payoff*.

With the addition of mixed strategies, this seminal existence result known as *Nash's theorem* holds: Every finite game has at least one Nash equilibrium in mixed strategies.

Multiple Nash Equilibria

Nash equilibrium eliminates some rationalizable strategy profiles, but a game may still have many Nash equilibria. The canonical example is the game of pure coordination, shown in Table 3, which has two pure-strategy (and one mixed

Table 2 A Game With No Pure-Strategy Equilibria: Matching Pennies

		Player 2	
		Heads	Tails
Player 1	Heads	1, −1	−1, 1
	Tails	−1, 1	1, −1

Table 3 A Game With Two Pure-Strategy Equilibria: Pure Coordination

		Player 2	
		A	B
Player 1	A	1, 1	0, 0
	B	0, 0	1, 1

strategy) equilibria. Without additional assumptions—concerning, for example, iterated play and dynamics—game theory proper has nothing further to say about which equilibrium would be chosen. In applications, the historical or cultural context in which a game is played might afford the players additional information about what each other will anticipate, resulting in a *focal point*, a choice among equilibria that players can arrive at more often than random chance or symmetric mixed strategies would predict. Games with multiple equilibria demonstrate the difference between rationalizable and Nash strategy profiles: If Player 1 chooses A based on the belief that 2 will choose A, and Player 2 chooses B based on the belief 1 will choose B, this is a rationalizable profile of strategies and beliefs. But the result disconfirms the players' beliefs and disappoints their expectations.

Evolutionary Game Theory and Learning in Games

Evolutionary game theory offers an additional set of assumptions and tools to say more about the conditions under which various Nash equilibria will be selected. These tools are used in biology to study actual evolution through natural selection (usually with "selfish genes" filling the role of rational players). Individuals whose phenotypes—strategies—yield them higher reproductive fitness in one generation have more progeny in the next. A distribution of genotypes stable in the resulting dynamic system corresponds roughly to equilibrium in the game.

In the social sciences, the tools of evolutionary game theory are more commonly applied to models of "learning in games," in which individuals play games many times against different opponents, occasionally switching strategies to adopt a new one observed to have been more successful. The abandoning of one strategy in favor of another takes the place of the biologist's process of natural selection. This learning process can be quite myopic and error ridden, but generally the result is that a population of individuals may reach a *stable point*, a whole-population profile of strategies in which little further systematic improvement is possible. Stable points correspond under general conditions to a subset of Nash equilibria. Models of learning in games are significant to game theory overall because they demonstrate that the strong assumptions used to construct basic games—perfect and common information, perfect ability to select optimal strategies, and an a priori coincidence in the selection among multiple equilibria—are not remotely necessary to produce choices that correspond to classic Nash equilibrium. What is required is a sufficient opportunity for players to gain experience in playing.

Imperfect Information in Strategic Games

The assumption of perfect information is obviously an extreme idealization of strategic interaction. Even in classical game theory (as opposed to evolutionary or population learning models), a major preoccupation is the generalization of this ideal case. This is accomplished by specifying probability distributions that describe the state of a player's knowledge, including knowledge about the state of other players' knowledge. In general, imperfect information about the set of players, the strategy sets, or the utility functions in a strategic game can all be expressed in terms of uncertainty about the utility functions alone: An unavailable strategy can be represented by an extremely low utility for any profile in which that strategy is used, and an absent player can be assigned a singleton strategy set. Often, the true payoff function of a player is called the player's *type*.

Once each player's imperfect information is expressed in the form of a probability distribution over payoffs, the criterion of best response can be expressed in terms of expected-payoff maximization. Nash equilibrium generalizes directly to this form of best response. An important complication is that, in calculating best responses, a player's subjective probabilities about other player types must be updated to account for the circumstances under which the first player's action will affect his or her payoff. For example, in models of instrumental voting, only the cases in which a player's vote will be *pivotal* have any importance for maximizing payoff; but the fact of being pivotal carries implications about what the other players' types might be in those circumstances.

Sequential Games

Strategic games abstract away players' opportunities to react to other players or to anticipate their future decisions, burying such activity implicitly within each player's strategy. Sequential games, by contrast, offer an alternative model designed to emphasize this aspect of interactive decision making. Political processes are usually sequential decision processes, and political scientists have exploited this in numerous ways. Crisis bargaining and the inception of war were early and important objects of study through sequential games; later models of ethnic conflict and cooperation involve an approach similar in spirit. In the study of policy formation through voting, agenda-setting models such as committee gatekeeping have been widely employed, and the theory of legislative bargaining has achieved the status of a general-purpose tool for legislative politics, political parties, and group choice generally. Sequential game models are prominent also in the study of delegation of powers to an agency or committee and of decision making within a system of separated powers. Games of sequentially repeated interaction are often applied to the formation and maintenance of community or of collective action, in settings ranging from the theoretical study of polities to the stability of international organizations. With the incorporation of incomplete information, sequential games have also found important applications to all manner of political communication phenomena, such as policy advice from biased experts, lobbying, and informative political debate.

General Formulation

The following elements are necessary to specify a basic sequential game; for special purposes, additional elements may be needed, and these will be described in the subsequent sections. Just as with strategic games, every sequential game has a set N of players and, for each player i, a utility function u_i over outcomes. The difference lies in the description of player decisions and, thus, of outcomes. A sequential game also consists of a description of turns on which a given player has the chance to act and the actions among which that player may choose. A game need not simply describe the turns as alternating regularly among players; in general, the coming of a player's turn, as well as the actions available to that player, may depend on the prior actions of all players. The description of the game must also fully specify the sequences of player actions that determine the various outcomes of the game. As with strategic games using this description, any outcome may be simply specified by the sequence of actions that led to it, although in applications the outcomes usually correspond to substantive results.

Traditionally, and in most small games, the whole description of turns, actions, and outcomes is accomplished through the specification of a *game tree*. The "tree" terminology refers to a *rooted tree* in the mathematical theory of graphs. In that theory, a *graph* consists of a set of *nodes* and the *edges* that connect some nodes directly to other nodes; a *tree* is any graph that is both *connected* (any node can be reached from any other node via a sequence of edges that does not retrace itself, called a *path*) and *acyclic* (has no cycles, i.e., no path from a node back to itself); and a *rooted* tree has one node designated as the *initial* node (or *root*). The properties of connectedness and acyclicity then imply that for any two paths leading away from the initial node, once those two paths diverge onto different edges they never reconnect—giving the graph the shape, schematically, of the branches of a tree.

The initial node represents the beginning of the game. The path leading from the initial node to any particular node represents a partial or complete *history* of play of the game (including the "null history" at the initial node); at each node along any path from the initial node, either it is one player's turn to move or else the path outward from the root ends. These nodes along any path are called *nonterminal* and *terminal* histories of the game, respectively. The edge connecting the node of a nonterminal history, h, to the next node outward from the root represents an *action* chosen by the player $P(h)$ whose turn came at h. Each terminal history represents an *outcome* of the game, the result of a particular *path of play*.

This description of a sequential game as a game tree is just a way of forcing the specification of turns, action choices, potential histories, and outcomes to satisfy appropriate regularity conditions, making the description unambiguous and internally consistent. With the addition, described below, of chance moves, simultaneous moves, and information sets, the structure is remarkably versatile and yet amenable to powerful proofs concerning the general properties of types of games and their solutions. Figure 1 shows an example of a simple game tree, a so-called entry or incumbency game. In the figure, the payoffs of the two players are shown by a label on each terminal history x, with $u_1(x)$ written above $u_2(x)$. This is sometimes written instead as $(u_1(x), u_2(x))$.

Note, however, that the general form of a sequential game may involve trees that cannot be literally portrayed in a tree diagram such as Figure 1. For many applications, analytic tractability is improved by allowing a player i at a given history h to have a set of available actions $A_i(h)$ that is infinite, as in games of bargaining over the division of a stock or in a spatial model of electoral competition. Also, it is often important that there be no a priori limit on the possible length of a path of play, so that some terminal histories are infinitely long, as in alternating-offer bargaining processes or in repeated games. A well-specified model must somehow limit the payoff to such an infinite "terminal" history (e.g., by a low reversion payoff in bargaining or by discounting in a repeated game). An infinitely long path of play is nevertheless, of course, unrealistic as an outcome; but the ever-present possibility of continuing the game is strategically critical. A game having at least one terminal history of infinite length is said to have "infinite horizon." A game having no such history, and in which the set of available actions at every turn is finite, is a "finite game."

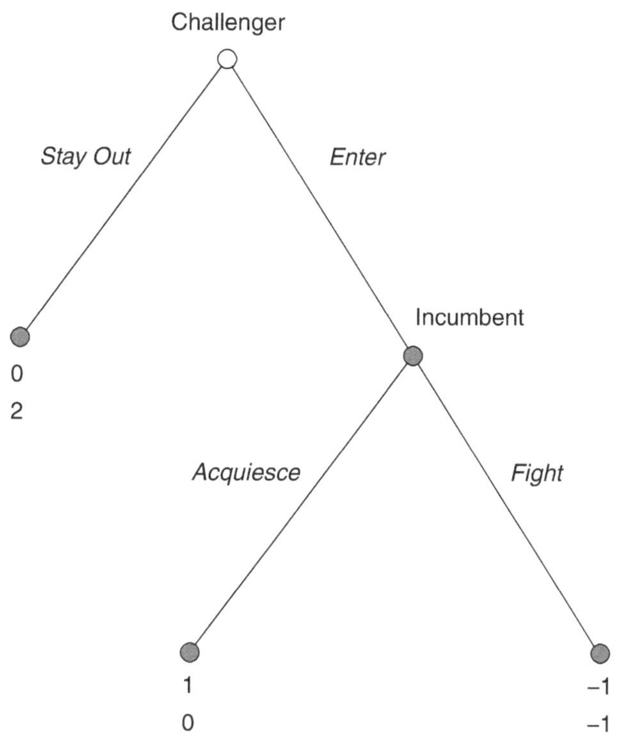

Figure 1 A Typical Game Tree: The Entry Game

Strategies and Solutions in Basic Sequential Games

A strategy for player i in a sequential game consists of a *function* s_i specifying, for each h having $P(h) = i$, an action $s_i(h)$ from i's set of available actions at that history. A strategy profile is a list of such functions, one for each player. As with strategic games, a strategy profile is written equivalently as s, $(s_1, s_2, \ldots, s_n)$, or (s_i, s_{-i}).

Backward Induction

For any finite basic sequential game, a simple and appealing solution concept is available: the method of *backward induction.* Consider an "ultimate" nonterminal history, that is, a history h such that every action taken by player $P(h)$ will end the game. Since there is a finite number of such actions, at least one of them yields a maximum payoff. Here at the end of the game, the only relevant implication of this player's choice is to determine his or her own payoff; clearly the rational choice is one yielding that maximum. Backward induction begins by identifying one such payoff-maximizing action for every ultimate nonterminal history. Now consider a "penultimate" history: a history h' for which (h', a') is an "ultimate" history no matter which action a' is chosen by player $P(h')$. For a given a', let a be the action that will then be taken at the resulting ultimate history (h', a'). In that case, using our analysis of ultimate histories, player

$i = P(h')$ will receive a predictable payoff from a', namely, $u_i(h', a', a)$. Proceeding in this fashion, backing up the tree to the initial node specifies an action choice for the choosing player at every nonterminal history, defining a strategy for every player. This strategy profile defines the sequence of actions that will transpire when the game is played—a terminal history or complete path of play through the game tree—as well as the actions that would be chosen following any arbitrary departure from that path. This strategy has the property that all actions chosen, both on and off the path, are payoff maximizing, given all the subsequent choices by all players. Call this strategy profile the *solution by backward induction.*

Nash Equilibrium: The Strategic Form of a Sequential Game

Alternatively, a sequential game can be converted to an essentially equivalent *strategic form* and solved by specifying a Nash equilibrium. For a finite basic sequential game, consider the strategic game defined by (a) the same set of players N; (b) for each player i, the strategy set consisting of all full sequential-game strategies for player i; and (c) for every profile of such strategies, a payoff equal to the sequential game payoff corresponding to the terminal node that would result from applying that strategy profile to the sequential game. A Nash equilibrium of this strategic form is defined as a Nash equilibrium of the original sequential game; the strategic form is also known as the *normal* form or occasionally the *matrix* form. The sequential form is also known as the *extensive* form or occasionally the tree form of the game.

Notice that every solution by backward induction is a Nash equilibrium of the game. In a backward-induction solution, no player has any incentive to change *both* an ultimate and any penultimate moves because all the ultimate moves are optimal regardless of how those ultimate histories were arrived at, and the penultimate moves were optimal given those. Backing up through the game tree, similar reasoning establishes that no player would want to change any subset of his or her moves in the backward-induction solution; hence the profile is a Nash equilibrium.

Not every Nash equilibrium is a backward-induction solution, however. Consider the Challenge Game shown in Figure 1. Backward induction yields a profile in which Incumbent Acquiesces, and Challenger Enters, which is also a Nash equilibrium. Consider another strategy profile in which Challenger chooses Stay Out and Incumbent chooses Fight. Clearly, Challenger would not prefer to Enter if Incumbent will Fight; moreover, given that Challenger will Stay Out, Incumbent has no incentive to Acquiesce. This too is a Nash equilibrium, but it violates backward induction. Such a flawed Nash equilibrium is sometimes called "imperfect."

Subgame-Perfect Equilibrium

A subgame of a sequential game G is the part of the game that follows any nonterminal node h, and thus, it is a game in its own right. Its set of histories corresponds to the set of all histories of G that begin with h; its payoffs are the corresponding payoffs from G; and its player set is the same, although some may have no moves to make in the subgame. (For games of imperfect information, defined below, this definition is modified to exclude putative subgames whose set of nonterminal histories would contain an incomplete portion of any information set.) When a game is solved by backward induction, a backward-induction solution on every subgame is induced as well. Thus, backward induction induces a Nash equilibrium on every subgame.

This property can be applied as well to a game with infinite horizon, which cannot be solved via backward induction. For any sequential game, a Nash equilibrium that induces a Nash equilibrium on every subgame avoids the "imperfection" described above; hence, it is called a *subgame-perfect equilibrium.* Since not every Nash equilibrium is subgame perfect, subgame perfection is also referred to as a *refinement* of Nash equilibrium. (The qualification "subgame" perfect distinguishes this refinement from other refinements treating alternative notions of imperfection.) Where backward induction is not possible or feasible, other methods may be employed to derive subgame-perfect equilibria. Such methods are often based in one way or another on Bellman's principle of dynamic programming: An optimal strategy is identified by always taking the optimal current action, assuming that the subsequent actions are optimal. Other Nash equilibrium refinements in a similar spirit use criteria based on rational behavior when choices are known to be subject to small errors or *trembles*, both in sequential and in strategic games. Examples include *trembling-hand perfection* and *proper equilibrium*.

Extending the Basic Formulation

The basic formulation of a sequential game, whether finite or infinite, can be extended in several ways. Backward-induction and subgame-perfect equilibrium extend as well, making the sequential game a powerful all-purpose modeling tool. This section examines how to generalize the formulation of sequential games to include simultaneous moves, chance occurrences, randomized actions, and imperfect information.

Simultaneous Moves

Suppose that, following some histories, two or more players are to choose actions simultaneously, after which the game may continue. This can be represented by letting the player function P designate a set of players, $P(h) \subseteq N$, rather than a single player. For each $i \in P(h)$, we still let $A_i(h)$ represent the set of actions among which i is to choose; this may, in general, be a different set of actions for each player in $P(h)$. The description of a history accommodates such simultaneous moves by allowing the sequence of actions defining h to include, where appropriate, a profile of actions by a set $P(h)$ of players, in place of the move by a single player. For example, if action a^1 by Player 1 is followed by a simultaneous choice by Players 2 and 3, who choose a^2 and a^3, respectively, then resulting history may be written unambiguously as $(a^1, (a^2, a^3))$. Player i's strategy in a sequential game can still be represented in the same form as before, letting $s_i(h)$ represent the action i would take at history h regardless of whether other players are simultaneously making choices at h. A basic sequential game is one in which $P(h)$ is always a singleton $\{i\}$. A strategic game now becomes a special case of a sequential game, in which the null history $\varnothing$ is the only nonterminal history, with $P(\varnothing) = N$.

Finally, it is natural to extend backward induction to simultaneous-choice situations as follows: when, in the process of backward induction, a history h is reached at which $P(h)$ has more than one player, then construct a special strategic game in which the set of players is $P(h)$; player i's strategy set is $A_i(h)$; and player i's payoff to strategy profile $s(h)$ in the special strategic game is identical to i's payoff in the overall sequential game from the terminal history defined by h, followed by $s(h)$, followed by continued play according to the backward-induction steps already completed. The backward induction is continued, then, by designating a Nash equilibrium $s^*(h)$ in the special strategic game at h, and then continuing up the tree under the assumption that if h is reached, the players in $P(h)$ will choose according to $s^*(h)$. As in backward induction in a basic sequential game, if a simultaneous-move history has more than one Nash equilibrium, the implications of each must be traced out for the remaining steps of backward induction, yielding several different backward-induction solutions. Extending the method of backward induction in this manner preserves the definition of strategic form, the definition of Nash equilibrium for sequential games, and the correspondence between backward-induction and subgame-perfect equilibrium all in the same form as defined for basic sequential games.

Example: Repeated Games

An important application of sequential games with simultaneous moves is the case of *repeated games*. Let G be a strategic game (players N, strategy sets S_i, and utility functions u_i). In a repeated game, the same set of players plays G, known as the *stage game*; all learn the outcome; and all play G again, and so on. The players know that G will be repeated a specific number of times or indefinitely. The payoff to this entire sequence is the sum of the payoffs to the successive instances of G, perhaps discounted (i.e., multiplied by some "discount factor" between 0 and 1 for each repetition) due to time preferences or to the probabilistic termination of the sequence.

Consider for instance the Prisoners' Dilemma shown in Table 1 as the stage game, to be repeated infinitely with discount factor w. This forms an infinite-horizon sequential game, in which at every nonterminal (i.e., every finite) history h, $P(h) = \{\text{Player 1, Player 2}\}$ and $A_i(h) = \{\text{Cooperate,}$

Defect}. A terminal history is an infinite sequence of the form $((a_{10}, a_{20}), (a_{11}, a_{21}), (a_{12}, a_{22}), \ldots)$, where each $a_{it} \in$ {Cooperate, Defect}. The payoff to player i from such a terminal history is

$$\sum_{t=0}^{\infty} w^t u_i(a_{1t}, a_{2t}),$$

where t represents time.

Finally, a strategy takes the form of a rule telling what action would be chosen at every possible nonterminal history. Actual strategies of interest are usually expressed in the form of a relatively simple rule. For example, the strategy of Tit for Tat in the repeated Prisoners' Dilemma can be described as follows: Cooperate at $t = 0$; and for all $t > 0$, imitate the other player's action at $t - 1$.

A repeated-game strategy profile can be proven to be a subgame-perfect equilibrium by showing that at no possible history (on or off its path of play) could payoff be increased by changing the action taken at that history and nowhere else. This method is derived from Bellman's principle. Notice that the profile in which both players use Tit for Tat is a Nash equilibrium for sufficiently large w but is not a subgame-perfect equilibrium for any value of w. This is because if one player ever commits an unexplained Defection, then, under the assumption that both players would adhere to Tit for Tat in the future, it would be better for the other player to forgo punishing the defection (incurring a punishment in turn). If the strategy for both players is modified, however, to include an "apology"—namely, Cooperate twice regardless of the other player's action—for any unprovoked Defection, it becomes a subgame-perfect equilibrium (again, for sufficiently large w). Thus, although Defect is a dominant strategy in the unrepeated game, full cooperation can be maintained in equilibrium in the indefinitely repeated game.

Moves by Chance

The interactions we subject to game theoretic analysis sometimes depend in part on intervening events best understood by the players as being random. Such phenomena can be included by allowing the player function to specify that at some histories h, instead of a player or players choosing an action, a random event occurs before subsequent player actions or payoff determinations take place. This is denoted by writing $P(h)$ = Chance or $P(h)$ = {Chance} and such an h is casually referred to as a "move by Chance" or by "Nature." In describing the game, any such instance must be accompanied by a set of possible outcomes of the random event, which we might as well write $A_{\text{Chance}}(h)$, and a probability distribution p on $A_{\text{Chance}}(h)$. The outcome of a Chance move is part of the sequence of actions defining any history.

If Chance moves are encountered in the path of play under a profile s, then s determines not a particular terminal history but rather a probability distribution over terminal histories. For a game involving moves by Chance, then, the backward-induction process must be modified by maximizing *expected* payoffs, computed in the appropriate way using the probability distributions for the Chance moves to determine the probabilities of various payoffs given a strategy profile.

Behaviorally Mixed Strategies

Mixed strategies are usually treated in a different way for sequential games than for strategic games. Game theorists use the term *behavioral* (or *behaviorally*) *mixed strategy* to refer to a strategy in a sequential game in which the player randomizes over the actions. (Where the context is clear, the modifier "behavioral" is usually dropped.) Unless otherwise specified, these randomizations are always taken to be independent across players; they are represented as independent across histories too, although of course different actions at an earlier history lead to different subsequent histories, at which the player may use different randomizing probabilities.

Obviously, a strategy profile involving randomization will determine a probability distribution over outcomes, and expected utility is the criterion for backward induction. Analogous to deriving mixed-strategy equilibria in strategic games, the procedure in a sequential game for finding subgame-perfect equilibria involving behavioral mixed strategies depends on the fact that a player who maximizes expected utility can rationally randomize if and only if each of the actions accorded positive probability would, if used alone, also maximize expected utility. In the backward-induction process, this means that a single player $P(h)$ could use either no randomized action or a continuum of randomized actions at h. However, many of these possibilities will often be ruled out of the eventual subgame-perfect equilibrium, since randomizations by more than one player or at more than one history will require multiple indifference conditions that (again as in strategic games) constrain the feasible values of the probabilities used.

Imperfect Information

Perhaps the single most important extension of the basic formulation is to represent games in which players do not have full information about the previous actions of other players. This is, after all, an important feature of many parlor games as well as a key feature of real-world interactions. The state of player i's knowledge about previous moves in a sequential game is represented by distinguishing, as an *information set* of player i, any subset of histories at which player i is required to move but among which i is unable to distinguish at the time they are reached. Thus, for all histories within the same information set, the player is required to choose the same action. The whole collection of such information sets for a player is that player's *information structure.* To define equilibrium in a game with imperfect information requires that we incorporate a notion of player i's probabilistic beliefs about previous actions. These notions are formalized below to facilitate defining the relevant equilibrium concepts.

For each player i, let $H(i)$ be the set of histories for which i is in the player set. Let I_i be a partition of $H(i)$—that is, a set of nonempty subsets of $H(i)$ such that each history in $H(i)$ is an element of exactly one of those subsets. Denote by $I_i(h)$ the partition element containing h, called i's *information set* at h. In what follows, the symbol Z denotes a typical information set without reference to a particular history in it; but for any h in Z, $I_i(h) = Z$. I_i is a valid *information structure for i* if and only if, for each information set Z in I_i, player i has exactly the same action choices at every h in Z. (In any application, the names or labels of the actions for each history in an information set should be identical as well. From a theoretical standpoint, however, the labels on the actions are irrelevant; hence, the only real restriction is that the action sets be of the same size.) This restriction is needed since i must be aware of the available choices at the present history; it must be impossible for the player to infer from this whether that history is h or h'. Thus, we may as well write $A_i(I_i(h))$ for the actions available at every h in information set $I_i(h)$. Finally, for any history h at which player $i \in P(h)$ does know the entire sequence of previous actions, $I_i(h) = \{h\}$, just that one history.

This approach requires a slight redefinition of a strategy. Since player i cannot distinguish between h and h' in an information set Z, a strategy must specify the same action at both histories. Thus, in general, a strategy for player i can be fully described as a mapping not from each history into its action set but simply from each information set $Z \in I_i$ into its action set; thus, instead of $s_i(h)$, we keep track of the accounting by writing $s_i(Z)$, which automatically reminds us that $h, h' \in Z$ implies $s_i(h) = s_i(h')$. As noted above, the presence of information sets restricts the applicability of the notion of subgame-perfect equilibrium. In a proper subgame, every h within the subgame must have the property that the subgame contains *all* the histories in $I_i(h)$. That is, no information set can be "shared" between two subgames. Thus, in a game of imperfect information, not every nonterminal h gives rise to a subgame. With this restriction on what qualifies as a subgame, the definition of subgame-perfect equilibrium remains the same as before.

To go further in assessing the choice of a rational strategy requires that we devise some method of handling a player's uncertainty at any nontrivial information set Z. As usual, we represent the state of the player's knowledge about what is the actual history in Z with a probability distribution over Z. Now, the payoff from choosing action a from $A_i(Z)$ is the expectation over the histories in Z of the payoffs from choosing a. Each of these payoffs, in turn, may be an expectation based on subsequent moves by nature or randomized actions to be chosen by i or by other players subsequent to that. We thus wish to equip each player i with a probability distribution over each nontrivial Z in I_i. Let $\mu_Z(h)$ represent i's subjective probability that the current history is h given that the current information set is $Z \in I_i$. The distribution μ_Z is known as player i's *beliefs* at Z, and μ as defined over all Z for all players is a *system of beliefs*. Using this notion of beliefs, we can generalize subgame-perfect equilibrium to the imperfect-information setting. There are several such extended definitions, each having the following form: An equilibrium consists of an *assessment*, that is, a profile of strategies s and a system of beliefs μ, obeying two conditions:

1. *Sequential rationality*: For each i and each $Z \in I_i$, $s_i(Z)$ maximizes the expected value of u_i given s_{-i} and μ.
2. *Consistency*: Each μ_Z is consistent with s and with the probabilities placed on Chance moves, given the laws of probability and other considerations.

The sequential rationality condition is just a restatement of the criterion we have been using all along, that each action maximizes expected payoff. The consistency condition varies according to the "other considerations" imposed as conditions, and this gives rise to different solution concepts.

The simplest consistency condition—and the least restrictive while still being consistent with the laws of probability—is that beliefs must comport with Bayes's rule wherever it is directly applicable. That is, for every information set Z that can actually be reached with positive probability given s, for every history h' in Z, we must define $\mu_Z(h')$ according to Bayes's rule, namely, as the conditional probability of reaching h' given that Z is reached, given the players' strategies and the game's Chance-move probabilities. This amounts to

$$\mu_Z(h') = \Pr(h')/\Pr(Z) = \Pr(h')/\Sigma_{h \in Z} \Pr(h),$$

for all h' in Z. Each marginal probability $\Pr(h)$ is calculated by multiplying all the mixed-strategy action probabilities and Chance-move probabilities along the sequence of actions that make up h. An assessment (s^*, μ^*) satisfying this form of consistency, as well as sequential rationality, is a *weak sequential equilibrium* (WSE).

Game theoretic models frequently invoke a related equilibrium concept called *perfect Bayesian equilibrium* (PBE). A sequentially rational assessment (s^*, μ^*) is a PBE if and only if it induces a WSE on every subgame. The only difference between PBE and WSE occurs when there is an information set Z that is not reached by s but for which other off-path actions or chance moves intervene between the point where s diverges from Z and Z itself. In such cases, WSE consistency imposes no restriction on beliefs in Z, but PBE consistency requires that the probabilities in Z comport with the probabilities of reaching Z conditional on the initial departure from the path of s. Other, stronger consistency conditions produce further *belief-based refinements* of WSE, such as sequential equilibrium and divine equilibrium. In general, such refinements are used to rule out equilibria thought to be based on "unreasonable" beliefs.

Example: Signaling Games

The important example of "semipooling" equilibrium in certain *signaling games* provides important applications of chance moves, behavioral mixed strategies, and imperfect information. In a signaling game, a Sender learns the value of an initial Chance move and then sends one of a set of feasible signals to a Receiver, who must choose an action. The players' payoffs depend in different ways on the combination of the true chance move and the Receiver's move. If the Sender's payoff does not depend directly on the Sender's signal, the game is one of "cheap talk"; otherwise it may be a game of "costly signaling." Depending on the details of the conflict between the players' interests, in equilibrium the Sender's signal may be (a) ignored by the Receiver, called "pooling" since the Sender's behavior is the same regardless of the Chance move; (b) perfectly informative about the Chance move, called "separating" since the Sender's signal perfectly distinguishes the possible Chance moves; or (c) partially informative, called "semipooling" since the Sender uses a mixed strategy, reporting truthfully with some probability less than 1.

Figure 2 shows the game tree for a signaling game that minimally embodies all these features. The game begins (in the middle of the diagram) with Chance determining whether Policy A or Policy B would be best for Receiver; A is best with probability $p < .5$. Sender learns the truth and signals either a or b. Receiver knows p but does not know the Chance move; thus, Receiver has two nontrivial information sets, one reached when Sender signals a and the other when Sender signals b. These are indicated in the game tree by the dotted lines connecting histories that Receiver cannot distinguish. After hearing the report from Sender,

Receiver must choose either α (implement Policy A) or β (implement Policy B). At each terminal history, each pair of payoffs in the diagram shows Sender's payoff above Receiver's payoff. Thus, Receiver's preferences simply favor Policy A when A is best and B when B is best, with equal intensity. We assume that Sender's payoff parameters obey $x > w > y > 0$, so Sender has a preference for A regardless of which policy is best for Receiver. Since $w > y$, Sender's message has a direct impact on Sender's utility: if B is best and B is implemented, Sender's utility will be reduced (by $w - y$) for having falsely reported that A is best. This is, therefore, a game of costly signaling rather than cheap talk.

This game has a semipooling equilibrium defined by the following assessment, which incorporates a behavioral mixed strategy:

- Sender signals a when A is best; when B is best, Sender signals a with probability $r = (1 - 2p)/(1 - p)$ and b with probability $1 - r$.
- Following a signal of b (the left-hand information set), Receiver believes that B is best with probability 1. Following a signal of a (the right-hand information set), Receiver believes there is a probability $m = p/[p + (1 - p)r]$ that A is best and a probability $1 - m$ that B is best.
- Following a signal of b, Receiver chooses β with certainty. Following a signal of a, Receiver chooses α with probability $s = (w - y)/(x - y)$ and chooses β with probability $1 - s$.

To see how the belief m is derived from Bayes's rule, notice that the top history in the right-hand information set is reached with probability p (Chance probability that A is best, times Sender's probability 1 of truthfully reporting that) and the bottom history is reached with probability $(1 - p)r$ (the Chance probability B is best times Sender's mixed-strategy probability of falsely reporting A is best). Notice that this formulation of m is equivalent to the usual form of Bayes' rule: m is the conditional probability that A has occurred, given that Sender has reported a, so Bayes' rule says $\Pr(A|a) = \Pr(A)\Pr(a|A) / [\Pr(A) \Pr(a|A) + \Pr(B) \Pr(a|B)]$, which is just $p / [p + (1 - p)r]$, as given above.

As with any signaling game, there are also pooling equilibria in which Sender uses the same signaling probabilities regardless of Chance's move; and Receiver chooses β in all cases, believing B is best with probability $1 - p > .5$ regardless of the signal.

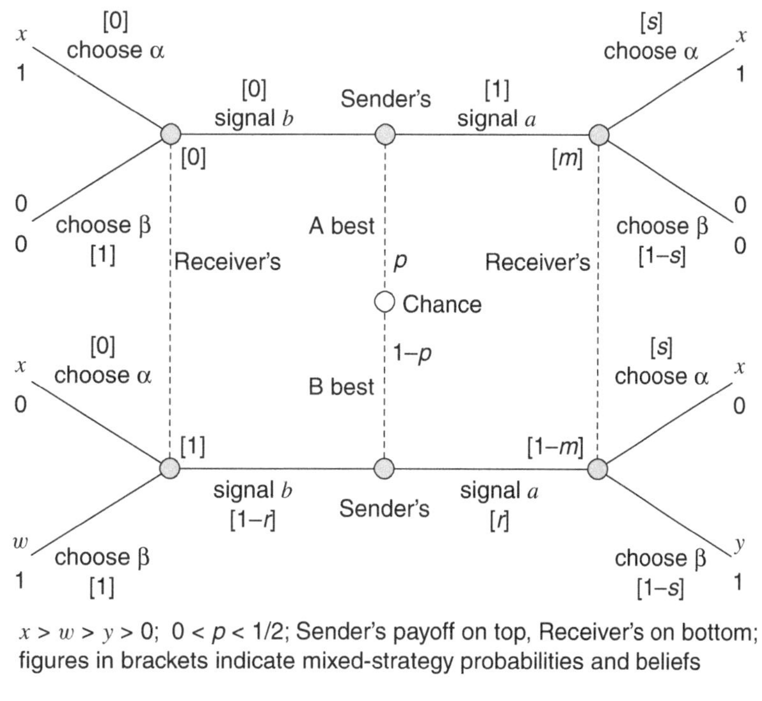

Figure 2 Semipooling Equilibrium in a Signaling Game

These are often referred to as "babbling" equilibria, since the Sender's signaling is meaningless.

Cooperative Game Theory

The term *cooperative game theory* should be understood to cover a variety of fairly distinct approaches, including axiomatic bargaining theory and spatial voting theory; but the central and original branch of the theory is that of games in *characteristic function* form or simply *coalition games*. A brief treatment will serve to illustrate the approach and its differences from and similarities to the noncooperative theory.

As the emphasis on coalitions might lead one to expect, some of the original applications of game theory to politics used cooperative game theory. The cooperative game formulation provided the basis for the calculation of *power indices* that, in a 1950s conceptual breakthrough, clarified the difference between voting weights and voting influence for small weighted-voting bodies and for voting bodies with complex veto rules, notably the United Nations Security Council. The earliest models of voting competition also took the form of cooperative games, being based on the specification of winning and blocking coalitions; this approach is still used productively, both in theoretical analyses and in the empirical study of multiparty election systems. A related early political science use of game theory was in the study of parliamentary government formation, where coalition patterns were analyzed using both party size and the restriction that coalitions include ideologically compatible partners.

The theory of coalition games originated with the attempt of John von Neumann and Oskar Morgenstern to theorize about zero-sum games with more than two players. In such games, a coalition of players could act in concert to assure themselves certain outcomes regardless of the efforts of the remaining players; the question is, "what coalitions will form to take advantage of their capabilities?" The original formulation assumed, contrary to our previous assumptions, that payoffs have meaning across players and can in fact be combined and voluntarily transferred from one player to another in a simple additive fashion. This class of coalition games is today called *transferable utility* (TU) games; in nontransferable utility (NTU) games, by contrast, one keeps separate account of the payoffs chosen by the coalition for each player.

Formally, let $N = \{1, 2, \ldots, n\}$ be a set of players. For every subset of players C, let $v(C)$ be the total payoff that those players can ensure receiving regardless of the actions of the remaining players; each nonempty C is a possible *coalition*, and v is the *characteristic function*; strictly speaking, v completely describes the game (since it implicitly includes a specification of the set of players). A valid characteristic function should be *superadditive*: For any two disjoint coalitions C and D, $v(C) + v(D) \leq v(C \cup D)$ since, acting together, the members of the two coalitions could do anything they could have done by acting separately, and perhaps more. Let $x = (x_1, x_2, \ldots, x_n)$ be the distribution of payoffs that ultimately results from the play of the game, after any transfers of utility to which members of coalitions have agreed. The aim of the characteristic function formulation is to predict the distribution of payoffs among the players, given the capabilities of the coalitions that they might enter into. Notice that the particular actions taken by individuals, acting alone or in concert, are completely abstracted away, and that it is implicitly assumed that a coalition can perfectly accomplish any desired commitment, cooperation, or coordination to achieve its potential total payoff. The definition of $v(C)$ as the most that C's members can ensure themselves embodies a pessimistic viewpoint that is really appropriate only where the underlying game is zero sum (so $v(N) = 0$), although that restriction is not always imposed when the coalition theories are applied.

The first, very weak, solution concept is the set of *imputations* of a game v. This is the set of payoff distributions satisfying two properties:

1. *Individual rationality*: For every player i, $x_i \geq v(\{i\})$, since the player has no reason to accept a payoff lower than what he or she could ensure himself or herself by acting alone.
2. *Efficiency*: $x_1 + x_2 + \cdots + x_n = v(N)$, since by definition the grand coalition can get any feasible total payoff, and there is no reason to settle for less.

The addition of one more condition defines the fundamental solution concept for coalition games, the *core*. Let x and y be two imputations; x is said to *dominate* y if there is some coalition C such that

(a) $v(C) \geq \Sigma_{i \in C} x_i$, that is, members of C have the power to impose x, and (b) $x_i \geq y_i$ for each $i \in C$, and strictly so for some $i \in C$, that is, each member of C is at least as well off, and some better off, under x than under y. The core of v then consists of the set of all undominated imputations. In many games of interest, the core is empty; consider, for example, three players who divide a dollar by majority rule. The Bondareva-Shapley theorem gives a *balance condition* ensuring the core will be nonempty. Alternative conditions on imputations yield other solution concepts, such as the *von Neumann-Morgenstern solution*, the *kernel*, and the *nucleolus*.

Randall Calvert
Washington University in St. Louis
St. Louis, Missouri, United States

See also Analytic Narratives: The Method; Bargaining; Cooperation; Coordination; Experiments, Laboratory; Prisoners' Dilemma; Rational Choice; Social Choice Theory; Spatial Models of Politics

Further Readings

Camerer, C. P. (2003). *Behavioral game theory: Experiments in strategic interaction.* Princeton, NJ: Princeton University Press.

Fudenberg, D., & Levine, D. K. (1998). *The theory of learning in games.* Cambridge: MIT Press.

McCarty, N., & Meirowitz, A. (2007). *Political game theory: An introduction.* Cambridge, UK: Cambridge University Press.

Morrow, J. D. (1994). *Game theory for political scientists.* Princeton, NJ: Princeton University Press.

Osborne, M. (2004). *An introduction to game theory.* New York: Oxford University Press.

Peleg, B., & Sudhölter, P. (2007). *Introduction to the theory of cooperative games* (2nd ed.). Berlin: Springer-Verlag.

Weibull, J. W. (1997). *Evolutionary game theory.* Cambridge: MIT Press.

Young, H. P. (1998). *Individual strategy and social structure: An evolutionary theory of institutions.* Princeton, NJ: Princeton University Press.

Gender

Today, *gender*—a term that is also used in languages other than English—is used in the context of gender relations or as a social construction of sexuality. It is comparatively a new term, with *gender* originally being used until the 1960s only as a grammatical category to allocate nouns into different categories—feminine, masculine, and neutral. Since then, the term has been fully engrained in the social and cultural sciences discourse and has also established itself in the political discourse of different societies, as the concepts of gender mainstreaming and gender budgeting show. The expansion of the term and its widespread use can be seen as a sign that gender inequality is perceived in many areas of society and is examined as a social–organizational form. This entry discusses the origins of this concept, its relevance in social discourses, and its implications for contemporary political science.

Background

As opposed to the biological term *sex*, the term *gender* refers to the "social" or "psychological" gender of a person, where "sex" and "gender" should be seen as analytically independent of each other. Gender refers to a historically specific practice of social classification. It focuses on the special perceptions and patterns of interpretation by which the binary structure of "male" and "female" is viewed, dealt with, and institutionalized. In doing so, it deals with the symbolic order of sexes in a society, as well as with the self-attributions and identification of the individual, which focus on it but are not identical to this symbolism. In most societies, categorizing into male and female gender categories takes place on the basis of the shaping of primary and secondary gender characteristics. Disambiguations and the one-sidedness of "male" and "female" are associated with the two-gender classification, as well as with social relations of symmetry and asymmetry, equality and hierarchy, of inclusion and exclusion. These relationships are embedded in concrete social relations and structural connections. At the same time, the fact that classifications do not simply exist but constantly need to be reacquired points to their instability and dependency on having to be updated at a practical level. Based on the realization that social gender differentiation is not based on anthropological, biological, or physiological conditions but on the result of social classifications, it can be inferred that the hierarchical relationship of the sexes to one another is not an expression of a "natural" order that cannot be changed.

Stages in the Discourse

The sociological debate on inequality between women and men and the category of "gender" began around the middle of the 1960s and is closely linked to the so-called second wave of the women's movement emerging at that time in many Western countries. The studies, mainly compiled by female academics, first concentrated on unmasking science as "male oriented" and criticizing the lack of awareness of women's lives and active dealings in research and teaching. A close connection between the women's movement and feminist criticism in science was established, and it resulted in criticism of the discrimination against women in academia and society and of the one-sidedness of research that was mainly conducted by men and that often treated women as objects.

Feminist criticism of science highlighted the facts that cultural, political, and socially dominant gender images influenced the scientific theories of the time. Based on this, the much lauded scientific objectivity was often distorted by a male point of view. The primary aim in women's studies was, therefore, to make the ignored contributions of women in academia visible by coming to terms with and analyzing the social setting of the time and women's thoughts and actions. In doing so, women's studies were viewed at first as biased research that placed the focus on women and on the changes in their life situations.

This view was gradually broadened, however, and increasingly women's thinking and actions were analyzed in relation to men's with the intention of identifying differences and hierarchies. It was in this context that the discussion began about what sex and gender really mean. In gender and women's studies, gender is no longer treated as something natural but as a social or structural category with subsequent social roles. People are assigned or denied specific characteristics, attributes, and places in society on the basis of their sex. Sociological gender studies since the 1980s, therefore, speak of gender as a structural category. What is meant is that the separation and hierarchization of social spheres such as reproduction and production, and, consequently, the public and private realms are significant characteristics of modern, industrial societies. This separation and hierarchization are accompanied by an engendering of different spheres and social subdisciplines. Gender is regarded as a binary hierarchy that co-organizes the different levels of social organizations. Although study on the discrimination against women is frequently the point of departure for research, gender research now also addresses the social organization of gender relationships more broadly.

Based on the recognition that gender is a part and a result of a construction process in which "he" and "she" as individuals are involved, a sociological shift has occurred: Gender is no longer viewed as a structural category but also as a process category. Candace West and Don Zimmerman's concept of "doing gender," which was developed in 1987, differentiates itself from the current sex/gender distinction and the nature/culture concept transported with it. Doing gender understands gender attribution and gender identity as a continuous production process that is taking place in all human activities. This ensures that the gender discrepancy is generated by people continuously making themselves—and allowing themselves to be turned into—women and men in their everyday lives. It is a collective and individual process of construction through which, depending on the context and the situation, dual-gender classification is strategically implemented in practical social actions.

Similarly, a critical "men's studies" category is emerging that focuses on male disciplinary and normalization processes and calls into question the norms and realities of "hegemonic maleness." A central understanding within men's studies is the recognition that hegemonic maleness is responsible not only for the dominance of men over women but also for hierarchies among men. Beyond this, research on maleness has emphasized the fact that men are also subjected to one-dimensional gender assignations that are formative and do not at all represent the "general human being." An important difference from women's studies continues to be that the experience of injustice and discrimination has not formed the basis of research and the relationship between research and practice in the context of a "political" or partisan intervention—as was central in the early days of women's studies—has therefore had very little significance.

Gender studies further broadened in scope in the 1990s. The category of gender, which had until then been viewed as a "natural" classification, even if culturally and socially formed, was questioned. *Gender Trouble*, a book by the American philosopher Judith Butler published in 1990, evoked a comprehensive discussion on the identity-giving category of "woman." What had widely served as an unquestionable basic assumption in women's studies—the natural existence of two exclusive genders—increasingly became an object of academic examination. The binary distinction between two—and only two—genders is now frequently understood as an ideological construct of a discursive power system. Gender affiliation of persons and the two-sex model as a social classification and functional differentiation principle do not refer to the law of nature but are the result of social constructive processes.

This construction of gender cannot, however, be viewed as a neutral form of determination; rather, it is already part of the social determination of gender relations and therein also of the social inequality between men and women. The factitiousness of gender not only affects gender, however, but also applies to the biological category of sex. As the latter is also not free of a sociocultural construct, the "prediscursivity" of sex and the norms and regulations tied to biological sex must be debated.

Gay theory also focused the spotlight on the connection between gender and heteronormativity, or the social norm of heterosexuality. Academic studies continue to take up heterosexuality as a power configuration, which gender studies has barely researched and has not acknowledged as hetero-normatively composed. Normative reference points in women's and gender studies are put up for discussion with the transformation and broadening of knowledge on the category of gender as a binary construct.

In the beginning, gender studies were oriented—as was the women's movement—toward the issue of how equality between women and men could be attained in all areas and which barriers are an obstacle to this goal at the political, legal, symbolic, and other levels. At a practical political level, equality was seen as nondiscriminatory, but this view raised the issue that equality leads to a cementing or even strengthening of inequality according to the different points of departure and socially created differences. In addition, there was a criticism that the concept of equality was targeted toward aligning the position of women—their social and individual possibilities—with those of men. The measure of equality is thus "the man" and the options, values, and concepts of work, life, and politics ascribed to him.

As a patriarchal devaluation of the female is latently connected to this view of equality, the difference perspective articulated the suggestion that women should be treated differently from men. Connected to this is the challenge to go beyond stereotypical attributions to reflect on the ways in which women are different or unique. Furthermore, the characteristics, lifestyles, and so on of women should not be viewed as deficient but as parts of one and the same concrete whole. Associated with this, however, is a fear of a codification of typical female characteristics and gender roles that tend to become gridlocked. The discussion on equality or difference has become a never-ending story; nonetheless, it is clear that the deconstruction of gender has led to a shift from the selection of one of these two positions to a concern with analyzing the connections between equality and difference. For some years now, the perspective has broadened, and in addition to the gender imbalance, differences among women are also increasingly being taken into consideration—especially class-specific or ethnic differences that resulted from American theory-building discourses and Black feminism, as well as the debate surrounding women (co)perpetrators during National Socialism.

As all individuals not only belong to *a* group but always belong to multiple groups at the same time, how the category of gender interacts with other categories of inequality is analyzed below. Both legally and politically, this is codified in the concept of multiple discrimination. At a theoretical level, gender studies subsume this phenomenon as a crossing over between different categories of inequality under the term of *intersectionality*, a term that the American legal specialist Kimberlé Crenshaw coined in 1987 in the context of Black feminism. The debate surrounding intersectionality and the interdependencies among race, class, and gender has so far been mainly theory driven and is only gradually being enhanced by empirical studies. In general, it is argued that the question of whether sex or another category has a larger influence on discrimination, which has been raised in the discussion on gender as a "master category" from time to time, should remain open in the analysis.

Gender in Political Science

In comparison with other social science disciplines, political science was relatively late in focusing on gender as a category. In the beginning, solely the field of "women and politics" was the object of study. Within this context, the question of the political representation of women and how it was reflected in political issues was especially interesting. The feminist perspective first took up this analytical perspective and questioned the reasons behind the formal and informal exclusion of women from politics.

A reconceptualization and expansion of the research field to include "gender and politics," however, was initiated relatively quickly. In this context, maleness/masculinity as a measure and norm is inscribed in all political processes in a more or less subtle manner. In most countries, a quantitative overrepresentation of men in politics exists that is oriented on the biological sex. Politics is not, however, male because almost all political decision-making bodies are dominated by men, but because male interests are systematically presented as hegemonic, representing and giving preferential treatment to interests that most closely correspond to the everyday lives of this social group. In addition, there is a substantive masculinity: as Joan Acker highlighted with the term *gendered organizations*, institutionalized male patterns are integral components of political organizations that influence political rules, values, norms, and structures.

Thus, gender-critical discourse within political science generally takes place at two levels. First, it occurs at the sociopolitical level and expounds on the limited number of women in the discipline. The underrepresentation of women results in the fact that women receive less attention as actors and, at the same time, the androcentric scholarly conception of women, sex, and sexuality is maintained. The other level focuses primarily on epistemological and conceptual questions and delivers a critical inspection of political science paradigms and terms at a theoretical analytical level with the goal of making the gender subtext visible. Based on this deconstruction of apparently gender-neutral normative premises, terms, and research interests in mainstream political science, the political was broadened and reformulated to include a gendered view. Part and parcel of this was a critical revision of its core areas and subdisciplines, among others the fundamentals of political scientific thinking. Among these, especially, are the fundamental categories of the public sphere, privacy, and politics.

The Public Versus the Private Sphere

The central point of departure for a gender-critical political science is the challenge of the separation and polarization between the public political and the private nonpolitical spheres. Every debate concerning this distinction deals with the problem of participation at its very core or the possibilities and conditions of women's presence in politics. In the history of political ideologies, "women, together with other groups such as slaves, servants (to which a large number of women belonged) and landless men, were described as incapable of leading a moral life or able to participate in the justice system" (Seyla Benhabib & Linda Nicholson, 1987, p. 514). The differences and inequalities between the genders were substantiated on four assumptions: First, the natural, anatomical, and physiological differences were used to justify inequality by claiming that the ability to give birth as well as other apparent characteristics of women were decisive criteria for participating in political life. Second, it was assumed that men are both physically and intellectually superior to women, which brought with it a hierarchy of naturalized differences that was also reflected in the significance of the spheres. Third, the so-called female sphere is irrelevant for political life. This is accompanied by the fourth point—the assumption that the domestic sphere, although it takes place outside the political arena, is nonetheless controlled by politics and is inferior to it (Benhabib & Nicholson, 1987, p. 515). In sum, this means that male reason and rational conduct are attributed to the public sphere, while the private sphere is seen as being characterized by irrational, unpredictable patterns.

Criticism is targeted at the double separation of the public and the private, which has traditionally influenced theory formation in political science. By distinguishing state and (private) economy on the one hand, and economy and (private) households on the other, gender inequalities are left out of sight in many respects. The gender-specific division of labor that is constitutive for the (private) economy (paid/unpaid) eludes state and political regulation, such as gender-hierarchical appraisal of labor (well paid/badly paid), which essentially represents a continuation of this labor division in a semipublic space in its differentiation between women's and men's activities. The entire vocabulary used in political science is built on this dichotomy. Feminist welfare state research especially points to the fact that gender-specific labor division is not only a constitutive element of the (welfare) state—as Carole Pateman (1988) showed with the "sexual contract" approach—but that politics is also gendered and supports gendered processes: "In a society in which there is a gendered division of labour there is almost no area of policy in which women and men are not differently affected" (Joni Lovenduski, 1992, p. 610). The discourse on the separation of public and private highlights the fact that a close connection exists between the two spheres, and that, at the same time, these are placed in a hierarchy (e.g., important–unimportant, inclusion–exclusion) that is constructed and has an ideological basis.

Broadening of the Definition of Politics

The division between the public and the private sphere has also become engrained in the field of politics and the political. The classic definition of politics views politics (*politikos*) as the administration of the affairs of the *polis*, the community. In contrast, the areas of housework, household administration, the house (*oikos*), and the family, or in other words those areas in which women were traditionally active, were not seen as political. Even if this classic political understanding in political science does not dominate (anymore), and many different political definitions exist, the political is commonly positioned in the public sphere. Feminist political science, therefore, calls for a widening of a public and institutionalized definition of politics that only sees gender relationships and gender relations as un- or prepolitical but not as a political expression or object.

The American political scientist and philosopher Nancy Fraser, for example, distinguishes between an official political and a discursive political definition. The former views a matter as political if it is represented in official government institutions or, in other words, in parliaments, administrations, and other bodies. As Fraser (1989) notes, "the discursive political definition comprises everything that is disputed beyond a range of different discursive arenas and among a range of different discourse publics" (p. 166). Between the political definitions is a close connection, as an issue usually only turns into an object of legitimate state intervention once it has been discussed among the broader public. The border between both attributions is not defined but is an object of conflict and changes within social discourses.

The expansion of political contents and spaces is accompanied by criticism against forms, norms, processes, and practices linked to a governmental political definition. This would lead to the fact that women not only as a group of people but also concerning women's interests (even if these are not necessarily homogeneous interests) would insufficiently be represented or not be represented at all.

A further important aspect in the discourse surrounding the definition of politics concerns the question of how gender relations and gender relationships can be viewed as political objects.

When politics govern social relationships, they also embody identities and interests and the relationships between men and women, as well as between different groups of women or men. If this understanding is pursued, the field of activity of political science is broadened to include a debate and analysis of politics as the regulation of bipolar hierarchical gender relationships. Birgit Sauer (2005) outlines the meaning of gender categories for political science as follows:

> As a structural category in politics and political science, gender is constituted at the subjective individual and objective levels—a culturally formed, socially shaped relationship that is loaded with purpose and meaning, that possesses structural and institution-building potency. (p. 381)

Gender is to be understood as a structural and structuring category. This means that gender, on the one hand, is a political institution and that, on the other hand, institutions "have" a gender and reproduce genders. The following five levels are relevant to the analysis of gender in political science: first, the level of political cultures and symbols; second, the level of state organizations and rules (polity); third, the policy level; fourth, the level of political processes and their actors (politics); and fifth, the level of political subjects.

Status Quo

Nowadays, a gendered view of the discipline can be found in nearly all areas of the field, such as international relations, political theory, political systems, or policy research. Similar to this profiling, a partial institutionalization of feminist or gendered political science as an area of research and as a teaching subject has taken place. Nevertheless, a problem that Virgina Sapiro (1995) identified almost 15 years ago continues to be true:

> Despite the size of the gender politics community, and despite the fact that most political science departments now offer at least one course in this area, gender politics has not been fully integrated into political science; its theories, questions, and conclusions have not been "mainstreamed" to any significant degree. (p. 292)

This means that gender relations beyond the feminist and gender-oriented branch of the discipline are not, or are barely, conceptualized as social relations that structure politics.

Alexandra Scheele
University of Potsdam
Potsdam, Germany

See also Feminism; Feminist Movements; Feminist Theory in International Relations

Further Readings

Benhabib, S., & Nicholson, L. (1987). Political philosophy and the question of women. In M. Lotsch & W. Preller (Eds.), *Piper's handbook of political ideas* (Vol. 5, pp. 513–562). Munich, Germany: Piper.

Carroll, S. J., & Zerilli, K. M. G. (1993). Feminist challenges to political sciences. In A. W. Finifter (Ed.), *Political science: The state of the discipline II* (pp. 55–76). Washington, DC: American Political Science Association.

Fraser, N. (1989). *Unruly practices: Power, discourse, and gender in contemporary social theory.* Cambridge, UK: Polity Press.

Lovenduski, J. (1992). Gender and politics. In M. Hawkesworth & M. Kogan (Eds.), *Encyclopedia of government and politics* (Vol. 1, pp. 603–615). London: Routledge.

Pateman, C. (1988). *The sexual contract.* Stanford, CA: Stanford University Press.

Sapiro, V. (1995). Feminist studies and political science—and vice versa. In D. Stanton & A. Stewart (Eds.), *Feminism in the academy* (pp. 291–310). Ann Arbor: University of Michigan Press.

Sauer, B. (2005). Limitation and transgression of the political gender studies in political sciences. In H. Bußmann & R. Hof (Eds.), *Genus: Geschlechterforschung/gender studies in den Kultur- und Sozialwissenschaften* [Genus: Gender studies in cultural studies and social sciences] (pp. 366–401). Stuttgart, Germany: A. Kröner Verlag.

Generalized Least Squares

See Weighted Least Squares

Genocide

While the term *genocide* is new, the phenomenon is old. Genocide has a long history, going back to at least the 12th century BCE and continuing into the present. The 20th century can be considered an "age of genocide," with numerous examples of genocide throughout the period claiming as many as 70 million lives (some scholars would say many more than that). After the Holocaust, the watchword was "Never again," yet since 1945 the lives claimed by genocide exceed those killed in international and civil wars combined. But with so many genocides, different situations, motives, and victim groups, it has been difficult to define *genocide* in ways that everyone would accept. Moreover, the term is widely used in a rhetorical fashion to attract attention and to further political and social demands.

Nevertheless, the definition of genocide that is contained in the United Nations (UN) Convention on the Prevention and Punishment of Genocide, though widely criticized, is the one that prevails among scholars. To complicate matters further, the concept of genocide could be described, following Ludwig Wittgenstein, as a concept with "blurred edges." Here, the family resemblances and differences between genocide and other concepts, such as ethnic cleansing, must be taken into account. There is still a core meaning: Genocide consists of acts that intentionally threaten the existence of human groups. Yet this statement itself is incomplete: What acts? What level of threat? What is a group? Who defines it? And how is intentionality determined?

Before the term *genocide* existed, mass killings were referred to as *massacres*, *race extermination*, and so on. Perpetrators had very different terms: *victory*, *self-defense*, *purification of society*. It was not until 1944 that the term *genocide* was created by the Polish Jewish lawyer Raphael Lemkin in his book *Axis Rule in Occupied Europe*. The term was based on the Greek *genos* (race, group) with the Latin *cide* (killing). Lemkin used the term to describe not so much the destruction of individuals but "the destruction of a nation or ethnic group." Political and social groups, such as classes, were not included in his definition and nor was the partial destruction of a group. He stated, "Genocide is a coordinated plan of different actions aiming at the destruction of the essential foundations of the life of national groups, with the aim of annihilating the groups completely" (p. 79). For him, the core of the crime was the destruction of groups, not individuals; he believed that groups were the bearers of civilization and culture, of identity, of diversity, and thus in special need of protection. Pieter Drost (1959) countered with a definition that focused not on the destruction of groups but of individuals: "Genocide is the deliberate destruction of physical life of individual human beings by reason of their membership of any human collectivity as such" (p. 125).

Lemkin pressed the UN to declare genocide a crime against international law. From 1946 to 1948, the UN debated the wording of what would become, by unanimous vote in December 1948, the UN Convention on the Prevention and Punishment of Genocide. With sufficient ratifications by member states, the Convention entered into force in early 1951. But despite the occurrence of numerous examples of genocide in the years following, not a single case of genocide was tried under international law until the opening years of the 21st century. The International Tribunals for the former Yugoslavia and Rwanda have now both charged and convicted several individuals for genocide. One problem with this, however, is that a vast, state-organized process, with deep societal involvement, is treated as if it were simply a trial for murder.

The Convention makes genocide and related crimes, such as incitement to genocide, crimes under international law, "whether committed in time of peace or in time of war." But the heart of the Convention is found in Article II, where the crime of genocide is defined and where many of the problems with the concept lie:

> In the present Convention, genocide means any of the following acts committed with intent to destroy, in whole or in part, a national, ethnical, racial or religious group, as such:
>
> (a) Killing members of the group;
>
> (b) Causing serious bodily or mental harm to members of the group;
>
> (c) Deliberately inflicting on the group conditions of life calculated to bring about its physical destruction in whole or in part;
>
> (d) Imposing measures intended to prevent births within the group;
>
> (e) Forcibly transferring children of the group to another group.

Many important issues arise from this conception of genocide. First, not all groups are protected; political and social groups, such as classes, lie outside the boundaries of the definition. The reasons for this are that (a) only groups would be covered that were "stable and permanent" and (b) many countries wanted to keep open their right to suppress by violence any political or social challenge to the authority of the ruling power. Second, not only must there be intent to destroy a group, but there must also be "specific intent," that is, the intent to destroy the group must be because of its particular characteristics (national, ethnical, racial, or religious). Destroying such a group for, say, economic reasons, would not count as genocide. Third, the question of destroying a group "in part" has raised issues about how large a part and whether it is a matter of numbers or a percentage of the overall group that counts. In general, these issues have now been dealt with by saying a "substantial part," leaving it to courts to decide just where to draw the boundaries. Some legal scholars, however, would add that "in part" could mean a "significant part," in some functional sense—for example, culling the leadership elements of the group.

A fourth issue concerns the problem of what constitutes a group. For example, the Tutsis in Rwanda were neither a national nor an ethnic group, but they were perceived by their killers to be members of a group. In the UN Rwandan tribunal, the court decided that groups and membership in them are defined by the perceptions of the perpetrator. Finally, the acts that are listed as constituting genocide are physical, biological, and cultural may not matter, but of the five acts, any one of which constitutes genocide, only one of them actually involves killing, though all aim at the destruction of the group. The UN definition focuses on intent, not on results. That genocide could occur with few or even no deaths is a surprising conceptual outcome of the UN's approach and contrary to both scholarly analysis and public understanding of what is meant by genocide.

There are other concepts that bear a family resemblance to genocide but also can be distinguished from it—for example, war. Many genocides occur within the context of war, but apart from ancient warfare, which was synonymous with genocide, war traditionally was a battle between armed combatants not between perpetrators and largely unarmed civilians. In the 20th century, war has often been total war, and waged against civilians as well as soldiers, but not with the idea of eliminating the "enemy" as a group. Genocide, on the other hand, is a species of total war: It is aimed at a particular group, most of whom are unarmed, and the intent is not the subduing of the group but its elimination, if not in whole, in substantial part.

Massacre also can be part of how genocide is carried out, but more often it is geared toward revenge or repression, not annihilation. It tends also to be episodic and isolated rather than sustained and pervasive as in genocide.

The term *ethnic cleansing*, on the other hand, has gained so much traction since the war and genocide within Bosnia that it has almost displaced the idea of genocide or, alternatively, is treated as another term for genocide. In practice, ethnic cleansing is often part of the genocidal process; the term is also a euphemism used by the perpetrator to disguise what is actually taking place. But in theory, ethnic cleansing means using violence, rape, terror, and forced deportation to drive out or remove a particular group from a common territory. The emphasis is on creating a homogeneous society through fear and expulsion, not as in genocide on annihilating the group.

There are legal and institutional developments that also relate to the status of genocide within international law. In 1998, the Statute of Rome created an International Criminal Court, with the following crimes within its jurisdiction: genocide, crimes against humanity, war crimes, and the crime of aggression. The very term *crimes against humanity* arose out of the Young Turk genocide of the Armenians, when the Allies in May 1915 warned the Ottoman rulers that they would be held accountable and tried for "crimes against humanity and civilization." In the statute, "crime against humanity" is defined in terms of a number of particular acts, including murder, extermination, and deportation or forcible transfer of population but more widely, torture, apartheid, and "other inhumane acts of a similar character intentionally causing great suffering, or serious injury to body or to mental or physical health." Any of these acts "when committed as part of a widespread or systematic attack directed against any civilian population" constitutes a crime against humanity. The key category here is "civilian population," not particular groups as indicated in the Genocide Convention; and the question of intent is different from that required under the Convention: Here, no specific intent is required.

Though one can differentiate "genocide" and "crimes against humanity" in important respects, the two concepts overlap in many ways. But it is much easier to prosecute actions as crimes against humanity than as genocide; the former also have a wider reach, not being restricted to crimes against particular groups named in the Convention. Some international legal scholars suggest that with the increased emphasis on crimes against humanity, the international community could dispense with the Genocide Convention. Prosecution of crimes against humanity would thus provide alternatives to the conceptual confusions and limitations of the Convention.

Roger W. Smith
College of William and Mary
Williamsburg, Virginia, United States

See also International Law; Violence; War and Peace

Further Readings

Chalk, F., & Jonassohn, K. (1990). *The history and sociology of genocide.* New Haven, CT: Yale University Press.

Drost, P. (1959). *The crime of state: Vol. 2. Genocide. United Nations Legislation on International Criminal Law.* Leiden, Netherlands: A. W. Sijthoff.

Lemkin, R. (1944). *Axis rule in occupied Europe.* Washington, DC: Carnegie Endowment for International Peace.

Schabas, W. (2000). *Genocide in international law.* Cambridge, UK: Cambridge University Press.

Smith, R. (1987). Human destructiveness and politics: The twentieth century as an age of genocide. In I. Wallimann & M. Dobkowski (Eds.), *Genocide and the modern age* (pp. 21–39). Westport, CT: Greenwood Press.

Straus, S. (2001). Contested meanings and conflicting imperatives: A conceptual analysis of genocide. *Journal of Genocide Research, 3*(3), 349–375.

United Nations. (1948). *United Nations Convention on the Prevention and Punishment of Genocide.* Geneva: Author. Retrieved November 19, 2010, from http://www.hrweb.org/legal/genocide.html

United Nations. (1998). *Rome statute of the International Criminal Court.* Geneva: Author. Retrieved November 19, 2010, from http://untreaty.un.org/cod/icc/statute/romefra.htm

Geopolitics

Geopolitics denotes, generically, strategic power struggles among states over the political control of territories and resources. More specifically, it suggests that politics is primarily defined by geographical location, territorial expansion, and interstate competition over finite spaces. The late-19th-century interimperial rivalries provided the historical context for the rise of geopolitical thought across the core countries of the imperial zone, rearticulating the relation between economic expansion and territorial control. The final division of the last extra-European vacant spaces generated an acute awareness of the closure of absolute space in a new "planetary" age. Interimperial relations came to be regarded as intensified zero-sum conflicts over the redivision of an occupied planet. This closed spatial horizon prompted a reconceptualization of the state as a territorial phenomenon in space, locked into a permanent struggle for survival. The revalorization and politicization of geography and its absorption into a reconceptualized science of politics forged the new field of political geography—geopolitics' direct precursor. Today, particularly with increasing globalization, geopolitics is more and more challenged and questioned: Territory has lost its classical relevance, as transnational relationships imply a new vision of the global world, which is less compatible with geopolitics. Critical geography points out the ideological and political background of geopolitics.

The concept of geopolitics was invented by the Swedish political scientist Johan Rudolf Kjellén (1864–1922) and developed in *The State as an Organism* (1917)—a critique of the prevailing legal positivism in constitutional and international law. The radicalization of political geography into *Geopolitik* as a specifically German theory of international politics was prosecuted—most notably by Karl Haushofer (1869–1946) and his school and, from a different angle, by Carl Schmitt (1888–1985)—during the revisionist conflicts over the Versailles Settlement in Weimar Germany. Geopolitics had a lasting, though not exclusive, impact on Nazi foreign policy. Intellectually, it positioned itself as a counternarrative against Marxist theories of imperialism (Rosa Luxemburg, Nikolai Bukharin, Vladimir Lenin) and against the Wilsonian liberal internationalism, represented by Isaiah Bowman (1878–1950). Basic elements of geopolitical thought infused, if in a semantically altered and politically sanitized form, the American Cold War discourse of neorealism in a new binary world-political geography. The proliferating but often indiscriminate contemporary invocations of the term *geopolitics* reflected the shifting post–Cold War strategic geography—globalization, multipolarity, hegemony, unipolarity, empire—and a renewed urgency of resource politics in times of natural resource depletion and environmental degradation. Simultaneously, the new approaches of critical and Marxist geopolitics sought to recover, respectively, the cartographic discourses that shape the construction of geopolitics and the efficacy of geopolitical conflicts that mediate European and worldwide socioeconomic and political developments.

Friedrich Ratzel (1844–1904), a professor of political geography and the cofounder of the *Alldeutscher Verband* (Pan-German League), was cross-nationally the most influential figure in the development of the geopolitical tradition. Applying ideas from biology, evolutionism, and human geography, he contended that state behavior—the expansion and contraction of states in space—is primarily determined by geographical properties and geostrategic location. Space, as a political category, is no longer conceived as a geometric, neutral, and empty expanse (the absolute space of nonhuman geography) but as a concretely ordered and constructed territory (the historical-relational space of political geography). Fusing an organic-biological conception of the state with principles of Darwinian natural selection in interstate relations, Ratzel claimed that states come to life, grow, and die in the struggle for space. Borders are temporary phenomena in a pulsating geopolitical environment. Preoccupied by the quest for a "scientific" legitimation of Wilhelmine Germany's expansionist policies, his *Politische Geographie* (1897) suggested that states enjoy a natural right to an adequate *Lebensraum* (living space) grounded in variations between soil fertility and population growth. Population "density pressures," established by a calculus between state territory and demography, are formalized in the "laws of the spatial growth of states." Differences arise in the prewar era between ethnocentric and geopolitical conceptions of states and the goals and limits of their foreign policies. While the ethnocentric notion defines nations as cultural-linguistic units (*Volksnation*), leading to a self-limiting territorial correspondence between a nation's area of settlement and the scale of state territory, the latter conception (*Staatsnation*) prioritizes territorial aggrandizement over ethnic-racial homogeneity, although it may also involve an active policy of ethnic settlement (Germanicization). *Volksnation* and *Staatsnation* are not synonymous and constitute rival points of reference. This tension between "race" and "space" resurfaced later in differences between the original program of German geopolitics and Adolf Hitler's racial ideology.

Contemporaneously, Alfred T. Mahan's (1840–1914) anti-isolationist navalism and Halford Mackinder's (1861–1947) heartland theory formed the core of political geography in the United States and Britain. Admiral Mahan's *The Influence of Sea Power on History, 1660–1783* (1890) identified the fleet-based domination of seaborne commerce as the decisive factor in world politics, exemplified by Britain's early modern oceanic hegemony. In an age of pre-aerial warfare and limited mechanization of terrestrial military technology, a major battle fleet secures a mutually reinforcing and self-sustaining relation between naval domination and commercial supremacy—the geostrategic axis of history. Mackinder drew the opposite conclusion in his lecture *The Geographical Pivot of History* (1904). Naval power, after unifying the world into a closed political system during the Columbian age (1500–1900), was superseded during the post-Columbian age by land power. According to Mackinder's trizonal global geography, a geostrategically immune inner-Eurasian heartland—the pivot of history—is surrounded by an inner crescent (the European periphery, Near/Middle East, India, China), enclosed, in turn, by an outer crescent (England, the Americas, Africa, Australia, Oceania, Japan). The contemporary global balance between land and sea power was decisively altered by the infrastructural penetration of the pivot area (Central Asia, Russia) through the construction of transcontinental railway networks. The future belonged to a German–Russian alliance, strategically invulnerable in its territorial heartland against sea power. Only a grand coalition of sea powers could prevent Eurasian world domination. Both conceptions had to be situated in the transition from cosmopolitan free trade imperialism to protectionist neomercantilism.

During the passage from the 19th-century European pentarchy to the new constellation of world politics, flanked by the rise of the United States and the former USSR, political geography turned into German geopolitics. Kjellén's antilegalistic *The State as an Organism* contrasted the norm-oriented concept of the state as a legal subject, most notably represented in Weimar Germany by Hans Kelsen, with an "empirical viewpoint" of the state as a geographic organism commanding space. Foreign policy was elevated to an existential condition. Geopolitics was redefined as an auxiliary science of statecraft in the international struggle for survival. Ratzel's and Kjellén's thoughts received a wide and enthusiastic reception in Weimar Germany during the revanchist intellectual struggles against the Versailles *Diktat* and as a key legitimation for national-socialist *Großraumpolitik*. The rise of the geopolitical tradition in the 1920s was marked by the foundation of the Institute of Geopolitics in Munich (1922), the *Geopolitische Seminar* at the *Deutsche Hochschule für Politik* (1924) in Berlin, and the launch of the high-circulation *Journal of Geopolitics* (1924). Haushofer, who was professor of geography at the University of Munich (1919–1939), director of the Institute of Geopolitics, president of the German Academy (1934–1945), and a close confidant of Rudolf Hess, emerged as the most influential figure in the German discourse. Its intellectual core was premised on

1. an organic-biological conception of the state and a Darwinian view of interstate rivalry;
2. a critique of Western, liberal, and "mechanistic" conceptions of state and society, contrasted with the *völkisch* "ideas of 1914" that recast states as expressions of culturally defined and homogeneous peoples, organically rooted in specific territories;
3. a revaluation of agriculture, mystified as "chthonic" and "organic," coupled with a neo-Malthusian understanding of population growth, leading to demands of an autarchic *Lebensraum*;
4. the rejection of international law (League of Nations) and its replacement by a new *Großraumordnung* (Grand Spatial Order);
5. a geostrategic determinism premised on the dualism between land power and sea power, informing the programmatic policy prescriptions for a Eurasian power bloc under German leadership;
6. the promotion of geography as the key science of statecraft and the dissemination of "suggestive cartography" for the collective preparation of the nation in its struggle for survival; and
7. the combination and political radicalization of these elements in Anglophobia and anti-Semitism.

Geopolitics matured from 1933 onward into the official German science of the state. Scientific pretense and normative orientation blended into a highly politicized literature. Attacking the "liberal" system of European *Kleinstaaten* (ministates), the juridicization of international politics and the fixing of borders, the geopoliticians invoked during the 1930s the "law of growing spaces." Buoyed by the first Nazi foreign policy successes, the new spatial order envisaged no longer sovereign nation-states as the units of the international system—the defunct Westphalian System—but a plurality of *Großräume* (Pan-regions). Schmitt, although institutionally unconnected to the geopolitical school, emerged as the sharpest critic of the League of Nations project and advocate of a new *Nomos of the Earth* (1950). He argued that all conceptions of international law are ultimately grounded in metajuridical foundations—the power projections and land appropriations that underlie state formations and expansion, exemplified in relation to the Spanish and English conquests of the Americas. Anglo-American international law was based on a structural correspondence tying the postwar promotion of liberal-constitutional *Kleinstaaten* on the European continent and beyond to their capitalist penetration by private economic forces and integration into the world market. Their incorporation into the League obliterated their political essence—the right to define an enemy and to wage war—due to the turn toward a discriminatory concept of war. The apolitical "spaceless universalism" of universal law—the flattening of differentially organized polities and their submission to common legal principles—sanctioned a constitutive dualism between the proliferation of liberal-constitutional states and the expansion of a borderless private world market. This strategy represented a concrete political project of global domination—the rationalization of global space driven by a nonterritorial capitalist imperialism for American *Lebensraum*.

The architect behind this project was Bowman, director of the American Geographical Society (1915–1935), key adviser to Woodrow Wilson at Versailles and, later, to Franklin D. Roosevelt. Wilson's moralistic liberal internationalism was commensurate with the American national interest in an attempt to move international order "beyond geography." Simultaneously, Schmitt contended that U.S. hemispheric policy toward the Pacific, Middle, and South America (Monroe Doctrine, 1823) and the British Empire constituted legal precedents for his multi-*Großräume* vision. The Monroe Doctrine manifested Anglo-American double standards in international law and politics. Against this background, Schmitt set out the historico-legal argument for the pluralization and regionalization of diverse, coexisting, and mutually exclusive legal spheres. *Großraumwirtschaft* (Grand Economic Order) and *Großraum*—not a biological, but a political-juridical category—merged into a supranational hegemonic order in Central and Eastern Europe under German leadership, located between the Soviet bloc and the Western powers' spheres of interest. Schmitt remained vague on the inner structure of Pan-regions and silent on inter-*Großraum* relations, excepting the principle of nonintervention for foreign powers. Similarly, Haushofer pleaded with reference to Mackinder's heartland theory for the construction of a continental bloc, comprising Germany, the former USSR, and Japan. This conception informed the German-Japanese Anticomintern Pact (1936), the German-Soviet Non-Aggression Pact (1939), and the division of Poland. The contradiction between Haushofer's anti-Bolshevism and his demands for an Eurasian bloc remains irresolvable. During the late 1930s, the term *geopolitics* became recharged with *völkisch* terms and was finally subordinated to racial policies.

Benno Teschke
University of Sussex
Brighton, United Kingdom

See also Anarchy; Balance of Power; Biology and Politics; Capitalism; Fascism; Imperialism; International Law; International Relations, Theory; International System; Marxism; Power and International Politics; Realism in International Relations; Sovereignty; State; Territory; War and Peace; Westphalian Ideal State

Further Readings

Bowman, I. (1921). *The new world: Problems in political geography.* New York: World Book Company.
Ratzel, F. (1897). *Politische geographie* [Political geography]. Munich, Germany: Oldenbourg.
Schmitt, C. (2003). *The nomos of the earth in the international law of the ius publicum Europaeum.* New York: Telos Press. (Original work published 1950)
Smith, N. (2003). *American empire: Roosevelt's geographer and the prelude to globalization.* Berkeley: University of California Press.
Teschke, B. (2003). *The myth of 1648: Class, geopolitics and the making of modern international relations.* London: Verso.

Globalization

Globalization refers to the integration of separate nations, regions, or even individuals into a wider global system. It is characterized by increasing the linkages and connections between peoples and countries and by the growing knowledge of these interactions. This integration process can affect the economy, polity, society, or culture; that is, the definition of the process is very general and can refer to economic, political, social, or cultural integration. The question of who is being integrated is also left open, although in political science it is mostly the countries themselves that are at issue. The way in which such integration operates is also variable. The most common form of globalization in the literature involves the economic integration of national economies into a wider global one, usually through international trade, capital flows, labor movements, and global production networks. For some authors, this means the integration of countries into a global capitalist system—that is, one based on private property, limited government intervention, and the use of markets to allocate economic value. Some term this *neoliberal globalization.* Capitalism, international capitalist groups, and neoliberal practices all spread throughout the world as globalization proceeds. Whether this is good or bad for countries and individuals greatly depends on a scholar's perspective. Some associate globalization with the homogenization of distinct groups; one example is the loss of many local languages and the increasing diffusion of the use of English. Others associate it with the domination of American (or Anglo-American) values, beliefs, and practices. The global turn to liberal democracy is often cited as an example. Globalization is not complete at this point. Countries have different levels of integration into the world system. The extent to which a truly global system—whether economic, political, or social—exists is a point of debate. The causes and consequences of globalization are also debated.

Globalization has both secular and cyclical aspects. For some, the roots of globalization are in technological changes, such as the lowering of the costs of communications and transportation, which make the movement of people, ideas, goods, services, and capital faster and less costly. These changes are irreversible and often increase over time. While countries and their governments may try to put up barriers against such changes, it is very difficult for them to successfully fend off the pressures of globalization. In this view, globalization has been increasing steadily over time as technological change makes the world ever smaller. Sometimes technological change is treated as exogenous—that is, it has sources other than countries' policies or global integration. Other times, globalization itself, especially via trade of capital flows, is seen as having an impact on technology; it usually is conceived of as helping induce innovation and speeding its transfer around the world. Globalization and technological change may then go hand in hand, each encouraging the other.

On the other hand, globalization has been viewed as cyclical; high levels of global integration have been associated with two distinct periods in recent history. In the mid- to late 19th century, a global economy emerged as the European powers, especially the British, forged an open economy using both military power and economic policy. The development of colonies around the globe and the extension of European trade, capital, values, and political power undergirded this period of globalization. In the late 19th century, the world economy attained levels of openness that had never been seen before. In some areas such as the movement of labor, such levels of integration have never been achieved since. This open economy collapsed in the early 20th century with the two World Wars and the Great Depression. From 1914 to 1945, globalization was in retreat. Protectionism became the dominant trade policy for many countries; trade and currency blocs formed regionally, often around one powerful country, and military conflict was prevalent. Nationalism, isolationism, and regionalism marked this 30-year period. Globalization thus declined during this period.

However, after 1945 the United States picked up the mantle from the British and began to forge a world economy through the creation of international institutions, an open economic policy, and an internationalist foreign policy. The global system, however, was divided into at least two blocs with the United States on one side and the former Soviet Union on the other; hence, globalization would always be limited in this Cold War system. The United States pressed ahead with the organization of an open, capitalist economy guided by principles embodied in various international institutions. It worked to encourage democratization in certain regions and then to include democracies in this integration process. The creation of the General Agreement on Tariffs and Trade (GATT) and the subsequent development of the European Community started a process of trade liberalization among developed countries. The Bretton Woods monetary system supported by the International Monetary Fund (IMF) and the World Bank helped countries establish currency convertibility and a fairly stable world monetary system based on the dollar. This stability provided the conditions for the development of private international capital markets, and over time these markets have come to dwarf those for goods and services. The removal of capital controls from many advanced economies in the 1970s and 1980s, after the termination of the Bretton Woods fixed-exchange rate system, opened these economies even more to global markets. While labor flows never became as free from government intervention as those of capital and goods, largely because of immigration restrictions in the developed world, there was some return to the greater mobility of labor that had prevailed in the late-19th-century period of high globalization. The extension of the European Union (EU) to new sets of countries and new issues also characterized this integration movement. By the 1980s, most of the advanced industrial world, except the former Soviet Union and its satellites, had joined the world capitalist economy. Globalization was only partial in this period.

From the 1980s onward, the rest of the world's countries began opening their markets and borders even more and joining the world economy. The end of the Cold War, the collapse of the former Soviet Union, and the economic reform movement in China all added impetus to the globalization process, as the former communist countries and China all began to integrate their economies into the global capitalist one. In the 1990s and early 2000s, the world's developing countries began joining this world economy and its international institutions in large numbers. Most countries in the world now belong to the World Trade Organization (WTO), the IMF, and the World Bank. Democracy was also spreading throughout much of the world at this time. Countries also increasingly chose to join a wide variety of international organizations and treaty systems. Conventions on labor standards, human rights, environmental issues, and other areas became widely adopted by countries around the world. By 2009, most of the world's countries had become part of a global system that had become increasingly organized around a series of common principles and values governing numerous issues. Economic shocks, such as the 1998 Asian financial crisis and the 2008 financial crisis begun in the United States, spread across the globe rapidly. The second period of globalization had arrived. A major issue is to what extent globalization was purposefully constructed, rather than unintentionally realized. Whether globalization is reversible or not is also at issue.

Globalization has been studied from two general perspectives. On the one hand, the causes of globalization have attracted much attention. Why has there been a movement toward increasing contact and interaction between states and peoples all over the globe? Why has this occurred more at certain times than others? Why have some regions or peoples been more involved in this process than others? Why have certain aspects of globalization such as international trade moved faster than others? Many questions have been raised about globalization as an outcome that in itself needs explanation. On the other hand, the impact of globalization has also received great attention. What effects does this process of increasing contact and interaction among states and peoples have on the economy, politics, society, and culture? Are these effects large or small? Negative or positive? Delineating the myriad effects that globalization might have and developing evidence for these has been central to the literature. Once we understand more about globalization, we can then address the question of how to manage the process and its effects.

The Causes of Globalization

A question of much import has been how globalization has developed, and why it has developed the way it has. If one adopts the secular view of globalization, then its advance can be explained by how fast technological change occurs and spreads. In periods where such change is very rapid and when the adoption of new ideas and techniques is quick, globalization will progress rapidly. Many seem to feel that this was the case in the mid- and late 19th century, when critical innovations such as steam power, railroads, and the telegraph changed political, social, and economic life around the globe. Spread in part by military competition and imperial control, these technologies helped integrate distant regions of the world. Technological change did not stop in the interwar period when globalization was in retreat; indeed, war tends to spur such innovation. But the spread of such technologies in this period was much more limited since many borders were closed and countries guarded their new secrets, which were often tied to war fighting. The development of nuclear weapons is a case in point. The period after World War II has again been viewed as one when rapid technological change was fostered by governments, when the spread of new processes and products was unhindered, and when the adoption of innovations at least in the noncommunist countries was embraced by states. Globalization thus sped up after 1950 because technological change accelerated.

It is important to note that technological change is not just about the economy; such changes have major ramifications for society, culture, and the polity. Electricity, the telephone (not to mention the mobile phone), radio, television, refrigerated shipping containers, automobiles, airplanes, and now the Internet—to name just a few of the major innovations of the last century and a half—have affected social, political, and cultural life in enormous ways. They have all contributed to globalization by reducing the cost of transportation and communication among individuals across the globe. In this secular story of global integration, countries can try to impede innovation and slow its spread, but they cannot ultimately halt such change. To the extent that technology reduces transportation and communication costs, technological innovation provides an irrepressible force for globalization. The pace of globalization may be affected but not its forward movement.

In the cyclical view of globalization, other factors are often cited as being of great importance to the changes we see. One theory focuses attention on the salience of having one country lead the globalization process. Hegemonic stability theory (HST), developed in the 1970s and 1980s, argued that a single world leader was necessary for an open, stable world economy. Without such a leader, even technological change would not bring globalization. Two versions of this theory exist. In one, the hegemon, who has overwhelming capabilities in all areas relative to other countries, exercises a benign influence over the rest of the world by organizing and paying the costs for such openness and stability. It plays the role of leader and others benefit from its efforts. The United Kingdom (UK) and the United States are cited as two examples of this in the mid- to late 19th and mid- to late 20th centuries, respectively. The loss of British leadership capacity and the failure of the United States to exert leadership in the interwar period were seen as the leading causes of the closure and turmoil of that period. Without such benign leadership, the world would not be able to integrate and countries would remain in an isolationist stance trying to beggar their neighbors. The hegemon solves the problem of trust and competition for the smaller states and thus allows everyone to emerge better off through its provision of global public goods. It acts as lender of last resort and tries to provide an open market in difficult economic times. By creating international institutions to help countries in difficult times, the hegemon can also promote stability and bind itself to reassure other countries of its benign motives. Globalization requires leadership from the world's strongest power. Some note that perhaps a small group of powerful countries could provide this same leadership, but concerns about disagreement or buck passing within this group have shed doubt on this view.

In a second view, the role of the hegemon is not seen as selfless. Here the global leader seeks to maximize its own interests and uses its superior resources to bribe and coerce others into following it. British and American hegemony is seen as a coercive process by which the country imposes its will on others; the hegemon gains, while everyone else submits. In the British case, imperialism combined with open markets and the dominant role of the pound helped it induce others open their markets and join the international trading and financial system. Even international law as developed in this period served to enable globalization as the European powers used it to force open the colonies. British domination ran into increasing difficulty, however, as other countries grew and became competitors. Once Britain could no longer dictate the terms of engagement with the world economy, regional blocs developed around the strongest powers. Britain could no longer force countries, including the United States and Germany, to follow its preferred practices, such as joining the sterling system or opening their markets to international trade. The decline of British hegemony then ended the period of globalization as powerful rivals developed their own spheres of influence.

In the case of the United States, its dominance in all domains after World War II helped it establish a system of international governance that has maintained American hegemony for over 60 years. Unlike the British earlier, the Americans set up a series of international institutions to embed the U.S. global order. The GATT/WTO, IMF, World Bank, and regional development banks have, among others, been a means for the United States to exercise its domination without having to do so directly. These institutions have pushed countries to adopt capitalist practices, to open their markets to flows of goods, services, and capital, and to follow the so-called Washington Consensus in other economic matters. Allowing or encouraging countries to become indebted and then imposing conditions on them when they are unable to service their debts has allowed international institutions to open the developing world to the global economy. More recently, pressure for democratization has also come from these institutions. Thus, the American method for controlling the global system has differed from the British one, but it has also involved coercing others to join the global economy. The use of soft power has been perhaps more evident in the case of the United States. But American military intervention around the world has been plentiful, and this view has served to enforce its global vision. In this view of coercive hegemony, first the UK and then the United States gained much from their exalted position at the center of the global system; ironically, however, in both cases their decline seems to be connected to their leadership role. This view of the malign hegemon is associated with both a realist and a Marxist approach to international relations. Substantial debate exists as to whether the coercive or benign view of hegemony is more evident. This debate includes controversy over the extent to which the countries other than the hegemon have been hurt or helped by this globalization process.

A more constructivist account of the globalization process would focus on the way ideas and norms about the global community and modernity shape state behavior. It would identify the dominant ideas of the past 60 years and how these have been legitimated and spread throughout the system. Beliefs in liberal democracy, human rights, capitalism, and neoliberalism, for instance, have diffused across the globe; these institutions and practices have become legitimated and viewed as the "modern" way to manage a country. Countries thus aspire to introduce and develop them in order to be a part of the global community. International institutions embody and diffuse these ideas, as do norm entrepreneurs from global civil society. The focal effect of these ideas, however, is to reduce diversity and contribute to homogenization. Scholars are often divided as to whether this normative globalization is beneficial or not. Clearly, the spread of some ideas (e.g., democracy and human rights) is seen in a more positive light than the spread of others by some scholars (e.g., capitalism and neoliberalism). There is also debate over how certain ideas come to be dominant. Is it through coercion or inducement by a powerful country, such as the United States, that others espouse these ideas? Is it more the zeitgeist of the time that makes certain ideas fit the situation better? Or is it the impact of international political entrepreneurs who give legitimacy and moral suasion to certain views, independent of countries?

Another reason given for the rise of globalization is much less intentional. The uncoordinated actions of countries over time have simply resulted in an increasingly open and interconnected system. No country desired such a result, but each one acting on its own best interests adopted policies that resulted in a globalized world. This view has support since the reasons for and sequencing of many countries' decisions to globalize were nationally distinctive. The advanced industrial countries liberalized trade and then their capital markets back in the 1960s to 1980s. The EU was a major force for movement in this direction; however, European countries joined and expanded the Union for reasons other than globalization, such as domestic politics or international security. China then launched its economic reform program in the late 1970s and early 1980s for internal reasons, and political reforms have not been forthcoming. The former communist countries only moved toward a more open and capitalist economy after the end of the Cold War and the demise of the former Soviet Union in 1991, and for many of them, joining the EU had important domestic political and international security motivations. In the developing world, democratization often came before economic liberalization. Many poor countries did not liberalize economically until the late 1990s and later. Indeed, the most striking is the different paths that countries have taken since the 1970s. The manner in which and the degree to which countries are integrated into the world system are remarkably varied. While the overall trend has been toward greater contacts and openness, there has been substantial diversity in how states realized this. For instance, English is spoken much more in most countries today than 30 years ago, but the penetration of English varies greatly from country to country. In this view, this uncoordinated process has been driven by different causes in each country. Globalization has developed differently for each; and the fate of globalization lies with the (somewhat independent) decisions of countries. The reactions to the global financial and economic crisis of 2008 to 2009 underline this view since governments have failed to coordinate and have instead responded distinctly.

Consequences of Globalization

In addition to the debates over the causes of globalization, there is much debate about its consequences. There are at least three distinct views in the literature: (1) Whereas some see its consequences as negative in all aspects, (2) others see its effects as positive on the whole, and (3) still others stand firmly in the middle and see it as having both costs and benefits. Globalization is said to have many different effects. The approach here is to look at a number of those effects and sketch out the different opinions scholars hold on each. At this stage, there is little consensus on its effects. Substantial literatures exist on whether (and how) globalization has affected economic growth rates, poverty, inequality, democracy, conflict, state capacity, policy and institutional convergence, cultural diversity, volatility and the diffusion of crises, and balance of power between capital and labor. Assessing the impact of globalization implies that one must hold other factors constant, which is a difficult task. Since globalization is an ongoing process, definitive answers to these questions cannot be given. What is striking, however, is the wide range of views and evidence that exists for each of these outcomes.

Economic Growth

Globalization is alleged to have had a variety of effects on economic growth. Growing integration of national economics into a wider global one has usually been achieved through trade liberalization and the pursuit of foreign investment, and sometimes through capital market liberalization. The consequences of these policies for economic growth are still debated. Some research supports the idea that all of the policies increase growth; there is probably more evidence that trade and foreign investment support growth than does capital market liberalization. Research also shows evidence that countries that globalized in the past 30 years grew faster than those that did not. Many expected that the integration of developing countries into the world economy would promote economic convergence—that is, it would make the poorest countries grow faster and hence catch up over time with the richest. There is some evidence that this has occurred in parts of the world—mainly Asia—but not much support for it globally. The North–South divide does not seem to have closed much over the past few decades. In part, this is because the North has had faster growth rates than some developing countries. For a wide range of countries, however, globalization does not seem to have fostered faster growth. Scholars point out that for parts of Latin America and Africa growth rates were higher in the decades before the 1980s than after. The impact of trade on growth for many countries has also been ambiguous; some, especially in Asia, seem to have gained from it. But many others, in Latin America and Africa, for instance, do not. Foreign direct investment has tended to flow to the most rapidly developing economies and so it is associated with fast growth, but this may not be causal. Finally, there is much skepticism that capital market liberalization for developing countries is or has been good for economic growth. Some of the problems associated with globalization, such as inequality and volatility, seem to have affected its capacity to deliver growth.

Poverty and Inequality

A large debate centers on the impact of globalization on poverty and inequality. World Bank data suggest that from the early 1980s to roughly 2005, poverty declined globally. The number of extreme poor (those living on less than $1.25/day) decreased from 1.9 billion in 1981 to 1.4 billion in 2005, which is equivalent to a decrease from 50% of the developing countries' population to 25% thereof (*World Bank Annual Report 2009*, p. 61). Also, for example, in the East Asia and Pacific regions, the percentage living on less than $2 a day fell from 69% in 1990 to 25% in 2007. Nevertheless, 2.5 billion people in the world still live on less than $2 a day (*World Bank Annual Report 2008*, pp. 14, 34).

Other measures of the quality of life in developing countries have also improved: Literacy rates, life expectancy, and infant mortality, for example, have ameliorated in most regions except where HIV/AIDS has struck hardest. Was this decline due to globalization? Some countries that have lowered trade barriers and promoted foreign investment, such as China, Taiwan, and Vietnam, have experienced significant declines in poverty in the past decades. However, even for these countries, it is not clear that within-country inequality has been reduced; the growing rural–urban divide in many developing countries suggests rising inequality. Many other countries have seen little change in poverty levels, and inequality has either remained fairly constant or risen.

The World Bank associates greater globalization with increased growth, declining poverty, and falling inequality—especially globally. But other data call this optimistic scenario into question. A number of studies of trade have shown that its liberalization in developing countries does not reduce poverty or inequality. The so-called skill bias associated with trade and foreign investment today often means that more highly skilled workers gain more from international integration than do low-skilled ones, which tends to exacerbate the degree of within-country inequality. Interestingly, inequality seems to also have risen recently in the developed countries. This outcome was not unexpected. Standard models of trade suggest that in rich countries, high-skilled workers should gain the most from globalization and low-skilled ones should be the losers; this is the opposite of what should happen in the poor countries. This seems to have occurred in a number of developed countries, although it has probably been tempered by the redistributive effects of the welfare state. Inequality has thus risen in a number of developed countries.

The more surprising outcome has been that low-skilled workers in the developing world have not done better. While there are now numerous reasons articulated for this result, it is a problem for poverty reduction and equity in the developing world, especially since these countries by and large do not have well-developed welfare states. The impact of financial crises and their diffusion in a global system are also concerns with regard to poverty and inequality. Some argue that such crises are more likely, more intense, and spread more broadly in a globalized world. Others point out that with an open economy domestic and international shocks may balance each other out and actually make the system more stable. There is little doubt, however, that these financial shocks can have negative consequences for countries. The Asian financial crisis of the late 1990s and the recent global financial crisis have both increased poverty and inequality. How governments shape the globalization process in their countries seems to be important in influencing the way globalization affects poverty and inequality. This suggests that countries will have quite different experiences with globalization.

Politics and Democratization

Globalization has also been credited with having effects on politics. Some argue that it has helped spread democracy and put pressure on leaders to democratize. Democracy has certainly increased globally since the 1980s. But has this been due to globalization? Globalization through an open economy or through international pressure generated by international institutions or norm entrepreneurs may induce leaders to adopt more democratic forms of governance if they want to be members of the international system. Some argue the reverse: Democratization was necessary for the change in policies in many countries that led to greater globalization. The causal connection between democratization and globalization is much debated. There is also the difficult question of whether democracy and globalization are compatible. Political regimes practice democracy within their boundaries, and publics see their governments as responsible for the outcomes they experience. But in a globalized world both of these may be compromised. Democracy may have little meaning if the most important outcomes result from global forces and if governments can do little to affect these forces. The supposed democratic deficit in the EU is one manifestation of this problem. The growing number of international institutions may also be a related concern. Many of these institutions are established to facilitate international cooperation and prevent countries from pursuing beggar-thy-neighbor policies. But if they take decision-making power away from governments, they may undermine democracy at home and the public's faith in it. Others have argued that democracy may be enhanced by such international institutions. The spread of democracy and this wave of globalization seem to have gone hand in hand; how countries react over time to a highly globalized world may or may not be propitious for democracy.

Conflict

Globalization may have an impact on conflict as well. The frequency of international wars has declined steadily since the World Wars, but civil wars had risen in frequency until recently. Some research suggests that aspects of globalization can reduce conflict, especially interstate war. Research has shown that increased trade among countries, increased foreign investment, and trade agreements are all associated with less international conflict. The so-called international capitalist peace is one example of this argument. International institutions also seem to have a similar relationship: The more of them a country joins, the less likely it is to get into military conflicts. There do not seem to be similar connections for civil war. On the other side of the ledger, however, as countries trade and invest more with each other, they become more likely to have trade and investment disputes. Over time these can exacerbate, if not create, conflicts. Furthermore, as distant countries and peoples are brought into ever closer contact, the potential for misunderstandings and disputes rises as their different cultures, values, and beliefs clash; the so-called clash of civilizations is more likely in a highly interdependent world. As their interdependence increases, countries also become more vulnerable to the actions of other states. International economic ties have the potential to be used as political leverage. An interesting example is the case of China and the United States in the early 2000s. The growth of trade and investment ties between the two countries has resulted in very large and imbalanced flows of capital and trade from China to the United States; these economic linkages can serve as potential political levers for both sides. The relationship has become much more complex and fraught with political stress. Some think that these ties will dampen any propensity to engage militarily; others see them as potential sparks for a future conflict. Globalization may reduce tendencies toward conflict by making it more costly since countries will have to break their economic ties if they fight; or it may induce conflict as they have more and more linkages that can lead to disputes.

State Capacity to Govern and International Cooperation

Questions have arisen about the impact of globalization on state capacity. That is, does globalization weaken countries and erode their capacity to govern? States are often judged by their capacity to manage their economies, to respond to crises, and to provide public goods such as health care, national defense, and education. As they become increasingly intertwined in a global economy, states may lose the ability to manage their economies. The smaller the national economy relative to the world economy, the more likely is this outcome. Countries will experience the externalities of other countries' policies but will often be unable to manage these negative consequences. Losing control over monetary policy, especially if a country opens its capital account and lets its currency float, is a well-known example of this. Tax competition among states in a globalized world is another concern, since taxes provide the resources for governments to provide public goods. The race-to-the-bottom phenomenon in general that is associated with globalization can signal a country's increasing loss of control over its economy and perhaps its polity. As noted above, for democracies this loss of control can be especially worrisome as it may induce a loss of public faith in the government and in democracy overall.

On the other hand, international cooperation and international institutions may help states alleviate the problems associated with globalization. State behavior can create negative externalities for others even in a system that is not very globalized. But without globalization it may be very hard for states to cooperate to address these externalities. Globalization may awaken states to the need for organized cooperation. It may induce the creation of international institutions that help states deal with these externalities and thus provide greater political capacity than otherwise. One can think of the EU in this light. The states within the EU may now have greater capacity as a group to affect their economies than they did before joining the EU. Individually they might not be able to manage the pressures of globalization but with an institutionalized cooperative regime they may be much better able to do so. The recent interest of countries such as Iceland in joining the EU after the 2008 financial crisis suggests such an outcome. Globalization no doubt creates or exacerbates problems that do not respect national borders, but it may also contain pressures that allow countries to better respond to those problems.

Convergence Among States

Globalization has also been associated with policy and institutional convergence among states.

Some have suggested that as countries open their economies they become more likely to adopt similar policies and institutions. This convergence process can be driven by different pressures. Some attribute it to the power of the world's hegemon; some, to the increased vulnerability of states to the pressures of international institutions; some, to increased competition among states; others, to a learning process undertaken by countries. Whatever the cause, this convergence seems to have occurred in economic policy and institutions. The widespread adoption of neoliberal policies, or the so-called Washington Consensus, has been notable since the late 1980s. Other examples are the decisions by many countries to create independent central banks and to allow their currencies to float. This process has been remarked in other areas, from the creation of bureaucracies to deal with science and technology issues to the turn to democracy itself. Globalization may narrow the choices that states have and pressure them to adopt similar institutional forms and practices. To the extent that these forms and practices result in better outcomes, this process may be welcomed. However, if they are not productive for states, then this convergence process may be a negative for governments everywhere.

When this convergence pressure extends to cultural and social life, it is often seen as a negative force. Losing the cultural and social diversity that are associated with distinct regions, ethnic groups, languages, and nations is an often remarked effect of globalization. The disappearance of many languages and the increasing use of English are two such examples. For some, this is a benefit since transaction costs are greatly reduced if all people speak the same language, and the dream of a common global language has a long history. The pressure on countries or peoples to curtail certain practices and rituals that are not considered "modern" or "civilized" is said to be growing as well. Debate rages over whether countries have the right to condone all types of practices within their borders or whether there exist certain minimal standards that all countries must follow. And the end of some practices, such as slavery, has been widely applauded. The decrease in both communication and transaction costs in a globalized world has obviously helped intensify such convergence. External pressures to conform to global norms may be stronger today than ever but such pressures have always existed. Today they are less likely to be imposed through the use of force or conquest but that does not mean these pressures are less powerful.

Scholars also worry that a global system is an increasingly interconnected one where problems in one country or region can spread more rapidly, forcefully, and widely than in a less interconnected environment. The increasing ease of transportation, for example, makes the spread of disease much faster and perhaps deadlier. The communications revolution does much the same for new ideas and fads. Information cascades are more likely in such systems. This means that instability may be greater as well. Small changes to the system radiate out in all directions and can lead to large consequences. There is a concern that crises are also more likely and more contagious in such a globalized world. The Asian financial crisis of the late 1990s and the recent global financial crisis of 2008 to 2009 are two such examples. Some have argued that the world's largest economies have experienced a "great moderation" since the 1970s with a dampening of business cycles and decreasing inflation due partially to greater international exposure. Others see an international economy beset by rising volatility over time, as crises multiply and spread. Globalization may stabilize a system by spreading problems out and bringing counterbalancing forces to bear, but it may also destabilize a system by creating a network of linkages among all countries and across all sectors that transmits and magnifies problems.

Domestic Economies

In addition to the question about which countries gain and lose from globalization, there is the issue of which groups gain and lose domestically. Many see globalization as strengthening the hand of capital owners and right-wing political parties as opposed to labor owners and left-wing parties. With a global economy where capital can move relatively freely, it becomes advantaged domestically. Globalization changes the domestic balance of power between business and labor. When owners of capital do not like a government policy or fear labor has become too strong, they can often move to a new political environment that is more accommodating. This process can then generate race-to-the-bottom pressures as governments try to retain capital in their country by deregulating and adopting more business-friendly policies. Some claim that globalization has helped undermine labor unions and other forms of labor market organization. This process can then influence the political system. If right-wing parties represent business interests more, they may be strengthened by globalization. Left-wing parties and their programs may seem increasingly unattractive as they "scare" capital away and perhaps slow down growth. Evidence for this effect is mixed. Some claim that left-wing parties and governments actually do a better job wooing capital and thus are not disadvantaged by globalization; they may even make better partners for international business than right-wing parties. Some scholars see no effect of globalization on domestic politics; they claim that domestic political institutions filter and shape such external pressures so that their ultimate effects are a function of domestic politics. Preexisting domestic institutions and practices then govern whether and how globalization affects internal politics. The impact of globalization on political power within and between countries is a topic of debate and great importance for future research.

Limits of Current Research

The consequences of globalization could thus be widespread. They might affect economics, politics, society, and culture. Existing research points out that globalization has affected economic growth rates, poverty, inequality, democracy, conflict, state capacity, policy and institutional convergence, cultural diversity, volatility and the diffusion of crises, and balance of power between capital and labor. But it provides little consensus on the direction or magnitude of these effects.

Globalization and the Future

Given the many consequences that globalization might have, one question that is often raised is whether countries can manage its impact. This is especially important to the extent that globalization has negative consequences. Many types of problems that have been endemic to countries for centuries have taken on a new perspective in a globalized world. Problems that were national have become transnational. The ability of countries to realize many of their basic goals has become more and more tied to the actions of other countries. Economic prosperity domestically often depends now on international trade and capital movements around the globe; national security from all sorts of threats depends on the behavior of other countries and nonstate actors; environmental conditions rely on the behavior of other agents globally; and public health relies more and more on transnational factors and the behavior of international agents. Countries have always faced such problems; it is just that their impact and resolution depend more and more on agents outside the state itself. Globalization is intimately connected to this process. By increasing contacts and interactions among countries and peoples, it helps make many issues transnational in character, rather than national.

Given that governance is largely the domain of nation-states, is there anything that can be done to address these transnational problems? One country can rarely dictate another's economic, environmental, security, or public health policy, for example. But to deal with transnational problems, coordination of policies may be the best way forward. In particular, cooperation where countries coordinate their policies to arrive at mutually preferable outcomes may be essential. Globalization may facilitate cooperation; it may make the costs of failing to cooperate so high that countries are more willing to try. But it may also make the stakes of cooperation much higher and thus render it less likely.

International institutions may be one way to address these concerns. In a globalized era, some see such institutions as essential for dealing with transnational problems. Countries alone cannot successfully deal with them; they require changes in the behavior of other states. International institutions that states voluntarily join and comply with may help them. Such institutions may help states realize cooperative outcomes; they may provide transparency and lower transaction costs for negotiating solutions to transnational issues; they may embody global norms and practices that allow states to identify focal points for cooperation and/or help them enforce compliance with international norms and cooperative agreements. These are the potential benefits of global institutions. They may have costs as well. Not all international institutions function adequately; some have serious internal defects that cause them to operate poorly. Others are deadlocked by internal divisions. Some are dominated by one or two states that coerce others to adopt their preferred norms and practices even if these are not very beneficial for the others. International institutions cannot be seen as a costless and efficient solution to all transnational problems. But many of them have shown some ability either to prevent transnational problems for worsening (e.g., the WHO and the WTO in times of crisis) or to allow states to cooperate in order to better manage problems in a globalized world (e.g., the EU).

A related issue is concern over globalization's future. If one adopts the secular view of it, then little chance exists that the increasing contact and interactions among peoples and countries can be reversed. Indeed if there is technological progress, there is likely to be increasing globalization; more and more contact and interaction are inevitable as technology brings people in the world closer together. On the other hand, the more cyclical view suggests that globalization comes and goes in waves depending on political, economic, and social reactions. We may now be experiencing the height of this period of globalization. Forces for a backlash against the pressure exerted by increasing contacts and interactions among peoples and states may be gaining strength. The economic and financial crisis of 2008 to 2009 may be a prelude to this type of backlash. In this view, governments can respond in ways that curtail or reverse globalization; they can protect their economies, close their borders, end participation in international institutions, and take other steps that seal them off from the rest of the world. The period between 1914 and 1945 is one example of this. The question, of course, is what would be the costs and benefits of such a course of action and would governments be able to achieve any kind of meaningful autonomy or autarchy, given the technologies we now have and the public expectations about their connections to the rest of the world. Whether globalization is reversible or not is a question of great import; the costs of doing so would be a key factor. More realistic, perhaps, are questions about whether globalization can be slowed down or managed in ways that are better for all concerned.

In conclusion, debate rages about globalization. A number of theories exist about its sources. Technological change, international political hegemony, global normative convergence, and/or independent country reactions have all been cited as major causes of globalization. Globalization's effects have been debated in even greater intensity and breadth. Substantial literatures exist on whether globalization has affected economic growth rates, poverty, inequality, democracy, conflict, state capacity, policy and institutional convergence, cultural diversity, volatility and the diffusion of crises, and balance of power between capital and labor. Agreement on the nature of its effects on any of these is scarce. For some, the balance of its impact has been negative in almost all domains; for others, it is seen as largely positive, especially in the economic and political areas; and for yet others, it has costs and benefits that are hard to calculate and summarize overall. One fact not in doubt is that globalization is an important feature of our world these days; it seems to have consequences for all domains of economic, political, social, and cultural affairs. How to manage it in order to make states, peoples, or the world better off is thus of central importance.

Helen V. Milner
Princeton University
Princeton, New Jersey, United States

See also Capitalism; Colonialism; Conditionality; Democracy, Theories of; Development, Political; Governance; Hegemony; Human Rights, Comparative Perspectives; Human Rights in International Relations; Inequality, Economic; International Monetary Fund (IMF); International Organizations; International Trade; Multinational Corporations (MNCs); Neoliberalism; Power; Realism in International Relations; Trade Liberalization; World Bank; World Trade Organization (WTO)

Further Readings

Bhagwati, J. (2004). *In defense of globalization.* New York: Oxford University Press.

Cox, R. W. (1987). *Production, power, and world order: Social forces and the making of history.* New York: Columbia University Press.

Eichengreen, B. (2008). *Globalizing capital.* Princeton, NJ: Princeton University Press.
Frieden, J. (2008). *Global capitalism.* New York: W. W. Norton.
Garrett, G. (1998). *Partisan politics in the global economy.* New York: Cambridge University Press.
Greider, W. (1997). *One world, ready or not: The manic logic of global capitalism.* New York: Simon & Schuster.
Hirschman, A. O. (1980). *National power and the structure of foreign trade.* Berkeley: University of California Press. (Original work published 1945)
Hoogvelt, A. M. M. (1997). *Globalisation and the postcolonial world: The new political economy of development.* Houndmills, UK: Macmillan.
Keohane, R. O., & Milner, H. V. (Eds.). (1996). *Internationalization and domestic politics.* New York: Cambridge University Press.
Kindleberger, C. P. (1973). *The world in depression.* Berkeley: University of California Press.
Milanovic, B. (2007). *Worlds apart: Measuring international and global inequality.* Princeton, NJ: Princeton University Press.
Polanyi, K. (1957). *The great transformation: The political and economic origins of our time.* Boston: Beacon Press. (Original work published 1944)
Robinson, W. I. (2004). *A theory of global capitalism: Production, class, and state in a transnational world.* Baltimore: Johns Hopkins University Press.
Rodrik, D. (1997). *Has globalization gone too far?* Washington, DC: Institute for International Economics.
Stiglitz, J. E. (2002). *Globalization and its discontents.* New York: W. W. Norton.
Strange, S. (1988). *States and markets.* London: Frances Pinter.
Wolf, M. (2004). *Why globalization works.* New Haven, CT: Yale University Press.
Woods, N. (2006). *The globalizers.* Ithaca, NY: Cornell University Press.
World Bank. (2008). *The World Bank annual report 2008: Year in review.* Washington, DC: Author.
World Bank. (2009). *The World Bank annual report 2009: Year in review.* Washington, DC: Author.

GOVERNANCE

Amid the debate on globalization and its influence on domestic politics and institutional arrangements, it is intriguing to note the resilience of national institutions, policy styles, and perceptions of the role of the state in society. True, many countries that displayed significantly different governance arrangements a few decades ago today present a more common governance model. Even so, however, the legacy of—or more correctly, perhaps, the continued support for—traditions of statehood, governance, and collective action loom large. These traditions can be seen as value systems that have evolved over an extensive period of time, continuously reproduced in public policy and public discourse. If there is strong resilience in institutions and policy, this in part can be attributed to strong political and administrative tradition. This entry examines the nature of the contemporary state and then examines the different governance models as means of solidifying policy preferences.

Although it makes sense to think of these value systems as traditions, they can mostly be traced back to specific political contexts and policy choice (see, e.g., Francis Castles, 1993). For instance, the Asian "developmental state" (Chalmers Johnson, 1982) and the Scandinavian and continental European welfare state models (Gøsta Esping-Andersen, 1990) evolved through a series of political choices about the role of the state, the market, and civil society. Against this backdrop, the purpose of this entry is to explore the linkages between policy choice and models of governance. Conventional wisdom holds that policy choice is largely a product of institutional arrangements. The immediate interest in this entry is to see to what extent those institutions, in turn, can be related to a more overarching set of values and beliefs about the role of the state. (*Value* refers to everything that is considered to have a value, be it material, ideological, ethical, or other, by most people/citizens.) Should that be the case, we will be well under way to connect a typology of governance arrangements to broad categorizations of policy. There has been some work done on the relationship between different types of policy, drawing on the familiar typology developed by Ted Lowi, and the institutional arrangements of the state but this is a vast research field and much more work remains before we have a more complete account of the linkages between governance arrangements and policy styles.

This entry then looks at a couple of different governance models as a form of institutionalization of overarching policy choices in terms of constitutional and institutional arrangements. The underlying premise of this entry is that the institutions framing policy choice are themselves "locked in" by fundamental policy choices concerning the role of the state in society and its centrality in governance. The predominant governance model of a particular country is not a given but reflects entrenched notions about the role of the state, the market, and civil society.

These values and perceptions become deeply institutionalized over time and elevated into political culture above and beyond day-to-day policy making. Even so, however, when observed over a longer stretch of time distinct changes in these value systems can be observed. The role of government in the United States changed fundamentally from Lyndon Johnson's Great Society project in the 1960s to Ronald Reagan's neoliberal policy style in the 1980s; in Britain, Labour under Tony Blair and Gordon Brown looked significantly different from Labour under Harold Wilson; in Japan, the relationship between the Liberal Democratic Party (LDP), the bureaucracy, and the corporate sector has changed profoundly since the 1960s; and in Scandinavia, the welfare state today has very different organization and modus operandi from those of the 1960s or 1970s, and so on. Thus, however entrenched and institutionalized these values may be, they do nonetheless change, sometimes abruptly, sometimes more subtly.

The hypothesis that specific cases of policy making are embedded in more overarching values and norms, perhaps even a social theory, concerning what should be the role of the state in society opens up for potential theoretical circularities. It could be that the more general values are simply defined as the sum of specific policies, in which case the argument about embeddedness and institutionalization becomes circular. And, even if different specific types of policies can be theoretically linked to different governance arrangements, a causal mechanism is still needed to explain how and why that would be the case. A more plausible way of looking at such relationships would be to suggest that policy and governance tend to foster and reinforce each other. For instance, "big government" service models tend to emphasize redistributive policies and equality and equal treatment in service delivery, while neoliberal policies emphasize economic growth and a customer-oriented, market-like model of public service. Thus, different aspects of public policy and public administration practices are closely related.

This entry first looks at four broad dimensions of governance that relate to different aspects of the role of the state in society. It then discusses three different models of governance: state-centric, liberal-democratic, and network-based governance. The third section merges these two analyses to elaborate the features and logics of the three governance models. Since issues related to institutions, institutionalization, and deinstitutionalization are central to the present analysis, these issues are discussed before a concluding section sums up the entry.

Dimensions of Governance

Nation-states around the world offer a wide variety in terms of how they organize their governance. Perhaps the most obvious and striking differences relate to the fundamental aspects of state organization in terms of their institutional arrangement. Thus, there are federal states and unitary states, centralized states and decentralized states, and states with a long tradition in regulating markets and social behavior while other states see their role as enabling and facilitating markets and free individuals.

These institutional arrangements are highly path dependent. They evolved as constitutional systems defining the model of governance, which were believed to reflect popular expectations and the requirements of a political system to govern the country. Thus, for instance, American or Canadian federalism was the model that was believed to provide the optimal balance between national interests and regional autonomy in those vast territories, while the unitary state was the preferred arrangement in smaller European countries. These are complex issues to capture analytically because they are shaped by the history of the country and its unification process, its state tradition, the homogeneity of the population, and its geopolitical context.

One strategy to approach these issues is to relate them to a set of dimensions of governance. If we conceive of governance as the pursuit of collective interests, with the state as a coordinating and enabling actor, we can clearly see that governance is both a process that is endogenous to the state—division of labor, competencies, jurisdictions, and resources—and a process in which the state interacts with other actors in society. Therefore, we will want the dimensions of governance to capture both the internal and external aspects of governance. Below, four such dimensions of governance are briefly outlined. These dimensions describe different relationships between the state, the society, and the market.

The governance dimensions speak to very basic issues about the organization of the state and its role in society. Therefore, it should not be surprising to find that they are normatively charged and are frequently topics of political disunity in many countries.

Popular Representation Versus Institutional Autonomy

The first governance dimension measures the degree to which the state is responsive to popular demands and expectations, and it places that responsiveness in juxtaposition to a high degree of autonomy for the state's political and administrative institutions. For governance to qualify as democratic, it is essential that the state responds to popular demands and incumbent political parties are allowed to shape the policy agenda and to engage in public discourse. At the same time, however, institutions need to have some integrity and autonomy, both in relationship to partisan ideologies and to direct popular pressures in order to be able to fulfill their role in the policy process. Institutions that develop close and bilateral relationships with parochial societal interests can develop networks as alternative instruments of policy implementation, but they will have problems in implementing policies that discriminate among policy targets. This is, thus, a dimension where both extremes are unsatisfactory from a governance perspective; democratic governance is contingent on both popular input on public policy and some degree of institutional autonomy allowing those institutions to pursue policies that might not enjoy popular support but are necessary to the state.

Another example of the complexities associated with this dimension can be seen in the relationship between politicians and bureaucrats. On the one hand, we expect the civil service to be responsive to the government of the day, implementing its political wishes without prejudice. On the other hand, we expect the public administration to be guided by values such as impartiality and by due process and public law, and a "politicization" of the administrative system is often seen as a controversial development that could compromise the integrity of the bureaucracy. Again, both extremes on the dimension are problematic in a governance perspective whereas some form of combination of the two positions fosters democratic governance or is indeed integral to governance.

Societal Integrity Versus Institutional Capacity

A second dimension of governance refers to the tension between fundamental values related to individual freedom, on the one hand, and the need for institutions to encroach on that freedom in order to ensure collective interests and values, on the other. This dilemma and the question it raises on forms of justification for political control over individuals is a major field of research and discourse in political philosophy, and the finer details of that debate are not probed too deeply here. There are obviously values related to the individual qua an individual and other values derived from the individual as a member of a polity. The tension between these two types of values plays out almost daily in a variety of policy sectors such as environmental policy and climate change, crime prevention, social welfare, and tax policy. The government's need to collect information about individual behavior has become a major issue, particularly in matters related to national security where the need for surveillance stands against personal integrity. A similar debate has surrounded means-tested welfare state programs where government agencies require beneficiaries to submit detailed information about their standard of living and income.

The degree to which government should have access to private information or regulate personal behavior is ultimately a normative issue where different interests are weighed against each other; it is not possible to objectively delineate the pursuit of individual interests aggregated into government action, on the one hand, and the rights of individuals to act freely, on the other. The point here is instead that some encroachment on individual freedom is necessary for government to govern society, while the precise extent to which such encroachment can be justified remains a normative issue that reemerges fairly regularly on the political agenda. Meanwhile, constitutional reform and institutional design have to wrestle with this issue in a more mundane and pragmatic fashion.

Institutional capacity is a key variable in a broader governance perspective. According to one perspective, contemporary society has become too complex for any single actor to provide effective steering or coordination. Even if government previously had the capacity to fulfill those roles, the growing complexity has undermined the governing capacity of the state. As a result, governance is conducted through networks, partnerships, and other interactive instruments of coordination and collective action. In terms of institutional capacity, this perspective argues that in contemporary governance, such capacity is not so much a matter of constitutional mandates as a continuous process of reproducing institutional leverage through cooperation with societal actors.

National Interests Versus Subnational Autonomy

All systems of government integrate political and administrative action on different institutional levels. Exactly how that integration is organized is, however, a matter of substantive cross-national variation. Thus, subnational political systems are granted some degree of autonomy in relationship to central government (for an overview, see Alan Norton, 1994).

The basic logic of organizing government in this way is one of efficiency and expediency, but there are also important aspects of these arrangements that speak to the development of democratic governance. The efficiency argument is fairly obvious; it simply does not make any sense to have the national government organize water and sewage system maintenance or garbage disposal service in every town and village throughout the country. The democracy argument holds that participation in local public affairs socializes citizens into the democracy form of governance. For that socialization to work, local government must have some autonomy, some jurisdiction, within which the local demos can make decisions pertaining to public matters in their locale. Also, the democratic theory of local government holds that the role of elected officials should be to cater to the interests of the populace in a nonpartisan way. Ideology and division should not be imported from national politics and brought onto the local political scene.

This somewhat cozy account of local government is troubled by the existence of national interests, which play out in the local territory. In issues such as infrastructural development, the location of windmill parks, or the deposit of nuclear waste, national interests frequently encounter fierce opposition from local governments. The question then becomes under what conditions should the central government be allowed to override the will of a local demos? The problem is larger than simple not-in-my-backyard (NIMBY) politics; it relates ultimately to the problem of two competing *demoi*: the national and the local.

Again, the two extremes of this dimension—complete dominance of national interests and extensive, unconditional local autonomy—raise serious questions in terms of the quality and, indeed, the prospects, of governance. Instead, some middle ground position characterized by dialogue between central and local government with respect for both the national and local *demoi* should provide for better governance.

As is the case with the previous dimension, this dimension, too, speaks directly to governance issues in several different ways. If central, regional, and local governments have overlapping competencies and jurisdictions, that is, if policy making involves several levels of government, the policy process will be characterized by a significant vertical dimension of resource allocation, control, and bargaining. If, on the other hand, policy sectors are largely divided among institutional levels so that central government is in control of some policy sectors, regional government of other sectors, and local governments of yet other sectors, the process becomes less complex and will not involve much interaction among institutional levels. It is thus essential to acknowledge the political nature of state–local relationships; while a formal institutional analysis depicts those relationships mainly as one of division of labor, a closer inspection of central–local interactions will uncover struggles over control, financial resources, and policy.

Another example of the governance ramifications of central–local relationships is that they define to a large extent the relationship between a city and key players in the local environment. Urbanists would refer to this as the interplay between horizontal and vertical dimensions of autonomy where the vertical dimension defines much of the preconditions for horizontal, urban governance.

Autonomous Markets Versus Regulation

The degree to which government regulates markets is often seen as a fundamental aspect of the left–right division in political life. Parties on the political right typically insist that markets work best if they are left alone; market regulation chokes the market, rendering it an inefficient instrument of resource allocation. Government regulation in this perspective distorts market mechanisms, perverts pricing, and removes incentives for risk taking and entrepreneurialism. Leftist parties, on the other hand, maintain that markets need to be brought under some public control partly in order to ensure that they do not create politically undesirable outcomes such as vast differences in wealth and life chances. Many of the areas of society that are essential to the type of social reform that parties on the political left pursue (e.g., housing, education, health care, and work), operate under market control. Therefore, market regulation is an important instrument to insert political objectives into markets.

Market regulation, as mentioned earlier, is politically controversial. While there may be agreement among political actors on long-term policy goals such as economic growth, issues become charged as soon as the role of the market toward those political goals is to be defined. Parties right of center will argue that markets left alone will deliver the highest economic growth, whereas parties on the political Left will insist that markets cannot deliver a socially acceptable economic development or that markets are simply unable to solve collective problems.

That having been said, however, there is also a fair amount of pragmatism surrounding the issue of market regulation. The American political culture has historically, albeit with few but important exceptions, heralded the notion of free markets and small government. Meanwhile, the economic history of the United States is replete with examples of publicly driven large-scale infrastructure development projects and public service delivery, according to Jeff Madrick (2009). More broadly, there is an understanding from Adam Smith's classic book in the field, *On the Wealth of Nations*, onward that markets need a regulatory framework to function properly. Furthermore, the evidence supporting the argument that nonregulated markets perform better than markets under some degree of government regulation is agnostic. The key problems seem to revolve around issues such as designing the governance of a market economy that generates growth at the same time as it solves problems of coordination and provides consumer protection and sustainable development.

This leads us to consider the critical distinction between regulation *of* and *within* markets. The regulation of markets means providing a regulatory framework defining property, contracts, and so on and a mechanism for settling disputes among market actors. Regulation in a market refers to political and administrative control of market mechanisms such as price or supply by regulating entrance to the market. The former type of regulation is nondiscriminatory, while the latter form is discriminatory and targeted to ensure collective interests in the markets such as consumer protection and price caps on specific goods provided by the market. Such public presence in the market could also manifest itself in taxes or incentives to sanction or encourage different forms of market behavior.

From a governance perspective, this dimension provides important information about the political economy of governing. Peter Hall and David Soskice's (2001) distinction between "liberal" and "coordinated" market economies suggests that the degree to which the capitalist economy is embedded in domestic governance varies considerably among different countries. In coordinated market economies, with the continental European, Scandinavian, and several Asian countries as leading examples, interactions between the state and private capital are institutionalized, making concerted governance less complicated and politically sensitive than in the Anglo-American liberal market economies. Also, market regulation is a policy instrument defining a political objective in the market. That objective could, however, also be implemented in less obtrusive ways, thereby facilitating a higher degree of concerted action among public and private interests.

As is the case with the other governance dimensions, both end points of the dimension—completely free or completely regulated markets—are neither efficient from a market point of view nor perhaps desirable from a democratic governance perspective.

Governance Models

Let us now turn to a brief presentation of a few stylized models of governance. In 2005, Jon Pierre, together with Guy Peters, outlined a theory of governance drawing on a typology of governance models. The basic assumption sustaining that analysis was that all governance arrangements have to fulfill a number of roles or functions, but different governance models accord the state and societal actors widely different significance for those roles. The authors found that both the most state-centric governance model and, at the other end of the spectrum, network-based governance had problems with defining a state–society interaction that blended institutional autonomy with openness to the interests and expertise found among societal actors. Instead, governance models between the two extreme positions on the continuum, such as the corporatist governance model, fared relatively well; they were capable of blending some indigenous capacity to steer with a fair openness in state–society exchanges.

The defining feature of governance theory, as opposed to more traditional government-centric accounts of governing, is the centrality of exchanges between the state and actors in its external environment. The three models outlined here describe different types of such relationships and interactions. However, the present space only allows for very brief accounts of complex and multidimensional governance arrangements.

State-Centric Governance

The first governance model portrays the state exercising firm control over its territory and population. The state has few contingencies to other societal actors and does not have to be concerned about any lack of institutional capacity to impose its will on society. The typical governing style of government in state-centric governance is to use policy instruments sufficiently distinct to ensure the desired change in social behavior. That includes securing tax revenues of sufficient level to sustain those projects that the state wishes to implement. The state, in this model of governance, sees little reason to engage in collaborative forms of governance or service delivery.

If we accept Joel Migdal's (2001) argument that state and society mutually constitute each other, democratic forms of state-centric governance occur where there is a societal expectation for such a leading role of the state. That means that although government will not refrain to use obtrusive policy instruments, the societal submission to the state suggests that the state does rarely have to throw much weight to impose its will on society. Whether it is because the state sees it as its role to provide distinct leadership or because society expects it, state-centric governance is built on the centrality of the state. That centrality is obviously a significant asset in terms of being able to steer and control societal development. However, it tends to entail a fairly unidirectional process of state–society exchange whereby the state executes its preferences on society. States in this model of governance easily become self-referential and arrogant vis-à-vis societal actors and may thus be unaware or oblivious of societal change.

France is historically seen as a prime example of state-centric governance although that state predominance is today somewhat less articulated. We also find examples of state-centric governance in many Latin American countries such as Argentina (not least under Juan Perón) and Uruguay. Note that state-centric governance does not correlate with the existence of leftist political regimes. The legitimacy of state encroachment on society stems from a symbiotic notion of the state embodying the people and catering to its interests like parents look after their children. In this model of governance, nationalism plays a significant role and it is legitimate, and expected, of the government to intervene in markets if it can be justified with reference to interests of the state.

Liberal-Democratic Governance

The previous model of governance is a relatively rare phenomenon in time and space. Liberal-democratic governance is a much more common creature. The Anglo-American democracies and the continental European countries belong to this category as do some of the Asian countries, particularly with regard to their post-2000 model of governance. Thus, although the fundamental features of the governance model cover a fairly narrow section of the spectrum of different governance models, we should expect to find a fair degree of empirical heterogeneity as we inspect this model in more detail.

In terms of democratic theory, liberal-democratic governance rests on a notion of a distinct separation between state and society. The state is not expected to interfere in markets and to honor values of individual freedom and personal integrity. However, the state is expected to play a key role in the regulation of markets by upholding a regulatory framework for markets and ensuring free competition. Thus, in the spirit of Adam Smith, the "regulatory state" model sees the government enforcing antitrust legislation to protect markets from cartels and other forms of improper market behavior. Thus, there is an emphasis of regulation *of* the market and an equally strong normative belief that government should regulate *within* markets. In the parlance of economic theory, it is the role of the state in this governance model to prevent market failure. It should not, however, pursue political objectives through regulation within markets.

The state in liberal-democratic governance is more deeply embedded in society than state-centric governance, yet it is able to maintain some degree of institutional integrity in relationship to policy targets and other social interests. The state is not alien to collaborative forms of governance but insists on playing the role of a primus inter pares in those arrangements. That means that government will consult with social partners in policy making but will reserve the right to make the final decisions on policy design. Thus, in some ways liberal-democratic governance could be just as intrusive on society as state-centric governance, but the mechanisms and processes sustaining that capacity of the state are less derived from institutional strength and more a result of social bargaining.

The different forms of corporatism that have been a trademark of state–society exchanges in several European countries and also in Japan fit nicely into this model of governance. This applies in particular to the tripartite arrangements between the state, private capital, and labor where the state can be both an arbitrator as well as a negotiating party. The significance of these corporatist arrangements has declined in several countries remains strong in, for instance, Denmark.

Network Governance

Some time ago now, Rod Rhodes gave new momentum to the emerging debate on contemporary governance by arguing that policy networks were the key instrument of governance, hence governance of policy sectors saw government as one of a large number of actors. Indeed, cohesive policy networks had the capacity to resist government policy and were basically capable of governing the sector themselves. Coupled with the growing literature on the governance problems that stemmed from the increasing social complexity and multilevel institutional arrangements of the political and administrative sphere, networks and other interactive forms of governance became the key focus of a large group of governance scholars.

Network governance scholars deliver a powerful argument about the lack of institutional capacity and integrity of the state. Short of those features, segments of the state embark in a range of different interactive arenas where collective solutions are designed and implemented in concert with social partners. Policy becomes reflective of the contextualized process from which it evolves; interactive governance forms have difficulties with imposing unpopular policies on those social actors and collective action becomes to a large extent defined by the least common denominator among the network participants. That said, network governance provides public officials with a multitude of social contacts that ensures up-to-date information about social change. Network governance therefore provides quicker and more effective linkages between changing societal problems and a political response to those changes.

It is difficult to think of any national context where networks do not exist. The intriguing question is how such forms of governance are integrated with more traditional, hierarchical governance and administrative arrangements and what the consequences are of blending different governance models. Network governance is predicated on substantive autonomy and empowerment for lower-level civil servants so that they can engage in meaningful dialogue with social partners. Thus, network governance challenges traditional top-down channels of communication in public sector organizations, both in terms of policy implementation and in bringing information from networks to the attention of the senior levels of the organization.

Governance as Institutionalization of Policy Choices

Following these discussions about dimensions and models of governance, this entry now presents a more elaborated account of different stylized models of governance with regard to how they score on the overarching dimensions of governance.

It is particularly challenging to look at the dynamic nature of these interactions. The dimensions of governance described earlier could easily produce a functionalist analysis of the roles of government in governance with all that entails in terms of static modeling. However, thinking about how government resolves these issues and tasks in a governance perspective yields a highly dynamic account of the role of the state since the core assumption in governance theory is that collective objectives are pursued in a variety of different concerted and collaborative process between state and society. The key assumption being explored in this analysis is that the degree to which political actors and institutions shape the governance process determines much of how specific governance arrangements relate to the three dimensions of governance.

State-Centric Governance

With the leading role of the state in this model of governance, we would expect that its institutions enjoy a high degree of autonomy in relationship to societal actors and interests. Since those institutions have very little collaborative interaction with societal actors, there is little incentive for them to make concessions on policy. Also, given the centrality of the state and its insistence on "going it alone" in terms of policy implementation and service delivery, government institutions will have the administrative and financial resources required to play those roles.

State-centric governance is also likely to display a priority for national interests over local autonomy. It is interesting to note that many of the empirical contexts that we associate with state-centric governance, again with France as a leading example, have weak and fragmented local government systems. This is obviously not a feature only of countries with state-centric governance—consider for the sake of comparison the equally fragmented local government system in the United States—but it makes sense to stipulate that state-centric societies do not develop strong subnational government as that could create or exacerbate central–local conflict.

State-centric governance easily translates into strong regulation of markets. This is because these states have a path-dependent political and administrative behavior according to which they rarely yield to the interests of societal actors. The state defines its interests and objectives in the market and implements whatever regulation is required toward those ends.

All these features of state-centric governance—strong, insulated institutions, central government control, tight market regulation, and so on—are in fact reflections of society as much as of the state. It is very difficult to think of a democratic state ascending to such societal predominance without the consent and indeed expectation from society. While this is a governance model that may appear to be highly obtrusive and insensitive to societal actors, a closer inspection of specific governance processes indicates that coercive policy instruments are not always necessary for the state to control society; societal actors anticipate the preferences of government and act accordingly. A case in point is the Japanese developmental state, which throughout much of the postwar period was a case of state-centric governance. Governance was coordinated within the tripod of the Liberal-Democratic Party, the bureaucracy, and leading corporate players. The chief ministry driving the economic modernization programs could ensure compliance for its plans by formulating "visions"; it rarely had to employ its institutional capacity to ensure corporate compliance with its policy, according to Johnson (1982).

However, as we look at the dimensions of governance, we can see that the case of Japan offers some intriguing patterns. For instance, although national interests were paramount through the history of Japan, not least during the postwar economic recovery, and although central–local relationships have been predominantly hierarchical, the relationship between central and subnational government has been replete with ideological conflict. Central government actively promoted the ascension of Tokyo to a global city status, triggering rivalries with several other metropolitan areas. National interests have translated into Tokyo interests, arguably at the expense of other cities.

The paradox of state-centric governance is thus that although the state has all the instruments and resources necessary to impose a strict regime on society, it rarely needs to use all that muscle as societal actors readily submit to more subtle forms of governing. Society expects the state to play a leading role in governance. When we bring state–society exchanges that are integral to governance theory into the analysis, it becomes clear that the more formal power bases that a state controls, the less it will have to use those forces.

The governance approach to these issues also suggests that states remain strong but that the sources of that strength have changed. State-centric governance, embedded in norms that legitimized such governance and prescribed long-term policy goals, defined overarching policy choices that continued to shape public policy for decades. Economic development has seen a distinct role for the state either as a coordinator of private business or as a leading player in research and development or as safeguard against overseas competition or all of the above. State-centrism has also had a major influence on the policy instruments typically employed in policy implementation. Again, this rather self-referential modus operandi proved to be a significant problem in times of rapid external change such as when globalization caught momentum, opening up society to new political, financial, and cultural influences.

Liberal-Democratic Governance

If state-centric governance presents a pattern of a state that enjoys extensive capabilities to impose its will on society but rarely has to use that leverage, an almost opposite pattern is found in liberal-democratic governance. In this governance model, the state has some political and institutional capabilities but the exercise of those power bases is more contested than is the case in state-centric governance. Thus, this governance model displays a medium level of institutional autonomy and an institutional capacity that is more contextualized than in the previous model.

The portrayal of the state in liberal-democratic theory is an idealized account of the state as distinctly separate from society. It could be seen as an extension of the Wilsonian model of public administration as firmly separated from the political sphere of the state. That model has lost much of its empirical accuracy in contemporary public administration and a similar development can be seen with regard to the separation of state and society. Migdal (2001) describes this development of the state nicely:

> Various parts or fragments of the state have allied with one another, as well as with groups outside, to further their goals. Those practices and alliances have acted to promote a variety of sets of rules, often quite distinct from those set out in the state's own official laws and regulations. These alliances, coalitions, or networks have neutralized the sharp territorial and social boundary that the first portrayal of the state has acted to establish, as well as the demarcation between the state as a pre-eminent rule maker and society as the recipient of those rules. (p. 20)

With the border between state and society thus compromised by parochial interests inside and outside the state, governance theory offers a new and promising approach to understanding the process of governing. Indeed, Migdal's account of the contemporary liberal-democratic state is an apt illustration of the contemporary liberal-democratic state, involved in collaborative governance and a rule taker almost as much as a rule maker. It might be argued that the state–society division that this model of governance departs from has become a normative myth. This myth may at some previous time have defined what constitutes proper exchanges between the state and its external environment, but given the complexities of contemporary governance the state–society separation has become impossible to sustain. That having been said, normative models still matter. As the rules of the political game, normative models provide definitions of roles for political actors and institutions. Those norms are also the foundation on which constitutions are written and amended.

In the liberal-democratic governance model, the state itself has moderate institutional capacity but makes up for that through collaboration with social partners. This can take place through corporatist models of interest representation and mediation but it can also be generated through more ad hoc models of joint ventures such as public–private partnerships. Also, states in liberal-democratic governance tend to define their chief role as a "regulatory state," providing market stability without necessarily being committed to extensive service delivery.

It is interesting to note that liberal-democratic governance would encompass both liberal and coordinated market economies. Government plays a distinctly different role in those two models of the capitalist economy, with a higher profile and more accentuated political presence in the market in the case of the coordinated market economy. According to Hall and Soskice (2001), there is also more legitimacy for articulating collective interests in economic development in the coordinated market economy than in the liberal market economy where government is expected to provide a regulatory framework for the economy but not to itself be a player in the market. Corporatism is clearly related to the coordinated market economy. This stronger legitimacy for market intervention in the coordinated market economy links it strongly to welfare state models and to overarching policy choices that give a higher priority to distributive or redistributive types of policy than to promoting economic growth.

Network Governance

This model of governance could be summarized as characterized by low institutional autonomy; its institutional capacity is to a large extent contingent on societal consent and a low degree of regulation or even self-regulation. In a model of governance where concerted action is the typical strategy to govern, the issue of institutional autonomy becomes moot as institutions do not require autonomy to engage social partners. Indeed, such autonomy could be an obstacle to creative problem solving since it suggests that there are rules defining the forms and conditions for institutions' exchange with their external environment.

The institutional capacity in network governance is limited; it is part of the logic of network governance that action is based on consent and therefore institutions can only implement those programs that other actors in the network agree to, which frequently comprises important policy targets. That having been said, however, when there is consensus for the execution of a policy, implementation is likely to be swift and efficient since interaction between institutions and their social partners continues throughout the implementation process.

The regulatory capacity of networks is high within the network itself but less so outside the network. In network governance theory, primary attention is on networks as instruments of self-regulation within a policy sector. In that perspective, networks offer regulation that, by definition, is reflective of the interests of the participants in the network.

This is not a model of governance that defines large-scale political projects such as welfare states or developmental states. It lacks the social inclusion and capacity to resolve conflicts between the network and other social constituencies. Rather, it operates within the parameters set by long-term policy objectives.

Change and Resilience in Models of Governance

The three governance models discussed in this entry are manifestations of social norms and values related to individual versus collective action, state versus market, and proactive versus reactive policies. They become institutionalized in the system of government so that state-centric governance draws on extensive institutional capabilities and a strong legitimacy of political encroachment of society, or in liberal-democratic governance where there is a search for a balance between political capabilities and individual and societal freedom.

These norms and values are reinterpreted over time. What constituted a free market in the early 20th century was different from what is today considered a free market. The developmental state was the Japanese state's response to a situation of national urgency. It became deeply institutionalized in the Japanese society for decades but was weakened during the 1980s when the downsides to aggressive progrowth policies surfaced and the most acute problems had been resolved. The Scandinavian welfare state enjoyed massive political support for several decades but has lost some of that support along with growing social affluence and increasing tax levels. The Great Society in the United States had a shorter life span and was put to rest with the election of Ronald Reagan as president in 1980.

Thus, although governance models are, by definition, institutionalized, they change over time. It is a major task in itself to account for what drives those changes. Given their institutionalization, redefining the role of the state or the market is a slow and incremental process. One type of change is where values and norms and expectations on the state are not fundamentally reassessed but instead rearticulated and given a new meaning in a new political and economic landscape. In other cases, new governance models emerge to solve new types of societal problems. Network governance could be seen as a response to growing social complexity and a lacking capacity or knowledge within the state to effectively and appropriately address those problems. If the state cannot solve such problems, actors closer to the source of problems may spring into action themselves.

Another driver of change is international influences and the diffusion of strategies and instruments for problem solving. Globalization has brought with it seamless and instant communication spreading ideas and expertise across national and jurisdictional boundaries. This means that models of problem solving, including the best agents of those measures, are imported and implemented in another national or local context, something that in turn triggers a reassessment of which actors are best equipped for such action.

Conclusion

We should not expect broad definitions of models of governance to provide clues about policy choices; as any textbook in public policy will testify, policy evolves through complex and contextualized processes. More important than promoting specific policy choices, it appears as if the governance models are manifestations of previous choices of policy styles and the role of government in solving collective problems. State-centric governance does not, in and of itself, define any long-term policy objectives. However, it does define a particular policy style. Also, the governance models define different institutional arrangements in the state, which in turn define the preconditions for broader policy choices. It is, to give an example, difficult to think of extensive welfare state policies managed overwhelmingly through network governance arrangements.

This brings us back to a comment made earlier in this entry about causal mechanisms. Do overarching policy choices such as welfare states or developmental states lead to the emergence of a particular model of governance, or is it rather the case that the entrenched governance model that is typical to a country is conducive to a particular set of broad policy goals? A tentative and preliminary answer to these questions is that there could well be causality in both directions, that is, processes of mutual reinforcement of values and norms through which one fosters the other. Megapolicy choices such as between a developmental state and a welfare state must by necessity include the creation of an institutional system equipped to coordinate and implement such large political campaigns.

Equally important, for such projects to be successful, they must draw on political and social sentiments of the significance of such projects to the country. There will only be a welfare state if dominant social constituencies support such a massive undertaking in terms of government effort and treasury, just as a developmental state requires all political, administrative, and corporate actors to commit themselves to such a national priority. Such commitment is reflective of fundamental social values such as national security or, in the case of the welfare state, social justice. Thus, social norms are directly or indirectly instrumental in fostering both overarching policy choices and predominant governance models.

The analysis presented here represents the first few steps in what appears to be a rather long journey toward a better understanding of why and how different national contexts or what Castles called "families of nations" develop different models of governance. This entry explored only a few conceivable explanatory factors. It is likely that state traditions, the trajectory of state building, political culture, and national prosperity provide important additional clues to answering those questions.

Jon Pierre
University of Göteborg
Göteborg, Sweden

See also Institutions and Institutionalism; State

Further Readings

Bell, S., & Hindmoor, A. (2009). *Rethinking governance: The centrality of the state in modern society.* Cambridge, UK: Cambridge University Press.

Castles, F. (Ed.). (1993). *Families of nations: Patterns of public policy in Western democracies.* Aldershot, UK: Dartmouth.

Esping-Andersen, G. (1990). *The three worlds of welfare capitalism.* Princeton, NJ: Princeton University Press.

Hall, P. A., & Soskice, D. (Eds.). (2001). *Varieties of capitalism: The institutional foundation of comparative advantage.* Oxford, UK: Oxford University Press.

Johnson, C. (1982). *MITI and the Japanese miracle.* Stanford, CA: Stanford University Press.

Kenworthy, L. (1995). *In search of national economic success.* Thousand Oaks, CA: Sage.

Madrick, J. (2009). *The case for big government.* Princeton, NJ: Princeton University Press.

Migdal, J. S. (2001). *State in society.* Cambridge, UK: Cambridge University Press.

Moran, M. (2002). Review article: Understanding the regulatory state. *British Journal of Political Science, 32,* 391–413.

Norton, A. (1994). *International handbook of local and regional government: A comparative analysis of advanced democracies.* Cheltenham, UK: Edward Elgar.

Peters, B. G., Doughtie, J. C., & McCullogh, M. K. (1977). Types of democratic systems and types of public policy. *Comparative Politics, 9,* 327–355.

Pierre, J., & Peters, B. G. (2005). *Governing complex societies: Trajectories and scenarios.* Basingstoke, UK: Palgrave.

Rhodes, R. A. W. (1997). *Understanding governance: Policy networks, governance, reflexivity and accountability.* Buckingham, UK: Open University Press.

Sörensen, E., & Torfing, J. (Eds.). (2007). *Theories of democratic network governance.* Basingstoke, UK: Palgrave.

Vogel, S. K. (1996). *Freer markets, more rules: Regulatory reform in advanced industrial countries.* Ithaca, NY: Cornell University Press.

Governance, Administration Policies

Some decades ago, in the early 1950s, Harold Lasswell defined politics as "who gets what." This simple but powerful definition emphasizes the fundamental point that virtually all political action is directed toward using the power of the public sector to allocate goods and services among the members of a society. Some politics is symbolic and emotive, but to some extent even those components of political action may help legitimate the political system and the decisions it must make about allocations of costs and benefits among citizens. Citizens may be willing to accept allocations with which they do not agree in part because of their emotional attachment to their government and the legitimacy associated with that attachment. This entry examines basic questions about making and implementing public policy in contemporary political systems.

Perhaps the broadest possible manner in which to consider this process of allocating goods and services through the public sector is to employ the concept of *governance*. As explained more fully below, the meaning of governance is contested rather vigorously in the academic community, but the fundamental notion of governance is that there is a need for some form of collective decision making to steer the society. This functionalist conception of governance emphasizes that although the market may be an efficient mechanism for making individual choices, there is a need to make some decisions for the society as a whole. Furthermore, those decisions may need to take into account a range of human values, not just economic values, and also attempt to accommodate influences from a range of actors. (*Value* refers to everything that is considered to have a value, be it material, ideological, ethical, or other, by most people/citizens.)

The idea of *governance* therefore is to provide some means of collective steering for the economy and society, and the word is derived from a Greek word for steering that also is the root for cybernetics. This steering activity is usually associated with government and with the formal institutions of the public sector, but this entry presents an argument for seeing the concept as neutral about the manner in which steering occurs, as suggested by Jon Pierre and Guy Peters in 2001. Although those formal institutions of the public sector continue to have a role in governing, social actors—both market and societal—also have an influence. This involvement of social actors certainly occurs in democratic societies but may also operate in less democratic systems that have sought to co-opt those social actors as part of their legitimation strategies.

The activity that we generally conceptualize as public policy making is a major component of governance. Governments exercise that steering function mainly by making policies and then putting them into action. The policy choices made through the state, and also involving actors from the civil society, are directed at a range of targets, involve the use of a number of instruments, and reflect a variety of political, economic, and social values. Furthermore, the process through which governments make policy (and again this typically is done with the involvement of other actors) is complex, often taking years to complete, and involves a large number of actors, many of whom may be able to exercise a virtual veto over the actions as suggested by George Tsebelis in 2002.

The emphasis on who gets what from political action is sometimes considered to be technical and apolitical, focusing on economic values of efficiency, or on the legalistic application of the law through public administration. Public policy is, however, anything but apolitical and reflects the convergence of a wide array of political forces, all attempting to influence the policy choices in ways that will benefit them and their constituents. According to Margaret Hill in 2005, these political forces play themselves out through complex processes that move from recognizing policy problems to deciding what good policy would be and then to evaluating the consequences of public action.

Although it is only one component of the policy-making process, governance depends heavily on the implementation of policies through a variety of political and social institutions, notably the public bureaucracy. Although much research in contemporary political science is directed at organizations and actors involved in making inputs into the political system—through voting, political parties, policy networks, legislatures, and so on—the public bureaucracy remains the largest component of the public sector, and arguably the most significant for policy choices. Not only does the expertise of the public bureaucracy inform policy making, but the bureaucracy is, in fact, more often in touch with citizens than are other parts of the public sector.

Following the implicit outline already presented, this entry begins with the most general concept of governance, moves on to the policy-making process as a major component of public action in governing, and concludes by discussing public administration and its importance in implementing, as well as making, public policy. All these aspects of governing are necessarily linked in the "real world" and in theory, but each of them also must be considered separately to understand better how the three interact. The three perspectives all combine to provide a picture of what the public sector actually does and how it affects the lives of citizens.

Studying these three aspects of political science involves the relationships between policy and administrative issues that occur in the reality of public governance and in the analytic and theoretical approaches that social scientists employ to interpret and understand those problems. Although the objective problems in these areas have considerable practical relevance, the role of theory must also be emphasized. This emphasis on theory is especially important given that some of the same strands of theory, for example, institutionalism and bounded rationality, can be applied across these areas. Therefore, the entry is a tour d'horizon designed to identify the principal issues and approaches in these parts of the discipline of political science.

Governance and Political Science

The basic idea of governance has been part of political science as long as there has been such a discipline, but the concept has become more central to studying politics over the past several decades. The exact date and source of the revival of the term is perhaps not important. What is more important is that the discipline has been supplementing its general concern with individual political behavior with greater concern with what the political processes and all that individual behavior produce by working through institutions and processes. The outcomes of governance can be conceptualized to include not only policy choices but also the general management of the political and social systems. These outcomes would therefore include the capacity to involve members of the public in the governance process, the building of trust and social capital, and what Canadians might recognize as the maintenance of "peace, order and good government," as identified in the Constitution Act of 1867.

At its most basic level, governance means the capacity to steer the economy and society toward collective goals. That definition does not privilege any particular actors or any particular institutions, but, instead, it recognizes the functional need to provide that steering and then attempts to understand how the process is carried out. One of the most important distinguishing features between governance and other forms of social action, for example, markets, is the notion of collective goals and their centrality in steering. Other forms of social action, for example, markets, assume that individual goals are sufficient, or that goals emerge through interaction, but a governance perspective assumes that goals emerge through collective choice of some sort.

Governance models in political science therefore are at their heart functionalist explanations for the processes of governing writ large. In this way, the governance approach to political science has some affinity with the structural-functionalist approaches used in comparative politics during the 1960s and 1970s. In those approaches, there was an assumption that some form of collective choice is necessary, but the specific actors to be involved in making that choice were not identified, and the variations in the way in which decisions were made were the loci for comparison. The same assumption concerning the need for collective choice is made about governance, and the approach, in the view of some political scientists, should be agnostic about how it is performed and about what activity should be subject to collective control and what is better left to the market and society.

The major contrast concerning governance that has been made in contemporary political science is between *government* and governance. The traditional assumption in political science was that governance almost inherently was the appropriate province of the institutions within the formal public sector. To the extent that nongovernmental actors were involved in the process, they were to different degrees suspect. The degree of suspicion concerning nongovernmental actors varied with political cultures. For example, the pluralist traditions in Anglo-American countries have tended to assume that interest groups pursue "the private use of public power." On the other hand, however, most of the countries of Northern and continental Europe have some tradition of corporatist involvement of private sector actors in making and implementing policy, and these countries tend not to denigrate but often laud that involvement.

This contrast between government and governance (see, e.g., Seppo Tiihonen, 2004) has emerged as a central analytic question for scholars concerned with governance. Many scholars advocating the governance perspective have argued that the formal institutions of the public sector have become increasingly incapable of providing that scarce commodity called governance. The formal organizations of the public sector are characterized as bureaucratic, clumsy, and incapable of coping with the rapidly changing societies with which they are confronted. There is ample evidence of policy failure (for a variety of evidence, see Mark Bovens, Paul 't Hart, & Guy Peters, 2001) and the underperformance of the public sector in many countries that has been used to justify the position that governments are not able to provide governance.

Critics of conventional forms of government have argued that as well as being weak in terms of efficiency, they are also weak in democratic terms. The institutions of representative democracy appear unable to capture the enthusiasm of many citizens, and levels of voting in most industrial democracies have been decreasing. Likewise, membership in political parties and many other political organizations appears to be dropping rather inexorably. Much of the successful political mobilization that has occurred has been around "flash parties" that are developed around an individual or around a particular political issue. The advocates of the "new governance," therefore, believe that providing other loci and methods of political participation will make public action more democratic as well as more capable of solving collective problems.

Even if citizens were engaged in the mass politics of representative democracy, the limited capacity of those institutions to translate their preferences into effective policy choices is clear. Richard Rose pointed out in the mid-1970s that even in majoritarian Westminster systems, voting was an extremely blunt instrument to use to control policy choices. In addition, the divided-government literature helps explain the extent to which coalition governments further complicate democratic control over policy. These constraints on governance become even more apparent as governments move away from direct ministerial mechanisms for service delivery that are driven more by market and social actors than by political controls.

The lack of agreement about what the term *governance* actually means has been addressed in part by adding various adjectives to the basic concept. One of the most important of these more circumscribed terms has been *network governance* (Eva Sørenson & Jacob Torfing, 2007), and indeed a good deal of the movement toward governance as an approach to political life has been focused on the capacity of networks to provide governance. The basic conviction of network governance is that self-organizing networks of social actors are better suited to coping with the complexity of contemporary governing demands than are hierarchical mechanisms. The "new governance" of networks is assumed to be better able to cope with that complexity and respond to changing social conditions.

Another way of limiting the meaning of governance has been to focus on "good governance," generally meaning the reduction of corruption and the creation of greater accountability, especially in less developed political systems. This version of governance has been dominant in much of the international donor community that is seeking not only to describe governance but also to improve public sector performance. Some scholars, however, have begun to focus on the quality of governance in a more general vein, attempting to understand what features of political systems may be associated with the capacity to improve the quality of life of citizens.

The linkages between institutional and behavioral characteristics of political systems and the quality of public decisions is often tenuous, but establishing that linkage can both help develop understanding governance within comparative politics and enhance the actual performance of the public sector. There is as yet very little discussion of the design of governance systems, but the accumulation of evidence may provide that version of "constitutional engineering" just as knowledge about formal public sector institutions has generated some design principles.

Governance has been discussed primarily at the national level, but the concept can be used to discuss steering capacity at all levels. For example, "global governance" has been used to describe steering at the international level. At this level, the state often ceases to be the major actor in governance, much as national governments cease to be the principal actors in some models of governance. Instead, regimes composed of nongovernmental actors are often central to providing some control over policy areas that governments may not be able to or want to. Although states have attempted to exert some control over areas such as climate control, the nongovernmental actors may prove to be more effective.

Urban areas, as well as other subnational levels, also require governance, and these regions experience all the problems of mobilizing consent and exercising control over policy choices that the national level may encounter. Indeed, networks and other forms of social actors may be more significant at the local level than at the national level, and much of the study of local politics has revolved around these interactions between formal and informal actors. Perhaps more than at other levels of government, urban areas have developed complex patterns of service delivery that correspond to the governance ideas of involving a range of private sector actors in the process of steering.

As Ian Bache and Matthew Flinders noted in 2004, one of the more important aspects of the development of governance as a means of understanding comparative politics has been the development of *multilevel governance*. While students of federalism, such as Thomas Heuglein and Alan Fenna (2006), and of intergovernmental relations more generally might consider that this term has to some extent reinvented a very old wheel, the prominence of the concept of multilevel governance has emphasized the complexity of the processes through which public programs are made and implemented. The basic point of multilevel governance is that most attempts to govern in the early 21st century involve interactions among multiple levels of government, as well as interactions between the public and private sectors.

The multilevel governance approach also points to the extent to which the contemporary state has been disaggregated and the linkage between the structure of states and the governance being provided. Christopher Pollitt and Colin Talbot noted in 2004 that as the public sector has moved a large number of its activities to agencies and quangos or has developed mechanisms such as public–private partnerships to deliver services more efficiently, the capacity for control from the center is reduced. Liesbet Hooghe and Gary Marks in 2003 pointed to the variable consequences of the different mechanisms for disaggregating the central state, but the general consequence has been to reduce the steering capacity of the center of government.

The need to understand reactions to disaggregation and the empowering of nonstate actors in governance has led to consideration of the capacity to restore some direction from the center. The concept of "metagovernance" has been coined to reflect the need for central steering the context of a more decentralized and devolved world of political action. Metagovernance is the governance of governance, or the attempt to provide or create some coherence out of very decentered policy processes. Metagovernance does not imply a return to the command and control style of governing associated with the hierarchical state but rather reflects an attempt to steer through frames and guidelines instead of through hierarchy and formal rules.

Metagovernance also represents an attempt on the part of many political leaders to reassert the primacy of politics. If networks and other forms of devolved political action are increasingly dominating political life, then the connection between voting and policy choices is becoming more attenuated. Political leaders therefore have felt the need to control policy without necessarily undermining the efficiency and legitimation gains achieved by using the devolved and marketized methods of governing. In some cases, these attempts at control have involved overt politicization of the public service, but others have involved softer forms of steering and control.

Even if one accepts that a great deal of the action of governing has been shifted away from formal institutions in the public sector and toward devolved and delegated action, it is important to remember that this activity is always being done in the "shadow of hierarchy," as noted by Fritz Scharpf (1997). That is, if the market or social actors being given grants of power fail to perform adequately in making and implementing policy, then the state can always revoke its delegation and resume control over the policy. The reassertion of hierarchical control would go beyond the softer controls associated with metagovernance to recapture direct control of policy and a more direct imposition of the priorities of elected politicians.

At the same time that governing is carried on in the shadow of hierarchy, to some extent, more formal patterns of governing are carried on in the "shadow of governance." The policy-making processes of the public sector do fail all too often; creating policy arrangements that rely more heavily on nonstate actors provide political leaders an opportunity to correct for, or perhaps avoid, those failures. In part, the capacity to move activities that may fail within the state out of the center is an important means of blame avoidance for politicians. Using market and nonstate actors can, of course, be a less "political" strategy and more a reflection of the capacity of those institutions to act in ways that the public sector cannot—whether that is being less bureaucratic in the pejorative sense of the term, being able to respond more nimbly to changing conditions, or being able to leverage human and financial resources that are out of the reach of government.

In summary, the governance turn in political science has brought the discipline back to some of its roots in thinking about the capacity of the public sector to provide coherent direction to society. Clearly, in the case of failed states, this type of governance is not possible, and even for some more successful political systems, it can be sporadic and inconsistent. Furthermore, governance is not just about the success or failure of the formal public sector but also involves the capacity of those institutions to interact successfully with social actors and also increasingly the capacity to interact with the global environment.

Public Policy

Public policy studies are the second major body of work to be considered when thinking about the outputs of the public sector. Most political scientists do not think of themselves as "policy scientists" of the type advocated by Harold Lasswell and Abraham Kaplan in 1950, but in essence they are. The individualistic turn in political science, reflected in both behavioral and rational choice approaches to the discipline, has diverted attention from the output side of the political system toward aspects of political life where institutions and processes are less dominant features. For many political scientists taking those approaches, public policy is better left to economists or to professions such as planning.

Although the two aspects of political science—policy and individual behavior—are in fact more complementary than competitive, they tend to ignore each other and to press the primacy of one or the other. This is most unfortunate, given, that it is individuals, working singly or collectively, who must make policy decisions; we need to know more about how they make those decisions. Likewise, public policies frame a good deal of the political action by individuals, so that voting may be voting for or against specific policy choices.

The Policy Process

The study of public policy in political science has several important but somewhat disparate dimensions. The largest single body of research has been on the policy process, notably the work of Charles O. Jones. This approach to policy is inherently political, arguing that the policy choices made by government are primarily a function of the political process through which they are made. The majority of the process models attempt to explain policy choices by understanding the actors who are involved at each of these stages, as well as by understanding linkages among the stages. These models are, however, far more useful as heuristics for describing the process than they are as means of explaining outcomes.

The conventional process model of policy making begins with agenda setting or problem definition and then proceeds through a series of steps such as program design, legitimation, resource attachment, and evaluation; typically, it did not have any strong assumptions about the political mechanisms that were used to manage that movement. Although some elements within the general model, for example, agenda setting, relied on the role of policy entrepreneurs to provide agency within the process, the general models tended to be largely devoid of that animation.

Furthermore, the process model as generally used in political science did not reflect the degree of conflict that might exist in these crucial political processes; rather, the process appeared to move along rather smoothly to its conclusion. One important addition to process models that did contain that conflict was Paul Sabatier and Hank Jenkins-Smith's (1993) "advocacy–coalition framework." This model was concerned explicitly with policy change and suggested that policy change came about through the clash of ideas, as manifested in an existing policy coalition and a potential replacement. These conflicts could be worked out through bargaining processes, often generating a new synthesis about policy, which would in turn be institutionalized, setting the stage for the next round of policy change.

In addition to the general model of the policy process, there has been a substantial degree of theorizing about various components of the policy process. In particular, political scientists have been concerned with agenda setting, budgeting, implementation, and, at one point, evaluation. These process considerations have, however, often been divorced from concerns about the quality of policies being adopted. Each of these process areas has produced a large body of literature that has influenced more general studies of policy. That having been said, with the exception of the study of agenda setting, these areas of research have declined in political science to some extent, reflecting the general decline in the importance of policy studies in the discipline.

Implementation

The first of these components of the policy-making process to emerge as a distinctive field for research was *implementation*. Although the term is hardly new, it was brought to center stage in policy studies by Jeffrey Pressman and Aaron Wildavsky in 1974. They focused attention on the difficulties of taking legislation and making it work in "the real world" and especially the difficulties in making it work in the manner intended by the framers of the legislation. They developed this analysis by identifying the number of clearance points that had to be passed successfully if the program were to go into effect. While their analysis of the difficulties of implementation was perhaps excessively pessimistic, it did help frame a fundamental policy problem in a strong analytic model.

The Pressman and Wildavsky framework for understanding implementation is a top-down perspective on the process, while the process may also be analyzed from a bottom-up perspective. The bottom-up perspective assumes that programs might be better designed from the perspective of the prospective of implementation. This "backward-mapping" perspective assumes that programs might ultimately be more effective if their final implementation were central to their formation. Although criticized as putting implementation ahead of policy goals, this approach does emphasize the key role of implementation in making programs actually work.

A third wave of implementation research emphasized quantitative studies of the success and failure of implementation efforts, relying heavily on measures that were in many ways difficult to sustain in the face of the complexity of the implementation process. If anything, the complexity of implementation has become even greater. For example, implementation increasingly involves multiple actors at multiple levels of government, as described by Laurence O'Toole in 2004, or perhaps also actors in the private sector.

Budgeting

Wildavsky was also central to the emergence of public budgeting as an area of concerted research in political science in the mid-1960s. In contrast to economists who looked at the public budget as a search for a Pigovian optimal allocation, Wildavsky saw budgeting in a much more political manner, emphasizing the importance of structure and process in producing the outcomes. In particular, the repetitive nature of budgeting and the multiple organizations involved in the process (at least in the United States) tended to produce incremental outcomes. There was also some individual element involved in this model of incrementalism, given that many of the actors involved played the "game" year after year and their memories and their interpersonal trust also influenced the outcomes.

After his initial insights into the American budgetary process, Wildavsky and his colleagues, Otto Davis and Michael Dempster, made a number of other important contributions to a political understanding of budgeting. First, they formalized and tested the incremental model of budgeting in 1966 and demonstrated that there was a great deal of predictability in the decisions made for the U.S. federal budget. Furthermore, Wildavsky and colleagues developed alternative models that could describe budgetary choices in other types of political systems. Finally, Hugh Heclo and Wildavsky in 1974 provided a detailed analysis of budgetary decision making in the British Treasury, again emphasizing the importance of trust in these deliberations.

The seminal work by Wildavsky sparked a number of interesting elaborations of budgeting and critiques of the incremental model. Unfortunately, however, that interest in budgeting has not been maintained, even given its centrality in governing. The interest in budgeting that remains has been largely on the part of rational choice scholars who see the budget as a logic locus for actors to seek to maximize their own benefits and to pursue interesting strategies in order to do so.

As Charles Lindblom (1965) notes, the incremental ideas that have been central to understanding budgeting in the United States, and to a lesser extent elsewhere, are related to more general analytic approaches emphasizing the likelihood, and the desirability, of incremental decision making. In this view, the public sector will produce better governance through successive limited comparisons rather than through attempting to make a single, correct, and comprehensive decision. While such a pattern of governing can be condemned as excessively conservative, the logic also corresponded well to the American political style from which it had evolved.

At a more theoretical level, beginning with Herbert Simon's (1947) work, the logic of *bounded rationality* has been a powerful contender in the attempted domination of more rationalistic approaches to policy, and to politics more generally. In this view, any attempt at comprehensive rationality in public decision making is doomed to failure, so the more appropriate course of action is to make a series of smaller decisions, examining the outcomes of those decisions in turn and adjusting. Furthermore, the objective of the policy-making exercise is better understood as *satisficing* rather than maximizing utilities, so that all that decision makers must find is a decision that is good enough rather than one that is optimal.

Agenda Setting

Agenda setting is the final element of policy process that has achieved a great deal of prominence in the discipline. Roger Cobb and Charles Elder were responsible for bringing the idea of agenda setting to a central place in the study of policy in the early 1980s. The basic argument is, of course, that nothing can be done about a problem in society unless it is identified and transferred to the active agenda of a political institution. Thus, one of the most important aspects of political mobilization is generating awareness of the issue and commitment on the part of politicians to attempt to deal with it.

Cobb and Elder's approach to agenda setting was largely purposive, but later approaches to this stage of policy making emphasized the almost random elements of the process. In particular, Kingdon's (1995) work emphasized the need for a "policy window" to open before an issue can be put on the agenda. This idea is not dissimilar to the garbage can model of decision making proposed in 1972 by Michael Cohen, James March, and Johan Olsen in the bounded rationality literature mentioned earlier, which argues that decisions are largely the product of the fortunate confluence of opportunities and ideas and actors. This is, of course, in marked contrast to the usual rational assumptions about how social and political decisions are made.

The agenda-setting literature has been expanded significantly by Frank Baumgartner and Bryan Jones's (1993) discussion of patterns of movement of issues on and off active agendas. They used some of the same terminology as historical institutionalism, such as "punctuations" to emphasize the rather abrupt changes in the visibility and the salience of policy problems. Their plotting of the dynamics of agenda in American politics has generated a large new area of inquiry in the United States and in other countries that has made significant progress in mapping the sources of policy change and the political foundations of policy choices.

Policy Causes Politics

A second strand of theorizing about policy in political science, developed or initiated by Theodore J. Lowi (1972), has to some extent reversed the logic of the process model, arguing that policy produces politics. This model involves the assumption that four fundamental types of policy tend to be associated with certain types of political action. They are distributive, constituent, regulative, and redistributive. For example, redistributive policies are assumed to be associated with the immediate applicability of coercion focused on the environment of conduct rather than on the conduct itself. In 1974 Robert H. Salisbury and John P. Heinz used a similar set of policy variables, although relating them more to the types of demands being placed on the policy-making system and the degree of fragmentation of that policy-making system.

The model developed by Lowi has motivated a great deal of empirical research as well as a number of theoretical critiques. Perhaps the most fundamental contribution has been, however, to make political scientists think about policies in more analytic categories. There is always the tendency to think about policies in terms of the names one finds on government buildings—agriculture, defense, housing, and so on. That manner of thinking is useful, but only up to a point, and it may mask some of the internal variations in individual policy areas.

A slightly different version of the "policy causes politics" approach is the argument made by Gary Freeman and others that the differences across political systems are not as great as the differences across policy areas. The technical and political foundations of a policy area such as health may be more similar across countries than are those foundations for disparate policy areas within a single system. As policy ideas spread across national boundaries, these common aspects of policy may become more similar. Pressures from globalization and from Europeanization have tended to homogenize policy across national boundaries, further reinforcing Freeman's argument.

Policy Styles

To understand public policy, it is important to consider the policy choices made by any one country (or subnational unit). It is also important to compare those choices with the choices made by other countries. This comparison could be done on a policy-by-policy basis, as described for the welfare state below, or the policy-making style of the political system in question could be typified. In this case, rather than policy being assumed to cause policy, policy is used to characterize the political systems; policy becomes the lens through which to compare those systems.

Jeremy Richardson made the first major analysis of policy styles in Western Europe, arguing that the policy styles in these countries could be characterized by two variables. One was an active–reactive dimension, assessing whether a county attempted to anticipate policy problems, and, if so, to what extent, or simply waited until the problem appeared. The other dimension was one of imposition versus negotiation, reflecting in part patterns of corporatist interest intermediation in some political systems.

Almost all the research on policy styles has been done on the industrialized democracies. This pattern has the advantage of holding some important variables, notably wealth and democracy, relatively constant. There have been some attempts to assess the policy styles of less affluent countries, generally attempting to build something on the order of a model of policy making for one region or another. In particular, a great deal of work has been done on the policy styles of Asian countries and their relationship to economic growth.

Policy Instruments

Implementation studies have been concerned with the ability to transform stated policies into effective action. The ability to make the difficult translation from law to action involves a number of components; one of the more important elements is the choice of a policy instrument, or tool (Christopher Hood, 1976). The basic idea of policy instruments is that the public sector can achieve its goals using a variety of different types of programs—subsidies, regulation, vouchers, and so on—and each of these instruments will have distinct substantive and political characteristics that will influence the likely success of the program being implemented.

While it is common to think of these instruments in more or less technical terms, it is crucial to remember that they do have a strong political dimension. For example, as the politics of governing have changed to cast suspicion on direct public sector interventions, many of the conventional "command and control" instruments of the public sector, such as regulation, have been exchanged for softer instruments. The choice of policy instruments may also reflect the need to build coalitions needed to get legislation adopted. For example, much of the federal support for university students in the United States is provided through private bank loans guaranteed by government. While it might be more efficient to have the loans managed through the universities, it was important to create a political ally in the banking industry.

The study of policy instruments leads to a number of other, even more difficult, questions about public policy and the possibilities of effective public sector intervention. The most fundamental issue that the choice of instruments raises is the possibilities of policy design. Do policy analysts, whether in political science or not, have the ability to design better policies? To do so requires some understanding of the causation of policy problems, the relationship of those problems to the instruments available to address those issues, and some normative basis to evaluate the outcomes of the policy intervention (Pearl Eliadas, Margaret Hill, & Michael Howlett, 2005). The design issue also raises the question of whether the simple functional categories we generally use for policy are sufficient to capture the complexity of the challenges faced when attempting to match instruments to the underlying dimensions of policy problems.

Discourse and Deliberation

The majority of thinking about public policy has used a strongly objective model, attempting to measure policies as dependent variables and then finding the factors that explain those policy choices. Likewise, economic and utilitarian values tend to undergird much of this analysis, assuming that policies are best understood in terms of how they improve the economic well-being of the objects of the policy. One strand of reasoning in political science, however, argues that policy is best understood in more linguistic terms. The assumption of deliberative models as presented by Frank Fischer (2003) is that the discourse surrounding the policy, and the conflicts between alternative discourses, defines the ways in which policy choices are made. Of course, utilitarian values belong to a discourse, but they are only one among many possible sets of values that can guide policy choices.

Discourse and deliberative models are often best applied in areas such as science policy and some aspects of environmental policy where there are often widely diverging understandings of the nature of the policy. Herbert Gottweiss, for example, has examined the deliberative aspects of research on human biology, and there have been a number of studies of environmental policy that apply the deliberative approach to policy analysis. These studies have demonstrated the range of values that may be involved in complex policy issues as well as something of the ways in which those almost inherent conflicts may be resolved.

Welfare State

Although there are many policy areas, the discussion will focus attention on the development of, and then the challenges to, the welfare state. This special treatment is justified because not only have welfare state politics and policy been central to the legitimation of the contemporary political systems in Europe, and to some extent the rest of the world, but the welfare state has played a central role in theorizing about the politics of public policy. Furthermore, the study of the welfare state has to some extent integrated the study of policy, comparative politics, and normative political theory.

The development of the welfare state and the various forms that this policy regime has assumed has been a rich vein of research and theorizing. Gøsta Esping-Andersen's *The Three Worlds of Welfare Capitalism* (1990) is perhaps the most famous work of this sort. Esping-Andersen identified three types of welfare states, based on the extent to which labor was commodified, and the welfare system was seen as replacement for labor or simply as more of a right of citizenship. Although the Esping-Andersen work has been central to thinking about the welfare state, a number of other studies have attempted to explain patterns of development and differences in the contemporary systems. For example, Peter Flora and Arnold Heidenheimer constructed a development model to explain welfare policy choices, taking into account explicitly the differences between Europe and North America.

Although the welfare state project has been central to legitimating the states of Western Europe, and in improving the quality of life for most citizens of those countries, the model for building a social safety net for all members of society has been under a good deal of pressure since at least the late 1970s. The oil crisis of the 1970s brought the cost of these programs to greater public attention, and those costs have only continued to increase. Furthermore, the continuing aging of the societies with well-developed welfare states will exacerbate the financial problems. In addition to the manifest fiscal problems of the welfare state, this model of governing has been the source of large-scale ideological assaults driven by shifts in the consensus that had dominated policy. Those assaults came from both the political Right and, less predictably, from the political Left, which complained about the depersonalization and bureaucracy of the welfare state.

The pressures on the welfare state have engendered a number of important studies that have integrated the study of the policies themselves with the study of comparative politics. For example, Paul Pierson and his collaborators have been concerned with the role of demographic and fiscal pressures on the erosion, or at least recasting, of many welfare state programs, even in the countries that have been among the most committed to this style of governing. Rather than being a simple economic response, however, these transformations are considered in a very political light, reflecting the variety of pressures being exerted on government and the internal politics of organizations within the public sector itself.

The pressures on the welfare state reflect the confluence of political, economic, and social change and the impact of that juncture of forces on a set of very successful public programs. Somewhat ironically, the welfare state that had been crucial for legitimating the state has now become a source of delegitimation in many political systems. In an era of neoliberal economics and politics, these programs no longer have an uncontested place in governing but yet remain crucial for the well-being of many segments of society.

Public Administration

The third body of literature to be included in this entry, public administration, has been a component of public sector studies virtually since that inquiry began. Governments have always had to have some means of implementing their programs (see above), and the public bureaucracy has been central to that role. As important as public administration is in implementation, however, its role is not limited to that activity, and public administrators play a major role in shaping public policy and making public policy directly too. Finally, civil servants also play a role, and an increasing role, in linking the public sector and the public, so that public administration has become a central locus for emerging forms of democratic control over governing processes.

Bureaucracy

To this point, this entry has dealt with bureaucracy and public administration as virtually identical concepts, but the two should be differentiated. Public administration is the more general term, while bureaucracy refers to a particular organizational form, and especially to the ideal-type model of bureaucracy developed by Max Weber in 1946. That conceptual distinction does not, however, prevent *bureaucracy* being used as a word of opprobrium for public administration, referring to the perceived inefficiency and excessive formality of those public organizations.

As the concept was developed by Weber, bureaucracy was meant to be the highest level of development of rational-legal governance. Rather than oppressing the public, as is now often argued, the bureaucracy should provide both greater equality and greater transparency than the traditional forms of governance that it would replace. The reliance on law, the separation of the bureaucracy from political controls, and the development of files were assumed to allow citizens to know when decisions were being made in their case and to have some justification for those decisions. These patterns would be markedly different from the patrimonial administrations that characterized many governments at the time that Weber wrote and that also characterize many governments in the early 21st century.

Although the Weberian model of bureaucracy and associated model of the state were dismissed almost completely by reformers stressing markets (see the discussion of new public management [NPM] below) and/or social networks as alternatives to the hierarchy of bureaucracy, the bureaucratic model has made something of a comeback. Christopher Pollitt and Geert Bouckaert (2004) have argued for the emergence of a "neo-Weberian state" that would reassert some of the values of bureaucracy, albeit while retaining many of the reforms that have produced greater efficiency in the public sector. In particular, the neo-Weberian state is an attempt to recapture accountability for service delivery instruments that have become increasingly divorced from controls by legislatures and political executives.

The New Public Management

The Weberian style of bureaucracy not only produced a number of benefits for the public sector and for citizens, but it was also the focus of intense criticism. Rigidity, reliance on formal authority, impersonality, and overspecialization were but a few of the numerous criticisms leveled at formal bureaucracy. Beginning from the end of the 1970s, NPM (Hood, 1991) posed a series of challenges to the bureaucratic model and, to some extent, became a new paradigm for public administration.

NPM has been defined in any number of ways and has been argued to be both the salvation and damnation of the public sector. At its most fundamental, NPM implies at least (a) the use of market-type mechanisms for public policy and for public management and (b) an emphasis on the role of managers in the public sector, often using the mantra of "let the managers manage" (see Peters, 2001). To this core set of ideas in NPM might be added some notion of the citizen as an important actor in the process, although citizens are more likely to be conceptualized as customers than as full-fledged citizens participating in a democratic, political process.

As NPM has evolved, the style of governing has become one of *making* the managers manage rather than merely letting them manage. Performance management has been one of the principal instruments for that change in emphasis. The measurement of the outputs of individuals and programs, and using that information to make decisions about budgets, retention, and other important outcomes for the organization and its managers, places pressure on those managers to perform as well as possible. To be successful, however, that performance must be measured well and there must be a means of enforcing the results.

Public Personnel

The people who work for the public sector are one of the crucial elements explaining the relative success or failure of administration. There is little disagreement on the proposition that the public should, to the extent possible, employ the "best and brightest." Indeed, management in the public sector is almost certainly more difficult than in the private sector, given the absence of clear criteria for success and failure, the transparency of most of the operations, and the absence of control over many aspects of the personnel and budget systems.

Public personnel management raises a number of highly technical questions about the employment, training, and motivation of public employees, but there are several crucial political questions as well. The following sections focus on three political concerns: (1) the role of representative bureaucracy, (2) the politicization of the civil service, and (3) the importance of understanding the rewards of high public office, whether elected or appointed.

Representative Bureaucracy

Representative bureaucracy is one of the classic topics in public administration. The term was coined toward the end of World War II when it became clear that there would be a socialist government in the United Kingdom (UK) at the end of the war and that the implementation of what appeared to be a rather sweeping set of policy initiatives would be the responsibility of a civil service that was in cast of mind, if not of party membership, conservative. Could the new government expect support from this civil service, or would its social background prevent its whole-hearted support?

The question of to what extent membership of the public service mirrors the nature of society has both empirical and normative elements. The empirical questions require identifying the extent to which the members of the civil service are representative of the population, and especially the extent to which women and members of minority groups are included in government. The answers to these questions vary markedly depending on what level within the government is being considered. As a whole, the public sector in most industrialized countries does represent the society reasonably well, and often is more than half female. On the other hand, at the higher levels of the public bureaucracy, women, and especially minority group members, tend to be underrepresented.

The second part of the empirical question concerning representative bureaucracy is whether it really makes any difference. One version of the role of representation is a passive one, in which merely having women and minority group members in the public service is assumed to present a positive image to the public and to produce better outcomes. In a more active version of representation, those minority representatives would assume a more active role in governing and in attempting to use their positions to redress some of the inequalities that may exist in the social and economic benefits available from government.

The normative questions about representative democracy are based on the logic that the public sector should be a "model employer" and should demonstrate that more equitable hiring practices can be effective. They are further based on the logic of attempting to use the public sector as a means of addressing long-standing social and economic deprivations experienced by social groups, with public servants adopting a more active representational role in that process. These normative stances may not be as effective as their advocates might like them to be in improving the lot of members of society, but they do express some commitment toward social justice through administration.

Politicization

Another important political question about recruitment of public officials is the extent to which political criteria are, and should be, involved in the selection of public officials. The logic of bureaucracy and the civil service is that public administrators should be selected on the basis of merit and that political criteria should be irrelevant. On the other extreme, however, there is a perceived need by politicians to have advisors, and to some extent also managers, who will support their programs.

Although the norm of a professional and depoliticized public service is certainly accepted in the industrialized democracy, it is also under attack. The movements toward a more politicized public service are generally subtle and the argument in favor of the movement is difficult to press overtly, but politicians clearly want to have greater control over their public servants. The movement toward greater politicization reflects in part the consequences of adopting NPM, with many programs being moved from direct ministerial control. Furthermore, contemporary changes in personnel management, reflecting the logic of NPM, have made it easier for ministers to make decisions about hiring that are not done strictly on merit criteria.

For many of the less developed countries, politicization of the public service is quite common. The failure to institutionalize a merit-based civil service reflects the importance of public service employment in less affluent countries. For politicians in these often clientelistic administrative systems, the ability to distribute public office is an important means of building a political power base. In addition, political leaders may perceive the need for loyalty from their civil servants, as well as commitment to particular policy agendas, which is crucial for their vision of development as well as their political future.

Although merit recruitment is the usual standard for a "proper" civil service, all public sectors have some place for political recruitment. At one extreme among the industrial democracies, the United States has more than 4,000 political appointments in positions that in many other countries would be career positions. In France and Belgium, there is also large-scale use of political appointments in ministerial *cabinets* that advise ministers and help enforce their decisions. In a number of other cases, a parallel bureaucracy may be created with political appointees to some extent shadowing the actions of the career public servants.

Rewards

Decisions about the level of rewards for public employees are a final issue in personnel policy. Although there is a good deal of evidence that pay is not the prime motivation for individuals joining or remaining in the public service, it must be considered. Financial rewards are increasingly important because of the adoption of ideas from NPM concerning the opening of the public service to direct entry from outside. These rewards may be especially important for the top officials of the public sector, who may be responsible for extremely large organizations but receive very modest rewards. At the extreme, the Secretary of Defense in the United States, who is responsible for the largest organization in the world, receives a "princely" salary of $180,100, while his subordinates receive even lower salaries.

If we want to understand the importance of public rewards for the public sector, however, we need to move beyond formal salary levels. The formal salaries and visible benefits of public officials are but a small portion of the rewards for high public officials in many countries. At the extreme, the nominal salaries of the leaders of China are less than $100 per month, but that figure does not begin to take into account the huge range of housing, transportation, and other benefits from holding office. At the other end of the dimension of visibility, public officials in Australia and New Zealand receive few indirect rewards and are held to close account for the benefits they do receive.

The degree of rewards received by public officials, and especially those informal rewards received in addition to their formal salaries and benefits, is important for the legitimacy of the system as well as for recruitment. The relationship between rewards and legitimacy often represents a negative spiral in which low legitimacy makes it difficult for some governments to provide adequate resources to their employees, and therefore, those governments may choose to provide a number of intransparent rewards. They are almost inevitably exposed to public scrutiny, increasing public cynicism about government and reducing legitimacy.

Politicians and Bureaucrats

Thus far, this entry has considered the role of public servants primarily as the providers of public services to the public. That role is certainly their dominant image for most citizens, but senior public servants also play a crucial role in the political processes of their countries. Although both scholars and practitioners had understood for years the importance of civil servants in making policy and in advising their political masters, the understanding was largely anecdotal until Joel Aberbach, Robert Putnam, and Bert Rockman (1981) began to conceptualize and measure the relationships more precisely. Their work has been the foundation of a number of other studies on the roles of civil servants in a range of countries. Although there are a number of differences across political systems and across time, the research does find that the same roles appear in most countries, although they may be interpreted differently.

The Aberbach et al. approach to the relationships between politicians and bureaucrats is largely attitudinal, judging the extent to which both sets of actors have attitudes that are conducive to cooperation and to effective policy making. These relationships can, however, be considered in terms of structural relationships. For example, Peters identified five ideal types of relationships between politicians and bureaucrats and then used those models as a means of comparing the styles of executive politics in a number of countries. These models ranged from the formal Weberian/Wilsonian domination of governing by elected politicians to an administrative state in which experts in the bureaucracy dominate policy. All the models were conceived of as ideals, but there were certainly empirical referents in a number of countries.

Finally, the relationship between civil servants and politicians can be conceptualized as a bargain between the two sets of actors. It can be argued that politicians give up some of their personal powers in this bargain so that they could create a professional and career public service and thus gain the loyalty and commitment of an expert body of professionals. Likewise, the civil servants cede their capacity to complain publicly about policies in return for a more or less guaranteed position in the structures of governing and a predictable set of rewards.

Accountability

While public administrators have a powerful role in governing and exercise substantial control over the public as they implement programs, these officials also have substantial influence over public policy. In both their roles—implementing policy and making policy—bureaucrats have been able to exercise their power with little direct control from the public (but see below). The traditional model of accountability for public servants was that they were accountable to their ministers (or to some other political official), the minister was accountable to the legislature, and the legislature was accountable to the people. Even in nondemocratic regimes there has been some sense of the necessity of holding public officials accountable for their actions, often to the hegemonic party rather than to duly elected officials.

To make the hierarchical model of accountability function effectively, governments have developed a number of instruments that enable political officials, and the public, to detect malfeasance and to force some reckoning for failures (whether of commission or omission). These instruments are too numerous and beyond the scope of this entry, but some generalizations should at least be mentioned here. One is that many of the instruments for accountability are internal to the executive branch of government, and they require ministers (and other public servants) to exercise control over their subordinates.

A second generalization about hierarchical forms of accountability is that legislatures have played a central role. This role is easier for well-staffed legislatures with strong committees, such as the U.S. Congress, but it is true even for the less well-resourced legislatures. In addition, as cabinets and prime ministers come to dominate parliamentary systems, their legislatures appear to be using the enforcement of accountability as a means of recapturing some of the powers they may have lost. Legislatures appear to be adding staff and creating structures to facilitate this central function, but they still have a great deal to do to be effective controllers for the executive.

In addition to the revival of legislatures as a locus of accountability, public policy and administration have become increasingly influenced by law and the courts. Public administration has always been the implementation of law, and in some administrative systems such as that of France and those derivative of that tradition, there has been substantial *ex ante* judicial control. Legal means of control over administration have, however, become more central, especially in Westminster systems in which the courts had relatively little capacity to control the other branches of government. However, with the adoption of some constitutional instruments such as the Charter of Rights and Freedoms in Canada, and the UK's membership in the European Union (EU), the courts have gained a greater capacity to enforce accountability even in those systems.

To some extent, all these mechanisms for accountability, even those with a strong institutional foundation, depend on transparency and openness. If an administrative system can keep its practices hidden from the public and from political actors, then the possibilities for exercising control over that administration are very limited. The central role of transparency is at the heart of many efforts by international organizations, for example, the World Bank, to promote transparency and accountability in transitional and developing countries. Transparency is important for maintaining accountability in general, but it may be especially important in the ongoing war against corruption in these systems.

The traditional, hierarchical model of accountability was built on some heroic assumptions, and to some extent it is now being complemented by a range of other approaches to accountability that relies on a variety of different instruments. The most important addition to the repertoire of accountability instruments has been the use of competition both to identify problems in service provision and to find the means of enforcing control over less successful programs. This method of control is to some extent manifested in performance management (see above), and it further rely on the "customers" of programs paying attention to the success or failure of the programs that serve them and becoming mobilized politically if the programs perform poorly.

A final point concerning accountability is that we need to recognize the growing importance of output legitimation in many countries. The traditional democratic model of legitimation is that the political process, along with inputs such as voting, is central to legitimating government and its policy decisions. To an increasing extent, however, the public sector is legitimated by its ability to provide services. This change is, at least in part, a consequence of the NPM and its emphasis on service provision, but it is also in part a function of the declining centrality of political participation in many democratic systems. Furthermore, many scholars argue that the alleged democratic deficit in the EU, due to inadequate mechanisms of representation, has required output legitimation.

The Centrality of Administration

Although most citizens, and many political scientists, do not consider public administration as a central part of contemporary politics and government, it is difficult to understand what is happening in governance without understanding the central role of the public bureaucracy. Furthermore, the centrality of administration may be increasing as many political institutions lose some of their capacity for governance and the actions of public administrators become more important both for making substantive decisions and for linking state and social actors.

The increasing centrality of administrative actors in governing is to some extent a paradoxical result of some reforms of the public sector that were designed to transform administration and to make service delivery more market and customer driven. Although many of these reforms were directed ostensibly at the public bureaucracy as traditionally organized and managed, the net effect of the reforms has been to reduce the power of the political officials nominally in charge of government. In reality, NPM was a broader theory of governance as much as a theory of public administration per se. Its explicit demand was to let the mangers manage; its implicit recommendation was that politicians should absent themselves from the process of governing as much as possible.

Linking the Fields of Inquiry

The preceding discussion has considered three major fields of inquiry in political science somewhat in isolation from one another, namely, (1) the role of representative bureaucracy, (2) the politicization of the civil service, and (3) the importance of understanding the rewards of high public office, whether elected or appointed. While that strategy helps clarify each of the three fields individually, it does not capture the reality of governing and the close interconnections between policy choices, the administration of policies, and the overall governance capacity of these systems. The purpose of political science can be understood as finding ways to explain why certain policy choices are made, why they are effective, and what their consequences are for citizens. All these three fields focus on what governments actually do to improve the lives of their citizens.

If we adopt the basic Lasswellian principle that politics is about transforming the life chances for citizens, then we should begin with the study of public policies and work back from those outputs of the political process. These policy choices can be conceptualized both as a dependent variable for the political process and as an independent variable for explaining the steering capacity of the political system. That is, the nature of the policy process, as well as the demands being pressed on the system, may serve some purposes well but may not enable the governance system to steer effectively. For example, Scharpf has pointed out that the design of policy-making systems in the EU and in Germany tends to produce suboptimal results, and hence the steering capacity of these systems is not as great as it might otherwise be. There are mechanisms available to overcome those problems, but they too may present governance challenges. Furthermore, in other cases, the outputs of the political system may reflect the interests of dominant groups in society, but by ignoring other interests, they may complicate its steering and diminish its overall legitimacy.

When beginning to think about the broader processes of governing with making policy choices, however, it is important to remember that making and implementing policy is not a final set of choices. Almost all policy making in contemporary political systems consists of revisioning and attempting to improve older policies, sometimes incrementally and sometimes radically, but there tends to be a framework for public action that must be addressed. That is, remaking policy, or policy succession feedback from the earlier attempts to make policy, is a crucial part of assessing the success and failure of those interventions. For comparative political analysis, the capacity and willingness of political systems to respond to feedback is one crucial element for understanding the differences in policy making.

The feedback process places public administration in a central position. There are certainly political processes for providing feedback, but the connections between the bureaucracy and the environment are crucial. Hood (1976) noted that the tools of government (see above) included both detectors and "effectors" and that the public bureaucracy was central to both. The involvement of the bureaucracy in feedback occurs in part through its connections with clients, and especially because of the role of street-level bureaucrats. The public bureaucracy may also be important in detecting more "objective" problems in policy, given the wide range of data collection in which it is engaged.

As patterns of governing continue to shift toward the greater use of market and civil society actors, the bureaucracy may become even more important as a locus for steering. The public bureaucracy is crucial for managing instruments such as contracts and partnerships and in providing the linkage between networks of social actors and the public sector. Political leaders may not have the technical capacity for some of these aspects of contemporary governing and may not be willing to engage in the continuous bargaining and adjustment needed for coping with networks. These patterns of governing may therefore be uncomfortable for many public servants who believe that they are being forced to make too many policy decisions and for politicians who may feel they have lost control of governing.

In addition to being linked through some aspects of the common problems with which they are concerned, these three major components of political science are also linked through theory. Each area has its own particular theoretical and conceptual issues, as identified above, but there are also some common theoretical strands that unite them. Perhaps the most apparent of these is institutionalism, and the fundamental assumption that structure matters. These three bodies of research all recognize that agency is also a part of any explanation; however, at the heart of the three, and perhaps especially public administration, there is also a strong sense that structures to a great extent constrain that individual agency (Peters, 2001).

While institutionalist approaches may appear the most logical means to link these three sets of literature, they may also be addressed through other approaches, such as rational-choice models. Certainly, rational choice has been applied to both public administration (Murray Horn, 1995) and to public policy, providing a good deal of insight into these aspects of governing. Rational choice has, however, been applied to the more comprehensive issues associated with governance only to a limited extent. Although that has been the case, one can see how that application might be made. The design of governance structures can be considered from the rational perspective almost as easily as can the design of administrative structures or the choice of policy.

In addition to the central role of institutions in making and implementing public policy, a number of the central concepts in political science are relevant for understanding governing. Governing involves the use of power, as the public sector must impose its decisions on society and is often confronted by countervailing power within society. Power is often subtle and is seen as much in what does not happen as in what does. Governing also involves the use of authority and legitimacy, allowing governance without the overt application of power. The list of fundamental concepts could be extended, but the fundamental point is that public administration and policy are not distinct from the remainder of political science but rather may be at the heart of the discipline and its concerns.

B. Guy Peters
University of Pittsburgh
Pittsburgh, Pennsylvania, United States

See also Governance

Further Readings

Aberbach, J. D., Putnam, R. D., & Rockman, B. A. (1981). *Politicians and bureaucrats in Western democracies.* Cambridge, MA: Harvard University Press.

Baumgartner, F. R., & Jones, B. D. (1993). *Agendas and instability in American politics.* Chicago: University of Chicago Press.

Bovens, M., t'Hart, P., & Peters, B. G. (Eds.). (2001). *Success and failure in public governance: A comparative analysis.* Cheltenham, UK: Edward Elgar.

Eliadis, P., Hill, M., & Howlett, M. (2005). *Designing government: From instruments to governance.* Montreal, QC, Canada: McGill/Queens University Press.

Esping-Andersen, G. (1990). *The three worlds of welfare capitalism.* Princeton, NJ: Princeton University Press.

Fischer, F. (2003). *Reframing public policy: Discursive politics and deliberative practices.* Oxford, UK: Oxford University Press.

Heuglein, T. O., & Fenna, A. (2006). *Comparative federalism: A systematic inquiry.* Toronto, ON, Canada: Broadview Press.

Hood, C. (1976). *The tools of government.* Chatham, NJ: Chatham House.

Hood, C. (1991). A public management for all seasons? *Public Administration, 69,* 3–19.

Hooghe, L., & Marks, G. (2003). Unraveling the central state, but how? Types of multi-level governance. *American Political Science Review, 97,* 233–243.

Horn, M. (1995). *The political economy of public administration: Institutional choice in the public sector.* Cambridge, UK: Cambridge University Press.

Kingdon, J. W. (1995). *Agendas, alternatives and public policies* (2nd ed.). New York: HarperCollins.

Lindblom, C. E. (1965). *The intelligence of democracy: Policy-making through mutual adjustment.* New York: Free Press.

Lowi, T. J. (1972). Four systems of policy, politics, and choice. *Public Administration Review, 32,* 298–310.

Peters, B. G. (2001). *The future of governing: Four emerging models* (2nd ed.). Lawrence: University Press of Kansas.

Peters, B. G. (2005). *Institutional theory in political science: The new institutionalism.* London: Continuum.

Pollitt, C., & Bouckaert, G. (2004). *Public management reform: A comparative perspective.* Oxford, UK: Oxford University Press.

Sabatier, P. A., & Jenkins-Smith, H. (1993). *Policy change and learning: An advocacy-coalition framework.* Boulder, CO: Westview.

Scharpf, F. W. (1997). *Games real actors play: Actor-centered institutionalism.* Boulder, CO: Westview.

Simon, H. A. (1947). *Administrative behavior.* New York: Free Press.

Sørenson, E., & Torfing, J. (2007). *Theories of democratic network governance.* Basingstoke, UK: Palgrave.

Tiihonen, S. (2004). *From government to governance: A process of change.* Tampere, Finland: University of Tampere Press.

Governance, Global

Few terms are as insecurely defined or controversial in a normative sense as *global governance.* A major part of the problem is the word *governance*. How does this differ from traditional notions of government exercised by sovereign states and their legal subdivisions? Must governance be institutionalized and rest on national, legal, and moral authority? To the extent that governance exists beyond the state, must it be created by formal agreement among states? Or should governance be understood to include all forms and degrees of rule, exercised by states and nonstate actors, whether based on law and institutionalized or much less formal in nature? If governance is other than traditional government by states, from where does such governance derive its legitimacy? What is the relationship between authority and legitimacy? Indeed, does legitimacy actually matter if there exists a capacity to govern effectively? Does authority imply legitimacy or only effective governance?

Confusion is compounded by the word *global*. Is the analytical focus only on some form of world government—that is, a truly global manifestation of some form of rule that extends over all the territory and persons in the world? Or should global be understood as including all forms of governance, however narrow in function and limited in territorial reach?

The answers to each of these questions obviously affect the answers to still others: How old or new is global governance? How do present patterns of global governance differ from those of the past? This entry discusses several forms of global governance, including international governmental organizations (IGOs), international regimes, and nongovernmental organizations (NGOs), and the legitimacy of global governance.

International Governmental Organizations

Not coincidentally, even as *globalization* in the 1990s became a popular way to describe a vast acceleration in the volume and pace of transnational activities, so did global governance gain prominence in diplomatic and academic circles as a concept that seemed to capture the increasing challenge of managing issues that were beyond the geographical reach of individual states to address on their own.

The term *global governance* was associated early on in the decade with the Commission on Global Governance. In 1991, a group of distinguished public figures met in Stockholm and pledged to form an international commission intended to help build a more effective system of world security and governance. The United Nations' (UN) then– Secretary-General Boutros Boutros Ghali endorsed the initiative, and in 1992, the commission was established with 28 members from around the world, who served in their personal capacities. The commission issued its report *Our Global Neighbourhood* in 1994, making recommendations for the reform of the UN Economic and Social Council and certain other UN bodies. Few of the recommendations were implemented, so the report constituted more of a landmark than a watershed.

Be that as it may, the commission experience did seem to link global governance with the UN and, more broadly, with IGOs whose members are states. In the modern state system, growth in IGOs went hand in hand with the expansion of international law in the 19th and early 20th centuries. More than 20 times as many treaties from 1851 to 1950 took the multilateral form as in the period between 1751 and 1850 (Charlotte Ku, cited in Jan A. Scholte, 2005).

One trend was multilateral conference diplomacy, beginning after the defeat of Napoleon in 1815, with the Concert of Europe, an informal consultation mechanism of European government officials. The concert convened periodically to deal with perceived general European problems, including arms races and potential clashes over imperial expansion, which was the main focus of the 1884–1885 Berlin meeting. Over time, the number of countries attending multilateral conferences increased and included some beyond Europe. The Hague conferences of 1899 and 1907 banned aerial bombing, chemical warfare, and the use of hollow-point bullets; attempted to control the proliferation of submarines and armed merchant vessels; and established the Permanent Court of Arbitration. In addition, the two Hague Conventions, along with the later Geneva Conventions, profoundly shaped the laws of war and related matters, such as the treatment of prisoners.

Meanwhile, beginning with the 1826 Panama Congress, there was also a series of inter-American and Pan–Latin American conferences. The inter-American meetings eventually led to the creation of the Pan-American Union in 1910. Later inter-American conferences were overshadowed by U.S. military interventions in the Caribbean basin, but after the Roosevelt Good Neighbor Policy and as World War II loomed, the Americas forged an almost united hemispheric alliance against the Axis.

Another parallel trend in the establishment of IGOs was that of functional and/or regulatory organizations that from the outset concerned themselves about global matters within the area of their expertise. What is now the International Telecommunications Union (ITU) was created in 1865 and the Universal Postal Union in 1874. An agreement on universal time coordination (UTC) based on the Greenwich prime meridian was concluded in 1884. Technical standardization started with the International Electrotechnical Commission (IEC) in 1906. The International Labor Organization (ILO) was founded in 1919. Functional IGOs to date include a total of 19 UN-specialized agencies—among them, well-known organizations such as the World Health Organization (WHO), the Ford and Agriculture Organization (FAO), the International Civil Aviation Organization (ICAO), and the International Maritime Organization (IMO)—as well as numerous others outside the UN system, such as the Bank of International Settlements (BIS) founded in 1930, the International Atomic Energy Agency (IAEA), and any number of other regulatory bodies at the regional level.

The aftermath of the two world wars saw a momentous advance in universal IGOs: the League of Nations and then the UN. Both organizations institutionalized great power control at the council level that seemed to recall the earlier Concert of Europe and were primarily, although not exclusively, concerned with peace and security issues. The same, by definition, was true of post–World War II alliances such as the North Atlantic Treaty Organization (NATO), the Warsaw Pact, and the Organization of American States, which alone included a process for resolving disputes among its own members. On the other hand, economics was the focus of the Bretton Woods institutions—the International Bank for Reconstruction and Development (IBRD—the World Bank), the International Monetary Fund (IMF), the General Agreement on Tariffs and Trade (GATT), and its eventual successor, the World Trade Organization (WTO). Likewise, economic recovery and growth were the central motivation for post–World War II European institution building that over time produced the European Common Market and today's European Union (EU). Yet another area of concern for universal IGOs has been law and justice, including the Permanent Court of International Justice (PCIJ), the International Court of Justice (ICJ), and most recently the International Criminal Court (ICC).

Overall, the growth in the numbers of IGOs has been so rapid that *The Yearbook of International Organizations, 2004–2005* (Union of International Organizations, 2004, Appendix 3, Table 1) was able to list some 245 as "conventional" IGOs and another 1,743 under the classification of "other international bodies."

International Regimes

Foreshadowing later discussions about global governance, regime theory appeared in the 1970s and 1980s partly to explain how international cooperation might continue even as United States' post–World War II dominance gradually eroded. This was a concept of what has been described as "governance without government" that did not require a "hegemon," or at least one dominating the entire international system.

Regime theory postulates that states cooperate through institutional arrangements, rules, or shared practices. According to Oran Young, the capacity of these regimes depends either on the ability of a dominant actor or on jointly maximizing shared interests. Some authors point out the role of influential groups of experts, constituted as epistemic communities, who define the problem at stake and suggest solutions; others, in a more functionalist vision, consider the regime as spontaneously emerging when it is needed. According to this perspective, states succeed in cooperating when (and to the extent that) they are able to form institutional arrangements or sets of roles, rules, and relationships of the sort we have come to think of as international regimes. This perspective attempts to explain successes and failures in terms of whether such regimes are created.

Regime theory paradoxically, for all its emphasis on states, was important not least because it pointed away from an exclusively state-centric view of global affairs. Rather, as Hedley Bull (1977) suggested about the same time, cooperation and order are as commonplace in international society as competition and anarchy. Cooperation might result in the creation of constitutionalized IGOs—which themselves often proved to be more than the simple sum of their state parts—but equally significant were international treaties and other much less formal arrangements ("conventions" in a different sense) that shaped outcomes in particular issue areas. There were regimes to protect endangered species and transnational ecosystems, to curb nuclear proliferation and chemical warfare, and so on. Moreover, regime theory highlighted the prominence of epistemic communities linking experts inside national bureaucracies, IGO bureaucracies, and NGOs.

Postinternational Perspectives on Global Governance

Classical-realist international relations (IR) theory rested so firmly on the presumed egoistic behavior of states and assumptions about anarchy in world politics that it put little stock in international organizations and international law. Therefore, it is not surprising that IR theory was late in acknowledging the significant presence of NGOs, let alone in beginning to conceptualize their influence on and even direct involvement in governance both within and across state boundaries. In fact, there has been such a proliferation of NGOs in the past few decades that they have become increasingly impossible to ignore. James Rosenau (2003) describes this growth as a veritable "organizational explosion." Many of even the most "local" among the millions of NGOs are concerned with issues that also resonate at regional and global levels, and many if not most such NGOs are networked with others that advance their joint positions transnationally.

The same reference work on international organizations (Union of International Organizations, 2004, Appendix 3, Table 1) cited earlier for numbers of IGOs lists 7,261 "conventional" NGOs and an additional 13,590 under the heading of "other international bodies." Many of these NGOs have institutionalized relationships or are at least selectively engaged with IGOs. Rosenau (2003), for example, noted that NGOs were involved with some 70% of World Bank projects in 2002. The literature on globalization has tended to characterize the proliferation of NGOs and their transnational activism with the rise of "global civil society." A related body of writings has built on earlier work on nonstate actors and transnational corporations (TNCs) to spotlight the growing importance of "private authority" in global governance and international affairs generally (see, especially, A. Clair Cutler, Virginia Haufler, & Tony Porter, 1999; Rodney B. Hall & Thomas J. Biersteker, 2002).

However, the NGO and TNC dimension of the organizational explosion is only one of numerous sweeping changes in the global system identified by *Postinternationalists* like Rosenau, as well as Yale Ferguson and Richard Mansbach (2004, 2008). They argue that these changes are the fundamental trends that profoundly shape patterns of governance at all levels. The central analytical challenge, as Rosenau (1997) expresses it, is how to assess

> a world in which the [domestic-foreign] Frontier is continuously shifting, widening and narrowing, simultaneously undergoing erosion with respect to many issues and reinforcement with respect to others? . . . Under what circumstances does authority along the Frontier accrue to like-minded states, to global regimes, to transnational organizations, to subnational entities, or to coalitions of diverse types of actors? (p. 5)

Postinternational change is the product of simultaneous processes of fusion and fission of authority. The first is reflected in the growth of networks that connect and influence the behavior of persons geographically far from one another. As has often been observed, some associations are falling apart even as others come together. In his book *Distant Proximities: Dynamics Beyond Globalization* (2003), Rosenau describes this dual process as "fragmegration." The main argument is that "the best way to grasp world affairs today requires viewing them as an endless series of distant proximities in which the forces pressing for greater globalization and those inducing greater localization interactively play themselves out" (p. 4). The second tendency is the fracturing of existing political units into islands of self-identification that localize and often specialize authority and that may encumber efforts to deliver collective goods.

Postinternational theory sees the world today (also historically) as inhabited by countless actors of many different types that reflect different identities, are differentially engaged in countless issues, and exercise effective authority in particular domains and contexts.

Accelerating change is producing an increasingly complex universe of actors in global/local politics. Ferguson and Mansbach call them *polities*, while Rosenau prefers the term *spheres of authority* (SOAs). Polities are collectivities with a significant measure of identity and institutionalization, a degree of hierarchy in their organization, and the capacity to mobilize persons and groups for political purposes (value satisfaction). Some entities more clearly meet these criteria than others. For instance, most states, international institutions, TNCs, major NGOs, and criminal and terrorist organizations are polities. By contrast, most markets are not polities because they lack the requisite identity, institutionalization, and hierarchy.

Polities coexist, cooperate, compete, and clash. They often overlap, layer, and "nest" (Ferguson & Mansbach, 1996) and hence share some of the same "political space"—territory, institutions, issues, identities, markets, and/or cyberspace. Polities are all "becoming" in the sense that political evolution is constant, although they evolve at different rates and not necessarily in a unilinear fashion. In the postinternational framework, each type of polity is only an ideal type and assumes many different forms in practice. There are, for example, many variations in the structures and processes of cities and empires, and the same is plainly true of sovereign states, IGOs, NGOs, TNCs, and so on—not to mention hybrid polities such as public–private partnerships or polities arising out of networks or alliances. The "domain" of any polity—its "reach" in political space—consists of the persons and groups who identify with it and comply with its directives, as well as the resources it can therefore command.

All polities are authorities and govern within their respective and often overlapping domains. Thus, governance exists within, across, and beyond the jurisdictions of sovereign states. Global governance, in turn, refers to the totality of discernible polity authority domains in the world. It is important to understand that postinternational theory defines authority and governance as effective influence or control. Authority need not be legitimate to be effective, although almost every polity offers some sort of ideological justification for its existence and behavior, and those that are widely regarded as legitimate obviously tend, for that very reason, to be all the more secure.

A postinternational approach presumes that another related assumption of traditional IR theory—that the world is fundamentally anarchic—tells us little more than that there is no effective world government. Human affairs are largely governed—that is, ruled on a day-to-day basis—not only by states but also by a multitude of individual polities that exist within, crisscross, or transcend individual states. Some of these polities are internally dysfunctional or inclined to disruption and violence, but many if not most act individually and collectively in a peaceful, fairly effective, patterned, and often predictable manner. This is the "real world order."

The Legitimacy of Global Governance

Long before a global financial crisis triggered a major downturn in the global economy in mid-2008, there was a rising worldwide antiglobalization movement revolving around resistance to free trade and unregulated markets, to the Washington Consensus model for development, and to presumed threats to local culture, labor standards, and the local and global environment from more open borders and rapid economic change. The earliest mass demonstrations occurred in 1999 and ebbed and flowed in subsequent years at meetings of global economic institutions, the G7 (+1), G20, and the World Economic Forum at Davos. For most of the antiglobalization protesters, global governance was and continues to be a symbol of unrestrained economic liberalism and thus something that is *inherently* illegitimate.

Among scholars, policymakers, and attentive publics more favorably inclined to a globalizing world, there has also arisen a separate debate about the legitimacy of international institutions and other actors engaged in global governance. This discussion has usually been framed as concern about a "democratic deficit" in global governance. In sum, the ideal notion of governance in liberal democratic states has been that it derives from the "consent of the governed," expressed in elections and other democratic processes. How can such an ideal be translated to governance by international institutions and other nonstate actors? Indeed, should the same sort of ideal apply?

In fact, from one perspective, the entire problem is vastly overstated. First, except for a few high-profile institutions such as the UN, the World Bank, the IMF, and the EU, most global governance actors operate with little publicity and far off the radar except for those relatively few states and citizens most closely affected by their activities.

A second and important reason is that most of the states in the world are not democracies and many of those who claim to be have a serious democratic deficit of their own. It is not an exaggeration to say that most international institutions are paragons of democratic virtue by comparison with most states.

From a third perspective, the problem is minimal because states are the main actors in international institutions and regimes. In a legalistic sense, states thus "consent" at least to this governance on behalf of their citizens.

This third perspective is what Allen Buchanan and Robert O. Keohane (2006) term "the Pedigree View," that "legally constituted institutions, created by states according to the recognized procedures of public international law and consistent with it, are ipso facto legitimate or at the very least enjoy a strong presumption of legitimacy" (pp. 412–413). As they observe,

> The Pedigree View fails because it is hard to see how state consent could render global governance institutions legitimate, given that many states are non-democratic and systematically violate the human rights of their citizens and are for that reason themselves illegitimate. State consent in these cases cannot transfer legitimacy for the simple reason that there is no legitimacy to transfer. (pp. 412–413)

Moreover, as Michael Barnett and Martha Finnemore (2004) emphasize, many international institutions have a tendency to build on their initial mandate, which may itself be sufficiently ambiguous as to invite improvisation.

> Scholarship on organizations generally (not just IOs) has made it abundantly clear that organizations routinely behave in ways unanticipated by their creators and not formally sanctioned by their members. Organizations that start with one mission routinely acquire others. . . . They exhibit mission creep. They wander far from their original mandate. . . . They develop new rules and procedures in response to new problems they identify. They formulate rules that are politically safe and comfortably routine rather than efficient or effective. . . . [They act] like the bureaucracies they are. (pp. 2–3)

How, then, may we best understand the issue of the legitimacy of global governance? It is crucial to recognize that legitimacy is different from authority. Authority, for those inclined to a legalistic interpretation, rests on a legal right to exercise it. For the Postinternationalists and Constructivists Barnett and Finnemore (2004), authority is the capacity to "rule" effectively, which may be bolstered by—but does not depend on—law and general approbation.

Legitimacy, at root, is the widespread belief that a global governance actor has the *right* to exercise whatever authority it does. That belief may be influenced by an actor's constitutionality, state pedigree, and internal democratic character and processes, as well as matters such as the actor's reputation for moral authority or possession of expert knowledge. However, legitimacy derives *fundamentally* from a global governance actor's ability to deliver the goods that its constituents (members and wider publics) need and want. Success in doing so, over time, establishes a track record and tends to attract broader support, identity, and even loyalty. Consistent failure, obviously, courts the reverse.

Yale H. Ferguson
Rutgers University–Newark
Newark, New Jersey, United States

See also Authority; Governance; International Organizations; Legitimacy; Political Systems, Types

Further Readings

Barnett, M., & Finnemore, M. (2004). *Rules for the world: International organizations in global politics.* Ithaca, NY: Cornell University Press.

Buchanan, A., & Keohane, R. O. (2006). The legitimacy of global governance institutions. *Ethics & International Affairs, 20*(4), 405–437.

Bull, H. (1977). *The anarchical society: A study of order in world politics.* New York: Columbia University Press.

Commission on Global Governance. (1994). *Our global neighbourhood.* Oxford, UK: Oxford University Press.

Cutler, A. C., Haufler, V., & Porter, T. (Eds.). (1999). *Private authority and international affairs.* Albany: State University of New York Press.

Ferguson, Y. H., & Mansbach, R. W. (1996). *Polities: Authority, identities, and change.* Columbia: University of South Carolina Press.

Ferguson, Y. H., & Mansbach, R. W. (2004). *Remapping global politics: History's revenge and future shock.* Cambridge, UK: Cambridge University Press.

Ferguson, Y. H., & Mansbach, R. W. (2008). *A world of polities: Essays on global politics.* London: Routledge.

Hall, R. B., & Biersteker, T. J. (Eds.). (2002). *The emergence of private authority in global governance.* Cambridge, UK: Cambridge University Press.

Rosenau, J. N. (1997). *Along the domestic-foreign frontier: Exploring governance in a turbulent world.* Cambridge, UK: Cambridge University Press.

Rosenau, J. N. (2003). *Distant proximities: Dynamics beyond globalization.* Princeton, NJ: Princeton University Press.

Scholte, J. A. (2005). *Globalization: A critical introduction* (2nd ed.). New York: Palgrave.

Union of International Associations. (Ed.). (2004). *Yearbook of international organizations: Guide to global and civil society networks.* Munich: KG Saur Verlag.

Governance, Good

The concept of good governance has multiple meanings, but it most generally refers to a standard or model for how states or other political entities should govern and be governed. This usually includes a long list of normative principles to which these entities should adhere, such as transparency, accountability, inclusiveness, effectiveness, and impartiality. Quite commonly, good governance is defined in terms of its antonyms—that is, by referring to phenomena that indicate its absence, such as corruption, nepotism, favoritism, particularism, or patrimonialism. Within policy circles of the developmental aid community, the concept has been used as an agenda for reform of developing countries, such as civil service reforms, securing property rights, or installing judicial independence. Within the academic community, where close synonyms such as institutional quality or quality of government have been developed, the concept has been systematically linked to several highly desirable outcomes, most notably economic growth and long-term development.

The concept was first launched by the World Bank in the late 1980s and early 1990s in a series of reports that sought to develop a new strategy for aid conditionality. Previously, the Bank had refrained from taking political criteria into account in its donor policy. By demanding that recipient countries adhere to the agenda of "good governance reforms," this stance was changed. By the late 1990s, the concept started to surface on the research agenda of several academic fields in the social sciences, most notably in economics and political science. To a considerable extent, this development was propelled by the appearance of empirical measures, or worldwide governance indicators, made publicly available by the World Bank Institute.

To apprehend the scope of meanings attached to the concept, a series of distinctions is needed. First, good governance may be defined in terms of what it is (as a good in itself) or in terms of what it is good for (e.g., good for economic development). The former may be called an *internal* definition and the latter an *external* (or functionalist) definition of good governance. In the internal case, some properties of the governance system of a country must be singled out in advance, together with a notion of why these properties make the system better or of a higher quality. This could, for example, be the idea that good governance is to be equated with the rule of law. Countries abiding by this principle are then considered to have good governance, regardless of whether the rule of law leads to other desirable consequences. In the external case, empirical scrutiny is required to determine what properties of the system are considered to be good, namely, those that are found to exert an influence on some preferable, external outcome. In this case too, rule of law might be considered to be part of good governance but only to the extent that rule of law can be shown to influence, for example, economic growth or other desirable phenomena.

Second, good governance may be defined in terms of *procedures* or policy *content*. Procedural definitions refer to regulatory principles, codes of conduct, norms, or other value-laden criteria that constrain the forms in which politics may be conducted. Definitions demanding certain contents, by contrast, require certain policies to be enacted by the political system, such as market deregulation or state privatization.

Third, there is a fundamental difference between procedural definitions referring to the input and the output sides of the political system. The former, where *access* to public authority is regulated, is the realm of decision-making bodies, such as parliaments, cabinets, juntas, party executive committees, or royal councils. The output side concerns, instead, the *exercise* of public authority: how reforms are implemented, rules enforced, court cases decided, and so on. This is the realm of the public administration, the courts, and the law enforcement bodies of the state apparatus. Different regulatory principles guide our general thinking as to what makes different political systems better than others on these two sides of the political system. On the input side, democracy and the principle of political equality (one person, one vote; civil and political rights, etc.) is the most well-established norm. On the output side, key guiding principles are the rule of law, administrative effectiveness (or efficiency), and impartial policy implementation. The most comprehensive procedural definitions of good governance encompass all these normative views and facets of the political system, whereas other more specific notions concentrate on the output side, or even on certain aspects of the output side (such as administrative corruption).

The academic discourse has concerned itself with both the causes and consequences of good governance or quality of government. Starting with consequences, the strongest empirical regularity, as already mentioned, concerns the positive link to long-run economic growth. The theory underlying these findings posits that governance is key to shaping the incentives of key economic actors in society, in particular their propensity to invest in physical and human capital and technology, the key generators of growth. Most critical in this regard is the security of property and contract rights for a broad cross section of the population. Simply put, investments require transactions where a commodity at one time or place is traded for a return that occurs at another time or place. Key examples include borrowing and lending, a demander and supplier some distance apart, and the parties to an insurance policy. Secure contract rights (or contract enforcement) underpin beliefs among economic actors that their agreement will be carried out in these situations. Secure property rights, in addition, guarantees that the fruits of such transactions are not at some later point of time expropriated by the state or by other economic actors. Research on the determinants of economic growth has highlighted the importance of good governance or quality of government in securing these contract and property rights.

Other positive consequences of good governance have been uncovered in the literature. Some of these concern individual-level phenomena. Empirical studies show that corruption has a negative impact on ordinary people's feelings of trust, not only in political authorities but also in one another (the latter sometimes being referred to as interpersonal trust or social capital). The more general governance indicators published by the World Bank Institute have even been found to be strongly related to feelings of happiness or life satisfaction. Thus, people living in countries with better working government institutions are on average happier than those living in corrupt and ill-governed countries, other things being equal. Studies of peace and conflict have also taken interest in the quality of government institutions. It has been argued that dysfunctional government institutions make both civil war and interstate belligerence more likely.

The literature on causes of good governance or quality of government is most refined in the area of explaining the origins of corruption, but key insights from this work apply to other, broader governance phenomena as well. There are two general approaches to understanding the prevalence of corruption or other forms of illicit behavior on behalf of government officials. The first is the principal–agent model. According to this view, a collective body of actors (e.g., the top political leadership in a country) are the *principals* who delegate the performance of some government task to another collective body of actors (e.g., the bureaucracy), the *agents*. As in any situation where authority is being delegated, the problem from the perspective of the principal is that the agents may acquire specific information about the task at hand that they do not disclose to the principal, or that they may have other private motivations affecting their behavior than the goals of performing the delegated task. In the case of corruption, administrators delegated the task of collecting a tax, for example, may collude with firms and collect bribes rather than taxes. The principals will try to monitor the behavior of their agents by exacting legal remedies for those being caught collecting bribes. Seen from this principal–agent perspective, the level of corruption—or, more generally, the extent to which good governance is being upheld—in a country is primarily a function of the individual incentives and risk perceptions of the agents. The principal, in turn, may affect these individual motivations by use of control instruments such as increasing the effectiveness of the monitoring system and the severity of the legal punishment exacted.

The principal–agent model of corruption (or other forms of governance failures) has been a forceful tool for understanding this phenomenon, but it suffers from several limitations. The most serious flaw is probably the implicit assumption that the principals are benevolent—that is, that their overall goal is to promote good governance and quality of government in the country. In a more pessimistic (some would say, more realistic) scenario, however, everyone has something to gain personally from a dysfunctional system as long as a large enough body of actors continues to play foul. This may be called the collective action theory of good governance or quality of government. According to this theory, government officials at any hierarchical level (and even ordinary citizens) may reason as follows: True, the best solution for all would be to have a government free from corruption or other forms of dysfunctional behavior. But as long as most other actors take bribes, why should I play fair? As should be clear, this structure of incentives leads to a collective action problem: Despite the fact that everyone realizes that another outcome would be preferable, if most others are expected to play foul, everyone will play foul. To break the deadlock of the collective action dilemma, actors have to start believing that a large enough number of other actors will from now on play fairly.

The study of good governance or quality of government is a fairly new and rapidly growing field of research. The future of this field will in large part hinge on how well the literature resolves a number of tensions inherent in the concept itself. These include, above all, the tensions between narrow (e.g., corruption) and broader (e.g., impartial government institutions) concepts of good governance, between functionalist and internal understandings, between definitions referring to policy contents and those referring to procedures, and between definitions stressing the input and those stressing the output side of the political system.

Jan Teorell
Lund University
Lund, Sweden

See also Corruption; Corruption, Administrative; Rule of Law; State Collapse; State Failure; State Formation

Further Readings

Acemoglu, D., Johnson, S., & Robinson, J. A. (2005). Institutions as the fundamental cause of long-run growth. In P. Aghion & S. Durlauf (Eds.), *Handbook of economic growth* (385–472). Amsterdam: North-Holland.

Adserà, A., Boix, C., & Payne, M. (2003). Are you being served? Political accountability and quality of government. *Journal of Law, Economics, & Organization, 19*(2), 445–490.

Kaufman, D., Kray, A., & Mastruzzi, M. (2008). *Governance matters VII: Aggregate and individual governance indicators, 1996–2007* (World Bank Policy Research Working Paper No. 4654). Washington, DC: World Bank.

Nanda, V. P. (2006). The "good governance" concept revisited. *Annals of the American Academy of Political and Social Science, 603*(1), 269–283.

Rothstein, B., & Teorell, J. (2008). What is quality of government? A theory of impartial government institutions. *Governance, 21*(2), 165–190.

Governance, Informal

Many academic observers would argue that we have witnessed a shift from government to governance over the past decenniums, reflected in "softer" and more indirect steering mechanisms. Governance also involves more interaction between public authorities and other social actors. Still, from a distance, the discussion seems rather confusing, in that different meanings of the concept of governance are used in the literature. According a few European scholars, the term *governance* basically refers to "new" ideas related to the involvement of society in the process of governing. According to some American specialists, on the other hand, the term retains much of its original steering conception. To overcome this conceptual challenge, one may understand governance as consisting of four activities:

1. the process of articulating common priorities,
2. the process of bringing coherence to these priorities,
3. the process of and capacity for steering, and
4. the processes of establishing some form of accountability.

Based on this perspective, this entry explains the characteristics of informal governance and the different forms it takes and discusses how informal governance may be evaluated in terms of effectiveness and democracy.

Governance can assume many different forms and can be classified along different dimensions. Focusing on the extent of formality, one can argue that governance is formal when the production of authoritative decisions and actions takes place in a single hierarchical structure, such as a democratically elected legislative assembly and government.

Moving to the opposite pole, informal governance means that the production of public values arises from the interaction of a plethora of public and private and collective and individual actors. The mechanisms in use depend, moreover, to some extent on the cooperation of the involved nongovernmental actors. Informal governance means that participation in the decision-making process is not yet or cannot in fact be codified and publicly enforced. But it may also mean that a certain group of decision makers agree *informally* to advocate or enact particular policies, while still acting in *formal* decision-making contexts.

Informal governance is not new, nor should it be associated with specific institutions or levels of government. Governments have been engaged in informal governance since time immemorial, and informal governance can be found in institutions such as the European Union (EU), as in national, regional, and local policy processes.

Why Informal Governance?

Although not new, governments have come to rely more heavily on informal governance. Many reasons exist for this shift toward informality. One is the declining trust in, and respect for, government in many countries. As most formal instruments of governance rely on a government's legitimate authority to be effective, the waning of legitimacy makes traditional instruments less certain. Likewise, governments have experienced direct mechanisms as costly and inefficient, compared with the use of the private sector as partners in implementation. Governments are seldom the sole proprietors of expert knowledge, often needing to rely on other institutions' expert knowledge, and a wide range of stakeholders wish to participate in the policy process. Ideological changes toward "new public management" and a "network society" have also stressed the need to move away from direct government involvement to more indirect forms of governing and informal governance.

Some argue that informal governance is propelled by the EU, and to a significant extent, informal governance can be claimed to be a necessary part of the EU system, because the EU can often actually make policy by way of informal routes and networking. One example of this is the Eurogroup: the circle of finance ministers arguably shaping European economic governance by pre-agreeing on all critical decisions made by the council, deciding on overall orientation of economic governance in the euro area, and establishing common interpretations of the European Monetary Union's (EMU's) core policy instruments. In spite of its important role, the Eurogroup is seen as administratively precarious and only semirecognized by law. It is formally recognized that it should meet informally, and consequently neither a secretariat nor a Eurogroup mailbox exists in Brussels.

Forms of Informal Governance

Even if informal governance appears as a concept in the literature, one should not treat all forms as virtually identical. These interventions in the name of, if not by, the public itself need to be invested more carefully, and one should attempt to put into perspective the various political, economic, and administrative logics of choice involved.

One way to categorize different forms of informal governance, proposed by B. Guy Peters, is to divide informal governance into soft law, networks, partnerships, coproduction, multilevel governance, and the so-called open method of coordination.

The basic idea of *soft law* is that the public sector does not establish all the rules for action but permits social actors to bargain within a broader established policy statement. One example is negotiated rule making in the United States, where the affected parties and relevant government agencies are permitted to bargain among themselves with regard to the final and operating rules. This commonly discussed form of governance stands in contrast to the hard law of legal command and formal regulations.

Network is a second type of informal governance, covering mechanisms through which state and society have become more closely linked. Networks represent a broad and general category of interactions that is grounded in interdependency among actors simultaneously keeping their operational autonomy intact. These actors interact and negotiate over a period of time, creating an institutional framework of rules, norms, shared knowledge, and social imagination.

Public–private *partnerships* represent a distinct subcategory of networks and a common mechanism for implementing public programs. The basic idea of these arrangements is that a relationship is created between the public sector and one or more private actors, intending to deliver a specific service jointly. Most commonly, these arrangements materialize as written contracts between the involved partners. Building or using existing trust is arguably a necessary condition to make these partnerships work.

Coproduction is closely related to partnerships and departs from the idea that the public sector will cooperate with private actors in the delivery of a service, therefore running the risk of devolving the necessary authority to these actors. Public programs directed at "neighborhood watch" and different kinds of user boards consisting of, for example, school teachers and parents have served as examples of informal governance—in the form of coproduction.

Multilevel governance is usually understood in terms of public actors who, through bargaining, make decisions and coordinate their actions. But even if a clear hierarchy does not exist, multilevel governance still does not by definition include social actors. On the other hand, the use of these interactions, and the way they steer clear of the traditional hierarchy, may provide social actors with greater opportunities for influence.

The so-called open method of coordination, a distinct form developed in the EU, resembles to some extent the form of soft law discussed above. This cannot be defined as a single method, rather a variety of mechanisms, such as benchmarking and sharing best practices to change the behavior of the relevant actors (in the case of the EU, the governments within the union). But the basic ideas of benchmarking apply much more widely and indicate that this model should be understood as a more general form of informal governance.

Evaluating Informal Governance

Informal governance can be evaluated on different terms, and the specific forms mentioned above will to some extent score differently depending on which criterion is used. However, relevant literature on the subject tends to agree that informal governance has consequences for its steering capacity. Permitting a wider range of actors to become involved in, for example, policy processes means that their views will be known to actors with a formal capacity to make decisions. This may improve the quality of decisions and, thereby, prevent later problems when policies are actually implemented. However, this may also slow down the process and make bargaining among the different actors more complicated.

The most problematic aspects of informal governance are still related to democracy and accountability. Informal governance, whatever specific form it takes, means that some social actors become part of the public policy process, while others do not. To evaluate informal governance in democratic terms, questions need to be raised about authority, participation, and assurance: Who has the authority to invite participants? Who participates and on what terms? And finally, how are justice and reliability assured?

Just asking these questions leads one to draw the inevitable conclusion that the existence of informal governance definitely challenges core ideas about democracy. These challenges appear at two levels. From the viewpoint of representative democracy, we are entitled to ask whether informal governance can be developed in such a way that its foundation in representative government remains clear. But informal governance may also lead to a broader discussion about democracy and to whether the whole idea of democracy should be rethought in such a way that informal governance becomes less challenging.

Asbjørn Røiseland
Bodø University College
Bodø, Norway

See also Coordination; Governance, Multilevel; Networks; Soft Law

Further Readings

Christiansen, T., Føllesdal, A., & Piattoni, S. (2003). Informal governance in the European Union: An introduction. In T. Christiansen & S. Piattoni (Eds.), *Informal governance in the European Union* (pp. 1–21). Cheltenham, UK: Edward Elgar.

Goldsmith, S., & Eggers, W. D. (2004). *Governing by network: The new shape of the public sector.* Washington, DC: Brookings Institution Press.

Peters, B. G. (2007). Forms of informal governance: Searching for efficiency and democracy. In T. Christiansen & T. Larsson (Eds.), *The role of committees in the policy-process of the European Union* (pp. 39–63). Cheltenham, UK: Edward Elgar.

Pierre, J., & Peters, B. G. (2005). *Governing complex societies.* Hampshire, UK: Palgrave.

Puetter, U. (2006). *The Eurogroup: How a secretive circle of finance ministers shape European economic governance.* Manchester, UK: Manchester University Press.

Sørensen, E., & Torfing, J. (Eds.). (2007). *Theories of democratic network governance.* Hampshire, UK: Palgrave.

Governance, Multilevel

Multilevel governance gained prominence in the field of European Union (EU) studies, where it was applied to explain patterns of European integration and the way in which policy was made and implemented within an increasingly populated European political arena. Feeding into the broader governance debate, which seeks to understand the challenges to governmental capacity presented by processes such as hollowing out and fragmentation, multilevel governance highlights the vertical relations between actors and institutions across various territorial levels, alongside the transforming horizontal relationships between state and nonstate actors. Proponents of multilevel governance reject the state-centricity of many alternative accounts to highlight the blurring of boundaries between domestic and international politics, wherein authority is increasingly shared across levels. In turn, the growing multiplicity of both state and nonstate participants and of policy implementation is highlighted. A key empirical question underpinning theories of multilevel governance is therefore the extent to which central governments are subsequently losing their authority and capacity to achieve their policy preferences. This entry identifies the commonly understood strands that underpin accounts of multilevel governance before considering the various distinct forms that multilevel governance can assume. This entry then provides an account of multilevel governance's major strengths, while highlighting the weaknesses identified, to illustrate its utility as a theory of political science.

Historical and Theoretical Context

The intellectual origins of *multilevel governance* can be found in the study of the EU. Influenced by the emerging perspective of the EU as a distinct political system, the term was first used by Gary Marks in 1992 to capture developments in European policy making. Prior to the 1980s, the study of the EU and the process of European integration were dominated by approaches that were influenced by the field of international relations (IR). Drawing on the tradition of pluralism within IR studies, the neo-functionalist approach, which prevailed in the late 1950s and early 1960s, suggested that despite their initiation of the integration process, national governments were increasingly losing control in a complex network of state and nonstate actors. The neo-functionalist perspective was not unanimously accepted and was countered by the intergovernmentalist approach, which drew on the realist approaches in IR to stress the ongoing dominance of national governments within European structures. Its assumptions were strengthened by the reassertion of national authority and the continuance of national veto across the majority of policy areas, and the intergovernmentalist approach emerged as the dominant approach to EU studies from the 1960s onward. However, by the mid-1980s, the structures of the EU had begun to undergo a series of significant reforms, including the creation of a single market (the common market) following the 1986 Single European Act and the continued extension of qualified majority voting across a range of policy areas, which in turn reduced the scope of national veto. In particular, the ongoing shift toward qualified majority voting influenced new perspectives regarding the EU, wherein the EU was perceived as a distinct political system, with parallels to domestic political institutions, rather than simply as a vehicle, or process, of integration. In turn, greater attention was given to the role of subnational and supranational actors within EU policy making, which led to a reappraisal of traditional conceptions of center–periphery relationships. It was against this theoretical and empirical backdrop that Marks sought to move away from a two-dimensional analysis, centered on the upward flow of power from national to supranational actors, in order to highlight the effects of the downward seepage of power to subnational actors and their resultant impact on the policy process. He also drew on ideas regarding fragmentation, policy networks, and the role of nonstate actors to indicate the horizontal, as well as the vertical, flows of power.

Essence of Multilevel Governance

The burgeoning role of subnational governments as key actors in the European political arena has attracted increasing academic attention, within which multilevel governance has emerged as a key theoretical response. A central assumption of multilevel governance is that the process of European integration has meant that authority and policy-making influence are shared across multiple levels of government—subnational, national, and supranational. In contrast to the earlier state-centric views, multilevel governance has stressed the apparently independent role played by subnational actors in the European policy-making process, suggesting that regional governments have sufficient independence from national governments to shape their own preferences and directly influence the EU agenda. In turn, as Marks has noted, national governments are perceived as no longer representing the sole interface between the domestic and supranational arenas. The theoretical focus of multilevel governance can be located within the governance narrative, which has gained increasing currency since the mid-1990s as a way of understanding the challenges of steering and coordinating policy making and policy implementation within an increasingly complex social system. Central to the governance debate is the ability of national governments to assert their agendas on increasingly segmented polities, wherein concepts such as hollowing out and fragmentation have been applied to suggest that national governments have become simply one among a range of competing authorities. Multilevel governance thus refers to the negotiated, nonhierarchical exchanges between institutions at the supranational, national, regional, and local levels, highlighting the vertical layering of governance processes at these different levels.

As with so many concepts and theories in political science, multilevel governance is without an all-encompassing definition, and disagreement exists regarding its scope and utility. Nonetheless, there are several commonly agreed strands. A shared starting point is the acceptance that decision making occurs at various territorial levels and is characterized by the participation of state and societal actors. In turn, this has meant that the identification of the discrete and/or nested levels of decision making has become increasingly difficult in the context of complex, overlapping networks. Within this context, according to Ian Bache and Matthew Flinders (2004), the role of the state is under transformation, as emergent nonstate actors seek to develop new strategies of coordination, steering, and networking to protect, or even enhance, their autonomy. It is important to note that multilevel governance does not necessarily confront the sovereignty of states directly, and it casts national governments as the most important pieces of the European puzzle. Nevertheless, by highlighting the inability of national governments to monopolize the policy process, theories of multilevel governance make important judgments regarding state capacity, suggesting that the sharing of decision-making competencies among actors at various geopolitical levels has involved a significant loss of control for individual national governments. This has been compounded by the shift away from nested political arenas to increasingly interconnected policy networks, wherein subnational actors operate in both the national and international arenas, creating a range of transnational associations. Instead of being explicitly challenged, EU states are therefore

> being melded into a multi-level polity by their leaders and the actions of numerous sub-national and supranational actors, [and] one does not have to argue that states are on the verge of political extinction to believe that their control . . . has significantly weakened. (Liesbet Hooghe & Gary Marks, 2001, p. 27)

Reflecting on their changing capacity, many accounts of multilevel governance have identified the development of a gatekeeping role for state actors, wherein national governments act as a mediator between subnational and supranational actors to control access to the European policy arena in order to achieve or defend its preferred policy outcomes. Adopting the role of gatekeeper is perceived as enabling state actors to address strategic alternatives to zero-sum power struggles, as they seek to move away from "authoritative allocation and regulation 'from above' to the role of partner and mediator" (Beate Kohler-Koch, 1996, p. 371).

Competing Models of Multilevel Governance

In many respects, multilevel governance had assumed the guise of a conceptual umbrella, and it had been suggested that the breadth of its focus was sometimes at the expense of its explanatory power and analytical vigor. In particular, multilevel governance had been criticized for its focus on relationships between state actors across different levels rather than across different sectors, for being overly descriptive, and for overemphasizing the role of subnational actors in the policy process. Andrew Jordan (2001), for example, suggested that while multilevel governance (MLG) provides an "appealing picture of what the EU looks like," it was "weak at explaining which levels are the most important and why, and what actually motivated the experiment in governance in the first place" (p. 194). This led him to conclude that "the most we can currently say about MLG is that it needs to be subject to a great deal more case-study testing before it can be adopted as a general account of how (parts of) the EU operate(s)" (p. 204).

In response to such criticisms, Hooghe and Marks sought to delineate two contrasting views of the organization of multilevel governance, which they labeled simply Type I and Type II, summarized in Table 1. Type I multilevel governance focuses on formal intergovernmental relationships at a limited number of levels. These jurisdictions are general purpose, bundling together a range of policy responsibilities, and the membership boundaries of each jurisdiction do not intersect. Alternatively, Type II is composed of specialized jurisdictions wherein governance arrangements are organized around functionally specific governance networks (Hooghe & Marks, 2003).

As this brief overview suggests, Type I and Type II multilevel governance have different intellectual foundations, and therefore, they seek to explain different manifestations of the policy process. With its emphasis on power sharing among a limited number of formal governmental levels—international, national, regional, meso, and local—Type I multilevel governance has been influenced

Table 1 Types of Multilevel Governance

Type I	*Type II*
General-purpose jurisdictions	Task-specific jurisdictions
Nonintersecting memberships	Intersecting memberships
Jurisdictions at a limited number of intervals	No limit to the number of jurisdictional levels
Systemwide architecture	

Source: Hooghe and Marks (2003, p. 235).

by theories of federalism, which have been developed and applied beyond the parameters of individual nation-states. Type I multilevel governance is characterized as a "nested" or "Russian doll" model, wherein there is only one relevant jurisdiction at any particular territorial scale, which is intended to be stable for several decades or more. The bundling together of policy functions in a system of Type I multilevel governance is perceived to gain the benefits of varying territorial scale while minimizing the number of jurisdictions to be coordinated. Within this typology, nation-states remain of central importance, reflecting the emphasis given to national boundaries as a key organizer of political activity, and the focus of analysis is therefore on individual governments or institutions rather than on specific policies or issues. Alternatively, Type II multilevel governance reflects too many of the concepts associated with the governance narrative to present a fluid and complex picture of governance. Unlike the general purpose design of Type I multilevel governance, jurisdictions in Type II multilevel governance are task specific and organized around explicit problems or policy areas, their organization being flexible as governance demands change. These jurisdictions can entail intersecting memberships and can be organized across a range of jurisdictional levels, without being constrained by the nested hierarchical structures associated with Type I multilevel governance. Type II governance structures are intended to secure optimum efficiency in policy making and will be discontinued once they have served their purpose, in accordance with the emphasis on flexibility. Each typology is therefore based on a different conception of power. Type I is suited to dealing with zero-sum conflict about basic values, because it facilitates logrolling and cross-issue trading. However, Type II is effective in solving ad hoc coordination problems among individuals sharing the same geographical or functional space (Marks & Hooghe, 2004). Nonetheless, the two typologies are not mutually exclusive, and often, Type II governance is embedded within a Type I structure, for example, general-purpose jurisdictions can coexist alongside special-purpose jurisdictions; and formal institutions of government can actively assign functions to special-purpose bodies charged with addressing particular problems. The result of this has been described as a "baroque patchwork of Type II jurisdictions overlaying a nested pattern of Type I jurisdictions" (Hooghe & Marks, 2003, p. 238).

Strengths and Weaknesses

Multilevel governance has made an important contribution to political theory and has utility across a range of empirical settings. It has drawn on a range of ideas and concepts in political science—such as internationalization, regionalization, complexity, governance, and policy networks—to highlight the transdisciplinary approach that is needed in analyzing many contemporary issues and challenges. In particular, the theory bridges the traditional dichotomy between domestic and international politics to emphasize the "blurring of the distinction between the two through the process of European integration" (Bache, 2008, p. 28). Although developed in the context of EU policy making, multilevel governance has also gained increasing salience across a range of geopolitical settings, being perceived as a far more relevant way of understanding intergovernmental relationships by moving beyond the characterization of the zero-sum nature of intergovernmental relations implicit in previous approaches. While it remains contested, the broad appeal of multilevel governance reflects a shared concern with the role of nonstate actors, the growth of intersecting jurisdictions, increased complexity across the policy arena, and the challenges posed to state power. In this respect, multilevel governance has made an important contribution to the broader governance debate, providing a theoretical model, the robustness of which has been reinforced by the later distinction between Type I and Type II, which highlights the relationship between vertically organized territorial units of governance on the one hand and the interplay between task-specific, horizontally organized jurisdictions on the other. Multilevel governance has therefore been seen to provide a way of understanding the interaction of complexity within and between all jurisdictional levels, highlighting the role of state and nonstate actors. In this sense, multilevel governance can be seen as having been successful in moving beyond simplistic conceptions of the linear exercise of power that was implicit in earlier intergovernmentalist approaches by focusing attention on the impact of processes such as supranationalization, decentralization, devolution, and the dispersal of authority to semiautonomous bodies. In turn, multilevel governance can be used to sharpen questions regarding the mechanisms and strategies used to govern within a system of multilevel governance not just by national government actors seeking to ensure their influence in an increasingly complex policy arena but also by regional and subnational actors who similarly seek to ensure their influence.

Nonetheless, there have been several criticisms of multilevel governance as a way of understanding contemporary policy making and implementation. While posited as a counter to state-centric approaches, there are criticisms that multilevel governance has overstated the erosion of the governing capacity of nation-state actors, and it has been suggested that an emphasis on the plurality of competing interests has led to "fundamental questions" about the structure of power relations being "downplayed" (Paul Stubbs, 2005). It has also been suggested that multilevel governance has been overly descriptive at the expense of analytical vigor (e.g., Jordan, 2001). This was acknowledged by several exponents of multilevel governance, contributing to the delineation between Type I and Type II multilevel governance discussed above; see, for example, Hooghe and Marks (2003). Nevertheless, despite attempts at refinement, there is uncertainty regarding the ability of multilevel governance to "travel" across alternative geopolitical settings, with a distinction being made between the "theoretical vagueness" of multilevel governance as a concept, which can travel, and its precise and "rigid" modeling, which is unsuited to different contexts (Stubbs, 2005). A pronounced normative dimension has also been identified within several later accounts of multilevel governance. Despite suggesting that "there is no agreement about how multi-level governance should be organised," Marks and Hooghe (2004) have argued that

> the dispersion of governance across multiple jurisdictions is *both more effective than, and normatively superior to* [italics added], central state monopoly . . . that governance must operate at multiple scales in order to capture variations in the territorial reach of policy externalities. . . . To internalize externalities, governance must be multi-level. (p. 16)

The normative justification for the application of multilevel governance has been perceived as a "very dubious elision" of "what governance should be, whilst a legitimate question in normative political science, is of a different order to questions of what governance *is*" (Stubbs, 2005, p. 69). Thus, as Bache and Flinders have argued, it is therefore important to distinguish between multilevel governance as an analytical mode and a normative concept.

Role in Future Political Analysis

While some aspects remain contested, multilevel governance has emerged as an important way of making sense of policy making and implementation in an increasingly crowded polity. Although its roots are in the study of the EU, the way in which multilevel governance bridges the divide between the study of international and domestic politics has meant that its utility has extended beyond the field of Europeanization and into a range of alternative analytical areas. To promote the ongoing salience of multilevel governance, a key challenge will be in ensuring that it remains responsive to the organic evolution of the political world that it seeks to explain. Returning to the study of the EU, the 2004 enlargement saw 10 further countries formally join the EU, which were joined by Bulgaria and Romania in 2007; and accession negotiations are going on with several other states. As the EU continues to expand east, it is likely that questions will emerge regarding the possibility of stretching a Type I jurisdiction of an EU that comprises upward of 27 countries or the extent to which Type II governance arrangements will be used in policy making and implementation. Another emergent issue is the extent to which the changing context of policy making, as perceived within accounts of multilevel governance, has challenged traditional conceptions of democratic accountability. In turn, this necessitates their reappraisal, as while different forms of multilevel governance may add to the legitimacy of policy making through increased efficiency, this may reduce democratic legitimacy unless new means of connecting citizens with these shifting locations of power are identified. Finally, as noted by Bache and Flinders, there is some evidence that suggests the emergence of unintended consequences arising from forms of multilevel governance that are beyond state control, and a key future research agenda will entail making sense of their occurrence.

Matthew Flinders
University of Sheffield
Sheffield, United Kingdom

Felicity Matthews
University of Exeter
Exeter, United Kingdom

See also European Integration; Europeanization of Policy; Governance, Good; Governance, Informal

Further Readings

Bache, I. (1999). The extended gatekeeper: Central government and the implementation of EC regional policy in the UK. *Journal of European Public Policy, 6*(1), 28–45.

Bache, I. (2008). *Europeanisation and multi-level governance.* London: Rowman & Littlefield.

Bache, I., & Flinders, M. (Eds.). (2004). *Multi-level governance.* Oxford, UK: Oxford University Press.

Hix, S. (1994). The study of the European Community: The challenge to comparative politics. *West European Politics, 17*(1), 1–30.

Hooghe, L., & Marks, G. (2001). *Multi-level governance and European integration.* Lanham, MD: Rowman & Littlefield.

Hooghe, L., & Marks, G. (2003). Unravelling the central state, but how? Types of multi-level governance. *American Political Science Review, 97*(2), 233–243.

Jordan, A. (2001). The European Union: An evolving system of multi-level governance . . . or government? *Policy & Politics, 29*(2), 193–208.

Kohler-Koch, B. (1996). Catching up with change: The transformation of governance in the European Union. *Journal of European Public Policy, 3*(3), 359–380.

Marks, G., & Hooghe, L. (2004). Contrasting visions of multi-level governance. In I. Bache & M. Flinders (Eds.), *Multi-level governance* (pp. 15–30). Oxford, UK: Oxford University Press.

Marks, G., Hooghe, L., & Blank, K. (1996). European integration from the 1980s: State-centric v. multi-level governance. *Journal of Common Market Studies, 34*(3), 341–378.

Sbragia, A. (Ed.). (1992). *Euro-politics: Institutions and policymaking in the "new" European Community* (pp. 191–224). Washington, DC: Brookings Institution Press.

Stubbs, P. (2005). Stretching concepts too far? Multi-level governance, policy transfer and the politics of scale in South East Europe. *Southeast European Politics, 6*(2), 66–87.

Governance, Urban

The term *governance* is increasingly used in urban politics, policy, and administration to signify activities related to public policy that are undertaken jointly by multiple actors, including some outside government. Gerry Stoker (2000) defines governance as "working across boundaries within the public sector or between the public sector and private or voluntary sectors" (p. 93). Although the literature has dealt with governance at different levels, the idea has special relevance at the local level, where solving problems or creating the capacity to act often involves mobilizing support from other sectors and other levels of government. This entry first discusses the evolution and types of governance and then focuses on models of urban governance.

Why Governance?

Social and economic changes have increased the permeability of policy making. The literature points to forces such as globalization and fiscal pressures across advanced industrial democracies, particularly because of demographic change and economic competition. Jan Kooiman (2000) describes this complexity as the growing ungovernability of society. At the same time, the demands and expectations of citizens have increased. Rising education levels, more critical citizens, and decreased trust in government have increased pressures for reform and alternative service delivery.

These reforms have opened up government to the market, and in some cases it has led to more participation at the grassroots level. As Donald Kettl in 2000 and B. Guy Peters in 2001 note, the wave of privatization in the United States in the 1980s and trends such as new public management abroad or government "reinvention" here have produced new contractual relationships with private sector and nonprofit organizations. These changes have also multiplied quasi-governmental agencies and special districts. Most governance theory and research is concerned with describing, explaining, and managing *processes* within this new context, particularly processes of bargaining and cooperation.

While cities in the decentralized American system are particularly sensitive to business investment decisions, Stoker (2000) contends that fragmentation and interdependence are more generally high in urban policy across countries. Problems such as poverty and the redevelopment of distressed areas are not easily solved by government alone. Theories of local governance have evolved more broadly to embrace other types of local policy partnerships.

Types of Governance

Two general approaches to governance are identified by Jon Pierre (2000), and while these apply to governance at the national level, they are useful for thinking about models of local governance as well. One is governance as goal definition and policy making. Pierre and Peters (2005) define it in terms of four activities:

1. goal definition (articulating a common set of priorities for society),
2. coherence (consistency and coordination),
3. steering (finding ways of achieving goals), and
4. accountability.

In the literature on *local governance*, urban regimes or governing coalitions set the policy agenda and goals more generally within the community, in contrast to the more specialized governance relations in policy networks.

On the other hand, research on governance as networks emphasizes interactions within policy domains such as education, economic development, or public safety, as described, for example, by Walter J. M. Kickert, Erik-Hans Klijn, and Joop F. M. Kopenjan (1997), Laurence J. O'Toole (1997), Rod A. W. Rhodes (1997), R. A. W. Rhodes and David Marsh (1992), and Fritz Scharpf (1993). Interdependent and cooperative relationships in networks are often depicted as distinct from those in hierarchies or markets, as noted by Kooiman (2000) and Rhodes (1997). According to Pierre and Peters (2005) and Stoker (2000), collaboration, of course, entails costs in terms of time and effort, and processes of negotiation and compromise may also produce outcomes that are not congruent with the goals of all participating organizations. The research on urban governance as policy networks is often more prominent in European research, as local governments often have less autonomy from the central government and play an important role in delivering the services of the welfare state. But work on civic capacity and urban education in the United States also falls into this category.

Urban Regimes and Governing

Models of local governance arose in response to earlier debates on community power and contemporary debates over the role of economic development in American local government. In 1987 John Logan and Harvey Molotch, for example, depicted urban governance as occurring through local growth coalitions, composed of city officials and locally dependent businesses such as newspapers, utilities, banks, and developers. The most influential framework for understanding cross-sectoral governance at the local level has been urban regime analysis. A "regime" connotes a set of governing arrangements, and in its usage over the past few decades, it indicates cooperation across institutional boundaries, beyond the formal apparatus of government. According to Karen Mossberger and Gerry Stoker (2001), collaboration is a response to the fragmentation of authority and interdependence between the policy-making capacity of democratic institutions and the wealth-generating resources of the market economy.

Early versions of regime analysis emphasized cross-sectoral goal setting and steering rather than network, for example, historical variation in regimes, and suggest change over time in goals, resources, and partners in American cities. Their typology described directive regimes during the period of urban renewal, concessionary regimes in the 1960s, and entrepreneurial regimes that responded to later cuts in federal aid and capital mobility with economic development initiatives. For Stephen Elkin, regimes are also goal setting and steering in the most fundamental sense. They are "constitutive" or formative institutions that shape the interaction between the democratic state and the privately controlled market. Elkin also depicts historical and geographic variation in regime types.

According to Clarence Stone (1989), urban regimes are governing arrangements also; but more concretely, they are carried out by a governing coalition, "an informal yet relatively stable group with *access to institutional resources* that enable it to have a sustained role in making governing decisions" (p. 4). Stone's work echoes many of the same themes found in the network literature—interdependence, congruent goals, the mobilization of resources, negotiation, and mutual adjustment of goals through interaction over time. The social production model of power in regime analysis is necessary to overcome the fragmentation of authority and resources. Regimes embody the "power to act" or the "capacity to act" rather than simply domination over other actors. According to Stone, the goal-setting and steering aspects of regimes are significant—urban regimes are more than economic development coalitions: They are governing coalitions that set priorities for the city as a whole. Over time, Stone (2005) has broadened the concept, arguing that regimes may vary in their stability and that cross-sectoral participation does not require the presence of business. The participation of other groups varies with the policy agenda of the regime.

Stone and his collaborators on education reform have formulated the concept of "civic capacity," applied to cooperation within a more specific local policy network (rather than a governing coalition). Civic capacity is needed "to devise and employ formal and informal mechanisms to collectively solve problems," but it also engages a broader range of actors than governing coalitions, including neighborhood residents and community groups as well as policy professionals, universities, nonprofit organizations, businesses, and other stakeholders in the particular issue. Influencing policy requires changing governing arrangements within policy subsystems rather than winning sporadic victories through interest group pressure. Some other scholars have used elements of urban regime analysis to explain cooperation in local policy networks—for example, in AIDS policy. The range of actors, the motivations, and the difficulty of mobilizing resources and maintaining collaboration would be expected to differ across policy areas.

Other Models of Urban Governance

At the same time that urban regime analysis developed in the United States, economic restructuring and changes in the welfare state in many countries increased pressures at the local level and the possibility that urban regime analysis could explain new forms of governance appearing in many places. One study of 11 cities in the United States, Germany, and France found stable urban regimes in all three countries, particularly where there were locally dependent businesses. There are also instances where no stable regime has formed in any of the countries in the study.

The cross-national use of the urban regime concept poses some challenges, however (see Mossberger & Stoker, 2001). European institutional contexts offer markedly different patterns of resources, authority, and incentives for cross-sectoral collaboration at the local level. In Europe, greater fiscal support from central governments, more public ownership of municipal land, and other factors lessen the need for business involvement as a critical factor for the "power to" achieve development and support local services. In some countries, business is more centralized (as in the United Kingdom), or corporatist arrangements are largely worked out through the national parties. Stronger parties more generally lend a national character to political relationships at the local level, in contrast with the United States. Partnerships in small U.K. cities, for example, appear to be the result of top-down initiatives from central government rather than an expression of the social production model of power at the local level. Economic development partnerships are apparent in several Western European countries, but despite some parallels with urban regimes, the central government often played a large role in the formation and priorities of the partnerships. And European instances of cross-sectoral cooperation are not always setting agendas for the city as a whole. Furthermore, economic development policy in Britain tends to resemble a discrete policy network with strong vertical links to the central government as well as business participation. As such, it appears to be closer to the model of networks within policy domains rather than a governing coalition that influences citywide priorities.

Pierre (2005) and Alan DiGaetano and Elizabeth Strom (2003) have argued for a broader concept of urban governance that is more comparative. There has been a burgeoning literature on local governance across many countries, conceived of as a local multi-actor collaboration that fits either policy networks or governing models. Studies show evidence of trends toward governance at the local level in most advanced industrialized countries and in some other countries as well. One edited volume containing studies of a dozen Organisation for Economic Co-operation and Development (OECD) countries reveals the presence of public–private partnerships in 10 of them. The authors caution that these "may not look like urban regimes" but that there is increased local economic development activity and greater dependence on other organizations outside of government at the local and regional levels (see Robin Hambleton & Jill Gross, 2007).

Conclusion

Concepts of urban governance have been useful for describing patterns of urban policy making in both citywide agenda setting and in local policy domains. While forms of governance differ across countries, the concept has described trends toward policy making, mobilizing the resources of multiple actors in governing coalitions or networks. There are many questions about governance that bear further scrutiny—the role and legitimacy of actors outside of government, the costs and difficulty of coordination, the consequences of unequal power within coalitions and networks for representation and for problem solving, and diffused accountability for achieving public purposes. All of these are important questions for empirical investigation and for theory, across different countries, policy areas, and forms of urban governance.

Karen Mossberger
University of Illinois at Chicago
Chicago, Illinois, United States

See also Governance, Administration Policies; Governance, Informal; Governance, Multilevel; Regime (Comparative Politics)

Further Readings

DiGaetano, A., & Strom, E. (2003). Comparative urban governance: An integrated approach. *Urban Affairs Review, 38*(3), 356–395.

Hambleton, R., & Gross, J. (2007). *Governing cities in a global era: Urban innovation, competition, and democratic reform.* Hampshire, UK: Palgrave Macmillan.

Kooiman, J. (Ed.). (2001). *Modern governance.* London: Sage.

Mossberger, K., & Stoker, G. (2001). The evolution of urban regime theory: The challenge of conceptualization. *Urban Affairs Review, 36*(6), 810–835.

Pierre, J. (2005). Comparative urban governance: Uncovering complex causalities. *Urban Affairs Review, 40*(4), 446–462.

Pierre, J., & Peters, B. G. (2005). *Governing complex societies: Trajectories and scenarios.* Basingstoke, UK: Palgrave.

Rhodes, R. A. W. (1997). *Understanding governance. Policy networks, governance, reflexivity and accountability.* Buckingham, UK: Open University Press.

Stoker, G. (2000). Urban political science and the challenge of urban governance. In J. Pierre (Ed.), *Debating governance* (pp. 91–109). Hampshire, UK: Palgrave Macmillan.

Stone, C. (1989). *Regime politics: Governing Atlanta, 1946-1988.* Lawrence: University Press of Kansas.

Stone, C. N. (2005). Looking back to look forward: Reflections on urban regime analysis. *Urban Affairs Review, 40*(3), 309–341.

Governance Networks

Governance is usually defined as the processes through which a plurality of actors aim to produce and deliver public purpose in the broad sense of political visions, operative plans, problem definitions, policy solutions, infrastructures, regulations, resource allocations, and public services. Governance can be provided by unicentric forms of government based on hierarchical command structures. It may also involve forming multicentric forms of quasi markets where public and/or private actors compete to deliver goods and services on terms defined by elected governments. Finally, governance may take the form of pluricentric partnerships and networks in which policy decisions are reached through negotiated interaction among interdependent actors.

The study of governance networks constitutes a novel research field based on the "discovery" of nonhierarchical forms of governance involving networks of public and/or private actors. The basic argument prompting the recent surge in governance network research is that public policy, defined as common attempts to achieve a desired outcome, is the result of governing processes that are no longer controlled by the government, instead involving a wide range of relevant and affected actors engaged in ongoing negotiations that give rise to a stable pattern of horizontal interaction constituting a specific mode of coordination. It is this "heterarchic" mode of coordination that is dubbed "governance networks" in the academic literature.

The focus on governance networks has an empirical background in the widespread recognition of the increasingly fragmented, complex, and dynamic character of contemporary society. Fragmentation increases as a result of the functional differentiation of society into relatively autonomous subsystems and organizational entities. At the same time, the breakup of the sedimented forms of political alignment and identification spurs multiplication of political actors and identities. Complexity increases as a result of the growth and interweaving of crosscutting policy problems, and it is further augmented by the advent of new forms of risk and the blurring of the boundaries between institutions, sectors, and scales. Finally, new societal dynamics are created by the proliferation and interconnection of new spatial and temporal horizons of action. The contingent articulation and interaction of the different rationalities, procedures, and strategies for solving policy problems and exploiting new opportunities produces new and unpredictable developments. The result of the growing fragmentation, complexity, and dynamism is an increasing ungovernability of society that makes it difficult to meet the growing steering ambitions demanding that public governance be flexible, knowledge based, targeted, responsive, and inexpensive. The mobilization of the knowledge, resources, and energies of relevant and affected actors through governance networks offers a promising way out of this impasse.

Leading politicians and executive administrators seem to have taken governance networks to their hearts. Governments around the world and at different levels increasingly aim to govern at a distance by creating arenas for self-governance and self-regulation. Public agencies and managers are becoming linked through new initiatives aiming to promote joined-up government. Last but not least, public and private actors are brought together through the formation of different kinds of partnerships and collaborative governance.

After closer inspection of the definition of governance networks and a brief account of the theoretical roots of the concept of governance networks, some caveats regarding the discussion of governance networks are presented here. This is followed by an assessment of the merits and problems of governance networks in public policy making. Finally, some of the main theories of governance networks are presented before a concluding discussion of the major themes in the research on governance networks.

Defining Governance Networks

Governance networks can be defined as (a) a relatively stable horizontal articulation of interdependent but operationally autonomous actors, (b) that interact with one another through ongoing negotiations (c) that take place within a regulative, normative, cognitive, and imaginary framework; (d) facilitate self-regulation within the limits set by external forces; and (e) contribute to the production of public purpose. Other defining features might be added, but this definition captures the essence of what are commonly referred to as governance networks.

This entry attempts to unpack this dense definition of governance networks by considering each defining feature in turn. First, governance networks articulate a number of public, semipublic, and private actors who, on the one hand, are dependent on one another's resources and capacities to get things done and, on the other hand, are *operationally autonomous* in that they are not commanded by superiors to act in a certain way. The interdependent relations between the network actors mean that they are horizontally, rather than vertically, related. However, the horizontal relations between the network actors do not imply equality in terms of authority and resources. There might be an asymmetric allocation of material and immaterial resources among the network actors, but since participation is voluntary and the actors are free to leave the network—and since the actors are mutually dependent—no single actor can fully exercise its power to exert hierarchical control over anyone else.

Second, members of governance networks interact through negotiations that combine elements of bargaining and deliberation. The network actors may bargain over the distribution of resources to maximize outcomes; however, to facilitate some degree of cooperation, coordination, and collaboration, the bargaining process must be embedded in a deliberative process that facilitates trust building, reciprocal recognition, learning, and common understanding. Nevertheless, deliberation within governance networks will seldom lead to consensus, since it transpires within a context of power struggles that breed conflict and social antagonism. Hence, outcomes involve a collective agreement-based compromise and tacit acceptance of decisions despite grievances.

Third, the negotiated interaction between the network actors does not take place in an institutional vacuum. Rather, it proceeds within a relatively institutionalized framework that is shaped and reshaped in the course of action. In the beginning, when a governance network is formed, there is no agreed-on institutional framework that determines where and how a legitimate decision is to be taken. However, the ongoing interaction of network actors will lead to the formulation of an incomplete and precarious framework of rules, norms, values, and ideas that condition the future interaction in the network by defining appropriate action. (*Value* refers to everything that is considered to have a value, be it material, ideological, ethical, or other, by most people/citizens.)

Fourth, governance networks are relatively self-regulating, as they are not part of a hierarchical chain of command or components of markets. Rather, they aim at regulating a particular policy field or problem area based on their own ideas, resources, and dynamic interactions, and they do so within a regulative, normative, cognitive, and imaginary framework that is adjusted through negotiations between the participating actors. Nevertheless, governance networks always operate in a shadow of hierarchy as public authorities and other legitimate and resourceful actors aim to facilitate, shape, and constrain the network's preference and capacity for self-regulation. Governance networks that are metagoverned in this way only enjoy a bounded autonomy.

Fifth, governance networks contribute to the production of public purpose within a certain policy area. Public purpose is an ensemble of visions, values, plans, policies, and regulations that are claimed to be valid for, and directed toward, the general public. As such, the network actors are engaged in political negotiations about how to identify and solve emerging policy problems and provide new opportunities. Networks that do not contribute to the production of public purpose in this broad sense cannot be counted as governance networks.

Governance networks, as defined above, may have *different functions*. Some governance networks merely contribute to the exchange of knowledge, ideas, and experiences, while other networks aim to coordinate action in order to avoid conflicts and duplication of efforts. Some governance networks might even attempt to arrive at a common understanding of emerging policy problems and formulate joint solutions. Governance networks may also take *different forms* as they grow autonomously from below or are initiated from above, are open or closed, are loosely connected or highly integrated, are short-lived or relatively permanent, and have a sector-specific or society-wide scope. Finally, governance networks have many *different labels* as they are frequently referred to as planning cells, think tanks, public boards and committees, commissions, partnerships, and so on. The different labels, forms, and functions of governance networks attest to the broad relevance of the concept for describing contemporary interactive governance.

Theoretical Roots

The increasing prominence of governance network research is rooted in theoretical developments in organization theory, political theory, policy analysis, Europeanization studies, and international relations. The conception of organizations as open systems adapting to environmental changes—and the subsequent recognition that this environment consists of other organizations—paved the way for a new focus on the interorganizational exchange of information and resources taking place through relatively stable forms of network-based negotiation. Likewise, the recognition of the limits of the corporatist and neo-corporatist images of Iron Triangles, linking state agencies and social partners in tightly organized decision-making arenas, spurred the attempts of political theorists to distinguish between different kinds of more or less integrated policy networks that may include a broader range of public and private actors.

If both organization theory and political theory gradually arrived at some notion of governance networks, the real breakthrough for the new focus on governance networks came in the field of policy analysis. Decision-making theorists revealed the limits of the rational decision-making model in the face of the complexity of increasingly fragmented policy processes in which social and political actors struggle to link problems and solutions in highly contingent policy decisions, and implementation theorists demonstrated the failure of comprehensive planning and top-down programming in the face of the fierce resistance of street-level bureaucrats, user groups, and interest organizations. The inescapable conclusion was that public policy making becomes more efficient if the key actors are somehow included in the policy process and develop an ownership to joint decisions.

The empirical discovery and analytical description of the European Union as a networked polity in which public and private actors negotiate within and across multiple levels and the current transformation of international regimes into transnational networks where private actors play an increasingly important role in policy making have further contributed to the development of theories of network governance.

Some Caveats

Policy making and public governance are not congruent with the formal political institutions in terms of parliament and public administration but take place in and through interactive forms of network governance. Some scholars tend to describe the result of this apparent shift from government to governance as a hollowing out of the state. However, others note that the growth of interactive forms of governance in the shape of networks and partnerships has not mitigated the role and impact of the state. The state may have lost its privileged position in public policy making, but many of the former state powers remain in place and new capacities are developed as central and local state agencies take on the task of metagoverning governance networks at different levels. As such, state power is not reduced; rather, it is exercised in new and subtle ways.

A common misunderstanding is that governance networks are an entirely new phenomenon. In many countries and policy areas, there are long traditions for the corporatist involvement of the social partners in the formulation and implementation of policy, and interaction between public and private actors is a key feature of modern government and a constitutive trait of pluralist theory. What *is* new, however, is that political theorists and central decision makers increasingly view governance networks as both an efficient and legitimate mechanism of public governance. This is evidenced by the increasing reliance on governance networks at all levels of government.

When discussing governance networks, it is important to counteract the tendency to perceive governance networks as the perfect solution to all kinds of public governance problems. Governance networks are no panacea. When it comes to the exercise of public authority, there are good reasons for placing this task in the hands of public bureaucracies that can be held accountable for their action and inaction. Likewise, when it comes to the production of fairly standardized public goods and services, private markets might provide good value for public money. Governance networks have little to offer in relation to these public tasks, but they have their strength in relation to the large amount of "wicked problems" in public governance where the nature of the policy problem is uncertain, specialized knowledge is needed, and there are many relevant stakeholders from different sectors and levels and a high risk of conflict.

Merits and Problems of Governance Networks

Today, governance networks are increasingly perceived as a suitable response to the question of how to tackle complex and crosscutting policy problems and governance tasks. Hence, both political scientists and practitioners praise governance networks for their potential contribution to efficient governance. Efficiency gains derive from the distinctive features of governance networks. First of all, it is often claimed that ongoing negotiations among relevant and affected actors give governance networks a large potential for proactive governance. The network actors can identify policy problems and future opportunities at a relatively early stage and produce adequate responses that allow for adjustments in the face of new developments and changing conditions. This helps explain why small states with strong traditions for negotiated governance have done relatively well in the face of fluctuations in world markets.

Governance networks are also regarded as important instruments for the aggregation of information, knowledge, and assessments that can help in qualifying policy decisions. The network actors often possess specific knowledge that is relevant for political decision making, and when the knowledge of all of the network actors is pooled together, it represents an important basis for formulating and selecting innovative and yet feasible solutions or responses to the problems and challenges at hand.

In addition, governance networks are said to establish a framework for consensus building or, at least, for the civilizing of conflicts among the stakeholders. Governance networks tend to develop their own logic of appropriate action, which regulates the process of negotiation, the formulation of shared objectives, and the resolution of conflicts. Trust building through social interaction, through joint fact-finding, and through mutual learning further contributes to mediation of conflicts.

Finally, governance networks tend to reduce the risk of implementation resistance. If the affected actors are actively involved in the decision-making process, they will develop a sense of joint responsibility and ownership for the political decisions, even when they disagree with crucial aspects of these decisions. The shared ownership will oblige the stakeholders to support, rather than hamper, the implementation of public policy based on collaborative interaction.

The problem is that the potential efficiency and legitimacy gains of governance networks are only fully realized in well-functioning governance networks. Changes in the composition of a network and the presence of unresolved tensions and conflicts, weak and ineffective leadership, frustrations over the lack of clear and visible results, and external events that jeopardize the policy process tend to destabilize governance networks and turn them into inefficient talking shops. Careful institutional design and network management might prevent major dislocations and mitigate the impact of various disturbances, but optimizing the functioning of governance networks on all dimensions poses a daunting task. Even apparently well-functioning networks might cause problems for public policy making, either by enabling particular veto players to block new and innovative policy initiatives or by attempting to shift the costs of expensive policy solutions to third parties. To avoid such problems, elected governments and other forms of political agency must exercise their powers to overrule veto players and provide incentives for the networks to find responsible solutions.

Theories of Governance Networks

The concept of governance networks is descriptive, but the study of the emergence, functioning, and results of interactive forms of network governance certainly has explanatory ambitions, though not in the classical sense of aiming to establish deterministic causalities with a lawlike character. The ambition is to produce open-ended, context-sensitive knowledge that is relevant for the actors engaged in network governance. Explanation is established through theoretically informed empirical analysis of network-based policy processes and policy outcomes. The attempts of politicians and administrators to metagovern the relatively self-regulatory governance networks, the sociopolitical conditions and institutional design of governance networks, and the power struggles among the key stakeholders are central factors in explaining the outputs and outcomes of networked policy making.

Explanation of the formation, development, and impact of governance networks may draw on central insights from two of the main theories of governance networks: interdependence theory and governability theory. Both theories tend to view social action as driven by interest-based calculations, but they differ in their view on the prospect of overcoming conflicts and facilitating collaboration among multiple stakeholders.

Interdependence theory is inspired by historical institutionalism. It defines governance networks as an interorganizational medium for interest mediation between interdependent—but conflicting—actors, each with a rule and resource base. Governance networks are formed as a result of strategic calculations of independent actors who choose to interact because of their mutual resource dependencies. The formation of governance networks counteracts the institutional fragmentation caused by new public management reforms. Governance networks are formed through incremental bottom-up processes but are recruited as vehicles of public policy making by public authorities. The network actors pursue different interests through internal power struggles, but they are held together by their mutual interdependence, which facilitates negotiation and compromise.

Governability theory combines rational choice institutionalism with a systems theoretical view of societal development. It defines a governance networks as a horizontal coordination between autonomous actors who interact through different negotiation games. The formation of governance networks is seen as a functional response to the increasing societal complexity, differentiation, and dynamism that undermine the ability to govern society efficiently through hierarchy and market. Governance networks are viewed as gamelike structures that facilitate horizontal coordination among systems and organizations and are held together partly by the anticipated gains from resource pooling and joint action and partly by development of mutual trust that helps overcome collective action problems and mitigate conflicts.

Institutional theories of normative integration and theories of governmentality advanced by Michel Foucault and his followers also provide insights into the intricacies of interactive governance. These theories do not focus explicitly on governance networks, but they tend to view governance as a decentered process involving a plethora of public and private actors. While differing in the emphasis on the role of power and conflict in societal governance, both theories take an interpretative approach to social action, emphasizing the role of institutions and discourses in shaping the identity, perceptions, and actions of social actors.

Institutional theories of normative integration define governance networks as an institutionalized field of interaction between relevant policy actors who are integrated in a community defined by common rules, norms, and perceptions. Governance networks are regarded as a normative response to the twin problems of totalitarian overintegration and individualistic underintegration of social agency. They are formed through a bottom-up process whereby contacts established due to the recognition of interdependence are evaluated and extended on the basis of institutionalized logics of appropriateness. Over time, governance networks develop their own logic of appropriateness, and the network actors become normatively integrated through the construction of solidarity and common identities.

Governmentality theory implicitly defines governance networks as an attempt by an increasingly reflexive and facilitating state to mobilize and shape the free actions of self-governing actors. Governance networks are interpreted as a political response to the failure of neoliberalism to realize its key goal of less state and more market. The problematization of neoliberalism has led to the formulation of a new governmentality program, associated with advanced liberal government that aims to shift the burden of government to local networks in which the energies of social and political actors are mobilized and given a particular direction in order to ensure conformity. Governance networks are constructed and framed by particular governmental technologies and narratives that aim to recruit social and political actors as vehicles of the exercise of power.

Major Themes in First- and Second-Generation Research

Although the field of research is relatively new, it is possible to talk about first and second generations of governance network research. The first generation attempted to convince us that something new was occurring. As such, it was primarily preoccupied with explaining why and how governance networks are formed, how they differ from traditional forms of governance in terms of hierarchy and markets, and how they contribute to efficient governance within different policy fields and at different regulatory scales. The first generation succeeded in linking the rise of network governance to new societal trends, in fleshing out the distinctive features of governance networks vis-à-vis state and market, and in analyzing the formation and functioning of governance networks in different countries, in policy areas, and at different scales.

Slowly but surely, the research agenda has proceeded beyond the preoccupations of the first generation of governance network research. Governance networks no longer represent something new and exotic; rather, they are an intrinsic part of modern governance. At this stage, new and as yet unanswered questions have come to the fore and constitute the research agenda of a second generation of governance network research. The new generation does not constitute a clear break with the past as there is a considerable overlap in terms of scholars and research themes. However, the research agenda has been expanded to include a number of pressing questions. First, there is a growing number of researchers who are analyzing the sources of governance network failure and the conditions of success. Second, a large number of scholars are studying how public authorities and other legitimate and resourceful agencies can regulate self-regulating governance networks through different kinds of metagovernance. Third, the persistent critique of the tendency to view networked policy processes as depoliticized, managerial problem solving has prompted studies of the role of political conflicts and power struggles. Finally, political theorists and public administration researchers are paying increasing attention to the democratic problems and merits of governance networks.

Eva Sørensen and Jacob Torfing
Roskilde University
Roskilde, Denmark

See also Governance, Administration Policies; Governance, Global; Governance, Good; Governance, Informal; Governance, Multilevel

Further Readings

Dean, M. (1999). *Governmentality: Power and rule in modern society.* London: Sage.

Jessop, B. (2002). *The future of the capitalist state.* Cambridge, UK: Polity Press.

Kickert, W. J. M., Klijn, E. H., & Koppenjan, J. F. M. (1997). *Managing complex networks: Strategies for the public sector.* London: Sage.

Kohler-Koch, B., & Eising, R. (Eds.). (1999). *The transformation of governance in the European Union.* London: Routledge.

Kooiman, J. (Ed.). (1993). *Modern governance: New government-society interactions.* London: Sage.

March, J. G., & Olsen, J. P. (1995). *Democratic governance.* New York: Free Press.

Pierre, J. (Ed.). (2000). *Debating governance: Authority, steering, and democracy.* Oxford, UK: Oxford University Press.

Rhodes, R. A. W. (1997). *Understanding governance: Policy networks, governance, reflexivity and accountability.* Buckingham, UK: Open University Press.

Scharpf, F. W. (1997). *Games real actors play: Actor centered institutionalism in policy research.* Oxford, UK: West View Point.

Sørensen, E., & Torfing, J. (Eds.). (2007). *Theories of democratic network governance.* Basingstoke, UK: Palgrave Macmillan.

GOVERNMENT

Government is a key concept in comparative political science that has undergone frequent changes in terminology and has different importance in the intellectual traditions of democratic countries. Its core, more current definition refers to all activities of steering within human groups, from tribes to the state and to supranational and international organizations. This entry first discusses the meanings of the term *government* and then reviews the main functions of government. In the third section, the different contemporary models of government are illustrated. The subsequent two sections examine the key institutional aspects of government and the new approaches to the study of government, such as the so-called core executive models, the rational choice institutionalism, and governance studies.

Terminology

In the Middle Ages, the terms *regere* and *gubernare* were used as synonyms. The tradition of English- and French-speaking countries derived *to govern* and *government* or *gouverner* and *gouvernement* from the Latin term *gubernare*, whereas the German-speaking countries derived their main term *Regierung* from the Latin word *regere*. The French terminology preserved the notion of *régime*, which later was frequently used in a pejorative sense. The term ancien régime originally referred to the French system of government from about the 15th century until the French Revolution. Following Alexis de Tocqueville's 1856 work on the concept of ancien régime, the term was usually not used in a value-free and neutral way to refer to the prerevolutionary system under the Bourbon dynasty. Still, Max Weber, in his political writings, denounced the "regime" of his country as "half-patriarchical, half caesaristic."

In early-modern times, *government* and *administration* were rarely differentiated. Later, under the impact of the division of power theories of the 18th and 19th centuries, they were combined under the heading of the *executive*—as contrasted with the *legislature* or *parliament*. In the era of absolutist monarchy, *government*—defined as the auxiliary institution of a monarch—was the most important term. With the increasing constitutionalization of monarchy, government was no longer the leading institution in a political system but became a subsystem under the control of parliament and jurisdiction. Even in constitutional regimes with a dualistic structure but without a dominant parliament, as in Britain and the United States, the legal state or *Rechtsstaat* promoted the idea that government could not act without being empowered by a legislative decision. In Germany, positivist legal thinkers restricted the possibility of acting without mandate from parliament in the so-called *justizfreien Hoheitsakte* (governmental acts as an emanation of a sovereign will in the state, not underlying judicial review) in foreign policy and military affairs.

After the parliamentarization of monarchical regimes, the political power of government was increasingly differentiated from the mere technical execution of decisions taken by a common enterprise of legislature and government. New terminology arose due to the rise of the parties in parliaments. With the tenure of Benjamin Disraeli as prime minister in Britain, the term *party government* came to be used to demonstrate the integration of those politicians who are currently holding office. Parliamentary majorities and the prime minister and his or her ministerial crew were united by a common organization originally though not yet provided for in the statutes of the legislature—that is, the parties or parliamentary party groups.

Outside Britain or the United States, there is rarely one homogeneous majority party governing the country. Governmental coalitions or *Regierungskoalitionen* are directed by various office holders with quite different names, such as the British *prime minister*, the French *président du conseil*, or the *imperial* or *federal chancellor* in the German and Austrian traditions. In the hierarchy of government, there are normally two or more levels. In Britain, *the cabinet* constitutes only the inner core with ministers of state and parliamentary secretaries. In the United States, government is normally described as *the administration* or *the executive*.

Key Functions of Government

In parliamentary systems, the government has several functions. Most important is the function of *initiating policies*. Quite frequently, parliamentary bills are prepared by the executive offices. Moreover, government has the increasingly important function of *implementation*. Research on implementation has shown that laws and decrees are changed substantially by modes of implementation in the hand of bureaucracies under the guidance of governmental offices. A third function of government is *coordination*. The office of the government leader has to ensure that policies and bills and their implementation are complementary and do not contradict each other. With the growing power and fragmentation of parties in parliament during the 20th century, conservative political theorists frequently complained that countries were becoming increasingly difficult to govern. *Ungovernability* was a polemical term that became a popular exaggeration of political reality in the 1970s. The highly normative debate on governability was a reaction to the growth of the new social movements—the ecological and right-wing populists. The more progressive analysts who fought against the conservative doomsday scenarios accepted the new society of movements. They accepted the ecological movement as a promising source of change in society. These theorists came to less negative conclusions about the populist movements, which criticized "the system" but did not challenge the system as a whole, instead directing their criticism primarily at individual institutions and at the behavior of the "political class."

The postmodern cultural turn created other derivations. In France, Michel Foucault developed the expression *gouvernementalité*, which tried to link the mode of governing and regulations with the specific rationality of a decision. The mode of governing in this context aims less at direct influence of the individual and collective actors and focuses more on the indirect impact of action. *Gouvernementalité* tried to overcome the restrictions of an outlook that puts the sovereignty of state at the center of analysis. The dichotomy of notions, such as governing oneself and governing over others, is meant to strengthen the self-responsibility of modern citizens. Criticism in this theory is directed not so much against the existing governments and their institutions but against the underlying rationality of governmental aims and actions.

In the history of comparative research, the original term *comparative government* is rarely used anymore, and the dilemma of how to define government is avoided by adopting the new term *governance*, which came into use in the 1990s. In recent encyclopedias, "government" is no longer listed as an entry but is generally replaced by entries on "governance" and "governability" instead. In other professional dictionaries, only specialized articles such as "government regulation," "government budget constraint," or "government lawyers" and "government statistics" are included.

Models of Government

Government as a subject of comparative political science in recent years is no longer at the center of scholarly attention as it used to be until the 1970s. The literature on executive government in parliamentary systems is often not written by political scientists. Biographies and journalistic approaches dominate (Rod Rhodes, 2006). Government was defined as an institution that has the authority to allocate values within a legitimately recognized set of institutions. Experience increasingly showed, however, that government was no longer capable of making the desired allocations. Complex arrangements rest on horizontal forms of interaction between actors, independent of each other and no longer embedded in one hierarchical structure. Such horizontal relations have always been studied by political science, as in the "cozy triangles" of interest groups, administrators, and parliamentarians. In some European systems, the existence of federal actors and constitutional courts with certain veto powers complicated decision making. Postmodern polities developed this kind of cooperation with a certain regularity. Governance includes decision making not only via deliberation and negotiation but also through implementing bodies. Governance is no longer centered on the coercive power of the *state*—the incarnation of national sovereignty—although *governance* is not just another term for the *market*.

In a family tree of comparative politics, Philippe Schmitter in 2009 differentiated between three main branches of comparative politics: (1) *historical-sociological institutionalism* from Alexis de Tocqueville and Max Weber to Raymond Aron, Gabriel A. Almond, and David Apter; (2) *legal constitutionalism* from Maurice Duverger and Carl J. Friedrich to Klaus von Beyme; (3) *rational institutionalism* in the public choice tradition from Mancur Olson and Albert Hirschman to Anthony Downs, James Buchanan, and William Riker. Public policy and administration—no longer lumped together under the heading of "government"—could be studied under the auspices of both neo-institutionalism and rational institutionalism. Schmitter's plea was in favor of "complexification"—that is, of using different approaches depending on the problem to be addressed.

In spite of the dominance of the notion "governance" during past decades, the term *government* is still used in various ways. In a recent essay, the political scientist Jean Blondel concluded that the governments are a recurrent feature of all social organization. In a broad sense, government comprises—especially in the British tradition—the central institutions of decision making, such as parliament and government. In 1930s and later, *government* was used in the broader sense of a whole political system. The classifications of systems since Aristotle, such as "monarchy," "aristocracy," and "democracy," have been treated under the notion of "classification of governments." Later, government appeared in subtypes of representative democracies, such as "parliamentary government" and "presidential government." These prototypes were developed by Britain and the United States. In a parliamentary government, the cabinet is responsible to parliament. There is mutual dependence, contrary to the dualism in a presidential government; parliamentary majorities can topple the government by votes of nonconfidence, and governments can dissolve parliament and call for new elections. In general, there are parliamentary governments throughout the European continent and in the British dominions. Presidential government in many variations was developed in Latin America and Eastern Europe when those countries were making the transition to democracy. Presidential government tends to be less dependent on parties, especially the parliamentary party groups. Under Charles de Gaulle, a semipresidential government with a popularly elected president was reinvented in France, a system that had existed in the Second French Republic (1848–1851), in the Weimar Republic (1919–1933), and in Finland (since 1919). With the third wave of democratization since the early 1970s, new variations were created in Eastern Europe, such as in Poland and Russia. As suggested by Thomas Poguntke and Paul Webb (2005, pp. 8ff), in a postmodern media society the various types of executives are becoming more similar—that is, there is a "presidentialization of parliamentary government" that exists even in the United Kingdom.

Institutional Settings of Government

In a narrower sense, government "is" governmental organization, including the chief executive and his or her office, the cabinet, and the ministries. The varieties of governmental organizations depend on constitutional provisions, conventions, and standing orders of parliament and routine orders in the bureaucracy. In the governments of Great Britain and some Commonwealth countries, the government is dominated by the prime minister. In the French Third and Fourth Republics, the président du conseil was weak and ministers had more room for maneuvering. The British principle of "hire and fire" is rarely valid in continental government organizations because coalition parties and important politicians representing wings of the majority party limit the power of the head of government. The German chancellor system is somewhat closer to the British prime ministerial government, though it has always needed a coalition government—with one exception, 1957–1961 under Konrad Adenauer, and even in this case, the federal chancellor preferred a coalition to provide majorities for a case of less comfortable majorities in forthcoming elections. The cabinet or council of ministers was legally recognized for the first time, though rather late, in the constitutional laws of the Third French Republic (1875).

Beyond these legal principles, governments in most countries have developed informal traditions. In European parliamentary systems, governmental organization is hierarchical and bureaucratic. The collaborators of the chief of government are mostly experienced professional civil servants. The recruitment of politicians for important offices is determined by the strength of their parties. When the influence of parties is strong, the cabinet considers its leader as primus inter pares. This is, however, incompatible with the legal framework of the German government. Nevertheless, German history shows strong chancellors, such as Konrad Adenauer or Helmut Schmidt, and weak chancellors, such as Kurt Georg Kiesinger and Angela Merkel. These latter leaders were restricted in their power by a *grand coalition* of the two major parties. Such a chancellor has to set guidelines for all ministers, as mandated by Article 65 of the Basic Law. Some offices, such as agriculture or health, also attract exponents of important interest groups. Moreover, in the United States, the Senate has an important influence on the composition of government because it confirms the president's appointees for certain government offices.

Several years ago, it was common to identify the United States with having an "amateur type" of government and France with a "technocratic type" of leader who usually came from a few *grandes écoles* (elite schools). Most European parliamentary systems are somewhere in between. As noted above, Germany is relatively close to the British type of selection of government officers, which could be dubbed the "parliamentary party type." In systems with a high number of parties and the resultant fragmentation, coordination is more difficult, and governmental stability may be underdeveloped. The most important example was Italy before Silvio Berlusconi's period. In fact, the highly fragmented party government increased the number of offices. With a strong factionalism within parties, as in the case of the Italian *correnti*, the government apparatus expanded. In general, it was largely accepted that coalition governments increased the number of offices. But prime ministerial, single-party governments of the Westminster type contributed still more to the proliferation of offices, up to the point where one third of the governing parliamentary group in Britain held executive office. The "executivization" of parliamentary personnel had repercussions on parliament. When all the capable deputies held office, the remaining parliamentarians were weakened, and it was not easy to organize parliamentary activities independent of the government. Some systems, therefore, limited the number of ministers, as in Norway. The cabinet in a narrow sense and the government in a broader sense in parliamentary systems comprise a number of offices from a dozen to several dozens of governmental posts. In the presidential system of the United States, the patronage power of the president can result in about 4,000 nominations for government positions. In Germany, there are about 20,000 employees in the government in a broader sense, but only about 150 positions are held by secretaries of state and leading ministerial directors who can be dismissed at any time. German government in a broad sense includes also trustees for special tasks (about 27) and parliamentary secretaries of state who are parliamentarians, and as exponents of their respective parties, they connect government and parliament. Their main task is to support the views of government and to defend governmental propositions in parliament to find a majority of favorable votes.

Recent research on government in Europe increasingly turns to the study of multilevel government within the European Union (EU), characterized by the fact that most parliamentary legislation in member countries is the implementation of EU decisions and directives. The European influence on national government depends on the policy arena, most frequently in environment, agriculture, traffic, and communication. The least affected so far is the most important area for citizens—that is, social security (about 5%). According to Klaus von Beyme (1998), not more than one quarter of the laws in European countries are the absorption inside each country of decisions made by the EU.

New Approaches to the Study of Government

Three approaches have recently been used to study governments in order to overcome the conventional classifications of types of government: *core executive models*, *rational choice institutionalism*, and *governance studies*.

Core Executive Models

The six core executive models that have been differentiated by Robert Elgie (1997) more exactly indicate the true center of power than traditional notions such as parliamentary government:

1. *Monocratic government:* The key feature is personal leadership by a prime minister or president.
2. *Collective government:* Small, face-to-face groups decide policy, with no single member controlling.
3. *Ministerial government:* The political heads of major departments decide policy.
4. *Bureaucratic government:* Nonelected officials in government departments and agencies decide policy.
5. *Shared government:* Two or three individuals have joint and equal responsibility for policy making.
6. *Segmented government:* A sectoral division of labor among executive actors with little or no cross-sectoral coordination.

These "ideal types" are rarely found in modern democracies, but elements of them are combined in fluid patterns and sometimes one model succeeds another.

Rational-Choice Institutionalism

George Tsebelis (2002), in his approach to rational choice, posits that governments in order to change policies must get individual actors or veto players to agree. Institutional veto players are specified by the constitution and partisan veto players are specified by the party system. Tsebelis (2002) reverses the usual meaning of notions such as parliamentary and presidential government: "Agenda control most frequently belongs to governments in parliamentary systems and parliament in presidential ones." If the veto players are differentiated according to policy areas, the old taxonomy of representative systems is more or less irrelevant.

Governance Studies

The concept of governance (derived from the Latin term *gubernantia*) has a wider range than that of government because it includes all individual and collective interactions of governments with nongovernmental organizations, interest groups, social movements, and citizen groups. Even before the invention of the notion of governance, the governmental organization was integral to the communications network involving interest groups and expert bodies of political advice. Also included in the notion of governance are long-term policy networks and short-lived networks established for individual decisions. The increasing complexity of the decision-making process has contributed to a wide debate on "government overload," namely, a higher number of demands that are difficult or impossible for government to meet. This overload contributed to the discussion on ungovernability that occurred in the 1980s. Governance studies have shown that the generic analyses of ungovernability were misleading, given the new forms of overcoming crises and deadlocks that have been developed in postmodern societies.

The term *governance* was first widely used in the subdiscipline of international relations where "governing without government" (James N. Rosenau & Ernst-Otto Czempiel, 1995) played a major role. Moreover, in the subfield of international relations dealing with developmental politics in the Third World, the term *good governance* has been used. It aims at finding normative criteria for efficient aid to developing countries. This approach was directed against an ideological motivation for aid to developing countries in the times of the Cold War. Later, the instrumental combination of multilateral developmental strategies and the ideological preoccupation of developed democracies for the promotion of democracy in the Third World were criticized by the elites in the Third World. Building on the resolutions adopted by the United Nations since 1996, scientific criteria for good governance were developed.

Governance gained a central importance for the discipline when *network* became the central expression for a great variety of interactions beginning in the early 1980s. *Governance* is a new term for old approaches that started with theories of neocorporatism on guided cooperation of governments and interest groups and theories on governmental steering when the term *planning*, which dominated in the 1970s, became obsolete. Theories of the cooperative government and interdependence management in the science of administration also prepared the road for studies of governance. The older approaches were clearly centered on "actors." Governance was not only a new game of words but part of a neo-institutionalist turn in the social sciences. Governance approaches were built on the experience that policy formulation became more difficult in postmodern societies. There is more differentiation in the new century in the realm of interest groups and social movements than in neocorporatism—a dominant paradigm in the 1980s—aimed at cooperation between state agencies and main actors, such as organizations of business and trade unions. Self-organization in a civil society made "steering" less easy. The core executive was no longer dominant even in the area of traditional government because many governmental and para-statal agencies are involved in policy formulation and policy implementation and a new term—*agencification*—has been invented. In the name of new public management reform for greater efficiency, a separation of policies and operations was recommended by Christopher Pollitt and Colin Talbot (2003). Lobbying also changed in postmodern governments. Clientele relations grew up between ministerial and para-statal agencies and organized interests, as Marian Döhler (2001) pointed out. Think tanks and councils of experts gained an important role in many policy fields.

Moreover, the role of the media has increased. Public affairs agencies and international organizations of attorneys that do not permanently work for the same interests grew in importance against the traditional organized lobbies. Privatization and liberalization of former state monopolies in infrastructure (e.g., mail services, telephone, railroads, and energy supply) have created new profiles of governmental tasks. The old instruments of government such as laws, persuasion and propaganda, coercion, and regulation developed a different relative weight. As already suggested by von Beyme (1998), today, there is virtually no institution that is "sovereign," for example, "the legislator"—as an actor that includes both parliament and government.

These changes left political science with considerable pessimism as to whether institutional policies can create more efficient policies. There are two approaches to answering this question. One approach prefers the *transformative perspective* and accepts that institutional arrangements can be changed only by long-run changes in culture and outlooks. "Path dependency" of governmental institutions has been discovered and tries to explain why French centralization or German federalism is so difficult to be transformed because historical traditions and vested interests prevent radical change.

Another approach believes in the possibility of creating a deliberate design of a regulating system and that a kind of "metagovernor" (as described by Bob Jessop) or "third-order governing" (according to Jan Kooiman) survived in postmodern society.

In both approaches, government ceased to be "government" in the traditional sense in which it had been under the impact of theories on states and sovereignty for almost 500 years after Niccolò Machiavelli, Jean Bodin, or Thomas Hobbes.

Klaus von Beyme
University of Heidelberg
Heidelberg, Germany

See also Comparative Politics; Governance, Administration Policies; Governance, Good; Neo-Corporatism; New Public Management

Further Readings

Döhler, M. (2001). Institutional choice and bureaucratic autonomy in Germany. *West European Politics, 25*(1), 101–124.

Elgie, R. (1997). Models of executive politics: A framework for the study of executive power relations in parliamentary and semi-presidential regimes. *Political Studies, 45*(2), 217–231.

Finer, S. E. (1997). *The history of government* (Vols. 1–3). Oxford, UK: Oxford University Press.

Poguntke, T., & Webb, P. (2005). *The presidentialization of politics.* Oxford, UK: Oxford University Press.

Pollitt, C., & Talbot, C. (Eds.). (2003). *Unbundled government: A critical analysis of the global trend to agencies, quangos and contractualization.* London: Routledge.

Rhodes, R. A. W. (2006). Executives in parliamentary governments. In R. A. W. Rhodes, S. A. Binder, & B. A. Rockman (Eds.), *The Oxford handbook of political institutions* (pp. 323–342). Oxford, UK: Oxford University Press.

Rosenau, J. N., & Czempiel, E.-O. (1995). *Governance without government: Order and change in world politics* (2nd ed.). Cambridge, UK: Cambridge University Press.

Tsebelis, G. (2002). *Veto players: How political institutions work.* Princeton, NJ: Princeton University Press.

von Beyme, K. (1998). *The legislator: German parliament as a centre of political decision-making.* Aldershot, UK: Ashgate.

von Beyme, K. (2000). *Parliamentary democracy: Democratization, destabilization, reconsolidation, 1789–1999.* Houndmills, UK: Macmillan.

Granger Causality

Granger causality is the concept that if a variable causes another variable, it should help with the prediction of the latter variable. First, Granger causality is defined informally and formally. Next, the standard hypothesis tests used to evaluate the concept are presented. Third, the interpretations of these tests for Granger (non)causality are discussed. Then, some caveats and limitations are presented before turning to some common extensions and applications.

The statistical concept of Granger causality is related directly to the idea of causality and causal inference in the social sciences. In the (social) sciences, it is the case where two variables are causally related if

- the change in one variable temporally precedes that of the variable it causes,
- there is a nonzero correlation among the two (or more) variables, and
- the relationship among the variables is logically nonspurious.

Granger causality assesses the first two of these using a statistical test, leaving the third to the justification of the analyst. Granger causality analysis asks whether a variable helps in predicting another, which requires both temporal precedence and correlation. One of Clive Granger's seminal time-series papers on this topic developed the statement of the concept and presented the most common statistical tests used to assess causality.

If a variable Z at Time t Granger causes a variable X at Time t or Z_t Granger causes X_t then the following three statements are logically equivalent:

1. Z_t helps predict X_t (i.e., it lowers the error of the prediction),
2. Z_t is not exogenous of X_t,
3. Z_t is linearly informative about future X_t.

The assumption that makes these three statements equivalent is that there is a linear relationship between Z_t and X_t. Granger causality can be defined more generally and can also encompass nonlinear relationships. In this case, only the first two statements are relevant.

The formal definition of Granger causality is actually a statement of noncausality. A variable Z_t is Granger noncausal for X_t if the past values of Z_t do not help predict the current (or future) values of X_t over a prediction based on the past history of X_t alone. Under the assumption of linearity, then, this is the same as analyzing a dynamic regression of X_t on past values of X_t and Z_t, or

$$X_t = d + \sum_{i=1}^{p} \alpha_i X_{t-i} + \sum_{i=1}^{p} \beta_i Z_{t-i} + e_i,$$

where d is a constant, α_is are the coefficients for the p lagged values of X_t, and β_is are the coefficients for the p lagged values of Z_t. If Z_t Granger causes X_t, then some of the β_i coefficients are different from zero. Note that by including the lagged values of X_t, the variable Z_t must add more to the prediction of X than its own past (and thus help minimize the prediction error e_t) to deem it causal. Testing whether these are equal to zero is thus a test of Granger noncausality.

Statistical tests of Granger (non) causality depend on comparing the residuals of the model in the above equation with those of a model where X_t only depends on its past values, or where one assumes that $\beta_i = 0$ for $i = 1, \ldots, p$. Statistical tests for Granger causality are generally implemented as a comparison of the mean squared prediction error of the previous equation with

$$X_t = d + \sum_{i=1}^{p} \alpha_i X_{t-i} + u_t.$$

This amounts to comparing the variance of e_t with u_t. If the variance of the former is smaller than Z_t, Granger causes X_t under the earlier assumptions. A Granger causality test is done most commonly using either an F, Wald, or likelihood ratio test for whether $\beta_1 = \beta_2 = \ldots = \beta_p = 0$. These test statistics degrees of freedom are typically corrected by a factor of $T - 2p - 1$, where T is the sample size and p is the number of lags. This helps account for the estimation of the potentially large number of parameters in these equations.

While this test statistic is easily and commonly implemented, it depends on several assumptions. These include (but are not limited to) the following:

1. The relevant information and variables have been included in the model used to conduct the test. Any relevant omitted variables can lead to a biased test.
2. The relationship between the variables is linear and the errors in the equations are normally distributed. (The result can hold for nonlinear and nonnormal cases but requires other assumptions.) In this most common case, testing for Granger causality is reduced to the comparison of the minimum mean squared regression errors defined above.
3. There is no residual correlation in e_t or u_t, meaning that the lag length p is sufficient to remove any residual serial correlation from the regressions used to construct the test.
4. The variable Z_t is stationary. Nonstationarity could induce spurious correlation, since then there could be an error correction mechanism between the variables that naturally implies a Granger causality relationship among the variables. Extensions of the standard Granger causality tests exist for this case.

Finding that one Granger variable causes another depends on the information set or the variables that are included in a model. So if one were to introduce a variable Y_t that is causal for X_t and correlated with Z_t, one could find that the effects of Z_t on X_t work through this new variable. The same is not necessarily true for findings of Granger noncausality, since the existence of a variable that would turn a noncausal relationship into a causal one is nearly impossible.

It is important to note that tests for Granger (non)causality *do not assess the direction* of the causal relationship. The null hypothesis is that the past values of the variable Z_t do not help with predicting X_t. Rejecting this hypothesis could occur if there were a positive or negative correlation among the past values of Z_t and the current X_t. To interpret the causal direction of the effects of Z_t on X_t, one typically employs a vector autoregression model or computes the dynamic effects of changes in past Z_t on contemporaneous X_t. This is where theory helps identify that the relationship is nonspurious and provides some ideas about the expected direction of the effects of one variable for forecasting the other. Formally, impulse response functions or the vector moving average interpretation of a vector autoregression model are used to determine the direction of these effects. The vector autoregression model and its estimated effects will demonstrate the same causal relationships identified with a Granger causality test and provide the magnitude and direction of any causal effects.

The above definition of Granger causality is what is known as *bivariate Granger causality*. The concept can also be extended in several ways. The first involves the multivariate case. Suppose now that Z_t and X_t are vectors of observations at time *t*. Then, we say that Z_t is non-Granger causal or *block exogenous* of X_t if the past values of the matrix Z_t do not help in predicting the current values of X_t. The earlier test statistics can then be extended to their matrix equivalents and used to assess whether the past Z_t values help predict X_t.

A second extension is what is known as *contemporaneous Granger causality*. A variable Z_t instantaneously causes Granger X_t if the contemporaneous and leading or future values of Z_t help in predicting the current value of X_t. To test this hypothesis, one looks at the contemporaneous relationships (the e_t and u_t residuals for the vector autoregression) to see if there is a correlation among the current values of the series.

The third possible extension is to move beyond the assumption of minimizing one-step prediction errors. Multistep Granger causality can be defined by looking at the *h*-step residuals for a regression of X_t on past X_t and Z_t. If past Z_t minimize the *h* periods of forecast errors in X_t better than the past X_t alone, then Z_t is said to be multistep Granger causal for X_t. A final extension is to panel data. One can extend the same ideas used in assessing Granger causality in time-series data to collections of time series that are part of a panel of time series.

Granger causality is a useful test and tool for determining which variables help predict each other in multivariate time-series models. It is used commonly to justify which variables are included in a vector autoregression or other multivariate time-series models since it allows the analyst to justify different (weak) exogeneity assumptions. The point of a Granger causality test analysis is that one uses the results to support an argument about the predictive power of a variable on another in a time-series model.

Patrick T. Brandt
University of Texas at Dallas
Richardson, Texas, United States

See also Causality; Statistical Inference, Classical and Bayesian; Time-Series Analysis

Further Readings

Brandt, P. T., & Williams, J. (2007). *Multiple time series models*. Thousand Oaks, CA: Sage.

Freeman, J. R. (1983). Granger causality and the time series analysis of political relationships. *American Journal of Political Science, 27,* 327–358.

Granger, C. W. J. (1969). Investigating causal relations by econometric models and cross-spectral methods. *Econometrica, 37,* 424–438.

Hamilton, J. (1994). *Time series analysis*. Princeton, NJ: Princeton University Press.

Lutkepohl, H. (2005). *New introduction to multiple time series analysis*. Berlin, Germany: Springer.

Sims, C. A. (1972). Money, income, and causality. *American Economic Review, 62,* 540–552.

Graphics, Statistical

Statistical graphics provide visual displays of quantitative information. While graphs have been an important tool in the statistical sciences, their role and applications have evolved over time. In the past, graphical displays were generally employed for pedagogical purposes and to present the final results of an analysis. Currently, graphs are being incorporated more directly into data analysis itself, where they are used to provide insights and directions for further investigation. In this entry, the basic elements, major advantages, and recent developments of statistical graphics are presented.

Statistical graphs are used for several purposes. First, they provide a tool for exploring the contents of a data set; in effect, graphical displays enable researchers to interact directly with the "raw material" for their analyses. Second, graphs enable researchers to look for structure in their data; they provide a ready means to identify interesting features such as concentrations of observations at particular data values, covariance across variables, outliers in distributions, and so on. Third, graphical displays are useful for checking the assumptions of statistical models; for example, they can be used to examine distributional shapes of constituent variables or to search for systematic patterns among model residuals. Fourth, graphs remain an excellent vehicle for communicating the results of statistical analyses; they provide fairly intuitive representations of complex models that can be understood by broad audiences.

Of course, all of the preceding objectives could also be achieved through numerical methods, such as equations and tabular representations. But graphs have several advantages. For one thing, an enormous amount of information can be represented directly or summarized in a single well-constructed graph; therefore, graphical displays are useful for depicting large, complex data sets. At the same time, graphs are not as reliant on underlying assumptions as are numerical summaries of data such as descriptive statistics or model coefficients. And graphs almost inherently encourage greater interaction between the researcher and the data; interesting features stand out immediately and graphs provide the means to pursue them to gain further insights.

Historical Evolution

The earliest "modern" graphical displays, generated during the Enlightenment period of the 17th and 18th centuries, downplayed depictions of empirical data in favor of graphing the abstract functions that seemed to describe the dynamics of the observable universe. But a minor scientific revolution occurred at the end of the 18th century, when an iconoclastic Scottish political commentator, William Playfair, published *The Commercial and Political Atlas* (various editions were produced between 1786 and 1801) and the *Statistical Breviary* (1801). The substantive objective for each of these books was to provide information about the British economy, relative to other nations. But they are remembered largely because Playfair developed a number of graphical displays to illustrate his data and support his arguments. Playfair's innovations would be recognizable immediately to a modern reader; they include bar charts, pie charts, and line charts.

During the 19th century, graphs were used widely in scientific communications. This period is characterized by the use of creative pictorial devices to convey information as efficiently as possible. For example, a famous map by French engineer Charles Joseph Minard depicts Napoleon's march during the Russian campaign of 1812. It has been hailed as the finest statistical graphic, in large part because it encodes information about six different variables into a single display. Graphical representations of empirical information waned once again during the first half of the 20th century. During this period, statisticians turned their attention to confirmatory methods and hypothesis testing. These are strategies where the characteristics of the data need to be well understood before the tests are applied to gain insight about the values of specific parameters. And since assumptions about the processes that generated the data precede the tests, graphical displays tend to be less useful.

Beginning in the 1950s, and continuing through the first decade of the 21st century, there has been a strong resurgence of interest in statistical graphics. There are several reasons for this recent trend. First, there has been an increasing emphasis on exploratory methods, through the influence of the late John Tukey and his followers. Second, there has been productive research on the psychology of graphical perception, so there is greater understanding of the ways that people process visual information. Third, there have been major advances in graphical methodologies, providing new tools for pictorial representations of numeric information. Fourth, the widespread availability of powerful computing equipment and high-resolution, fast-refreshing, graphical displays means that scientists now have the means to render graphs quickly and easily. And fifth, the "data explosion" of recent years has encouraged broader reliance on graphical strategies for coping with the sheer volume of information confronting many researchers.

Graphical Information and Human Perception

A graph can be effective only if the information contained therein can be extracted easily and accurately by its intended audience. Understanding how to accomplish this requires some understanding of human graphical perception. An influential theory developed by William S. Cleveland holds that interpretation of graphs comprises two fundamental tasks: table lookup and pattern perception. Table lookup refers to the process of moving from the displayed geometric rendering of the data back to the numerical values that generated the display. This process is facilitated through careful attention to the axes and scales that define the plotting region(s) of a graphical display.

Pattern perception is, itself, composed of three more fundamental perceptual tasks: First, *detection* refers to the ability to perceive the individual elements of the data in a graph; it usually involves the selection of suitable plotting symbols to represent data points. Second, *assembly* refers to the ability to combine separate elements together in a way that facilitates recognition of nonrandom structure within the data—for example, the shape of a univariate distribution or functional dependence of one variable's values on another variable's values. Third, *estimation* is the ability to make quantitative comparisons across the geometric elements in a graphical display. For example, observers can typically make quite accurate judgments about relative differences when data points are plotted along a common scale. But it is more difficult to make similarly accurate comparisons of quantities that are represented as differences in angles, areas of geometric shapes, or gradations in color.

Theories of graphical perception are important because they provide standards for judging the quality of graphical displays. Relying on Cleveland's theory, the objective is to encode the data with geometric devices that optimize the three components of pattern perception. However, compromises are almost always necessary; for example, emphasizing the individual data points facilitates detection but may impede assembly. As a result, there is seldom any single *best* display for a given data set. Instead, different graphs may provide different useful perspectives on the same basic information.

Types of Graphical Displays

There are many situations in which the analyst is confronted with labeled quantitative values, such as the raw data values associated with individual observations or summary values calculated for subgroups within a data set (e.g., the conditional means on a variable or the percentage of observations within each subset). For such data, pie charts, bar charts, and dot plots can be used. Pie charts require relatively inaccurate visual judgments of angles and areas, while accurate interpretation of bar charts can be impeded by the arbitrary location of the origin on the scale that defines the lengths of the bars. Carefully constructed dot plots can overcome these problems, and they can be adapted to a wide variety of specific situations. Therefore, they are the preferred analytic graphical display for labeled data values.

Graphical displays for univariate data enable visual assessments of a distribution's most important features—center, spread, shape, and outliers. Again, there are several possibilities, including univariate scatterplots, histograms, smoothed histograms, quantile plots, and box plots. Univariate histograms are simple to construct and interpret; however, they are effectively limited to small data sets. Histograms are familiar and easy to interpret. However, the contents of a histogram can be affected by the definitions of the categories (or "bins") used to delineate its bars. Smoothed histograms overcome the problems caused by bin definitions, but they are similarly affected by technical aspects of the smoothing process. Quantile plots overcome all of the preceding problems, but they are cognitively demanding and probably not familiar to many social scientists. Box plots focus on the most important quantiles of a data distribution; they are easily interpreted and are especially useful for comparing univariate distributions.

There is really only one type of graphical display for bivariate data: the scatterplot. But careful attention to the details is critical for optimizing the information conveyed by this type of display. For example, the plotting symbol used to represent individual observations must be visually prominent and resistant to overplotting effects. And the plotting region should be fully enclosed by the scale rectangle, with none of the data points colliding with any of the axes. Grid lines should not be included within the plotting region. And if the objective of the graphical display is to assess the relationship between two variables, then there is usually no need to include point labels. Finally, a scatterplot smoother (i.e., a curve that traces out the conditional mean of the variable plotted on the vertical axis across the range of data values on the horizontal axis) can be used to summarize the relationship between the variables plotted in the display.

Multivariate data pose particular challenges for statistical graphics. While it is possible to draw a three-dimensional scatterplot, using an oblique orientation on the data space to simulate a perspective view, such displays are generally not very effective. Instead, other devices have been employed to represent multiple dimensions of variability in a two-dimensional display medium. For example, a scatterplot matrix is the graphical analog of a correlation matrix, showing scatterplots between all possible pairs of variables arranged in a regular, square layout. Conditioning plots and trellis displays show one- or two-dimensional graphical displays for subsets of a data set, where the subsets are defined by intervals of values on other variables. And finally, there are a number of related strategies for "touring" high-dimensional data, by taking projections of the data points into a smaller dimensioned subspace that can be visualized directly.

William G. Jacoby
Michigan State University
East Lansing, Michigan, United States

See also Data Visualization; Quantitative Methods, Basic Assumptions

Further Readings

Cleveland, W. S. (1993). *The elements of graphing data.* Summit, NJ: Hobart Press.

Cook, D., & Swayne, D. F. (2007). *Interactive and dynamic graphics for data analysis: With examples using R and GGobi.* New York: Springer.

Jacoby, W. G. (1997). *Statistical graphics for univariate and bivariate data.* Thousand Oaks, CA: Sage.

Jacoby, W. G. (1998). *Statistical graphics for visualizing multivariate data.* Thousand Oaks, CA: Sage.

Wainer, H. (2009). *Picturing the uncertain world.* Princeton, NJ: Princeton University Press.

Wilkinson, L. (2005). *The grammar of graphics* (2nd ed.). New York: Springer.

Greek Philosophy

Greek philosophy is often taken as synonymous with ancient Western philosophy, or as thought in the age of classical Athens, represented by Socrates, Plato, and Aristotle. Strictly speaking, however, it means the thoughts expressed and transmitted in Greek before the Byzantine period, except for Christian writings. It covers the period from the early 6th century BCE to 529 CE (the year of the closure of the Academy [a school founded by Plato around 385 BCE] by Justinian I). In a long tradition, it has formed our ways of thinking about the world and human beings and is therefore regarded as the basis of Western civilization. This entry first examines the essence of Greek philosophy and then reviews the development of Greek philosophy from its origin to the classical period, particularly the political philosophy of Plato and Aristotle.

Greek philosophy has four stages: (1) early Greek (or so-called Presocratic) philosophy (early 6th to mid-5th century BCE), (2) classical philosophy (late 5th to 4th century BCE), (3) Hellenistic philosophy (3rd to 1st century BCE), and (4) the philosophy of late antiquity (1st to early 6th century CE). In the first two stages, philosophers were active mainly in the Eastern Mediterranean region (Asia Minor, Greece, and southern Italy), and in the latter two, their activities were extended to the Near East and the whole Mediterranean region. It should be remembered that many philosophers living in the Roman Empire wrote their works in Greek (e.g., Plutarch, Epictetus, Marcus Aurelius, Plotinus, Galen, and Sextus Empiricus).

What we possess is the transmitted body of Greek philosophical texts, mostly of the classical and the Roman periods. While a large portion of the ancient books were lost, some have been transmitted to us first in manuscripts (earlier in papyri and later in codices) and then in printed books. Quotations or references included in those books are also edited as "fragments" or "testimonies" of Greek philosophers, for example, the Presocratics (*Die Fragmente der Vorsokratiker* by Hermann Diels) and the Stoics (*Stoicorum Veterum Fragmenta*, by Hans von Arnim). Luckily, a few important texts are also preserved in papyri, inscriptions, and so on. Therefore, studies of Greek philosophy consist of the intellectual excavation of original thoughts and the reexamination of their heritage.

Greek philosophy is by no means monolithic, but rather, it is characterized by variety and competitiveness. Greek philosophers provided polar ideas such as "monism versus pluralism," "materialism versus idealism," "absolutism, relativism, and skepticism versus agnosticism," "free will versus determinism," and "eudaimonism and hedonism versus asceticism." Nevertheless, they shared some essential features: inquiry into nature and being and open debate between different positions. Their philosophical inquiry was based on experience and reason—that is, the pursuit of truth through argument (logos). By pursuing rationality and universality, Greek philosophy achieved systematization of science and knowledge and thus participated in shaping political science. This feature dissociates it from the preceding cultures of Egypt and Babylonia and from the other cultures outside Europe. Therefore, Greek philosophy is often evoked as a source of the cultural identity of Europe and the West.

The Beginning of Philosophy

Philosophy (Greek *philosophia*, meaning "aspiring for wisdom") is generally thought to have started in Greece in the beginning of the 6th century BCE, with Thales of the Ionian city Miletus, whom Aristotle calls "the founder of philosophy." Although Thales, one of the Seven Wise Men, probably left no writings, he and his compatriots, Anaximander and Anaximenes, started a philosophical inquiry (*historia*) into nature. The early philosophers were interested mainly, but not exclusively, in natural phenomena, such as celestial motions and the structure of the universe. They asked what the "origin" or "principle" (*archê*) of the world and all things is and presented different candidates: water (Thales), fire (Heraclitus), air (Anaximenes, Diogenes of Apollonia), the unlimited (Anaximander), and the unchanging One (Parmenides). In the mid-4th century BCE, Empedocles from Sicily established the four-element theory (fire, air, water, and earth) and thereon explained the cycle of change of the universe, in terms of mixture and separation, by means of the two powers, love and strife. As Empedocles composed the religious poem called *Purifications* and the cosmological one called *On Nature*, arguably in a single work, inquiry into nature and moral thinking came together in the early philosophers. They often used metaphorical expressions, but the first crucial step can be clearly observed: They sought one or the smallest number of principles to explain the whole world.

The Ionian tradition of inquiry developed both natural sciences (astronomy, mathematics, and medicine) and social sciences (geography and history). Herodotus, in the investigation into the causes of the Greco-Persian Wars, collected a wide range of geographical and cultural information about the regions of Egypt, Asia, and Europe. His *Histories* (*Historiai*, meaning "inquiries") provided ample examples of the conflicting ethical and legal values adopted by different peoples and societies and thus introduced a multicultural and relativistic way of looking at the world, which was further developed by the Sophists.

The first stage of Greek philosophy is often characterized as a progression from *mythos* (myth) to *logos* (reason). This means that the way of understanding the world changed from mythical stories based on Greek religion to more rational or scientific explanation. Yet the actual development was not so straightforward. Philosophical theories and explanations still contain many mythical or irrational factors but philosophers at least share interest in the program of rational inquiry, and on this basis, they compete with each other to attain the truth.

The Sophists and Socrates

In the mid-5th century BCE, when Athens experienced democracy and prosperity under Pericles, professional thinkers and teachers called Sophists appeared and became influential in the society. These intellectuals played an important role in the democratic society, where free citizens sought power by cultivating their own ability and the Sophists taught young people how to succeed in society.

The greatest Sophist, Protagoras of Abdera, propagated the famous "Man measure thesis": "Man is the measure of all things: of those which are, that they are, and of things which are not, that they are not." This thesis, which bases moral values not on gods but on human beings, promoted a radical relativism fitting for democracy. Protagoras was successfully teaching virtues—that is, political excellence.

What the Sophists actually taught was rhetoric—the art or skills of speech—for it was crucial in the court or the assembly to speak persuasively in front of a large audience. Gorgias from Sicily developed the technique of public speech and reflected on the power of speech (*logos*), noting that it can move people and the country and therefore becomes a source of political power. The Sophists' appeal to the power of speech attracted people but was regarded as radical and dangerous to traditional morality.

The Sophists investigated the basis of society and the political system. One of their inventions was the contrast of *nomos* and *physis* (law or custom and nature), and based on this contrast, they put forward a social contract theory. This theory initially tried to explain how and why social and moral systems differ in societies, but it was later used to attack the current customs and morality. Antiphon, the Athenian politician, teacher of rhetoric and Sophist (though there is a controversy over his identity), wrote a treatise called *On Truth* (of which three large fragments have been preserved in papyri), where he insisted that while it is human nature to do harm to others in order to get more, laws and customs prevent one from doing so.

The work of Herodotus and Thucydides in their *Histories* contains the origin of Greek political thought. Their description and comparison of Persia, Sparta, and Athens reflected the serious discussions and controversies over the different political systems in the late 5th century BCE: monarchy, oligarchy (also called aristocracy, i.e., rule of the best), democracy, and tyranny. Several comparative studies on the Athenian and Spartan constitutions (*politeiai*) were written and circulated in this period. It is noteworthy that in democratic Athens, the oligarchic system of Sparta was popular among the intellectuals, including Socrates, Critias, Xenophon, and Plato.

Critias was an oligarchic politician and political thinker influenced by the Sophistic movement. A fragment of the tragedy *Sisyphus*, attributed to him, claims that gods were invented by a clever man to deceive people into obeying laws. The Sophist Prodicus expressed a similar rationalistic view on the origin of religion—that gods are personifications of the useful things and heroes. By casting radical doubts on traditional values, the Sophistic enlightenment movement contributed to re-forming the ideas of politics and ethics as distinct from those of traditional religion and to considering them objectively and scientifically.

Socrates belongs to the same generation as the Sophists and was regarded as a major Sophist by his contemporaries (as depicted in Aristophanes's comedy *Clouds*). It was his pupils, above all Plato, who distinguished him from the other Sophists and natural philosophers. Since Socrates did not write anything, it is difficult to determine his original thought, but a few philosophical contributions are generally ascribed to him. First, Socrates raised questions on moral issues, such as courage, justice, and goodness. He often began his inquiries with a request for a definition, and in doing so, he often revealed his interlocutors' ignorance. Second, he often drew a conclusion from a series of examples, thus making use of the logic of induction. Third, by this cross-examination, he urged people to take care of the soul (*psychê*)—that is, one's own self. However, his radical way of questioning was seen as dangerous and subversive of ordinary beliefs and traditional morality. Socrates was convicted of impiety and for corrupting youth and was executed in 399 BCE. But his way of life became a major subject of the later philosophers, and Socrates was made the model philosopher for Cynics, Stoics, Cyrenaics, and skeptics of the Academy.

Plato

Plato was born in a famous Athenian family, and in his youth, he wished to be active in politics, as was usual in his society. His life was changed by his encounter with Socrates, and particularly after seeing the trial and death of Socrates, he kept his distance from Athenian politics and concentrated on philosophy and scientific research in the Academy. It is reported that Plato visited Syracuse a few times to convert the despot Dionysius to philosophy, but in vain. Plato wrote some 30 works in the form of dialogues, most of which feature Socrates as the main speaker.

Plato made full use of the dialogue form. The author himself never appears or speaks in the dialogues. Readers are urged to think for themselves about the issues discussed in the dialogue. While it is often assumed that the main character, Socrates (or a few others), speaks for Plato's position, the opposition often has a good point to make. For example, when in the *Gorgias*, Callicles, the young Athenian, challenged Socrates and defended the life of politics by an appeal to "natural justice," some readers strongly sympathized with Callicles's position, despite Socrates's eventual refutation. Friedrich Nietzsche is an obvious example of a later philosopher whose work reflects the perspective taken by Callicles. Nietzsche openly defended the "will to power" and tried to overturn Platonist morality. It is sometimes suggested that Plato himself experienced such a tension and conflict between the life of philosophy and the life of politics as depicted in the dialogue.

Plato's dialogues put forward several paradoxical arguments of Socrates—for example, that no one willingly does wrong and that it is better to suffer injustice than to do injustice. His emphasis on the need for a thorough examination of moral concepts and values appeared to ordinary men to turn their lives upside down. In urging people to take care of the soul, Plato makes a sharp distinction between the soul and the body and its desires. Then, the soul in itself is able to contemplate the essence of each thing—what it essentially is, or what Plato calls its "Form." The Forms are distinct from sensible things, and cause their being, while the sensible things partake of the transcendent Forms. For example, "Beauty" itself is different from beautiful things but makes things beautiful. This is Plato's theory of Forms, presented in the dialogues, including the *Phaedo*, *Symposium*, *Republic*, and so on.

Socrates himself was probably not interested in politics and lived a nonpolitical life as a private citizen. However, Plato's dialogues understand his life as engaging in true politics and present him as the ideal statesman. The trial of Socrates is reinterpreted as fundamentally political. His cross-examination of his accusers at his trial and his constant advice to his fellow citizens to take care of the soul and virtue, instead of the body, money, and reputation, constituted a true political activity to make the *polis* better, but they gave rise to misunderstanding and hatred toward Socrates and eventually led to his death.

Through the Socratic dialogues, Plato explores the tension between politics and philosophy and expresses the principle that justice in all its forms can be understood only through philosophy. In this way, the famous idea of philosopher-kings or philosopher-rulers is conceived and proposed in the *Republic* (the Greek title *Politeia* meaning the being of a state or a constitution). The main question of the dialogue is what justice is and whether a just person lives a happy life. The Sophist Thrasymachus first raises a radical claim of justice as the "advantage for the stronger"—that the stronger people exploit the weaker in the name of law and justice. Following him, Glaucon and Ademinatus (Plato's older brothers) reformulate this claim into a formidable challenge to morality: that people obey the law and do justice only because they think it necessary (while wanting to avoid it) on the basis of the social contract. Against this, Socrates has to demonstrate that justice is *good* both in itself and for its results. To consider justice and injustice more clearly, Socrates then suggests that they construct a state (*polis*) in argument and compare its justice with that of the soul. The basic principle of founding the state is that everyone does one's own work (labor division according to one's nature). If each class, namely, rulers, warriors, and producers, does its own work, the state is just. On the other hand, when someone transgresses this boundary, various types of injustice occur. The just state is discussed to show by analogy the justice of the soul. When the three parts of the soul, namely, reason, spirit, and appetite, harmonize to make a single whole, the soul is just. Thus, the *Republic* deals with political philosophy in the context of discussing justice.

The conditions of the ideal state are a focus in the central books of the *Politeia* (Books 5–7), where some original proposals are discussed, such as equality of men and women in ruling, abolishment of the family, and a common property system. Socrates' most challenging proposal for realizing the ideal state in this world is to unite philosophy and politics by either making the philosopher a ruler of the state or making the present ruler a philosopher, since the philosopher, who has knowledge of "Justice," "Goodness," and the other Forms, alone can make a state just and good in the proper way. To become a philosopher, however, one needs a long course of education and hard training, first in general education in literature and physical training and second in the mathematical sciences. The final stage consists of training in dialectic (the art of dialogue), which is said to deal with the reality or the Forms by *logos* (reason) alone.

Plato's idea of political science was criticized by his contemporaries and by later philosophers. Isocrates, Plato's rival teacher of rhetoric, insists that sound judgment is more important than the theoretical sciences, such as mathematics, in making one a good citizen and politician. Aristotle also criticizes Plato's idea of unity in Book 2 of the *Politics*. A state should not seek a strict singleness as proposed in the *Republic* but should be realized in a harmony of diverse elements. This echoes the modern criticisms of Plato as totalitarian. According to Karl Popper and other critics, Plato's notions of dictatorship, the "noble lie," eugenics, and censorship resemble the modern totalitarian ideologies of Nazism and Stalinism. Whereas in the 19th century Plato's *Republic* was read as a "utopian" work, in the 20th, there was greater emphasis on its political implications. However, it should be noted that Plato's main aim lies not in the political blueprint but in the ethical contrast between the tyrant, who rules for his own interest and greed, and the true philosopher.

Plato places the Form of the "Good" in the highest position in the realm of reality. This implies that the natural world and human activities have a common basis. This idea is developed in his later dialogue, the *Timaeus*, in which the origin and structure of the universe are explained as the god's (Demiurge's) creation by means of mathematical principles. Goodness and beauty are regarded there as the foundation principles of the universe. Plato's cosmology (which he called "a likely myth") was influential in late antiquity and the Middle Ages as a part of his political thought.

Plato wrote two other dialogues that deal with political philosophy: the *Statesman* (*Politicus*) and the *Laws* (*Nomoi*). The *Statesman* defines the art or knowledge of statesmanship as the interweaving of different elements in a state, particularly courage and temperance. Plato's last work, the *Laws*, discusses the principles and laws of a new colonial state. Although the differences between Plato's ideas in the *Republic*, *Statesman*, and *Laws* are matters of much debate among modern scholars, it is clear that Plato examines political science as a major subject in his whole system of philosophy.

Aristotle

Aristotle was born in Macedonia, the son of a medical doctor. Probably because of this background, he was more interested in biology and other natural sciences than in mathematics (which Plato ranks high as a more abstract and academic science). He joined Plato's Academy as a youth to study philosophy. After his master's death, Aristotle founded his own school, the Lyceum, and led scientific projects in biology and political science. Although he tutored the young Alexander the Great for some years, it is uncertain what influence he had on the prince.

While all his published works were lost, his lectures fortunately survived and were edited by Andronicus of Rhodes, the Peripatetic philosopher of the 1st century BCE. The *Corpus Aristotelicum* (Works of Aristotle) is the transmitted body of texts from this edition, and it is normally assumed that the order of treatises more or less represents Aristotle's original scheme of sciences: namely, logic, physics (natural philosophy), metaphysics, ethics, politics, rhetoric, and poetics. On the other hand, one must be cautious in using the lectures, since they are often sketchy and may seem to contradict each other. Modern scholars have tried to distinguish the different layers of composition within the *Corpus*, but no agreement has been reached so far.

Aristotle founds the logical system of syllogisms and discusses epistemology as the basis of the whole of science. In the *Posterior Analytics*, he defines the scientific demonstration as necessary reasoning from the true and primary premises. Whereas it remains controversial how much of this principle he applies to particular sciences, such as physics and ethics, the idea of a demonstrative and deductive system lays the basis for all scientific disciplines. Another important method in use is dialectic. In the academic fields where we cannot secure true premises, we should collect common opinions and reputable views of experts (called *endoxa*) first. Then, by examining the *exdoxa*, we can hope to find truth in them. The method of dialectic is applied in several places, mainly to provide the starting points for establishing his own theories.

While physics deals with the world of changing things and their unchanging causes, human practice and morality should be treated differently. As distinct from the causally necessary phenomena, human issues cannot be reasoned about or proved with the same strictness. Therefore, in studies of ethics and politics, we should be content with something true "for the most part." This clear distinction between the theoretical and practical sciences is one basic divergence from Plato's thought.

The aim of lectures in ethics and politics is practical, namely, to make the listeners good human beings and citizens. Every person seeks the good—that is, happiness (*eudaimonia*, not in the sense of modern "happiness" as a subjective feeling)—but its conceptions differ among people. Aristotle argues that since the *eudaimonia* of human beings is the realization of their natural activity, and since their essence lies in rationality, the human *eudaimonia* is sought in the activity of contemplation (*theôria*). Ethics is included in politics, which is the highest science for thc human good. Aristotle again bases his inquiry on human nature: Since a human being is by nature a political animal (i.e., animals that form a *polis* to live together), which is equivalent to the rational animal (the animal that has *logos*, i.e., reason and speech), the *polis* (political community) is the first completion of self-sufficiency of this political nature of human beings. In *Politics*, Aristotle then examines family, slavery (which he notoriously favors), citizenship, various constitutions, and education.

Aristotle is also said to have engaged in joint research on some 158 constitutions (*politeiai*) of Greek and foreign states. Perhaps the most important one was the Athenian Constitution, which was discovered in 1880 in the Egyptian desert. This work provides essential reports of the political system of Athens, collected in his school.

The philosophies of Plato and Aristotle spread throughout the world and formed a basic way of thinking about the world and life. The most important legacy of Greek philosophy is perhaps the whole system of our scientific and philosophical inquiry, which we now take for granted.

Noburu Notomi
Keio University
Yokohama, Japan

See also Normative Theory in International Relations; Political Philosophy; Political Theory

Further Readings

Ferrari, G. R. F. (2003). *City and the soul in Plato's Republic.* Chicago: University of Chicago Press.

Guthrie, W. K. C. (1962–1981). *A history of Greek philosophy* (Vols. 1–6). Cambridge, UK: Cambridge University Press.

Kraut, R. (2002). *Aristotle: Political philosophy.* Oxford, UK: Oxford University Press.

O'Meara, D. (2003). *Platonopolis: Platonic political philosophy in late antiquity.* Oxford, UK: Oxford University Press.

Rowe, C., & Schofield, M. (Eds.). (2000). *The Cambridge history of Greek and Roman political thought.* Cambridge, UK: Cambridge University Press.

Schofield, M. (2006). *Plato: Political philosophy.* Oxford, UK: Oxford University Press.

Green Parties

Green and alternative movements first emerged in several Western European countries in the 1970s accompanied by a more general generational change toward postmaterialist values. They were mostly concerned with environmental issues, such as the antinuclear movement, but also with peace and women's issues. Since then, the electoral as well as the parliamentary performance of green parties has improved remarkably in many democratic societies (mostly, however, in European countries). Thus, green parties were not just a temporary phenomenon—as many political observers had suggested in the early 1980s—but have developed into a stable element of many party systems around the world. In 2001, the green parties created a "global network" that consists of 61 member parties:

15 from Africa: Benin, Burkina Faso, Cameroon, Côte d'Ivoire, Guinea, Guinea-Bissau, Kenya, Mali, Mauritius, Morocco, Niger, Nigeria, Senegal, Somalia, and South Africa;

12 from the Americas: Brazil, Canada, Chile, Colombia (2), Dominican Republic, Mexico, Nicaragua, Peru, the United States, Uruguay, and Venezuela;

14 from the Asia-Pacific region: Australia, Japan, Mongolia, Nepal, New Caledonia, New Zealand, Papua New Guinea, Pakistan, Philippines, Polynesia, South Korea, Sri Lanka, Taiwan, and Vanuatu; and

32 from Europe: Austria, Belgium (2), Cyprus, Czech Republic, Denmark, Estonia, Finland, France, Georgia, Germany, Greece, Hungary, Ireland, Italy, Latvia, Luxembourg, Malta, the Netherlands (2), Norway, Poland, Portugal, Romania, Russia, Slovakia, Spain, Sweden, Switzerland, Ukraine, and the United Kingdom.

Most green parties outside Europe developed later, in the mid- or late 1990s, and have remained relatively minor players in terms of electoral success. Consequently, comparative research and scholarly debates focus mainly on Western European green parties. The central scholarly contributions revolve around four topics: (1) the rise and development of the Greens in Europe (Ferdinand Müller-Rommel, 1989; Michael O'Neill, 1997; Dick Richardson & Chris Rootes, 1995), (2) their political profile (Kitschelt, 1989; Rihoux, 2001), (3) their electoral and parliamentary performance (Pascal Delwit & Jean M. de Waele, 1999), and (4) their participation in national governments (Ferdinand Müller-Rommel & Thomas Poguntke, 2002).

This entry documents the rise of green parties and describes their political profile, performance, and participation in national governments. Last, this entry discusses the impact of green parties, both as a voice for those whose views are not represented by established parties and as a way of bringing attention to issues these parties have not addressed.

From Social Movements to Green Parties

The early 1970s saw the rise of new social movements in many countries of the Western world. Most of these movements emerged spontaneously from politically independent citizen initiative groups. These groups were generally interested in specific issues such as the provision of parks, and they protested against urban renewal, new highways, or the construction of nuclear power plants. They mobilized public opinion via unconventional political behavior characteristic of earlier student movements, such as demonstrations and occasional sit-ins, information campaigns, and other similar tactics.

In the mid-1970s, one particular issue became dominant in several European countries: nuclear energy. At this time, heavily influenced by the oil crisis, most European governments had decided to expand their nuclear energy programs. It was precisely the issue of nuclear power that stimulated the rise of environmental movements at the national level, since governmental decisions on nuclear power expansion could not be resolved at the local level. Thus, more and more local action groups formed national "anti–nuclear power" umbrella organizations to concentrate their impact on policy making. In addition to issues of nuclear energy and environmental protection, the debate over the North Atlantic Treaty Organization's (NATO's) dual-track decision on intermediate nuclear forces and the stationing of cruise missiles and Pershing II rockets in Western Europe in the late 1970s strengthened these movements. This debate created considerable solidarity among the new social movements across Europe.

In the early 1980s, most national social movements expected the established left-wing parties to act as effective safeguards against unlimited growth, environmental degradation, and the deployment of nuclear weapons. Yet, for different reasons, these parties could not accommodate these demands. Hence, one of the main reasons for the foundation of the Greens was their negative experience with existing left-wing parties, as well as the perceived inability of established political parties and institutions to come up with a fundamentally different policy approach.

Political Profile

Green parties in Western Europe can be characterized by three elements: First, most of these parties follow the idea of the concept of New Politics (emphasizing quality of life, citizen participation, and self-actualization rather than material affluence and economic growth). They generally embrace a left-wing standpoint consisting of fervent egalitarianism (equal rights for minorities), strong ecological and antinuclear power orientation, and solidarity with the Third World. They campaign for a genuine sharing of wealth between rich and poor nations and for assistance to underprivileged countries in creating their own self-sufficient economies, free of financial domination by industrial nations. In a nutshell, green parties introduced a new form of programmatic and ideological thinking that is less consistent with the traditional ideological Left–Right dimension. Instead, they offer a set of alternative values that differ significantly from the established parties.

Second, green parties display a much stronger preference for participatory party organization than established parties. Their organizational structure gives local party branches more autonomy in decision making and a maximum of interest articulation from grassroots initiatives. Thus, the process of decentralization is considered an essential precondition for meaningful participation.

The third and last characteristic that sets green parties apart is that they have an electorate with attributes that differ significantly from those of established parties. Comparative data on the electorate of the Greens have, for instance, shown that followers of new social movements are among the majority of green party voters. They are for the most part young, highly educated, and occupy white-collar and government jobs where the traditional class conflict is virtually nonexistent.

Although there was some diversity in the programmatic demands, and in the degree of participatory party organization, green parties developed rapidly: Between 1980 and 1984, new green parties were founded in 12 Western European countries. By the late 1980s, these parties had gained significant electoral and (in some countries) parliamentary success.

Electoral and Parliamentary Performance

The electoral performance of green parties in Western Europe has varied markedly across countries over the past 3 decades. Most of these parties have participated by now in six or more national elections and have therefore stabilized their electoral performance in major European countries. Overall, the average electoral results of green parties range between 1.5% and 7.3% of the total suffrage. In six countries, Austria, Belgium, Finland, Germany, Luxembourg, and Switzerland, electoral support for the Greens was higher than 5% of the overall vote in the past three national elections.

This comparably low electoral support for the Greens is also reflected in their parliamentary representation. During the period ranging from 1978 to 1984, only three green parties (in Germany, Luxembourg, and Switzerland) have succeeded in passing the electoral threshold for gaining representation in national parliaments. Between 1985 and 1997, the number of green parties in parliaments has increased from three to nine: Austria, Belgium, Finland, France, Germany, Luxembourg, Netherlands, Sweden, and Switzerland. Meanwhile, green parties were also represented in the Italian, Irish, Greek, Czech, and Portuguese parliaments. However, compared with most other parties, the absolute number of green party members in parliament is rather low. The average parliamentary strength ranges from 0.3% in Greece to 6.5% in Luxemburg. In sum, the electoral and parliamentary performance of green parties in Europe has remained marginal except for the green parties in Austria, Belgium, Germany, Luxembourg, and Switzerland.

Participation in National Governments

The majority of green parties in national parliaments serve as opposition parties and therefore have no impact on government formation or policy making. Outside Europe, the Greens in Brazil are the only green party to have participated in government after the 2002 national elections. In Europe, seven green parties have entered governments as coalition partners: The Greens in Finland were the first to become a member of the ruling government coalition (1995), followed by the Greens in Italy (1996), France (1997), Germany (1998), Belgium (1999), Ireland (2007), and, last, the Czech Republic (2007). Interestingly, the parliamentary duration of these parties prior to government participation varied substantially. The Greens in Belgium and Ireland held the longest representation in national governments (18 years each), followed by the German Greens (15 years), the Finnish Greens (12 years), and the Italian Greens (9 years). The French and the Czech Greens were immediately invited to participate in government after having entered parliament in a national election. Thus, we can differentiate between three types of governing green parties: First, the *professionals*, defined as green parties with a long duration of preparliamentary and parliamentary participation before entering government (e.g., in Germany and Finland); second, the *parliamentary experienced* Greens who have accumulated long experiences of parliamentary participation but low duration in preparliamentary activities (e.g., Belgium, Italy, and Ireland); third, the *preparliamentary experienced* Greens who had some extraparliamentary experience before entering parliament and government (e.g., in France and the Czech Republic).

The Impact of Green Parties

The individual and collective political relevance of the green parties can be summarized in two points: First, green parties mobilize many citizens with new value orientations by making it possible for them to find expressions for their views at the ballot box. The Greens therefore serve as political vehicles for those citizens whose grievances have been ignored by the larger established parties. By making themselves the spokespeople of the dissatisfied, green parties also stimulate a process of change of party loyalties and are paving the way for increasing volatility within Western European party systems. Second, green parties affect political issues and the tone of political life by bringing controversial matters into the public debate. If the issues prove popular, they are adopted by one or more of the larger established parties. This led to changes in the programs of major European parties. Finally, and by means of conclusion, the political impact of green parties to a very large extent depends on the emergence of New Politics issues influencing mass public opinion and the inability of larger left-wing or right-wing established parties to harness these issues and integrate them into their political agenda.

Ferdinand Müller-Rommel
Leuphana Universität Lüneburg
Lüneburg, Germany

See also Environmental Issues; Postmaterialism; Social Movements

Further Readings

Delwit, P., & de Waele, J.-M. (Eds.). (1999). *Les Partis verts en Europe* [Green parties in Europe]. Brussels: Editions Complexe.

Kitschelt, H. (1989). *The logic of party formation: Ecological politics in Belgium and West Germany.* Ithaca, NY: Cornell University Press.

Müller-Rommel, F. (Ed.). (1989). *New politics in Western Europe: The rise and the success of green parties and alternative lists.* Boulder, CO: Westview Press.

Müller-Rommel, F., & Poguntke, T. (Eds.). (2002). *Green parties in national governments.* London: Frank Cass.

O'Neill, M. (1997). *Green parties and political change in contemporary Europe.* Aldershot, UK: Ashgate.

Richardson, D., & Rootes, C. (Eds.). (1995). *The green challenge: The development of green parties in Europe.* London: Routledge.

Rihoux, B. (2001). *Les partis politiques: Organisations en changement. Le test des écologistes* [The political parties: Organizations in change. The test of the ecologists]. Paris: L'Harmattan.

Grounded Theory

Developed by the sociologists Anselm L. Strauss and Barney Glaser at the University of California at San Francisco in the late 1960s, grounded theory (GT) has become one of the foremost research styles in qualitative and interpretative social, political, and educational research. Aiming at empirically GT generation rather than at theory testing or mere description, GT provides the researcher with a rich set of research heuristics, the so-called constant comparative method. GT is, unlike ethnography or interviewing, not a method of data generation. It is also, despite its somewhat confusing name, not a theory. Instead, it is a general model for certain types of research designs, the results of which are substantive theories of the field under scrutiny. This entry discusses the origins of GT, basic procedures, its role in political science, and recent developments.

Origins

Epistemologically, as well as in terms of social theory, the origins of GT are primarily in early American pragmatism and interactionism as represented by Strauss. At the sociology department of the University of Chicago, he was trained in the pragmatist logic of inquiry (of Charles Peirce, John Dewey, and George H. Mead), with its strong notion of reality being brought forth constantly in interactively dealing with the physical and social restraints of the "world out there." By the same token, Strauss was influenced by the empirical fieldwork practice of E. C. Hughes, a descendent of Robert E. Park's human ecology approach. A second strand of origin lies in the Columbia School and its leanings toward the development of middle-range theories—a heritage brought into the project by Glaser, who was trained under Robert K. Merton before he worked with Strauss in San Francisco. While Strauss advocated the need of a research style that allows for creativity to be brought into the scientific process, Glaser represented the call for rigor in qualitative and interpretative research and theory development.

Developed in practice during an organizational ethnography on death and dying in hospital wards, the first monograph on GT, instead of being a method textbook, served more as a political statement against the orthodox consensus of structural-functionalist theories and logico-hypothetical methods. Published in 1967, amid the political uprising of the civil rights and student movements, *The Discovery of Grounded Theory*, and its methodological statement, was meant to support these new ways of thinking among young researchers. Since GT was among the first qualitative research styles spelled out in its practical details and at the same time offered a way to systematically develop empirically grounded scientific theories, it was quickly adopted by a broader group of social science researchers. While originally developed in the field of medical sociology, GT has gained a standing in most areas of sociology, psychology, education, ethnography, and social anthropology.

Basic Procedures and Heuristics

Though advocating rigor in theory development, the most basic rule of GT is that it is not to be understood as a rigid set of rules. Researchers are meant to grasp the general guidelines of GT in an interpretative and flexible manner in order to adapt its heuristics to the circumstances of practical research. Among these basic guidelines is the call for understanding the entire case—that is, instead of either comparing single items on various cases (as in quantitative research) or interpreting in depth single cases (as in hermeneutic approaches), GT developed a heuristic that integrates key features of both strategies into its constant comparative method. A second basic rule underlines not only the inevitability but also the need for and the advantage of the researchers' subjectivity and creativity. Following Dewey's notion of research as iterations of problem-solving cycles, it is the creativity of abductive processes that bridges the gap between a problem systematically laid out in processes of logical reasoning and results obtained in experimental practice. The notion of creativity goes hand in hand with the pragmatist claim that there is no universal reality to discover. Third, research is seen as a joint endeavor of a community of practice comprising not only the research team but also the scientific community. In terms of GT, this endeavor is understood as a work in progress, which gives scientific activities a down-to-earth flavor of practical day-to-day activities that need to be organized and articulated interactively among research participants. Finally, GT assumes social reality to consist of complex phenomena requiring a similarly rich theoretical understanding that primarily accounts for variation. This includes the notion of theory as a never-ending process.

In GT, both analysis and theory building start immediately with scrutinizing the material produced in investigating a first case. Thus, analysis here is thought of as a continual interplay of data generation, data inspection, and theoretical reasoning in an iterative-cyclical procedure. Single incidents of phenomena occurring in the data are compared with each other to develop a conceptual, theoretical understanding of what these incidents mean with respect to the research question under scrutiny. No a priori hypothesis drives this process. The researcher starts from a research question that in the beginning is more like a vague research curiosity: What is going on here? It is the interplay of data analysis and conceptual thinking that at the same time allows for a step-by-step stating of the research question more precisely.

The comparative analytical mode employed in GT is called *coding*—that is, occurrences of a certain phenomenon in the data are compared with other occurrences of the same or a similar phenomenon. Here, two comparative heuristics alternate. Whereas in the first phase the analyst compares incidents where the phenomenon occurs that are as similar as possible (homogeneous cases), in the second step, he or she will compare these with incidents as different from the first ones as possible (heterogeneous cases). The first step serves to develop the theoretically relevant properties of the concept to be constructed on the basis of the empirical data. While still adding to the development of properties, the second step is more dedicated to determining the scope of the concept. The aim is to find out under which conditions and in which contexts the concept still holds and which variations of the concept are necessary in order to account for the complexity of the phenomenon in reality. This scope is called *conceptual representativeness*.

The coding process consists of different modes. As the GT procedures of Strauss and Glaser have been developed in different directions over time, there is a Glaserian two-mode procedure and a Straussian three-mode procedure. Both Glaser and Strauss start with *open coding*, which tries to break up the data in a line-by-line analysis and develop those units into theoretical concepts that in light of the research question appear to be relevant. Glaser on his part continues with a coding mode called *theoretical coding*. Here, the concepts derived inductively from the data are compared with and linked with theoretical codes chosen among a larger number of code families (e.g., dimensions, cultures, and types). The aim of this procedural step is for the researcher to come up with a central core category. Viewed from the perspective of this core category, the analytical structure developed in the course of the project should answer the research question. Strauss in his more widely used approach instead suggests two further coding modes: axial and selective coding. In *axial coding*, researchers seek to establish empirically grounded relations between different concepts, often by using a so-called coding paradigm that offers a set of basic questions to answer for a phenomenon under scrutiny. These questions serve to account for contexts, intervening conditions, causalities, strategies, and consequences. Though not operating with theoretical code families, *selective coding* likewise aims at discovering a core category, thereby integrating the variety of concepts into a coherent theoretical perspective.

As analysis does not limit itself to a single case, empirical material on further cases is integrated in a step-by-step procedure called *theoretical sampling*. Different from random sampling, this selection strategy draws on the basic findings of the theory under construction. By posing generative questions derived from open ends in the theory-building process, the researcher determines which material on which types of cases is needed to continue the relevant comparative strategies at a certain point in the project. Thus, not only homogeneous and heterogeneous sampling strategies on cases and materials but also on incidents within the material alternate flexibly. The criterion for switching from one strategy to the other is called *theoretical saturation*. A certain comparative step ends when the researcher does not gain any more conceptually relevant insights from it.

An important issue in most qualitative strategies is the question of how to deal with previous practical and theoretical knowledge. Right from the beginning, GT has underscored the importance of studying social phenomena unbiased from pregiven theoretical frameworks and has encouraged researchers to start their empirical investigations right away. At times, this has been critically interpreted as a tabula rasa—a critique that was encouraged by the late Glaser's naïve inductivism. However, even in the early writings, Glaser and Strauss denied starting with a tabula rasa and Strauss for his part repeatedly advocated the advantages of a knowledge-based *theoretical sensitivity* as opposed to the definiteness of pregiven theoretical frameworks.

Grounded Theory and Political Science Research

Compared with other social sciences, the usage of GT in political sciences is less widespread. This is true not only for GT but also for all kinds of sound and systematic qualitative research methods. Overall, qualitative research is not yet well established in political science. This might be due to the fact that this field has a long tradition of normative, value-driven theorizing, which fits well both with theory-testing procedures—as a test whether the reality of political systems indeed behaves as maintained in normative theories (e.g., theories of democracy)—and with presenting exemplary evidence in an illustrative manner. The place of GT, in contrast, lies in the domain of developing explanatory theories of interactions between political actors as representatives of, for example, political parties, nongovernmental organizations (NGOs), legal institutions, or lay groups. It can be observed, however, that young scholars from the field of political science are increasingly attracted by GT, for example, for studying policy making, community power structures, or empowerment processes.

Variants and Add-Ons of Grounded Theory

Over the more than 40 years of its existence, GT has developed into a number of variants: some of them challenging the original claim, others representing add-ons to the basic model. The most important split happened between the two originators of GT during the early 1990s, when Glaser accused Strauss and his coresearcher Juliet Corbin of forcing the data into preconceived concepts (e.g., by using the coding paradigm). Glaser himself proposed a purely inductive version of GT and rejected both the use of previous knowledge and the verification of data. Strauss on his part regards previous knowledge as an inevitable and useful precondition of empirical research but only when it is used in a sensitizing instead of a definitive manner. Also, he insisted on the need for a constant process of experimental verification to come up with scientific theories based on which predictions of future developments can be made. Recently, some of Strauss's students came up with alternative or additional concepts of how to do GT. Adele Clarke, for example, suggests further developing GT into a situational analysis by using a set of mapping techniques to better represent the various perspectives occurring in the data. Another strand of discussion introduced by Kathy Charmaz centers on the notion of a constructivist GT as opposed to older, objectivist versions of GT.

Jörg Strübing
Universität Tübingen
Tübingen, Germany

See also Case Studies; Constructivism; Hermeneutics; Qualitative Versus Quantitative Methods

Further Readings

Clarke, A. (2004). *Situational analysis: Grounded theory after the postmodern turn.* Thousand Oaks, CA: Sage.
Corbin, J., & Strauss, A. L. (2008). *Basics of qualitative research: Techniques and procedures for developing grounded theory.* Thousand Oaks, CA: Sage.
Glaser, B., & Strauss, A. L. (1967). *The discovery of grounded theory: Strategies for qualitative research.* Chicago: Aldine.
Strauss, A. L. (1987). *Qualitative analysis for social scientists.* New York: Cambridge University Press.
Strübing, J. (2007). Research as pragmatic problem-solving: The pragmatist roots of empirically-grounded theorizing. In A. Bryant & K. Charmaz (Eds.), *The SAGE handbook of grounded theory* (pp. 581–601). London: Sage.

Groupthink

The rather Orwellian-sounding word *groupthink* is one of those pieces of social-scientific terminology that has entered popular usage, where it is now used rather loosely and colloquially to refer to defective or dysfunctional group decision making in general; the U.S. Senate Intelligence Committee concluded in 2004, for instance, that there was evidence of groupthink in the mistaken assessment that there were weapons of mass destruction (WMD) in Iraq prior to the 2003 American invasion. The chairs of that committee were using the term to refer to a kind of generalized or collective misperception. In the study of public policy, foreign policy analysis, psychology, and management, however, groupthink has a rather more precise usage. It was originated by the late social psychologist Irving Janis in his book *Victims of Groupthink*, first published in 1972 and later reissued in a revised form 10 years later as simply *Groupthink*. Although Janis himself did apply his theory to domestic cases such as the Watergate scandal—and the theory has also been used to explain management fiascoes such as the 1986 decision to launch the space shuttle *Challenger*—within political science it has exerted its greatest impact on the study of foreign policy decision making. The theory has been heavily criticized in recent years for reasons that are detailed below, but Janis's basic assumption that individual behavior can be altered by group pressure is supported by a substantial body of empirical research.

Janis defined the groupthink phenomenon as a process through which a group reaches a hasty or premature consensus and then becomes closed to outside ideas or alternative thoughts within. The effort to achieve unanimity and agreement overrides the desire to consider a full range of policy alternatives. High group cohesion or excessive camaraderie lies at the heart of the groupthink phenomenon and may develop where the members think too much alike or have developed powerful links of friendship or collegiality that inhibit the challenging of assumptions. While Janis did not feel that groupthink was inevitable in such a situation, he maintained that this kind of group can fall victim to groupthink where members of the group come to prize "concurrence seeking" (unanimity or agreement) over the comprehensive, rational consideration of all available courses of action. Janis illustrates his theory with a range of examples in which he claims that groupthink played a central role in the decision making, including the 1941 decision by U.S. admirals at Pearl Harbor to ignore reports that the naval base was about to be attacked by Japan, the 1961 Bay of Pigs fiasco, and the 1965 escalation of the Vietnam War. He contrasts this with what he calls *vigilant appraisal*—in which decision makers do rigorously and thoroughly consider all possible options—and holds up the Cuban missile crisis of October 1962 as a notable instance of a case in which this kind of superior process occurred.

According to Janis, groupthink has a number of antecedent conditions in addition to high group cohesiveness. For instance, it is encouraged where the group is insulated from outside advice, where an aggressive or opinionated leader prevents meaningful debate, where norms requiring the use of methodical procedures are absent, where most members of the group come from a similar social and educational background and/or think alike, where the group is confronting high levels of stress, and where its members are experiencing temporarily low levels of self-esteem. Janis also identifies a number of symptoms that can be used to diagnose the presence of groupthink. These include the presence of an illusion of invulnerability among the group; collective rationalization about the risks of a chosen option; a belief in the inherent morality of the group, in which members come to believe in the exclusive moral rightness of their cause; the appearance of stereotyped views of outgroups or "the enemy"; the exertion of direct pressure on those who dissent from the majority opinion; self-censorship, where doubters fail to express their true feelings; the false perception of unanimity, where in fact some members may harbor personal doubts about the policy option chosen; and finally, the emergence of self-appointed "mind guards," where members of the group take it on themselves to protect the group and its leader from dissenting views (guarding minds much as a bodyguard guards us physically).

It is important to realize that groupthink is essentially a theory about the policy process; it does not necessarily tell us about the outcomes of decision making. In other words, a process free of groupthink will not guarantee policy success, nor will procedures fraught with groupthink necessarily lead to policy disaster (although Janis argued that the *likelihood* of an undesirable outcome was greatly increased by the presence of groupthink). It is possible that sheer luck, for instance, will intervene in a rather fortuitous fashion to break the general causal chain between process and outcome.

In the years since Janis's book was first published, the theory of groupthink has been subjected to a variety of criticisms, and it has been adapted and reformulated in various ways. Probably the most common criticism of Janis's theory is that it is too vague and imprecise—allowing almost anything that might be labeled poor collective decision making to be categorized as an instance of groupthink—and some have critiqued the theoretical coherence of the model Janis developed. As Philip Tetlock and his colleagues have suggested, four broad criticisms can be raised against Janis's work in this vein: First of all, Janis relied on qualitative case studies, a method that frequently tempts the researcher to emphasize evidence that "fits" a theory; second, there is a suspicious correlation between the presence of groupthink and flawed decision making in Janis's book, even though Janis concedes that process is not everything; third, critics have noted an equally suspicious all-or-nothing quality to the way in which Janis's case fits so conveniently into the categories of groupthink or vigilant decision making; and last, there are various conceptual problems with the model itself, especially those having to do with distinguishing the causes from the consequences of groupthink. Certainly, Janis lumps together a bewildering variety of factors; some have questioned the inclusion of a belief in the inherent morality of the group and the stereotyped views of outgroups in his list of antecedent factors, for instance, since these appear to have little to do with consensus formation.

Others have critiqued the model on empirical grounds, and later analysts have challenged Janis's interpretation of the Bay of Pigs and Vietnam case studies, the two centerpieces of the book *Groupthink*. The contention that Lyndon Johnson did not receive competing advice on Vietnam, or that he and others felt "an illusion of invulnerability" on this issue, has been strongly questioned in recent years. The evidence we now have suggests that Johnson himself agonized quite extensively over the decision to escalate the war. The recent declassification of secretly taped phone calls that Johnson made in late 1964 and throughout 1965 reveals a president who was deeply troubled by the issue of Vietnam and quite pessimistic about the chances of winning the war. Similarly, it has also been argued that Janis's interpretation of the Bay of Pigs episode sits poorly with what we now know. In giving the go-ahead for the invasion of Cuba, John F. Kennedy and his advisers may have been influenced not so much by a feeling that they could not fail as they were by faulty (and perhaps deliberately misleading) intelligence assessments provided by the CIA (Central Intelligence Agency). Rather than being influenced by group processes, Kennedy may have simply believed that a great World War II general like Dwight Eisenhower would not have advised him to go ahead with a plan that had little chance of success.

One response to these kinds of criticisms has been to reformulate Janis's original argument in the effort to lend it more theoretical rigor. Some have attempted to better specify the kind of leadership behavior that gives rise to groupthink. Paul 't Hart, on the other hand, argues in his study of the Iran–Contra decision making under the Reagan administration that groupthink is not one phenomenon but two. Noting that the decision makers in some of Janis's cases do not appear to be laboring under an illusion of invulnerability, 't Hart distinguishes between what he calls Type I Groupthink (or Collective Avoidance) and Type II Groupthink (Collective Overoptimism). 't Hart argues that the first kind of groupthink occurs when members perceive that the likelihood of successfully resolving the problem confronting the group is low, while the latter occurs when the likelihood of success is seen as high. Prompted by the desire to "look beyond groupthink," analysts of foreign policy decision making have also reexamined the wider literature on group behaviors within social psychology for clues as to how other theoretical frameworks might be developed. One such approach has become known as the *newgroup syndrome*. Paul 't Hart, Eric Stern, and Bengt Sundelius, the theory's major advocates, have proposed that in ad hoc or newly formed groups, the lack of well-agreed norms and the absence of any existing organizational culture create uncertainty among the members. Group conformity is especially likely under such circumstances, they argue, and members are particularly likely to accept strong direction from a leader or other dominant individuals.

Nevertheless, Janis's theory has also been supported by a large body of empirical research that has essentially confirmed his original claims about the ways in which group cohesion can lead to defective decision making. Perhaps the greatest strength of this approach is that it highlights the fact that groups are more than the sum total of the individuals who compose them; once policymakers form a group, the resultant body subsumes (and may overwhelm) its members. Individuals often behave differently in groups from how they do on their own, and the greatest contribution of groupthink has been the way in which it highlights the fact that even the "best and the brightest" can fall prey to dysfunctional group dynamics.

David Patrick Houghton
University of Central Florida
Orlando, Florida, United States

See also Consensus; Foreign Policy Analysis; Leadership; Policy Process, Models of

Further Readings

Janis, I. (1982). *Groupthink: Psychological studies of policy decisions and fiascoes.* Boston: Houghton Mifflin.

Kramer, R. (1998). Revisiting the Bay of Pigs and Vietnam decisions 25 years later: How well has the groupthink hypothesis stood the test of time? *Organizational Behavior and Human Decision Processes, 73,* 236–271.

't Hart, P. (1994). *Groupthink in government: A study of small groups and policy failure.* Baltimore: Johns Hopkins University Press.

't Hart, P., Stern, E., & Sundelius, B. (Eds.). (1997). *Beyond groupthink: Political group dynamics and foreign policy-making.* Ann Arbor: University of Michigan Press.

Tetlock, P., Peterson, R. S., McGuire, C., Chang, S., & Feld, P. (1992). Assessing political group dynamics: A test of the groupthink model. *Journal of Personality and Social Psychology, 63,* 403–425.

H

Health Policy

Health policy denotes normative and procedural dimensions of assuring physical, mental, and social well-being, including but transcending medical care. Spanning normatively and empirically contested domains, however, health policy means different things to different people. Sometimes it concerns content such as financing or organizing health services; sometimes it emphasizes the process by which valued ends are sought and occasionally attained; and sometimes it implies power and whatever else may influence the formation and implementation of health-related activities. This entry describes the values and practices intrinsic to health policy, focusing on six areas: (1) definitions of health, (2) values underlying responsibility for health, (3) the context of health care practices, (4) political actors in the health policy process, (5) options in providing health care, and (6) reforms in health care systems.

Definitions

Definitions of health range from perfect well-being through functional capacity to psychological perceptions. According to the World Health Organization, health is considered a state of physical, mental, and social well-being and not merely the absence of disease or infirmity. For the functionalist Talcott Parsons (1964), "Health is a state of optimum *capacity* of an individual for the effective performance of the roles and tasks for which he has been socialized" (p. 274). For the postmodernist Walsh McDermott (1977), "Health is a relative state that represents the degree to which an individual can operate effectively within the circumstances of his hereditary and his physical and cultural environment" (p. 136).

Health was originally an individual concern, then a concern of the family, and then of larger collectivities up to and including society. Given the changes in technology, health moved beyond physical encounters (the germ theory of disease) to socioeconomic concerns (contributions to productivity) and postmodern reconstruction of well-being (cultural coping with chronic disability).

Different societies perceive health in different ways and differ about the meaning of disease and ill health. Beliefs about health, disease, and illness also differ according to gender, socioeconomic status, profession, and social role. As definitions of health change over time, perceived health needs of people change. Paradigms about what constitutes health have been broadened by scientific investigations as well as the emergence of new ideas.

Prevention of illness is the first line of defense; restoration or rehabilitation of health through medical intervention is the remedial approach; and capacity to cope with chronic conditions is a third method. Systems of health services (which include a gamut of opportunities and interventions ranging from psychosocial supports through episodic pharmaceuticals to invasive therapies such as surgery) are valued in all societies and provide an arena within which occur struggles over the allocation of values as well as the pursuit and exercise of power that represent both policy and politics.

Values

Anthropologists note that the most important thing to know about people is what they take for granted. Unarticulated values guide behavior and generate consensus about its intrinsic propriety. Only when challenged by other deeply held views do such basic orientations become manifest—and then perhaps only dimly. But although elusive and pervasive, basic orientations serve as selective filters that inhibit or distort comprehension of alternative viewpoints based on other equally basic but unarticulated values.

Common values and beliefs determine the demands made on health policymakers. The more widely values and beliefs are shared, the easier and greater the public's acceptance of proposed policies. Public opinion sets the boundaries and direction of health policy, while the social system sensitizes policymakers about health demands and supports. Most countries share basic goals in health policy: universal (or near-universal) access to health services, equity in sharing the financial burden of illness, and good-quality health care. Given the ever-larger share of public money in funding health care, governments are increasingly concerned about cost control and efficiency. Patient satisfaction, patient choice, and autonomy of professionals are important goals too.

Normative preferences about responsibility for health care range from a commitment to individualism, where a person is the only one responsible for his or her well-being, to an abiding concern for general welfare, where the state (acting on behalf of all of society) ensures an all-inclusive system of health care for all. Empirical practice involves three dimensions of health care services: (1) equitable access, (2) effective quality, and (3) efficient production.

One cleavage that informs health policy divides those who stress an essential solidarity among all humans (at least those within a delimited territory) from those who espouse the individual responsibility of each human being (with perhaps concessions for age-specific categories such as children and the elderly). The former view is egalitarian or solidaristic; the latter is characteristic of libertarianism or radical individualism. As modern communications globalize Western orientations, their spread elicits challenges and responses from non-Western societies about how to regard, amend, or replace these values. "Great" traditions (to use Robert Redfield's term) such as the Confucian and Islamic as well as "little" traditions such as regional variants and local folkways provide options as they interact with the globalized values of a secularized Judeo-Christian culture.

Context

Health policy cannot be divorced from the situational and historical context in which it is made. The legacy of previous policies, including the absence of such policies altogether, provides a contextual limit on policy options. The situational environment provides demands for policy action plus support for as well as constraints on what policymakers can do. The environment within which policy is made as well as the substantive processes that underlie the formation and implementation of specific health policies must be understood.

Health policy analysis is applicable to all societies. Regularities in the policy process and similarities among actors who try to influence it transcend differences in levels or degrees of development. Within government are policymakers including politicians, advisers, judges, and administrators. Outside governments are groups with major stakes in policies that affect them; these range from organized institutions to social forces and latent interests, and even foreign entities. How far such groups participate in policy making depends on how open or closed the political system is. Even if the array of problems and their solutions are different, procedures and routines in policy making are comparable.

While empirical experience with goals and means for health policy indicates potential global convergence on patterns of performance, countries implement changes within their own historical legacies and within the constraints of existing national institutions and political boundaries. The timing and speed of change vary as well. Some governments implement major changes rapidly whereas others, including those characterized by well-organized stakeholders, adjust, delay, or even abandon health policies.

The health sector comprises a major share of the economy in each country. It employs many workers, accounts for a considerable portion of gross national product (GNP), absorbs large amounts of resources (including often unrecorded payments out of pocket), and generates vested interests. Since any expenditure is income for someone else, a "penny saved" deprives someone somewhere of his or her earnings.

Health is also influenced by public policies that initially appear to be unconnected with health care or services. Civic insecurity, political instability, environmental pollution, revenue generation, and economic regulation—all affect changes in morbidity and mortality, not to mention the provision of health services per se. Health policy draws on many sectors whose relevance is not at first glance self-evident.

Health policy is of global concern beyond the boundaries of the nation-state. Efforts to promote health cannot be restricted to a particular country because diseases do not confine themselves within geographical borders. They are transferred from one place to another through travel, migration, commerce, and social exchange. Efforts to prevent disease and to promote health require cooperation and collaboration among agencies at local, national, and international levels.

Actors

Structures and procedures of political institutions have important consequences for the adoption and content of health policy. Enduring institutions—both governmental and nongovernmental—interact in the policy-making process. Policy actors are individuals and groups, both formal and informal, that seek to influence the creation and implementation of public policies. Potentially such actors include everyone, but degrees of activity over time vary. Some potential players never enter the game; others dominate almost every stage of play. In the health sector, actors include branches of government, governmental agencies, commercial enterprises, nongovernmental institutions, organized interest groups, and professional associations. The role each actor plays, in combination with relationships among actors in formal and informal settings, determines health policy outcomes.

Interest groups are fundamental partners in policy making. To the extent that health policy interests are shared, collective pressure allows greater policy influence. But the dynamic of interest groups is not simple. While salient interests are represented by groups, the strength of representation is not tied to the salience of an issue. Some groups are already vested due to past history, and salience itself may be a consequence of interest group action. The study of health policy must identify the policy actors and their political resources. Common resources include information and bureaucratic knowledge, a network of contacts, citizen support (including size as well as strategic location of constituency), an ability to make political contributions, and an ability to mount a public relations campaign. While few groups ever use all such resources at all times, the profile of an organized group's ability to make use of some combination of them is critical for policy influence.

In addition to organized interests, political legacies matter as do key political processes. For example, the United States developed a health care system that relies on private financing and voluntary hospitals for the provision of health services. Public sector responsibility is confined to targeted financing for the poor, the elderly, and a limited public hospital network. Subsequent efforts to reform the American health system face increasingly vested interests and widely accepted routines of private health care.

Significantly for health policy, the American system of government is built on an enduring Madisonian system of checks and balances that gives well-mobilized interests the ability to impede or block policy initiatives. The American health system has numerous groups powerful enough to oppose any reform that might harm their own economic interests.

Robert Alford's classic conceptualization of health policy posits three categories of actors engaging in "dynamics without change": (1) professional monopolists, (2) corporate rationalizers, and (3) citizen-consumers—the latter getting the proverbial short end of the stick. While institutions of representation, government, policy making, and intergovernmental relations may be stable, processes by which health policy are shaped and implemented have undergone marked changes during recent decades. These changes challenge the notion that health policy is made by a unified center or by coordinated pillars at the helm of representative political regimes.

Options

Health care systems are characterized by country-specific mixes of public and private funding, contracting, and modes of providing services. The five main sources of funding are (1) taxation (general revenues, earmarked taxes, and tax expenditure), (2) public insurance, (3) private insurance, (4) direct patient payments (copayments, coinsurance, deductibles, and uninsured services), and (5) voluntary contributions. For some low-income countries, external aid is a major source as well.

Among the three basic contracting models, the integrated version places funding and ownership of services under the same (public or private) responsibility. The best known example is the British National Health Service (NHS) that provides tax-funded health care for all. The second contracting model allows governments or third-party payers (often administrative agencies for social health insurance but sometimes private health insurers) to negotiate long-term contracts with health care providers. The third model, common in private insurance, is reimbursement when a patient pays the provider and then seeks reimbursement from the insurance agency. Therefore, the ownership and management of health services can be public, private (both for-profit and not-for-profit), or a mix of those. Moreover, there are country-specific mixes of formal and informal care, traditional and modern medicine, and medical and related social services.

Combinations of those core elements—funding, contracting (including payment modes), and ownership—determine the allocation of financial risks and decision-making power among the main players in health care. Government ownership and tax-funded services require strong government influence, whereas private funding (insurance and direct patient payments) combined with legally independent providers restricts the role of the state even though governments can—and often do—impose rules to protect patients or safeguard the quality of and access to health care.

National arrangements for financing health care vary. In Scandinavia, Italy, and the United Kingdom, the major share of health care funding is financed by general taxation, whereas systems of health insurance are the major source of funds in Germany, France, and other continental countries. In all countries, patients are expected to pay a proportion of health care costs out of their own pockets through copayments or deductibles. In most cases, however, governments mitigate the effects of user fees by exempting certain groups or by setting annual limits on how much families must pay.

Variations in funding and contracting models in health care can be traced to country-specific historical developments, but two events in Europe played a crucial role as models for policy. The first was the introduction of mandatory social health insurance for industrial workers and their families in Germany in 1883. Several other countries in Europe followed the German example of state-sponsored (but not state-administered) mandatory social insurance to protect the family income of industrial workers against the risks of illness, disability, unemployment, and old age. Mandatory membership enforced by social insurance meant that the so-called sickness funds had stable revenue streams and could create wider pools of shared risk. In the past decades, these nongovernmental funds became core actors in the public policy arena by sharing the responsibility for social policy making but under ever-greater government regulation.

The second major innovation in the funding of health care was the establishment of Britain's NHS in 1948. The NHS extended the German insurance model by providing coverage to the entire population with costs paid out of general taxation. Although hospitals in the United Kingdom were nationalized, family physicians remained independent as practitioners. Postwar reconstruction in Europe was characterized by popular support for the expansion of state-sponsored schemes. Some countries followed the German example of employment-based schemes; others preferred the population-based NHS model.

The spread of the two models was not restricted to Europe. Nations throughout the world sought to implement policies to protect the incomes of their populations (or population groups) against the financial risks of illness, disability, and old age. By the end of the 20th century, funding for health care in most countries had become hybridized by adopting elements from both the British and German models. Employment-based arrangements for certain categories of workers were combined with population-wide and tax-based universal schemes.

Reforms

The 1970s saw a shift from expansion and popular support for welfare state arrangements to reassessment and retrenchment. Economic, demographic, and ideological factors contributed to the reshaping of the popular notion of the welfare state as a solution for social problems to that of an economic burden and a cause of economic stagnation. After the oil crisis, economic stagflation with persistently high levels of unemployment meant that state revenues stagnated or declined while public expenditures continued to grow. Moreover, as the end of the postwar baby boom became visible, demographers revised earlier demographic projections downward and future pension outlays upward.

Ideological views about the role of the state also changed. On both the left and right of the political spectrum, critics agreed that state powers had become too intrusive in the lives of individuals. Discontent over fiscal burdens and disappointing results of public programs, rising consumerism, and patient advocacy groups claiming a stronger say in the allocation and organization of health care—all challenged existing arrangements for providing welfare. Governments sought alternative models of governance to reduce the dominant role of the state and decentralize decision making, with more space for choice and entrepreneurial ideas. Some countries introduced market competition in health care by reducing state control over the funding and planning of health care services. They also sought to broaden patients' choice of provider and health plan. Other countries turned to traditional tools of controlling public expenditure by setting strict budgets, reducing the scope of public insurance, and increasing direct patient payments.

During the past few decades, attempts to change health policy have been stimulated by economic recession and by severe fiscal problems in the state treasury rather than by an ideologically driven taste for reform, although the 2010 health reform bill in the United States was intended to address not only economic concerns but also issues of social justice. Declining government budgets have adversely affected service delivery, even in countries that previously had reasonably well-performing systems for the public delivery of health services. Pressures for changes in health policy often emanate from central ministries such as finance and planning. In many cases, the ministries of health struggle to reinterpret and to respond to policy directives outside their control.

Economic realities of recession and fiscal crises affect not only the types of policies that are implemented but also reactions to them by the users, beneficiaries, and citizens. The stage of raising revenue through the introduction of user fees to supplement government budgetary resources was critical for many governments because of the endemic economic crisis. But the success of the policy, however logical in theory, was constrained by the dwindling capacity of citizens to pay for health care. Furthermore, the administrative cost of collecting user fees and of monitoring exempted categories of users often exceeds the revenue collected. Although well intended, the initial policy had not considered inevitable transaction costs.

For several decades, health policy reforms have been premised on the assumption that improving the ability of government to manage its business will lead to improved social and economic progress. The first generation of reforms sought to cut public expenditures and to revive the private sector. Measures included budget cuts, tax reforms, limited privatization, liberalization of prices, and, most conspicuously, efforts to downsize the public sector. The latter was invariably described as bloated and in need of surgery followed by a strictly enforced diet.

When it became evident that the transformation of government would require a long time and that the savings from reduced bureaucratic costs would be insufficient to provide even basic levels of public services, a second generation of policy reforms sought to improve the efficiency and effectiveness of government. While the first-generation reforms stressed downsizing, contracting, and improved control over budgeting and public expenditures, the second generation advocated decentralization to subnational levels, creation of semiautonomous agencies in the central government, and reforms of human resource management (recruitment, selection, and training).

Recently, the agenda of health policy refocused yet again as a third generation of reforms seeks to improve social outcomes through better service delivery. This strategy emphasizes sectorwide approaches, particularly in health and education, to produce a coherent program for delivery of services that involves both governmental and nongovernmental organizations. While these generations of policy reforms are overlapping rather than strictly sequential, all have been driven by a combination of external and internal agencies. Multilateral and bilateral aid entails conditionalities that require a (commitment to) change in governmental behavior before money can be transferred. In turn, national planning commissions and ministries of finance require line agencies to adopt reforms that may include a combination of these generations.

Policy reforms range across a repertoire of instruments: streamlined budgets, staff reductions, raised tariffs, contracting out, and other forms of privatization. Reform of the health sector has focused on four main options, none of which is mutually exclusive and all of which may occur at the same time. These are the establishment of autonomous organizations, introduction of user fees, contracting out of services, and the enablement and regulation of the private sector.

While these issues characterize features of health care systems and health policy, they do not explain the causes or effects of policy change. To understand why countries embark on particular reform paths, not only external and internal pressures for change must be investigated but also structural features of social policy making that enable politicians and policy entrepreneurs to change the system despite the fact that institutional legacies and popular support for existing policy arrangements create barriers to change.

James Warner Björkman
Institute of Social Studies
The Hague, Netherlands

See also Functionalism; Individualism; Institutions and Institutionalism; Interest Groups; Libertarianism; Policy Analysis; Policy Community; Policy Cycle; Policy Learning; Policy Network; Reform; Responsibility; Solidarity; Values; Welfare State

Further Readings

Alford, R. R. (1975). *Health care politics: Ideological and interest group barriers to reform.* Chicago: University of Chicago Press.

Altenstetter, C., & Björkman, J. W. (Eds.). (1997). *Health policy reform, national variations and globalization.* London: Macmillan.

Barker, C. (1996). *The health care policy process.* London: Sage.

Björkman, J. W., & Altenstetter, C. (Eds.). (1998). *Health policy.* Cheltenham, UK: Elgar.

Curtis, S., & Taket, A. (1996). *Health and societies: Changing perspectives.* New York: Wiley.

Cutler, D. M. (2002). Health care and the public sector. In A. J. Auerbach & M. Feldstein (Eds.), *Handbook of public economics* (pp. 2143–2243). Amsterdam: Elsevier.

Gatrell, A. C. (2001). *Geographies of health.* Oxford, UK: Blackwell.

McDermott, W. (1977). Evaluating the physician and his technology. In J. Knowles (Ed.), *Getting better and feeling worse: Health in the United States* (pp. 135–158). New York: W. W. Norton.

Parsons, T. (1964). *Social structure and personality.* London: Free Press.

Parsons, T. (1972). Definitions of health and illness in the light of American values and social structure. In E. G. Jaco (Ed.), *Patients, physicians and illness: A source book in behavioral science and health* (2nd ed., pp. 97–117). New York: Free Press.

Ranade, W. (Ed.). (1998). *Markets and health care: A comparative analysis.* New York: Longman.

Venkat Raman, A., & Björkman, J. W. (2009). *Public-private partnerships in health care in India: Lessons for developing countries.* London: Routledge.

World Health Organization. (1946). Preamble to the constitution of the World Health Organization. In *Official records of the World Health Organization* (No. 2, p. 100). Geneva: Author. (Adopted 19 June 1946 by the International Health Conference, New York; signed 22 July 1946 by representatives of 61 States, and entered into force 7 April 1948).

Hegel, Georg Wilhelm Friedrich (1770–1831)

Georg Wilhelm Friedrich Hegel was born in Stuttgart, Germany, on August 27, 1770. His political writings, including those on political philosophy, owed much to his reactions to the fragmentary nature of the German territories within the Holy Roman Empire and Napoleon's attempted forced unification of them under a common civil code, between the early 1790s and the Battle of Waterloo in 1815. Hegel's trenchant critique of the abstract universalism of the French revolutionaries in his *Phenomenology of Spirit* (1807) did not prevent him from celebrating every Bastille Day until his death on November 14, 1831. His alternative was a form of civic nationalism based on shared traditions and cultural attachments, an ideal that he championed against the ethnic nationalism espoused at the time by many German romantics. In itself, the fact that Hegel allied himself so clearly with the civic nationalists in this particular dispute should do much to unsettle the received picture of him as an apologist for Prussian authoritarianism and a forerunner of Nazism.

Today, Hegel is notorious for his claim, made most famously in the *Philosophy of History* (1831), that history is the gradual revelation of *Geist* (translated as "Spirit" or "Mind" and synonymous with God's temporal self-manifestation) in the world, a dialectical process that critics allege he believes occurs without the knowledge of individual human agents and largely through the brutal intervention of quasi-mystical "world-historical individuals." The meaning and significance of such claims are easily misunderstood and, in certain cases, apparently deliberately distorted. Hegel approaches the historical record as a philosopher, and in this role, he seeks to discover the rationality underlying the shifting events of the past. He explicitly distinguishes this "philosophical history" from the other forms of history, including those undertaken by the early chroniclers and those who would now be seen as historians, both of whom he acknowledges have legitimate functions to perform in providing an understanding of the past. The philosopher's primary task, however, is to try to arrive at knowledge of the fundamental processes at work in the world. According to Hegel, knowledge can only be of a rational system of related concepts and propositions; hence, knowledge of the fundamental structural processes of human action must presuppose the ultimate rationality of the world. It is partly because he holds this view that Hegel claims, most notably in the Preface to *Elements of the Philosophy of Right* (1821), that "what is rational is actual; and what is actual is rational." Knowledge is of reality and, Hegel argues, everyone presupposes reality to be structured by a coherent system of fundamental principles or laws. To "comprehend" something is to understand that particular thing as being underpinned in particular ways by such a coherent system of laws. A philosophical history attempts to discover those laws as they have been revealed through past actions and events.

This presupposition informs every branch of Hegel's philosophical system. Hence, in the preface to *Elements of the Philosophy of Right*, he states that the fundamental task of his political philosophy is "*to comprehend and portray the state* [Staat] *as an inherently rational entity*" [italics added]. It is this project that has led a great many critics to allege that Hegel is simply an apologist for the Prussian state. In reality, Hegel is seeking to discover the ideal type of the *Staat* that is implicit within the self-image of the world's most developed empirical politically organized communities. This project necessitates an attempt to rationalize certain negative features of the world, not least war. Nevertheless, the project has a profoundly critical thrust, in that some elements of empirically observable states do not cohere with the majority of the other elements of those states. In this sense, these wayward features of empirical states cannot be included within a conception of the state as an ideal type. The irrational elements must be excluded, which in practice means that the incongruent features of the world should be reformed, a process that may require radical changes to existent states. Hegel's most significant analysis of an incoherent social practice concerns slavery, in *Phenomenology of Spirit*. While the master treats the slave as a thing that can be owned and used, in giving him orders he treats him also as a being with capacities for cognition and practical reason—that is, as a person. More than this, the master seeks to gain a sense of his own power and status by dominating the slave. Yet he can never be satisfied with recognition from a lesser being. Similarly, the slave is denied the recognition that he seeks innately from his master. Hence, the master–slave relationship is self-contradictory and unsatisfying for both parties; the situation tends to drive each to destroy the other or to try to reconstruct their relationship on a more egalitarian footing. This struggle for recognition is the primary motor of human progress.

Hegel's project would have profound implications even if he had restricted his conception of the proper subject matter of political philosophy (the *Staat*) to the state as it is understood by many contemporary political scientists and philosophers: the formal legal-political organs, including the legislature, executive, judiciary, civil service, police, army, and so on. In fact, Hegel adopts a wider conception of the *Staat* understood as an order that encompasses conventional sociopolitical, economic, and legal practices and institutions in such a manner that, in essence, it represents a thoroughly modernized ideal of the ancient Greek polis. *Elements of the Philosophy of Right* analyses the relationships within the ideal type of the modern state through the interactions of its three "moments": (1) the individual will, (2) *Moralität* (translates very loosely as "morality"), and (3) *Sittlichkeit* (usually translated as the "ethical life"). In Hegel's view, the individual will is free when the agent acknowledges the determinate action that results from that will as an expression of a law that he (the individual) has set for himself. (Hegel is concerned with men, not women, as commented on below.) Institutions and practices are justified to the extent that they facilitate such freedom. Hegel explores this claim through his discussion of the individual right to private property, which he analyses as the means for the facilitation of the determinate expression of the individual's will in the world. This discussion leads him to an analysis of contract as a moment of the interaction of the wills of different persons. This leads him to the discussion of wrong action and the first stage of his analysis of punishment as the annulment of crime. Hegel conceives this "cancellation" of wrong action as the reharmonization of the individual's will with itself and with the social practices and institutions that provide the will with its initial content (its socialization) and background. Underlying Hegel's theory is a proposition that recurs throughout his writings: The reality of an object—in this case, the determinate individual will—is constituted by the coherent principles underlying it. If existent states were to embody their ideal type, then the criminal act would represent of necessity an internal contradiction within the individual. Punishment enables the individual's rational will to reassert itself in practice, by communicating the *Staat*'s disapproval thereby "reminding" the individual of the nature and legitimacy of the presupposed meanings and values that form the basis of his rational will.

Hegel titles this part of *Elements of the Philosophy of Right* as "Abstract Right." He argues that the lack of determinacy in such a (logical rather than temporal) "moment" is overcome through *Moralität*. Yet even this second "moment" is limited because it lacks an external referent, being concerned solely as it is with the individual's internal moral life, the qualities of his particular character, virtue, and conscience. The individual can overcome these limitations only by being an active participant in the *Sittlichkeit* ("ethical life") of his community. The first facet of ethical life in which the individual participates is the family. This is the realm of love and hence the unreflective honoring of one's duties to the members of one's family. In essence, in the family the individual acts without asking why or what is required of him; in this sense, Hegel calls the family the realm of "immediacy." This realm is limited, however, in that the person is treated as a facet of a group, rather than as an individual with his or her own desires, beliefs, values, plans, and will. The person moves closer to expressing his or her individuality through participation in civil society. In Hegel's view, this nonpolitical public realm encompasses the economic system, voluntary associations, and the like. The fruits of private property are realized here in the "system of needs," partly through employment and self-expression through work. (Yet Hegel appreciates that these fruits are associated with unemployment and poverty.) In civil society as a whole, individuals face each other as self-interested agents, bound together by contracts that they have entered into self-consciously and deliberately. In this sense, it is a realm of mediated action.

In spite of any appearance of pure self-determination, the individual's actions in civil society are necessarily conceived and executed within a shared framework of common modes of action, norms, conventions, and, ultimately, civil laws. These underlying structures are maintained through the action of the state, conceived as living interactions of citizens in the context of the formalized legal and political organs. To the extent that the state embodies its ideal, it enjoys the self-conscious loyalty of its citizens. This is true patriotism: the self-conscious emotional identification of individual citizens with the community as the latter is embodied in the state, with this identification being based on an uncoerced recognition that one's own highest good is realized through respecting the good of one's *Staat. Elements of the Philosophy of Right* concludes with pregnant discussions of the tragic inevitability of war and various forms of imperialism, with the latter in particular anticipating many Marxist theories. Finally, Hegel argues that progress is inherently tragic, in the sense that human development is driven by world-historical individuals, such as Napoleon, and world-historical states (here, one might think of the contemporary United States), who in driving the world forward, inevitably bring about their own fall from grace.

Hegel's claim that the *Staat* should be conceived organically has led many to argue that he sees individual human beings as mere adjuncts of the state qua political-legal institutions or as organs and limbs to be directed not by their own individual wills but by the automatic functioning of the state as some form of collective whole. On this view, Hegel held the state to be the determining agent and the individual to be valuable only to the extent that he or she served the state's interests and will. This unappealing picture is crowned literally by Hegel's retention of the monarch as the embodiment of the state, exercising the sole function of signing bills into law. In reality, Hegel holds that individuals in a well-ordered state would be active, self-conscious, and critical patriots; organized through various civil society associations; and represented politically through their membership of corporations that are integrated formally into the state apparatus. To the extent that they fail to be so in practice, the particular state fails to live up to its ideal. Throughout, the guiding principle of Hegel's political philosophy is "to be a person, and respect others as persons" (*Philosophy of Right*, Part 1, sec. 36).

Certainly, problems remain. Even though Hegel describes polygamy as slavery for women, he excludes women from full citizenship, claiming that they are incapable of freedom in that they are guided by emotion rather than reason. Other critics have baulked at his corporatism and retention of the monarch, even if in only a largely ceremonial role. Hegel himself acknowledges different contradictions within his rationalization of the world: Free economic activity seems to result inevitably in poverty for some respectable workers, and self-interested states remain the primary actors in an international system thereby destined for conflict and war. Despite the claims of both friends, such as Alexandre Kojève, and critics, such as Karl Popper, Hegel never claimed that the world that we have now is perfect. Rather than believing that we have reached the "End of History," Hegel insists that philosophical insight always comes too late: The philosopher can only rationalize a stage of the world when it is in its death throes.

Colin Tyler
University of Hull
Hull, United Kingdom

See also Citizenship; Civil Society; Constitutionalism; Idealism; Identity, Social and Political; Individualism; Liberty; Nationalism; State

Further Readings

Beiser, F. C. (Ed.). (1993). *Cambridge companion to Hegel.* Cambridge, UK: Cambridge University Press.

Bradley, A. C. (1965). Hegel's theory of tragedy. In A. C. Bradley (Ed.), *Oxford lectures on poetry* (pp. 69–95). London: Macmillan. (Original work published 1909)

Hegel, G. W. F. (1991). *Elements of the philosophy of right* (A. W. Wood, Ed.; H. B. Nisbet, Trans.). Cambridge, UK: Cambridge University Press.

Hegel, G. W. F. (1999). *Political writings* (D. Laurence & H. B. Nisbet, Eds.; H. B. Nisbet, Trans.). Cambridge, UK: Cambridge University Press.

Inwood, M. (1992). *Hegel dictionary.* Oxford, UK: Blackwell.

Pinkard, T. (2000). *Hegel: A biography.* Cambridge, UK: Cambridge University Press.

Pippin, R. B. (2008). *Hegel's practical philosophy: Rational agency as ethical life.* Cambridge, UK: Cambridge University Press.

Tyler, C. (2006). *Idealist political philosophy: Pluralism and conflict in the absolute idealist tradition.* New York: Continuum.

Hegemony

Hegemony derives from the Greek term *hēgemonía* (ἡγεμονία), referring to the predominance of one of the city states (e.g., Sparta or Athens) over the others and its related leadership in issues of common interest. In modern times, it has come to be used in reference more generally to the predominance of one actor over others. In contemporary political science, we can distinguish two traditions in the use of the term *hegemony*. In international relations theory, hegemony has been used more or less directly in reference to the original Greek meaning, where it refers to the predominance (primarily in terms of economic and military power) of one state over others. Alternatively, in Marxist-inspired political science, hegemony refers to the predominance (especially in an ideological sense) of one social group over others. Finally, Robert Cox has established an approach in critical international relations theory in which the differences between these two traditions are transcended.

Hegemony in International Relations Theory

In international relations theory, the concept of hegemony has been applied to the phenomenon of one state's being strong enough to maintain an international order that is beneficial to (most) other states as well. Two main traditions can be distinguished here, the neorealist theory of hegemonic stability and the theory of historical cycles of global hegemony and leadership.

Hegemonic Stability

The theory of hegemonic stability (developed in the 1970s by Charles Kindleberger and subsequently subscribed to by many neorealist authors) argues that the interstate system will be relatively peaceful and stable if there is a hegemonic state that provides certain public goods to the system (most basically prosperity and security). A state will be a *hegemon* if it has both the capability and the will to perform this function. The capability of a state depends on the (relative) size and level of development of its economy, its ability to dominate certain key technological sectors, and its political and military power. During much of the 19th century, Great Britain dominated the world economically, politically, and militarily. Through its role as a stabilizer in the European balance of power and through its management of the gold standard, it was able to secure a measure of stability in interstate relations, which was beneficial to the growth of a liberal world economy. Similarly, after 1945 the United States became the hegemon: It emerged out of the war as by far the strongest military and economic power, and it used its power to create the institutional framework (the Bretton Woods system), which facilitated the unprecedented expansion of the world economy in the following decades.

When the Bretton Woods system collapsed in the early 1970s and the hegemony of the United States weakened, hegemonic stability theory predicted the erosion of the liberal regime established by the hegemon as well. However, no such development took place. This gave rise to an alternative interpretation. In his *After Hegemony* (1984), Robert Keohane argued that collaboration between states needs to be based not only on the exercise of hegemony but also on the recognition by states that voluntary cooperation can be beneficial to them. Crucial to this approach is the concept of complex interdependence, which explains why states engage in cooperation through the creation and reproduction of international regimes.

World Systems Theory

Very similar conceptions of hegemony have been developed by scholars who started theorizing interstate hegemony from adjoining disciplines such as historical sociology (e.g., Immanuel Wallerstein) or political geography (e.g., Giovanni Arrighi and Peter Taylor). Wallerstein (1980), the intellectual founder of world systems theory, defines hegemony as that "short moment in time when a given core power can manifest simultaneously productive, commercial and financial superiority over all other core powers" (pp. 38–39). According to Wallerstein, there have been three instances of hegemony in the history of the capitalist world economy: (1) the United Provinces (1620–1672), (2) England (1815–1873), and (3) the United States of America (1945–1967). All these powers displayed some common characteristics. First, they initially achieved a relative advantage in agro-industrial production, then in commerce, and finally in finance. Second, hegemonic powers tended to be advocates of global "liberalism" in economic and political terms. Finally, in all three cases military power rested primarily on naval capabilities. The conditions that determine the rise of a particular country to hegemony in the system are manifold: Geographic location and size, the strength of the state apparatus, the availability of new technologies capable of giving the country in question a competitive advantage over other core powers, the availability of sufficient investment capital and human capital (skilled labor), and a productive agricultural sector can all contribute to the attainment of hegemony.

Some authors with intellectual roots in international relations, such as George Modelski and William R. Thompson, have taken a historical view and arrived at insights very similar to those of world systems theory (although without using the word *hegemony*). Modelski's "long cycle of world leadership" consists of four phases: the phase of (1) *global war* among major powers in the system, resulting in the emergence of a (2) *world power* assuming the leadership role; after a period of 2 to 3 decades, the world power's leadership starts to wane in the phase of (3) *delegitimation* so that eventually a strong challenger rises in the phase of (4) *deconcentration*, whose challenge results in a new global war. According to Modelski, there have been five such cycles in the history of the world system: the Portuguese cycle (1494–1580), the Dutch cycle (1581–1688), the first (1689–1791) and second (1792–1913) British cycles, and finally the American cycle (1914–present). Decisive for the attainment of world leadership is the "capacity for global reach": The aspiring power must be securely located, preferably on an ocean; it must possess ocean-going sea power (potentially more than half of all available sea power); it must have sufficient financial resources to pay for its navy; and it must have a political structure that can lend coherence to a global enterprise. The principal challengers have been land powers: The French challenged the Dutch leadership only to find the English taking over the lead, and similarly the French and German challenges eventuated in leadership by (again) Britain and the United States.

Ultimately, these different approaches to hegemony are in agreement on one fundamental point: They all conceptualize hegemony as a relationship between states. This contrasts sharply with the original definition of hegemony in Marxist thought.

Hegemony in Marxist Political Theory

Hegemony in the Marxist tradition is usually associated with the name of Antonio Gramsci, the leader of the Italian Communist Party between 1924 and 1926, when he was arrested by the Fascist regime. In fact, the term was already used extensively by various Russian socialist leaders in the decades leading up to the Bolshevik Revolution of 1917. In this early debate, hegemony referred to the leading role that the proletariat might play in the revolutionary struggle against the feudal order, provided it could transcend its internal divisions and develop a coherent ideological project. Gramsci was concerned to rethink political strategy in light of the very different experiences of the Russian and the West European revolutions of 1917–1919. In Russia, the capture of state power gave the revolutionary forces a sufficient grip on society at large to implement their political program. In the West (as the failed revolutions in Germany and Italy showed), the political power of the ruling class did not rest primarily on the control of the coercive apparatus of the state but was diffused and situated in the myriad institutions and relationships in civil society. In reflecting on these historical experiences, Gramsci developed his understanding of hegemony beyond its early forms by emphasizing the importance of intellectual and moral leadership and of the hegemonic group being able to bind other social groups and by recognizing the possibility of hegemony being exercised by any social class (in particular the bourgeoisie).

No social group can rule by force alone. In any class society, the ruling class, that is, the social group that has the ultimate control over the primary means of production, organizes, reproduces, and reinforces its position of economic power through a complex mix of noneconomic mechanisms. These include ideological or religious power, institutional forms, and ultimately the (threat of the) use of force. Under certain historical conditions, the balance between force and persuasion can move from one end of the continuum to the other (without either ever completely disappearing). Hegemony, in the classic Gramscian sense, is then defined as a form of class rule based primarily on consent by the subordinate groups (produced by the political, intellectual, and moral leadership of the hegemonic group) rather than on *coercion* (resting on the application of physical force).

Ernesto Laclau and Chantal Mouffe have critiqued Gramsci's thought, and in particular the adoption of Gramsci's ideas by more recent

Marxist authors, as being marred by a lingering materialist determinism. They have argued for a radical reinterpretation of Gramsci's theory of hegemony on the basis of discourse theory: Hegemony then becomes a strictly subjective phenomenon. Their intervention has led to continuing debate in Marxist thought between those committed to further developing historical materialism and those arguing for a constructivist (or post-structuralist) turn.

Transnational Hegemony

Robert Cox became the founder of an approach that became known as neo-Gramscianism or transnational historical materialism in which he brought the earlier two traditions together by applying Gramsci's understanding of hegemony to the analysis of international politics. He argued that to understand global politics we need to abandon the idea that is central to the classic paradigm in international relations theory, namely, that the state is the key unit of analysis. Basing himself on a materialist position, he argued that it is social relations of production that are key and that therefore the basic unit of analysis should be the state–society complex rather than the state conceived as a black box. Cox enlarged the scope of his project by making the crucial claim that Gramsci's core ideas can fruitfully be applied to the analysis of a globalizing *international* capitalism even though Gramsci himself was primarily concerned with analyzing politics in national contexts.

Hegemony, in Cox's understanding, is simultaneously a relationship between social forces as well as a relationship between states: The international hegemony of states such as Great Britain and the United States is in fact the outward projection of the domestically grounded hegemony of a particular configuration of social forces. American hegemony in the post-1945 era was grounded in the hegemony of the class coalition (or in Gramsci's terminology *historic bloc*) of internationally oriented transnational corporations and the organized industrial working class. The longer-term historical dynamics of the global system are determined by the patterns of interaction of hegemonic and nonhegemonic state-society complexes: societies characterized by the predominance of consensual and coercive forms of class rule, respectively. The international order can be characterized as hegemonic when a specific national configuration of class forces is able to project its predominant influence externally, thus supporting a leading role for its state; or it can be characterized as nonhegemonic (Cox speaks of "rival imperialisms") when such leading class coalitions remain "domestic" because they are too weak to project their influence outwardly.

Henk Overbeek
Vrije Universiteit Amsterdam
Amsterdam, Netherlands

See also Civil Society; Class, Social; Constructivism; Interdependence; International Regimes; Marxism; Power; World Systems Theory

Further Readings

Cox, R. W. (1987). *Production, power and world order: Social forces in the making of history.* New York: Columbia University Press.

Gramsci, A. (1971). *Selections from the Prison Notebooks.* New York: International.

Keohane, R. O. (1984). *After hegemony: Cooperation and discord in the world political economy.* Princeton, NJ: Princeton University Press.

Kindleberger, C. P. (1973). *The world in depression 1929–1939.* Los Angeles: University of California Press.

Laclau, E., & Mouffe, C. (1985). *Hegemony and socialist strategy: Towards a radical democratic politics.* London: Verso.

Modelski, G. (1987). *Long cycles in world politics.* Seattle: University of Washington Press.

Wallerstein, I. (1974, 1980, 1989). *The modern world-system* (Vols. 1–3). New York: Academic Press.

Hermeneutics

As one might expect of a concept and tradition of thought that traverses vast expanses of history and a variety of disciplines, the term *hermeneutics* is inconducive to short summary or univocal definition. In the broadest of terms, hermeneutics refers to the theory and methodology of interpretation, that is, the theory and methods of understanding, or making sense of, an object of investigation. The proper objects of interpretation are taken to be "texts" or "text analogues" whose meanings are unclear, strange, puzzling, confused, fragmentary, incomplete, or seemingly contradictory. The primary aim of hermeneutical investigation is to provide a reading or interpretation of the text that removes or mitigates its obscurity or puzzling aspects by disclosing its underlying meaning and coherence. Additionally, hermeneutical inquiry involves systematic reflection on questions about the very nature of interpretation: What is interpretation? What makes one interpretation better or more correct than another? What is the proper scope of interpretive inquiry? What are its social and political implications? One's stance on these and other questions will decisively shape one's conception of hermeneutics. This entry discusses its history, various meanings, and possible applications in political science.

History and Meanings

Consistent with the varied contemporary understandings of the term, the etymological roots of the word *hermeneutics* are equally rich and complex. The word first appears in ancient Greek as the verb *hermēneuein* ("to interpret") and the noun *hermēneia* ("interpretation"). Specifically, its origins point to Hermes, the wing-footed herald of the gods who traveled between the mortal and immortal worlds, delivering messages from the latter to the former. As such, Hermes is associated with activities that are later regarded as central to the hermeneutical enterprise, namely, the activities of interpreting and illuminating alien or opaque systems of meaning (in Greek, a *hermēneus* was an interpreter), of translating meanings from one world or language into another, and of mediating between different people or worlds. At the same time, Hermes's reputation as the discoverer of writing, music, and poetry points to the strong emphasis that advocates of hermeneutics place on the role of language in human life. Coming to an understanding of some phenomenon, hermeneuticists contend, inevitably requires a grasp of the linguistic practices and symbolic systems through which the meaning of that phenomenon is expressed. Finally, the connection between hermeneutics, interpretation, and language is apparent in the title of Aristotle's work on the relationship between language and logic, *Peri Hermeneias*, which was later translated into Latin as *De Interpretatione*.

Although originating in the classical world, the concept of hermeneutics is sharply altered during the modern period. With the advent of the Protestant Reformation and its shift of responsibility for interpreting the Bible from the Church Fathers to individual Christians, hermeneutics, especially in Germany, becomes increasingly identified with efforts to expound the proper principles and methods of Biblical interpretation. This notion is broadened over time to include methods of philological and legal interpretation but nonetheless remains the dominant understanding of hermeneutics into the 19th century, when the philosopher and theologian Friedrich Schleiermacher advances a view of hermeneutics as a universal discipline that encompasses all fields of study in which the interpretation of texts (in the extended sense of the term) is a central concern. According to Schleiermacher, universal hermeneutics aims to articulate the general principles of all understanding that constitute the foundation of the specialized fields of hermeneutical inquiry.

Perhaps the most significant shift of meaning occurs in the late 19th century, when the philosopher Wilhelm Dilthey conceives of hermeneutics as providing the methodological and epistemological foundation of the *Geisteswissenschaften* (the social sciences and humanities). Contending that the central task of the *Geisteswissenschaften* is to understand lived experience in all of its abundant richness and diversity, Dilthey differentiates the mechanistic and nomological forms of explanation characteristic of the natural sciences from the types of hermeneutical understanding that in his view constitute the methodological and epistemological foundations of the human sciences. While the former strive to explain the behavior of physical objects through the discovery of causal laws, the proper aim of the latter, Dilthey argues, is to understand the historically constituted mental life and lived experience that is an essential aspect of human reality.

Consequently, the human sciences are both irreducible to and partly independent of the sciences of nature. Not only is their subject matter ontologically distinct from that of the natural sciences, but this ontological difference yields a methodological distinction. One of Dilthey's central projects was to develop a view of hermeneutics as providing the proper methods for the study of human existence. This project is taken up and variously reformulated by several leading representatives of hermeneutical thought in the late 19th and 20th centuries, including figures as diverse as Max Weber, Robin George Collingwood, Hans-Georg Gadamer, Martin Heidegger, Peter Winch, Paul Ricoeur, Jürgen Habermas, Charles Taylor, Clifford Geertz, and Quentin Skinner.

Hermeneutics and Political Science

Although Dilthey is the first writer to argue that hermeneutics, or interpretation, provides a firm foundation for the human sciences and constitutes its central task, it is only during the later decades of the 20th century that hermeneutical perspectives become a significant part of the discourse of Anglophone political science. Largely in response to the growing prominence of positivist epistemologies, the champions of hermeneutics simultaneously criticized many of the central claims of positivism and outlined their own post-positivist conceptions of political inquiry. Importantly, hermeneutical critics held that positivist orthodoxies not only sustained a model of scientific explanation that was inappropriate for the social sciences, but they also obfuscated important issues of power and politics that could only be identified through careful attention to the interpretive dimensions of political affairs.

On the one hand, hermeneuticists challenged the central commitments of positivism: that the covering-law model of explanation constitutes the only valid model of scientific explanation; that sense data can be directly perceived and represented in a neutral, noninterpretive observation language; that empirical data can be neatly divorced from theoretical frameworks; that scientific explanations are necessarily value-free; and that the methods of the mature natural sciences provide the proper model for the study of political affairs. Although articulated in various ways, the hermeneutical critique of positivism generally turns on an analysis of a key task of social and political inquiry that has no echo in the physical sciences, namely, the radically reflexive and doubly hermeneutical task of interpreting interpretations. Because human beings are self-interpreting animals whose individual and social self-interpretations constitute an essential part of social reality, no investigation of social or political phenomena can neglect this task on pain of distorting the phenomena it purports to explain or understand.

At a minimum, hermeneuticists maintain, social and political inquiry must begin by understanding agents' self-understandings and self-interpretations. It is only on the basis of such understanding that one can, first, identify properly what stands in need of explanation and, second, combat the often fatal tendency of social scientists and laypersons to project their own languages of understanding onto the agents, cultures, traditions, and practices they study. More generally, because self-interpretations partly constitute human and social reality yet typically change over time and vary across cultures, the conceptual unity that is a central feature of the covering law model and a necessary condition of precise prediction rarely, if ever, obtains in social science. In short, the inherent mutability and instability of social reality undermines the positivist imperative to develop a nomological and predictive science of society and politics.

On the other hand, hermeneuticists have developed their own accounts of the proper practices of political inquiry. The central premise of hermeneutical approaches is that interpretation takes place within specific backgrounds or contexts that are conceived, for example, as traditions, webs of meaning and belief, constellations of social relations, or practices embedded in what Ludwig Wittgenstein calls a "form of life." In the act of interpretation, both the interpreter and the text (or text-analog) are "situated" within one or more of these contexts or backgrounds. The relationship between them is therefore not one of a disinterested, disembodied observer in search of objective, context-free knowledge. Rather, it involves a dialogical and fallible process of navigating within and between often disparate linguistic, cultural, historical, and political contexts to better understand or make sense of the text or texts under investigation.

Most significantly, interpretation involves movement within what is called the hermeneutic circle. Hermeneuticists contend that an adequate interpretation of the meaning or sense of a text requires an analysis that is circular in a double sense: first, any effort to establish the meaning of a text must proceed by moving back and forth between a reading of particular parts of the text and the text as a whole, with the latter being read in light of the former and vice versa; and, second, both the individual parts of the text and the text as a whole must be located within a larger context, background, or field of conventions and assumptions from which they derive their meaning and to which they contribute. The process is therefore unavoidably holistic and circular—there is no privileged standpoint outside the circle of meanings from which one might establish the meaning of a single element within the text or of the text as a whole. This, however, does not imply that the standards for assessing interpretations are subjective or arbitrary. Because even individual beliefs and attitudes are only intelligible against a background of publicly available "intersubjective" and "common" meanings, the latter provide a publicly accessible evidential basis for evaluating the adequacy of an interpretation.

Although hermeneutical writers argue that interpretation is an indispensable part of all social inquiry, the deliberate appropriation of hermeneutical methods is more common in some areas of political inquiry than in others. Hermeneutical approaches are most frequently deployed in political theory and legal interpretation and in scholarship that examines the historical development and transformation of ideas, concepts, and institutions. They have also gained considerable currency in areas of comparative politics and international relations where scholars explore issues of nationhood and national attachments, the politics of recognition, and a host of problems involving cultural, ethnic, religious, and class differences and conflicts. Finally, they have acquired prominence among a wide range of scholars—including scholars who use multiple or mixed methods—who investigate the multiple dimensions of empowerment and disempowerment that reside in language, social practice, and the complex legacies of cultural and political traditions. These scholars have found hermeneutics to be a valuable resource for analyzing how language can conceal and distort relations of power yet also open new possibilities for enhanced understanding, resistance, social transformation, and political renewal.

Keith Topper
University of California, Irvine
Irvine, California, United States

See also Constructivism; Discourse Analysis; Methodology; Positivism; Thick Description

Further Readings

Bevir, M., & Rhodes, R. (2003). *Interpreting British governance*. New York: Routledge.

Gadamer, H.-G. (1989). *Truth and method*. London: Continuum.

Rabinow, P., & Sullivan, W. (Eds.). (1987). *Interpretive social science: A second look*. Berkeley: University of California Press.

Taylor, C. (1985). *Philosophical papers II: Philosophy and the human sciences*. Cambridge, UK: Cambridge University Press.

Topper, K. (2005). *The disorder of political inquiry*. Cambridge, MA: Harvard University Press.

Hierarchical/Multilevel Models

See Multilevel Analysis

Hinduism

Hinduism is more a civilization than a religion: not only because it is associated with a full-fledged social system, the caste system, but also because it is closely linked with an ancient culture spread over a clear-cut territory (today's India) and endowed with a language (Sanskrit). As a civilization, Hinduism does not display much cohesion and homogeneity. At first sight, it seems to possess the classic duality between what Robert Redfield calls a "great tradition" and a "little tradition," which one may call "popular Hinduism," composed of local practices. According to Shyama Charan Dube, however, this schema is complicated in the Hindu case by the lack of unity in the great tradition itself.

A Religion of "Unity in Diversity"

Most Hindus traditionally share a common belief in reincarnation, consider the seven sacred cities

(Ayodhya, Mathura, Haridwar, Benares, Kanchipuram, Ujjain, and Dwarka) as pilgrimage centers, worship god according to similar rituals in their respective temples (*pujas*), and celebrate the same festivals, including the *Kumbh Mela*, for which people gather together in millions every 9 or 12 years. Yet Hinduism does not have an orthodoxy enshrined in one book and guarded by an ecclesiastical body but encompasses several religious streams founded by gurus who pay obeisance to any one of the many gods of the Hindu pantheon (Shiva, Vishnu, or one of his avatars, or the *Shaktas*, who worship the Goddess under one form or another). Thus, the Hinduism of the great tradition appears as a "conglomeration of sects" (Romila Thapar, 1989, p. 207), known as *sampradaya* (from the Sanskrit *samprada*, to transmit); indeed, the essence of the sect lies in "the uninterrupted transmission from one master to another" (Catherine Clémentin-Ojha, 1990, p. 19) of the message of the founding guru, which itself derives from a revelation. (However, a Hindu sect may also take the form of a *panth* [way], where the founder is not considered as having been the recipient of a divine revelation.) Isolated from one another, these sects are also rivals to the extent that they compete for patronage and for the preeminence of their particular teachings.

The main, if not the only, current of Hinduism—which became formalized in a way that approximates to an "ecclesiastical structure" (Thapar, 1985, p. 17)—was that of Shankara. This ascetic reformer of the 8th century responded to the spread of Buddhism by establishing monasteries (*math*) in the four corners of India—Sringeri in the south, Dwarka in the west, Badri in the north, and Puri in the east—at the head of which were placed *shankaracharyas*, ordained to exercise a spiritual authority comparable with that of the Buddhist clergy.

The Making of Hinduism

In spite of the common features listed above, the remarkable diversity of Hinduism prevailed for centuries, to such an extent that until the 16th century there was no single religious tradition known as "Hinduism." The development of a collective Hindu consciousness was inhibited not only by the extreme social and religious differentiation within Hinduism but also by a tendency to discount the importance of the Other and therefore to ignore the need for solidarity in the face of that Other. In the process of sociocultural integration, a capacity for assimilation in the caste system is revealed: Insofar as the hierarchy represents a system of gradation based on the notion of ritual purity, everyone can find a place in it, below the *Brahmins*, according to the degree of conformity with the exalted values personified by *Brahmins*. As a result, invaders such as the Huns found themselves classed as *Kshatriyas* (warriors), observing the ritual practices prescribed for these castes and recognizing the authority of the *Brahmins*.

Paradoxically, the ability to integrate newcomers also reflected an inability to recognize the Other as such. Brahminical texts assume that the indigenous social order has a homologous relationship to the cosmic order, the *dharma*; and it is the preservation of this relationship in equilibrium that tends to demand the assimilation of foreign elements into the social system. The same texts describe this society as endowed with a language and territory with unique attributes and thus enable the rites necessary to perpetuate the *dharmic* order to be performed. Sanskrit is that language par excellence, and other languages are seen as, at best, degraded forms of it. Parallel to this, North India—*Aryavarta*—is considered to be the land where the rites necessary for the maintenance of *dharma* are fulfilled.

This belief in a privileged connection between India and *dharma* underlies the logic of the social system of the *varnas*, which consists of *Brahmins*, *Kshatriyas*, *Vaishyas* (merchants and artisans), and *Shudras* (the servile castes). In a foundational myth of the Vedas—the basis of the *Brahmanical* great tradition—these *varnas* are described as owing their origin to the sacrificial dismemberment of the cosmic Primeval Man, the *Virat Purushan*, when the *Brahmin* proceeded from this mouth, the *Kshatriya* from his arms, the *Vaishya* from his thighs, and the *Shudra* from his feet. This division of the social structure into four parts reflects the belief in a correspondence between Hindu society and the totality of the cosmic order, a correspondence that hampers the development of a distinct identity. Nothing outside it can have any meaning or be worthy of interest. In the absence of "them," there cannot be "we" and "us."

The term *Hindu* was originally derived from the name *Indus* and was used successively by the Achaemenids, the Greeks, and the Muslims to denote the population living beyond that river. However, it was not appropriated by the people who themselves bore this designation, nor did they use it themselves till the medieval period. This development has to be seen in conjunction with the penetration of the subcontinent by Muslim invaders, who were the first to put up a sustained resistance to the capacity of the indigenous culture for assimilation. For example, to be integrated into the *Kshatriya varna*, Muslim leaders would have been obliged to recognize the natural superiority of the *Brahmins*; in fact, they refused to give up the practices required by Islam and indeed were prepared in certain circumstances to clash with the Hindus, such as over cow slaughter. Such antagonism contributed to the emergence of a Hindu consciousness.

The Hindu consciousness apparently found its principal expression in the 17th and 18th centuries in the empire of Shivaji and then in the Maratha confederation. In 1720, *Brahmins* took over the latter kingdom, in which they had formerly served as chief ministers (*Peshvas*—a name they retained when they became the ruling dynasty) and military chiefs. These two political institutions were formed in Maharashtra in opposition to the Mughal Empire and in the name of *dharma*; the slaughter of cows, which the Muslims sometimes offered as a sacrifice, was thus forbidden there. However, according to Christopher Bayly, the conquests of the Marathas in the direction of the Gangetic plain were not examples of religious war based on ethnic or communal consciousness. They resulted from a motivation that was ritual in character—to restore to the Hindus certain holy places, such as Varanasi, which were revered throughout India.

From Hinduism to Neo-Hinduism

Things changed after the establishment of the British Raj in the mid-19th century. The proselytizing activities of the Christian missionaries and the (selective) reformist zeal of the administration fostered a reaction from the Hindu upper castes, mostly from the *Brahmins*, who were the custodians of the Hindu tradition.

The Brahmo Samaj was founded in 1828 not as a conservative movement but as the instrument of Hindu revivalism. Admitting that Hinduism had lost its pristine purity—as the European Orientalists were arguing since the 18th century—its leaders claimed that it could regain it through a reform process drawing its inspiration from a Golden Age that was associated with the Vedic period. This invention of tradition was the touchstone of a new Hindu nationalism that acquired its definitive shape in the late 19th century and early 20th century. In 1875, the Arya Samaj claimed that the Hindus descended from the first people of the earth—the Aryans—whose language, Sanskrit, was the mother of all languages. In 1915, this movement was the crucible of the first Hindu nationalist party, the Hindu Mahasabha. A few years later, Vinayak Damodar Savarkar gave an ideological charter to Hindu nationalism in a book called *Hindutva: Who Is a Hindu?* (1923).

The Muslim mobilization in defense of the *Khilafat* (caliphate) had a catalytic effect, and from then on, the Muslim minority was the real bête noire of the Hindu nationalists because of its Pan-Islamic solidarities and its reluctance to assimilate into the Hindu civilization. The Hindu identity had crystallized primarily in reaction to this so-called threatening Other. Its contours were further hardened by the census operations, which enumerated religious communities from 1871 onward, and by the politicization of religion under the impulse of populist politicians.

The erosion of the traditional inner diversity of Hinduism continued during the 20th century under the influence of these different forces. Among them, the most powerful was—and still is—the Rashtriya Swayamasevak Sangh (The National Volunteers Corps), which was founded in 1925 and has developed several fronts after independence, including a student union, a labor union, and a political party, the Jana Sangh, whose heir, the Bharatiya Janata Party (Indian People's Party), led the ruling coalition from 1998 to 2004. While Hindu nationalism has stagnated in the early 21st century, its social activities (including free medicine and education) and its proselytizing zeal (aiming to reconvert Christian communities especially) have increased.

Christophe Jaffrelot
CERI-Sciences Po/CNRS
Paris, France

See also Buddhism; Christianity; Islam; Religion

Further Readings

Clémentin-Ojha, C. (1990). *La divinité conquise: Carrière d'une sainte* [The divinity conquered: Career of a saint]. Nanterre, France: Société d'Ethnologie.

Dube, S. C. (1965). The study of complex cultures. In T. K. N. Unnithan, I. Deva, & Y. Singh (Eds.), *Towards a sociology of cultures in India* (pp. 404–426). New Delhi, India: Prentice Hall.

Jaffrelot, C. (1996). *The Hindu nationalist movement and Indian politics*. New York: Columbia University Press.

Purasher, A. (1982, July–1983, January). Attitudes towards the *mleccha* in early northern India—up to AD 600. *Indian Historical Review, 9*(1–2), 1–30.

Redfield, R. (1953, March). The natural history of folk society. *Social Forces, 31*(3), 224–228.

Thapar, R. (1978). *Ancient Indian history*. New Delhi, India: Orient Longman.

Thapar, R. (1985). Syndicated moksha? *Seminar, 313*, 14–22.

Thapar, R. (1989). Imagined religious communities? Ancient history and the modern search for a Hindu identity. *Modern Asian Studies, 23*(2), 215–225.

Historical Memory

The concept of "historical memory," often expressed as "collective memory," "social memory," or for political scientists, "the politics of memory," refers to the ways in which groups, collectivities, and nations construct and identify with particular narratives about historical periods or events. Historical memories are foundational to social and political identities and are also often reshaped in relation to the present historical-political moment. In this entry, the origins and uses of this concept in contemporary political science are discussed. This applies particularly to recent transitions from authoritarian rule and the formation of newly democratizing political cultures.

The study of memory has a long tradition in other social science disciplines. Yet until fairly recently, political scientists tended to dismiss historical memory as a conceptual or research arena. There seemed to be three general reasons for this: First, political scientists saw memory as too subjective, as properly the realm of psychology, difficult to measure, quantify, and operationalize in ways that could be compared and generalized. Second, political scientists tended to hold that "relevant" memory belongs to the discipline of history, of sorting facts, validity, and particularities, and that particularities were simply not what was driving the discipline of political science. It was for the historians to decide what constituted the dividing line between memory and history. Third, political scientists tended to view collective memories as codified in social and political institutions, and therefore it was more useful to study institutions than memories. Institutions enshrine memories.

Despite these biases against the study of memory as a lens on politics, political scientists have come to appreciate that historical memories powerfully influence politics in observable as well as subjective ways; that they are constructions of fact, myth, and interpretation; and that they fall outside the rubric of institutions as usefully understood. Historical memories are the less conventionally institutionalized dimensions of politics—symbols and sites for contestation, associations, palpably expressed through representations, testimonials, imagery, the media, public opinion, and political discourse.

In political contexts that involve transitions from conflict, war, and repression, all of which involve traumatic individual and collective experiences, collective memories prove difficult to ignore politically. Memories often become mobilized to challenge opponents, including the state. States themselves can be aggressive as purveyors of national memory, illustrated by the recent proliferation of officially sponsored truth commissions and "museums of memory" around the globe. Implicitly, the nation-state has always been preoccupied with developing a national memory that exudes unity, continuity, stability, and purpose. This is often expressed through commemoration, educational textbooks, and official political rhetoric. There is a significant and growing set of debates on statecraft, the nation and memory, or the memory-nation.

History of the Term

The French sociologist Maurice Halbwachs is widely regarded as the founding father of collective memory studies. His work *On Collective Memory*, originally published in 1925, broke new ground in the sociology of knowledge. Halbwachs emphasized social interaction as foundational to individual memory—as formed in relation to groups and collectivities—and remembering itself as a process subject to the needs of society as a whole. Both classic and more contemporary works in sociology and history argue persuasively that memory is reconstructed over generations to fit particular social and political contexts.

Following this vein in the 1980s, the French historian Pierre Nora made a major contribution to reawakening interest in Europe concerning the relationships between memory and history. Together with a team of well-known researchers, Nora produced a seven-volume study locating and classifying a host of French *lieux de mémoire*, or "sites of memory," that evoke or symbolize, in an emotive sense, the modern French nation. In the past, according to Nora, history and memory blended together fairly seamlessly. Historic *lieux de mémoire*, including monuments, the national flag, school history textbooks, commemorative dates, national museums, and others, served to project a shared sense of civic values and an allegiance to the French Republic. Nevertheless, Nora claimed that such cohesive projections had given way in postmodernity to particularistic, fragmented, subnational identity sites. Nora claims that a psychologization of memory, an individual psychology of remembering, has increasingly replaced the memory-nation and the social rituals and emotive symbols that accompany a shared, master past.

Memory scholars often charge that Nora's analysis leans toward sentimentalizing the notion of a national memory or lamenting the loss of shared national narratives, of some kind of master memory. Postcolonial, subaltern studies scholars note with irony such lament or nostalgia. Scholarly work on voices and memories of the subaltern, including memories of the French colonial past and French practices in Algeria, Haiti, and elsewhere, prove powerful correctives to any tendency to romanticize the French nation. In addition, studies of Vichy France, including most prominently that of the French historian Henry Rousso, emphasize the deliberate efforts of the post–World War II political elite to recraft a national memory of French collusion with the Nazi regime as a memory of resistance to Nazism. In his history of the evolution of memories regarding France and World War II, Rousso termed the French preoccupation with this period the *Vichy syndrome*, a constantly erupting societal neurosis about French failure to prevent or, for the most part, even to challenge the fascist takeover of government.

The British international relations theorist Jenny Edkins emphasizes the violent production and reproduction of the state through commemoration, particularly in the aftermath of wars, genocides, famines, and terrorism, when states attempt to erase memories of atrocities committed and compelled by the state as well as against other states. Yet Edkins also shows that citizens do not accept such erasures lightly. Edkins's work on World War I, the Vietnam War, the Holocaust, and September 11, 2001, demonstrates how in spite of states' intentions, families and groups in society frequently challenge states to mourn and to be held accountable for atrocities. Edkins terms societal challenges to state erasures an *encircling* of traumatic memory. Recent historical memory scholarship warns against neat divisions between state and society in battles over memory. Rather, scholars emphasize negotiation, tense collaborations, complementarities, as well as struggles within civil society over memory itself.

Historical Memory and Transitions From Authoritarian Rule

Historical memory began to make an impact in political science when it came to be recognized as an important dimension in regime transition during the latest "wave" of democratization since the 1970s. The first political science transitions theorist to study historical memory in an intensive way was the Spanish scholar Paloma Aguilar, who documented how political discourse was gradually reinvented to allow for a more consensualist elite interpretation of past conflicts across the political spectrum, thereby facilitating the mid-1970s Spanish transition from authoritarianism to democracy, involving a consensus between the moderates on both sides—the "old" elite and the opposition. More than a quarter century after the Spanish transition from Franco (1939–1975), however, long-repressed memories of the Spanish Civil War (1936–1939) have resurfaced and produced a range of collective action, debate, and legislation. This is illustrative of the nonlinear nature of historical memory, where generations-old events and phenomena can be recalled and deployed as if they occurred far more recently.

Scholarly debates on the politics of memory have emerged in several transitioning regions of the world, including Latin America, Eastern Europe, and the former Soviet republics. In the case of Chile, for example, the American political scientist Brian Loveman and the Chilean social psychologist Elizabeth Lira traced a powerful pattern of conflict and subsequent political elite amnesia, manifested chiefly as postconflict congressional declarations of amnesty, from the 19th century to the very recent past. Drawing a good deal from Holocaust studies, the Argentinian sociologist Elizabeth Jelin conceptualized and led a major collective memory social science research initiative. The project produced 12 volumes on what Jelin framed as "state repression and the labors of memory" in the aftermath of dictatorships in Argentina, Chile, Uruguay, and Brazil, as well as in Peru at the close of the Alberto Fujimori (1990–2000) regime. The purpose of the project was both to define a memory studies field in Latin America's Southern Cone, Brazil, and Peru and, implicitly, to contribute to rebuilding the social sciences in the wake of their devastation by dictatorship. Like most scholarship on historical memory, the agenda was thus ethical and practical as well as intellectual and interdisciplinary.

Historical memory studies emphasize the fitful process of what is (or as Nietzsche once said, what must be) forgotten to forge a viable politics of the present. Framed in an instrumentalist way, historical memory is at the service of political actors and institutional processes. Embedded in many of the historical memory studies, however, is a serious critique of officialist approaches and policies of "forget" to move on. Common to historical memory works are at least three arguments: first, that different generations are entirely capable of interpreting the same political events differently; second, that political ideology or partisanship continues to weigh heavily on interpretations of past political events; and third, that in the aftermath of traumatic conflict, a significant number of both citizens and political elites profoundly desire consensual collective memory images, crafted by the political class, that convey national unity and peace. Such consensual images can have the ability to overcome ideologically driven memory divides, at least for a while. The studies remind us that though national political trauma may have occurred decades ago, memories of such trauma continue to influence politics at several levels.

At the same time, memories can be powerfully enduring in spite of social change or dominant political discursive attenuation. Official memories can be perceived as being imposed far more than embraced. And on the ground, in countries such as Chile, state actors and institutions are in constant reactive mode to grassroots memory mobilizing. Social historians document how individual and collective memories part dramatically and are not obviously reconcilable and that distinct communities temporalize traumatic memories quite distinctly.

While calls to remember atrocious pasts have been consistently embraced by grassroots sectors, there is also considerable a desire to forget. This desire is not limited to the political elite, for whom resurrecting painful pasts can prove contentious and costly. The wish to forget can also be heard from communities affected most directly by armed conflict, including formerly displaced families that have lost loved ones and are uncertain whether they can return either physically to their former communities or mentally and spiritually to their memories of violence and loss.

In their studies of communities in Ayacucho, Peru, the region in which confrontations between the Peruvian military and the Shining Path most frequently occurred (1980–2000), the scholars Ponciano del Pino and Kimberly Theidon reveal a pattern of narration in indigenous accountings of the recent past that they have termed *toxic memory*. Toxic memory emerges from experiences of intense, direct violence within a community for which there is no recourse, no sense of the possibility of social justice, or remorse from the perpetrators. Public memory debates in such settings are explicitly constrained by the knowledge of what violence particular agents are capable of exacting and by power dynamics that make no guarantees that such violence will be prevented in the future.

Today, the term *politics of memory* is most often associated with studies that assess human rights politics and policies—prosecutions, truth telling, commemoration, reparations—as well as with what is commonly referred to as the "transitional justice" literature. Transitional justice studies analyze how particular political institutions, policies, and actors hold human rights violators of previous regimes accountable for their crimes. Such studies focus on the judiciary, the military, and civil society organizations, as well as the executive and legislature. Government-sponsored truth-telling processes, for example, are largely symbolic exercises to produce official and societal acknowledgment of past atrocities and to drive home the message of never again. Such processes are fraught with debate over political intent: What truths should be privileged and what downplayed? Where should remembering begin? Should testimonies be private or public? Can witnesses be subpoenaed? How will the findings be deployed? Truth-telling designs have significant political implications, some anticipated, but some, such as the irruptions of memories themselves, unanticipated.

The anthropologist Richard Wilson argues that government-sponsored truth commissions attempt to craft narratives of the past that render the present more governable and that "manufacture bureaucratic legitimacy" for the state. At first glance, such would appear to be the case for the truth commissions of Chile (1991) and Peru (2003), both of which include the term *reconciliation* in their official titles, suggesting an intention to build consensus and foster national unity. The United Nations–sponsored Guatemalan truth commission, in contrast, defines itself as a body for "historical clarification," explicit in its intent to examine long histories of violence and injustice that make even the concept of reconciliation more distant. The proliferation of truth commissions, memory debates, and the like can be interpreted as a sign of leaders striving for a new kind of credibility. In contrast to an earlier period in which political leaders attempted to move on, to "turn the page" on painful memories, politicians are increasingly resorting to political manipulations of memory, championing explorations of the past, and instrumentalizing memory to serve their agendas or to enhance their status.

The transitional justice literature brings international institutions and actors deliberately to the fore, marrying international influences with local power dynamics. Yet a politics of memory literature is a more apt conceptual frame than transitional justice for such policies, given that much of the movement to hold human rights violators accountable, and to bring an important measure of justice, is taking place in posttransitional rather than transitional contexts. In addition, a politics of memory frame allows us both to reach back in historical terms and at the same time, therefore, to reach beyond the focus on human rights violations of repressive regimes, to violence and/or dramatic phenomena that mark distinct temporalities for distinct collectivities. It is clear in the Chilean case, for example, that the indigenous Mapuche communities possess deep historical understandings of what constitutes trauma, as well as what constitutes continuity in Chile. In contrast, the Chilean right consistently evokes memories of the 1960s land reform and takeovers during a democratic regime as a haunting traumatic memory. Politics of memory studies heighten our analytical sensitivity to distinct temporalities as well as more broadly to the role of timing in political processes.

Katherine Hite
Vassar College
Poughkeepsie, New York, United States

See also Accountability; Conflict Resolution; Democratization; Genocide; Human Rights, Comparative Perspectives; Political Culture; Transition

Further Readings

Aguilar, P. (2002). *Memory and amnesia: The role of the Spanish civil war in the transition to democracy.* New York: Berghann Books.

Edkins, J. (2003). *Trauma and the memory of politics.* Cambridge, UK: Cambridge University Press.

Halbwachs, M. (1980). *The collective memory.* New York: Harper & Row.

Jelin, E. (2003). *State repression and the labors of memory.* Minneapolis: University of Minnesota Press.

Mallon, F. E. (2005). *Courage tastes of blood: The Mapuche community of Nicolás Ailio and the Chilean state, 1906–2001.* Durham, NC: Duke University Press.

Nora, P. (Ed.). (1984). *Les lieux de mémoire* [The places of memory]. Paris: Gallimard.

Olick, J., & Robbins, J. (1998). Social memory studies from "collective memory" to the historical sociology of mnemonic practices. *Annual Review of Sociology, 24,* 105–140.

Rousso, H. (1991). *The Vichy syndrome: History and memory in France since 1944* (A. Goldhammer, Trans.). Cambridge, MA: Harvard University Press.

Wilson, R. (2001). *The politics of truth and reconciliation in South Africa: Legitimizing the post-apartheid State.* Cambridge, UK: Cambridge University Press.

Young, J. (Ed.). (1993). *The texture of memory: Holocaust memorials and meaning.* New Haven, CT: Yale University Press.

Historical Sociology

History and sociology have been, since the 19th century, two completely separate fields based on different views of society. History was supposed to deal only with the main political or military events, with important people shaping the world, its battles, its diplomatic quarrels, while sociology was supposed to be concerned with the evolution of the society as a collective body changing through various stages. Sociology was frequently ahistorical, neglecting individuals and their values, outlining, on the contrary, the structures and the functions of crucial institutions, their role within the process of modernization leading all societies toward some kind of progress. History and sociology were competing, excluding each other from the realm of social science. History was the noble science, often building a kind of philosophical approach accepted by everyone on the meaning and the destiny of random events. Increasingly, though, these two fields have intersected, resulting in the discipline of historical sociology, which studies sociology within a historical framework. This entry describes the historical foundations and the contemporary historical sociology, including its subfields, is discussed.

Historical Foundations

From Auguste Comte to Émile Durkheim, sociology was mainly based on positivism and an objective knowledge of society excluding ideologies, values, and even cultures from the variables explaining social phenomena. Even though Durkheim, the father of contemporary sociology, once said that sociologists need historians trained as sociologists, he nevertheless saw history as a chronology of dates and singular events unrelated to any more general social laws. For example, in a comparative study of suicide, Durkheim acknowledged the role played by religion; however, his explanation of the rate of suicide did not consider the role of history or of political crises.

The Marxist tradition was also built outside any real historical explanation. Historical materialism, a theory explaining changes based on contradictions occurring between class interests structured by capitalism, did not in fact focus on the impact of specific historical events but instead simply described these contradictions as created by the nature of ownership. History was therefore seen as an objective result of social contradictions. Karl Marx, like Durkheim, was also a positivist and advocated a form of functionalism. He did not deal with religion, regarding it as a means of alienating the working class; he did not compare religions and their influence on the emergence of a specific kind of capitalism or political system. His work, like Durkheim's analysis, did not contain any serious comparative research that would have shown how, in the long run, cultures, religions, and values shape almost all social phenomena, such as the state and the public realm, the occurrence of conflicts or revolutions, the process of secularization, the nature of education, and even different kinds of capitalism. Although Marx was aware of this need for a historical and comparative dimension, and although he looked seriously at the values of various individuals in *The Eighteenth Brumaire of Louis Napoleon* (1852) and short articles written for various newspapers, he ignored history and culture in his main works, such as *Das Kapital* (1867). Thus, the Marxist movement's neglect of crucial variables such as states and religions resulted in a reluctance to look seriously at other elements of culture, such as loyalty to a nation, which is shared by most citizens; deeply rooted traditions and the molding of cultures; and the values and behavior of all individuals, regardless of their position in the economic structure. This weakness had important consequences for contemporary sociology, which was largely shaped by Marxism or by a Durkheimian positivist view looking at correlations between purely morphological variables.

Therefore, to find traces of historical sociology in previous centuries, one must look at Alexis de

Tocqueville's work. During the first part of the 19th century, far from his own society, Tocqueville discovered the culture, history, and religion of the United States. He also traveled to Algeria and Ireland. He was keen to learn as much as he could about India's caste system and values. At the core of his work is a historical comparative sociology dealing with different kinds of states, religions, and cultures and numerous interpretations of individualism and even of liberty and equality within societies based on almost the same kind of capitalism. In his main book *Democracy in America* (1835), Tocqueville implicitly compared France with the United States and showed that everything was quite different within the same socioeconomic system; comparative histories (presence or complete absence of feudalism and therefore of nobility) and cultures (Catholicism vs. Protestantism) therefore matter deeply. Tocqueville also raised the kind of issues that are much discussed today: Is it possible to import some institutions, such as democracy, into another culture molded by a different religion? At what cost? With what kind of collective movement leading, in reaction, toward nationalist anger? He foresaw this crucial contemporary discussion related to the importation and exportation, through soft or military means, of various regimes and institutions in societies shaped by contradictory histories and values. Tocqueville was mainly a politician; unfortunately, he never built a systematic model laying the foundation of historical sociology. He remained alone in his comparative historical attempt, and not until almost the end of the 19th century did the real birth of modern historical sociology appear through Max Weber's work.

In Weber's main books, such as *Economy and Society* (1920) or *The Protestant Ethic and the Spirit of Capitalism* (1905), and in his numerous studies of ancient Judaism, China, Japan, or even the Muslim world (looking seriously at Judaism, Hinduism, Buddhism, and Islam), he was clearly comparing sociologically different societies shaped by various histories, religions, and cultures. Deeply concerned by the values of each actor, by their degree of rationality or irrationality, and looking at the interactions among all of them, the way they met and organized their world together, Weber can be seen as the founder of historical sociology. Among sociologists, he was the first to deal extensively with questions of power, state, and authority in different historical frameworks, from sultanism to feudalism, patrimonialism, and modern rational bureaucracy in the context of capitalism. Far from any positivist methodology and avoiding an evolutionist interpretation common among most authors studying the process of modernization, Weber permanently underlined the intentions of every individual and tried to understand his or her decision and his or her reasons for acting in a particular way. Weber's interpretative approach to historical sociology finally provided a valuable comparative methodology. For example, Weber was the first to call attention to charismatic authority—the fact that some individuals possess personal and almost magical qualities that allow them to lead people, crowds, political parties, or even a nation. Neither Marxist economic analysis nor Durkheim's positivist methodology was able to interpret this personal quality (charisma) of some leaders in ancient as well as modern societies and in authoritarian states as well as in democratic ones. Even though he argued that a process of rationalization or bureaucratization was increasingly shaping all modern societies, he kept a non-evolutionist view by outlining the unpredicted individual power of some individuals within different cultures.

Contemporary Historical Sociology

Weber's interpretative sociology has many heirs and, today, one can argue that he remains at the core of contemporary historical sociology, which became, in the 1960s, a legitimate subfield. His influence on most issues is obvious. Four different fields within this subdiscipline are considered below.

State

Alone among the founding fathers of sociology, Weber gave us a convincing theory of the state as an institutionalized and differentiated institution serving the general interest, recruiting its own ruling elite through meritocratic competition, and concentrating in itself all means of violence previously controlled by specific social groups or by forces located at the periphery. Today, to bring back the state as a crucial variable, one can look either at Tocqueville or, even better, at Weber's analysis. The contemporary rediscovery of the state began, in fact, mainly thanks to a kind of revision of an evolutionist Marxism.

Immanuel Wallerstein and Perry Anderson then, while remaining Marxists, nevertheless were the first to introduce a strong comparative perspective into their work during the 1970s. Wallerstein, an American sociologist, in the three-volume *The Modern World System* (1974, 1980, 1989), described, on the one hand, the birth of the state located in the core of Europe, on its Atlantic facade, where the bourgeoisie needed a state to protect its economic interests and its wide-ranging foreign economic relations, and, on the other hand, Eastern Europe, unaware of either capitalism or the birth of the state. In his *Lineages of the Absolutist State* (1974), Perry Anderson, the director of *The New Left Review*, contrasted Western and Eastern Europe. He showed that the state was born before capitalism, in those Western regions where an intense feudalism, in the context of Roman law, led to an extreme pluralism favorable to the earlier differentiation of a state that made it easier to protect the dominant economic interests. In the East, on the other hand, a mighty nobility kept its power, using it against the peasantry's revolts. These analyses, while keeping to an instrumentalist view of the state, clearly belong to comparative historical sociology; nevertheless, they remained quite schematic in their use of history, and they completely ignored the cultural element.

Stein Rokkan, a Norwegian sociologist, drew many conceptual maps of Europe based on two different axes: the first one, East/West, dealing both with the economy and, in a new approach, with territorial aspects and the second, North/South, based on a broad opposition between Protestantism, Catholicism, and regions of Counter-Reformation. It was immediately clear that the neo-Marxist conception of the state had been supplemented by a more rigorous, comparative, Weberian interpretation. Rokkan's innovative work brought us to the core of historical sociology because he was able to compare different paths of state building in the context of meaningful territorial variations, thus raising a definitive argument against any kind of evolutionism. Rokkan was clearly following Weber's comparative lesson when he described the absence of state building in the core of Europe, from Hamburg to Barcelona through Geneva, Bern, and Milan, where the market was predominant and each strong city was unable to conquer its surrounding territory. This comparative approach was also evident when he showed how Protestantism, in the North, allowed the early building of the nation through a common consensus while Catholicism led to an internal split of the nation in the South. However, Rokkan remained focused only on a sociological approach; his interest in history was still too limited.

Rokkan did not base his work on a deep knowledge of English, French, German, or Russian history. If he had, he likely would have shown, for instance, the incredible strength of the French state as a reaction against the formidable power of the Catholic Church; he would have acknowledged the weakness of the state in the strong and consensual English society; and he would have described more precisely, following Weber, different types of states. This task had been initiated by Charles Tilly in his comparative work on the European state-building process. Tilly, both a historian and a sociologist, showed the crucial influence of wars on the growth of the state's bureaucracy. This perspective has also been taken by Samuel Finer, Shmuel Eisenstadt, Joseph R. Strayer, Theda Skocpol, and other specialists on the state. Thus, according to Bertrand Badie and Pierre Birnbaum, one can use the broad opposition between strong and weak states as useful ideal types based on a comparative history of state-building processes explaining not only different kinds of strikes, collective actions, and new social movements but also various importation and exportation of types of states in another cultural context. At last, sociologists are themselves becoming historians, working like them on archives and primary resources while raising specific sociological questions.

Citizenship

The Weberian sociohistorical approach has also been applied to the question of citizenship. In a lecture in London given just after World War II, Thomas Humphrey Marshall, an English economist, presented a famous evolutionist interpretation of citizenship based on three dimensions of citizenship (civil, political, and social) corresponding more or less to three different centuries (the 18th, 19th, and 20th) and illustrating mainly the

British case. However, this model was criticized for not applying, for instance, to the German or French cases and for being even less applicable to Eastern European societies. In some societies, such as Germany, citizenship emerged first in the social dimension, while the civil and political dimensions emerged only recently, with the creation of the Federal Republic after World War II.

Other contemporary societies still ignore most dimensions of citizenship. Marshall's notion of citizenship also implied a strong consensual and democratic nation with a near absence of strong political and religious cleavages, a weak state, and an efficient representative political system bringing a deep feeling of loyalty, with citizens sharing a common interest.

In France, on the contrary, serious internal cleavages led to deep ideological conflicts: among them, the permanent antagonism between the state and the Catholic Church, which led to a divided loyalty. Citizens were supposed to be loyal to the state, while confining their religious identity to the private sphere. Until the middle of the 20th century, some Catholics did not really feel at home in the strong republican universalist state. Moreover, a strong radical right arose, wishing to destroy the strong state that it viewed as an artificial source of French identity, while the real French identity was Catholic. The Jacobin culture battled against religious beliefs that challenged the nation's common culture and that prompted the birth of a unique public space open to meritocratic procedure. In a context such as this, any private identity of the citizen is supposed to be hidden from the public realm. In such a historical context, one cannot hold two identities, such as French and Catholic, so far as public allegiance is concerned. Any multiculturalist identity is largely ignored and fought within such a strong republican state. For instance, in Turkey and in France, this militant notion of citizenship may explain the willingness to ban the veil from the public sphere. Thus, a comparative approach to the concept of national identity based on different historical paths to emancipation can explain why citizens are expected to show their religious, cultural, and/or gender identities in one case, whereas in another, they are barred from doing so. The French principle of *laïticé* is thus shaped by a long history through which politics was built by separating it from private life: In the public sphere, the French citizen is not permitted to show up his or her religious, cultural, or familial allegiances; his or her commitment to French citizenship is prior to any other sources of identity and may even exclude them from public life. This is the main basis of the culture of the Jacobin state. The multiculturalist approach of North American authors such as Charles Taylor, Michael Walzer, Michael Sandel, and Will Kymlicka cannot be easily imported into France, Turkey, or Tunisia or into societies molded by a thick conception of culture such as Japan, a country eager to keep a homogeneous culture and reluctant to open itself to diversity. In the same perspective, one can also make a comparative study of Jewish emancipation. For example, Jews in France are openly asked to assimilate completely when entering the public sphere, thereby quickly submitting their collective identity to their citizenship; whereas in the United Kingdom, the United States, or in various empires such as the Austro-Hungarian Empire where collective identity is seen as legitimate, they are able to keep it.

Elite

The comparative study of the recruitment of elites to positions of power is also more and more bound to a historical sociology approach. To understand why the circulation of elites is shaped by a specific network, one must take a comparative approach in studying both the state and the ruling class. The stronger the institutionalization of the state, the stronger its differentiation; the weaker the penetration of business or private interests within the state structure and the state elites, the weaker the penetration of the political parties, of the churches, of any recruitment of the elites based on some kind of affirmative action. In such a secularized public realm, civil servants, like a strong civil army, are protected by their role and status within the state from any political, religious, or economic pressures coming from outside. The reverse is also true: The weaker the state, the stronger are those kinds of penetration within the elite. Thus, the horizontal circulation of elites is shaped by the actual presence of different kinds of states resulting from a long history.

To summarize this point, the stronger the state, the weaker and less homogeneous is the upper (ruling) class. In addition, the stronger the state, the more open the vertical circulation. For example, where there is a state-owned educational system that is not subject to clientelist or other social intervention, there is greater meritocractic recruitment across all social strata. One can thus not only outline the remarkable differences in the elite recruitment circulation within almost the same capitalist societies but also study the recruitment, for instance, of political elites in African societies where even now, the state is often shaped by different long-term histories framed by thick cultures that have not experienced the process of differentiation.

Nationalism

Nationalism has also been studied through a new kind of historical sociology approach. According to some main theorists, nationalism is a normal and functional phenomenon within strong industrialized societies in which collective identity has been threatened by individualism and a process of atomization. Nationalism—as defined by the British sociologist Ernest Gellner and as viewed by most authors whose ideas have been framed by a developmentalist interpretation—is supposed to be a normal process of socialization controlled by the state in order to bring citizens together in a sort of nationalization of the mind owing to mass communication and the educational system. Gellner's interpretations (and also the important contributions of Karl Deutsch and Elie Kedourie on nation building) are largely evolutionist, ignoring nationalism as a historical phenomenon implying the use of violence, the impact of ideologies, the cultural reaction against Enlightenment, or a contemporary colonial domination. Following the work of the English philosopher Isaiah Berlin, nationalism can, in fact, be described as a "bent twig" reaction based on a neglected cultural identity. Thus, to understand its appearance, one again needs a historical comparative approach explaining why German or Russian nationalism in the 19th century was mainly a cultural reaction against the French state imposing its domination in the name of Reason; why during the 20th century, the struggle for decolonization was also a kind of collective nationalist protest; and why, for instance, Algerian nationalism took such a bloody form in reaction to the violent form of colonization imposed by the strong French state while countries colonized by England or the Netherlands were more frequently able to liberate themselves without a violent reaction to violent repression. This approach can tell us the following: (a) why this type of nationalism may suddenly appear from within a society, as a collective reaction of a repressed culture usually organized by the radical right—a populist uprising against the establishment as a political target, seen as an almost foreign power cut off from native culture; (b) why one cannot find an obvious nationalism in pluralist societies, such as the United States, wherein populist collective actions are quickly exhausted; (c) why civic and ethnic forms of nationalism grow in different historical contexts; (d) why not only "imagined communities" but also realms of memory and rediscovery of the past feed nationalist movements and to what extent nationalism and patriotism are distinct phenomena; (e) why transnationalism can penetrate a society with a weak state that is more open to globalization than a strong nation-state; and (f) why loyalty to a diaspora remains more alive when immigrants are spread within weak state societies in which immigrants are able to keep their identity and are not required to assimilate into a homogeneous whole.

Nevertheless, historical sociology must avoid the pitfalls of relativism and culturalism. By outlining the impact of different cultures or types of states as a crucial factor, this comparative perspective must be careful not to invent a new kind of determinism conditioning each specific history. It must only try to discover regularities, collective behaviors, and processes initiated by various participants but occurring similarly even within different historical contexts.

Tocqueville and Weber used essentially historical secondary works to ask those comparative sociological questions. Today, as "sociology meets history," to use Tilly's famous phrase, social scientists must become increasingly aware of the necessity to build their work within a long-term historical framework. They themselves must look at various kinds of historical data, through which they can ask sociological questions. If, in turn, historians are to be trained as sociologists, in the spirit of the French Annales School, the two fields will meet more and more frequently, with historians recently starting to study the transformation of contemporary societies.

Pierre Birnbaum
Université Paris 1
Paris, France

See also Citizenship; Durkheim, Émile; Elites; Nationalism; State; Weber, Max

Further Readings

Anderson, P. (1974). *Lineages of the absolutist state.* London: New Left Books.

Badie, B., & Birnbaum, P. (1992). *Sociology of the state.* Chicago: University of Chicago Press.

Delanty, G., & Engin, I. (Eds.). (2003). *Handbook of historical sociology.* London: Sage.

Déloye, Y. (2007). *Sociologie historique du politique* [Historical sociology of politics]. Paris: La Découverte.

Gellner, E. (1983). *Nations and nationalism.* London: Blackwell.

Mahoney, J., & Rueschmeyer, D. (Eds.). (2003). *Comparative historical analysis in the social sciences.* Cambridge, UK: Cambridge University Press.

Rokkan, S. (1999). *State formation, nation-building and mass politics: The theory of Stein Rokkan.* Oxford, UK: Oxford University Press.

Skocpol, T. (Ed.). (1984). *Vision and method in historical sociology.* Cambridge, UK: Cambridge University Press.

Smith, D. (1991). *The rise of historical sociology.* Philadelphia: Temple University Press.

Tilly, C. (1981). *As sociology meets history.* New York: Academic Press.

Wallerstein, I. (1974). *The modern world system.* New York: Academic Press.

History of Political Science

The idea of politics as a subject of science is as old as Aristotle, but, as Bernard Crick stressed, political science as a distinct academic discipline and branch of social science originated as a uniquely American invention. Although there were, in many respects, functionally equivalent studies of politics in other countries, the history of political science, from the mid-19th century to the mid-20th century, was primarily a story of the "American science of politics." Notwithstanding its universal scientific aspirations, its emigration, and export to other countries, especially subsequent to World War II, and the waves of foreign influence that have at times significantly contributed to shaping the field, political science has borne a unique relationship to American political life and to American democratic ideology. Although the history of the discipline could be written from many perspectives, an important dimension of that history is the democratic narrative. The field has always been committed to creating a truly scientific study of politics, but, despite changing images of science, there has been a consistent search for a discipline that would contribute to realizing and enhancing democratic values and institutions. In this respect, as well as with regard to matters of methodology, the genetic imprint of the American form has remained manifest in the extended speciation that now characterizes so many other countries within which the field has taken root and evolved.

There has, however, been a constant ambivalence about the discipline's practical relationship to politics, and it has often been suggested that the simultaneous commitments to science and democracy have not always been in harmony. Although this tension has in part involved the problem of reconciling scientific and political criteria of judgment, it has also been the consequence of a longstanding assumption that only by remaining aloof from politics and establishing its claim to scientific objectivity could the discipline gain the cognitive authority that would facilitate practical purchase. Such distance was viewed as necessary in part because many, particularly in the late 19th century, who attempted to speak politically from the podium discovered that politics was often a dangerous object of inquiry, particularly when inquiry involved advocacy. Consequently, it is not surprising that some have suggested that the discipline has at times become alienated from the realities of political life, but self-consciousness about its relationship to politics has significantly informed political science's successive crises of intellectual identity. Despite sometimes contradictory claims about the extent to which claims about politics and government produced by political science have influenced political ideas and behavior, the images produced by the discipline have, in various ways, such as through diverse levels of pedagogy and through their influence on a variety of media, been reflected in the practices of citizens and political actors.

There was, from the point of the formation of the American Republic, a theoretical paradox that has been the central axis in discussions of popular government. This paradox, which was bequeathed to the field of political science, emerged with respect to validating American democracy—and validating America as a democracy. While it was assumed that a republican or democratic regime was predicated on the existence of an intelligible and autonomous people, it was, at the same time, difficult, after the American Revolution, to identify any such entity. This search for a "people," and for democracy, was, and has been, through the end of the 20th century, confronted, and conducted, in two distinct ways. One approach has been to argue that, despite great social diversity, there is an American people that has been the author and subject of democratic government. The other approach has been to argue that the existence of such a national community is not necessary to achieve the ends of popular sovereignty. One persistent aspect of the democratic vision in America, represented in both of these approaches, has, however, been its accommodational character. The tendency has been to adapt the concept of democracy to changes in the perceived realities of American politics.

This paradox of democracy was first exemplified in the *Federalist Papers*, which were devoted to a defense of the proposed 1787 Constitution. While the authors maintained that the Constitution, manifesting the accrued wisdom of Western political thought regarding a science of politics, created a popular government that was republican, or representative, rather than purely democratic, they had difficulty clarifying and defending their continued allegiance to the basic idea of popular sovereignty. The concept of a people that had been at the core of revolutionary ideology, as well as essential to the arguments of certain of the anti-Federalist criticisms of the new document, seemed to have an anomalous ring when juxtaposed to the images of American politics advanced by James Madison and Alexander Hamilton. The Federalists and anti-Federalists shared the worry that there was not an identifiable American people, which transcended the smaller communities of the various states. From one perspective, the genius of the authors of the *Federalist* was to invent the very idea of a unified people that encompassed more local constituencies and that was to be represented in and by the new national government. To the extent, however, that the oft-mentioned "people" had a concrete meaning for Madison, as voiced in *Federalist No. 10*, it seemed, in the end, to refer either to the sum of self-interested individuals or to diverse and divisive factions that were characterized by their attachment to their own rather than a public good. In place of the traditional republican notion of an organic people, Madison conceived of a virtual people that would arise out of an institutional and social balance of conflicting interests. He argued that the disease of republican, and now American, government was factionalism but that it could be transformed into its own cure through an intricate constitutional design combined with fortuitous demographic and geographical circumstances. Political discourse and commentary, however, kept alive the civic republican image of a people capable of, and the subject of, popular government, which lay beneath the surface of American diversity. The origins of political science were closely involved with vouchsafing that image.

The Science of the Democratic State

During the 19th century, academic publicists produced their own version of the people, which was represented in the concept of the "state." While today many tend to look back on this concept as an archaic formalistic and legalistic artifact or as an intellectual reflection of American state building, it was in fact the nucleus of a theory of American democracy. Apart from a reference to the American states, the word *state* had, by the beginning of the 19th century, little currency in the language of American politics. The introduction of the concept of the state was largely through the work of the German émigré Francis Lieber, beginning about the time that his acquaintance, Alex de Tocqueville, visited America. Tocqueville had noted that the new world of American democracy demanded a "new science of politics," and Lieber can reasonably be designated the founder of American political science. There was already a nascent program of civic education within the traditional American college and university curriculum of moral philosophy, which was devoted to practical ethics and to educating the American elite in the principles and duties of public life. Lieber focused on expanding this field of study by integrating German, largely Kantian and Hegelian, philosophy and images of world history (*Manual of Political Ethics*, 1839). He applied that philosophy to the circumstances and traditions of the United States and to devising a solution to the perennial democratic paradox. His adaptation of the German philosophy of the state (*Civil Liberty and Self-Government*, 1853) paralleled the work of individuals such as the German theorist Johann K. Bluntschli (*The Theory of the State*, 1895), and, for nearly a century, it provided the intellectual, institutional, and professional foundation of academic political inquiry in the United States.

After a period in South Carolina, Lieber, who was a strong supporter of the Union cause, was appointed, in 1857, as the first professor of political science at Columbia College in New York. His work was perpetuated and refined by second-generation theorists such as Theodore Woolsey at Yale, Herbert B. Adams at Johns Hopkins, and, above all, John W. Burgess, who was Lieber's successor at Columbia. What Lieber, and the later American state theorists, who were educated abroad and imbibed the German paradigm of *Staatswissenschaft* (in German, "political science"), created was the image of a democratic people as well as a history of democratic institutions that sprung from ancient Teutonic origins, passed through English government, and culminated in the American polity. Although Americans had at first been wary of the word *democracy*, it had, by the middle of the 19th century, been largely divested of its radical overtones and become a general term of approbation in the United States as well as in many places abroad. Unlike some of his European counterparts and correspondents, such as Edouard Laboulaye in France, as well as the American historian George Bancroft, who all commented extensively on American political society and contributed significantly to the 19th-century democratic narrative, Lieber, still feared "democratic absolutism" and, like Tocqueville, majoritarian rule. He inveighed against ideas such as women's suffrage and tended to eschew the word *democracy* in favor of phrases such as *self-government* and *hamarchy* by which he basically meant representative institutions. His vision of the state, however, was essentially that of an associationally and institutionally diverse but organic people and its pedigree that gave theoretical substance to the idea of democracy.

Although the "state talk" of 19th-century political inquiry, as well as that of public intellectuals such as Orestes Brownson and Elisha Mulford, paralleled the discourse of democracy in political life, it remained, like many later constructions of political science, far removed from the language of politics in the United States. The most essential feature of the concept of the state during this long and formative period in the evolution of American political science was that it did *not* refer either to forms of government or to the institutions of government but rather to a community whose voice expressed a will and interest that was expressed through the agency of government but preceded, in both time and authority, both the constitution and the government. This vision often reflected and abetted the conservative ideology of theorists such as Burgess, who wished to propagate and justify limited government as well as to curtail democratic populism while maintaining the ethic of popular sovereignty, and it was in some ways both inspired by, and functioned to legitimate, the cause of the Union before and after the Civil War. But it was also embraced by social scientists on the political left, such as the economist Richard Ely, who perceived the state as authorizing government intervention in social life. The theory of the state provided a scientific identity for the discipline and sublimity for its subject matter, but, above all, it offered a distinct answer to the congenital paradox of American democratic theory, and it was an answer that extended well into the Progressive Era after the turn of the century. The 19th-century American state theorists, despite their attachment to a certain conception of individual natural rights, all rejected contract theory and its implications. They claimed that there was, from the outset, a primordial people who both authorized and placed limitations on government. Burgess (*Political Science and Comparative Constitutional Law*, 1891) validated this picture with a singular and ingenious account of American history. He argued that modern states, and particularly the United

States, were the prime examples of those founded on a national unity and that they represented a self-conscious democracy that was the apex of political history. Nations, as ethical and geographical units, he claimed, tended, at least in the West, to become states—that is, a people with a government—and the highest examples of the latter were those that had achieved the popular or democratic form.

Burgess's interdisciplinary School of Political Science at Columbia (1880) represented an attempt to replicate the form of scientific education that characterized German universities, and his aim was both to educate an American administrative and political elite and to influence government policy. The imprint of this curriculum is still evident in contemporary political science programs, and Columbia produced the first professional journal of political science, *Political Science Quarterly* (1886), which was devoted to the assumption that the "domain of political science" was the study of the state and that among the social sciences concerned with this subject, political science occupied the "dominant position." Similar institutional developments took place under Adams at Hopkins, which published *Studies in History and Political Science* and which was the site of the first professional Political Science Association, and in Europe, there was the beginning of institutions such as École Libre des Sciences Politiques in France and the London School of Economics in England. By this point, political scientists were still not always clearly distinguished, either intellectually or professionally, from historians and economists, but it was primarily the theory of the state that bound them together. The third generation of political scientists, which included Bernard Moses at Berkeley, Woodrow Wilson at Hopkins and Princeton, and Westel W. Willoughby at Hopkins, did much to institutionalize further the field of political science in American universities during the last years of the 19th century and early years of the 20th century, but by the last decade of the 19th century, a significant theoretical transformation had begun to take place. Theorists such as Wilson (*The State*, 1889), who established the department of politics at Princeton, continued in many ways to affirm some aspects of the traditional theory of the state, but, in part as a consequence of urging a more active administration, they began to blur the line between state and government. The problem, in a country of great and increasing complexity and multiplicity, was to specify the locus of the invisible community that putatively constituted the American people, and eventually, no one did more than Willoughby (*An Examination of the Nature of the State*, 1896) to empty the word *state* of its original theoretical meaning and transform it into an analytical or juristic category and synonym for government. This, however, precipitated a crisis in democratic theory.

Although it has often been assumed that there was a fundamental break between the state theory of the 19th century and the conceptions of both political inquiry and politics embraced by early-20th-century political scientists, the continuities in many respects exceeded the innovations. One might very well ask how the largely conservative academic culture that dominated 19th-century universities, such as Columbia, produced progressive, reform-minded scholars, such as the historian and political scientist Charles Beard and, particularly, Charles Merriam, who might well be considered the father of 20th-century political science and who contributed so significantly to transforming the discipline. In addition to retaining commitments both to the idea of scientific inquiry and to its application to practical ends, one thread of continuity was a persistent belief in, and dedication to, the national state as encompassing both government and community. During the early part of the 20th century, Progressive politics as well as political and social thought continued to be predicated on the belief, such as in the case of sociologist Charles Horton Cooley (*Social Organization: A Study of the Larger Mind*, 1909), that there was at least an incipient national political community or, like Herbert Croly (*The Promise of American Life*, 1910), that such a community could be created and mobilized and in whose name government could legitimately and authoritatively act. It was, however, eventually out of the ruins of both traditional state theory and the Progressive vision that a new account of democratic government in America emerged. The decline of the state as a theory of democracy was paralleled by the beginning and evolution of the theory of democratic pluralism and by the account of science and forms of research that the latter entailed.

During the last years of the 19th century, professional social science associations began to break away from the umbrella of the American Social Science Association, which had its roots in a variety of reformist causes, such as the abolition of slavery, and to affiliate more directly with academic institutions, under the assumption that this would provide scientific authenticity and authority. The American Political Science Association (APSA), with the leadership of individuals such as Willoughby and its first president, Frank Goodnow, was formed in 1903, when it broke away from its affiliation with the more conservative American Historical Association, and the *American Political Science Review* began publication in 1906. The practical concerns of the previous generation were perpetuated in the creation of this organization, but it represented an emerging progressive ideology as well as a commitment to endow the discipline with yet greater scientific authority by embracing what was viewed as the methods of modern empirical science. For individuals such as Wilson and Goodnow, who were dedicated to more efficient and effective government, the goals were still ultimately practical. There was, however, something of a theoretical hiatus regarding both democracy and the nature of politics as the original concept of the state continued to wane, and, at the same time, departments of political science and government continued to emerge at major universities such as the University of California, Berkeley; University of Illinois; University of Wisconsin; Harvard University; and Stanford University.

Pluralism and the Liberal Science of Politics

The demise of the theory of the state was in part a reaction, in the context of World War I, to its German, and now allegedly authoritarian, origins, but it was also a consequence of the dimming Progressive hope of awakening or creating a democratic public, which could rise up and take power back from corrupt politicians and a capitalistic economic hegemony. Social scientists, in the wake of immigration and growing cultural and class differences, became overwhelmed with evidence of social and economic diversity and contentiousness. There was an increased sense that there was no homogeneous American public but rather only complex congeries of interests and groups that exceeded even Madison's account. In 1907, Harvard historian Albert Bushnell Hart, after presenting an exhaustive account of discarded theories of popular government in the United States, noted that even though the idea of the state as the basis of a theory of popular sovereignty seemed to still hold sway, it really did not fit the present circumstances of American politics. Although he expressed faith that America was a democracy, he could no longer, any more than most of his contemporaries, account for it theoretically. To provide such an account was the task of pluralist theory as it evolved during the first third of the 20th century. Individuals such as Lawrence Lowell (*Public Opinion and Popular Government*, 1913), and, later, Walter Lippmann (*The Phantom Public*, 1925) questioned the existence of an actual public or even the reality of a public opinion that commentators such as James Bryce (*The American Commonwealth*, 1890) had emphasized as constituting the heart of democratic society in America.

Despite the publication of William James's *Pluralistic Universe* (1904), the term *pluralism* had not, at this point, in any substantial manner, entered the discourse of American political science. Although Arthur Bentley's pointed critique of the concept of the state and his analysis of interest groups as the essence of politics (*Process of Government*, 1908) would become a central reference for later pluralist theory, it had very little immediate impact, and Bentley never employed the term *pluralism*. It was during Harold Laski's brief sojourn in the United States, subsequent to World War I, that the term was introduced into the conversation of political science, as part of his attack on the idea of state sovereignty and centralized authority and his propagation of the notion that the state was merely one association among many in society. Laski's principal concern, as in the case of Tocqueville, was his own country, but he, as well as other English theorists such as Ernest Barker and A. D. Lindsay, helped instigate a debate about pluralism that focused on whether political reality consisted of anything more than an endless process of group interaction with the government functioning as an arbiter and whether this could add up, empirically and theoretically, to democracy. It was difficult, however, for American political scientists to give up the idea that the state was nothing more than government and that government was not the agent of a general popular will.

Merriam embraced certain democratic values associated with cultural diversity and political pluralism, but he was equally impressed with the divisiveness inherent in such difference and with the antidemocratic sentiments and practices of certain groups. He retained the assumption that democracy ultimately required unity, even if, in his view and that of his student Harold Lasswell, it was necessary to introduce it from the top down through social control, civic education, and even the judicious use of propaganda. They transferred their hopes for a democratic society to the actions of governmental elites informed by social-scientific knowledge, but no articulate image of American democracy and the American political system appeared, for example, in Merriam's principal work of this period (e.g., *New Aspects of Politics*, 1925), even though he sponsored much of the research and modes of inquiry that seemed appropriate for a changing image of politics.

The strongest riposte to the normative theory of pluralism associated with Laski and other writers of the period, as well as to empirical political scientists and sociologists whose work increasingly lent support to the notion that politics was irreducibly pluralistic, was the work of William Yandell Elliott (*The Pragmatic Revolt in Politics*, 1928). He spoke for many of his generation when he argued that to give up the concept of the state as an organic public was, in effect, to give up democracy as well as the autonomy of political theory and political science. Elliott did not reject the reality of pluralism, but he believed that it tended to undermine the communal basis of democracy. He argued that in an age dominated by empiricism and pragmatism, as well as by the threat of foreign doctrines such as fascism and communism, it was still possible to perceive, and suggested that it was at least necessary to believe in, what he called a "co-organic" community in American political life, which was the basis of constitutional government. A somewhat similar, but ideologically different, position had been advanced by Mary Parker Follett (*The New State*, 1918). It was difficult, even for someone such as John Dewey (*The Public and Its Problems*, 1927), who along with Laski was perceived by Elliott as a purveyor of relativism and its destructive implications for democracy, to sever the idea of popular government from the existence of a national community that transcended the complexity of modern "great society."

By the end of the 1920s, however, the concept of pluralism had become Americanized and formed the basis of an empirical account of American politics, a normative image of democratic practice, and closely connected to what G. E. G. Catlin, a transplanted British scholar who championed both pluralism and the work of Merriam, referred to as *The Science and Method of Politics* (1927). For the first time since Madison, a description of social diversity and conflict and of group pressures on government was transformed into a theory of popular government that would provide much of the content of a new and widely embraced image of democratic identity. The group theory of political reality became deeply entrenched in political science as it evolved into an argument about how the process of interest-group politics constituted a form of both democratic interaction and representation. This had been implied by the early research of individuals such as Pendelton Herring (*Group Representation Before Congress*, 1927), but, during the late 1920s and early 1930s, a number of individuals such as Peter Odegard (*The American Public Mind*, 1930) and John Dickinson ("Democratic Realities and Democratic Dogma," *American Political Science Review*, 1930) elaborated a pluralist theory of democracy that contained all the essential theoretical elements that would be rearticulated and reconstructed a generation later in the work of individuals such as David Truman and Robert Dahl.

At the core of this theory was the claim that all societies consisted of groups seeking their self-interest and that this, at any stage of social evolution, required mechanisms for compromise and adjustment. In the context of modern society, such adjustment was achieved through the medium of government that functioned as an umpire acting pragmatically in response to the needs of the situation and with respect to matters of intervention and control. It was through participation in groups that individuals realized their goals and achieved identity, and it was through groups gaining access to influence, more than through formal institutions, that democratic representation was most essentially effected. Stability in society was achieved through a balance of conflicting social pressures constrained by appropriate enabling institutions and a basic consensus on the rules of the game. Majoritarian democracy was viewed as a myth that belied the fact that majorities were little more than aggregations of individual preference that were democratic only in the sense that they had the capacity, through elections, to effect a circulation of elites.

From the 1920s to the 1940s, political science continued to be institutionalized and expand as a part of higher education in the United States, and during this period, the membership of the APSA tripled. The work of Merriam and Lasswell, at the University of Chicago, represented the most important development, but early forms of political science were emerging in England, France, and Germany. During the later part of the 1930s, there was little in the way of a further explicit statement or elaboration of pluralist theory, but it became, in both politics and the academy, the basis of an account of the United States as a democratic society, and it was advanced as distinguishing the American polity from the growing number of totalitarian regimes that seemed to be characterized by excessive unity. The name for this new democratic identity was liberalism, and the manner in which pluralism was transfigured as liberalism is a crucial chapter in the story of the evolution of democratic theory in American political science.

Although common in Europe, the term *liberalism* had seldom been systematically invoked in either American politics or political science before the 1930s. While politicians such as Woodrow Wilson, and later Franklin Roosevelt, began tentatively to court this label for a variety of policy initiatives, everyone eventually seemed anxious to adopt this synonym for democracy. A variety of individuals, including Herbert Hoover, claimed to be the "true" liberal, but Roosevelt won the title, and his opponents eventually accepted the name he had originally pejoratively bestowed on them—Conservatives. The term *liberalism* gravitated into the language of political science, often via those such as Dewey who were sympathetic to the New Deal, but eventually political theorists, such as George Sabine in his paradigmatic *A History of Political Theory* (1937) emptied the concept of its concrete political meaning and began writing the history of Western political thought and institutions as a story of the progress of liberalism that, despite the temporary aberrations of totalitarianism, found full expression in American society. Although in the work of Dewey, as well as a number of political scientists, there continued to be a certain correspondence between the academic and lay visions of liberalism, two quite distinct traditions of discourse began to evolve as liberalism, in the language of political science, was reified, provided with a philosophy and history, and reimposed as a description of American politics. To the extent that liberalism had a definite conceptual meaning in the literature of political science and political theory, other than a name for American government and society, it tended to stand for pluralism and attendant values such as individualism, social freedom and difference, bargaining, and compromise. Philosophers, such as T. V. Smith at Chicago (*The Promise of America*, 1936) took the position that what characterized democracy was less any absolute doctrine and regime than a commitment to toleration and the propagation of diversity within a procedural framework for settling conflicts.

By the early 1940s, on the eve of World War II, the basic elements of this vision were extracted from the research of mainstream political science, systematized by individuals such as Herring, and presented as the *Politics of Democracy* (1940). Herring saw his task as taking all that was often considered bad about politics—from pressure groups to bosses and soft money—and demonstrating that they were all, if understood scientifically, part of a democratic process. One reason for the rearticulation of pluralism qua liberalism was to provide a response and counterideal to the doctrines of totalitarianism. For Lasswell, political science continued to be part of "The Developing Science of Democracy" (*The Future of Government in the United States*, edited by Leonard D. White, 1942).

The Behavioral Era and the Reconstitution of Science and Democracy

Just as the discipline was expanding in the United States after World War II, it was proliferating abroad. In 1949, the International Political Science Association (IPSA) was formed in Paris, which brought together national associations from numerous countries in Europe and elsewhere. The emerging national forms of the discipline were in many respects increasingly responsive to and reflective of the social and cultural milieu in which they were situated, even though the American commitment to empirical and quantitative studies was widely accepted and promulgated along with more traditional historical and institutional forms of research. In the United States, David Easton's *The Political System: An Inquiry Into the State of Political Science* (1953) set the agenda for the next decade by defining political science as the study of the "authoritative allocation of values" and making the case for moving beyond mere factual research as well as traditional historical and institutional forms by advancing empirical theory and adopting the methods of natural science. The behavioral "revolution," for which Easton was often the principal spokesperson, significantly transformed the practice of political science and increased in large measure the substantive and methodological contributions on a variety of subjects, including survey research and voting behavior. It was, however, in many respects, less a revolution than a recommitment to the visions of both the scientific study of politics and liberal democracy that had informed the discipline for nearly half a century, and it was also in part a response to the first significant challenge to those visions.

By the 1950s, the academic image of liberalism had become increasingly dominant as individuals such as Daniel Boorstin (*The Genius of American Politics*, 1953) and Louis Hartz (*The Liberal Tradition in America*, 1955) set out to demonstrate that although there might not be an American public, there was, for better or worse, in addition to the institutions that held the fragments of society together, a historically rooted liberal value consensus and tradition that gave credence to the concept of e pluribus unum. This notion of a liberal consensus that transcended and reconciled group differences became an essential element of the revived group theory of politics. The continuing attempt to give meaning to the idea of liberalism, and to equate liberalism with democracy, was, however, catalyzed and galvanized by a persistent but often still somewhat submerged attack on liberalism that had begun to influence what had been, since the 1920s, a thoroughly American political science. By the 1950s, liberalism, because of both doubts about interventionist government and events such as the McCarthy hearings, had become a highly contested concept in American politics. Often, for quite different reasons, it was also losing its positive valence in academic discourse as a somewhat subterranean critique of liberal democracy, and political science began to infiltrate the discipline and form a counterpoint to the postwar behavioral movement in political science and its rededication to a scientific study of politics based on emulating what was assumed to be the methods of natural science.

This critique, largely conceived and mounted by émigré scholars, was gaining a place in the literature of political theory, and it was manifest in journals such as the *Review of Politics* with its theological antiliberal perspective as well as in the perspective of the president, Robert Hutchins, and those involved in the Committee on Social Thought at the University of Chicago who set themselves directly against the Chicago image of social science. What emerged was a new mode of political theory that would eventually lead a number of scholars to make an identity choice they had never previously been confronted with—that is, a choice between political science and political theory. The confrontation between this critique and the reconstituted pluralist account of liberal democracy in political science made up the dialectic of democracy in the postwar generation. At this point, what really separated mainstream political scientists from political theorists was less a commitment to science, as opposed to a commitment to normative theory, than holding two quite different ethical positions on the issue of democracy.

The predominantly German scholars who emigrated to the United States, beginning in the 1930s, were in many respects a philosophically and ideologically diverse group, which included Hans Morgenthau (*Scientific Man and Power Politics*, 1946), Eric Voegelin (*The New Science of Politics*, 1951), Leo Strauss (*Natural Right and History*, 1953), Hannah Arendt (*The Human Condition*, 1958), and members of the neo-Marxist Frankfurt School such as Herbert Marcuse, Theodor Adorno, Otto Kirchheimer, and Max Horkheimer. What they had in common, however, was a suspicion of, if not antipathy toward, liberalism, which as a political theory they believed was philosophically flawed and which as a political form, they claimed was inherently pathological and represented political institutions that historically, as in the case of Weimar Germany, were on the threshold of totalitarianism. This form of antimodernism, rooted in the politics and intellectual context of early-20th-century Germany and in various transcendental philosophies such as that of Heidegger as well as forms of socialist thought, was a strange and difficult body of ideas for Americans to absorb. These theorists, who rejected scientism and who were wedded to images of the decline of Western civilization, represented a profound challenge to a conception of democracy based on commitments to empiricism, relativism, liberalism, and historical progress, which had characterized American political science for half a century. By the end of the 1950s, the work of these foreign scholars and indigenous fellow travelers had largely begun to define the subfield of political theory, which heretofore had been an integral dimension of mainstream American political science and the principal vehicle of its vision of democracy. This challenge, coupled with the continuing concern about presenting a coherent image of democracy as a counterpoint to totalitarianism, prompted the postwar reconstitution of group theory and the pluralist account of democracy.

David Truman's *The Governmental Process* (1951) and Earl Latham's *The Group Basis of Politics* (1952) revived the relevance of Bentley's work, and Robert Dahl's *Preface to Democratic Theory* (1955) established the genre of empirical democratic theory that was devoted to vouchsafing the image of pluralist democracy. The latter work was in one respect less a "preface" than an "epilogue" and codification of ideas that, during the 1930s, had become an essential part of the identity of political science. Dahl returned to Laski's and Barker's term *polyarchy* as a synonym for a form of democracy that Dahl contrasted both with majoritarian or "populist" types and with what he claimed was Madison's excessive emphasis on constitutional checks and balances at the expense of adequate attention to the informal and social dimensions of group interaction where, in effect, minorities ruled. In *Who Governs?* (1961), Dahl explicitly embraced the term *pluralism*, and his theory of pluralist democracy was offered in part as a counter to the claims about elitism and the structure of community power advanced by individuals such as C. Wright Mills (*The Power Elite*, 1956) and various sociologists such as Floyd Hunter. But it was also an attempt, during the Cold War, to systematize and accentuate an image of Western liberal democracy that supported the faith of those who opposed the political ideas and institutions of the East. Dahl, like those after him such as Gabriel Almond and Sidney Verba (*The Civic Culture*, 1963), argued that we should begin by examining the character of those countries that we know to be democracies and by extracting an empirical basis for a normative theory that, Dahl claimed, was most fully represented in the "American hybrid."

The critique of liberalism and pluralism was, however, perpetuated by a wide range of political theorists in the 1960s, and the "end of ideology," which had been proclaimed by sociologists such as Daniel Bell and Seymour Martin Lipset as the future of the dominance of pluralist liberal democracy, failed to materialize. While the debate that precipitated between political theory and behavioral political science during this period has often been represented as a conflict between "scientific" and "traditional" theory, the underlying issue was the nature of democracy. The émigré-inspired critique was at this point joined by theorists such as Sheldon Wolin (*Politics and Vision*, 1960) as well as by the persistent progressive statist countertradition that had remained alongside pluralist theory in political science and that was now represented in a new form by individuals such as Elmer E. Schattschneider (*The Semisovereign People: A Realist View of Democracy in America*, 1960). Schattschneider argued that interest-group politics had an upper-class bias as well as a corrosive effect on party democracy. Grant McConnell (*Private Power and American Democracy*, 1966) and Theodore Lowi (*The End of Liberalism*, 1969) mounted sustained attacks on what they claimed democratic and institutional pathologies of the theory and practice of "interest-group liberalism." Despite their similarities, the critiques of behavioralism and liberalism that were inspired by the émigré theorists and those that were rooted in the American tradition were sometimes uneasy allies, such as in the Straussian-inspired *Essays on the Scientific Study of Politics* (1961), but a growing intellectual split between political theory and mainstream political science characterized the 1960s and evolved through the 1980s.

From Postbehavioralism to the 21st Century

Although in 1961 Dahl had proclaimed that with respect to the behavioral movement it was possible to write "An Epitaph for a Monument to a Successful Protest," both the commitment to pure science and the pluralist theory of democracy continued to be the target of widespread criticism from both political theorists and a number of more mainstream political scientists. This dissatisfaction sprung in part from what seemed to many to be political science's lack of relevance for and attention to political events such as the Vietnam War, the crisis of American cities and problems of civil rights, and Cold War politics. The Caucus for a New Political Science challenged the authority of the APSA, and in 1969, Wolin pitted the "vocation of political theory" against what he claimed was the apolitical "methodism" of behavioral political science. At the same time, the president-elect, Easton, repudiated the tenets of much of what had represented the behavioral movement when he announced a "new revolution in political science," a "postbehavioral revolution" that would recognize the deficiencies of the pluralist theory of democracy and embrace a new "credo of relevance" that would give precedence to research on pressing contemporary political issues rather than to the immediate advancement of scientific theories and methods.

By the early 1970s, concerns about practical issues led the mainstream discipline to seek an identity for the postbehavioral era by a return to what Lasswell had championed as policy science, and a more ecumenical spirit was apparent as the debate about behavioralism wound down and the issue of maintaining professional inclusiveness became more prominent. Although the controversy about behavioralism had created an intellectual breach between mainstream political science and the subfield of political theory, it also had the effect of relocating, or dislocating, the discussion of American political identity and democratic theory. While political science continued, in various ways and degrees, to validate the traditional liberal vision, it tended, after the 1970s, to concede to political theory the role of normative theorizing. The conversation about democracy and liberalism increasingly became the property of the interdisciplinary and relatively autonomous enterprise of political theory and absorbed into an eclectic conversation that was determined more by the reigning academic philosophical authorities than by any direct relevance to the particularities of American politics. Debates about liberalism, often centering on philosophical arguments such as those of John Rawls, Robert Nozick, Jürgen Habermas, and Richard Rorty, became a large part of the focus of political theory, while both political science as a whole and political theory as a subfield became increasingly pluralized.

By the mid-1980s, it was increasingly difficult to speak in general of political science as a discipline and of the history of the field as a whole. Although the debate about behavioralism had fractured the field, it had also constituted the terms of a common conversation that in some respects defined the discipline. The centrifugal forces of specialization, increased concerns about social and gender diversity within the profession, and other internal tendencies toward pluralization in the field were accentuated by the need to recognize the growing distinctions among national practices of political science. In 1982, the IPSA Study Group on the Comparative Sociology of Political Science was formed, and in 1986, it was supplemented by the International Committee for the Study of the Development of Political Science. These two groups merged in 1988, forming the IPSA Research Committee for the Study of Political Science as Discipline, which was formally recognized as IPSA Research Committee 33 (RC 33) in 1989. Since its formal establishment, RC 33 has been active in all of the IPSA Congresses, and it has also undertaken a number of inter-Congress workshops, conferences, research projects, and publications devoted both to the study of the history and character of political science in various countries as well as to features common to the field as a whole. The research sponsored by this endeavor has made it clear that despite many similar concerns and research programs, political science is no longer consistently the science of politics as it evolved in the United States.

The beginning of the 1990s was a watershed for political science. The public policy orientation inspired by the events of the 1960s began to fade, and many believed the growing popularity of what Anthony Downs had referred to as *An Economic Theory of Democracy* (1957) and what came to be referred to as rational choice analysis promised a new methodological basis for disciplinary identity and a reconstruction of democratic theory. This trend, however, was paralleled, and challenged, by those who had begun to advocate new directions in institutional and historical research (e.g., *Bringing the State Back In*, edited by Peter B. Evans, Dietrich

Rueschemeyer, & Theda Skocpol, 1985). There were calls for more diverse approaches to the study of politics as the enthusiasm for rational choice declined (e.g., *The Economic Approach to Politics: A Critical Assessment of the Theory of Rational Choice*, edited by Kristen Monroe, 1991). The collapse of communism and the bipolar world of the Cold War also heightened the sense of plurality as the basic condition of both politics and political science, and it catalyzed a renewed concern with the theory of democracy as a variety of national communities sought to define, and redefine, themselves as democratic societies. In this context, pluralism emerged once again as a dominant theme. Not only had politics become internationally more diverse but concerns about multiculturalism and philosophies such as postmodernism accentuated the value and reality of diversity.

After its intellectual estrangement from mainstream political science, a unifying and driving force in the increasingly dispersed conversation of political theory continued to be a critique of the liberal/pluralist vision of democracy and an attempt to resurrect some version of participatory democracy. By the early 1990s, however, there was a subtle, but in some ways quite fundamental, shift in perspective. Although the idea that democracy must be rooted in unity was still evident in the work of individuals such as Robert Putnam (*Bowling Alone*, 2000), who stressed the importance of social capital and a communal basis of democracy, the concept of pluralism once again appeared in the discourse of political theory as the centerpiece of the democratic imagination. The concept was seldom any longer that of the interest-group liberalism of the 1950s, but theorists such as Robert Dahl and Charles Lindblom, despite some critical emendations, maintained their faith in social diversity as the ultimate value of democracy. Both John Rawls (*Political Liberalism*, 1993) and Jürgen Habermas (*Facts and Norms*, 1992) manifested an increased acceptance of the social realities of liberal democracy, and the many and various versions of both deliberative and radical democracy embraced the ethic of pluralism.

The manner in which the critique of pluralist liberalism by democratic theorists gave way, during the closing years of the 20th century, to the idea of pluralism as the core of democracy uncannily mirrored the path of conceptual transformation that occurred in the first quarter of the century. And the new pluralism, like the emergence of the old pluralism, seems in large measure to be a response to the ineluctable realities of the sociology of contemporary society. Dahl took it as a virtue that in a polyarchial society one might say that no one governs or that minorities govern, but the problem always was that if this is the case, then it also means that democracy, as the mediation of public decisions through the general citizenry, is difficult to identify. Plurality, one might argue, is surely a necessary condition of any realistic concept of democracy, but it may not be a sufficient condition. In the last analysis, the philosophical reconciliation of pluralism with democracy has been no easier than it was at the time of Madison.

By the beginning of the 21st century, it was difficult to discern any clear basis of unity in the discipline (*Political Science: The State of the Discipline*, edited by Ira Katznelson & Helen V. Ingram, 2002), and by the end of the first decade, it is still not easy to specify what trends may be most significant. In the United States, concerns about methodological diversity surfaced once again in what came to be known as the *Perestroika* debate, but, unlike the conflicts of the late 1960s and early 1970s, the issues appeared to be more professional than political. The discipline's origins were closely tied to a definite practical mission of political reform and political education, and, like the meaning of democracy, the relationship between political science and politics remains unresolved. In addition to noting the continuing tendencies toward specialization within and among subfields, it is necessary to recognize that in taking account of the history and current practices of the field, the story of political science, despite some intimations to the contrary (*A New Handbook of Political Science*, edited by Robert Goodin & Hans-Dieter Klingemann, 1996), is no longer simply the story of the American science of politics.

John G. Gunnell
State University of New York
Albany, New York, United States
and University of California, Davis
Davis, California, United States

See also Behavioralism; Democracy, Theories of; Interest Groups; Liberalism; Paradigms in Political Science; Pluralism; Political Science, International Institutionalization; Political Theory; State

Further Readings

Ancar, D., & Berndtson, E. (Eds.). (1988). *Political science: Between past and future*. Helsinki, Finland: Finnish Political Science Association.

Andrews, W. G. (Ed.). (1982). *International handbook of political science*. Westport, CT: Greenwood Press.

Collini, S., Winch, D., & Burrow, J. (1983). *That noble science of politics*. Cambridge, UK: Cambridge University Press.

Crick, B. (1958). *The American science of politics: Its origins and prospects*. Berkeley: University of California Press.

Easton, D., Gunnell, J. G., & Graziano, L. (1991). *The development of political science: A comparative survey*. London: Routledge.

Easton, D., Gunnell, J. G., & Stein, M. B. (1991). *Regime and discipline: Democracy and the development of political science*. Ann Arbor: University of Michigan Press.

Farr, J. (2003). Political science. In T. M. Porter & D. Ross (Eds.), *The Cambridge history of science: Vol. 7. The modern social sciences* (pp. 306–328). Cambridge, UK: Cambridge University Press.

Farr, J., Dryzek, J. S., & Leonard, S. T. (1995). *Political science in history: Research programs and political traditions*. Cambridge, UK: Cambridge University Press.

Farr, J., & Seidelman, R. (1993). *Discipline and history: Political science in the United States*. Ann Arbor: University of Michigan Press.

Gunnell, J. G. (2004). *Imagining the American polity: Political science and the discourse of democracy*. University Park: Pennsylvania State University Press.

Haddow, A. (1939). *Political science in American colleges and universities, 1636–1900*. New York: Appleton-Century.

Ricci, D. M. (1984). *The tragedy of American political science: Politics, scholarship, and democracy*. New Haven, CT: Yale University Press.

Ross, D. (1991). *The origins of American social science*. Cambridge, UK: Cambridge University Press.

Seidelman, R. (with Harpham, E. J.). (1985). *Disenchanted realists: Political science and the American crisis, 1884–1984*. Albany: State University of New York Press.

Sigelman, L. (Ed.). (2006). "The evolution of political science" essays. *American Political Science Review, 100*(4), 479–486.

Smith, R. M. (1997). Still blowing in the wind: The American quest for a democratic scientific political science. *Daedalus, 126*, 253–287.

Somit, A., & Tanenhaus, J. (1967). *The development of American political science: From Burgess to behavioralism*. Boston: Allyn & Bacon.

Hobbes, Thomas (1588–1679)

Thomas Hobbes is regarded as one of the greatest political thinkers in the Western tradition for his contribution to the development of the concepts of political obligation and state sovereignty. His theory is often associated with absolutism in domestic politics and with realism in international relations. A long line of interpreters, however, have questioned such associations.

Hobbes was born in Malmesbury, England, on April 5, 1588. For much of our knowledge of Hobbes's early life, we have to rely on the notes of his contemporary and friend John Aubrey. Hobbes was of humble origin; his education at Magdalen Hall in Oxford was sponsored by an uncle. For most of his life, Hobbes worked for the earls of Devonshire. In his capacity as tutor, he travelled extensively in Europe and came in contact with the finest minds of the time, including Galileo, Descartes, and Leibniz. Hobbes fled to France during the English Civil War and was tutor of mathematics to the future King Charles II, who was also in exile.

The intellectual context of 17th-century Europe inspired Hobbes to plan a comprehensive system of philosophy that explained everything that could be explained, resorting to one basic principle, namely, "motion." Hobbes's project was made up of three parts, the first on metaphysics, the second on man's physiology and psychology, and the third on politics. The political crisis in his country induced Hobbes not to follow the order of the original project but to begin his investigation with the study of the rights and duties of citizens. Indeed, the political climate also explains why Hobbes translated Thucydides' *History of the Peloponnesian War* in 1628. According to Hobbes, Thucydides' work affords us important insights into the weaknesses of democracies and was relevant at a time when there were growing tensions between Charles I and Parliament.

It is not from history, however, that Hobbes thought that political science should take inspiration for its methodology. In *Brief Lives*, Aubrey relates an anecdote that sheds some light on the method that Hobbes used in his political writings. Apparently, Hobbes was 40 years old when by chance he came across the 47th proposition in the first book of Euclid's *Elements*. Although at first the proposition appeared counterintuitive to Hobbes, its demonstration convinced him of its truth. This, Aubrey tells us, was the beginning of Hobbes's love affair with geometry.

Hobbes believed that it was possible to apply the formal rigor of geometry to the study of politics and demonstrate logically, proceeding from assumptions to conclusions, the causes of civil war and the conditions for "immortal" domestic peace. Hobbes firmly believed that he had succeeded in his endeavor, and he famously claimed that political science was not older than his book *De Cive*. The concepts and ideas put across in *De Cive* are very close to those expanded in *Leviathan*, which was published in English in 1651, after the execution of Charles I (in 1649). *Leviathan* is regarded as one of the masterpieces of Western political science. In addition to being brilliant in style, *Leviathan* brings to light in an unparalleled way the protection–obedience principle that lies at the foundation of the Western concept of political obligation: Citizens obey the political state in exchange for protection.

Hobbes explains the sources, nature, and limits of political obligation in three steps. In the first step, Hobbes describes some immutable characteristics of human nature. To begin with, he emphasizes that every man regards self-preservation as *summum bonum* and fears violent death at the hands of others "as the greatest mischief that can arrive to nature" (*De Cive*, Epistle Dedicatory); he stresses that all men are capable of rationality and that "every man by reasoning seeks out the most appropriate means to achieve his ends" (*De Cive*, chap. 14, sec. 16). Furthermore, he stresses the natural equality of men, in the sense that "the weakest has strength enough to kill the strongest" (*Leviathan*, chap. 13, sec. 1) and remarks that some men (who we cannot easily identify) are not satisfied with natural equality but want dominion over others and are in perpetual contention for power, honor, and riches.

In the second step, Hobbes imagines a state of nature where there is no authority, no private property, no industry, and no common definition of just and unjust, right and wrong. Under such conditions, everyone's means of survival are very limited and unprotected. Hobbes puts it to his reader that the combined effect of the action of men living in such conditions is a war of all against all: Driven by a fear of being attacked, all individuals, who are rational and concerned with self-preservation, and who are equally vulnerable and equally dangerous, attack each other in anticipation. Hobbes points out that life in such conditions is "solitary, poor, nasty, brutish and short" (*Leviathan*, chap. 13, sec. 9). He claims that reason makes man understand the first and fundamental law of nature, namely, that he ought "to seek peace" (*Leviathan*, chap. 14, sec. 4) if he thinks he can obtain it, and that if he cannot obtain it, he may use his right of nature and defend his life by all means.

Finally, having argued that the result of the joint action of natural men and women living in the state of nature is a state of war "of everyone against everyone," Hobbes examines the conditions that would bring about the opposite result, namely, a state of "immortal peace." As the nature of man cannot be changed, Hobbes argues that the only way to avoid the horror of anarchy is for individuals to "lay down their right to all things," to enter a social contract with one another, and to appoint a sovereign with the primary task of protecting their lives and bodily integrity. The sovereign, Hobbes stresses, is not part of the social contract but simply retains the original natural right to all things. Hobbes explains that sovereign power can reside in one man (or woman) or an assembly, but its characteristics are the same: It must be absolute, unconditional, unlimited, irrevocable, and indivisible. Hobbes maintains that it would be irrational to impose restrictions on the sovereign power as it would restrict its ability to protect its citizens. He also claims that if there were to be someone who could restrict the sovereign power, then this person would, in fact, be the sovereign. Hobbes leaves virtually no scope for resistance to the state: A Hobbesian citizen can only disobey to protect his own life. Because of his notion of sovereignty, Hobbes is regarded by many as the champion of the absolute state.

In the 20th century, David Gauthier led the camp of those who suggested that game theory (prisoners' dilemmas, coordination games, supergames, etc.) sheds light on Hobbes's political argument. On the one hand, game theory has been used to support Hobbes's claim that from a set of undemanding assumptions he demonstrated that the state of nature turns into a state of war; on the other hand, the game-theoretical armory has also been deployed to claim that Hobbes's enterprise ultimately fails in that rational agents cannot escape from the state of war and cannot create the Leviathan in the way suggested by Hobbes.

Critics of game-theoretical applications to *Leviathan* have pointed out that Hobbes stresses that, historically, states are rarely born out of contracts. In this view, the state of nature is not meant to describe a state that precedes the creation of the political state but a state into which people might fall into as a consequence of civil disobedience. In other words, the state of nature describes a state of civil war.

There is textual evidence to support the view that, for Hobbes, fear of punishment alone cannot guarantee long-term order and stability and that citizens need to be educated. In *Behemoth*, Hobbes singles out popular ignorance as the primary cause of the English Civil War. The state of nature is a thought experiment used by Hobbes to teach citizens why we ought to remain in political associations and why bad governments are better than no governments at all.

In Chapter 13 of *Leviathan*, in addition to stating that the state of nature materializes into civil wars, Hobbes also claims that it occurs in some primitive societies and that it describes the relations between states. He famously compares states to "gladiators with their weapons pointing and their eyes fixed on one another" (*Leviathan*, chap. 13, sec. 12) in a constant posture of hostility and war. Such remarks have induced some interpreters to claim that Hobbes is one of the founding fathers of realism. It has been claimed that Hobbes's pessimistic view of human nature, his idea that men are self-interested and seek power after power, his concept of anarchy, and his notion of the sovereign state inspired the realist tradition of international relations.

Whereas there is universal agreement among interpreters of the importance of Hobbes's contribution to the development of the concepts of political obligation and state sovereignty, no such agreement exists as to the association of Hobbes with absolutism and with realism. Points of contention among the interpreters are Hobbes's views on natural law, morality, God, and religion. The dominant view maintains all or most of the following claims: (a) the laws of nature for Hobbes are prudential rules that recommend the creation of the absolute state; (b) the state is the source of all law, all justice, and all morality; (c) the detailed analysis of the Bible that occupies a large part of *Leviathan* is meant to support the claim that the ecclesiastical powers are totally subordinated to the civil power and that a citizen must obey the Leviathan in everything except if he or she is asked to renounce the belief that Jesus is the Christ.

In contrast to the above views, since the work of A. P. Taylor in 1938 and Howard Warrender in 1957, a long line of interpreters have argued that Hobbes's laws of nature are not just samples of prudential morality, that Hobbes makes the Leviathan accountable to God, that the sovereign power is absolute but not arbitrary, that not all justice in Hobbes's construct is legal justice, that Hobbes is ultimately committed to the individual and not to the state, and that the claim that Hobbes is a precursor of John Austin and legal positivism, or indeed a founding father of realism, is ungrounded.

The most renowned works on Hobbes in the 20th century are those by Carl Schmitt, Leo Strauss, Howard Warrender, Michael Oakeshott, C. B. Macpherson, David Gauthier, Jean Hampton, Quentin Skinner, Sheldon Wolin, and Noel Malcolm.

Gabriella Slomp
University of St. Andrews
St. Andrews, United Kingdom

See also Realism in International Relations; Sovereignty; State

Further Readings

Aubrey, J. (1982). *Brief lives.* Woodbridge, UK: Boydell Press. (Original work published 1696)

Hobbes, T. (1983). *De Cive* (H. Warrender, Ed.). Oxford, UK: Clarendon Press. (Original work published 1651)

Hobbes, T. (1990). *Behemoth* (F. Toennies, Ed.). Chicago: University of Chicago Press. (Original work published 1682)

Hobbes, T. (1994). *Leviathan* (E. Curley, Ed.). Indianapolis, IN: Hackett. (Original work published 1651)

Shaver, R. (Ed.). (1999). *Hobbes*. Aldershot, UK: Ashgate.

Slomp, G. (Ed.). (2008). *Thomas Hobbes*. Aldershot, UK: Ashgate.

Springborg, P. (Ed.). (2007). *Cambridge companion to Hobbes's Leviathan*. New York: Cambridge University Press.

Human Development

The term *human development* (HD) that came into prominence through the work of Amartya Sen denotes the development toward a more humane society in which a maximum number of people live in dignity. From a humanist position, a dignified life is a life that people have reason to value because they are free to shape it in accordance with their own and mutually agreed ideals. This notion of HD is inspired by an inherently emancipative idea of the "good life" that unifies republican, liberal, contractual, and democratic thought, as noted by David Held (2006). To be human in this perspective means to have the potential to reason, to judge, to choose, and, thus, to be an agent who is in control of one's actions and life. The most humane life is an emancipative life that one lives in self-determination.

Human Development as Emancipation

Mastery, control, and autonomy are features of human emancipation emphasized in Edward L. Deci and Richard M. Ryan's psychological theory of self-determination (2002). In the evolution of our species, self-awareness became the most salient feature of the human intellect. Self-awareness creates a need to realize oneself in what one is doing, and this implies a need to act in self-determined ways. Self-determination is thought to become a dominant striving as soon as humans are existentially secure, so that the trying to thrive can replace the struggle to survive as the main director of human energies. Self-determination is an inherently emancipative striving that, if satisfied, creates feelings of being in unison with oneself. Because self-awareness is an evolution-shaped feature of *every* human being, self-determination is the most universally and most specifically human striving.

Sen also draws on the emancipative notion of HD in psychology, but he relates it to societies as the unit of reference. When the good life is an emancipated life, the good society is a society that makes a maximum number of people capable to live emancipative lives. Because, as members of the human race, all people are of equal existential value, every person has the same right to an emancipated life; opportunities to live in emancipation must be equally distributed in a humane society. In that sense, HD theory construes the ideals of freedom and equality as interdependent rather than contradictory.

Due to Sen's capability approach, the HD of societies can be measured by how widely emancipative capabilities are distributed. The United Nations Development Programme (UNDP) follows the capability approach in its annual Human Development Report, which publishes a Human Development Index (HDI). The HDI summarizes on a per-country basis information on the average person's life expectancy, educational attainment, and per capita income, assuming that longevity, education, and income increase ordinary people's capabilities to live an emancipated life.

In the perspective of HD, democracy becomes an integral part of the definition of development for the following reasons: Human emancipation requires freedom of choice in private and public affairs, and such freedoms are granted through the civil and political rights that define democracy.

The emancipative notion of HD has been criticized as prescribing a Western view of the good life. But supporters of the HD approach note that this criticism is defensible only on two questionable premises: The potential to live an emancipated life is not a universal human potential but one that only Western people possess, and emancipation is not a universal human value because non-Western people do not desire it. Neither of these positions is tenable. First, the potential for emancipation is anchored in a most general feature of the human mind, namely, self-awareness, which is not the sole property of Westerners. Second, the claim that emancipation is not a valued feature of life among non-Westerners has been empirically disproven. Whether people value emancipation can be seen in whether feelings of being free in shaping their lives impact satisfaction with their lives. Only if freedom over their lives increases people's satisfaction with their lives is emancipation of value for people. As Ronald Inglehart and Christian Welzel have shown, feelings of freedom over their lives increase people's life satisfaction in all cultures. Thus, HD's emphasis on emancipation does not prescribe a specifically Western view of the good life. It champions a particularly humane view.

The People Empowerment Framework

Christian Welzel, Ronald Inglehart, and Hans-Dieter Klingemann widened the capability approach into a people empowerment framework (PEF). The PEF specifies how economic conditions, cultural norms, and institutional rules interact in empowering people, relating each of these three areas of social reality to human emancipation as a common underlying theme. Figure 1 depicts the PEF.

In line with the emancipative notion of HD, people empowerment denotes ordinary people's potential to govern their lives themselves through the practice of personal freedoms in private matters as well as political freedoms in public affairs. The joint and equal emphasis on personal and political freedoms resonates with Isaiah Berlin's notion of "negative" and "positive" freedom: To be truly free, people must have the right to follow their personal preferences in private matters and to make their political preferences known, bargained, and counted in public matters.

Elements of People Power

To make freedoms practicable for people, social reality must meet three criteria. First, ordinary people must have command over participatory resources that make them capable to exercise freedoms. Participatory resources include material means, cognitive skills, and connective opportunities; these resources empower people on the level of capabilities, widening their objective-action repertoire. Second, ordinary people must have internalized self-expression values that make them

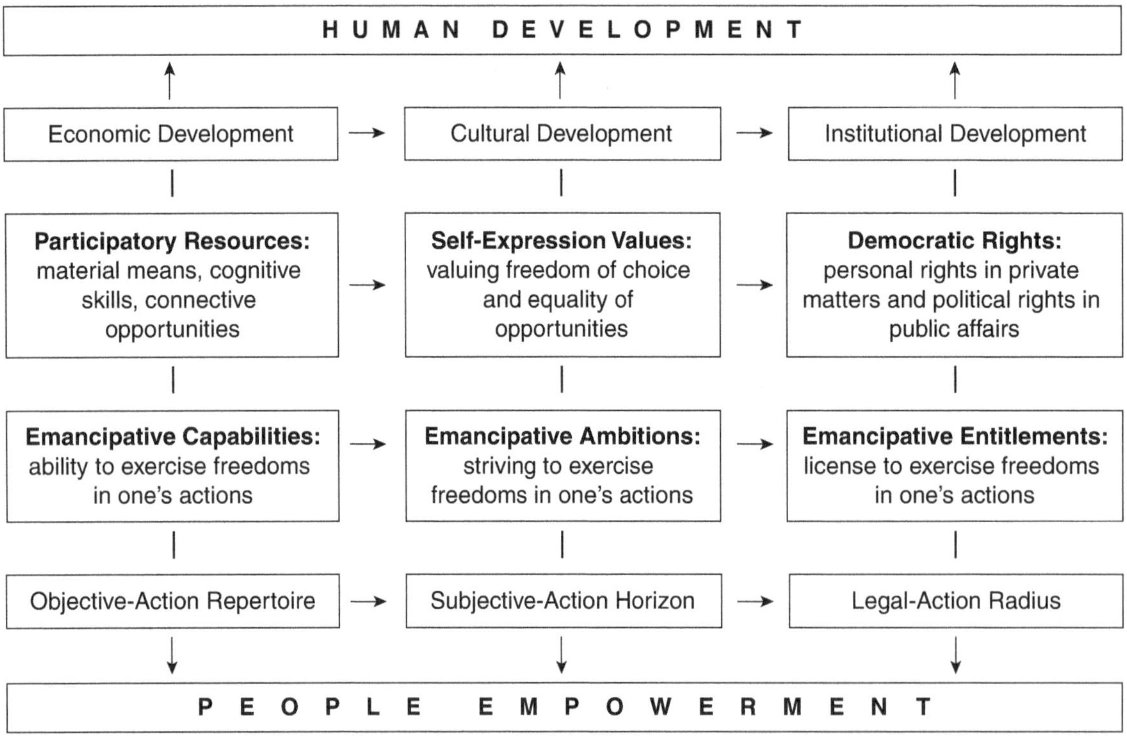

Figure 1 Human Development as People Empowerment

Source: Adapted from Welzel, C., Inglehart, R., & Klingemann, H.-D. (2003). The theory of human development: A cross-cultural analysis. *European Journal of Political Research, 43,* 379–401.

strive to exercise freedoms. Self-expression values emphasize freedom of choice and equality of opportunities; they empower people on the level of ambitions, widening their subjective-action horizon. Third, ordinary people must be granted *democratic rights* that license them to practice freedoms. Democratic rights establish equal personal and political liberties; they empower people on the level of *entitlements*, widening their legal-action radius.

Participatory resources, self-expression values, and democratic rights constitute three distinct, though interdependent, elements of people power. The pattern of their interdependence is governed by the "utility logic of freedom." This logic becomes evident when rethinking participatory resources, self-expression values, and democratic rights as, respectively, capabilities of, ambitions for, and entitlements to exercising freedoms. Doing so makes a number of logical connections obvious. For one, utility suggests that people become ambitioned to exercise freedoms only insofar as they find themselves able to exercise them. The utility logic also suggests that entitlements to exercise freedoms come into wide and frequent use only insofar as people are able and willing to use them. Together, these propositions suggest that self-expression values grow in response to grown participatory resources and, then, that popular pressures for democratic rights grow in response to grown self-expression values and participatory resources.

The three elements of human empowerment are interdependent not on conceptual grounds only. Empirically, as shown by Welzel, Inglehart, and Klingemann (2003, pp. 368–369), the interdependence is reflected in very strong correlations between societal-level measures of participatory resources, self-expression values, and democratic rights. The three elements correlate so strongly that statistically speaking they reflect one and only one empirical dimension. Content-wise, this dimension represents people empowerment—which is a unity of empowering capabilities, mentalities, and entitlements. Because of their interdependence, the three elements of people empowerment establish equilibria that resemble vicious and virtuous cycles of HD. Most societies are found on either consistently low or consistently high levels of HD in all three elements. HD is a syndrome of developmental conditions that is not easily disentangled. This is part of the reason why it is so difficult to get development started: It needs a synchronized effort to trigger economic, cultural, and institutional changes, as they mutually condition each other.

Democracy represents the institutional element of people empowerment and as such is highly conditioned by the economic and cultural elements of empowerment. No question, democracy can be imposed from the outside by foreign powers, or it can be adopted from the inside by unilateral acts of domestic power holders—irrespective of the social conditions. But in such cases, one most likely deals with a socially aloof version of democracy, in which case the freedoms that define democracy are not coming into wide usage by most of the people. Only when ordinary people are capable of exercising freedoms and only when they are willing to do so will the freedoms granted by democracy come into wide use. Only then do we witness socially embedded democracy.

Sometimes one finds democratic freedoms institutionalized at a level that goes beyond most people's capabilities and ambitions to struggle for these freedoms. When this is the case, power holders are free to corrupt formally enacted freedoms, and in general, they use this leeway to their benefit. Thus, when democracy is conceded by power holders in the absence of popular pressures, it is usually corrupted democracy. By contrast, when one finds democracy to be effective in the sense that its freedoms are really respected by those in power, this is usually a tribute to ordinary people's capabilities and ambitions to practice freedoms and struggle for them.

Strengths of Human Development Theory

Compared with other concepts in the social sciences, HD theory offers a broad perspective by integrating economic, cultural, and institutional aspects of social reality into a common framework. This breadth of perspective does not come at the expense of the analytical focus. Instead, HD theory sharpens the analytical focus by relating all three aspects of social reality to the empowerment of people as the lead theme.

The HD framework is inspired by an emancipative idea of the good society and the good life. This normative inspiration constitutes the framework's integrative core. However, the normativity of the concept is limited to providing a standard against which to evaluate a factual state of affairs as desirable or undesirable. Having a standard to evaluate reality does by no means mean to prescribe reality. Rather, it provides a basis for interventions to change it.

The only other concept in the social sciences comparable with HD in its integrative potential is social capital (SC). With its emphasis on *assets that facilitate collective action*, SC theory sets a focus similar to HD theory's emphasis on *assets that empower ordinary people*. Thus, the three assets championed in SC theory—networks, trust, and norms—resonate with the three assets highlighted in HD theory—capabilities, ambitions, and entitlements. However, SC theory lacks two properties of HD theory. First, SC theory lacks an evolutionary perspective that theorizes how development transforms different types of SC. Second, SC theory has little grounding in psychology and has hence difficulties to anchor SC in the human motivational system. By contrast, with its evolutionary perspective, grounding in psychology, and humanistic inspiration, HD theory offers an appealing integrative framework for the social sciences.

Christian Welzel
Jacobs University Bremen
Bremen, Germany

See also Democracy, Quality; Democracy, Theories of; Development, Political; Development Administration; Human Rights, Comparative Perspectives; Participation; Social Capital; Values

Further Readings

Deci, E. L., & Ryan, R. M. (2000). The what and why of goal pursuits: Human needs and the self-determination of behavior. *Psychological Inquiry, 11*, 227–268.

Held, D. (2006). *Models of democracy*. Palo Alto, CA: Stanford University Press.

Inglehart, R., & Welzel, C. (2005). *Modernization, cultural change, and democracy: The human development sequence*. New York: Cambridge University Press.

Sen, A. (1999). *Development as freedom*. New York: Knopf.

Welzel, C., Inglehart, R., & Klingemann, H.-D. (2003). The theory of human development: A cross-cultural analysis. *European Journal of Political Research, 43*, 379–401.

Human Rights, Comparative Perspectives

Human rights are inherently comparative. Empirical analysis on and advocacy for human rights are grounded in significant questions relating to human well-being and how such well-being varies across units, whether these units are individuals, groups, countries, or regions. Comparative politics is concerned with explaining variation in social and political phenomena across these very same units. Legal and normative frameworks for human rights have sought to establish rules and norms about how states and individuals ought to treat one another, and the human rights community has sought to make such a set of constraints on human behavior universal through the vehicle and mechanisms of public international law. Through the specification and testing of social theory on observed similarities and differences in the protection of human rights across individuals, groups, countries, and regions, comparative politics helps provide solutions to enhancing the promotion and protection of human rights. But it is crucial in this effort that comparison remains committed to methodological considerations of case selection and bias, measurement error and data availability, universality and particularity, and causal heterogeneity (see, e.g., Todd Landman, 2002). Absence of attention to these key issues can lead to insecure inferences and the possibility of perverse outcomes that can endanger human rights. This entry first examines issues related to methodology and describes some commonly used measures of human rights. It then discusses research on human rights and the contributions of comparative politics to such research. It concludes with a look at some of the challenges for future research in the field.

Methodological Considerations

Broadly speaking, comparative analysis variously includes large-*N* statistical analysis of many countries over time and space, small-*N* qualitative or quantitative analysis of most similar or most different countries, or single-country studies of human rights developments at the national or subnational level. Such comparisons have struggled to overcome significant ontological, epistemological, and methodological challenges in order to provide valid, meaningful, and reliable inferences in this burgeoning subfield of research. But there is now, however, a distinct subfield and strong community of researchers specifically dedicated to the application of the theories and methods in social science to significant human rights problems and puzzles that includes systematic comparative analysis. The American Political Science Association (APSA), the International Political Science Association (IPSA), and the International Studies Association (ISA) have all established specialized human rights sections. The European Consortium for Political Research (ECPR) hosted a joint workshop, The Systematic Study of Human Rights Violations, organized by Steve Poe and Sabine Carey in 2002; the *Journal of Peace Research* published a special issue dedicated to political science analysis of protecting human rights, while other mainstream journals in comparative politics and international relations have increasingly published empirical studies on human rights that adopt a comparative framework of some kind.

Comparative studies have tended to sidestep normative concerns over foundations for human rights and have adopted a pragmatic approach that seeks to conduct systematic research on the conditions under which such protections are (or are not) made possible. Such a focus can help us understand how best to prevent human beings from doing their worst to one another, as well as how to overcome some of the structural barriers to achieving greater human dignity for a larger cross section of humankind. Comparative analysis of human rights is thus essential for explaining and understanding the conditions under which human beings forge their existence, assert their dignity, and seek protections for their different identities, for the pursuit of self-determination, and for the exercise of agency and autonomy. Like the study of markets, social classes, and democracy, the study of human rights reveals much about human nature and the ways in which structure and agency interact to create extraordinarily different life experiences across the globe and provides valuable insights into the types of real protections that need to be in place.

Measures of Human Rights

Beyond its normative and ontological concerns, comparative analysis of human rights problems is predicated on the genesis and use of comparable measures of human rights either within states or across states. Such measures can be qualitative or quantitative, and both types of measures provide some gauge of the degree to which human rights are being respected, protected, and fulfilled by states (see Todd Landman & Edzia Carvalho, 2009). To date, such measures have included events-based data on violations of human rights, standards-based data on country protection of human rights in principle and in practice, survey-based data on perceptions and experiences of human rights, and socioeconomic and administrative statistics on government inputs, processes, outputs, and outcomes that have a bearing on human rights. These measures still tend to be biased toward the protection of civil and political rights, but progress has been made recently on providing comparable measures of some socioeconomic rights (see Landman & Carvalho, 2009).

Causes, Conditions, and Consequences of Human Rights

In using these various measures, much comparative research has been carried out in an effort to explain and understand cross-national similarities and differences in the protection of human rights. There is now a large body of large-*N* quantitative studies, small-*N* qualitative and quantitative studies, as well as a vast array of single-country studies that examine the causes, conditions, and consequences of human rights protection around the world. Extant global comparative studies on human rights protection have tended to focus on a narrow set of civil and political rights and carried out diachronic and synchronic analyses to estimate the effects of a series of important explanatory variables that account for their variation. Such explanatory variables have included economic development, population and population growth, democracy and democratization, multinational corporations, internal and external violent conflict, the end of the Cold War, U.S. and European foreign aid, domestic constitutional provisions, and religious differences and ethnic diversity. In addition to consideration of civil and political rights, other global comparative projects have focused on discrimination, minorities, and conflict; U.S. refugee policy; and the provision of basic human needs.

The most recent area of interest has been the examination of the growth and effectiveness of the international human rights regime. Linda Camp Keith (1999) and Oona Hathaway (2002) were the first scholars to analyze the relationship between ratification of human rights treaties and human rights protection, while controlling for a variety of other variables. Their analyses do not find robust support for such a relationship. Emilie M. Hafner-Burton and Kiyoteru Tsutsui (2007) added a layer of complexity to the relationship by specifying models that included an interaction effect between treaty ratification and democracy, which in turn has an effect on human rights protection. Landman's (2005) analysis included the level and timing of democratization, a feedback process between treaty ratification and human right protection, as well as a weighted measure of treaty ratification that took into account the filing of reservations across the main international human rights treaties.

Common Themes of Analysis

Analyses of human rights problems and puzzles that use a relatively small and intentional selection of countries address a number of common themes and adopt a wide range of comparative methods. The dominant themes at this level of analysis include the struggle for rights and the relationship between social mobilization, political liberalization, and repression (Thomas Risse, Stephen C. Ropp, & Kathryn Sikkink, 1999); the similarities and differences in the formation, function, outcomes and impact of truth commissions (e.g., Priscilla B. Hayner, 2002); the legacies of authoritarian rule (Luis Roniger & Mario Sznajder, 1999); nonstate violence, "uncivil" movements, and death squads (Leigh Payne, 2000); and the ways in which human rights norms have transcended state sovereignty through the use of transnational advocacy networks that help form alliances and informational networks between domestic and international human rights organizations that are able to put pressure on rights violating states (Risse, Ropp, & Sikkink, 1999). These various small-*N* studies have adopted a range of comparative-case or focused-comparison strategies, including most similar systems designs (MSSDs), which compare different human rights–related outcomes across similar cases; most different systems designs (MDSDs), which compare similar outcomes across different cases; and the mirror image of MSSDs, which compare similar variation across similar cases and even different outcomes across different cases.

Comparative Strategies

Single-country studies have long been an important part of comparative politics, and social science more generally, for their use in description and classification, in plausibility probes, in generating and testing hypotheses, and as crucial cases (i.e., the most likely and least likely examples) that can confirm, inform, or disconfirm existing theories. The human rights themes that are addressed in single-country studies vary little from those that have featured in the large-*N* and small-*N* comparative studies, but as in the comparison of a few countries, single-country analysis has allowed for much greater attention to process tracing and dynamic relationships between actors, conditions, and rights. The work of Darren G. Hawkins (2002) provides a good example of how process tracing provides a deeper insight into the causal mechanisms within a single county. In his study of authoritarianism in Chile and the response of the Pinochet regime to international human rights pressure, Hawkins shows that the rule-oriented factions within the regime grew increasingly wary of the possible delegitimizing power of international human rights pressure, gained ground over time, and were largely responsible for the various moves the regime made toward democratization and improvement in human rights protection; these lessons, as Hawkins shows, apply to an analysis of South Africa and Cuba.

Increasingly, the inferential logic of large-*N* studies has begun to be applied to single-country studies using subnational divisions within individual countries, such as democracy and human rights in the federal systems of Mexico and India and democracy and political violence across the administrative districts of Nepal. In these studies, the use of states in a federal structure as the basic units of analysis allows for a large number of observations (or increased degrees of freedom) for the analysis of variation in human rights protection while, at the same time, controlling for similarities, since these units are all from the same country. In this way, comparative research in federal systems is a form of MSSD and offers tremendous promise for research in the field of human rights.

Taken together, there is a natural synergy between human rights and comparisons, and the field of comparative politics brings much to bear on our understanding of the conditions under which human rights can or cannot be protected in the ways that are outlined in the international law of human rights. Systematic analysis of human rights problems is a burgeoning subfield in comparative politics and in many ways is a natural place in the larger discipline of political science in which to locate such analysis. While the international human rights regime seeks to use the mechanism of international law to govern the ways in which states relate to their citizens, it is within states and it is across states that the promotion and protection of human rights varies. This variation, which makes a reference to an ideal standard outlined within the many international human rights norms and instruments, is best analyzed through the various methods available to comparativists. These methods, which have developed through the analysis of many areas of research outside any concern for human rights, have served and will serve human rights well for the future.

Challenges

Despite the many virtues of comparative analysis for human rights research, there are many challenges that remain in the field. Comparative politics does not have its own distinct theoretical tradition but engages in rationalist, structuralist, and culturalist theorizing that can be developed more fully in ways that will prove fruitful for human rights research. The attention to rationalism in Neil Mitchell (2004) and Hawkins (2002) is laudable, especially since both afford an equally large role for ideational approaches. Mitchell's "principals" are motivated by material self-interest, as well as ideology, and it is precisely the differences in these motivations that help explain the differences in levels of atrocity that he observes across his three cases. Moreover, the model that he develops ought to travel to other cases both in the past and in the contemporary period. In a similar fashion, the different factions in Hawkins's analysis of the military regime in Chile are not only motivated by the quest to maintain power but also by a particular attachment to legal rules and standards both within and outside the Chilean constitutional order. This kind of innovative development and testing of theories is needed in future comparative research on human rights.

For example, the field has not yet developed a set of formal models of the kind found in the political economy literature that use the relative costs and benefits of attention to human rights to explain either domestic or international state behavior. At the international level, there are signaling and reputational factors that may explain why states ratify human rights treaties, while at the domestic level, human rights can be theorized as a set of public good for which states have different welfare functions. Moreover, spatial econometrics and simple gravity models can start to examine possible spillover and bandwagon effects, as well as the influence of large and powerful states on other states. In all of these examples, systematic comparative analysis of the variation in state behavior can provide the evidence base to test models that have been developed at a particular level of conceptual abstraction.

Finally, it is clear that more attention is needed on methodological issues. For questions of measurement, more attention is needed on the sources of human rights information, the procedures for coding human rights information, the development of measures of economic and social rights, and the provision of indicators that capture the many different dimensions of human rights (Landman & Carvalho, 2009). These measurement issues are pertinent to all forms of comparative analysis from large-*N* studies to single-country analysis. For studies that compare a few countries or a single country, more attention to the process of case selection is needed to avoid indeterminate research designs and severe forms of selection bias.

MSSDs and MDSDs offer good first solutions for case selection, while greater attention to negative cases and crucial cases is required to make the most of single-country studies of particular human rights problems. Human rights research is a field worthy of study within comparative politics, where the standards for high-quality and systematic rules of inquiry apply equally, while the need for a strong evidence base is paramount for policymakers and advocates interested in the promotion and protection of human rights across the world.

Todd Landman
University of Essex
Colchester, United Kingdom

See also Comparative Politics; Equality; Equality, Political; Human Development; Human Rights in International Relations; Liberty

Further Readings

Hafner-Burton, E. M., & Tsutsui, K. (2007). Justice lost! The failure of international human rights law to matter where needed most. *Journal of Peace Research, 44*(4), 407–425.

Hathaway, O. (2002). Do treaties make a difference? Human rights treaties and the problem of compliance. *Yale Law Journal, 111,* 1932–2042.

Hawkins, D. (2002). *International human rights and authoritarian rule in Chile.* Lincoln: University of Nebraska Press.

Hayner, P. B. (2002). *Unspeakable truths: Facing the challenge of truth commissions.* London: Routledge.

Keith, L. C. (1999). The United Nations International Covenant on Civil and Political Rights: Does it make a difference in human rights behavior? *Journal of Peace Research, 36*(1), 95–118.

Landman, T. (2002). Comparative politics and human rights. *Human Rights Quarterly, 24*(4), 890–923.

Landman, T. (2005). *Protecting human rights: A global comparative study.* Washington, DC: Georgetown University Press.

Landman, T., & Carvalho, E. (2009). *Measuring human rights.* London: Routledge.

Mitchell, N. (2004). *Agents of atrocity: Leaders, followers, and the violation of human rights in civil war.* London: Palgrave.

Payne, L. (2000). *Uncivil movements: The armed right wing and democracy in Latin America.* Baltimore: Johns Hopkins University Press.

Risse, T., Ropp, S. C., & Sikkink, K. (1999). *The power of human rights: International norms and domestic change.* Cambridge, UK: Cambridge University Press.

Roniger, L., & Sznajder, M. (1999). *The legacy of human rights violations in the Southern Cone: Argentina, Chile, and Uruguay.* Oxford, UK: Oxford University Press.

Human Rights in International Relations

Human rights is the soul of politics. The essence of human rights is the idea that all persons possess equal moral worth, that social order exists to preserve the essential humanity of its members, and that therefore the exercise of all forms of political authority is properly bounded by its impact on fundamental human dignity. In contemporary international society, this norm has become the theoretical basis for the legitimacy of all states—albeit poorly realized in practice. The emergence of the principle and practice of human rights is an essential area of international law, a hallmark of global civil society, and a response to the multilayered challenges of globalization, along with the persistence of state abuse. The politics of human rights also provides a fascinating test of the power of transnational citizen action and international cooperation to sporadically transform state sovereignty. This entry traces the evolution of this emerging norm, charts some systematic patterns of violation, assesses the range of international remedies, and discusses challenges to the concept and its application.

Historical Development and Emerging Consensus

While most cultures have had some historic standard of humane treatment for their members, the notion of universal and natural rights rises with modernity and increasing interactions across borders. The early arguments put forth by the Spanish theologian Bartolome de las Casas to recognize the essential humanity of the Indians of the Americas culminated several centuries later in the transatlantic movement against the African slave trade, which secured its abolition. During the 19th century, the increase in costly collisions among the rising European powers led to recognition of the horrors of war as a violation of universal standards, the establishment of the International Committee of the Red Cross, and the drafting of a series of codes of conduct for the treatment of civilians and prisoners: the Geneva Conventions (four treaties developed between 1864 and 1949). Meanwhile, new types of democratic regimes based on citizenship and social contract inscribed the protection of life and liberty as a requisite of rule within the state, a practice that was later exported. The British Magna Carta laid the foundation in limiting the sovereign's powers of coercion, France's Universal Declaration of the Rights of Man and the Citizen asserted rights that transcend social class and condition, while the U.S. Constitution's Bill of Rights established a normative hierarchy in which fundamental rights supersede even the democratic popular will.

The contemporary international human rights regime was established in reaction to the horrors of the Holocaust—the first modern-era genocide committed by modern means within Europe, coupled with border-crossing war crimes and international aggression. The Universal Declaration of Human Rights, signed on December 10, 1948, is widely considered to mark the birth of the modern norm of international human rights. Over the following decades, a global architecture was constructed, consisting of an expanding body of international law, global and regional monitoring and sanctioning institutions, an emerging practice of humanitarian intervention, humanitarian and governance foreign assistance, and a growing global network of human rights movements. Jack Donnelly has calculated that more than 140 states now subscribe to the foundational documents that delimit human rights in theory: the Universal Declaration and two International Covenants—the International Covenant on Civil and Political Rights (ICCPR) and the International Covenant on Economic, Social, and Cultural Rights (ICESCR).

While human rights began as a legal defense of the lives and physical integrity of political dissidents and religious or ethnic minorities from the malfeasance of dictatorships, its mandate has expanded in claims, subjects, and mechanisms. During the Cold War, the Western bloc sought to globalize civil and political rights via the ICCPR, while the socialist states emphasized social rights such as education and health care under the ICESCR. Meanwhile, developing nations added to the canon a concern with collective rights of development, identity, and, eventually, attempts to secure accountability of nonstate actors such as multinational corporations for abuses connected with globalization. From decolonization onward, the increasing presence of non-Western states in international society brought diverse calls for expansion of the human rights agenda to socially marginalized as well as politically oppressed groups, attention to government negligence as well as repression, and culturally based critiques of the liberal norms. Since the 1990s, the claims and subjects of human rights have been expanded to previously unrecognized groups such as children and indigenous peoples. Islamic and Confucian cultural critiques of the liberal Western basis of human rights were largely transcended at the global level at the 1993 United Nations' (UN) Vienna Conference on Human Rights, which declared a consensus that human rights are "universal, indivisible, and interdependent" (although such challenges reappear regularly in selected states' defenses against international criticism). By the 21st century, international human rights enforcement mechanisms had been strengthened significantly—but only in the core domain of massive and systematic violations of life and liberty by government action of pariah states.

Defining Rights and Setting Standards

Like other forms of international law, human rights standards are a mélange of explicit treaties, customary international law, pilot domestic standards, and scholarly interpretation. For example, in assessing Spain's 1998 request for the extradition of former Chilean dictator Augusto Pinochet from Britain to face charges of crimes against humanity, a British court considered its obligations under the Convention Against Torture, the European Court of Human Rights, Chile's own amnesty and claims of sovereignty, British legislation, and expert testimony. The Universal Declaration and the twin International Covenants are considered to encompass a comprehensive foundation, with more specific standards and jurisdiction developed by the more widely subscribed phenomenon-based treaties: the Geneva Conventions on war crimes, the Convention Against Torture, the Genocide Treaty, and the International Convention on the Elimination of All Forms of Racial Discrimination. Another set of treaties is linked to vulnerable populations; they establish valuable benchmarks and monitoring obligations but are less widely accepted and less effective sources of pressure on states: the Convention on the Elimination of Discrimination Against Women, the Convention on the Rights of the Child, and Refugee Convention. The most recent 21st-century international norms, the Universal Declaration on the Rights of Indigenous Peoples and the UN Convention on the Rights of Persons with Disability, establish new populations of international concern but still struggle for broad recognition.

The conceptual core of human rights standards is to provide protection and empowerment against evolving threats to human dignity. To meet this mandate, fundamental human rights must be universal and inalienable—immune from contingent variations in geography and political conditions. Such rights must be enforced by the international system that provides a safety net for uneven citizenship regimes, incorporates increasing numbers of displaced persons and noncitizens, and acts to check rogue states. But international rights are also meaningless without international duties. In this sense, the key emerging debate on enforcement is the Responsibility to Protect doctrine (approved by the UN in 2005), which proposes a broad but important obligation on member states to act collectively where the state cannot or will not, in cases of massive and gross violations of fundamental rights.

Patterns of Abuse

If human rights violations are a form of political pathology, the search for a remedy begins with the study of the symptoms and analysis of the causes. The study of patterns of abuse has become a subfield of international relations and several social sciences. Violations can be measured and monitored by a combination of testimonies of survivors and witnesses, government records, country case studies, statistical patterns of demographic records and potential correlations with determinants of abuse, and forensic anthropology of gravesites.

War crimes such as massacres of civilians and torture of prisoners of war are often associated with counterinsurgency struggles and participation of paramilitary forces on both sides, which constitute an increasing proportion of conflicts. While state-sponsored slavery was almost eliminated by the 20th century through international cooperation, state-tolerated forced labor by private parties along with associated trafficking in persons has actually increased in the 21st century, in tandem with the pressures of globalization. Genocide, the attempt to systematically eliminate a population defined by identity characteristics, has also experienced a lamentable revival in the aftermath of the Cold War. Genocide is associated with recent defeat in international war, the collapse of hegemonic influence, and competitive political mobilization by "ethnic entrepreneurs"—and can rarely be attributed primarily to "ancient hatreds." Moreover, mass expulsions of ethnic cleansing often spill across borders to create new zones of conflict, as Rwandan refugees contributed to the epochal war in the Democratic Republic of Congo (DRC). Massive numbers of political prisoners and gulag-like prison complexes are characteristic of dictatorships, especially totalitarian regimes such as communist North Korea or theocratic Iran, and increasingly concentrated within such regimes. However, Amnesty International estimates that around half of all states practice torture with some regularity, and this includes some democracies—especially recent democracies in the developing world. High levels of social inequality and low levels of judicial accountability are the leading factors associated with the systematic occurrence of torture, especially in Latin America. Discrimination by race, religion, caste, gender, and national origin is still endemic and often state supported in South Asia and the Middle East, while even some democratic developed countries generally respectful of their own citizens have responded to high levels of migration with discriminatory policies that violate international standards.

Remedies: The International Human Rights Regime

The ensemble of local, national, and global human rights organizations has been labeled an "international human rights regime"—an issue-specific pattern of global governance. There is no definitive enforcement of human rights, but critical combinations of various forms of transnational pressure have resulted in significant reforms, such as the demise of the apartheid system in South Africa. Human rights campaigns are often catalyzed by transnational issue networks that include social movements, international organizations, and experts, in fluid habitual exchanges that pressure states from above and below. Margaret Keck and Kathryn Sikkink depict human rights appeals as a "boomerang" launched by a powerless civil society that reaches around the state to secure transnational pressure, while Thomas Risse, Stephen Ropp, and Kathryn Sikkink propose a phased "spiral model" in which such pressure evolves through phases of state denial, normative lip service without policy change, then limited local empowerment, more systematic reform, and eventual state socialization and internalization of human rights norms.

At the global level, standard setting and monitoring by international organizations depend mostly on "naming and shaming"—but the vigor of China's efforts to avoid annual censure by the United Nations Human Rights Commission (UNHCR), including generous aid packages to influence the votes of member states, suggests that such symbolic diplomacy does have a diffuse impact on violators. In addition to the Commission (now Council), which considers country situations, each of the major treaties generates a member state reporting regime, such as the ICCPR's Human Rights Committee. Issue-specific UN rapporteurs conduct field visits and issue reports on abuses such as forced disappearance, which can be influential in international or bilateral sanctions, or even secure the release of prisoners highlighted by the reports. At the regional level, the European Union (EU), the Organization of American States (OAS), and the African Union also host Human Rights Commissions, which vary correspondingly from the highest to lowest level of activity, in accessibility to individual versus state complaints, and in mandated impact on member states' domestic policies. Bilateral diplomacy can also serve as an important source of signaling, especially by superpowers with influence over abusive regimes, and seems particularly useful in occasionally freeing prominent political prisoners or protecting officially stigmatized ethnic or religious groups (such as Soviet Jews). However, diplomatic pressure alone has proven relatively unavailing in addressing broader patterns of repression imbricated in the dominance of the target regime.

Transnational legal processes run the gamut from a global, to a regional, to a bilateral exercise of universal jurisdiction. The International Criminal Court (ICC), following the UN's postwar tribunals on Rwanda and the former Yugoslavia, is the only permanent universal body with jurisdiction over war crimes, genocide, and crimes against humanity. Its combination of an autonomous Prosecutor and Security Council referral, with the standard safeguard that it can act only when domestic remedies are exhausted, has secured the participation of more than 100 member states—but not the United States. The ICC has been used mainly for war crimes in Africa since its 2002 activation. The EU and OAS also have human rights courts with contentious jurisdiction and the ability to levy sanctions against member states. Since treaties such as the Convention Against Torture and domestic mechanisms such as the U.S. Torture Victims' Protection Act grant willing states universal jurisdiction to prosecute foreign nationals in their own domestic courts for crimes against humanity committed abroad, several states have also secured national-level criminal or civil judgments against fallen dictators and war criminals (such as Argentine generals). The Spanish judge Baltasar Garzon, who brought the Pinochet case, has been particularly active in testing the parameters of transnational legal accountability in a variety of cases.

Global economic sanctions have been issued in a few of the most egregious cases of gross violations by pariah states but have sometimes had a contradictory humanitarian impact even where consensus was achieved. Bilateral diplomacy and sanctions have been more widespread and influential, including trade and investment limitations, foreign aid conditionality, and limitations on military assistance to repressive regimes. While the U.S. Office of the Treasury sanctions dozens of states each year, only a proportion of sanctions are based on human rights violations—but they include gross violators such as Burma, North Korea, and Sudan. Although U.S. foreign assistance legislation, such as the Kennedy, Harkin, and Leahy amendments, specifies that neither development nor military assistance should be given to violators, these limits have been very unevenly enforced and often overridden on national security grounds by the executive; however, the *threat* of suspension of aid has occasionally secured investigations, accountability, and even a reduction in violations by client states. The corresponding carrot for the stick of economic sanctions is human rights–directed foreign assistance, such as governance aid and support for global or recipient country human rights organizations. The Nordic countries, the Netherlands, and Canada have vital and effective programs of human rights foreign aid, training, and civil society promotion.

The ultimate enforcement of human rights is armed intervention against the violating authority. While the UN Security Council can authorize intervention in response to massive crimes against humanity, in practice the UN has acted only in the aftermath of regime collapse or conflict resolution—and UN peacekeeping forces on the ground as violations unfolded notably failed to protect victims in Bosnia, Rwanda, or Timor. More muscular interventions by the North Atlantic Treaty Organization (NATO) against abusive regimes did halt violence and contribute to subsequent return of refugees in Kosovo and Afghanistan but with controversial civilian casualties. Attempts to regionalize intervention in African conflicts have foundered most recently in Darfur. Unilateral interventions without multilateral consensus are often questioned as a selective rationalization of national interest on spurious humanitarian grounds, but it must be noted that the countervailing interests of neighboring powers afflicted by spillover violence have been the only check on some of the worst violations, such as the Cambodian genocide halted by a Vietnamese invasion or the murderous regime of Uganda's Idi Amin displaced by Tanzania.

International human rights movements monitor, lobby, protest, and reform human rights around the world—usually in conjunction with local organizations and victims. The flagship global organization Amnesty International, established in 1961 to advocate for "prisoners of conscience," now comprises millions of members in more than 150 countries—and has secured the freedom of around one third of its subjects from diverse regimes. Along with peers such as Human Rights Watch, Amnesty's nonpartisan annual reports on country conditions and monitoring of conflict situations and emerging abuses often influence global and bilateral condemnations and sanctions. Country-specific campaigns, increasingly mobilized via the Internet, are credited with shielding some local advocates and pressuring vulnerable repressive governments for limited reform. An additional element of advocacy mobilizes transnational identities, such as trade unionists defending their threatened colleagues in Colombia, Christians pressing for religious freedom in China, and women's groups campaigning to have genocidal rape designated as a war crime by the International Criminal Court. Local human rights movements generally seek to transcend political and ascriptive identities and derive their power from a combination of Gandhian nonviolent collective action and globalized information politics. Such protests contributed strongly to transitions to democracy in many Latin American countries, South Africa, and the Philippines, and former political prisoners became the first democratic leaders of Poland, the Czech Republic, South Korea, and Timor. Human rights campaigns dedicated to identifying new genres of transnational abuse have introduced new forms of leverage through boycotts and new mechanisms of global governance such as codes of conduct for multinationals to limit labor abuses and an international certification scheme to stem the trade in "blood diamonds," whose illicit export contributed to war crimes in several notorious African conflicts.

Human Rights Reform

When the international human rights regime is successful, states engage in human rights reform. Human rights reform can be studied from a policy design, comparative, or transnational perspective—since such reforms have often been diffused or implemented by global as well as national institutions. Retrospective accountability for abuses committed in a prior war or dictatorship is labeled "transitional justice" and generally consists of some combination of investigation ("truth commissions"), adjudication, and reparations. Human rights literature is replete with debates on the effectiveness and impact on regime stability of different forms of transitional justice, from Argentina's maximalist trials of former military rulers that led to rebellions to South Africa's explicit trade-off of truth for justice. Postconflict accountability is increasingly implemented by a hybrid blend of global and national institutions, as in Cambodia and Sierra Leone, which marks an evolution of sovereignty and international law.

New democracies and regimes responding to civil rights campaigns against chronic discrimination also establish forward-looking institutions and policies to improve citizen rights. National human rights institutions for domestic monitoring of policies as well as practices relevant to human rights, mandated by the UN under the Paris Principles, were originally established by Western European democracies but have diffused to dozens of states in Latin America and Asia. Such human rights institutes sometimes overlap with and sometimes replace ombudsman offices, which are empowered to independently investigate and represent citizens (and in some cases, migrants) against allegations of abuse by any government agency. Finally, programs of human rights education for agents of authority, vulnerable groups, schoolchildren, or the general population are promoted by global agencies such as the UN High Commissioner for Human Rights, regional bodies such as the Organization for Security and Co-operation in Europe's High Commissioner on National Minorities, and national governments seeking to implement international human rights norms.

Challenges

While the struggle for fundamental human dignity has advanced tremendously in the years since the Universal Declaration, challenges to the theory and practice of human rights continue. Since human rights are based in a liberal legal model of the primacy of the public individual, cultural, sociological, and even feminist critiques of universalism question the rights' relevance for the pursuit of disparate collective social goals and identities. During eras of renewed conflict, especially the unconventional transnational threat of terrorism, states revive old arguments about national security trumping inalienable rights—and human rights scholarship contests the rationale and record of such logics. Critics and campaigners alike note the increasing salience of abuses committed by private actors who are not accountable under the "government and opposition" model the international human rights regime was created to address: from multinational sweatshops, to private security contractors, to patriarchal religious authorities. Moreover, many abusive situations result from a lack rather than a surfeit of state authority. Human rights advocates and theorists respond that these concerns suggest the need to expand human rights norms and mechanisms, not abandon them. While human rights has not halted "death by government" or other systematic abuses of power, it has proven to be a resilient tool for the voiceless and vulnerable to often endure and occasionally prevail.

Alison Brysk
University of California, Irvine
Irvine, California, United States

See also Civil Society; Ethics; Genocide; Governance, Global; Human Rights, Comparative Perspectives; Indigenous Peoples' Rights; International Law; International Regimes; Intervention, Humanitarian; Normative Theory in International Relations; Rights; Rule of Law; Sovereignty

Further Readings

Brysk, A. (2005). *Human rights and private wrongs.* New York: Routledge.

Donnelly, J. (2007). *International human rights.* Boulder, CO: Westview.

Falk, R., Elver, H., & Hajjar, L. (2007). *Human rights: Critical concepts in political science.* New York: Routledge.

Forsythe, D. (2006). *International human rights in theory and practice.* Cambridge, UK: Cambridge University Press.

Keck, M., & Sikkink, K. (1998). *Activists beyond borders.* Ithaca, NY: Cornell University Press.

Landman, T. (2006). *Studying human rights.* New York: Routledge.

Risse, T., Ropp, S., & Sikkink, K. (Eds.). (1999). *The power of human rights.* Cambridge, UK: Cambridge University Press.

Steiner, H. J., Alston, P., & Goodman, R. (Eds.). (2008). *International human rights in context: Law, politics, and morality.* Oxford, UK: Oxford University Press.

Hybrid Regimes

The notion of hybrid regimes—that is, regimes that were characterized by the presence at the same time of key aspects of different models or types of regimes—has been present in the classic political science literature for years (Samuel E. Finer, 1970). The basic change in recent decades is the increase in the number and variety of hybrid regimes as a side effect of the widespread phenomenon of democratization in all areas of the world. This entry clarifies the notion, points out how to distinguish hybrid regimes from transitional phases, and builds on existing empirical research to show the varieties of hybridism in contemporary times.

Meaning

As regards the term *regime*, consideration is given here to all government institutions and norms that are either formalized or are informally recognized as existing in a given territory with respect to a given population. While formal and informal institutions may no longer configure some form of nondemocracy and do not yet configure a complete democracy, they still bear traces of the previous political reality. In addition, to have something that may be labeled a regime, at least minimal stabilization is needed. This is the key aspect differentiating a regime from transition phases, which are characterized by short duration. The precise length of time that is considered necessary before classifying something as a regime rather than a transitional phase is arbitrarily—but reasonably—stipulated.

Such a regime does not fulfill the minimalist requirements of a democracy, such as (a) universal suffrage, both male and female; (b) free, competitive, recurrent, and fair elections; (c) more than one party; and (d) different and alternative media sources. One important aspect of this definition is that in the absence of just one of these requirements, or if at some point one of them is no longer met, there is no longer a democratic regime but another political and institutional setup marked by varying degrees of uncertainty and ambiguity. Moreover, in a democracy, be it only minimal, institutions and rights should not be subject to, or conditioned by, nonelected actors or exponents of other external regimes. The former refers to the armed forces, religious hierarchies, economic oligarchies, a hegemonic party, or even a monarch with pretensions to influencing decision-making processes or the overall functioning of the democracy; in the latter case, a regime might be conditioned by an external power that deprives the democracy of its independence and sovereignty by pursuing nondemocratic policies.

In addition, such a regime does not have the key aspects of nondemocratic regimes, and a basic reference must be made at least to traditional and authoritarian regimes. The former are based on the personal power of the sovereign, who binds his underlings in a relationship of fear and reward; they are typically *legibus soluti* regimes, where the sovereign's arbitrary decisions are not limited by norms and do not need to be justified ideologically. Power is thus used in particularistic forms and for essentially private ends. In these regimes, the armed forces and police play a central role, while there is an evident lack of developed ideology and mass mobilization. Basically, then, the political setup is dominated by traditional elites and institutions. As for the authoritarian regimes, the definition advanced by Juan Linz is still the most useful one: a political system with limited, nonresponsible political pluralism; without an elaborated and guiding ideology but with distinctive mentalities; without either extensive or intense political mobilization, except at some points in their development; and in which a leader, or, occasionally, a small group, exercises power from within formally ill-defined, but actually quite predictable, limits. However, with respect to such a definition, which identifies five significant dimensions—limited pluralism, distinctive values, low political mobilization, a small leading group, ill-defined but predictable limits to citizens' rights—we need to stress the constraints imposed on political pluralism within a society that has no recognized autonomy or independence as well as no effective political participation of the people, with the consequent exercise of various forms of state suppression.

Having considered definitions for minimalist democracy, traditional regime, and authoritarianism, it is now possible to define *hybrid regimes*. As suggested by Terry L. Karl (1995) in relation to some Latin American countries, they may be characterized by "uneven acquisition of procedural requisites of democracy," without "civilian control over the military," with sectors of the population that "remain politically and economically disenfranchised" and with a "weak judiciary" (p. 80). But this definition refers only to authoritarianisms that partially lose some of their key characteristics, retain some authoritarian or traditional features, and at the same time acquire some of the characteristic institutions and procedures of democracy. A hybrid regime, on the other hand, may also have a set of institutions where, going down the inverse path, some key elements of democracy have been lost and authoritarian characteristics have been acquired. Thus, an adequate definition has to be completed by, for example, including some of the aspects that can be recurrent in authoritarian situation, such as the existence of incumbents who routinely abuse state resources, deny the opposition fair media coverage, harass opposition candidates and their supporters, and in some cases manipulate electoral results.

This discussion, however, prompts reflection about two elements. First, a hybrid regime is always a set of ambiguous institutions that maintain aspects of the past. Second, it is, consequently, a "corruption" of the preceding regime, lacking as it does one or more essential characteristics of that regime but also failing to acquire other characteristics that would make it fully democratic or authoritarian. Consequently, the term *hybrid* can be applied to all regimes preceded by a period of authoritarian or traditional rule followed by the beginnings of greater tolerance, liberalization, and a partial relaxation of the restrictions on pluralism or all regimes that, following a period of minimal democracy in the sense indicated above, are subject to the intervention of nonelected bodies—the military, above all—that place restrictions on competitive pluralism without, however, creating a more or less stable authoritarian regime. Moreover, in disentangling empirical realities that fit the previously formulated definition of the hybrid regime from different transitional situations, it should be stressed that there has been some sort of stabilization or duration, perhaps at least a decade, of those ambiguous, uncertain institutional setups. Consequently, to avoid a misleading analysis of democratization processes, a hybrid regime can be defined as a set of institutions that have been persistent, whether stable or unstable, for about a decade; have been preceded by authoritarian rule, a traditional regime (possibly with colonial characteristics), or even a minimal democracy; and are characterized by the breakup of limited pluralism and forms of independent, autonomous participation, but with the absence of at least one of the four aspects of a minimal democracy.

A Classification

On the basis of the previous definition, then, a crucial aspect of hybrid regimes is that there may be (or there may emerge) veto players—that is, individual or collective actors who are influential or decisive in maintaining the regime in its characteristic state of ambiguity and uncertainty. These actors may be an external, foreign power that interferes in the politics of the nation; a monarch or authoritarian ruler who has come to power through more or less violent means; the armed forces; a hegemonic party run by a small group or a single leader; religious hierarchies; economic oligarchies; and other powerful groups or a mixture of such actors, who are either unable or unwilling to eliminate other prodemocratic actors, assuming that in the majority of current hybrid regimes the alternative is between democracy and nondemocracy.

From this perspective, an effective classification should focus on the legacy of the previous regime and the constraints preventing a country from becoming a minimal democracy. Thus, the types of hybrid regimes that develop depend directly on the classifications of authoritarian regimes and democracies that have already been established and the factors that prevent democratic change. The core assumption of this typology is that traditional and democratic regimes can, by virtue of their characteristics, give rise to different results, while it is more likely that the survival of authoritarian veto players points toward a single solution.

However, when switching from theoretical hypotheses to empirical analysis (see Leonardo Morlino, 2009), three analytic axes emerge with clarity: a first one where electoral process, political pluralism and participation, freedom of expression and beliefs, and freedom of association and organization are grouped together closely; a second where state functioning stands alone; and a third one, conceptually close to the second one, where rule of law and personal autonomy are also strongly connected. Additional empirical analysis shows how three models can result by merging the second and third components also. Thus, the first model of hybrid regime, termed *limited democracy*, derives from the first component and is characterized by universal suffrage, a formally correct electoral procedure, and elective posts occupied on the basis of elections and a multiparty system but where civil rights are constrained by the police or other effective forms of suppression. Consequently, there is no actual political opposition and, above all, the media are compromised by a situation of monopoly to the point that part of the population is effectively prevented from exercising their rights. The notion of limited democracy is also well developed by Wigell (2008). The second empirical model is that of *democracies without law* or *democracy without a state*, as the state can be conceived of as a government based on the primacy of the law, where there are no relevant legacies or powerful veto players or any forms of state suppression or nonguarantee of rights but simply a situation of widespread illegality in which the state is incapable of performing properly due to poorly functioning institutions. Limited democracies and democracies without state are confirmed as empirically relevant classes for which different, contrasting elements need to be stressed: on the one hand, the lack of an effective guarantee of rights despite the presence of state institutions and, on the other hand, the lack of the rule of law and of a functioning state, with laws that are not applied because the judiciary has no effective independence, there is widespread corruption, and the bureaucracy is flawed and inefficient. The third model suggested by empirical research is that of *quasi democracies* characterized by regimes where all main aspects mentioned above are deeply rooted in ambiguity: There is illegality and at the same time partial constraints in the effective guarantee of rights. This model is the most empirically relevant one (see Morlino, 2009).

Conclusion

On the grounds of existing empirical analyses, hybrid regimes are a reality and empirically support an autonomous model of regime vis-à-vis democracy, authoritarianism, and the traditional regime. The three models of hybridism developed through empirical analysis suggest that the most significant empirical problem is to ensure the existence of institutions that are capable of performing their functions. Hence, there are countries where strengthening of the state and/or promoting more effective guarantee of rights might transform the regimes into democracies.

Leonardo Morlino
LUISS Guido Carli
Rome, Italy

See also Authoritarian Regimes; Democracy, Theories of; Democratization; International Regimes; Transition

Further Readings

Diamond, L. (2002). Thinking about hybrid regimes. *Journal of Democracy, 13*(2), 25–31.
Finer, S. E. (1970). *Comparative government.* Harmondsworth, UK: Penguin.
Karl, T. (1995). The hybrid regimes of Central America. *Journal of Democracy, 6*(3), 72–86.
Morlino, L. (2009). Are there hybrid regimes? Or are they just an optical illusion? *European Political Science Review, 1*(2), 273–296.
Wigell, M. (2008). Mapping "hybrid regimes": Regime types and concepts in comparative politics. *Democratization, 15*(2), 230–250.

Hypothesis Testing

The primary means of conveying the strength of empirical findings in political science is the null hypothesis significance test (NHST). This paradigm, along with its strengths and weaknesses, is therefore important for nearly every quantitative study in political science. This entry reviews the current hypothesis testing paradigm and its history, discusses the underused idea of statistical power from tests, and points out some common misinterpretations of hypothesis testing.

The Current Paradigm: Null Hypothesis Significance Testing

The current approach to hypothesis testing in all of the social sciences is a synthesis of the Fisher test of significance and the Neyman-Pearson hypothesis test. In this 20th-century procedure, two hypotheses are set forth: a null or restricted hypothesis, H_0, which is set against an alternative or research hypothesis, H_1. Thus, they are supposed to describe two complementary notions about some political science phenomenon of interest. The research hypothesis is the probability model that describes the author's belief about this phenomenon and is typically operationalized through statements about an unknown parameter $\theta \in \Theta$. In the most basic and common setup, the null hypothesis asserts that $\theta = 0$, and the research hypothesis asserts that $\theta \neq 0$. Such a two-sided test is the overwhelming default in assessing the statistical reliability of individual regression parameters.

Once the hypotheses are established, a test statistic T, some function of θ and the data, is calculated and assessed with the distribution under the assumption that H_0 is true. Commonly used test statistics are sample means, $\bar{X}$; chi-square statistics from tabular analysis, χ^2; and t statistics in linear and generalized linear models. Note that the sample space of the test statistic must correspond to the support of the specified null and alternative distributions. The key idea is that test statistics that appear to be "unusual" for the null distribution (e.g., those in the tails) cast doubt on the original assumption that this is the true distribution.

The test procedure ϕ assigns one of two decisions, D_0 and D_1, to all possible values in the sample space of the statistic T, corresponding to supporting either H_0 or H_1, respectively. The p value (also called the associated probability) is equal to the area in the tail (or tails) of the assumed distribution under H_0, which starts at the point determined by T on the horizontal axis and continues to positive or negative infinity. If a predetermined significance level α has been specified, then H_0 is rejected for p values less than α; otherwise, the p value itself is reported. More formally, the sample space of T is split into two complementary regions, S_0 and S_1, such that the probability that T falls in S_1, causing decision D_1, is either a predetermined null hypothesis cumulative distribution function (CDF) level (α = size of the test, Neyman-Pearson) or the CDF level corresponding to the value of the test statistic under H_0 is reported as follows:

$$p \text{ value} = \int_{S_1} P_{H_0}(T = t)dt \quad \text{(Fisher)}.$$

Thus, decision D_1 is made if the test statistic is sufficiently atypical given the distribution under H_0. This process is illustrated for a one-tailed test at $\alpha = .05$ in Figure 1.

Historical Background

The current NHST is a blend of two extremely important but incompatible schools of thought in 20th-century statistics. R. A. Fisher developed a procedure that gives significance levels from the data with the intention of possibly "nullifying" a straw man hypothesis, but Neyman and Pearson set up a very rigid decision-making process to arrive at one of two possible competing conclusions.

Fisher's Test of Significance

Originally Fisher, in 1935, developed his test of significance in the context of randomized experiments, where the physical act of randomization of units to treatment and control group is the basis for unbiased inference. Fisher posited a single and sharp null hypothesis, H_0. The simplest and most popular H_0 is that the treatment effect is zero for all units. Note that this H_0 is more restrictive than the usually tested null hypothesis that the *average* effect is zero across the sample. Under the sharp H_0, all (potential) values of the outcome variable under treatment and control can be either observed or inferred for each unit. Hence, the distribution of

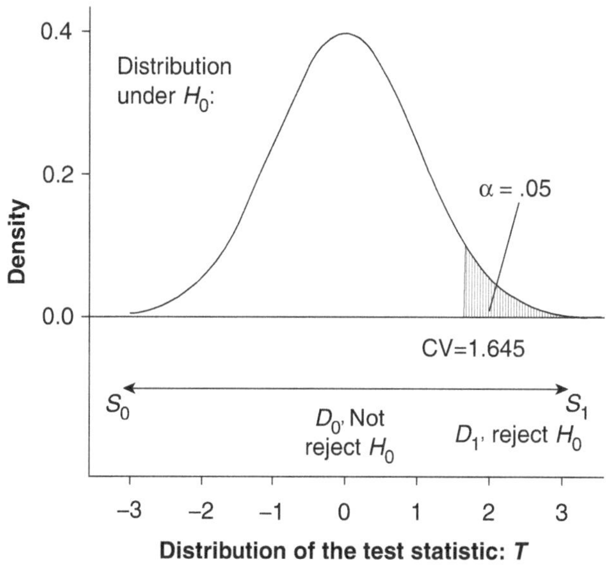

Figure 1 Null Hypothesis Significance Testing Illustrated

the statistic T is assumed to be known. Since the distribution of T is solely determined by randomization, it is called the *randomization distribution* of T. Using this distribution, one can compare the observed test statistic against its distribution under the null hypothesis. An observed value that is "very unlikely," given the null hypothesis and the implied randomization distribution, is taken as evidence against the null hypothesis in what is essentially a stochastic version of the "proof by contradiction," according to Guido Imbens and Don Rubin. More specifically, as the statistic moves away from its conditional expected value, $E(T|H_0)$, H_0 becomes progressively less plausible (less likely to occur by chance). However, as is shown below, the stochastic nature of this proof by contradiction creates some logical fallacies. The relationship between T and the level of significance produced by the test is established by the density outside the threshold established by T (one- or two-tailed), going away from the density region containing the expected value of T given H_0. The outside density is the p value, also called the *achieved* significance level. Fisher hypothesis testing is therefore summarized by the following steps:

1. Identify the null hypothesis.
2. Determine the appropriate test statistic and its distribution under the assumption that the null hypothesis is true.
3. Calculate the test statistic from the data.
4. Determine the achieved significance level that corresponds to the test statistic using the distribution under the assumption that the null is true.
5. Reject H_0 if the achieved significance level is sufficiently small. Otherwise, reach no firm conclusion.

The Fisher construct naturally leads to the question of what p value is sufficiently small as to warrant rejection of the null hypothesis. This measure of extremeness or what is considered as unlikely should be based on the specific application but involves necessarily some arbitrary judgments. Fisher established the CDF thresholds of .10, .05, and .01 as "convenient" and nothing more. Therefore, there is absolutely no scientific basis for making hypothesis test decisions at these levels whatsoever; they have merely become convention. This suggests a great amount of caution about making decisions about, say, .049 versus .051, a difference that is typically swamped by measurement error in the social sciences anyway.

Neyman and Pearson Hypothesis Testing

During the same period when Fisher was developing his exact test of significance based on the sharp H_0, Neyman and Pearson were interested in methods to estimate *average* treatment effects, such as $\theta = 0$ over the sample, and to construct confidence intervals around this estimate. They rejected Fisher's idea that only the sharp null hypothesis needs to be tested. Since only the assumption of the sharp null hypothesis allowed Fisher to derive the exact randomization distribution of T, Neyman and Pearson can only derive certain properties of this distribution. This is the price they have to pay to allow "nonsharp" hypotheses about average differences between, say, treatment and control groups. Neyman and Pearson argue that a more useful procedure is to propose two complementary hypotheses: Θ_A and Θ_B (or a class of Θ_B, such that $\Theta_A \cup \Theta_A = \Theta$), which need not be labeled "null" or "alternative" but often are purely for convenience. Furthermore, Neyman and Pearson point out that one can posit a hypothesis and consecutively test multiple admissible alternatives against this hypothesis. Since there are now two competing hypotheses in any one test, Neyman and Pearson can define an a priori–selected α, the probability of falsely rejecting Θ_A under the assumption that H_0 is true, and β, the probability of failing to reject Θ_A when H_0 is false. By convention, the first mistake is called a Type I error, and the second mistake is called a Type II error. Note that α and β are probabilities conditional on two mutually exclusive events: α is conditional on the null hypothesis being true, and β is conditional on the null hypothesis being false. A more useful quantity than β is $1 - \beta$, which Neyman and Pearson (1933, 1936) call the *power* of the test: the long-run probability of accurately rejecting a false null hypothesis given a point alternative hypothesis.

In this setup, we want to develop the test that has the highest power for a given a priori α. To state this more precisely, let the test function ϕ take on the values 1 if D_1 is reached under Θ_B and 0 if D_0 is reached under Θ_A. Hence, the set of data points or values of T for which $\phi = 1$ is equal to the region of rejection (this is only approximately true for randomization tests). For a given significance level α, the problem is to select a test ϕ such that $1 - \beta$ is maximized for all θ belonging to Θ_B subject to the condition that $E_\theta[\phi] \leq \alpha$ for all θ belonging to Θ_A.

To accomplish this goal, the researcher considers the fixed sample size, the desired significance level, and the research hypothesis, then employs the test with the greatest power. Neyman and Pearson's famous lemma shows that under certain conditions (a sufficient condition is that the probability density tested has a monotone likelihood ratio) there exists a "uniformly most powerful" test that has the greatest possible probability of rejecting a false null hypothesis in favor of a point alternative hypothesis, compared with other tests. Formally, this comparison employs the *power function* that is based on Type I and Type II error rates. Again, the probability of a Type I and Type II error can be stated as follows:

$$P(\text{Type I error}) = P(\text{reject } \Theta_A | \Theta_A \text{ is true})$$

$$P(\text{Type II error}) = P(\text{accept } \Theta_A | \Theta_B \text{ is true}) = 1 - P(\text{reject } \Theta_A | \Theta_B \text{ is true}).$$

The last expression gives the probability to reject Θ_A as a function of θ and builds the basis for the power function. If θ belongs to Θ_B then the power function gives the probability of making the right decision, that is, reject Θ_A. If θ belongs to Θ_B, then the power function gives the probability of a Type I error rate, which is smaller than or equal to α. Ideally, a power function of a one-sided test would be a step function, equaling 0 as long as θ belongs to Θ_A and equaling 1 as soon as θ belongs to Θ_B. It is already clear from the discussion above that this sharp and error-free distinction between Θ_A and Θ_B is impossible. However, the better a test, the steeper the slope of the power function between accepting Θ_A and accepting Θ_B. In general, the power of a test increases with the preset level α, the sample size, and greater difference between values from Θ_A and Θ_B. Figure 2 illustrates the power functions for a one-sided test. We use a normally distributed sample of size $N = 10$. We estimate the power function at $\mu = 105$ for Θ_A: $\mu = 100$ against Θ_B: $\mu > 100$ with a standard deviation of $\sigma = 10$ and varying values for α (.05, .01, .001).

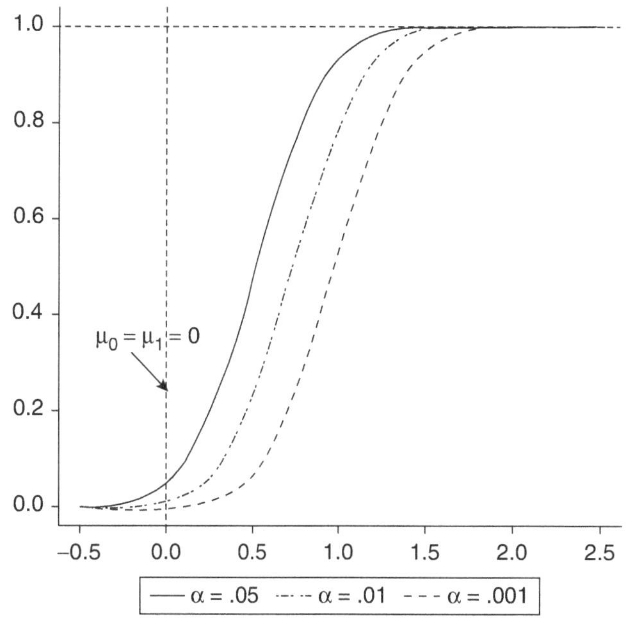

Figure 2 Power Function for a One-Sided Test; $\alpha = .05, .01$, and $.001$

Figure 3 illustrates the power functions for a normally distributed sample of varying size with $N = 10$, 20, and 100. Again, we estimate the power function at $\mu = 105$ for Θ_A: $\mu = 100$ against Θ_B: $\mu > 100$ with a standard deviation of $\sigma = 10$ and a fixed $\alpha = .05$. Again, the power functions are based on a one-sided test. The influence of the sample size on power is further discussed below.

In comparing the Neyman-Pearson approach with Fisher's exact test of significance, note how different the following steps are from Fisher's previously described steps:

1. Identify a hypothesis of interest, Θ_B, and a complementary hypothesis, Θ_A.
2. Determine the appropriate test statistic and its distribution under the assumption that Θ_A is true.
3. Specify a significance level (α) and determine the corresponding critical value of the test statistic under the assumption that Θ_A is true.

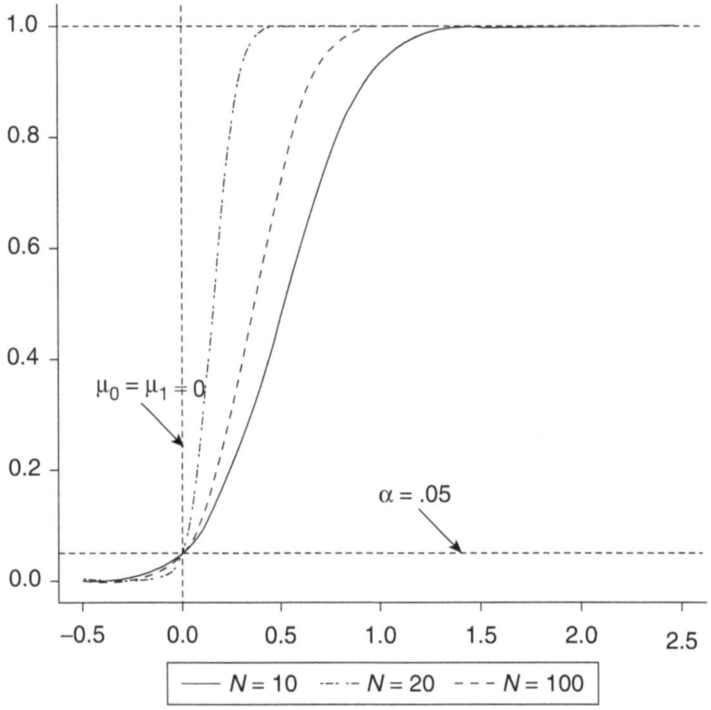

Figure 3 Power Function for a Normally Distributed Sample of Varying Size; $N = 10, 20,$ and 100

4. Calculate the test statistic from the data.
5. Reject Θ_A and accept Θ_B if the test statistic is more extreme than the critical value from the expected value of the test statistic (calculated under the assumption that Θ_A is true). Otherwise, accept Θ_A.

The Neyman-Pearson approach is important in the context of decision theory where the decision in the final step above is assigned a *risk function* computed as the expected loss from making an error. Most political scientists are surprised to see the word *accept* in this context since they are trained not to accept a null hypothesis, but Neyman and Pearson do not have a null; they have a partition of the decision space.

The Synthesis of Fisher and Neyman-Pearson

The NHST attempts to combine the two approaches described above giving a synthesized approach. There is no attributed authorship for this notion, and it appears to have come from textbook writers in the mid-20th century who may have been afraid to offend either Fisher or Neyman-Pearson (the conversation between these powerful voices was unusually vitriolic).

Neyman and Pearson's hypothesis test defines the significance level a priori as a function of the testing procedure and not as a function of the data. Conversely, Fisher's test of significance defines the significance level afterward as function of the *data* after the test. The current paradigm in the social sciences mixes these two approaches by pretending to select α a priori but actually using p values (or asterisks next to test statistics indicating ranges of p values) to evaluate the strength of the evidence. Thus, the NHST allows inclusion of the alternate hypothesis but precludes a search for a more powerful test.

The NHST also tries to reconcile the two differing perspectives on how the hypotheses are actually defined. It adopts the Neyman-Pearson convention of two explicitly stated rival hypotheses, but one is always labeled as the null hypothesis as in the Fisher test. In some introductory texts, the null hypothesis is presented only as a null relationship: $\theta = 0$ (no effect), whereas Fisher intended the null hypothesis simply as a straw man to be "nullified." The NHST pretends to use the Neyman-Pearson decision process except that failing to reject the null hypothesis is treated as a quasi decision: "modest" support for the null hypothesis assertion. There is also confusion in the synthesized test about *p* values as long-run probabilities. Since the *p* value or range of *p* values, indicated by asterisks, is not set a priori, it is not the long-run probability of making a Type I error but is typically treated as such, even with a single sample and a single test. Neither Fisher nor Neyman and Pearson would have been satisfied with the synthesis. Fisher objected to Neyman and Pearson's preselection of the significance level as well as the mandatory two-outcome decision process. Neyman and Pearson disagreed with Fisher's interpretation of *p* values.

Underlying Problems With the Null Hypothesis Significance Test

The basis of the NHST rests on the logical argument of *modus tollens* (denying the consequent) but adds a necessary probabilistic aspect:

If *X*, then *Y* is highly likely.

Y is not observed.

Therefore, *X* is highly unlikely.

This logic seems at first to be plausible. Yet it is a fallacy to assert that obtaining data that are atypical under a given assumption implies that the assumption is likely false: Almost a contradiction of the null hypothesis does not imply that the null hypothesis is almost false. This means that the NHST rests on a fundamentally flawed logical basis. The remaining issues in this section are merely common misinterpretations.

The Inverse Probability Problem

A common interpretive problem with null hypothesis significance testing is a misunderstanding of the order of the conditional probability. Many people have a belief, which stems directly from Fisher's perspective, that the smaller the *p* value, the greater the probability that the null hypothesis is false. This incorrect interpretation is that the NHST produces $P(H_0|D)$: the probability of H_0 being true given the observed data *D*. But the NHST first posits H_0 as true and then asks what the probability of observing these or more extreme data is. This is clearly $P(D|H_0)$. In fact, a more desirable test would be one that produces $P(H_0|D)$, because then we could simply search for the hypothesis with the greatest probability of being true given some observed data. Bayes's law clarifies the difference between these two unequal probabilities:

$$P(H_0|D) = \frac{P(H_0)}{P(D)} P(D|H_0).$$

The two quantities, $P(D|H_0)$ and $P(H_0|D)$, are equal only if $P(H_0) = P(D)$, and there is absolutely no theoretical justification supporting such an equality.

Significance Driven by Sample Size

There are two misinterpretations about the role of sample size in null hypothesis significance testing. First is the belief that statistical significance in a large sample study implies real-world importance. Many have observed that an NHST based on a large sample size almost always results in statistical significance (Macdonald, 1997). This is a concern in political science research since we do not want to infer that some subfields have greater legitimacy just because the corresponding data sets tend to produce smaller *p* values: "a prejudice against the null" (Greenwald, 1975, p. 1).

The second misinterpretation is that for a given *p* value in a study that rejects the null hypothesis, larger sample sizes imply more reliable results. This is false: Two studies that reject the null with the same *p* value are equally likely to make a Type I error even if they have dramatically different sample sizes. This mistake results from a poor understanding of Type II errors. Unlike the case above, two studies that fail to reject the null hypothesis are identical in every way except that the sample sizes are qualitatively different. The test with the larger sample size is less likely to make a Type II error since the sample size is always in the denominator of the equation for statistical significance. To show why this is true, Figure 4 displays two tests for H_0: $\mu = 0$ versus H_1: $\mu > 0$, with sample sizes of 9 and 12, respectively, and the true distribution normal (3, 3). The shaded region is the area under the true sampling distribution of $\bar{X}$ to the left of the area determined by setting $\alpha = .05$ under the false assumption that H_0 is true.

Thus, the shaded region is the probability we would fail to reject the false H_0 (i.e., $\beta = P(\text{Type II error})$). It is clear from Figure 4 that the probability of a Type II error is much lower for the test with a larger sample size, even though the probability of a Type I error is identical. The area under the true sampling distribution of $\bar{X}$ in either panel of Figure 4 not shaded is equal to $1 - \beta = 1 - P(\text{Type II error})$, which is the power of the test. It follows from above that the second test with a larger sample size has greater power.

Replication Fallacy

Another misinterpretation of null hypothesis significance testing is the belief that one minus the p value is the probability of replication (producing significant results in repeated iterations of the same study). This is equivalent to the two misconceptions: $P(H_0) = \alpha$ and $P(H_1) = 1 - \alpha$. The term *replication fallacy* describes the wrong belief that a low p value such as $p = .05$ implies that 95 out of 100 replications will be statistically significant. The error is obvious when one recalls that $p = P(D|H_0)$ and is thus a function of a single data set producing a single test statistic.

Asymmetry and Accepting the Null Hypothesis

Failing to reject the null hypothesis does not rule out an infinite number of other competing research hypotheses. Null hypothesis significance testing is asymmetric: If the test statistic is sufficiently atypical given the null hypothesis then the null hypothesis is rejected, but if the test statistic is insufficiently atypical given the null hypothesis then the null hypothesis is not accepted. This is a double standard: H_1 is held innocent until proven guilty, and H_0 is held guilty until proven innocent. Despite the fact that it is very risky to accept implicitly or

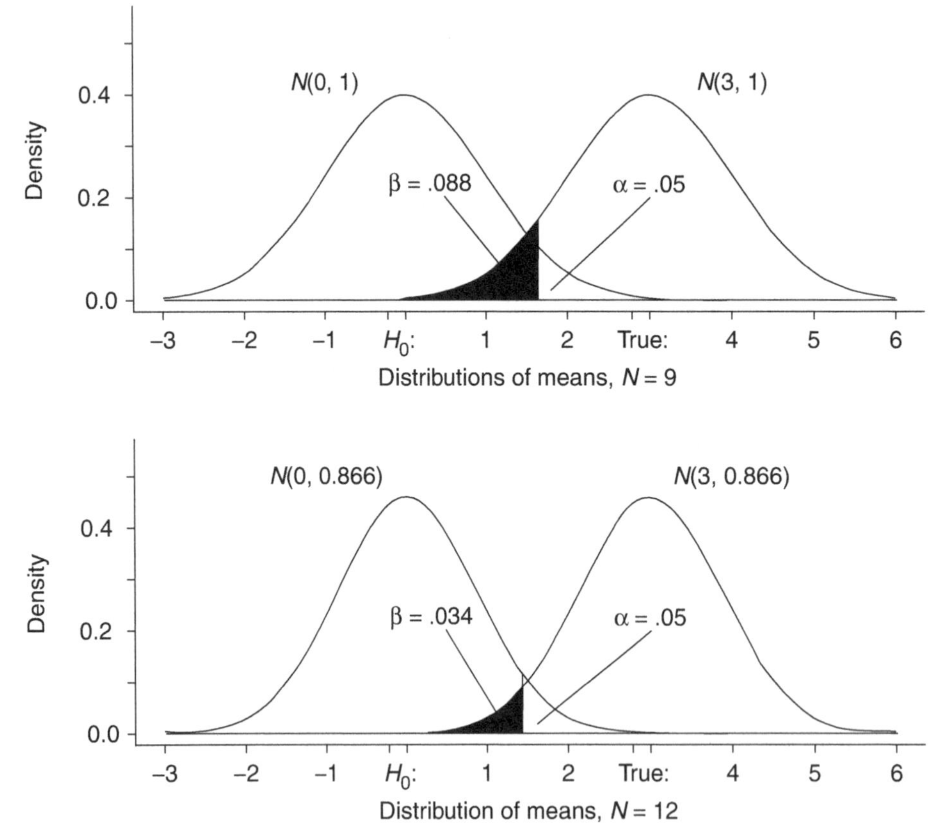

Figure 4 Type II Errors for $\bar{X}$, Differing Sample Sizes

expressly the conclusion from a nonrejected null hypothesis, such instances are common.

There are two problems that develop as a result of asymmetry. The first is a misinterpretation of the asymmetry to assert that finding a nonstatistically significant difference or effect is evidence that it is equal to zero or nearly zero. This acceptance of the null hypothesis is damaging because it inhibits the exploration of competing research hypotheses. The second problem pertains to the correct interpretation of failing to reject the null hypotheses. Failing to reject the null hypothesis essentially provides almost no information about the state of the world. It simply means that given the evidence at hand one cannot make an assertion about a relationship: All you can conclude is that you *can't* conclude that the null was false (Cohen, 1962).

Dominik Hangartner
University of California, Berkeley
Berkeley, California, United States

Jeff Gill
Washington University in St. Louis
St. Louis, Missouri, United States

See also Quantitative Methods, Basic Assumptions; Sampling, Random and Nonrandom; Statistical Significance; Statistics: Overview

Further Readings

Cohen, J. (1962). The statistical power of abnormal-social psychological research: A review. *Journal of Abnormal and Social Psychology, 65,* 145–153.

Fisher, R. (1935). *The design of experiments.* Edinburgh, UK: Oliver & Boyd.

Greenwald, A. G. (1975). Consequences of prejudice against the null hypothesis. *Psychological Bulletin, 82,* 1–20.

Imbens, G. W., & Rubio, D. B. (in press). *Causal inference in statistics and social sciences.* Cambridge, UK: Cambridge University Press.

Macdonald, R. R. (1997, May). On statistical testing in psychology. *British Journal of Psychology, 88*(2), 333–349.

Neyman, J., & Pearson, E. S. (1933). On the problem of the most efficient test of statistical hypotheses. *Philosophical Transactions of the Royal Statistical Society, Series A, 231,* 289–337.

Neyman, J., & Pearson, E. S. (1936). Contributions to the theory of testing statistical hypotheses. *Statistical Research Memorandum, 1,* 1–37.

I

Idealism

As a category in metaphysics, "idealism" usually refers at the most general level to the proposition that "reality" is in some sense mental rather than material. In political philosophy/theory, idealism refers to theories that hold concepts and propositions to be the constitutive and determining factors in politics, a claim that includes the belief that "material" processes are actually mental at root. Normatively, idealists tend to hold that the values by which personal and political conduct should be judged are in some sense "spiritual," usually founded on some notion of human nature that individuals are innately driven to realize in their daily lives. They also tend to reject utilitarianism, claiming that it celebrates man's animality rather than his inchoate humanity or, in many cases, immanent "divinity." That noted, idealists have tended to hold theological beliefs that were heterodox at best or even atheistic. Beyond these very general claims, little is shared by those political theories that are commonly labeled "idealist," aside from certain common misinterpretations made by nonidealists. For example, there is no necessary requirement to understand the world "idealistically"—that is, as ultimately "good," peaceful, or providentially ordered. Similarly, there is no common tendency to deny the existence of the external world outside of thought (the denial that is most associated with Berkeleyian solipsism). Instead, what is characteristically at issue is one's understanding of the concept of "reality," especially social reality. Idealists tend to hold that the closest one can get to any mind-independent world "out there" are the various (interpreted) sensations excited by (it seems) that world in our consciousnesses. Consequently, one can only analyze with even a modicum of precision those sensations and the ideas to which they give rise. Hence, the realms of human conduct such as social life, politics, aesthetics, and economics are constructs of the mind but are no less real for that (in fact, they are real because they are such constructions). Counterfactually, humans have no direct access to an underlying material world, meaning that the only "reality" that one can become aware of and can analyze and criticize rationally is the mental reality of interpreted thought.

Plato (ca. 428–348 BCE) was the first recorded idealist political philosopher. He claimed the world that we perceive is made up of imperfect ideas, which are themselves copies of a world of purely mental entities, each of which forms part of a single eternal coherent system of concepts, ordered with reference to the "Form of the Good." Only that single system is real, and our actual, imperfect ideas at best imitate what is real, and do so only to the extent that they reproduce elements of that system. To the extent that our beliefs do not match the eternal system of concepts, they trap us in mere opinion and error. This claim has highly significant ethical and political implications. According to Plato, the good life is one lived in accordance with the virtues of wisdom, courage, moderation, and justice, with the last of these being achieved through the correct ordering of the first three virtues within the individual's soul and within the life of the ancient Greek city-state or polis. Possibly on grounds of its impracticality rather than on philosophical grounds, Plato's later political works (*The Laws* and *The Statesman*) replaced the *Republic*'s system of rule by "guardians" with systems relying on greater constitutional checks. Nevertheless, many scholars have seen even these later books as totalitarian models.

There were many philosophically significant idealists in the centuries after Plato, most notably Neo-Platonists such as Plotinus (ca. 205–270 CE) and Iamblichus (ca. 250–325 CE), Cambridge Platonists including Ralph Cudworth (1617–1688) and Richard Cumberland (1631–1718), and the solipsistic idealist Bishop George Berkeley (1685–1753). Nevertheless, after Plato, the next significant idealist political philosopher was Immanuel Kant (1724–1804). Johann Gottlieb Fichte (1762–1814) sought to develop what he saw as the leading "spirit" of Kant's critical philosophy, placing particular stress on the significance of the self-expressing will as the basis of practical reason. His early individualism gave way to an increasingly collectivist political position, reinforcing Kant's earlier rejection of Fichte's self-proclaimed discipleship. Fichte's *Closed Commercial State* (1800) advocated an autarkic, corporatist, quasi-military state, while his *Addresses to the German Nation* (1808) stressed the need for state control of education as a precondition of the orderly development of the German people, the (allegedly predetermined) stages of which he set out in his *Characteristics of the Present Age* (1806). Idealism's next great philosopher was the much misunderstood Georg Wilhelm Friedrich Hegel (1770–1831).

Idealism was imported into the United States via the writings of the St Louis Hegelians, whose most important political philosophers were William Torrey Harris (1835–1909), Denton J. Snider (1841–1925), and Thomas Davidson (1840–1900). Their greatly modified form of Hegelianism emphasized the role of education in creating the conditions for the individual to enjoy a stable and worthwhile social existence. Yet members disagreed over the relative weight to be given to individual will and conscience, on the one hand, and social conventions and norms, on the other, and the movement dissolved into its current obscurity. A more lasting idealist heritage is found in Britain. Even though there were some idealist philosophers with an interest in politics in England in the 19th century—most notably, John Grote (1813–1866) and John Hutchison Stirling (1820–1909)—idealism first held sway in Anglo-American political philosophy (for approximately 50 years from the 1870s to the 1920s) through the dominance of British idealism. The origins of this tradition as an identifiable intellectual movement can be traced to Oxford University, especially the writings of Thomas Hill Green (1836–1882). His *Prolegomena to Ethics* and "Lectures on the Principles of Political Obligation" were published posthumously (in 1883 and 1886, respectively). Green defended a perfectionist ethics developed along the lines of Fichte's early philosophy. This ethics was founded on the claim that individuals experienced an inherent if often imperfectly articulated need and drive to develop their higher capacities through social citizenship and an active commitment to the Aristotelian virtues of temperance, wisdom, courage, and justice, with the latter spelled out as the honoring of Kant's categorical imperative and the realization of a "kingdom of ends" in a society orientated around a determinate ethically and aesthetically enriching common good (what later idealists called a "concrete universal"). In this way, Green claimed that individuals would manifest the "eternal consciousness" (which he saw as an immanent God) within their individual minds. This ethical perfectionism did not issue in a political perfectionism, however, largely because Green held that no one can be forced to act ethically. The most the state or any other group or individual can do is help foster the conditions under which individuals can develop, primarily through educational opportunities for all, employment contracts, and temperance reform. He invoked the medieval notion of a legitimate (according to Green, enabling) political order as a "societies of societies," much in the way that John Rawls was to invoke it 100 years later.

Green's preference for local democratic politics and his endorsement of the "rights recognition thesis" were shared by followers such as Bernard Bosanquet (1848–1923) and David George Ritchie (1853–1903). Bosanquet was especially sensitive to the individual character's vulnerability to state interference, whereas Ritchie saw more danger coming from socioeconomic factors and thereby saw more opportunities for beneficial state action. Ritchie sought to combine some form of utilitarianism with evolutionary theory, as a socialist alternative to the social Darwinism of Herbert Spencer, and in this sense his thought pointed toward the New Liberalism of Leonard Hobhouse and John Hobson. It is notable that Bosanquet's analysis of the ideal type of the modern state anticipated much of the contemporary literature on the state versus failed or quasi states.

Outside its Oxford heartland, idealism was also influential through the Coleridgeian idealism of Frederick Denison Maurice (1805–1872), the quasi Hegelianism of John McTaggart (1866–1925), and the personal idealism of Andrew Seth Pringle-Pattison (1856–1931), James Seth (1860–1924), and Hastings Rashdall (1858–1924), among others. Idealist philosophy was also influential in the subsequent decades in India (primarily through Sir Brajendra Nath Seal [1864–1938], whose humanism emphasized the parity of Eastern and Western cultures, and the philosopher and statesman Sarvepalli Radhakrishnan [1888–1975], who emphasized intuition over the rational consciousness of the earlier idealists), Canada (primarily through John Watson [1847–1939] and Leslie Armour [born 1931]), Australia (primarily through Francis Anderson [1858–1941], Mungo MacCallum [1854–1942], Ernest Burgmann [1885–1965], and Garnet Portus [1883–1954]), and South Africa (primarily through Arthur Ritchie Lord [1880–1941]). The leading Italian idealists differed significantly in their political persuasions: Benedetto Croce (1866–1952) was an outspoken liberal who was persecuted by Mussolini; Giovanni Gentile (1875–1944) was explicitly the philosopher of fascism, with his *Theory of Mind as Pure Act* (1916) being an attempted philosophical justification of the authoritarian nation-state as the protector of the people and the developer of their being as a corporate person.

Even though John Dewey defended Greenian ethics when young, at this time America's most significant defender of idealist political philosophy was Josiah Royce (1855–1916). While Royce denied any significant debts to either Hegel or Green, he acknowledged similarities between his own position and those of Green and Kant. Royce held conflict and struggle to be preconditions not merely of an ethical life for the individual but of a meaningful life. Only by orientating one's life around some worthwhile end could life be given purpose and value and even then only if that orientation is made freely by the individuals themselves. The end, however, must be one valued within one's community, for in that way one's orientation toward it represents an act of loyalty, which Royce argued was a necessary feature of a worthwhile life. Ultimately, Royce held that every valuable human society developed through the action of a spirit within it that transcended the minds of individual citizens.

Several subsequent political philosophers have exhibited idealist tendencies, most notably Robin George Collingwood (1889–1943) and Michael Oakeshott (1901–1990) in Britain, both of whom, along with the other British idealists, attract significant scholarly attention today. The main themes defended by these idealist philosophers form the heart of much contemporary political philosophy and social theory, including the social construction of reality; the interrelationship of personal self-realization and cultural forms; the politics of recognition and identity politics; the state as an ideal type (in opposition to what is now called the "quasi state" or "failed state"); the defense of the participatory enabling, welfare state against attacks from advocates of the competition state; and the critique of utilitarianism as a dehumanizing theory of public policy. What is most remarkable is the extent to which many of the idealists discussed above provide more extensive and deeper insights into these very live political issues than one finds in most mainstream contemporary political philosophy.

Colin Tyler
University of Hull
Hull, United Kingdom

See also Citizenship; Common Goods; Communitarianism; Hegel, Georg Wilhelm Friedrich; Hermeneutics; Individualism; Kant, Immanuel; Liberalism; Normative Political Theory; Patriotism; Rights; State

Further Readings

Boucher, D. (Ed.). (1997). *British idealists.* Cambridge, UK: Cambridge University Press.

Croce, B. (1913). *Philosophy of the practical: Economic and ethic* (D. Ainslie, Trans.). London: Macmillan.
Fichte, J. G. (2009). *Addresses to the German nation* (G. Moore, Ed.). Cambridge, UK: Cambridge University Press.
Hughes-Warrington, M., & Tregenza, I. (2008). State and civilization in Australian new idealism, 1890–1950. *History of Political Thought, 29*(1), 98–108.
McDermott, J. J. (2005). *Basic writings of Josiah Royce.* New York: Fordham University Press. (Original work published 1969)
Tyler, C. (2006). *Idealist political philosophy: Pluralism and conflict in the absolute idealist tradition.* New York: Continuum.

Idealism in International Relations

Idealism in the field of international relations has usually been identified with the perspectives, theories, and methods derived from the Wilsonian tradition. Referring to the ideals espoused by U.S. President Woodrow Wilson, idealist perspectives such as liberalism and neo-conservatism assume that there are universal political and economic ideals that humans should aspire for. In international politics, these ideals are said to be liberty, freedom, democratic systems of representation, free markets, and capitalist trading systems. Certain forms of idealism also see international institutions (economic and political) as ensuring transparency and reinforcing the incentives for states to cooperate. Post–World War II idealism also incorporated some of the tenets of scientific positivism in the hope of first studying and then isolating variables that contaminated the ability of nation-states to cooperate so that such variables could be eliminated over time. For much of idealism's history, it has been contrasted with realist international relations theory, which sees national ideals as relative and pluralist, derived from an anarchical order of international politics founded on power and an order that cannot be transcended. There are two forms of idealist approaches usually considered in international relations—liberalism and neo-conservatism. This entry discusses these two approaches as well as the relationship between idealism and realism and the political nature of the term *idealism*.

Idealist Approaches

Liberalism

Liberalism assumes that while states operate within anarchy, and that states are indeed primarily self-interested, this self-interest lends itself to cooperation rather than conflict. Since the end of World War II, liberal idealism has had three branches. *Institutional liberalism* posits that international organizations and regimes facilitate cooperation by reducing uncertainty among states and increasing transparency. Some institutional idealists, sometimes termed *neoliberal institutionalists* or even *institutionalists*, may not even consider themselves "liberal" in the sense that they would argue that international institutions can facilitate cooperation regardless of the type of domestic political system of a nation-state. *Economic* or *commercial liberalism* asserts that open trading systems make cooperation more likely because the benefits of trade outweigh the costs of going to war. *Political liberalism* assesses the likelihood of cooperation or conflict as based on the nature of a country's political system. Political liberalism has developed into a separate research program of democratic peace theory—which posits that democratic countries are less likely to go to war with one another because of the structural and cultural nature of democratic decision making. While many liberals would disagree with the "idealist" moniker, they still see certain ideals as universally valid and posit that an international community where those ideals were allowed to flourish would be a much more peaceful and stable one than the unstable one we currently have.

Neo-Conservatism

Neo-conservatism began as a domestic political movement in U.S. politics, but toward the conclusion of the Vietnam War and thereafter it became an approach to U.S. foreign policy and has now emerged as an approach to international politics. Neo-conservative argues that the United States bears a "special burden" because of its unique status as a nation-state and eventual great power. What has made the United States unique is the moral vision on which it was founded—liberty, human rights, democracy. These are universal principles, unlike those constituting past great power enterprises. Furthermore, these principles have made the United States powerful by—as the neo-conservative sees it—"right making might."

Neo-conservative idealism differs, however, in two major respects from liberal idealism. First, the neo-conservative emphasizes action—in U.S. politics it is sometimes termed *movement conservatism*. The United States' imperative to act may sometimes outweigh its imperative to cooperate with multilateral organizations, which constrain nation-states in their abilities to act. Against threats not only to U.S. national security but also to the ideals of Western civilization, neo-conservatives argue that certain liberal institutional restraints can be dangerous in that they get in the way of an effective, expedient, and forceful American action. Second, neo-conservatism maintains a skeptical stance toward the scientific positivism of liberals. Neo-conservatives argue that while scientific studies can provide us with generalizations, and even statistical evaluations, they do not give meaning to these evaluations, nor could such studies serve as a guide toward moral action. In using "value-free" lenses in these scientific studies, such studies missed certain qualitative features of emerging threats, such as ideological and cultural attributes that made certain regimes or groups more of a challenge to the West than others. Furthermore, such scientific evaluation, and judicious reflection in general, could get in the way of action. Nevertheless, some of the most prominent neo-conservatives in both policy circles (such as Paul Wolfowitz) and intellectual circles (such as Joshua Muravchik) readily admit the connections between neo-conservatism and liberalism.

Idealism and Realism

The term *idealism* in international relations is an old one. Idealism emerged as a dominant force in thinking about the world largely as a reaction to the World War I. In that conflict's wake, it was assumed that war was senseless and hardly effective at obtaining national objectives. This thinking became a centerpiece during the so-called First Debate among international relations theorists between realists and idealists during the interwar period of 1919 to 1939. Idealism permeated many of the peace movements, the push and eventual construction of the League of Nations, as well as some of the political initiatives (such as the Kellogg-Briand pact) to use legal means to outlaw war. This First Debate has been depicted as one in which idealists, putting their faith in Enlightenment principles such as reason, naively assumed that war could be legislated or collectively securitized away through international organizations such as the League of Nations. Ultimately, the depiction goes, interwar realists such as Edward Carr and Reinhold Niebuhr, and post–World War II ones such as Hans Morgenthau, John Herz, Arnold Wolfers, and Kenneth Osgood, "won" this debate when World War II disconfirmed much of the basis of interwar idealism.

Morgenthau, in *Scientific Man Versus Power Politics*, positioned scientific approaches to international relations as a form of idealist theory. Morgenthau asserted that such approaches approximated particularist bourgeois ideals (liberty, property, wealth, etc.) as universals, using those as a barometer to measure the "progress" of nations in global politics. According to Morgenthau, because these were abstract ideals, the study of these by the social scientist ignored the realities of power politics. Nevertheless, these scientific approaches toward the study of international relations became dominant during the 1950s and 1960s behavioral revolution of American social science, and thus, positivist frameworks because of their "problem-solving" approach to social action are considered by many classical realists to be another form of idealism.

Neo-conservative Joshua Muravchik has justified calling both liberalism and neo-conservatism forms of Wilsonianism with the helpful binary of possession versus milieu goals. Realists argue that the ordering principle of international politics—anarchy—by definition implies that there is no overarching or policing supranational authority. Thus, nation-states have possession goals—they seek to acquire as much power as possible to ensure their own survival. Both neo-conservatives and liberals, on the contrary, argue that the environment of international politics is subject to change if the political and economic institutions of members change; therefore, democratic states, such as the United States, can and should have milieu goals that seek change in the international environment. That is, a world constituted by economically and politically liberal democracies is much more stable and inclined to cooperation than a world constituted by totalitarian or authoritarian regimes. Or, in another realm, a world where international trade can occur openly without tariffs or other forms of national economic protectionism is one where cooperation is more likely than in a world where trade occurs in isolated pockets, if at all.

As such, both liberalism and neo-conservatism have at their core a faith in the idealist "democratic peace" account, which posits that democratic countries are less likely to go to war with one another because of the structural and cultural nature of democratic decision making. They have also spawned a number of evaluative institutions, such as Freedom House and Transparency International, which assess nation-states' economic and political development trajectories using operationalized liberal ideals as a metric.

Realist scholars and analysts have issued vibrant criticisms of both liberal and neo-conservative assumptions and policies. In addition to the realist–idealist debate in the interwar period, debates between realists and liberals in the 1980s and 1990s centered on the primary motives of nation-states and the implications such motives had for cooperation. Liberals posited that nation-states sought absolute gains and thus would cooperate with other states in certain interactions (such as trade) so long as both would gain, even if certain states gained more than others. Realists argued that nation-states sought gains relative to other states, and thus nation-states were more cooperation-averse because power was more important to nation-states in relative terms rather than absolute terms.

Since the beginning of the 21st century, realists and neo-conservatives have disagreed about the conception of U.S. foreign policy interests and acutely quarreled over the strategy of U.S.-led democratization of nondemocratic areas. Realists have argued that democratization is a fool's errand, one that wastes U.S. resources for little, if any, strategic gains. Ideals such as freedom, liberty, and capitalism are complex, arising in the West from a particular constellation of factors, and thus, such ideals are hardly transferable to every global region. Neo-conservatives posit that fostering democratic regimes, which sometimes necessitates U.S. assistance through force, not only promotes universal ideals but also serves as a demonstration to the international community that these ideals are worth fighting for. This realist/neo-conservative debate over democratization as a U.S. foreign policy strategy can be considered part of the larger debate realists have had with all forms of idealism over the past century.

Political Nature of the Term

It should be noted that many liberals and neo-conservatives would eschew the label "idealist." Often, idealism has been equated to a naive form of belief that peace is just around the corner if certain principles were implemented to amend the anarchical state of international politics. Both liberals and neo-conservatives have argued against their realist critics that their views, far from being naive, are derived from pragmatic social and historical patterns of human existence. For example, liberal democratic peace proponents would point to the many statistical studies proving that no two fully formed democracies have ever gone to war with one another. Neo-conservatives have also suggested that there is very little about realism that is "realistic," since it fails to recognize the inherent threats to U.S. interests that pure power calculations cannot predict—for instance, the hostility that originates within and from volatile rogue regimes.

As evidence for the political purpose behind the label *idealism*, one can consider that the term was deployed in the 1990s by realist scholars, such as John Mearsheimer, against the then emerging perspective of constructivism in international relations. Other scholars have argued that constructivism, which sees intersubjective understandings, identities, perceptions, discourse, and social structures as central to international relations, reflects a liberal bias. While it is highly debatable that constructivism is a form of idealism, this attempt by realists and other scholars to label it as such is reflective of the more generally pejorative aura the term *idealism* still conjures in some circles of international relations. This is problematic, simply because all international relations perspectives, even realism, can be considered idealist in the sense that they approximate a world of particular ideals and seek mechanisms through which humans can realize those ideals for a more stable existence.

Brent J. Steele
University of Kansas
Lawrence, Kansas, United States

See also Conservatism; Constructivism; Democratic Peace; Democratization; Realism in International Relations

Further Readings

Brown, M. E., Lynn-Jones, S. M., & Miller, S. E. (Eds.). (1997). *Debating the democratic peace.* Cambridge: MIT Press.

Carr, E. H. (2001). *The twenty-years crisis, 1919–1939.* New York: Palgrave

Mearsheimer, J. (1994/1995). The false promise of international institutions. *International Security, 19*(3), 5–49.

Morgenthau, H. (1946). *Scientific man versus power politics.* Chicago: University of Chicago Press.

Muravchik, J. (1992). *Exporting democracy.* Washington, DC: American Enterprise Institute.

Identity, Social and Political

Identity is a somewhat ambiguous term and a contentious concept. With regard to individuals, groups, and societies, a differentiation between personal, social, and collective identity is common. In popular language and essentialist concepts, *personal identity* is used to denote an individual's self-concept: certain typical traits and meanings that are perceived as relatively stable over different situations and over time and that distinguish the self from other persons. Although some have questioned the universality of this concept, the idea of an essential inner self of the individual dominates at least contemporary Western concepts of the person. *Social identity* refers to societal or cultural influences on the development of the self, to memberships of individuals along a continuum of interaction groups (e.g., families, sports teams, political parties, and other networks), and to social categories (e.g., according to social roles such as mothers, teachers, sports fans). As such, social identity is also part of the personal identity. The terms *cultural identity* and *collective identity* mostly denote social identities of a large scale (e.g., gender, age, ethnicity, class) and sometimes are also used to describe a relatively long enduring stability of values, institutions, symbols, and aims of a group, a society, or a nation-state (e.g., represented in national consciousness). *National identity* is a special form of a collective, political identity, which consists mostly of a self-image based on certain assumptions about common features as descent, history, language, culture, subjective feelings of belonging, and/or citizenship. Furthermore, the term *identity* is used not only with regard to the microlevel and its aggregates but also to describe certain traits at the meso- or macrolevel (e.g., the identity of the Americans, the British Empire, or the Eastern world).

For some, *identity* means absolute sameness of human beings; thus, if used in a social or political context, it carries connotations of strong homogeneity between persons and a collective. From a normative democratic perspective, this meaning is rejected because it is linked to ideas of a homogeneous people, authoritative leadership, and dictatorship as well as a sharp definition of insiders and outsiders and a demarcation of friend and foe.

Others use *identity* to depict scientific concepts that play a certain role in the humanities and social sciences. Most of them point to the fact that identity usually has multiple facets, which can gain different salience in different situations and thus may also change over time in intensity and meaning. In addition, the term *identification* is used to denote a feeling of sameness with another person or group and loyalty toward its motives, ideals, aims, leaders, and so on.

Since, in the human sciences, there are many differing concepts of social and political identity, this entry concentrates on concepts referring to the levels of individuals and groups as holders of identity. After a few remarks concerning the historical roots of the concept of identity and a brief mention of some concepts referring to personal identity, the entry discusses selected major approaches to social identity. The final section deals with questions of political identity with respect to societies, especially at the level of national identity, and considers its relationship to subnational and supranational units of identification. Other aspects of political identity such as party identification or identity of social and political movements are not dealt with here. Similarly, this entry also does not deal with identity politics at the macrolevel (e.g., affirmative action in multicultural societies).

Historical Roots of Identity Research

Early concepts of identity primarily dealt with the self as personal identity from a psychological perspective and concentrated on the development and consistency of the psyche. By contrast, sociology is concerned with social identity and its structural determinants, and social-psychological research focuses on human fundamentals in differing social contexts and thus on the interplay between cognitive, affective, and evaluative processes and social, cultural, and political influences and on their respective consequences for subsequent behavior.

The history of concepts of social identity in modern social sciences begins toward the first third of the 20th century. Early protagonists such as William James, Charles Horton Cooley, and George Herbert Mead had in common the view of identity as a product of constructions and perceptions of reality in social interactions. This was a main basis for the theoretical link between the individual and society. They argued that consciousness and self-knowledge are not natural, a priori characteristics of human behavior but features that both originate from and influence the processes of social interaction. Cooley's metaphor of a "looking glass self" describes how persons take their ideas about themselves from their perceptions of other persons' opinions about them. Somewhat later, James and Mead differentiated the self into the components "I" (internal perspective) and "Me" (external perspective). The component "Me" is determined by culture and society; it reflects social roles and expectations from others toward the person. These are learned and internalized in processes of socialization and identification with other persons or collectives. The component "I" means the spontaneous, active, more autonomous part of the self, which is not only a presupposition for the ability to identify with others and to learn social roles but also a necessary condition for the ability to keep a critical distance to the social self. This approach was further developed in theories of symbolic interactionism and phenomenology. Peter L. Berger and Thomas Luckmann conceptualized the socialization process as a dialectical one between identification by others (objective) and by self (subjective); they see this process as a mirror of a broader societal dialectic between subjective and objective reality.

In subsequent research, some authors concentrated on the "I" (personal identity) and linked this to ethno-methodological concepts, such as that of Alfred Schütz, or to the cognitive-structural approach of Jean Piaget and Lawrence Kohlberg. These approaches also distinguish an "ideal self," which means culturally framed ideas of how the self ought to be. The fit between these normative ideas and the perception of how the self actually is strongly affects a person's self-esteem.

Another approach, schema theory (e.g., Susan Fiske and Shelley Taylor), in part also deals with personal identity and its cognitive components. Schemata are highly generalized and organized cognitive structures in memory that guide perceptions and interpretations of new information and memory recall and thus help reduce the amount of necessary cognitive processes of orientation. Identity is defined as a system of possibly hierarchically and context specifically ordered self-concepts. Situations that fit an individual's self-schemata are more likely than contrary information to be processed and stored in memory and thus form a consistent and relatively stable self-schema. Research shows that individuals' schematic identities are different in intensity and amount. Highly complex, multifaceted self-schemata may contribute to psychological health in situations that threaten part of the identity (e.g., if a person's identity as a worker is threatened because of unemployment, the psychological activation of other identities such as being a good father and a gifted singer in church might help uphold his self-esteem). Critics of schema theory argue that—because of its emphasis on learning effects and automatic cognitive processes—it leads to a too passive and static perspective of identity.

Cognitive dissonance theory (Leon Festinger) and social attribution theory (Philip E. Tetlock) additionally integrate the affective motivational basis of identity, namely, the desire for a positive self-esteem, in their models of information processing. Thus, if cognitions or attitudes become dissonant with each other or with behavior because of new information, individuals try to reach consonance by cognitive strategies such as downplaying the inconsistent new information or changing its meaning. In this way, an individual's self-serving bias is activated when positive events or outcomes of actions are attributed to the self, whereas for negative ones the situation or others are blamed.

Social Identity

Approaches of Role Identity

Other authors concentrated on the "Me" component of the self. In this context, Ervin Goffman laid the foundations of role theory. He distinguished between a personal identity (individual uniqueness of life experiences) and a social identity (role expectations and roles) of the individual. Both confront the individual with demands in daily interaction, which he conceptualized as a kind of role play on stage. It is assumed that persons do not identify totally with their different roles, because of ever-changing social interactions. A reflexive and somewhat distant relationship toward one's own role identities is seen as especially characteristic for modernity. Thus, in traditional, relatively static societies, the "I" is strongly determined by the identification with (often primordial) social collectives (e.g., family, tribe, and guild) and, therefore, keeps close to the "Me," possibly throughout one's entire life. In modern societies, as Norbert Elias has argued, processes of social change, societal differentiation, and mobilization as well as globalization lead to an ongoing individualization. On the one hand, this is linked to rising freedom for the "I." There are more role models to choose from, identity facets can change often from situation to situation, and multiple aspects of identity can coexist. On the other hand, they can also compete or even come into conflict with each other and thus result in identity crises. Erik Erikson defines a (healthy) identity as one that guarantees sameness and continuity of the self throughout life in one's own perception and that includes the expectation that others will recognize this self. But modern societies can also produce problems such as a negative identity (e.g., identification with roles that are evaluated negatively by society and the individual him- or herself, because a positively evaluated role takeover was too difficult and failed) or competing identities (diverging structures of personality because of status inconsistencies in complex societies). Thus, modern societies produce more dangers and uncertainties concerning an individual's identity and thus create the need for life-long reflection about the relationship between the "Me" and the "I."

Some criticisms of this approach were directed toward the differentiation between personal identity as an ostensibly "true" one and role/social identity as a "false" one or as a "calculating" perspective on the self.

Whereas in earlier concepts the self was related to interactions with other persons, in role theory the self is related to features of the social structure. Role identity depicts a certain position or status within a social system. All role theories share the assumption that society is differentiated into social roles, which carry behavioral norms, and that identity entails the internalization of these roles by individuals laying the ground for patterned, structured, and routinized action. In their concepts of identity, some theorists combine the symbolic interactionism approach with role theory. In this kind of theory, society is seen as a rather stable structure that results from repeated patterns of behavior of individuals and groups. Macrolevel structures are seen as the product of the multiple roles that individuals perform in day-to-day interactions. The self and its identity are created by these interactions and by the meanings that the multiple roles have for the actors, and—in a reflexive process—identities provide the meanings of the roles.

There are various approaches for a systematization of multiple roles and identities. For instance, Peter Burke's taxonomy is oriented along different social situations: *Person identities* denote self-meanings, the meanings that characterize the individuality (as being active or passive, ambitioned or unpretentious). Individuals carry around these identities across different situations and they are activated frequently. *Role identities* are activated in specific situations where individuals perform in certain functions (e.g., being a daughter, a mother, a wife, an artist, or a sports fan). The meanings linked to such roles or functions are determined by culture and socialization as well as the individual perceptions and assessments of these roles. *Social identities* emerge from the identification of individuals with social groups or categories. They define the belonging of insiders as well as of the outsiders on the basis of similarity/difference and they may lead to common bonds and actions. Individuals have identities of all three types and usually more than one of these types is invoked in social interactions.

Peter J. Burke and others also examine internal processes of an individual concerning his or her identity and its influence on behavior. Identities here are seen as meanings attached to the self. The process of identity invoking is conceptualized as a perpetual control system, a circular process of self-definitions of identity meanings and their attachment to experiences in a feedback loop. This is assumed to lead to a permanent verification of the meanings of one's identity. Behavior is thought of as a function of the relationship between situations and identities.

Sheldon Stryker's analyses of the psychological organization of identities led him to a hierarchical concept of saliency and commitment. The main idea is that an individual's behavior is shaped by how often and how intensively his or her identities are activated. *Identity salience* refers to the probability that a specific identity is activated by others or by oneself. A salient identity is one that is invoked frequently and across different situations and contexts. The saliency of an identity determines the probability that the individual will enact roles that are consistent with this identity, that he or she will interpret situations as suitable to perform such roles, and even that an individual will seek opportunities to perform these roles. *Identity commitment* refers to the dependency of an individual's relationships to others on certain roles. The strength of the commitment defines the extent and intensity of an individual's attachment to other persons to whom he or she is linked by an identity. Strength of commitment and saliency usually go hand in hand, and the higher the position of an identity in the hierarchy, the greater is the probability the identity will be activated and thus shape behavior, which in turn reinforces its salience.

Others concentrate more on social positions as basis of roles and identity. George McCall and Jerry Laird Simmons distinguish between a conventional and an idiosyncratic component of role identity (similar to Erving Goffmann's distinction between social and personal aspects). The conventional component refers to expectations and internalized meanings linked to social positions; the idiosyncratic component refers to the individual meanings the respective roles have for the person. In this approach, a *prominence hierarchy* orders the identities according to their importance for an ideal self, which is seen as a result of the support an individual gains from others for a certain identity, an individual's commitment to an identity and reward for activating an identity. A *salience hierarchy* is seen as a function of the identity prominence, a psychological need for support and rewards, and the perceived opportunities for the activation of identities in specific situations and thus is important for concrete behavior.

Social Identity Theory and Social Categorization Theory

Two other closely related theories in social psychology have gained much importance in identity research, namely, the so-called social identity theory by Henry Tajfel and the social categorization theory by John Turner and colleagues, both together often denoted as the social identity approach. This approach was developed in the 1960s as a cognitive theory of group identity to explain prejudice, discrimination, and conflicts between members of social categories or groups and has since generated a huge body of research to test its basic assumptions and to generate new hypotheses. In part, it rests on earlier research and also shares some assumptions with other approaches to explain prejudice and conflict, but in other aspects it clearly departs from them.

Earlier research to explain prejudice focused on psychological traits and defects of the unconscious of individuals (e.g., the concept of the authoritarian personality in the work by Theodor Adorno, Else Frenkel-Brunswick, Daniel Levinson, and Nevitt Sandford or on attitudinal predispositions learned in early childhood (as in the concept of symbolic racism of Donald Kinder and David Sears). But both approaches are limited with respect to identity insofar as they remain restricted to the personal level and cannot explain changes in discrimination and conflict. Another concept, the theory of social dominance (e.g., James Sidanius), not only goes beyond personal identity but also has difficulties in explaining why and under what conditions discrimination and conflicts arise in certain situations. It claims that all societies are hierarchical and have at least one hegemonic and one subordinate group that usually hold prejudices against each other. This social dominance orientation reflects a normal psychological desire to belong to a high-status group. Thus, individual and institutionalized discrimination is seen as a normal feature of societies, which are perpetuated by processes of social identification, self-esteem maintenance, and social comparison. Realistic group conflict theory (e.g., Muzafer Sherif) assumes that conflicts between groups are based on competition for scarce resources and thus follow the principle of individual rationality. The conflicts are seen as the basis for ingroup identification and for ongoing psychological processes of stereotyping and discrimination of the outgroup. A recommended solution for such conflicts is to alter the group identification by imposing superordinate common goals. Critiques of this approach emphasize that the framing of the group conflict and the proposed solution undermine its rational choice basis. Furthermore, a change of identity by imposing superordinate goals may be possible only in very restricted situations, not in real-life conflicts of a broad range such as conflicts between ethnic groups or even nation-states, which may lead to war.

The social identity approach suggests that identification with an ingroup and distinction from/discrimination against outgroups are two sides of one coin and that competition for scarce resources is not a necessary condition for these processes. The empirical roots of this research are based on the minimal group paradigm. Here, in laboratory experiments, artificial groups were formed on the basis of overtly senseless tests (e.g., whether somebody preferred Paul Klee or Wassily Kandinsky as a painter) or even by lot, which was known by the participants. The participants had no interaction, there was no competition, and they did not know anything about each other. When asked to reward members of their own and of the other group, they consistently favored their own group and thus showed bias against the other group. Moreover, this ingroup favoritism did not occur in a way that maximized the benefit for one's own group (which would have supported the realistic group conflict model), but led to a maximum difference between both groups. Thus, a distinction of groups based on purely cognitive belonging produced ingroup favoritism and outgroup discrimination.

Social identity theory also rests on claims about psychological needs: Individuals strive for positive self-esteem, which leads them to identify with groups that will enhance their self-image. This is only possible if the ingroup is distinct from other relevant groups in a positive way. Moreover, a need to reduce uncertainty compels persons to compare and categorize groups as well as the self in relation to such groups. This social-psychological approach also takes a perspective on identity that differs from the sociological symbolic interactionist concept, because it does not conceptualize all identities as inherently social. Rather, it argues that group identity is formed in contrast to personal identity, claiming a continuum between both, along which behavior can move. Thus it assumes that group psychology and behavior are qualitatively distinct from the intra-individual and individual ones. The central aim is to explain under what conditions and how group bias occurs. For this process, three main tenets have been defined—namely, the salience of group membership, the situational context, and the individual's beliefs. Thus, for a social identity to affect perceptions, cognitions, attitudes, and behavior, the mere awareness of group membership is not enough. As long as the personal identity is more salient than social identity, the individual will behave in an interpersonal manner that takes account of personal traits and relationships between the actors. But if social identity becomes psychologically more salient, group behavior will occur. Since everybody develops multiple group memberships and corresponding social identities, the objective context is also relevant for defining which special social identity fits the situation best. Subjective interpretations of the situation as well as beliefs about the group memberships intervene in this process. The most important beliefs refer to chances for individual mobility or chances for social change, both of which represent the poles of a continuum. These imply corresponding strategies, if the outcome of a comparison between one's own membership group and another one is negative. For example, if a person thinks that it is possible to leave the ingroup and become a member of a comparable group with a higher status, he or she will act in this direction. This presupposes a belief in an open social structure or society. By contrast, if the personal strategy does not promise an enhancement of self-esteem, an action as a group member will be undertaken to change collectively the status of the ingroup, which includes a high saliency of social identity. Such actions can include social creativity (e.g., a change of the dimension of comparison, a change of the evaluation of the compared attributes, or a change of the group of comparison) or social competition/confrontation.

Whereas the ingroup favoritism/outgroup bias has been demonstrated consistently, empirical support for the self-esteem motive has been less strong. This may have contributed to a rise in interest in the cognitive dimension of the theory during the 1980s in the work of John Turner et al. They understand their self-categorization theory as an extension and elaboration of the social identity theory. Here, social identity is defined as a set of cognitive representations of the self. Two contributions are mentioned here, namely, the concept of multiple levels of inclusiveness and that of prototypicality. The idea is that self representations are organized along a hierarchy of categories, which are defined by similarity within classes and dissimilarity between classes, based on the metacontrast principle (this means, the interesting dimensions of categorization are classified in a way that minimizes the differences within a category and maximizes them with regard to other categories). Meaningful comparisons and classifications presuppose a similarity of the interesting traits and respective categories at a higher level. Thus—instead of a continuum between the personal and the social self—they suggest at least three main levels of identity. The most inclusive and therefore superordinate level is that of human beings against other forms of life (animals, plants); the intermediate level comprises membership in social groups as against other comparison groups (e.g., men and women, Europeans and Americans, the political Left and Right); and the subordinate level focuses on the individual and the differences from other ingroup members. Obviously, on the level of social groups, these again can show different patterns of inclusiveness, which can be seen as hierarchical or nested patterns (e.g., women, European women, left-oriented European women as against their respective counterparts). A group prototype is someone who shows the highest value of metacontrast on a certain dimension of comparison. Thus, prototypicality can change depending on the situation. Prototypes can serve as a model for other group members and thus can foster self-stereotyping of ingroup members and stereotyping outgroups. This depersonalization contributes to ingroup homogeneity and distinctiveness as well as to outgroup bias and is seen as central to all group processes.

From a sociological point of view, a general critique is that the ontological assumption of an independent person fluctuating between personal and social identities restricts the possibilities to account for social processes, especially with respect to the influences of political and economic macrofactors, because these can only be taken into account as specific traits of the situation. Another problem is that most research in this field relies on laboratory experiments and thus cannot simulate the complexity of the real-life world, which questions the external validity of such findings. From the perspective of political science, another deficit is the relative neglect of motivational factors and emotions linked to identities and their consequences.

Narrativity of Social Identity

Recent research in understanding social identity is also linked to social constructivism and the discursive approach, resting on poststructuralist perspectives and the interpretive paradigm. It is not concerned with individual or social-psychological processes of identity but concentrates on narrative, linguistic constructions of identity. A central assumption is that a person's identity is not a stable outcome and entity but has to be conceptualized as a permanent process of construction in language and talk in changing situations. Within this process, prevailing ideologies are said to be powerful mechanisms to determine identity so that an individual only has the illusion of an actively and freely chosen concept of the self. An example is Michael Billig's work on the link between thinking and arguing. Narratives are also seen as a person's self-representation toward others, which may appear stable and continuous but in fact can change (e.g., Kenneth Gergen and Mary Gergen). On the whole, these different approaches toward social identity have laid the ground for and can contribute ever more to the understanding of political identity as well.

Political Identity

National identity is one among other collective identities, and—in contrast to many other political identities—it is linked to a political as well as a territorial point of reference, a political community at the level of the nation-state. This community usually is thought of as one that encompasses people of both sexes, from all age-groups, and from all social strata. Typically, national identity also rests on beliefs about certain commonalities among the members of the group, such as a common ancestry, ethnicity, language, religion, culture, and values; a sense of belonging; political rights; participation, and so on. These are often thought to overcome contrasting and competing utilitarian interests of the members (e.g., those between different classes) and thus are crucial for the integration of society. Some of these characteristics also apply to sub- (local, smaller regional) and supranational identities (encompassing more than one nation in bigger regions ranging from border areas over continents to the whole human race or referring to supranational political units such as the European Union [EU]). Problems of national identity are most prominent in research, whereas sub- and supranational identities are often discussed only in their relation to national identities.

In political science, diverse subdisciplines deal with national identity, national movements, nationalism, and nation-building processes. With respect to national identity in the more restricted sense of the topic, research is based mainly on political sociological and political cultural approaches resting on behaviorism and working with surveys, although it is less linked than the topic of social identity to certain authors or research schools. In contrast to sociology and social psychology, political science is also less concerned with the cognitive basis of identity and more with affective components and its determinants and consequences. Moreover, identity is rarely treated as a cognitive categorization but rather as an attitude, as identification. Especially when dealing with national identity on a microlevel, the purely cognitive categorization seems self-evident, because there is almost no one who does not know to which nation he or she belongs. But categorization processes become a topic when dealing with stereotyping between different nationalities within a country or between countries. Here, questions concern the intensity of collective identification, the relationships between identifications with different collectives, and reference objects as the content and meaning of identity.

Intensity of Political Identification

People have been and still are ready to fight for their country. Wars in the name of country and nation again and again have shown unbelievable cruelties and destruction. Usually the losses and pains are not only on the side of the losers but also on the side of the winners. So the question is why people fight voluntarily and willingly in wars. Yet all nations and societies can function only for a time on the basis of common instrumental aims and interests; in the long run, they probably need a basis of common values and norms, which underlie a common identity. Moreover, most interests and identities are not mutually exclusive but work as reinforcing foundations of integration. Without these forces of integration any nation will fall apart, inner conflicts may arise, and civil war can be a consequence.

The different scenarios of war between nations or civil war within a nation may depict the poles of a spectrum from extreme national identification (highly salient cognitive national identity and strong affective identification) to a total loss of a common national identification (be it against a background of other interests or identities, such as in class struggles, race riots, or religious confrontations, or against a background of other national identities, such as in secessionism and separatist movements). Diverse national as well as cross-national survey research findings show that a purely cognitive identification with a nation (knowledge about one's national belonging, also called national consciousness) usually does not go along with a bias for one's own nation and aggressiveness toward others. Yet a purely cognitive identification is seldom seen. More often national consciousness is accompanied by positive feelings toward one's nation—for example, those expressed in national pride. In most, but not all countries and periods of research (also depending on the kind of measurement and the indicators used), the strength of positive feelings toward one's own nation shows links to ingroup bias and outgroup discrimination. Thus, for example, with the increasing intensity of national identification, it is not only the probability of constructive patriotism (seen as critical loyalty to one's own nation) that increases but also the probability of blind nationalism (designating an attitude that puts one's own nation on top of everything, regardless of its state of affairs: "Right or wrong, my country"). Moreover, this often coincides with skeptical or hostile attitudes toward immigrants and immigration per se and mistrust of other countries and peoples. Research has also shown that an extremely strong national identification often is accompanied by low identification with other political collectives and social groups and even more private roles—a loss of other identities giving place to the national one or the national one replacing the others. With regard to determining factors, within Western democracies a high level of education and a favorable socioeconomic position often lead to only moderate levels of national identification, at least in times of peace. By contrast, fast social change, feelings of anomie, and sometimes feelings of relative deprivation foster national and nationalistic attitudes. A perceived threat from immigrants and from other nations often contribute to a rise in national identification. This also points to the fact that national identification is also dependent on the political context. Thus, for instance, in Eastern European countries, national identification today is much stronger than in most Western countries as a consequence of their newly won freedom from the former Soviet empire Similarly, intellectuals and higher status groups in non-Western societies, as in the Middle East, often exhibit a higher level of nationalism (or religious fundamentalism) because of feelings of relative deprivation and of being dominated by the West, as noted by Bettina Westle and Paolo Segatti (2011). Historical facts and contextual events may also lead to periods where great parts of the population show only low levels of national identification or even negative feelings toward their own nation. This has been observed in countries that have been occupied or were defeated in war (e.g., Belgium) and in countries where many in the population felt guilty or ashamed about former wars and war crimes (e.g., West Germany).

Thus, all in all, it is known that some collective national identification is necessary for the inner cohesion of nation-states, but there is no straightforward answer to the question of how much intensity of national identification is needed and at which point it might become harmful. It can be said that the possible effect of national identification not only depends on the intensity of these feelings but also on the question of how far the national identity is accompanied by other identities or is exclusive. Moreover, it varies with the self-image of the nation, the content, meaning, or objects of national pride (which reflect the dimensions of the ingroup definition). Finally, strong positive feelings toward one's own nation are a precondition for nationalistic attitudes, but such feelings do not automatically result in nationalistic attitudes. And those feelings are per se neither helpful nor harmful, unless they become politically mobilized and lead to action. In Western democracies, mostly populist and right-wing parties mobilize traditional nationalistic attitudes on the basis of economic problems, which then typically are not directed against other countries but against the perceived cause of the economic problems—for example, immigrants or, in Europe, the European Union.

Relationships Between Nonpolitical and Political/National Identifications

National identity usually coexists with other diverse social and political identities. As political psychology shows, one can feel, for example, as a woman, a mother, a scientist, a dancer, and a member of a nation. Such identities belong to different domains of life and therefore usually do not compete or conflict with each other. Rather, they can be activated differently in diverse situations; for example, talking with children will activate one's identity as a mother, going to a party will highlight the salience of one's identification as a dancer and probably as a woman, teaching students a lesson will activate one's identity as a scientist, and getting confronted with the problems of foreign students or going to an international meeting may activate not only one's identity as a scientist but also one's own national identity. In the same way, national identity is compatible with various other political identities within a country, such as party identification or being a trade unionist, and even with identities that go beyond the nation-state, such as being a member of Amnesty International or identifying with Greenpeace. In the latter cases, the activation of the international identity may compete with the national identity, but it also can strengthen it, depending on the concrete conditions of the situation. Because national identity is rather close to the collective end of the continuum of possible identities between personal and collective, it can include many other identities. But situations that will primarily or even exclusively activate national identity are rather rare, as in the case of a national celebration or in cases of international conflicts.

Relationships Between Different Political/ National Identifications and Between Subnational and National Identities

More difficult are the relationships between national identity and other political identities, which also refer to nationality and/or to potential or real territorial-political collectives. Thus, there are many countries that can be called multinational states, because people who identify with more than one nation live within such countries. This is caused by different historical developments, which often underlie different situations and relationships between the respective nationalities.

A typical example for a historically multinational country is Switzerland, where French, German, and Italian populations (and even a small Ladino one) live together, in different parts of the country, with a great deal of autonomy and without major problems. Most of the Swiss citizens feel as though they are Swiss citizens, though they may have French-, German-, or Italian-Swiss identities as well. Another example is Belgium, with a Walloon (French speaking), a Flemish (Dutch speaking), and a small German-speaking population. Though these populations live in different parts of the country and there are highly complex political institutions for representation, conflicts between Wallonia and Flanders arise again and again. One example of aggressive conflicts and the desire for separation is Northern Ireland, though Britain has decentralized its political structures. Spain is another example where decentralization of political structures was undertaken to give people of different historically rooted nationalities, who also live in different parts of the country, more autonomy. This was partly successful, for example, in Catalonia. But other parts now also strive for more autonomy, and Euskadi (the Basque part) especially has a separatist movement, with the aim of creating a separate state together with the Basques living in France. On an individual level, these examples show that citizens tend to identify more intensively or even exclusively with their (officially) subnational identity than with their national one and sometimes strive to form a sovereign nation of their own. Historically rooted feelings of national identity that accompany contemporary distinguishing features with regard to other parts of the population or that even lead to political cleavages (e.g., a different religion or language, translated into politics) and/or that go along with feelings of economic deprivation are factors that often lead to inner conflicts and secessionist or separatist movements. But a favorable economic situation can also contribute to the wish for more national autonomy to avoid having to share welfare benefits with the poorer parts of a country, as is the case with northern Italy. Yet to satisfy the desires associated with such political identities through institutions of territorial autonomy is evidently possible only if the respective populations with a common we-feeling live predominantly in different internally homogeneous parts of the country or belong to a diaspora in which national minorities live in adjacent territories of another country.

In countries that are made up of many different ethnicities/nationalities and/or in countries where the populations of different nationalities are spread over the territory, such solutions are not possible. Such countries also show quite different histories and current situations with respect to questions of national identity. One typical situation is produced by nation-building processes in postcolonial countries. Often boundaries were drawn that did not respect traditional (prenational) we-feelings, such as in Africa, and therefore may lead to inner conflicts as well as to conflicts between countries. In other postcolonial cases, such as in India, huge populations with quite different ethnicities, traditions, languages, and cultural customs have succeeded in forming a common political identity.

Another constellation could be found after the dissolution of greater political entities, as in Eastern Europe in the 1990s with the breakdown of the Soviet empire. The Soviets have tried for almost a century to build a common communist identity that should overcome earlier ethnic and national identities. Yet this was only partly successful, and today these countries attempt to rebuild their earlier national identities in a situation of newly gained political sovereignty. This situation also produced new national, territorially concentrated, as well as dispersed minorities and diasporas. Thus, the split of former Czechoslovakia into two states is an example of a peaceful solution for the national self-determination of two populations with different identities and living in different parts of a country. The Baltic countries are an example of relatively peaceful ways of dealing with minorities, especially the large Russian minorities (mainly members of the former military and their families) by granting them certain minority rights and possibilities to gain full citizenship. By contrast, in the former Yugoslavia, extremely violent conflicts especially between (mainly Catholic) Croats, (mainly Orthodox) Serbs, and (mainly Muslim) Bosniaks developed, which destroyed the country and led to a division into several parts.

Other typical contexts in which different national identities play a role are caused by migration. Today there are so-called immigration countries—those where immigrants dominate an indigenous population, such as Australia, or where national subcommunities are formed from different subpopulations, including indigenous populations, descendants from early settlers, and new immigrants, as in the French- and English-speaking regions of Canada. Another example is the United States, where the population includes not only the indigenous American Indian population but also the descendants of immigrants from Europe, Latin America, and Asia, as well as the descendants of African slaves. These different populations come together with quite different backgrounds with respect to their identities—in some cases with a strong national identity, in others with a negative national identity with regard to their countries of descent, and in some with a nonnational but mainly ethnic identity based on race, language, or religion. Against this background of different ethnic or national identities and the feeling that a common political national identity is necessary to guarantee societal integration and stability of the political system, different ideas have developed (which in more or less moderated forms also have influenced other immigration countries): the perspective of a melting pot; the concept of a multicultural, ethnic pluralist society; and the group dominance and assimilation perspective. The melting pot concept suggests that all citizens regardless of their ethnic or ancestral national background form a common political identity and in the long run mingle with each other in such a way that the different identity backgrounds lose importance and form a new common composite identity. The multicultural concept, often associated with the metaphor of a salad bowl or mosaic, implies that the different ethnic and national groups keep their distinctive characteristics and identities but are respected as equal and as complementary reinforcing loyalties. The group dominance concept articulates that in multiethnic and immigration countries, there is one dominant group that claims to have preeminent rights and can legitimately expect newcomers to adapt to their rules and lifestyle and in the long run adopt the dominant group's national identity. These ideas are also linked to different identity politics. The melting pot concept disregards ethnic and former national identities. By contrast, the multicultural concept is linked to policies such as affirmative action in order to support the different identities, especially in cases where some groups have historically been deprived of social or political rights and chances of economic advancement. The assimilation concept is linked to politics that promote but also demand that immigrants adapt to the dominant group. As different and contrary as these concepts are, they all are intended to ensure peaceful relations between groups with different identities. However, there is no uncontested evidence that shows which concept works best. For example, in some cases the respect and support of different identities have helped pacify conflicts between groups, but in others they have led to a reinforcement of ethnic, exclusive identities with aggressive potential toward groups of other identities. Also, when individuals and groups keep their former national identification in addition to the new one, their national loyalty may be questioned, especially if the country of origin and the country of immigration should become involved in a conflict. Thus, identity politics in multiethnic and multinational contexts (with dispersed settlement) may involve a choice between two hazardous alternatives—like the one the sailors confronted between Scylla and Charybdis.

Finally, a new form of multiple national identity seems to arise with processes of globalization and migration, namely, so-called transnational identities. They may become characteristic for persons who live in more than one country, perhaps because they work in more than one country or because they have their family in one country and work in another, who migrate and re-migrate. With regard to multicultural societies, evidence and speculations about this kind of multiple identity are rather diverse, reaching from the expectation that for such individuals national identity will lose any relevance and they will develop into cosmopolitans to the contrary expectation that the different identities may reinforce each other permanently or to the expectation that those identities permanently will conflict with each other and cause individual identity crises.

Relationship Between National and Supranational Identity: The European Union

The idea of a cosmopolitan identity as well as concepts of a supranational identity mostly remained apolitical, because they did not have any specific political object of identification. Yet this is changing in the EU, as it develops from a mainly economic community to a political unit. Protagonists of European integration increasingly see a European identity as necessary for the chances and stability of this multilevel political community. A crucial difference from other situations such as nation-building or immigration countries is that the EU consists of countries that have developed their national identities for a long time. Thus, if a common European identity is to develop, it should not be in competition with the primarily ethnic or ancestral national identities but should be formed against the background of current national identities. Therefore, and before the foundation of the European Community (EC) was based on the aim of overcoming national rivalries and securing peace between its members, many supporters of the EC/EU expected that the national identities would lose importance for the sake of a developing European identity. Yet empirical data (mainly collected in the Eurobarometer surveys) show no decrease in national loyalties and no rise of European identity. They also reveal, from country to country and time to time, differing relationships between national and European identifications, with correlations ranging from negative to none to positive. Thus, the idea of a compatibility of national and European identity gained ground, which some researchers conceptualize as a hierarchical system (similar to identifications with one's town, one's region, and one's nation in federal countries) and others as a nested structure (like a Russian matryoshka doll), which is more apolitical and refers to territories, or as a structure like a marble cake, in which national and European components might mix and blend. Although compatibility of both identities can be shown for most of the member countries, the national identities until now remain by far stronger than the European one. Moreover, it seems as if changes in the relationship between the two identities follow a pattern, which has to do with the EU policy itself. Times of enforced integration and policies, which bring to mind a competition between member countries or between the national and the EU level, tend to reduce the European identification and to strengthen the national ones perhaps because of fears about a loss of national achievements. Thus, it is still an open question how far the existing European identity may reach in times of stress, and there are doubts about an EU-wide loyalty, for instance, in case of redistribution policies. Reasons for the difficulties in developing a strong European identification are manifold—for instance, the absence of a common history, a common language, culture, religion, media system, and so on, as well as the absence of clear boundaries and a clear aim with regard to common political structures. Researchers who conceptualize European identity in strong analogy to national identities therefore are mostly pessimistic about its chances, whereas others hope for the possibility that a common democratic culture might arise out of the heterogeneous general cultures and that this demos-based identity can be become sufficient for future political cohesion

Content and Meanings of Political Identities

The intensities of national, subnational, and supranational identifications and the links between them tell something about the relevance of these identities but nothing about their content or meaning. For a long time, answers to the question about the meaning of national identity were primarily informed by historical and macrosociological research. These mostly formulated dichotomous typologies, for instance, state-building nations versus nation-building states, cultural versus political nations, or ethnic versus civic nations. Sometimes, the former were linked to an Eastern model and the latter to a Western model. Additionally, the former ones are seen as less compatible than the latter ones with democracy, with openness toward immigration and with peaceful relations to other countries. Thus, the ethnic nation is associated with a high potential for aggressive nationalism, whereas the civic nation is linked to a loyal and constructive, but not fanatical, patriotism. Although these dichotomies have become somewhat contested in recent years, on the individual level they are mirrored, albeit not in a perfect way, as shown by diverse national survey data and by two studies in 1995 and 2003 of the International Social Science Programme (ISSP). An ethnic national identity mostly refers to primordial, ascribed features such as ancestry ("blood"), place of birth, and place of living and religion, whereas a civic identity builds on achievable and voluntary characteristics such as subjective feelings of belonging and political rights and institutions. Additionally, both kinds of identity can be linked to cultural objects, for example, language and way of life. Yet these types of identity do not distinguish between nations but rather between different strata of the population within countries. Furthermore, in some countries something like a postnational identity, denying the relevance of nationality and instead referring to the humanity as such, can be found. In any case, the ethnic type of national identity tends to go along with a more closed concept of the nation, in respect to immigrants as well as to other nations and supranational communities.

Finally, recent research questions also deals with the meaning of European identity. Some works on public narratives and discourse analyses find that national identity and European identity are intertwined in a strong way. Either they assume that the image of Europe has already influenced nation building in the early historical phases, or others find that different narratives about Europe are built into the national narratives. But again, analyses of ordinary citizens' thoughts about their national identity and their European identity (on the basis of the Europe-wide survey data of the project "Integrated and United" in 2008 and 2009) do not support these assumptions. Thus, both the national and the European identity concepts, and the links between them, do not distinguish different nations but rather different groups of individuals within nations. An ascribed national identity mostly goes along with a concept of European identity, which rests on the same characteristics, as is the case with religion as a basis of both identities and political rights, whereas cultural features are seen as a dimension that differs in the respective nations and in Europe as a whole. With the ongoing processes of modernization, internationalization, and globalization, the meanings of political identities and their consequences will remain a major field of research in the future.

Bettina Westle
Philipps-Universität Marburg
Marburg, Germany

See also Citizenship; Civil Society; Democratization; Ethnicity; European Integration; Individualism; Multiculturalism; Nation Building; Nationalism; Nationalist Movements; Patriotism; Political Culture; Political Integration; Political Socialization; Racism; Regional Integration (Supranational); Secession; Social Cohesion

Further Readings

Bar-Tal, D., & Staub, E. (Eds.). (1997). *Patriotism in the lives of individuals and nations.* Chicago: Nelson Hall.

Billig, M. (1995). *Banal nationalism.* London: Sage.

Diez Medrano, J. (2003). *Framing Europe: Attitudes to European integration in Germany, Spain and the United Kingdom.* Princeton, NJ: Princeton University Press.

Duchesne, S., & Frognier, A. (2008). National and European identifications: A dual relationship. *Comparative European Politics, 6,* 143–168.

Herrmann, R. K., Risse, T., & Brewer, M. B. (Eds.). (2004). *Transnational identities. Becoming European in the EU.* New York: Rowman & Littlefield.

Howard, J. A. (2000). Social psychology of identities. *Annual Review of Sociology, 26,* 367–393.

Huddy, L. (2001). From social to political identity: A critical examination of social identity theory. *Political Psychology, 22*(1), 127–156.

Jones, F. L., & Smith, P. (2001). Diversity and commonality in national identities: An exploratory analysis of cross-national patterns. *Journal of Sociology, 37*(1), 45–63.

Laitin, D. D. (1998). *Identity in formation.* Ithaca, NY: Cornell University Press.

Malmborg, M., & Strath, B. (2002). *The meaning of Europe.* Oxford, UK: Berg.

McLaren, L. (2006). *Identity, interests and attitudes to European integration.* Basingstoke, UK: Palgrave Macmillan.

Medrano, J. D. (2003). *Framing Europe: Attitudes to European integration in Germany, Spain, and the United Kingdom.* Princeton, NJ: Princeton University Press.

Smith, A. D. (1991). *National identity*. London: Penguin.

Smith, T. W., & Seokho, K. (2006). World opinion: National pride in comparative perspective: 1995/96 and 2003/04. *International Journal of Public Opinion Research, 18*(1), 127–136.

Tajfel, H., & Turner, J. C. (1979). An integrative theory of intergroup conflict. In W. G. Austin & S. Worchel (Eds.), *The social psychology of intergroup conflict* (pp. 33–47). Monterey, CA: Brooks-Cole.

Turner, J. C. (with Hogg, M. A., Oakes, P. J., Reicher, S. D., & Wetherell, M. S.). (1987). *Rediscovering the social group: A self-categorization theory*. Oxford, UK: Blackwell.

Westle, B., & Segatti, P. (Eds.). (2011). *European Identity in the context of national identity*. Oxford, UK: Oxford University Press.

Ideology

The word *ideology* was coined by the French philosopher Destutt de Tracy, who defined it as the "science" of the "intellectual faculties" of animals, therefore as a component of zoology but a component crucial for man, an animal for whom thought is fundamental. What Destutt de Tracy called *idéologie*, he might have named *psychology* (*psyche*, "soul" in Greek) if, as an empiricist and a utilitarian, he had not disapproved of this term. Ideology as he meant it was not just a general grammar but a form of logic that should enable men to think better and therefore to live better together in society. This entry first examines the evolution of ideology in Marxist thought. It then describes the development of the concept of ideology in 20th-century thought—for example, in the analysis of education, the elaboration of structuralism from a Marxism perspective, the explanation of totalitarianism, and the analysis of the relationships between ideology, science, and religion.

Ideology in Marxist Thought

This meaning was radically transformed by Karl Marx (and Friedrich Engels). In their theory—devised for the political purpose of bringing about a liberating revolution—ideology constitutes a sphere of society to be conceptually distinguished from the other two spheres, the economy and politics. Marx took up the word *ideology* and used it negatively to criticize the understanding that the driving force of history is ideas; Marx claimed that the driving force is not ideology but labor. Dividing thinkers into idealists and materialists, Marx declared that ideology was the idealist's illusion. However, despite the fact that society depended on the economy, ideological illusion was an essential part of that society, necessary to its operation. According to Marx, professional thinkers—that is, philosophers, clerics, jurists—believed that the world is governed by ideas. This belief had to be overturned, for in fact effective history was the history of production, labor, and modes of production. Men's consciousness, which was formalized in philosophy, religion, and law, amounted to a mystifying derivative of their material practices. In sum, Marx explained, ideology was "false consciousness," and in their false perception, men turned reality upside down: "If in all ideology men and their circumstances appear upside-down as in a *camera obscura*, this phenomenon arises just as much from their historical life-process as the inversion of objects on the retina does from their physical life-process" (Marx, *The German Ideology*, Pt. 1, sec. A). The error could be corrected, but the victims of the illusion were caught in a formidable trap: They did not know they were under the spell of false representations—hence Marx's stigmatizing of religion as "the opium of the people." The same applied to belief in political representation (universal suffrage, elections, parliaments); such belief mystified men by denying the reality of class differences. Marx's theory of ideology is thus inseparable from a theory of domination (*Herrschaft*): Ideology works to stabilize the existing social order, wherein one group necessarily dominates all others. The dominant class dominates economically (as the labor-exploiting class), politically (it holds state power), and ideologically (its ideas impose themselves as a general belief system).

The Concept of Ideology in 20th-Century Thought

Marx's analysis of ideology as illusion was explicitly reused by Pierre Bourdieu and Jean-Claude Passeron in their theory of how pedagogical and political authority is legitimated. The initial target of their critique was the ideology of giftedness, a model for their critique of ideology as legitimation of authority. In the modern French educational system, Bourdieu and Passeron explained, teachers, pupils, and parents all believe that scholastic success depends on having a gift, when in it fact it depends on the "cultural capital" a person has inherited. False belief in giftedness was what enabled the system to function, objectifying the failure of some pupils and legitimating the success of others in psychological terms when in fact that success was the product of the schooling system's "symbolic violence." Domination is all the more effective because the social mass of "the dominated" is blind to the principle of domination. Theories of ideology thus became linked to theories working to criticize and combat illusion and alienation.

In Marx's thinking, the polemic aspect was crucial because while criticism was an active practice amounting to revolutionary mobilization, it was also an intellectual one (the subtitle of *Capital* is "Critique of Political Economy"). Ideology was to be criticized in the name of science, which combated ideas that were derived not from true knowledge but from mere opinion (or the *doxa*, a Greek term Bourdieu liked to use). But ideology was not just false; it was also linked to the interests of the respective classes battling each other. The ideology of the nobility in ancien régime France (according to which the social order was founded on three hierarchically ranked groups: the nobility, on top, followed by the clergy, and then the third estate) ran up against the ideology of the bourgeoisie, a class fighting in favor of its own understanding—corresponding to its own interests—that all men had equal rights. This egalitarian, individualist ideology triumphed with the French Revolution, and it allowed the market system to develop and spread. But the revolutionary proletariat, declared Marx, could free itself from all such illusions and attain true knowledge. The various Marxist theories could therefore present themselves as true knowledge that coincided with the only true ideology: the ideology of the proletariat.

While ideologies divided society, they also played a functional role: It was precisely because ideology was an illusion that it enabled the given social order to maintain itself. In Louis Althusser's structural Marxist perspective, developed in the mid-1960s, ideology is the sphere of representation, and it could be an efficient cause of some forms of social organization, though in the last analysis, that role was determined by economic organization. An example of this relation between the sphere of representation and the economic sphere is Christianity in the feudal mode of production. The feudal arrangement known as the corvée amounted to blatant exploitation in that the serf had to work for the feudal lord for a certain amount of time every year, receiving nothing in exchange. By sanctifying this social order, Christianity enabled the feudal system of extorting "surplus value" to remain in place, whereas in the capitalist economy, that same extortion was masked by the form known as the wage. Moreover, in the capitalist economy, the ideology of equal human rights allowed for the perpetuation of a system based on radical inequality—the inequality between those who had to sell their labor power and those who were in a position to buy it. Revolutionary struggle, then, in Marx's understanding, was first and foremost an ideological battle whose ultimate purpose was to dispel illusion.

The understanding that ideology stabilizes existing social power relations was used in various forms by all communist regimes. In these regimes, ideology—in the form of propaganda and dogma that can be changed at any moment by the political power—would promote "true" doctrine. This in turn explains why for Hannah Arendt and Carl J. Friedrich, the existence of a single mass party with an official ideology was one defining attribute of the totalitarian syndrome. There was no need for people to believe in the ideology; in a totalitarian system, ideology of itself forbade all discourse except the one emanating from the party, and it did not matter that people knew that discourse to be a false one. Here, ideology has been virtually emptied of content, becoming little more than an obligation to lie and to acclaim the party and its leader.

In Maoism, on the other hand, ideology was conceived of as the ultimate condition for the triumph of the revolution. Ideological combat was the driving force of Mao Zedong's Cultural Revolution, launched in 1966. The understanding here was that the political and economic revolution had not been enough to transform China radically, lastingly; what was needed was a revolution in belief that would replace the bourgeois ideology with a new, people's ideology (wherein a sense of the collective would put down individualism, for example). As Mao saw it, having pure, radical revolutionary ideas was more important than having experience or expert knowledge. The ideological superstructure was presented as a force with the power either to slow down the revolution or to drive it forward. This explains the attacks in Mao's China against such doctrines as revisionism and Confucianism and also the violence against people who bore these "deviations" or traditions within them: They were stigmatized as—and treated like—vermin that had to be eradicated. In this way, Maoism actually reversed Marxism: The structure of social power relations was understood to *depend* on representations—that is, doctrinal purity. The Chinese Cultural Revolution can be understood as a war waged by one component of the political elite against other components, but it did not bring ideological struggle to an end; it continues in post-Maoist China. The party's hold on the means and content of communication has been the determinant for keeping it in power, and it does not hesitate to use strong coercive means. In any case, the collapse of Soviet communism definitively devalued the prestige of communism in the West. The "end of ideology" announced by Daniel Bell in 1960—namely, the end of the prestige of communist millenarianism—affected not only communist sympathizers but also the communist parties themselves. Some authors say that religious belief has returned to fill the void left by communist ideology, as if a society needed ideology. The claim leads to establishing an equivalency between a political program such as communism and systems of representation that are not necessarily linked to programs for transforming the world. This brings up the question of the political meaning of Islamism and its relation to theocratic programs.

The role played by Marxism as dogma in the Soviet regime led analysts to describe it as an "ideocracy": Because the communist party and its leaders had to justify any and all decisions with reference to an absolute truth whose prescriptions had to be followed in all circumstances, communist ideology has been described as a millenarian religious thought system. The same term has been applied to Nazism, but this disregards the real difference between the rudimentary totalitarian language of Nazism—the Nazi *Weltanschaung*, comprising *Führerprinzip*, hatred of democracy and Marxism, and anti-Semitism—and communist ideology, structured by abundant and in some cases sophisticated doctrines and numerous cultural references. Communist ideology has been compared with church ideology, and the term *ideocracy* has been extended to include power systems such as Islam in which religion structures social life. The anthropologist and political thinker Ernest Gellner grouped together communism and Islamism as ideocracies but specified that Islamic regimes do not impose a single economic form on their societies (as communist regimes did) and, thus, they allow the development of the market and industrial society. From this perspective, ideology appears a universal social dimension that can take a variety of forms, depending on the content of its doctrine and institutions. For example, scriptural religions such as Protestantism, where all individuals are called on to read the Bible in their vernacular language, have an effect on the social system as a whole: They foster national cultural homogeneity in countries where they are the dominant religion. The social sciences' use of the notion of ideology presents insoluble epistemological problems. Distinguishing ideology from true scientific knowledge presupposes that those who set out to do so (such as Althusser and Bourdieu) are in possession of a differentiation criterion. Marx believed he had one; he believed that history itself was the movement of a self-affirming, self-deploying truth. As Bourdieu saw it, sociology—which implies doing sociology of sociology—would provide such a criterion. This claim may seem similar to Georg Wilhelm Friedrich Hegel's that he possessed absolute knowledge in the form of "the science of science."

The belief that ideology stands opposed to true knowledge, that it is false consciousness as opposed to knowledge of objective truth, may thus appear the result of a paradox, since what is assumed to be science (historical materialism for Marx and Marxists, critical sociology for Bourdieu and Bourdieusians) is understood to be beyond critical suspicion.

Dominique Colas
Institut d'Etudes Politiques de Paris (Sciences Po)
Paris, France

See also Liberalism; Marxism; Political Philosophy; Theocracy; Totalitarianism; Utopianism

Further Readings

Althusser, L., & Balibar, E. (1967). *Reading capital* (B. Brewster, Trans.). London: Verso.

Bell, D. (2000). *The end of ideology: On the exhaustion of political ideas in the fifties*. Cambridge, MA: Harvard University Press.

Bourdieu, P., & Passeron, J.-C. (1977). *Reproduction in education, society and culture* (R. Nice, Trans.). London: Sage.

Gellner, E. (1994). *Conditions of liberty: Civil society and its rivals*. London: Penguin.

Marx, K., & Engels, F. (1972). Excerpts from *German ideology*. In R. C. Tucker (Ed.), *The Marx-Engels reader* (pp. 146–200). New York: W. W. Norton. (Original work written 1845–1846)

Immigration Policy

The migration of people from one territory to another is one of the oldest practices of mankind. However, immigration policy is a broad label encompassing a range of different and formally unrelated issues as diverse as the Viking settlement of Anglo-Saxon England following the Roman withdrawal in 410 CE; the triangular trade in slaves up to the 19th century; European immigration to the New World in the 19th and 20th centuries, and large-scale resettlements following conflicts such as World War II, the 1947 India–Pakistan War, and the Rwandan genocide of 1994. The first part of this contribution sets out what these issues are in the countries listed above before moving on to consider how they have been analyzed in political science.

Defining Immigration Policy

Conventionally, immigration policy is considered to refer primarily to the responses of governments in developed countries to migratory pressures from less developed countries post-1945. These essentially "rich" developed countries can be further subdivided into three broad categories. First, predominantly Anglo-Saxon immigration countries such as the United States, Canada, Australia, and New Zealand have traditions of accepting immigration that long predate 1945. Second, Western European countries have since 1945 been transformed from countries of emigration to countries of immigration. This transformation has not been uniform: Thus, France, the United Kingdom (UK), West Germany, the Netherlands, Belgium, and Austria all experienced large-scale immigration during the 1950s and 1960s, while countries such as Spain, Italy, and Ireland have only become destinations for immigration since the end of the Cold War. Lastly, the countries of Central and Eastern Europe have themselves also become destinations for migration since the turn of the millennium and especially since becoming member states of the European Union (EU) in 2004 and 2007. Notably, the developed countries of Asia, particularly Japan, Taiwan, and South Korea, have only experienced comparatively minimal levels of immigration.

Despite constituting just a relatively small element of human migrations both historically and contemporarily, immigration to developed countries has become one of the most sensitive, controversial, and therefore important domestic political issues. For this reason, the area has attracted increasing attention from scholars across a range of cognate disciplines, including economics, sociology, development studies, anthropology, geography, demography, history, education, psychology, and political science. Within political science, scholars of public policy, political theory, comparative politics, political economy, and international relations have all contributed to our understanding of this field.

At its most elementary level, immigration policy addresses the control of entry to a state's territory. The physical control of borders, through passport controls, visa requirements, or quite simply a barrier, remains one of the key deliverables for any government and indeed constitutes one of the fundamental elements of state sovereignty. In this context, the EU's policy in recent decades of removing border checks between its member states (the so-called Schengen Agreement) and replacing them with a closely guarded external border vis-à-vis third countries is particularly significant. However, and especially in the modern age of global travel, a high degree of control over frontiers, although frequently promised in election campaigns, is seldom easy to deliver, and borders, whether they are the U.S. border with Mexico, the Israeli border with Gaza, or the EU's external borders in Eastern Europe and the Mediterranean Sea, are notoriously porous. In consequence, illegal immigration remains a major challenge, both from a humanitarian perspective of human trafficking and in the context of enforcement. Prevention and return have become a top priority in international diplomacy: Thus, the EU has signed readmission agreements with a range of countries, as well as seeking the cooperation of countries such as Libya in preventing boats from leaving for southern Italy in the first place.

Five Dimensions of Immigration Policy

When it comes to managing and shaping migration flows, as opposed to simply controlling their entry, it is possible to identify five principal constituent elements of this field: labor migration, the increased importance of political asylum, the growth of immigration of dependents, ethnic immigration, and issues related to the integration of immigrants into the host country.

Labor Migration

First, labor migration has perhaps been the single most important element of immigration policy, and it underpins much of the migration that developed countries have received over the past 60-odd years. This is hardly surprising given the existing and indeed growing differences in wealth between developed countries and their neighbors. The desire to work is also a major driving force behind illegal immigration and residence. While the authorities in developed countries do formally seek to clamp down on such activities, for instance, by raiding building sites and farms where illegal immigrants are known to work, they are also often tacitly tolerated as a useful contribution to the economy. Several countries, such as Spain, Italy, and the United States, have also instituted amnesties, sometimes repeatedly, to regularize the status of illegal immigrants.

Labor migration can be both high skilled and low skilled. For instance, much of the labor migration to Western Europe up to the early 1970s, which numbered millions of people, was low skilled, largely from Mediterranean countries such as Italy, Spain, Yugoslavia, and Turkey. In some countries, notably West Germany, such migration was explicitly expected to be temporary in nature, leading to the coining of the (pejorative) term *Gastarbeiter* ("guest worker"). Labor migration was radically cut back during the 1970s and 1980s, but high-skilled migration has witnessed a resurgence since the late 1990s, with a range of countries now introducing points-based immigration systems originally pioneered in Australia and Canada.

This resurgence has been linked to two key developments in Western societies: first, the twin phenomena of increasing life expectancy and falling birthrates has created a demographic imbalance and the prospect of falling populations in many countries, especially Germany, Italy, Spain, and Eastern European countries, and labor migration is one key option for redressing this. Thus, the UK's decision not to close its labor market to the new member states of the EU in 2004 led to large-scale labor migration of up to 1 million persons, as a result of which the UK's population is projected to increase rather than decrease over the coming decades. Similarly, the comparatively dynamic state of the U.S. population is also largely down to recent immigration. The second key development is skills shortages, which have emerged in a range of sectors, most notably information technology.

Political Asylum

The second element of immigration policy has been the rise in importance of political asylum. Asylum is a humanitarian policy designed to afford protection to those persecuted for their political views in their home countries and its legal expression, the 1951 Geneva Convention, constitutes one of the best known cornerstones of international law. With low numbers of claimants globally until the end of the 1970s, the ability to seek political asylum was initially largely notional. However, since then, numbers have risen strongly, generally affecting those countries with an already existing sizeable immigrant population. Thus, West Germany was the principal destination for asylum seekers in Europe during the 1980s; since then, the UK, France, Netherlands, Austria, Switzerland, and

Belgium have also all emerged as major recipient countries. With rising numbers have come rising costs and not infrequently social tensions, which in turn have propelled asylum up the political agenda. In response, governments have introduced a range of measures to restrict the ability of refugees to lodge asylum claims, such as visa restrictions for major countries of origin, the principle of the "safe third country" (i.e., transit country), and the "safe country of origin" principle. Refugee organizations such as the UNHCR (the Office of the United Nations High Commissioner for Refugees) criticize that such measures undermine the spirit, if not the letter, of the Geneva Convention.

The annual numbers of asylum seekers have fluctuated widely over the years. The early and late 1990s were major periods of asylum migration, although, since the early 2000s, applications have dropped back. In the case of Germany, which had hitherto been the world's most significant destinations for asylum seekers, these are now historically low levels. In processing asylum cases, government agencies have generally tended to take a restrictive view of claims, and initial recognition rates have generally been around 25%, although in some countries they are as low as 5%. Nonetheless, the tendency of rejected asylum seekers to appeal their decision through the courts, plus logistical difficulties in physically deporting such persons once legal avenues have been exhausted, has meant that many asylum claims take years to complete, which has in turn led to a considerable backlog of cases in many countries.

Immigration of Dependents

Third, most developed countries have since the 1970s experienced a rapid growth in the immigration of dependents. Such migration is considered "secondary" because it cannot take place without the immigration of a "primary" migrant—typically a labor migrant but also potentially a recognized refugee. The quantitative dimension of such secondary migration should not be underestimated, and dependent migration currently constitutes the largest form of legal migration to developed countries, exceeding both asylum and labor migration. Crucially, dependent migration is generally regarded as a human right and in consequence, many countries have not found it easy to impose restrictions on this form of migration. Nonetheless, the right to family reunification has certainly been circumscribed in recent years, with countries imposing conditions such as minimum living space, maximum ages for dependent children, and, most recently, the introduction by several European countries of pre-entry requirements such as the successful completion of language and integration courses.

Ethnic Immigration

The fourth aspect is ethnic immigration, which broadly speaking refers to privileged entry conditions sometimes granted by countries to persons of specific ethnic and/or cultural origins. For instance, Israel guarantees residence to Jews from all over the world, regardless of whether they have any active ties to Israel. Likewise, the origins of the Green Card Lottery in the United States (through which 50,000 permanent green cards are issued annually on the basis of computer-generated random selection) lie in a decision by Congress to privilege immigration from Ireland. But the single largest instance of this immigration has been to Germany, with more than 4 million ethnic Germans having immigrated since 1950. Initially, these came from Poland, Czechoslovakia, and Romania, but since the late 1980s these have come overwhelmingly from the countries of the former Soviet Union. Typically, such ethnic Germans had been living in these countries for centuries but had then experienced persecution at the hands of the communist authorities. Germany initially offered generous immigration conditions, including extensive financial assistance, but the very large numbers that arrived between 1989 and 1993 (more than 1.4 million) led to this being sharply curtailed. The relative weakness of the German economy since 2000 has caused ethnic German migration to fall back to much lower levels.

Integration of Immigrants

The final aspect of policy to be considered here is in fact one of the most difficult: the successful integration of immigrants into their new host societies. Strictly speaking, integration is not related to the process of immigration itself; however, because integration arises as a direct consequence of immigration, the two are conventionally viewed under the same rubric. The principal policy challenge here is that immigrants across the developed world broadly speaking show similar socioeconomic deficits compared with the indigenous population, including higher unemployment, lower educational outcomes, lower wages, and substandard housing. That said, there are significant differences in the socioeconomic profile of immigrant groups: For instance, in the UK, people of Indian origin are generally better integrated socioeconomically than those of Bangladeshi origin.

The challenge of integration encompasses a particularly wide range of policy fields, including education, labor market, housing, health, and law and order. It includes not only residence policy but also citizenship and naturalization policy. What is more, integration is a highly symbolic area and touches on powerful mobilizers such as cultural identity and belonging. For instance, the question of Muslim head scarves in France, and especially in its schools, has polarized public opinion for more than 20 years and is considered by some to be challenging the Republican emphasis on secularism. Similarly, populist politicians such as Pim Fortuyn and Geert Wilders in the Netherlands, and Jörg Haider in Austria and the French Front National, have often politicized what they see as incompatibility between Islam and the respective indigenous culture. In this way, integration covers both substantive and symbolic issues, and in political debate, perhaps unsurprisingly, the two often get (deliberately) blurred.

Certainly, since 2000, governments across Europe have imposed new, largely symbolic restrictions on the acquisition of citizenship by foreigners. Thus, most countries now require applicants for naturalization to pass a citizenship test and to attend a citizenship ceremony, often involving an oath of allegiance as well. Such practices are of course well established in traditional countries of immigration such as the United States, Canada, and Australia, and indeed these countries' experiences have explicitly served as a template for the introduction of these citizenship policies in Europe. At the same time, there has been a general liberalizing trend across Europe in the acquisition of citizenship at birth, with countries increasingly using *ius soli* (the territorial principle) as well as *ius sanguinis* (the principle of descent). In parallel, dual citizenship, which once was widely rejected in European citizenship policies, is increasingly accepted, if not formally then through far-reaching exemptions.

Political Science and Immigration Policy

Together, then, these five key dimensions illustrate the complexity and the multifaceted nature of this controversial policy field of immigration policy. Arguably, this explains why scholars have struggled so far to develop an integrated, multidisciplinary perspective on immigration that can address the holistic aspect of the field while still capturing the specificities of its individual constituent elements. Indeed, the dominant explanations for migration and integration have come from economics and sociology, respectively. For instance, economists argue that wage differentials between economies create incentives for labor migration from the lower wage (or poorer) country to the higher wage (or richer) country. Certainly, this is a powerful explanation and helps account for both formal and informal labor migration over the decades, including the guest worker migration to West Germany, illegal migration from Mexico to the United States, and Polish migration to the UK after its 2004 accession to the EU. But equally, straight economics encounters difficulties in fully accounting for why some countries receive more asylum seekers than others.

From the perspective of political science and its several subdisciplines, including public policy analysis, immigration policy is a relatively new object of study, and scholars have yet to bring its full analytical toolkit to bear on its various elements. To date, though, a number of key approaches can be identified in the literature. The first approach is grounded in political economy, regulation, and welfare, with Gary Freeman as its leading exponent. In his work, he emphasizes the role that organized interests, and especially business interests, play in structuring immigration policy, thereby creating a clear pressure toward liberalization. A second approach draws on the role universal human rights play in requiring states to accept "unwanted" immigration, including dependent migration. At the same time, as Christian Joppke (1999) points out, states have proved to be quite activist in responding to such challenges; for instance, Germany's 1993 constitutional amendment to limit asylum can be seen as a prima facie example of a state wresting back control over a policy are.

Joppke's analysis is particularly germane to the issue of state sovereignty, which in turn has underpinned the contribution of international relations to our understanding of immigration policy. Here, the question of control and the ability of states to exercise it have traditionally been dominant. However, more recently, other aspects have come to the fore, in particular globalization, as Saskia Sassen points out, and increasingly security, as Barry Buzan, Ole Wæver, and Japp de Wilde have described. Indeed, Samuel Huntington took the latter argument several steps further in an (in) famous article mapping out a "clash of civilizations" between Christianity and Islam—a relationship that of course lies at the heart of much of the debate, at least in Europe, about integration.

Beyond international relations and political economy, a number of seminal contributions have been grounded in political theory, reflecting the fact that asylum and citizenship are two issues that directly intersect with notions of equality, justice, ethics, and pluralism. As well as discussions of asylum from this perspective (e.g., Matthew Gibney, 2004), multiculturalism has emerged from the pluralist stable as an influential model for immigrant integration (Bhikhu Parekh, 2005). However, although multiculturalism remains popular in the New World and especially Canada and Australia, it has found fewer devotees in Europe: On the contrary, recent debates in the Netherlands and Germany have reemphasized the more assimilatory nature of integration.

Elsewhere in the study of citizenship and integration, Adrian Favell's exploration of the philosophies of integration in the UK and France remains an indispensable point of reference, as does Yasemin Soysal's provocative discussion of "personhood" and its implications for the "hollowing out" of national citizenships in Western Europe. Other authors, such as Randall Hansen (2000) and Simon Green (2004), emphasize the importance of history and path dependence in understanding the evolution and operation of citizenship policy in France, Germany, and the UK.

Last but not the least, a thriving subfield has sprung up in recent years examining the development and role of the EU in immigration policy. The creation of the Schengen area plus the importance of some common labor market policies has made immigration within the EU a more important concern. As well as important overviews of this field, especially that of Andrew Geddes (2008), security has been the focus of extensive attention.

Conclusion

Although a brief overview such as this cannot hope to do full justice either to the complexities of the field of immigration policy or to the rich variety of the scholarly canon dealing with this policy, this entry has sought to do two things. First, it has sketched out in broad terms the nature and challenges of immigration policy as well as political actors' and institutions' responses to it in comparative perspective. Second, it has introduced the principal scholarly contributions of political science to our understanding of immigration policy in all its forms. There is no doubt that collectively these contributions have served to emphasize the centrality of the discipline to the purpose of understanding this vital policy field more broadly. At the same time, much remains to be done. Leaving aside the perhaps rather lofty aspiration of developing an integrated, cross-disciplinary model of immigration, the challenge for political scientists in this field is to provide further insights at all levels, to include the roots of party political positions on immigration, psephological aspects of immigrant voters, the formulation processes of government policy, the development of cross-national migration responses, the evolution and formalization of citizenship and integration policy, and the process of administration of these policies.

Simon Green
Aston University
Birmingham, United Kingdom

See also Citizenship; Path Dependence; Racism; Security Apparatus; Sovereignty

Further Readings

Buzan, B., Wæver, O., & de Wilde, J. (1998). *Security: A new framework for analysis.* Boulder, CO: Lynne Rienner.

Favell, A. (2001). *Philosophies of integration* (2nd ed.). London: Palgrave.

Geddes, A. (2008). *Immigration and European integration* (2nd ed.). Manchester, UK: Manchester University Press.

Gibney, M. (2004). *The politics and ethics of asylum: Liberal democracy and the response to refugees.* Cambridge, UK: Cambridge University Press.

Green, S. (2004). *The politics of exclusion: Institutions and immigration policy in contemporary Germany.* Manchester, UK: Manchester University Press.

Hansen, R. (2000). *Citizenship and immigration in post-war Britain.* Oxford, UK: Oxford University Press.

Huntington, S. P. (1993). The clash of civilizations? *Foreign Affairs, 72,* 22–49.

Joppke, C. (1999). *Immigration and the nation-state: The United States, Germany and Great Britain.* Oxford, UK: Oxford University Press.

Messina, A. (2007). *The logics and politics of post-WWII migration to Western Europe.* Cambridge, UK: Cambridge University Press

Parekh, B. (2005). *Rethinking multiculturalism* (2nd ed.). London: Palgrave.

Sassen, S. (1996). *Losing control? Sovereignty in an age of globalization.* New York: Columbia University Press.

Impacts, Policy

The concept of policy impacts refers to the effects and consequences of public policy on individuals, groups, the broader society, and the natural world in which we live. All policies have intended targets but are more or less successful in attaining their stated goals. This entry examines the nature of public policy in political science, discusses several taxonomies for understanding the targets for public policy, and also discusses the linkages between the design of policies and their final outcomes.

Public Policy and Political Science

Public policies are the mechanisms used by governing authorities to allocate benefits, burdens, and regulations for the society. Public policies are what governments and their agents *produce*, including statutes, budgets, resolutions, proclamations, programs, and direct contacts with people. Policies must be understood as nested in one another. Thus, the U.S. Constitution is a fundamental public policy. Statutes passed by Congress or state legislatures also are policies, as are the guidelines written by agencies as policy is implemented. Court rulings may change a statute, and thus court rulings also are public policies. A program established by a local government to regulate or provide services is itself a part of the public policy chain. These policies are revealed as texts and also in the actual practices and discourse of those involved in crafting or implementing public policy. Policy as written may not be the way it actually is perceived and may or may not be put in place exactly as written. Policy may have intended as well as unintended consequences: direct effects and indirect ones.

Although the effects of public policy have always been of concern to political science, this field was slow to develop. Part of the reason is the sheer complexity of policy content and the difficulty in finding common elements across different levels and types of policy. Another reason for the slow development of theory about policy impacts is the assumption that policy consequences are guided mainly by policy-specific theory, which often is simply not an accurate understanding of policy effects. So, for example, it is sometimes assumed that the impact of environmental policy depends on what theory of the environment is embedded in the policy rather than on theories of human behavior and values.

During the past 20 years, however, political science has embraced the study of policy consequences to the point that some are advocating a "policy-centric" approach to the study of politics in which two major questions dominate the field. The first is how to explain and understand how and why governments produce the kinds of policy designs that they have, and the second is how to understand the impacts of those designs.

Theories of Policy Consequences

Theodore Lowi is generally credited with being the first to offer a systematic theory of policy impacts. He popularized the phrase *policy creates politics*, thereby reversing the common causal pattern in political science. Lowi contends that there are characteristics of policy that encourage affected people to mobilize and that without these characteristics, elites will dominate. His typology is based on two dimensions: the probability of coercion and whether the policy identifies specific targets or consists of general rules that affect the environment of groups. From these dimensions, he posits four types of policy: distributive, regulatory, redistributive, and constituent. Regulatory policy, involving the imposition of costs in the environment, will produce pluralist competition according to Lowi. Policy becomes a temporary compromise between competing groups, but if policy becomes too harsh on some, they are expected to mobilize and change the governing officials or change the policy. Redistributive policy, such as welfare policy, Lowi contends, does not produce pluralist forms of subsequent participation but instead is dominated by elites who lead major segments of society who act to insure social stability. Distributive policy is the classic pork barrel and is inherently elitist, according to Lowi's framework. His fourth type, constituent policy, produces individualistic claims on government.

James Wilson proposed an alternative to Lowi's typology. Wilson's typology begins with whether benefits are narrowly focused or broadly cast, and whether costs are narrowly focused or dispersed broadly among the public. When benefits are broadly distributed (e.g., national defense) and costs are broadly distributed (e.g., taxes supporting national defense), then all people have about equal incentives to incorporate this policy into their behavior. The result is majoritarian politics. In majoritarian politics, elected officials pay special attention to what the majority wants. When benefits are concentrated on just a few (such as welfare recipients) but costs are distributed widely among taxpayers, there is little incentive for those bearing the costs to pay attention to the policy itself but great advantage to potential beneficiaries. This produces what Wilson called a clientist style of politics in which elected leaders distribute favors to their clients while apathetic taxpayers do not pay attention. A third type of politics, entrepreneurial politics, occurs when small portions of society pay the costs to benefit large groups—for example, education. This type of politics results in virtually uncontrolled growth because of the strong political payoffs for distributing numerous benefits at the expense of so few. Since most policies are either entrepreneurial or clientist, government grows until it becomes inefficient and produces more goods and services than people actually want.

A third typology, which seems to explain more about attitudes and participation patterns, was developed by Anne Schneider and Helen Ingram. Their theory recognizes that public policy involves far more than the allocation of benefits and burdens, and that all aspects of policy design may be important. Policy design refers to the empirical characteristics of a statute, agency guidelines, or practices of street-level officials. They contend that policies contain common observable elements that influence the types of impacts of the policy. Policies typically have target populations—the people affected positively or negatively by the policy, goals or problems to be solved, benefits or costs or both that are being allocated, and rules that guide or constrain action or specify who is to do what to whom, when, and with what resources. Policies also contain tools that motivate agents or members of the general public to take the action recommended by the policy and rationales embedded in the policy text or used to legitimate the policy. Policies typically have an implementation "chain" in which one level of policy directs the actions of another at a "lower" level. Hence, policies contain people, whose behavior impinges on policy consequences. Policies also contain underlying assumptions about how people behave and what motivates them, about cause and effect, about scientific knowledge, and about the values that should be pursued.

Policies are not simply instrumental means, however, and contain symbolic and interpretive elements that are important in understanding their impacts. For example, policies that impose burdens on people may simultaneously show their respect for these people. Or policies that impose burdens may denigrate the target groups and blame them for their own plight. The consequences of these two types of policy are quite different.

Schneider and Ingram's theory contends that policy designs are sometimes produced in institutions dominated by divisive social constructions that stigmatize some and extol the virtues of others. These social constructions interact with vastly unequal political power of target populations producing policy designs that, in turn, produce distinctive political attitudes and participation. Schneider and Ingram posit four types of target populations. *Advantaged* populations have considerable political power and positive social constructions, such as being "deserving," "intelligent," hardworking," and so on. Advantaged groups mainly receive benefits from government, but even if regulations are imposed, they tend to be those supported by the advantaged populations themselves as necessary to sustain their social position. Politics is a "game," but it is winnable if played by the rules. Advantaged groups have high levels of traditional political participation.

Contenders also have a great deal of political power but carry negative social constructions. Contenders know that they are controversial and that their interests clash with others. The types of policy they receive tend to provide significant benefits that are however well disguised and protected from public view. The consequences of such designs are that contenders become suspicious and vigilant. They believe that the political game involves the raw use of power and is often crooked. Their participation patterns tend toward low mobilization but high levels of financial assistance to candidates and office holders, along with intense lobbying.

A third type of target group Schneider and Ingram called *disadvantaged* in that they have almost no political power and are socially constructed as helpless, needy, and unable to function effectively in a highly competitive society. Public officials need to be careful with disadvantaged groups, because there would be political damage if an official appears to be mean spirited; on the other hand, there is nothing much to be gained by providing benefits to these people. Hence, policy tends toward paternalistic assistance and considerable rhetoric about the needs of these people but inadequate resources to meet their needs. The results of such policy designs is that disadvantaged people come to believe that they are helpless and needy; that government "wants" to assist but does not have the resources to do so; and that their problems are best resolved through religious organizations, nonprofits, and local government. Traditional participation tends to be very low—low turnout, lack of contacting officials, and not much participation in interest groups.

The fourth type of target groups are *deviants*—people with almost no political power who are viewed negatively as dangerous, violent, a threat to "our way of life." Policy directed at these groups tends to be overly punitive, as policymakers realize that considerable political capital can be gained by punishing these groups and holding them responsible for most of society's problems, and the groups themselves have so little credibility that they are unable to respond. Traditional participation among deviants is very low but other forms—strikes, demonstrations, riots, terrorist attacks—will occur.

This typology also is useful in understanding policy consequences for social justice. The dynamics of degenerative democracy produces too many benefits for advantaged groups. The groups themselves support public officials who provide them with desired policy, and others will not complain because the positive social construction of advantaged groups means that they are viewed as "deserving." Often, their interests are characterized as being necessary for the public good. And punishment for deviants will also become excessive as political leaders seek to outdo one another in being "tough." In degenerative politics, where divisive social constructions interact with power to produce distinctive types of designs, disadvantaged people continue to suffer from limited access to opportunities—poor schools and unemployment producing a continuing underclass.

One primary contribution of political science to the study of policy impacts has been to broaden the discussion beyond the narrow emphasis on whether policy has been successful in solving problems or achieving its instrumental goals. Deborah Stone, for example, has been especially influential in addressing the many complexities of policy consequences. Policies typically have multiple goals, some of which may be in conflict with others. Additionally, a policy success in the eyes of one person may well be a policy failure in the eyes of another.

The question remains, however: Are there any systematic characteristics of policy designs that increase the likelihood of policy producing desired consequences? Implementation scholars disagree over this question, as some such as Paul Sabatier argue that strong statutes are more likely to produce desired outcomes. Strong statutes contain clear statements of objectives, strong tools such as mandates, and little or no discretion for lower level agents. Others contend that policy designs must be fit into context and that designs that permit greater discretion at lower levels enable local officials to use local knowledge and are more likely to produce desired results. Still others focus on an analysis of the context itself and argue that the characteristics of policy at a higher level need to differ, depending on context. For example, if cause and effect theory is uncertain or weak, or if the context varies extensively across locales, then policy should encompass a learning mode sometimes called *adaptive management* so that local-level agencies can adjust the policy as they learn more about its consequences.

Some political scientists question what constitutes "good" public policy. Many focus on economic criteria such as efficiency, although complexities in measuring societal benefits and costs typically prevent most policies being assessed in efficiency terms. Some propose that effectiveness is a guide—in the sense that it is effective in addressing problems. As mentioned above, however, there may be many different indicators of effectiveness and little agreement on which are more important. Others have added that justice (fairness) must be considered when assessing the desired consequences of policy and that support for citizenship and institutions also must be ascertained. Unintended consequences must be considered and weighed against the positive effects.

To summarize, political science has made major contributions to the study of policy impacts, particularly in proposing a more complex way of conceptualizing what is meant by public policy and by broadening the discussion beyond the narrow view that policy serves only to solve a specific problem. Policy has many consequences for democracy, and theories of policy impact need to embrace them.

Anne Schneider
Arizona State University
Tempe, Arizona, United States

See also Implementation

Further Readings

Lowi, T. (2009). *Arenas of power*. Boulder, CO: Paradigm Press.

Sabatier, P., & Jenkins-Smith, H. (1993). *Policy change and learning: An advocacy coalition approach*. Boulder, CO: Westview Press.

Schneider, A. L., & Ingram, H. (Eds.). (2005). *Deserving and entitled*. New York: State University of New York Press.

Soss, J., Hacker, J. S., & Mettler, S. (Eds.). (2007). *Remaking America: Democracy and public policy in an age of inequality*. New York: Russell Sage Foundation.

Stone, D. (2001). *Policy paradox: The art of political decision making*. New York: W. W. Norton.

IMPERIALISM

The term *imperialism* contains the prefix *imperial*, at once an adjective and a noun. As an adjective, *imperial* means pertaining to empire or the ruler, an emperor or empress, and this is used to refer to characteristics that befit a ruler, such as majesty, regality, or grandeur. The term *imperial* also conveys the character of rule by a sovereign state over its dependencies or a commanding quality or manner of that rule. For these reasons, the term *imperial* has been associated with despotic, high-handed, and/or authoritarian rule. As a noun and in the context of political authority, an *imperial* is a member of imperial party, including troops. Imperialism in the senses above implies the pursuit of grandeur or the desire, policy, practice, or advocacy of extending the power and dominion of one political entity over another. From the above perspectives, imperialism has a long ancestry in multiple traditions and thus may be found historically to exist on many continents. One could reasonably speak of imperialism in the contexts of historic China and France, the Moguls in India, the Roman and Holy Roman empires, the Ottoman, Mali, and Mayan empires, and the like. In most of these contexts, an imperialist would mean an adherent of an emperor or empress or an advocate of such an adherence. The associated irredentist processes and forms constituted imperialism in its present understanding. For instance, these empires necessarily originated from a locality before outward expansions that required the dismantling of competing governments and the subordination of the resident authorities. Still, their ideologies, policies, systems of law, and organizing principles and norms emerged from contexts that are different from those of modern imperialisms.

The shift toward modern imperialism began under Pax Britannica, the period when Great Britain set the terms of the European order (and by extension world order) owing to its defeat of France at Waterloo in 1815, its unchallenged sea power, and control of the key naval trade routes. Pax Britannica coincided with scientific and industrial revolutions, the rise of finance capital and consumer society, transformations in the material conditions of states, and advances in warfare and bureaucracy that set the context for unprecedented overseas British expansionism in Africa, Asia, and Latin America. Subsequently, Britain came to dominate overseas markets and managed to project its "influence" over most regions of the world. The terms and conditions of British expansionism gave modern imperialism its distinctive characteristics. Above all, the new British expansionism involved a worldwide colonial system. From Waterloo in 1815 to the 1870 Franco-Prussian War to the beginning of World War I in 1914, Great Britain helped set in motion processes, structures, and relationships under a colonial order consisting of zones of influence, colonies, protectorates, trusteeships, and the like. Moreover, Britain associated its own dominions (Australia, Canada, New Zealand, and South Africa), other European powers, most notably France, and Japan and the United States in the management of this order under distinct colonial systems. For the above reasons, the expansionist activities of the era extending from the 19th century to the early 20th century were dubbed the New Imperialism.

There is a long-standing debate in Britain and the West, particularly among politicians and academics, about the motivation, wisdom, and utility of *imperialism* as well as the usefulness of the term itself. Most authors would trace the debate back to John Hobson's 1902 critique of imperialism and questions raised about the factors contributing to the New Imperialism. Accordingly, the roots of the New Imperialism are found in policies linked to the resolutions of the following problems: the maldistribution of wealth and underconsumption, the requirements of finance capitalism; commercial competition among rival industrialized countries; the erosion of British hegemony and the subsequent breakdown of the concert of Europe; challenges to Britain's dominance in world trade; quest for a supply of cheap raw materials to support home industries as a means to recovery from the Long Depression of 1873 to 1896 and beyond; the abandonment of free trade by rival European powers; and the need to overcome the constraints of domestic markets through export opportunities. Furthermore, it has been argued that imperialism was an instrument of national cohesion in the face of domestic restlessness, working-class militancy, and the emergence of radical left-leaning parties after the Depression. For others still, the New Imperialism was a matter of national pride (France after defeat in the Franco-Prussian war): a sign of national grandeur and manifest destiny (Germany on industrialization and the United States under the Monroe Doctrine) or a marker of racial equality and nondiscrimination (Japan after Meiji).

The New Imperialism soon turned into formal colonial regimes under which imperial powers took administrative control of "foreign" lands and turned them into colonies and dependencies. Initially, imperial powers established control through chartered companies such as the British East India Company. These corporations were afforded semisovereign status under letter patents that afforded them rights and titles allowing them to acquire territories outside of Europe and to exercise within them the total monopoly of power. The transition to formal imperialism in India and elsewhere was thus effected when companies transferred their prior administrative functions to European governments. The new administrative arrangements also associated trained natives as civil service for colonial rule. Thereafter, Britain, France, Portugal, Spain, the United States, and others proclaimed sovereignty or overlordship of foreign populations under diminished legal and political capacities. Formal imperialism in Africa began dramatically with the Berlin Conference (1884–1885), which moderated competition between colonial powers by defining "effective occupation" as the criterion for international recognition of territorial claims. The Sykes-Picot (-Sazonov) Agreement of 1916 was the moral equivalent of the Berlin Agreement for the Ottoman provinces of the Arab World. A secret agreement, it defined the respective spheres of influence of the United Kingdom and France in West Asia with the assent of Imperial Russia and in anticipation of the downfall of the Ottoman Empire. The post–World War I mandate system revived the mythical "White man's burden" under a so-called sacred trust as the means to incorporate former German colonies into existing imperial orders.

Among observers and scholars, these activities led to multiple explanations about the advent of imperialism. Conservatives favored political and psychological factors and therefore linked imperialism to the need to preserve the social order. Liberals who had been reluctant backers of imperialism nonetheless branded its economic benefits despite contravening free trade. Marxists, however, were struck by the rivalry and mutual suspicion that characterized international diplomacy throughout the era. Imperialist ambitions and rivalries in East Asia inevitably came to focus on the vast empire of China whose sovereignty barely survived the unequal treaties imposed on it by European powers. In any case, some Marxists attributed World War I to imperial ambitions and rivalries. Among them, Vladimir Lenin (1916) advanced the thesis that imperialism was the highest stage of capitalism.

Since Lenin, the debate on imperialism crystallized around two central questions. First is the extent to which imperialism was necessary and inevitable given the nature of the international order and the uneven capacities of states and economic agents. The second, favored by some Marxists, gravitates around the preposition of a necessary relationship between capitalist developments and imperialism. The relevant theses have been taken up in different contexts by world system theorists who view imperialism as part of a general, gradual extension of capital investment from the "core" of the industrial countries to a less developed "periphery." With the globalization of capital and the ubiquitous importance of civil society, other Marxists puzzled about the persistence of critical dimensions of imperialism under Pax Americana (the relative peace in the Western Hemisphere as a result of U.S. leadership during the second half of the 20th century). They turned to Antonio Gramsci's theses on the advent of hegemony, particularly on the role of "spontaneous consent" in perpetuating what might reasonably be called imperialism. They also drew attention to the ideological function of education in order to gain insight into the expansion of capitalism and the associated market institutions and modes of government.

On decolonization and the formal transfer of power to the newly created independent states, increasing numbers of scholars and politicians have dismissed the utility of the notion of imperialism in today's world. The dismissal is founded on two orders of deficiencies. The first, found in conservative and liberal theories, is the focus placed on the outward bureaucratic and organizational dimensions of imperialism at the time of creation and maintenance of domination and subordination. The second, found in Marxism and other radical theories, is the focus on dated historical events, for instance, the modes of expansions that established unequal economic, cultural, and territorial relationships between imperial states and their formal dominions. Indeed, it is hard today to entertain the possibility of direct or outright imperialism in which any power could claim to be justified by law or providence to take over the government of a territory other than its own. Nor could any power insist on a right to unequal relations with other political entities.

Indeed, the focus on state identity and ideology or culture and discourses may be misplaced today. To be sure, the novelty of the New Imperialism and the formal colonial empires that followed it had to do with the scale of the colonial order. The construction of empire required a domestic ideology associated with state identity and rationalizing narratives (of destiny and providence). The imperial project also required self-justification—for instance, to right the wrongs done by others or to improve the lot through trusteeships or mandates. In these regards, imperialism had the backing of elements of civil society. These elements successfully articulated their own private desires, passions, and motives of acquisition, enrichment, and self-aggrandizement as the national interest and then caused legislators and executives to spring into colonial adventures as means of defending the latter. These private interests were comforted in their positions by ideologues such as consumer advocates seeking to advance the good life, liberal progressives (who once engineered mandate systems under the sacred trust), and so-called cosmopolitans and internationalists. Science helped define conceptions of the moral qualities of subjects, the status of individual societies within the moral order, and the entitlements or deserts due to them. International law, legal doctrines, and jurisprudence completed the discourses of the emergent international order by providing the norms and instruments of empire. Each discourse played a part in defining the morality and ethics of war and peace.

Thus conceived, imperialism is not an arbitrary act. Historically, it remains a reflex or realism that has been guided, according to material conditions, by the available logics of power, the permissible modes of interventions, the applicable political and ethical traditions, and a recurrent theology and ideology of a preordained but singular hierarchical order lodged in the West. From this sovereignty flow inherent rights and privileges, a notion of predestined leadership, an assumed legitimacy of interests, an a priori and necessary absolution of sins against others, and a singular expectation of access to the necessary resources of its chosen lifestyle, presently the good life. These imperial claims, which were once contested within colonial empires, are yet to disappear from international relations today. Indeed, real and aspiring imperial states continue to demand deference from others even in the postcolonial world. This is not done without contestations, but to underscore the point, we still witness occasional unilateral political and military interventions to remind us of the lingering presence of the imperium.

Siba N. Grovogui
Johns Hopkins University
Baltimore, Maryland, United States

See also Power; Power and International Politics; Superpower

Further Readings

Arrighi, G. (1978). *The geometry of imperialism: The limits of Hobson's paradigm* (P. Camiller, Trans.). London: NLB.

Hobson, J. A. (1972). *Imperialism.* Ann Arbor: University of Michigan Press. (Original work published 1902)

Lenin, V. I. (1939). *Imperialism: The highest stage of capitalism* (New revised translation). New York: International.

Schumpeter, J. A. (1951). *The sociology of imperialism.* New Haven, CT: Meridian Books.

IMPLEMENTATION

Implementation refers to the carrying out of policy or authoritative actions in support of policy goals. Implementation is closely affiliated with the classic political function of executing laws, but implementation research also focuses on the execution of authoritative policies other than laws, such as administrative rules issued by government and policies made by local governments. Several stages, factors, and actors are involved in the implementation process and affect its results. Implementation is a continuation of the policy formation process, but it also involves new actors. The implementation process and its results depend on whether the policy design is valid and on what policy instruments have been selected. Also, the number and interests of the actors that are involved in carrying out the policy and the relationships between them affect the implementation process and results. Managers have an important but difficult task in transforming and communicating the policy down to the frontline workers. Because of the discretion that these workers typically have, they play a key role in delivering the policy to citizens or firms and enforcing the rules associated with it.

While most implementation studies analyze the implementation of one particular policy or a set of related policies, some bottom-up implementation scholars are more interested in local problem solving. These problems are typically defined by the researchers themselves, for example, Christopher Hull and Benny Hjern. They would often focus on a set of policies that have an impact on a given policy problem, for example, chronic youth unemployment or helping small firms grow. The relevance of this kind of research depends on whether the reader accepts the definition of the problem. This entry focuses on official public policy goals and mandates as a standard for implementation is warranted from a democratic effectiveness perspective. Democracy concerns not only how policies are made but also whether or not they are executed. Policy goals formulated in legislatures, governments, and local governments have a particular legitimate status and are relevant for holding government accountable.

The start of implementation research was stimulated by evaluation research. President Lyndon Johnson's Great Society social policy reforms in United States in the 1960s and 1970s fostered a lot of evaluation research. The effects of the new welfare state programs were assessed and improvements in social engineering suggested. As most evaluation studies actually showed little or no effect of the social program interventions, the first interpretation suggested that the program was a failure and based on wrong program theory. However, gradually, another interpretation emerged that the causal theory behind the planned policy intervention might after all be valid, but the intervention had not taken place as intended. This led to an interest in studying the relation between planned and actual interventions and the administrative process in between policy making and social interventions.

Most people consider Jeffrey Pressman and Aaron Wildavsky's 1973 book *Implementation* to be the first major piece of implementation research. It was a case study of a federal economic development program in Oakland, California, that had been created to enhance minority employment. It failed to do so, however, due to the complexity of many actors having to work together and because it was based on an invalid causal theory of how to stimulate minority employment. The book certainly opened the field of implementation research, yet some pieces of earlier research by, for example, Herbert Kaufman and Jerome Murphy had actually focused on implementation problems.

The organization of this entry is based not on a chronological review of the implementation literature but on the Integrated Implementation Model (Figure 1). The model was developed by Søren Winter to integrate some of the theoretically most promising implementation factors identified by various implementation scholars into a common analytical framework.

For dependent variables, the model focuses on both the actions of implementers in delivering policies and the societal outcomes in relation to the official policy objectives. Implementation research was long dominated by stories of implementation failures. The implementation of policies typically failed to achieve the planned outcomes, and implementers failed to deliver the mandated services or in enforcing regulations. Or the process suffered from serious delays. Implementation research focused mainly on barriers to successful implementation. However, gradually, more optimistic studies were made. One of the important insights was that time horizons matter. Often, policy programs suffer from start-up problems that are gradually ameliorated over the years on the basis of experience. Sometimes, it may take a decade or more to carry out a successful implementation. Implementation results also tend to vary among localities at any given point in time.

The first set of factors, which affects implementation results, is the policy design. Even perfect implementation processes and outputs are not likely to be successful if the expected causal relationship between policy objectives and means is invalid. Second, implementation is affected by the commitment of authorities and organizations that are involved in implementing policies and by the interorganizational relations between them. Third, managers' transmission of organizational policies to the staff is crucial. While management matters, it is no simple matter! Fourth, this complexity is due to the discretionary behaviors of street-level bureaucrats in their interactions with target groups. These bureaucrats typically enjoy some autonomy vis-à-vis the legislation and their managers. Fifth, target groups not only are passive recipients of public policies but are often active in affecting implementation outputs as well as outcomes. Sixth, implementation results are conditioned by socioeconomic factors. What makes organizations, street-level bureaucrats, and target groups important political actors in the implementation process is that their contributions to implementation are affected by their action models, which for all three sets of actors analytically are made up of actor interests and the resources the actors master. After presenting the theoretical implementation framework in the following, some major implementation research strategies and methodologies will be discussed before the entry is concluded.

Policy Design

Too many implementation researchers have erroneously put the whole blame for any lack of goal achievement on implementation. This is in sharp contrast to the early evaluation scholars who had blamed the policy design for any lack of effect. As noted by Peter May, well-designed policies are necessary but not sufficient for improving implementation prospects. A policy design typically contains a set of goals, a mix of instruments for obtaining these goals, a designation of governmental or nongovernmental entities charged with carrying out the goals, and an allocation of resources for the

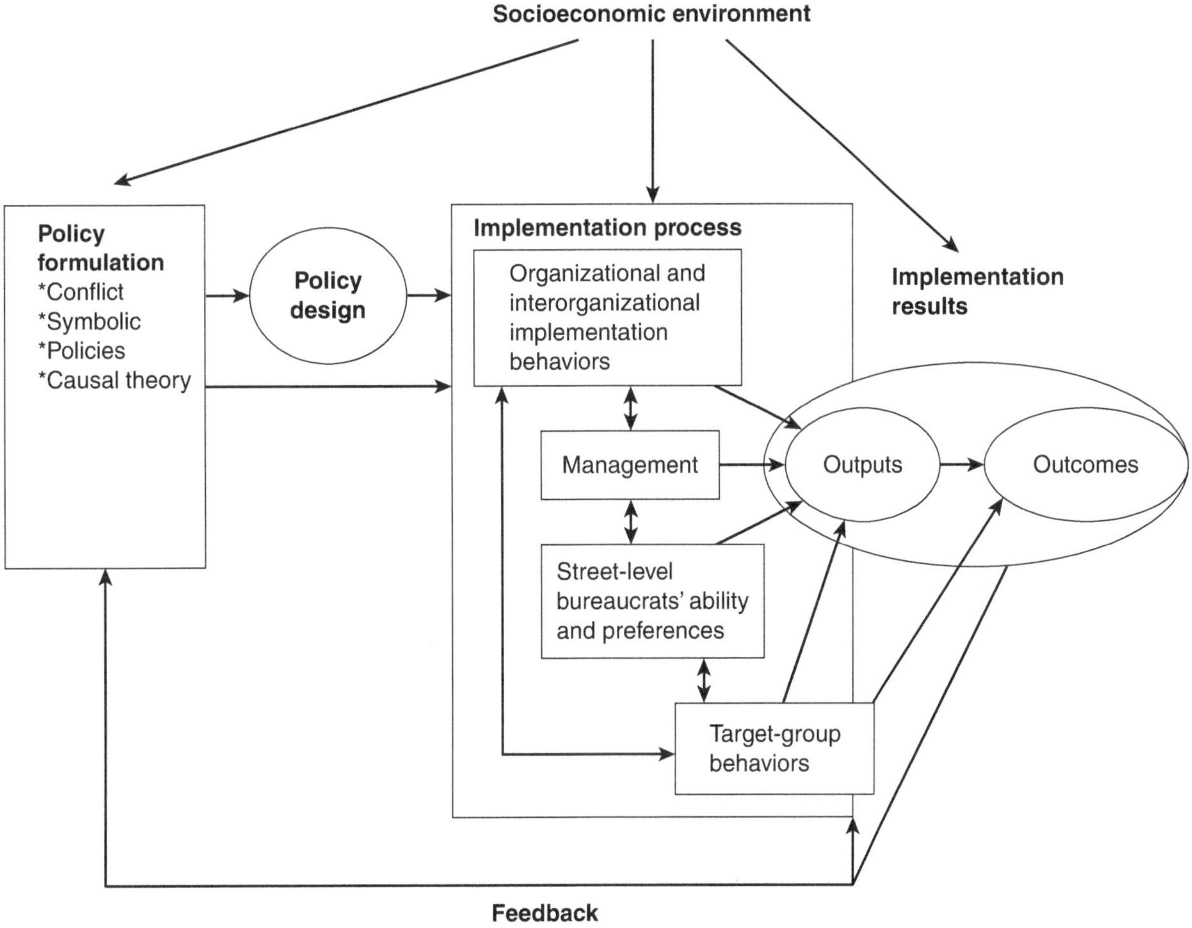

Figure 1 The Integrated Implementation Model

Source: Winter, S. C., & Nielsen, V. L. (2008). *Implementering af politik* [Policy implementation]. Copenhagen, Denmark: Academica.

requisite tasks. Policy design, and particular policy instruments, has received substantial research interest since the 1980s, for example, by Stephen Linder and Guy Peters, Lester Salamon, and May.

According to this literature, any policy can be disaggregated into one or a mix of few generic policy instruments. Unfortunately, the common research interest has not led to agreement on any typology of instruments. One simple classification focuses on rules (often combined with sanctions for noncompliance), economic incentives, and information, all of which aim at affecting the behavior of either target groups or intermediaries (implementers).

Policy designs may affect the implementation process and results in various ways. The pioneers of implementation research saw goal clarity as the key to implementation success. However, according to later research, conflicting, unclear, and ambiguous goals are the rule rather than the exception in public policies, and decent implementation results can be achieved even in theses circumstances. Different mixes of instruments are not equally effective in obtaining a given policy objective. In summarizing the scant empirical evidence in the field, May suggests that policy designs are important in affecting the incentives of intermediaries to carry out their requisite tasks, particularly through affecting their commitment and capacity and by signaling desired actions.

The selected instruments may also affect the overall implementation structure and process because certain instruments tend to favor the formation of particular implementation structures.

Mandates aimed at regulating the behavior of target groups normally require a staff for inspecting and enforcing the mandate and a set of sanctions. Information strategies and use of economic incentives such as environmental taxes can sometimes be implemented with less staff, although there is no one-to-one relationship between instruments and staff requirements. Some taxes are relatively automatic and easy to collect, such as an environmental tax per unit of gasoline sold, while others require a substantial staff for inspection and enforcing, for example, taxing diffuse pollution.

However, while, as already indicated by Pressman and Wildavsky, the validity of the causal theory linking instruments to objectives is crucial, the research documentation of instrument effects is still meager. One reason is that effects of instruments on implementation often depend on the context, including the political context. Consequently, designing good policies is not a simple, technocratic process such as selecting the best types of materials for building a bridge.

Policy design also involves organizational design, that is, what types of organizations are to be involved in implementing the policy, and what types of incentives can be used to increase their commitment to the policy and its objectives? Organizational implementation structures are often quite messy and uncoordinated. Some top-down implementation scholars like Daniel Mazmanian and Paul Sabatier hold quite optimistic views on the ability of policy proponents to structure the implementation process to provide more commitment and loyal implementation. Critics of their viewpoint, however, argue that policies are often political compromises that also include policy opponents with little interest in making an effective implementation structure.

The roots of problematic policy designs and implementation problems can often be found in the prior policy formulation process. For instance, conflicts in this process often create a policy with conflicting and ambiguous goals and an invalid causal theory embedded in a policy design that does not adequately connect the goals to the means. Furthermore, symbolic policies are sometimes adopted to address a policy problem without actually offering the means that could achieve the stated objectives. And as first claimed by Eugene Bardach, conflicts in policy formation often continue in the subsequent implementation process. It is important to understand that ineffective policy designs are not always due to lack of knowledge on the part of the policy designers. According to Terry Moe, policy design of instruments and organizational structure is first of all a political process, in which political actors—including both policy proponents and opponents—try to maximize their own interests. This includes the selection of an organizational structure that will maximize their long-term control of the implementation process.

Unfortunately, the research evidence on how different organizational arrangements contribute to implementation success or failure is rather modest. For example, we have very little evidence on the effectiveness or efficiency of using federal or state government field offices, local governments, nonprofit organization, or private firms for delivering public services. One study found that Danish central government field offices pay more attention to, are more committed to, and comply more completely with, the national employment policy rules on emphasizing quick job placements than is the case for local government agencies. May and collaborators show not only that cooperative regulatory strategies adopted by central or state governments toward local governments can provide more commitment and compliance at the local level by preventing flooding but also that these strategies can backfire for particular "bad apples."

According to many studies, outsourcing relatively technical public tasks is in most cases more efficient than public provision of services. However, the research on the effects of outsourcing of more classic social services to for-profit or nonprofit providers is much more limited and has more inconsistent findings. When comparing the effects of employment service provision of public, nonprofit, and for-profit organizations in the United States, Carolyn Heinrich and colleagues did not find any difference, while Danish analyses find that for-profit and nonprofit providers deliver both poorer outputs (e.g., in terms of job emphasis) and poorer employment outcomes with much higher unit costs than public providers. However, the overpricing may be due to large subsidies of outsourcing applied by the Danish government. More research is needed on how various types of organizations contribute to implementation success.

Interorganizational Relations

Implementation processes are characterized by organizational and interorganizational behaviors that represent different degrees of commitment and coordination. In their seminal implementation study, Pressman and Wildavsky (1973) focused on the "complexity of joint action," according to which successful implementation is likely to be negatively related to the number of actors, the diversity of their interests and perspectives, and the number of decision and veto points. Given the great number of actors, subsequent decisions, and veto points that is typical in policy implementation, Pressman and Wildavsky stated in their book *Implementation* that the fact that federal policies work at all is amazing. As an illustration, they suggested a series of subsequent implementation decisions with a relative high probability of success in each of, say, 90%. Yet, according to Pressman and Wildavsky, it only takes seven decisions to lower the cumulated chance of success to less than 50%.

One of their key insights was that the complexity of joint actions is not found only when implementing organizations fundamentally disagree with the policy objectives or with each other; it even takes place when implementing organizations generally agree about the reform goals but have slightly different perspectives on the implementation. For some authorities or organizations with implementation tasks, contributing positively to the implementation may be at odds with other commitments, or they may simply prefer other tasks that are more crucial to the core tasks of the organization. Or it may just be that organizations have different time lines for contributing to the implementation assembly process. However, serious conflicts of interest and bureaucratic politics tend to make implementation even more difficult.

Thus, how organizations contribute to the implementation process is strongly affected by their action model, which consists of their interests and their resources for pursuing them. Implementing organizations may have interests that are identical with the public policy. They agree both with its goals and means. Their interests may also be convergent. Although not agreeing with the goals, they agree with the means. An implementation success is more likely if organizations have interests that are identical or at least converge with the policy. However, implementation prospects are based not only on interests but also on the resources that organizations can use for pursuing their interests.

Bardach describes the implementation process as a series of "implementation games" that organizations play for promoting their own interests. The complexity of joint action and implementation games may lead to implementation failures, delays, or biases in the implementation outputs and outcomes that are produced. The notion of "the complexity of joint action" seems related to the proverb of "too many cooks spoil the broth." However, according to Laurence O'Toole, this problem applies only to certain kinds of interorganizational implementation settings. Decision points are not independent of each other. An early agreement on basic understandings can enhance implementation success by promoting "bandwagon effects" in later decisions, and decisions can be merged by crafting "package deals."

Implementation prospects also depend on the type of resource dependencies among participating organizations. The "complexity of joint action" is most relevant for a chain of sequential relations. Here, a particular organization, A, cannot produce its implementation contribution without receiving outputs from another organization, B, while B does not need any outputs from A. It is like Christmas tree lights where one dead bulb can put out all bulbs if they are connected on series rather than in parallel. The parallel connection resembles pooled relations where multiple organizations can produce implementation outputs independently of each other. This can produce relatively good implementation results although the coordination may not be optimal. Finally, reciprocal relations—where two or more organizations are dependent on each other—can decrease the likelihood of veto points because both organizations have incentives to cooperate. Reciprocal relations can be created based on exchange of services or money. Accordingly, better implementation results can sometimes be obtained by replacing sequential relations by reciprocal or pooled ones.

Interorganizational relations and the role of outsourcing and third parties in implementation have stimulated a substantial research interest under the labels of policy networks, governance networks, or implementation regimes. A common theme is the dependency of public authorities on resources from the private sector—for example, interest groups, associations, and firms—for implementing public policies. Perceived benefits for policymakers and implementers may be expertise, information, legitimization, or more cost-effective ways of providing services or enforcing regulations. In some countries—particularly the United States—private for-profit and nonprofit actors are involved so much in policy implementation that Brinton Milward talks about the "hollowing out of the state." Network studies focus on the character of networks and interdependencies, why networks are created, if and how they are sustained over time, and the democratic and participatory consequences of networks. This is also a key interest in corporatist research that studies the formal integration of major interest organizations into public policy making and implementation. Given the enormous research interest in networks, surprisingly few studies have so far examined the effects of different types of networks on implementation outputs or outcomes.

While interorganizational implementation research focuses on commitment and collaboration at the organizational level, managers have important roles in bridging inter- and intra-organizational levels when supervising street-level bureaucrats. However, much of the normatively based management literature fails to acknowledge the difficulties involved in this managerial task. The role of managers is considered below after discussion of the role of street-level bureaucrats in the implementation process.

Street-Level Bureaucracy

After the first group of implementation studies had focused mainly on the role of organizations in policy implementation, in 1980, Michael Lipsky turned the policy process upside down. He claimed that street-level bureaucrats are the real policymakers. His theory of "street-level bureaucracy" focuses on the discretionary decisions that each frontline worker is making when delivering policies to individual citizens. Often such decisions are made in face-to-face interactions with clients behind closed office doors or in the field as when an environmental inspector is inspecting a farm. It is not easy for managers to monitor bureaucratic behaviors in such encounters. Their discretion makes street-level bureaucrats essential actors in implementing public policies.

Although Lipsky emphasizes the individual role of street-level bureaucrats in implementing public policies, it is an ironic aspect of the theory that their similar working conditions make all street-level bureaucrats apply similar behaviors whether they are teachers, police officers, nurses, doctors, or social workers. It also means that organizational differences and bureaucrats' individual attitudes are not expected to have important implications for their behaviors.

Although trying to do their best, street-level bureaucrats are experiencing a gap between the demands they meet from legislative mandates, managers, and citizens on one side and their high workload on the other. In this situation, they all apply a number of coping mechanisms that systematically distort their work in relation to the intentions of the legislation. They ration services; make priorities between their tasks; process their clients through simple, standardized procedures, tending to favor the easier and more resourceful clients (creaming); and seek to control clients. Over time, street-level bureaucrats develop more cynical perceptions of the clients and modify the policy objectives that are the basis of their work. These coping strategies imply that the implementation of public policies is systematically biased compared with legislative mandates, for example, for individualized, yet equal treatment. According to Lipsky, even increasing staff resources is no solution to coping problems because more resources may lead to more demand for services.

A group of implementation scholars has a strong focus on these frontline workers. What unites them is a conviction that the behaviors of these workers have important implications for implementation that are inversely related to these workers' rank in the hierarchy. While Lipsky focuses on similarities in street-level bureaucratic behaviors, some implementation scholars seek to explain variation in the behaviors of these bureaucrats. They typically differ with respect to the aspects of frontline workers' behaviors they consider as dependent variables and to the concepts they apply. While Lipsky's coping strategies are reporting supposedly dysfunctional behaviors, John Brehm and Scott Gates suggest that street-level bureaucrats work, shirk, or sabotage. Bureaucrats persistently and loyally implement public policies when working. They do too little when shirking—either for leisure or because they disagree with the policy. Sabotage is a conscious attempt to actively counteract the aims of the public policy because these bureaucrats disagree with the policy mandate and follow another course of line. In their empirical work, Brehm and Gates find that street-level bureaucrats actually do work—not because of managerial directives and control—but because they fundamentally agree with the policy (refer to text below).

Other implementation studies examine the actions of these frontline bureaucrats, for example, in terms of the effort that they spend, the choices they make on what kind of clients and what aspects of their behaviors to focus on, and the tools that they employ, as well as the decisions they make. Particularly in regulation research, some research has focused on the styles that inspectors employ in day-to-day interactions with target groups (regulatees). Inspectors may, for example, differ in how legalistic versus flexible they are and how coercive versus trusting they are. However, style also seems to be a useful concept for social policy implementation, for example, when analyzing caseworkers' professional distance to the client versus personal involvement in addition to the above style dimensions. Studies of street-level bureaucrats typically find considerable variation in their behaviors, including both coping and styles.

This raises the crucial question of how this variation can be explained. Again, studies vary in the explanatory variables they consider. Some focus on the organizational norms by which frontline workers are socialized, which form their basis for treating clients. This research tradition has participants from both sociology (e.g., Pierre Bourdieu, Erving Goffmann, and Margaretha Järvinen) and political science (e.g., Jodi Sandfort, Steven Maynard-Moody, and Michael Musheno). Some studies within that tradition pay particular attention to how bureaucrats, often unconsciously, use power to make citizens comply with their directives. Through identity work, bureaucrats are trying to make citizens accept their identity and diagnosis as these are specified by the bureaucrat. Citizens must accept the frontline worker's definition of their problematic behavior and cooperate and improve to be perceived as a deserving client, which is often a precondition for receiving services. Thus, a client is "created." The function of identity work is to make each client fit the repertoire of measures that are available to the worker. These "institutionalization processes" are based on the norms of the organization.

While this perspective emphasizes the role of organizations for individual behaviors, other perspectives focus on the role of people. With inspiration from the classic theory of representative bureaucracy by Donald Kingsley, some studies suggest that street-level bureaucrats' behaviors are affected by their social background, for example, socioeconomic, ethnic, and gender as well as educational background. According to the classic theory on representative bureaucracy, the actions of public administration reflect the values of the social strata from where bureaucrats come. The theory was refuted for decades by studies of bureaucrats particularly in central government. However, recently some scholars—for example, Kenneth Meier and collaborators—have claimed that the theory might have more relevance at the front lines. Thus, social background and norms are likely to be more relevant when services are delivered and regulations enforced in direct interactions with citizens and firms and where bureaucrats typically have substantial discretion. According to some studies, gender does matter, for example, for prosecution and conviction in rape cases. By the same token, some studies indicate that minority students perform better in schools with a minority representation among teachers above a certain threshold.

Whereas the previous perspectives assume some kind of collective impact on the behaviors of street-level bureaucrats—that is, from the very job functions of street-level bureaucrats in general, organizational norms, or earlier socialization into the norms of a certain social group—some studies focus on the effects of individual differences among street-level bureaucrats in terms of their abilities and attitudes. Peter May and Søren Winter have found some empirical support for the importance of individual factors. They report substantially greater variation in caseworker behaviors within local employment service agencies than between these agencies. They also found that street-level bureaucrats' knowledge and attitudes have a considerable influence on the extent to which their behaviors are reflecting the policy mandate.

According to Winter, several kinds of attitudes can affect street-level bureaucratic behaviors, that is, their attitudes on (a) the policy, (b) the effectiveness of the tools that are available, (c) the target groups, and (d) their perceived workload. Bureaucrats' attitudes on the factors that are most closely related to their daily work—such as how they perceive and evaluate various tools, their clients, and their workload—appear to have stronger behavioral effects than their ideological—and more abstract—view on the overall policy. How street-level bureaucrats perceive the adequacy of their workload seems to have stronger behavioral effects—for coping and other kinds of behaviors—than have differences in their actual workload.

According to this research perspective, street-level bureaucrats are even more important as policymakers than implied by Lipsky's and the other street-level bureaucracy perspectives above because individual street-level bureaucrats are making important authoritative decisions on the content of the policies, which are delivered to citizens and firms, based on the bureaucrats' own individual preferences. However, although there is a substantial variation in their behaviors, Winter and May also found that Danish street-level bureaucrats show a considerable loyalty to the law.

Management

As indicated by the above analysis, managerial control of street-level bureaucrats is no easy task. The very nature of street-level bureaucrats' practices implies that they exercise considerable discretion in encounters with target groups that are normally not very visible to managers. While bookstores abound with simple recipes for excellent management, these are rarely based on systematic empirical research on public management. And the existing evidence is limited and suggests that managing street-level bureaucrats is by no means a simple but a difficult and complex task.

In a meta-analysis, George Boyne finds surprisingly few studies on effects of management on performance or outcomes. Yet he finds some evidence that management does matter. However, because such studies measure the direct link between management and outcomes, it is hard to know through what kinds of street-level bureaucratic practices managers can bring about better outcomes. Some causal links are missing. Unfortunately, so far, very few studies have examined the effects of management on street-level bureaucratic behaviors. Most studies indicate that these effects are limited and context contingent. The research challenge is to specify to what extent and how management affects street-level bureaucratic behaviors in given contexts. Such research has just begun, however. Some preliminary findings from studies of the implementation of employment policy by May, Winter, and associates can be mentioned.

Principal–agent theory offers a promising way for studying these relationships. According to its basic assumptions, a principal (manager) and his or her bureaucratic agents may not share all preferences, and the relationship is characterized by information asymmetry that systematically disadvantage principals. When applied to the management of street-level bureaucrats, managers' influence seems to vary with the visibility of street-level bureaucratic practices. Some are quite transparent and easy to measure and monitor, for example, social caseworkers' application of sanctions when clients are absent from mandatory employment promoting measures with no good cause. Other kinds of behaviors are more invisible, for example, coping behaviors and to what extent employment service bureaucrats emphasize immediate jobs in conversations with clients. Managerial objectives are likely to be better reflected in frontline practices when these are relatively visible.

Having an effective manager does not always result in better implementation. Sometimes street-level bureaucrats experience a multiple principal problem. Their local managers are not always loyal to the letter and spirit of the law. This may be reinforced if local political bodies resist national policies. Managerial tools also vary in the extent to which they are goal directed or capacity building. While capacity building through increasing staff or general information provision might generally improve the implementation of national policies, the effect of using the more goal-directed management tools may depend on whether local policies support or oppose national ones. Examples of highly goal-directed management tools are managers' clear signals of their expectations for frontline behaviors and recruitment of workers with a better fit with the goals of the organization. Greater application of such managerial instruments tends to induce poorer implementation of national policies among street-level bureaucrats when local policies resist national ones.

Finally, management is relational. This implies that the effect of management practices on street-level bureaucratic behaviors is often contingent on the characteristics of individual street-level bureaucrats, including their expertise, motivation, and perception of the applied management tools. In a study of the implementation of Danish employment policy, May and Winter found that all managerial effects on the extent to which caseworkers emphasized jobs in conversations with clients were contingent on caseworkers' perceived professional knowledge—for example, delegation improves implementation when workers have knowledge but weakens it when they do not. Similarly, in line with Bruno Frey's theory on motivation crowding in and out, Danish studies by Lotte Andersen and Thomas Pallesen show that performance pay and regulation of university faculty have positive effects on research publication productivity only if the faculty perceives these instruments as supportive of professional norms rather than as monitoring or control.

Although the direct and contingent effects of management on the behavior of street-level bureaucrats are often limited, indirect effects must also be taken into account. These include the impact that managers have on the attitudes of their frontline workers and on in-service training and the way in which managers by designing or changing organizational structures can shape bureaucratic attitudes and behaviors.

Target Groups

The target groups of a public policy have important roles both for the production of implementation outputs and outcomes. Target groups affect the implementation behaviors of agencies and street-level bureaucrats, and outcomes that achieve policy goals often require that target groups change their behaviors.

In depictions of the classic ideal type of the democratic chain of control, citizens are active when articulating political demands and electing political representatives but relatively passive and law-abiding subjects when it comes to the execution of the law. However, as much service production and regulatory enforcement take place in interactions between street-level bureaucrats and target populations, citizens and firms do often play an active role in shaping implementation outputs in a kind of coproduction of services and enforcement.

As noted above, clients can be relatively powerless in processes of coping, identity work, and creation of clients, but the power of target populations in implementation processes varies across and within policy areas. There is a huge difference between the position of nonunionized welfare minority clients in welfare and employment policy implementation on one hand and organized farmers in the implementation of agricultural support and environmental programs on the other hand. As is the case for street-level bureaucrats, the role of target populations in policy implementation depends on their action model in terms of their preferences and abilities. Relevant resources are cognitive skills, expertise, wealth, affiliation with other actors with resources including powerful interest groups (whether the group has a positive or negative social construction), and institutional arrangements and norms.

For decades it has been debated in the regulatory literature whether regulated industries tend to capture the public regulatory enforcement apparatus to make it a servant rather than a master. While capture was earlier the dominating research position, for the last couple of decades, the capture theory has found less theoretical and empirical support. The role of interest groups in implementation processes varies among political systems. Often strong interest representation is found in implementing committees in some European countries with strong corporatist traditions. According to Scandinavian studies, interest organizations still have a strong role in policy implementation, even though their formal inclusion in the policy-making process has been reduced during the past few decades, when their position apparently has weakened when compared with that of legislative bodies. In some more pluralistic political systems such as the United States, interest groups tend to be more fragmented in terms of representation, are generally less formally involved in policy making and implementation, and more often act as external pressure groups. Yet some recent research indicates that the role of U.S. interest groups in implementation—including administrative rule making—may be stronger than previously expected.

As Vibeke Lehmann Nielsen has found, the resources that individual firms and organizations can engage in conversations with regulatory inspectors can put pressure on these inspectors. This may affect their enforcement directly but also indirectly through the formation of the informal rules of the game for such interactions, which in turn affect how regulations are enforced. She found that regulations are more leniently enforced for public institutions, which speak the same language as the regulators, than for private firms. Also, big firms with substantial expertise in the regulatory area as well as local economic importance—tend to be more successful than small ones in negotiating enforcement terms.

For social policy implementation, some theories claim that clients with few personal resources are systematically disadvantaged in their interactions with the administrative system. According to the access theory originally developed by Bernhard Schaffer and Huang Wen-hsien, clients have to cross three thresholds to get access to the services to which they are entitled. The first is the registration threshold. For many services, eligible clients must apply themselves, which tends to disadvantage clients with poor educational background, poor knowledge about their rights, and low social status. This can be reinforced by some emotional factors, including stigmatizing. Some clients do not perceive themselves as deserving assistance, or they may hold personal ideals of dignity in fending for themselves.

Second, clients must cross the competence threshold, which requires that one can handle the interaction with the bureaucracy, including being acquainted with the formal and informal rules of the game and applied decision criteria and being able to formulate one's thoughts. This again disadvantages clients with a poor educational and social background. Finally, clients must be able to cross the efficiency threshold, and some do not make it because they do not fit with staffs' perceptions on how available services would be most effectively distributed among clients. Also, the efficiency threshold tends to bias the implementation systematically to the benefit of clients with more resources but disadvantages clients with a poor educational and social background (refer also to Lipsky's concept of "creaming" earlier).

Target groups have also important roles in relation to implementation outcomes. Most public policies aim at changing the problematic behaviors of—or conditions for—citizens or firms by either regulating their behaviors or providing services for them that will help them do better. Most policies build on an explicit—or often implicit—causal theory on how these behaviors and conditions can be changed by public intervention. However, as indicated above these causal theories are not always valid. Unfortunately, political science research has not paid much attention to the outcomes of public policies and the mechanisms that affect how citizens and firms respond to public policies and the way in which they are implemented. Some attention to these issues has been paid in regulation research in the borderline between sociology, economics, psychology, and political science. While developed for regulatory policies, the theorizing seems to have some relevance for social policies as well.

Citizens' and firms' responses to public policy implementation are based on their individual action model according to which their behaviors are influenced by their ability and motivations (refer to the above text). Among abilities, cognitive skills are very important. This first includes knowledge of the rules, which may be one of the most important factors in explaining how citizens and firms respond. When people do not comply with regulations or get their rights, it is often not because of lack of will but lack of knowledge of the rules. For decades, many parents of handicapped children in Denmark have not been compensated for taking care of their child at home because they are not aware of their legal rights. Second, favorable outcomes also depend on whether people know how to translate rules into concrete action. Farmers may know the agro-environmental rules but may not know what a particular rule implies for their farming practices. Financial capacity and resilience can also be important—not least for firms in regulatory policies.

Three main types of motivations can be identified. Economic motivation concerns the perceived net utility of different courses of action including compliance/noncompliance. For regulatory and criminal policies, deterrence theory involves a calculation of costs and benefits of not complying. Into that calculus enter both the perceived risk of being detected and the risk of being punished if violating the law, the costs of required additional investments and other production costs for complying, and the expected profits from different courses of action. Studies seem to converge on finding substantial effects of perceived detection risk, while most studies find no or weak effects of perceived sanction risk. Economic motivations also seem relevant for target groups in several social policies.

Social motivation builds on the wish of citizens and firms to get respect and social recognition from peers by following their social expectations. Thus, people comply not because they agree with the policy but because "significant others" expect them to comply. Those may be peers, friends and family, or customers and other firms, for example, trade organizations. For example, the fact that drunk driving has become socially less acceptable has helped the implementation of anti–drunk-driving programs. By the same token, some anti–drunk-driving information campaigns have successfully targeted young women rather than young men to encourage women to tell male drivers to avoid drunk driving.

Even street-level bureaucrats may affect the behaviors of target groups by setting up social expectations, for example, based on their styles of interaction with clients or firms. Legalistic rather than flexible enforcement styles may signal to regulatees that rules and instructions must be taken seriously, and legalistic styles may provide more certainty for firms when making decisions on investments in technology that would allow more compliance.

Normative motivation is based on moral and conscience. People or firms follow the law not because significant others expect them to do so but because they agree with the law or because they at least feel a general moral duty to obey laws even if they do not agree. The latter civic duty varies substantially between and within countries and is important for achieving policy goals. Because of the role of different motivations and resources in shaping citizens' and firms' action models, target populations' responses to policy implementation can involve a complex weighing of economic, social, and normative motivation along with abilities.

One implication of the different types of motivations is that public agencies and their street-level bureaucrats may not always be the most effective agents for implementing public policies. Third parties may sometimes be perceived as more important, competent, or trustworthy by target groups, and third parties may trigger more social and normative motivation. The anti–drunk-driving information campaign above with young girls as a third party is one example. Another is that in a study on agro-environmental regulation in Denmark, Winter and May found that advice from third parties (e.g., farmers' associations and their agricultural consultants, who are highly respected among farmers) enhance farmers' normative motivation to comply with the rules. In contrast, similar advice from public inspectors did not have such effect even when farmers listened to them.

Socioeconomic Environment

The task environment in terms of socioeconomic conditions is important for implementation processes and successes. It is quite a different challenge to implement an employment policy program in a recession than in a boom, and often substantial regional variations can be found as well at any given point in time. It is also a different challenge to implement an agro-environmental program in areas with a high livestock density with many large pig farms and a much greater risk of nitrate pollution than in areas with little animal husbandry. Consequently, it is important to isolate the effects of implementation from effects of task environments. As an example, no less than 60% of the variation in labor market integration of refugees and immigrants among Danish municipalities in the beginning of this century can be explained by differences in task environments. This is because the social composition of the target groups and the local labor market situation varied substantially among local governments.

Research Strategies and Methodologies

In the early 1980s, two opposing implementation research strategies were developed. Top-down implementation scholars with Mazmanian and Sabatier as the leading ones saw implementation as a control problem. They typically focused on the implementation of one particular law according to its official goals. These scholars tended to focus on the role of organizations in the implementation process and on how policy statutes could be structured to increase the clarity of goals and the commitment of implementing organizations.

Bottom-up researchers on the other hand examined mainly interactions between street-level bureaucrats and citizens or firms in a given problem area. Some of the leading scholars were Benny Hjern and Richard Elmore. They focused on the capacity of street-level bureaucrats to change the problematic behaviors of or conditions for citizens or firms. This capacity includes an experience-based knowledge of the incentives and conditions that operate on citizens or firms. While such information is crucial for problem solving, it is rarely systematically provided and used in lawmaking and implementation processes at higher levels. They also focused on the discretion and autonomy that these street-level bureaucrats have versus higher level officials. They emphasized the lack of central control over the decisive implementation processes that are taking place at the bottom. As mentioned above, some bottom-up scholars even disregarded official policy goals as an evaluation standard and instead used problem solving as defined by themselves or local actors as a standard.

A problem for these research strategies was that top-down scholars tended to ignore the bottom—particularly the discretionary role of street-level bureaucrats—and that bottom-up scholars tended to remain at the bottom and rarely got far enough up to focus on implementation mechanisms at an organizational level of analysis. Many bottom-up studies were very descriptive and added little to theory building. In the debate between the two contending perspectives, theoretical, methodological, and normative arguments were mingled together. Attempts of synthesizing the two strategies were made without much success, and the theoretical conflict among implementation scholars was not very fruitful for theory development. Although the integrated implementation model that has organized the previous part of this entry focuses on both top and bottom, it is not a real synthesis of the two strategies. It rather seeks to integrate some of the most promising theoretical elements from the implementation literature into a common framework.

The first generation of implementation studies relied on case studies, and most of these used mainly qualitative research methods such as document analysis and loosely structured interviews. These were sometimes combined with quantitative analyses of, for example, program intake and the social situation of target groups after program participation. Exploratory case studies were natural in an early stage of implementation research when knowledge about implementation mechanisms was very limited and when the main purpose of the research was to generate hypotheses and research ideas.

However, as first claimed by Malcolm Goggin, the case study tradition gradually became a barrier to theory testing, generalization, and the accumulation of theory and knowledge on implementation. Most implementation studies focused on many explanatory variables. As an example, the implementation model by Mazmanian and Sabatier has 21 different variables. Often key variables varied from one study to another. Implementation research ran into the "too many variables but too few cases problem." The single-case-study methodology did not allow isolating the crucial variables for implementation success. Accordingly, Goggin recommended greater use of comparative case studies and big-"*n*" studies to allow for statistical control for third variables.

From the mid-1980s, more quantitative research designs with many cases and the application of statistical designs have gradually been employed in implementation research and in the affiliated research fields of public management, regulatory enforcement and compliance, and recently also in a few network studies. This has lead to more systematic testing of theories and hypotheses with control for third variables including task environment. Gradually, statistical methods have become more advanced with the introduction of methods that take the hierarchical or multilevel character of data into consideration (e.g., street-level bureaucrats nested in organizations), use of instrumental variables, and time-series data for examining causal directions.

However, the case study tradition still continues parallel to the application of quantitative research designs. It is particularly popular in network studies and in studies of power relations between street-level bureaucrats and clients.

Conclusion

Policy implementation is neither an automatic nor dull process. It is a genuine political process for which the achievement of outputs or outcomes that match policy objectives cannot be taken for granted. Implementation results are affected by the chosen policy design and the validity of the causal theory behind it. The results are also affected by the commitment and cooperation of organizations that are involved in the process. Managers have a difficult role in transmitting policies to street-level bureaucrats that have a key discretionary role when delivering policies to target populations. The latter are not passive subjects but participate in shaping implementation outputs as well as outcomes.

Parallel analytic action models have been constructed for explaining the behaviors of implementation actors and target groups based on the interests and resources of the actors. Particularly in the first decades of implementation research, scholars sought to take steps to create a general implementation theory. This process led to very diverse analytical frameworks and research strategies but to little theory accumulation. Implementation is too complex to be accounted for by one theory. Different theories are relevant for explaining different stages or parts of the implementation process, outputs, and outcomes. Rather than a general theory of implementation, the integrated implementation model presented here can be perceived as a framework for analysis or as a series of spotlights that shed light at some key aspects of the implementation process that are worth examining more closely if one wants to understand what implementation is about.

Some observers have claimed that after a peak in the early 1980s, implementation research has come to an end. However, as shown by Harald Sætren, this is far from the case. The number of publications on *implementation* using that term has continued to grow exponentially since the 1970s. However, the growth has taken place particularly in journals and publications outside the core of political science, public policy, and public administration. Implementation studies have become widespread in education, health, environment, law, and economics and much more so than in the former core publications. However, even within the core journals, the number of implementation articles applying the *implementation* term has stabilized at a level not far below the peak of the 1980s.

However, implementation research as it has been presented here is often performed under labels other than "implementation," such as (new) governance, policy design and instruments, network studies, outsourcing, public–private partnerships, street-level bureaucracy, management, "new public management," principal–agent studies, performance, regulatory enforcement, and compliance. Accordingly, the total amount of implementation relevant research has increased considerably and continues to do so yet under various labels. At least two reasons for the described development can be identified. First, fashions are important for research interests and how they are labeled. Second, when for good reasons more and more implementation scholars gave up constructing *the* general implementation theory, several scholars got interested in partial aspects of implementation under various labels.

Søren C. Winter
Danish National Centre for Social Research
Copenhagen, Denmark

See also Bureaucracy; Bureaucracy, Street-Level; Collaboration; Effectiveness, Bureaucratic; Performance; Regulation

Further Readings

Goggin, M. L., Bowman, O'M, Lester, J. P., & O'Toole, L. J., Jr. (1990). *Implementation theory and practice: Toward a third generation.* New York: HarperCollins.

Hill, M., & Hupe, P. (2009). *Implementing public policy: An introduction to the study of operational governance.* London: Sage.

Lipsky, M. (1980). *Street-level bureaucracy: The dilemmas of the individual in public services.* New York: Russell Sage Foundation.

Lynn, L. E., Jr., Heinrich, C. J., & Hill, C. J. (2001). *Improving governance: A new logic for empirical research.* Washington, DC: Georgetown University Press.

Maynard-Moody, S., & Musheno, M. (2003). *Cops, teachers, counselors: Stories from the front lines of public service.* Ann Arbor: University of Michigan Press.

Mazmanian, D. A., & Sabatier, P. (Eds.). (1981). *Effective policy implementation.* Lexington, MA: Lexington Books.

Pressman, J. L., & Wildavsky, A. (1973). *Implementation*. Berkeley: University of California Press.

Sætren, H. (2005). Facts and myths about research on public policy implementation: Out-of-fashion, allegedly dead, but still very much alive and relevant. *Policy Studies Journal, 33*(4), 559–582.

Winter, S. C. (Ed.). (2003). Implementation. In B. G. Peters & J. Pierre (Eds.), *Handbook of public administration* (pp. 205–255). London: Sage.

Winter, S. C., & Nielsen, V. B. (2008). *Implementering af politik* [Policy implementation]. Copenhagen, Denmark: Academica.

Indigenous Peoples' Rights

The concept of "indigenous" as used in United Nations (UN) documents seeks to clarify a diffuse relationship between the modern sovereign state and a special type of traditional community that does not itself constitute a political entity. A report to the UN by Martinez Cobo in 1987 describes indigenous peoples as people who have a historical continuity with preinvasion or precolonial societies, who consider themselves distinct from other sectors of the societies now prevailing in those territories, who form at present nondominant sectors of society, and who are determined to preserve and transmit to future generations their ancestral territories and ethnic identity. This early description is rephrased in different forms maintaining the core criteria of priority in time, cultural distinctiveness, experience of marginalization and dispossession, and self-identification. The terms *first nations*, *first people*, and *aboriginal* convey a similar meaning. This entry analyzes the notion of indigenous peoples' rights, its global recognition, why they contest rights, the legal use and control of territories, and the most recent developments.

The Two Rights

The notion of indigenous peoples' rights may be interpreted in two ways. Most generally, it refers to a moral entitlement, perceived as restoration and redress of previous wrongs, and as such it has developed as a part of the decolonialization process and the global agenda for human rights. These rights are expressed most clearly in the UN Declaration on the Rights of Indigenous Peoples, passed by the General Assembly in September 2007. This nonbinding declaration states that indigenous peoples have the individual and collective right to the full enjoyment of all human rights and fundamental freedoms as recognized in the charter of the UN, and other human rights mechanisms, and that indigenous peoples have the right to self-determination.

A second understanding refers to the legal rights most clearly expressed in the International Labour Organization (ILO) Convention No. 169 of 1989, *Indigenous and Tribal Peoples Convention*, which is binding for the signatories and sets out procedures for how rights should be implemented in agreement between the state and its citizens. Rights granted within the legal structures of sovereign states through treaties and court decisions are creating a precedence expressed as a customary international law.

Global Recognition

The two kinds of rights are mutually reinforcing. The driving force behind a global recognition has been an indigenous movement initiated from the 1970s onwards among American Indians, Sami, Inuit, Maori, and Australian Aborigines, who found similarities in their situation across widely different continents and historical contexts. A common theme among emerging national and transnational organizations was the experience that the expanding social and economic domain of modern states ignored the life ways and livelihood of indigenous minorities; hence the first claim was for recognition.

A seminal event in the debate on indigenous rights was the establishment of the UN Working Group for Indigenous Populations (WGIP) in Geneva in 1982. The Working Group proper consisted of five experts who met yearly in July and allowed representatives from indigenous peoples worldwide to attend and give brief presentations. These meetings developed as significant meeting places for hundreds of delegates and advocacy organizations, which spoke at the plenary session and used the corridors and lounges and meeting rooms to forge new networks, exchange experiences, and develop strategies. By 1993, the WGIP had developed a draft for the Declaration on Indigenous Rights, and indigenous issues were raised in documents from conferences such as the Rio Conference on Sustainable Development (1992) and the World Conference Against Racism in Durban 2001. A Special Rapporteur position on the Situation of Human Rights and Fundamental Freedoms of Indigenous Peoples was created in 2002. The same year saw the establishment of the UN Permanent Forum for Indigenous Issues in New York composed of eight state representatives and eight delegates from indigenous organizations.

Contested Rights

The rights of indigenous peoples are contested in many ways. It has been relatively easy to identify who are indigenous on continents where colonizers arrived from across the water as in the Americas and Australia. But Africa and much of Asia represent special conceptual challenges. The dominant position of White colonial forces left all of Black Africa in a subordinate position that in many respects was similar to the position of indigenous peoples elsewhere, as first comers, nondominant and different in culture from the White intruders. The important difference from most settler states is that formally White colonial forces withdrew from Africa. Accordingly, many politicians argue that all Africans are indigenous, or alternatively, that this distinction does not apply to the African continent.

In addition to inevitable problems, then, in defining who are indigenous, another challenge is that any procedure for singling out one group for special treatment or affirmative action goes against a cherished liberal principle of equal treatment of all citizens. It also goes against administrative preferences for clear-cut and unambiguous target groups and routines for equal treatment. Some opponents claim that indigenous rights represent a new form for racism, distributing favors according to descent, while the main argument for special rights is a compensation for previous injustice.

Legal Rights

A crucial aspect of indigenous rights relates to the use and control over territories. The ILO Convention No. 169 goes far in recognizing, in Article 14, "the rights of ownership and possession." However, this convention has so far been ratified by only 20 countries and has occasioned extensive legal debates on implementation.

In a few cases, indigenous groups have been delegated control over larger territories and formed a governing body/parliament. The Inuit of Greenland achieved home rule as early as 1979. Nunavut was separated from the Northern Territory in Canada in 1999 with jurisdiction over territorial matters. Some northern indigenous peoples of Siberia control their own autonomous republics within the Russian state.

Land rights issues most commonly come up in negotiations with governments or are taken to the courts. An important judgment in Australia, the *Mabo* case in 1992, established the concept of "native title." Native or aboriginal title reflects the entitlement of the indigenous inhabitants, in accordance with their laws and customs, to their traditional lands, in the cases where it has not been explicitly extinguished. The judgment thus denounced the doctrine of *terra nullius*—that before the colonialization the land belonged to nobody. The subsequent Native Title Act 1993 attracted considerable international interest and established a precedent that has been argued in court cases in many parts of the world, even though later amendments reduced its scope.

In New Zealand, the Court of Appeal, in a case in 1987 that revisited the interpretation of the rights inherent in the Treaty of Waitangi from 1840, laid down the notion of "fairness" as a guiding principle for relations between the Maori and the Crown.

In Canada, forms of self-determination have been recognized in a series of treaties. The Nisga'a of British Columba went to court in 1969 for a declaration that their title to land had never been surrendered by treaty or otherwise extinguished. An agreement in support of aboriginal title was reached in 2000. The James Bay Cree reached an agreement with the Government of Quebec in 2002 in a treaty symbolically perceived as a nation-to-nation agreement.

Another case with wider impact was the decision by the Inter-American Court of Human Rights in 2001 in the case of *Awas Tingni Community v. Nicaragua*. The Court found that the Nicaraguan government had granted concessions to a foreign transnational company for logging on traditional lands without prior consultation and consent from the community. Thus Nicaragua had failed to implement the land rights provision of its own laws, and in violation of the Inter-American Convention on Human Rights. The decision set a regional precedent that is potentially applicable to similar struggles elsewhere against the incursion of transnational corporate interests.

In Botswana, a group of San indigenous peoples took the government to court after they were relocated from their traditional territory, the Central Kalahari Game Reserve. In 2006, the court ruled in favor of the applicants that they were lawfully in possession of the land they occupied and that they were deprived of it forcefully and without their consent. This was seen as a victory, as the case was argued as an "indigenous rights" case. However, while the verdict recognized rights based on continuous occupation, the Botswana government's violation of existing statutory laws was the main justification. In effect, a ruling that prohibited access to water in a desert environment has prevented the enjoyment of "possession."

In many of these cases, the courts have stressed the significant connection between indigenous land rights and indigenous identity. It is in the nature of these cases that the court has ruled against aspects of the development policies of their own governments, and verdicts may be counteracted by state policies. But such cases are supported by—and contribute to—an emerging body of international law. As argued, for instance, by James Anaya, the essence in this process cannot be reduced to a set of rules with fixed meanings but is a normative system that has developed "however grudgingly and imperfectly" to support indigenous peoples' demands.

Further Developments

Indigenous peoples are tied to their land by way of making a living. They also have spiritual connections to territories where ancestors are buried, and harvesting, herding, or hunting creates ties between people and nature and enhances a sense of belonging. An enduring and dynamic relation to land is best achieved through a measure of self-determination. The struggle for recognition of territorial rights (of ownership or possession) is an ongoing concern that has brought tangible results in some cases, while in other parts of the world it has only just begun.

However, this option is not always possible to implement. In many cases, the mix of indigenous and settler populations is such that it will not be possible to identify an indigenous ownership without discriminating against nonindigenous neighbors. Moreover, economic factors increasingly mean that the exercise of traditional adaptations often on a reduced territory can only carry a small population. Indigenous peoples find themselves as part of the global migration from countryside to urban areas and part of the pool of landless laborers and squatters.

The challenge for the future, then, in following up the intentions of self-determination as captured in the UN Declaration on the Rights of Indigenous Peoples will be to find ways to develop instruments for nonterritorialized self-determination. This will mean devolution of power within defined areas of activities, most obviously matters of language, culture, and education, but theoretically a broad range of areas can be included. Procedures for election of a representative body would have to be worked out based on self-identification and some criteria of descent. Such systems are in operation, for instance, for elections to the Sami assemblies in Scandinavia.

Sidsel Saugestad
University of Tromsø
Tromsø, Norway

See also Human Rights in International Relations; Identity, Social and Political; International Law; Multiculturalism; Self-Determination; Sovereignty

Further Readings

Anaya, J. (2004). *Indigenous peoples in international law* (2nd ed.). Oxford, UK: Oxford University Press.

Daes, E.-I. (1996, July). *Standard-setting activities: Evolution of standards concerning the rights of indigenous people* (Working Paper on the Concept of Indigenous People: U.N. Doc. E/CN.4/Sub.2/AC.4/1996/2). Geneva: Office of the United Nations High Commissioner for Human Rights.

Minde, H. (Ed.). (2008). *Indigenous peoples: Self-determination, knowledge, indigeneity.* Delft, Netherlands: Eburon.

Thornberry, P. (2002). *Indigenous peoples and human rights*. Manchester, UK: Manchester University Press.
Van Genugten, W., & Perez-Bustillo, C. (2004). The emerging international architecture of indigenous rights: The interaction between global, regional and national dimensions. *International Journal of Minority and Group Rights, 11*, 379–409.

Individualism

The concept of individualism comprises at least three basic ideas in the political realm. First is the dignity of man: Following the Kantian formula, each individual being exists as an end in himself or herself and not merely as a means for arbitrary use by this or that will. Second, the idea of autonomy holds that an individual's thought and action are his or her own and not determined by agencies or causes outside his or her control. Third comes privacy, according to which each human being should enjoy a private life, an area in which the individual should be untroubled by others and able to act and think in accordance with his or her own free will.

This concept of individualism is indissociably bound up with the tenets of modernity and with the conviction that meaning, truth, and value originate in—and exist for the benefit of—mankind. What we call our "modern societies" are no longer *holistic*, to use Louis Dumont's term. Holistic societies were understood as the units that existed before the individual, in which individuals had only to occupy their designated place. In individualistic societies, this relationship is turned on its head: Man's role is to grow into his or her autonomy and to learn to judge independently by detaching himself or herself from entrenched customs and prejudices.

However, this first brief overview of the concept should not hide the fact that individualism continues, as it always has, to lend itself to widely divergent interpretations. In a seminal book on this topic, Steven Lukes identified not less than 11 forms of individualism and added that they were not mutually exclusive or jointly exhaustive. As Pierre Birnbaum and Jean Leca have also shown, the notion of individualism can be interpreted in innumerable different ways that are not always in harmony with one another, whether we are referring to *utilitarian individualism*—a vision of independent units motivated by a common quest for well-being, *romantic individualism*—that of individuals inspired by their search for the most authentic form of the self, *juridical individualism*—which makes the individual the source and end of all law, *ethical individualism*—taking individual conscience as the supreme judge of the validity of moral norms, *sociological individualism*—emphasizing the distance between the subject and the plurality of his social functions, or, finally, *epistemological individualism*—which makes the individual a conscious subject distinct from his object.

This entry proceeds in four steps. The first two parts sketch a series of semantic histories that reveal alternative uses of the concept of individualism, ranging from a pejorative meaning to a positive conception associated with the defense of autonomy and the spirit of individuality. Both of these interpretations continue to feed into contemporary discussion. The next section proposes an explanation of methodological individualism since the concept has a distinct meaning when it is used in an epistemological sense. Finally, the fourth part examines the current debate on the relationship between political liberalism and individualism.

Individualism and the Dissolution of Society

As shown by Lukes, individualism has long carried and still carries a pejorative connotation, a strong suggestion that to elevate the individual is to harm the superior interest of society. The first uses of the term in the French form *individualisme* grew out of the general European reaction to the French Revolution and to its alleged intellectual source, Enlightenment thought. The Catholic counterrevolutionary Joseph de Maistre might have coined the term when, in 1820, he spoke of this "deep and frightening division of minds, the infinite fragmentation of all doctrines, political Protestantism carried to the most absolute individualism." It was the followers of Henri de Saint-Simon who were the first to use the term systematically and associate it with the perceived evils of the contemporary age—namely, disorder, antagonism, atheism, and anarchy. In that sense, Saint-Simonians shared the counterrevolutionaries' critique of the celebration of the individual and their revulsion for social atomization. However, unlike the counterrevolutionaries, they applied these ideas in a historically progressive direction: Social order was to be not the ecclesiastical and feudal regime of the past but rather the industrial order of the future. As pointed out by Koenraad Swart, these anti-individualists held that the 18th century had been successful in breaking down the traditional values but had failed in developing a new positive philosophy. In part because of the great influence of Saint-Simonian ideas, *individualism* came to be a widely used term over the course of the 19th century to describe a serious evil undermining social and political order.

However, it was a liberal thinker, Alexis de Tocqueville (2009), who was to give the most comprehensive definition of individualism. In *Democracy in America*, he opposed the egoism of our fathers—"a passionate and exaggerated love of oneself"—with individualism,

> which is a considered and peaceful sentiment that disposes each citizen to isolate himself from the mass of his fellows and to withdraw to the side with his family and friends; so that after thus creating a small society for his own use, he willingly abandons the large society to itself. (Book 2, sec. 2, chap. 2)

Above all, we owe to Tocqueville the idea that individualism would be inextricably bound up with democratic revolution: "Aristocracy had made all citizens into a long chain that went from the peasant up to the king; democracy breaks the chain and sets each link apart" (Book 2, sec. 2, chap. 2). Tocqueville was also one of the first to call attention to the paradox of democratic times: the combination of individualization (in the sense of a withdrawal into the self) and conformism (the subjection of all individuals to identical codes of behavior). While pointing out the danger of isolation inherent in increasing individualism, Tocqueville therefore also took care to counterbalance this term with a celebration of what he saw as its opposite: the spirit of individuality.

In a similarly pejorative vein, socialists such as Pierre Leroux have contrasted individualism with an ideal cooperative social order. Identified with the twin concepts of anomie and egoism, individualism came, for these authors, to encapsulate the social, moral, and political isolation of individuals and their dissolution from social purposes.

This usage of the term—associating *individualism* with a form of conformist withdrawal into the self—continues to hold sway in contemporary literature. In *The Lonely Crowd*, David Riesman thus described mass conformism by positing three character types—*tradition-directed*, *inner-directed*, and *other-directed* individuals—linked to three models of society. The last type relies on the judgment of other individuals, basing their conduct on that of those around them and on the model of mass communication. This hypothesis was critiqued by Richard Sennett, who argues for a reversal of Riesman's schema: Rather than moving from an inner-directed to an outer-directed model, the West—according to Sennett—is in transition between a society directed by others to a society ruled by the desires of individuals' inner life. According to this analysis, the risk today is that the predominance of individual private life might eventually destroy the public sphere.

This diagnosis is echoed by Christopher Lasch's theory of the narcissistic individual, which notes that society is being taken over by the "self" and particularly by a new form of therapeutic sensitivity in which individuals are excessively preoccupied with their own health, safety, and well-being. According to these thinkers, the danger of our times is that collective life might gradually wither away with the rise of the individual. In addition, they hold that the modern democratic wave has elevated the individual to ever new heights, leading to neglect of the collective effort that democracy should properly involve. Individualism is amalgamated in this view with a form of social atomism believed to destroy all possibility of social cohesion, as well as all democratic and civic participation in community life. In a similar vein, a number of theorists have recently challenged individualism in the name of community, with its appeal to rootedness, belonging, fraternity, and harmony. It is interesting to note the high degree of convergence between different critiques of individualism coming from disconnected historical periods and completely opposing political stances—one need only point out that the critiques outlined above come from thinkers as different as De Maistre, Karl Marx, and Carl Schmitt or contemporary communitarian thinkers.

Autonomy and the Spirit of Individuality

Nevertheless, individualism is not always understood in the sense of conformist egocentrism described above. It may also take in the ideas of a quest for autonomy and defense of a spirit of individuality. Defined in terms of *autonomy*, individualism is understood as the conviction that no natural subordination of the human being is possible and that every individual must be free to decide for himself or herself in the face of moral, religious, and political authority. This unlimited sovereignty of the individual is consequently based on a conception of human nature as being "individuated" before being social. In other words, every human being is a unique individuality with the capacity for self-definition, reasoning, and autonomous decision. The thesis at the heart of this individualism, originating in the English Protestant tradition of the 17th century—Milton, Hobbes, Locke—and continuing, in different incarnations, in the work of Rousseau, Paine, Kant, Jefferson, or Madison—is that every one of us is, partially at least, independent of our positioning in a particular social context and capable of freeing ourselves from it. Norms thus originate in the individual and not the group, an idea that legitimates the right to resistance against political power. The conception of the individual as a presocial being is not to be taken in a descriptive, temporal, or historical sense: It would be clearly absurd to deny that human beings need a social context in order to develop. The principle has a merely normative meaning, as a thought experiment that allows (at least partial) independence of the human being from his or her social group to be asserted as a legal principle.

The defense of a form of individualism adapted to democratic times, meanwhile, can be found in the work of many different authors. Tocqueville, for instance, distinguished two forms of individualism. The first indicates the withdrawal of individuals into their own private sphere; the second, however, introduces the idea that individuals may be led, by way of personal interest, to devote themselves to the public good. As Tocqueville demonstrated in his analysis of the rise of associations in the United States, "You first get involved in the general interest by necessity, and then by choice; what was calculation becomes instinct; and by working for the good of your fellow citizens, you finally acquire the habit and taste of serving them" (Vol. 3, Pt. 1, chap. 4a).

It is John Stuart Mill above all who must be credited with the idea, outlined in his book-manifesto *On Liberty* (1859), that the free development of individuality is one of the first requirements for the well-being of humanity and the condition for civilization, instruction, education, and culture. Mill transforms the atomist notion of the individual by emphasizing the collective advantages inherent in the development of individuality and diverse points of view: Pluralism is thus seen as indissociable from the defense of the individual, since it is the only state of affairs that allows every individual to exercise truly free choice. Mill thus opens the way to a form of individualism that is not only social but also encourages solidarity: What he advocates is not a denial of the relationship between individual and society but instead an optimization of this relationship to ensure the free development of all individualities. In the 19th century, socialists such as Louis Blanc similarly saw individualism as a major cultural principle. Like many other concepts, individualism was initially introduced by its opponents but gradually adopted by its tenants. The disciples of Charles Fourier denied any basic opposition between individualism and socialism and Joseph Proudhon openly claimed himself as an individualist. At the end of the century, Jean Jaurès posited that socialism was the logical completion of individualism. Less than a century later, Lukes likewise argued that a humane form of socialism would be the only viable means of realizing the values of individualism.

The output of John Rawls can also be situated in the tradition of Mill. The principles formulated in *A Theory of Justice* (1971) are highly individualist in that they are based on an absolute priority accorded to individual liberty, which Rawls argues must not be sacrificed to the broader well-being of society. However, Rawlsian principles are also egalitarian; they envisage a system of cooperation based on an equitable distribution of opportunities between individuals and acknowledge that the success of justice in a given society must be judged on the situation of the least privileged. In a similar vein, other authors have attempted to clarify the conditions for individual autonomy. The writings of Zygmunt Bauman, for instance, emphasize the gulf between the individual de jure and de facto: For individuals to be capable in real terms of choosing a life path and acting autonomously, the lack of provisions for collective protection of those in insecure situations must be remedied.

In more recent times, other more optimistic approaches than those outlined in the first section have been formulated, emphasizing the link between individualism and democracy. Anthony Giddens, for instance, argues that the erosion of traditional modes of coherence also generates democratic effects. The progress of gender equality and sexual tolerance should encourage us to relativize worries about individualism, since individualization should not be confused with selfishness. The crisis of the political domain is thus explained less by the apathy of individuals than by a mismatch between traditional politics and more societal, postmaterialist aspirations (environment, sexuality, etc.).

Methodological Individualism

One should be aware that individualism has a very different meaning when it occurs in the context of ethics or sociology from when it is used in an epistemological sense. In ethical terms, individualism is a doctrine that holds the person to be the supreme point of reference. Sociologically speaking, we define a society as individualist if its law, customs, and social constraints grant a broad autonomy to individuals. The methodological interpretation of individualism, meanwhile, is completely distinct from other forms: It is an attribute of the researcher and his or her methodology, not of the object of study. Elaborated primarily by Karl Popper and subsequently systematized by authors such as Raymond Boudon, the theory of methodological individualism posits that to explain a given social phenomenon—whether in the domain of methodology, political science, sociology, or any other branch of social science—it is essential to reconstruct the motivations of the individuals concerned by the phenomenon in question and to understand it as the outcome of an aggregation of individual actions governed by these motivations. In this sense, as Jon Elster has written, methodological individualism is a form of reductionism since it holds that any social phenomenon can be explained by the characteristics of the individuals who make it up. For Elster, explanation always works by opening up "black boxes," and this can only be done at the level of interacting individuals.

One should clear up two common misunderstandings. First, methodological individualism is not the same thing as an atomist concept of society: It may very well demonstrate that individual actions have meaning only in a specific social context and that individuals judge, decide, and act according to the social situation in which they find themselves. As pointed out by Lukes, explaining phenomena in terms of the microlevel does not preclude reference to holistically characterized causes. In another sense, however, it is true that methodological individualism is clearly distinct from methodological holism in that it rejects any representation of social structures as real and autonomous collective beings. Second, methodological individualism does not mean adhering to economic liberalism or ethical individualism. Boudon and Elster demonstrated that Marxist theory, for instance, often draws on a typically individualist methodology: Social phenomena are analyzed as the consequences of aggregation and interference effects between the actions of individuals each pursuing his or her own interest. One should therefore underline, as Birnbaum and Leca do, that employing an individualist methodology is not the same thing as suggesting that all societal forms are governed by individualist values. Conversely, arguing that modern society is imbued with individualist ideology does not preclude using a holistic methodology. There is therefore no reason why one might not reject methodological individualism while remaining a firm believer in the supreme importance of respecting persons and valuing their autonomy, privacy, and self-development.

Individualism and Political Liberalism

Despite these caveats, methodological individualism has often been reduced to an economic (monetary or rational choice) model, elevated to the status of a theory that is not merely explanatory but also prescriptive of a comprehensive system of social mechanisms. Over the past half-century, individualism has thus come to encapsulate a cluster of ideas propagated by libertarians or neoliberals. For Cold War liberal thinkers such as Friedrich

Hayek or Ludwig von Mises, individualism was considered as a protective bulwark against the dangers of ideological thinking from both right and left.

Consequently, authors such as Lukes now consider that defense of individualism's core values inherent in the ideals of liberty and equality has been hijacked and harnessed to various doctrines that embody libertarian thinking and promote market-favoring policies. The argument suggests that libertarians have captured the high moral ground from which liberal critiques of the market and arguments for redistribution can come to look concessionary and defensive. Colin Bird goes a step further in claiming that it makes no sense to clarify liberal values as individualist (rather than collectivist) in the first instance and ends up declaring the unhelpfulness of the dominant idiom of individualism and even the obsolescence of the label "liberal individualism." Lukes also views individualism as an ideological construct in the double sense that it embodies and conveys illusions and that these illusions serve partisan interests.

However, it is one thing to say that liberalism need not be identified with an atomistic model of human conduct and that there is no single or eternal view of the relation between the individual and society—that the liberal distinction between public and private spheres is neither permanent nor unalterable since, in Judith Shklar's words, the important point for liberalism is not so much where the line is drawn as that it be drawn somewhere, and under no circumstances be ignored or forgotten. It is quite another thing to claim that the individualist/collectivist dichotomy should be discarded altogether, as if it were possible to conceive of political liberalism without a firm commitment to individualism seen in its fullest sense.

Consequently, some liberals argue that the neoliberal approach is an incorrect interpretation of individualism and that the liberal commitment to individuality has resources that can be opposed to the libertarianism of economic conservatives. For instance, this commitment might be reformulated—as Jeremy Waldron did with the concept of liberty—as a commitment to equal individualism. This would give rise to a principle justifying social policies that do not infringe on the primacy of the individual but that rather—quite the opposite—aim at creating the necessary conditions for the full development of individuality by all persons concerned.

In a similar vein, George Kateb argues that a proper perspective should include two types of individualism. The first is the individualism of personal and political rights; the second is democratic individuality. These two types of individualism are closely connected since democratic individuality is, according to Kateb, the best achievement that can grow out of a culture in which personal and political rights are recognized. Put differently, democratic individuality could not exist without rights-based individualism, and any attack on the centrality of rights should be considered as an attack on democratic individuality.

Justine Lacroix
Université Libre de Bruxelles
Brussels, Belgium

See also Anomia; Citizenship; Communitarianism; Democracy, Types of; Equality; Human Rights, Comparative Perspectives; Liberalism; Libertarianism; Tocqueville, Alexis de

Further Readings

Bauman, Z. (2001). *The individualized society.* Cambridge, UK: Polity Press.

Bird, C. (1999). *The myth of liberal individualism.* Cambridge, UK: Cambridge University Press.

Birnbaum, P., & Leca, J. (Eds.). (1990). *Individualism: Theories and methods.* Oxford, UK: Clarendon Press.

Boudon, R. (1981). *The logic of social action: An introduction to sociological analysis.* London: Routledge.

De Maistre, J. (1870–1873). *Oeuvres complètes* [Complete works]. Lyon, France: Pélégaud.

Dumont, L. (1983). *Essays on individualism: Modern ideology in anthropological perspectives.* Chicago: University of Chicago Press.

Elster, J. (1982). The case for methodological individualism. *Theory and Society, 11*(4), 453–482.

Kateb, G. (1989). Democratic individuality and the meaning of rights. In N. Rosenblum (Ed.), *Liberalism and the moral life* (pp. 183–206). Cambridge, MA: Harvard University Press.

Lukes, S. (1973). *Individualism.* Oxford, UK: Blackwell.

Mill, J. S. (1974). *On liberty.* Harmondsworth, UK: Penguin.

Popper, K. (1960). *The poverty of historicism*. London: Routledge.
Riesman, D. (1950). *The lonely crowd: A study of changing American character*. New Haven, CT: Yale University Press.
Swart, K. W. (1962). Individualism in the mid-nineteenth century. *Journal of the History of Ideas, 23*(1), 77–90.
Tocqueville, A. de. (2009). *Democracy in America* (J. T. Schleifer, Trans.). Indianapolis, IN: Liberty Fund. (Original work published 1835 and 1840)

Inequality, Economic

Inequality is a complex multidimensional phenomenon, depending on many factors and lending itself to a great variety of explanations and evaluations. The existence, shape, and origins of inequalities are significant both from a positive perspective, owing to the fact that the economic, political, and psychological attitudes and behavior of individuals or groups are affected by the relative position they occupy in the distribution of meaningful resources, and from a normative one, as a consequence of the fact that in general a situation characterized by inequalities compares unfavorably with one of equality or with lesser inequalities. In this entry, a brief overall survey is provided that can be summarized in the following questions: Inequality of what? How large are the inequalities? Inequality among whom? Inequalities due to which causes?

Inequality of What and How Large?

The qualification of inequalities as economic lends itself to various interpretations: In a narrow sense, it regards the differences in the levels of personal income or wealth; in a broader sense, it includes all the values that directly or indirectly derive from economic activities, which can be used in obtaining them or can be exchanged with them. In the first case, its interpretation is straightforward, in the second, it requires the integration of different systems of inequality that include, besides income and wealth, elements such as health, knowledge, power, or availability of public services, and so on, whose distribution among individuals does not coincide with that of income. In the case of income and wealth, the size of the inequalities can be determined in terms of monetary units and in ways that are sufficiently precise, although not stable and exposed to a certain margin of error. For other aspects that can be broadly termed *economic*, this is not possible, and the differences between the positions can be described only in ordinal terms of *larger* and *smaller* (possibly with qualifications such as *much larger* or *much smaller*); in still other cases, even this is impossible, and one is limited to an incomplete or partial ordering. The measuring of inequalities raises problems even in the case of items that are directly expressed in monetary terms: In international comparisons, the per capita incomes of different countries are usually translated into a single currency through purchasing power exchange rates, whose value is affected by the choice of national baskets of representative consumption goods. Even more serious are the problems arising from the presence of externalities and of goods whose production counts as income when they are sold in the market but not when they are consumed by the producer or within his or her family, an occurrence that is usually more frequent in poorer countries or among lower income groups. To face these problems, a number of alternative and broader notions of economic welfare have been suggested, among them that of *net economic welfare*, proposed by Joseph Stiglitz, which adjusts gross domestic product (GDP) by subtracting from it negative factors ("bads") such as pollution and by adding the contribution of beneficial nonmarket activities such as leisure, household production, child care, or looking after sick people.

There are good reasons both for treating the inequalities existing in the various spheres separately and for pooling them in a single comprehensive notion of economic inequality. The reason for treating them separately is that the pattern of inequalities of one sphere does not coincide with those of others; that their economic and political consequences as well as the moral criteria for evaluating them are different, according to Michael Walzer, and that the instruments available for redressing them are usually specific to each sphere (redistributing income has no immediate impact on inequalities in health, education, or power). The reasons for pooling them is that the shortcomings in one sphere can, at least partly, be compensated for by advantages in another and that the overall condition of people depends on the positions they have in each of the relevant ones.

There have been many attempts at finding criteria for combining the individual positions in a number of separate spheres to form an overall indicator of their standing both in absolute terms and relative to each other. One of the most relevant of these is the one proposed by Amartya Sen (1993) with the term *capabilities*, defined as "combinations of *functionings* a person can achieve, and from which he or she can choose one collection" (p. 31), which represents an all-encompassing notion of what has value for an individual and covers the whole range of possible valuable life experiences that are within reach of a person (including alternatives that are mutually exclusive). The solution Sen put forward can be applied both to individuals and to groups or whole populations; in this second form it has inspired the adoption by the United Nations of the Human Development Index (HDI), as a benchmark for the evaluation of social policies and policies for development, an index that is calculated for each country on the basis of data concerning income per head, the expectation of life at birth, and the level of education. For each of these variables, each country is given a score corresponding to the point in which it is placed in the interval that separates the position of the country that ranks first from that of the country that ranks last, the general index being formed by the simple average of the indexes concerning the individual variables.

Inequality Among Whom?

A system of inequalities is defined

1. by the choice of the particular sphere, or groups of spheres, to be considered;
2. by the identification of the population about which the comparisons are made and of the units within it whose positions are compared; and
3. by the specification of the moment or span of time that is taken into consideration.

For the sake of simplicity, we shall limit ourselves to consider a single sphere of value (that of income) and to a static approach, considering a single moment in time. The definition of the population for which inequalities are assessed requires on the one hand that its members have a sufficient number of elements in common to make it relevant, and on the other that they present sufficient differences to make it interesting; both conditions depend on the nature of the problems examined.

The most frequent cases are those in which the population is defined on a national level, but Branko Milanovic notes that an increasing number of studies make reference to the broadest possible definition of the population, which of course corresponds to the whole of humanity. At the other extreme are populations that are formed by specific groups (such as the workforce of a single factory or the members of a single union), local communities, or even single families. As a general (but by no means universal) rule, we can say that the size of the inequalities increases with the size of the population but that its significance can move in the opposite direction, because individuals or groups living close together or having much in common tend to have a sharper perception of what makes them different.

We have a disaggregated representation of inequalities when the population is seen as formed by single individuals and an aggregate one when it is seen as formed by groups of individuals having in common certain characteristics such as gender, age, living in the same area, working in the same sector, having a similar professional qualification, belonging to the same ethnic group, or even belonging to the same bracket or fraction (decile, quintile, etc.) in the distribution of income. The case of families is in some ways ambiguous in that they can be considered both as elementary units and as groups. Aggregation is of course a matter of degree insofar as any group can be split into a number of subgroups or lumped together with others to form a wider group. When the aggregate approach is adopted, the systems of inequalities present both an external and an internal side: In the first case, the position of a group is considered in terms of a representative figure or parameter (typically the average or the median value) and compared with that of other groups; in the second, comparison is made of the position of each single individual or subgroup with those of other individuals or subgroups that make up the larger one.

The aggregate and disaggregate approaches are more often complementary than alternative, given that the position of single individuals in the larger populations is usually the joint result of factors affecting the position of the group to which they belong compared with that of other groups and of factors affecting their personal position in the former. The choice of an aggregate or disaggregate approach is far from neutral and can have relevant ethical and political implications: Presenting world income inequalities in aggregate terms through a comparison of the per capita incomes of different countries leads naturally to development policies that work through transfers of resources to governments; more disaggregate approaches lead to policies that are directly targeted to individuals or local communities. Similarly, policies of affirmative action addressed to disadvantaged groups (like women or ethnic minorities) often take the forms of reserving to members of those groups coveted positions or privileged conditions for obtaining them, measures that do in fact improve the average position of the targeted group but tend to increase the inequalities within it and often do little to improve the conditions of its most disadvantaged members.

Another meaningful distinction, according to Larry Temkin, is that between analytical and synthetic representations of inequalities. In the first case, we have a set of separate data regarding the differences between the position of every single element (individual or group) into which the population has been divided and that of each of the others; for a population of N elements, this representation takes the form of an $N \times N$ symmetrical matrix. The synthetic versions take the form of a single numerical indicator, whose value reflects the dispersion of the positions of the various elements, or more exactly the extent to which the distribution of values within the population diverges from equality. The most well-known and frequently used measure is the Gini index, which is especially sensitive to the variations of the extreme positions and takes on a zero value in the case of full equality and a value of 1 in the case of maximum inequality, when all resources belong to just one individual or group.

Synthetic representations may be thought of as the expression of inequalities in the singular, describing properties of entire populations or collective entities: analytical representations, on the other hand, as expressions of inequality in the plural, describing the relative positions of different individuals or groups. Analytical representations are closer to what might be called the direct perception of inequalities, that is, the actual conditions of individuals and the way they compare themselves with other individuals: Richard Wilkinson and Kate Pickett, for example, have shown that individuals are often more concerned with how much more or less than others they earn than with the absolute level of their income and that less wealth can be as painful (or even more painful) than actual poverty. The empirical descriptions of systems of inequalities combine in general synthetic and analytical aspects, as well as aggregate and disaggregate ones.

The systems of inequalities characterizing a given population can show at the same time stability and variability: stability, as the pattern of relative positions remains basically the same, and variability, as the individuals occupying the different positions keep changing all the time. A high degree of variability or mobility tends to dampen significantly the economic, social, political, and psychological impact of any given system of inequalities.

The Causes of Inequalities

The factors that give shape to a raw system of economic inequalities among individuals, by which is meant those that precede any corrective intervention by the state or other authorities, normally operate within a general competitive framework and can be grouped into three broad categories:

1. macrofactors, which determine the relative levels of average incomes of whole communities (typically countries);
2. personal factors, which determine the relative positions that individuals living in the same country can attain through their choices and actions; and
3. microfactors, which correspond to gaps in the general framework and provide privileged conditions for particular organizations or individuals within them.

The individual positions in a given system of inequalities are to a varying degree affected by each of the aforementioned factors.

The general framework is that of a competitive capitalist market economy in which the income people earn broadly corresponds to the contribution they have given to marketable production through their work and the resources they have made available. The rule applies fully and directly only to units (persons or firms) that sell their products in the market and are motivated by the maximization of income (or profit, in the case of firms). When production is organized by public bodies, or by nonprofit organizations, the rules are different, but still subject to the indirect influence of those of the capitalist sector, owing to the fact that individuals and resources can move or be transferred from one to the other. Before reaching individuals, the flows of income (mainly capital income but to a certain extent even incomes from labor) deriving from the sale of production can be partially modified by intermediate actors (corporations, financial institutions, insurance companies, families, etc.), which pool different flows and redistribute them among their members or associates.

The macrofactors are those that affect the position of a country in the world economy; they include the nature of the goods it produces, their prices, the efficiency of its firms compared with those of other countries, and its currency's exchange rate; they play a crucial role in determining the relative level of its per capita income and, owing to their frequent fluctuations, its variation through time. Each of them has a direct positive effect on relative per capita income that is sometimes accompanied by indirect negative ones; an appreciation of the exchange rate, for instance, reduces the competitiveness of national firms, making the goods they produce more expensive in terms of foreign currencies.

The personal factors are those that determine the precise position of individuals and the roles they perform in the economic system of the country they live in; these include their natural gifts (in terms of intelligence, health, and physical dexterity), the social milieu in which they were born and grew up, the choices they made regarding their development and during their working life, how much they worked and the effort and commitment they put in, how much they saved, the risks they took, and the luck they had. Mainstream explanations of income inequalities among persons living in the same country see them as arising from competitive market interactions of individuals having different personal characteristics.

The microfactors are mainly sociological and usually "local," in the sense of having a direct influence on specific sectors or locations; they reflect the structure of organizations (firms, unions, etc.) or networks within which and between which elements of power, monopoly, and discrimination play a significant role: They typically offer to insiders privileged channels of access to valuable resources from which outsiders are excluded or that they face obstacles in accessing. The inequalities they produce are sheltered from the competitive forces that are characteristic of the basic framework and have a "durable" nature insofar as they affect individuals' conditions throughout their lives and are often transmitted vertically through generations and horizontally among persons who share some easily recognizable and permanent traits (such as gender, ethnic origin, or faith). These microfactors can be grouped into the three broad categories of hierarchization, exclusion, and exploitation, which perform different but often complementary roles, according to Charles Tilly.

Hierarchization has been defined by Göran Therborn (2006) as "institutionalized ranking of social actors": The subjects occupying the higher ranking positions, usually limited in number, have at their disposal a variety of resources (finances, prestige, power, etc.), the access to which is subject to their control and approval, or from which those of lower rank are excluded; inequalities of this kind are generally codified by rules that are both formal and stable in time, and sometimes transmitted to designated heirs.

Exclusion occurs when access to positions associated with wealth and prestige is barred to subjects who would otherwise qualify, on the basis of characteristics such as gender, race, or religion, which are easily ascertained by the insiders and cannot easily be modified by the excluded.

Exploitation has been examined from various points of view: the Marxist one, for which every relationship based on the separation between workers and the means of production involves exploitation, is both too broad and insufficiently comprehensive; more limited versions refer to the presence of elements of monopoly and/or of coercion, which alter the distribution of the fruits of labor to the advantage of those who control them.

According to Tilly's version, similar to Marx's but more sociological and not limited to relationships between capital and labor, exploitation "operates when powerful, connected people command resources from which they draw significantly increased returns by coordinating the effort of outsiders whom they exclude from the full value added by that effort" (*Durable Inequality*, p. 10). Common to all these versions is the idea of a systematic and long-lasting distortion of relationships in favor of the exploiter, which (a) could be removed without significant loss of efficiency and (b) is accompanied by forms of "categorical inequality," that is, by the attribution to the exploited and exploiter of distinctive characteristics (in terms of race, gender, culture, or class) that tend to both consolidate and justify the exploitation. Alongside exploitation, and sharing some of its traits, Tilly proposes the category of "opportunity hoarding," which arises when groups of people sharing some recognizable characteristic establish preferential relationships that ensure them the control of resources, which they take advantage of to the exclusion of outsiders but without exploiting the latter.

Eugenio Somaini
Università degli Studi di Parma
Parma, Italy

See also Class, Social; Inequality, Political; Social Stratification

Further Readings

Milanovic, B. (2005). *Worlds apart: Measuring international and global inequality.* Princeton, NJ: Princeton University Press.

Sen, A. (1993). Capability and well-being. In M. Nussbaum & A. Sen (Eds.), *The quality of life* (pp. 30–53). Oxford, UK: Clarendon Press.

Temkin, L. S. (1993). *Inequality.* Oxford, UK: Oxford University Press.

Therborn, G. (Ed.). (2006). *Inequalities of the world.* London: Verso.

Tilly, C. (1999). *Durable inequality.* Berkeley: University of California Press.

Walzer, M. (1983). *Spheres of justice.* New York: Basic Books.

Wilkinson, R., & Pickett, K. (2009). *The spirit level: Why more equal societies almost always do better.* London: Penguin.

Inequality, Political

Political inequality is the unequal influence of the citizens on the collective decisions. It stems from a situation in which one person or one group within a community differs in its impact on the decisions that affect the whole community. Defined as an antonym, political inequality is the absence of political equality, a fundamental attribute of democracy. The principle of political equality departs from the idea that decisions can only be adopted by the persons who are subject to them, and that all preferences must be taken into account before deciding. From the point of view of the quality of democracy, addressing the levels of political inequality in a democracy is therefore essential. There are, however, two contradictory conceptions of political inequality, which frame differently the study of democratic quality. After a brief contextualization, this entry reconsiders these two main conceptions of political inequality and underlines the principal implications for the quality of democracy.

Discussions on the concept of political equality are intrinsically linked to democratic discourse. As such, the scope of political equality has gradually been changed, in parallel to the development of Western democracies. In the early 19th century, few men and almost no women were usually entitled to participate in the political sphere. Political equality existed but only for a reduced group of men from the high socioeconomic strata. It was not put into question, however, that suffrage should be extended to women, slaves, or the lower social classes. Only late in the 19th century was universal suffrage steadily introduced in most democracies and political rights expanded to the whole population. The new status of citizenship enabled all citizens to be political equal. Although by the end of the 20th century most societies labeled as democracies had incorporated universal suffrage as a basic norm, the ideal of political equality is far from being realized in many countries, and there are significant differences across them. Political inequality remains for that reason a major field of research.

Formal Versus Substantial Inequality

Further development of the liberal and republican theories resulted in two competing understandings of political inequality, which roughly reflect the distinction between formal and substantial inequality.

Formal Inequality

For formalists, universal suffrage and universal entitlement to participate in public matters are the basic features of political equality—a set of rights that allows citizens to equally influence collective decisions. Political equality is legally and formally guaranteed through the existence of these rights. In most democracies, indeed, the law endorses all citizens with the same rights and the same opportunities to participate in political decisions, and public institutions and administrations are prevented to avoid any type of discrimination against any of the citizens. Following this conception, political equality is equivalent to liberty, as the freedom to choose whether to participate or not. Once political equality is formally established, citizens might freely decide to become politically unequal. Freedom provides in fact with the opportunity to become unequal. As a logical result, freedom is only possible if there is political inequality; in other words, political inequality is a reflection of the citizen's decisions, an expression of their liberty. From this theoretical perspective, the principle of freedom is clearly superior to the equality principle.

Substantial Inequality

From a drastically different perspective, political inequality basically refers to the unequal distribution of political resources among the citizens. It comprehends not only formal equality but also substantive equality. Hence, formal equality is not a sufficient condition in a democracy, as its existence does not guarantee effective influence in the collective decisions of all the citizens. Unequal distribution of political resources—based on differences of income, education, skills, gender, race, and so on—undermines political equality; those who collect more political resources have a greater capacity to affect political decisions. Political inequality in this second meaning is inextricably linked to social inequality and social stratification. Because there normally is correspondence between a citizen's position in the stratification scale and his or her capacity to influence politics, there is an overlap of the concept of political inequality with social inequality. As an attempt to delimitate the former from the later, political inequality has been defined as the sum of three components: participatory inequality, unequal responsiveness, and unequal policy delivery. Participatory inequality is unequal political participation among the citizens, which might be caused by unequal rights to participate (formal equality), unequal capacity to participate (unequal distribution of resources), or unequal disposition to participate. Unequal responsiveness is uneven attention by the government, biased because of economic, ideological, or political factors. Unequal policy delivery is asymmetrical redistribution of favorable policies among the citizens, benefiting some groups more than others.

Implications for the Quality of Democracy

Addressing political inequality from either a formal or a substantive point of view has important implications with respect to the quality of democracy, regarding both how it should be measured and what goals should be attained through political equality.

Measures of formal political equality are based on objective indicators of the available rights and freedoms in a given society. Higher democratic standards can be achieved if there exist more alternatives to participate in collective decisions, if there are more freedoms and rights that citizens can enjoy, and if these rights and freedoms are more inclusive. Most democracies qualify high in this dimension, which is an indicator that formal equality is broadly extended.

However, a measure of the quality of democracy in terms of formal political equality has an important limitation with respect to political participation. There may be citizens who would like to participate in political decisions, who have the will to participate and freely decide to do so, but who lack the necessary resources to do so—they may not know how to participate, they may not have the time, and so on. A country may have a high degree of formal political equality, but there may be no guarantee that all citizens who wish to influence politics can effectively participate. There must be a minimal standard of life to ensure that all citizens are able to make their democratic choices. Restricting political inequality to a formal conception might therefore provide a partial picture of democratic quality.

When the substantive dimension is added to the definition of political inequality, measures of the quality of democracy are confronted by further critical dilemmas. Assessing levels of substantive political inequality is an extremely complex task, as measures of political inequality rely most of the time on subjective interpretations, which make them more difficult to control. Two indicators have generally been used to measure substantive inequality: levels of political participation (turnout, number of people working for a party, number of people who demonstrate, etc.) and political concentration (the extent to which office holding is monopolized by a group of individuals). Contrary to the measure of formal political inequality, though, many countries with relatively high ranks of formal equality rank relatively low on substantive political equality, with low levels of participation and high levels of political concentration. Formal equality does not in fact guarantee substantive equality.

Nevertheless, increasing substantive equality might also have a negative impact on the quality of democracy. Two main arguments have been developed against an increase in effective participation. First, the quality of the decisions is questioned. If all citizens are obliged to participate in the decision-making process, those with little interest in politics and low levels of education will be entitled to a voice. It is not certain, then, that they will be able to choose what is best for the whole community. A second concern is that increasing equality might endanger a basic principle of democracy: freedom. There are two possible ways to increase equality: Either citizens' socioeconomic status is equalized to avoid inequality based on unfair distribution of political resources, or citizens are obliged to participate. Although empirical studies are not always consistent in their results, the first option seems unfeasible in a reasonable period of time. The only sound option for increasing participation, therefore, is to make participation compulsory. Yet compulsory participation directly damages freedom, because it constrains individual liberties. In this situation, citizens do not freely decide whether or not to participate, but they are obliged to do so by the state; put differently, political participation—an act that is meant to be the expression of maximum liberty—is transformed into an obligation. Compulsory participation is hardly reconcilable with freedom, as it is extremely difficult to find the limits that do not harm individuals' liberties. There is, therefore, an unsolvable contradiction between increasing equality and ensuring freedom.

Inequality, Citizenship, and Immigration

A final issue concerning political inequality deals with the concept of citizenship and, as an extension, with immigration. Whether from a formal or substantive perspective, political inequality is at the core of the debate on citizenship. First, the status of citizenship is required to enjoy political equality. Political rights and freedoms are guaranteed only to the citizens, those who belong to the community and are legally recognized as such. Although substantive political equality cannot be ensured by the state, in contemporary democracies all people who have *full* citizenship formally should enjoy the same rights and freedoms. Second, and as a consequence, because immigrants do not have full citizenship, they constitute a specific, sometimes very large, group in the community that lacks basic political rights, such as the right to vote. While much discussion has been done on the extent to which political rights should be expanded to immigrants—that is, on the inclusiveness of the political rights—the right to vote is normally restricted to citizens. Formal inequality is therefore a feature of many democracies. Indeed, even if immigrants belong to the political community, they are not entitled to the status of citizens. Accordingly, and from the point of view of the quality of democracy, political inequality in a democracy may be addressed from three alternative outlooks: (1) Is there formal equality for citizens? (2) Is there formal equality for citizens and noncitizens? (3) Is there both formal and substantive equality?

Mónica Ferrín
European University Institute
Florence, Italy

See also Citizenship; Democracy, Quality; Equality, Political; Liberty

Further Readings

Dahl, R. A. (2006). *On political equality*. New Haven, CT: Yale University Press.

Rueschemeyer, D. (2005). Addressing inequality. In L. Diamond & L. Morlino (Eds.), *Assessing the quality of democracy* (pp. 47–61). Baltimore: Johns Hopkins University Press.

Schlozman, K. L., Benjamin I. P., Sidney, V., & Fiorina, M. (2004). *Inequalities of political voice* (Subcommittee report of the American Political Science Association Task Force on Inequality and American Democracy). Retrieved September 17, 2010, from http://www.apsanet.org/imgtest/voicememo.pdf

Sen, A. (1999). *Development as freedom.* New York: Knopf.

Verba, S. (2006). Fairness, equality and democracy: Three big words. *Social Research, 73*(2), 499–540.

Inference, Classical and Bayesian

See Statistical Inference, Classical and Bayesian

Inference, Ecological

The ecological inference problem is a long-standing problem that encompasses a rich set of intriguing puzzles. Scholars with diverse backgrounds and interests have a stake in approaches to ecological inference problems, which appear as frequently in political science as they do in medicine, geography, economics, or sociology. The problem occurs, for instance, when one is interested in the behavior of individuals, but has data only at an aggregated level (e.g., precincts, hospital wards, counties). In other words, a data limitation creates a situation where the behavior of individuals must be surmised from data on aggregated sets of individuals rather than on individuals themselves. Since the goal is to make inferences from aggregate units that are often derived from an "environmental level" (i.e., geographical/ecological units such as a county or precinct), the term *ecological inference* is used to describe this type of analysis. More generally, the problem manifests itself whenever one has data at one level of aggregation (e.g., the state level) but is interested in inferences at another level of data aggregation (e.g., the county level). Accordingly, the term *cross-level inference* is often used as a synonym for ecological inference. This entry discusses the nature and implications of this problem.

A classic example of the ecological inference problem in political science occurs when one tries to determine how members of different racial groups cast their ballots. Because the United States employs the secret ballot, the only data available for solving this inquiry are at the precinct level, where vote totals and racial demographics can be obtained but not vote totals broken down by racial categories. Epidemiologists confront identical methodological issues when they seek to explain which environmental factors influence disease susceptibility using only data from counties or hospital wards, rather than individual patients. Economists studying consumer demand and marketing strategies might need to infer individual spending habits with an analysis of sales data from a specific region and the aggregate characteristics of individuals in that region, rather than from data on individuals' characteristics and purchases. These different queries are substantively varied, and it would be simple to identify a host of other equally unique queries that fit into the ecological inference mold.

In addition to substantive applications that span many fields, the mathematics of the ecological inference problem are also related, sometimes isomorphic, to inferential problems in other disciplines, even when the subject matter is not substantially related. For instance, geographers have long been intrigued with the modifiable areal unit problem (MAUP). MAUP occurs when the estimates at one level of aggregation are different from the estimates obtained at a different level of aggregation. Many statisticians and mathematicians have been captivated by Simpson's paradox, which is the reversal in direction of association between two variables when a third ("lurking") variable is controlled. Described in this way, Simpson's paradox (and consequently ecological inference) is akin to the omitted variable problem discussed in virtually all econometrics and regression texts. While notation and terminology may differ, the similarities of the underlying problems cannot be denied.

The main difficulty with cross-level inference is that not only might the estimates at different levels of aggregation be different, they could be substantially different and even lead to different conclusions. William Robinson (1950) was among the first to point out this conundrum with correlation coefficients. He examined the relationship between nativity and illiteracy. At the individual level, the correlation coefficient was .118. If the data were aggregated at the state level, the correlation coefficient reverses sign and becomes −.526. If the data were aggregated at the census geographic divisions, the correlation coefficient remains negative at −.619. The same phenomenon occurs when race and illiteracy are examined. The correlation at the individual level is .203. At the census division level, the correlation is .946. At the state level, the correlation is .773. While these correlation coefficients do not change sign, they vary widely and imply different substantive conclusions. In fact, such wide discrepancies are common, and worse, in a given application, a researcher is unable to determine if his or her aggregated results bear similarity to the true individual-level relationship.

Let us consider the challenge of inferring how individuals voted from election returns aggregated at the precinct level. Because U.S. elections employ the secret ballot, individual vote choices are unknown. Election returns, however, are reported at the precinct level, and aggregate individual racial categorizations can usually be obtained and merged with the voting data. Hence, for any given precinct, the available data include how many votes each candidate received as well as the precinct's racial composition. The simplified problem can be summed up with a 2 × 2 contingency table.

	Candidate 1	*Candidate 2*	
Group 1	$\beta_{11}z_1$	$(1 - \beta_{11})z_1$	z_1
Group 2	$\beta_{21}z_2$	$(1 - \beta_{21})z_2$	z_2
	y_1	y_2	

The known elements of this problem are the proportion of voters in each group, z_1 and z_2, and the proportion of votes received by each candidate, y_1 and y_2. The unknown elements are the proportions of each group that voted for each candidate, β_{11}, β_{12}, β_{21}, and β_{22}. If we assume that Group 1 and Group 2 are mutually exclusive and exhaustive, then z_2 is simply $(1 - z_1)$. Similarly, if we assume that all votes were cast for either Candidate 1 or Candidate 2 and there were no abstentions, then $y_2 = (1 - y_1)$. Such contingency tables are usually available to describe each areal unit in the data set. In our voting application, since a set of precincts comprises the voting district in question, one might index these values with a further subscript to identify the precinct. For each precinct i, then, we have the following relationship:

$$y_{1i} = \beta_{11i}z_{1i} + \beta_{21i}(1 - z_{1i}).$$

This relationship holds exactly for each of the I precincts in the district, yielding a system with I equations (one for each precinct) and $2I$ unknowns (two parameters, β_{11i} and β_{21i}, for each precinct). From basic algebraic properties, we know that there is not enough information to solve for these parameters given these equations. The fundamental indeterminacy is that multiple values of the parameters satisfy these restrictions. Note as well that adding observations of further precincts does not change the indeterminacy. Each new precinct adds one more equation to the system and two more parameters to be inferred.

The ecological inference problem is an example of an ill-posed inverse problem, or an inverse problem with many "solutions," that is, a problem that encompasses a fundamental indeterminacy. Although one may wish to obtain a point estimate or "solution" to the problem, there is not enough information to narrow down the feasible set of estimates to one particular point estimate. This type of problem has been described as "partially identified" because while the available information does not allow one to identify the parameter of interest without the imposition of strong assumptions, it does often allow one to identify a "region" within which the parameters must lie, thus partially identifying the problem. How to proceed with partially identified problems such as the ecological inference problem is not obvious.

There are various strategies for pursuing problems of the partially identified ilk. However, for any particular application, how to proceed in identifying an estimation strategy is not straightforward and rarely obvious on the basis of theory alone. The key criterion involves the costs and benefits associated with different types of inferential errors. Every assumption involves an acceptance of potential error in estimation. Some of these assumptions may be more palatable than others. Importantly, one must never allow excitement over the possibility of a point estimate to override careful and explicit consideration of attendant assumptions. There are no pat answers, no generic solutions.

Many methods have been proposed for obtaining estimates for ecological inference problems. Although the multifarious approaches to this problem have been distinct, they can be seen as lying along a continuum. The left end of the continuum is characterized by a lack of assumptions and, concomitantly, high credibility. Even when no assumptions are imposed, the data can allow one to narrow the range in which the true values of the parameters of interest lie. The best known procedure for obtaining a range of possible estimates comes from Oris Duncan and Beverly Davis's method of bounds. The ideal situation occurs if the bounds are sufficiently informative. If they are not, one might choose to move along this continuum, but then assumptions, which may or may not be true, must be made. At the right end of the continuum are approaches that lead to a precise point estimate for each parameter. There are, to be sure, many different approaches clustered on the right, in the region of strong and numerous assumptions. Indeed, the bulk of the effort has been directed toward obtaining point estimates or to somehow identify a problem that is only partially identified. In general, one cannot zero in on precise estimates without making restrictive assumptions and thus trading reduced credibility for increased precision. Empirical researchers should be aware that no solution comes free. Every method yielding point estimates necessarily rests on assumptions that are strong enough to remove the indeterminacy of ecological inference. Researchers contemplating application of any method should carefully consider whether the associated assumptions are credible in their applications.

In practice, it is rare that one can accept point-identifying assumptions with great confidence. The prudent researcher should then resist the temptation to embrace any particular estimation method. Instead, the analysis of aggregate data should be a process. First, one should determine what one can learn from the data alone without imposing any assumptions. Then, one should consider various assumptions that have identifying power. A productive approach is to "layer" the assumptions, imposing them sequentially in order of decreasing plausibility. As more assumptions are imposed, one will be able to draw conclusions that are increasingly sharp but decreasingly believable. This process of inference illuminates the respective roles that data and assumptions play in empirical research. Moreover, it enables both researchers and their consumers to adjudicate how best to reconcile the inevitable tension between the strength of conclusions and their credibility in ecological inference problems.

Wendy K. Tam Cho
University of Illinois at Urbana-Champaign
Champaign, Illinois, United States

See also Aggregate Data Analysis; Measurement, Levels; Multilevel Analysis; Statistical Inference, Classical and Bayesian

Further Readings

Achen, C. H., & Shively, P. (1995). *Cross-level inference.* Chicago: University of Chicago Press.

Cho, W. K. T., & Manski, C. F. (2008). Cross-level/ecological inference. In J. Box-Steffensmeier, H. E. Brady, & D. Collier (Eds.), *Oxford handbook of political methodology* (pp. 547–569). Oxford, UK: Oxford University Press.

Duncan, O. D., & Davis, B. (1953). An alternative to ecological correlation. *American Sociological Review, 18,* 665–666.

Goodman, L. A. (1953). Ecological regressions and behavior of individuals. *American Sociological Review, 18*(6), 663–664.

Robinson, W. S. (1950). Ecological correlations and the behavior of individuals. *American Sociological Review, 15*(3), 351–357.

Information, Political

See Political Communication

Institutional Theory

Institutional theory has been grappling with one major problem: how to explain the dynamics of change in institutions. Scholars in the three long-standing "new institutionalisms"—(1) rational choice institutionalism (RI), (2) historical institutionalism (HI), and (3) sociological institutionalism (SI)—have increasingly sought to "endogenize" change, that is, explain it "from the inside." In response to criticisms that their analytic frameworks could account for continuity but not for change, which they explained mainly "from the outside," as the result of exogenous shocks, these neo-institutionalists have increasingly sought to explain the origins of and shifts in interest-based preferences, historical paths, or cultural frames. Whereas many of these scholars have sought explanations using one or other of the two existing alternative approaches, others have turned instead to ideas and discourse. For some of these neo-institutionalists, this was but a brief encounter, in particular for RI scholars, since taking ideas and discourse "seriously" undermined many of the very premises of their approaches. Others, however, broke with some of the fundamental premises of their own institutionalist tradition with their turn to ideas and discourse. Because these latter scholars have come to have as much if not more in common with one another than with those in the institutionalist tradition from which they emerged, they have come to be seen as part of a fourth new institutionalism, discursive institutionalism (DI)—sometimes also called the ideational turn or constructivist institutionalism.

The three long-standing neo-institutionalisms, although very different, tend to share one common assumption: Institutions serve primarily as constraints. RI focuses on rational actors who pursue their preferences following a *logic of calculation* within political institutions, defined as structures of incentives; HI details the development of political institutions, described as regularized patterns and routinized practices subject to a *logic of path dependence*; and SI concentrates on social agents who act according to a *logic of appropriateness* within political institutions, defined as socially constituted and culturally framed rules and norms. By contrast, DI focuses on sentient agents who convey substantive ideas through the interactive processes of discourse in given meaning to contexts following (contextualized) *logics of communication*. Institutions, here, rather than static external rule–following structures, are dynamic structures and constructs of meaning internal to agents who have the ability not only to create (and maintain) institutions but also to communicate critically about them and to change (or maintain) them through collective action. But while institutional context in DI therefore refers first and foremost to the structure, construction, and communication of meaning, it can also be understood in terms of the background information provided by the other three neo-institutionalisms in political science, with which discursive institutionalists may engage and from which they often emerge. This background information is all about the structures, understood in terms of historical institutional rules and regularities, sociological institutionalist cultural rules and frames, and rational choice institutionalist incentives and power asymmetries, that constitute the context within which collective action occurs and that affect the ways in which discursive institutionalist meaning structures are constructed.

Thus, the four institutionalisms share with one another a core focus on the importance of institutions, but they differ in their definitions of institutions, in their objects and logics of explanation, and in the ways in which they deal with change (see Table 1). This entry turns first to the examination of attempts to endogenize change and the move to ideas in RI, next in HI, and then in SI, before exploring the same in DI, in particular through the interactive dimension of discourse. The entry concludes with a consideration of the interrelationships among the four new institutionalisms.

Endogenizing Change in Rational Choice Institutionalism

RI posits rational actors with fixed preferences who calculate strategically to maximize their preferences and for whom institutions represent the incentive structures that reduce the uncertainties resulting from the multiplicity of individual preferences and issues. The very premises of RI about the fixed nature of preferences and the stability of institutions ensured that preference formation was long of little interest to RI scholars, while institutional change was ruled out analytically a priori, given equilibrium-based assumptions that entailed that change could only come from the outside, through exogenous shocks. The inability of RI to deal with institutional change from the inside and

Table 1 The Four Institutionalisms

	Rational Choice Institutionalism (RI)	*Historical Institutionalism (HI)*	*Sociological Institutionalism (SI)*	*Discursive Institutionalism (DI)*
Object of explanation	Behavior of rational actors	Structures and practices	Norms and culture of social agents	Ideas and discourse of sentient agents
Logic of explanation	Calculation	Path dependency	Appropriateness	Communication
Definition of institutions	Incentive structures	Macrohistorical structures and regularities	Cultural norms and frames	Meaning structures and constructs
Approach to change	Static—Continuity through fixed preferences, stable institutions	Static—Continuity through path dependency interrupted by critical junctures	Static—Continuity through cultural norms and rules	Dynamic—Change (and continuity) through ideas and discursive interaction
Explanation of change	Exogenous shock	Exogenous shock	Exogenous shock	Endogenous process through background ideational and foreground discursive abilities
Recent innovations to explain change	Endogenous ascription of interest shifts through RI political coalitions or HI self-reinforcing or self-undermining processes	Endogenous description of incremental change through layering, drift, conversion	Endogenous construction (merge with DI)	Endogenous construction through reframing, recasting collective memories and narratives through epistemic communities, advocacy coalitions, communicative action, deliberative democracy

Source: Schmidt, V. A. (2010). Taking ideas *and* discourse seriously: Explaining change through discursive institutionalism as the fourth new institutionalism. *European Political Science Review*, 2(1), 1–25.

its difficulties in accounting for preference formation have led scholars in the RI tradition in recent years to seek to endogenize change. For some, this has meant remaining within RI and seeking to explain change through shifts in political coalitions. For others, it has also entailed looking to HI approaches for the origins of preference formation, in particular for the origins of institutions, and for trajectories of change. For yet other scholars, however, endogenizing change has involved the turn to ideas—with most doing so in ways that did not undermine RI basic premises and a few moving to DI.

In their attempts to find new ways to account for preference formation and institutional shifts, RI scholars have mostly looked to political coalition formation, although they have also sometimes sought a rapprochement with HI. Those RI scholars concerned with political coalitions often focus on formal electoral institutions, arguing that these act as incentive structures to produce the political coalitions that implement certain kinds of policies. But whatever the value of this insight within purely RI analytics, the problem is that it remains highly deterministic, as institutions are portrayed as determining politics, which in turn determine political outcomes, and it still cannot explain the origins of the institutions or of the political coalitions that created them, let alone why institutions or policies might change over time. When RI scholars try to respond to the question of origins by turning to HI, they often go back to the founding moments of the electoral institutions. But in this case, institutional foundations serve to explain contemporary political institutions that explain current political coalitions that explain current policies. And where is endogenous change?

Instead of using HI to enhance substantive theorizing, RI scholars sometimes seek to build HI insights into game-theoretic analysis. Avner Greif and David Laitin, for example, redefine the goal of institutions—from self-enforcing to self-reinforcing or self-undermining institutions—and their effects as *parametric* in the short term, meaning exogenous and fixed for agents who act on self-enforcing beliefs, but only *quasi-parametric* in the long run, meaning endogenous and variable as individuals are led to act in a manner that does not reproduce the associated beliefs. The problem here is that although this may better account for change over time in game-theoretic terms, we are still left with the irrationality of the choice of institutions to begin with; the deterministic trajectory of change over time, now for better or for worse; and the limited rationality of these supposedly rational actors at any given point in time.

Relatively few RI scholars have turned to ideas to solve the problem of institutional change. Among those who have, the most significant RI engagement with ideas began in the 1990s, although it has remained rather circumscribed ever since. It never took ideas very seriously, since ideational explanation was deemed useful only when and if explanation in terms of objective or material interests was insufficient. This, RI scholars argued, would occur if ideas come before interests, as road maps—in which case ideas are little more than mechanisms for choosing among interests; if ideas come after interests, acting as focal points—in which case ideas serve at best as switches for interests; if ideas are embedded in institutions, in which case it is the institutions rather than the ideas that really matter; if ideas are after the fact legitimation of actors' interest-based action—in which case ideas are not really taken seriously at all; or even if, following the work of Douglas North, ideas are "shared mental modes"—in which case ideas would necessarily have an effect on the content of interests, undermining the very RI definitions of interests as separate from ideas.

The problem for RI scholars, then, and the reason most quickly abandoned the pursuit of ideas, is that they could not continue to maintain the artificial separation of objective interests from subjective ideas about interests, that is, beliefs and desires. Such subjective interests threatened to overwhelm the objective ones that are at the basis of the rationalists' thin model of rationality, by undermining the fixed nature of preferences and the notion of outcomes as a function of preexisting preferences. And without fixed preferences as well as neutral institutional incentive structures, RI scholars lose the parsimony of the approach and everything that follows from it, including the ability to mathematically model games rational actors play as opposed to, in the words of Fritz Scharpf, the "games real actors play." This helps explain why the foray into ideas for most dyed-in-the-wool RI scholars was short-lived. For those who persisted, however, a whole new approach to the explanation of interests and institutions has opened up.

For DI scholars engaged with the RI tradition, subjective interests replace the objective ones of RI, as ideas about interests that bring in a much wider range of strategic ideas and social norms. And these must be explained in terms of their meaning to the actors within a given meaning context rather than in terms of some set of universally identifiable interests. Material interests, economic in particular, which are at the basis of much of the institutional incentives in the rational choice institutionalist literature, are not ignored. But DI scholars tend to separate material interests analytically into material reality and interests rather than to conflate them, such that material reality constitutes the setting within which or in response to which agents may conceive of their interests. This makes for a DI ontology that is largely constructivist, much as in SI (see below), by contrast with the materialist ontology of most RI scholars, who assume that they can attribute material interests to actors, regardless of how those actors themselves construct their own ideas about their interests. And it makes for a different approach to epistemological questions of knowledge and certainty.

In DI, the kind of knowledge and degree of certainty agents may have with regard to their ideas about material reality may differ, depending on the aspect of material reality with which they are concerned. Illustrative of this epistemological observation is Ludwig Wittgenstein's little noticed distinction in *On Certainty* between language games based on our everyday experiences in the world, which tend to admit few doubts or mistakes, and language games based on our (social) scientific pictures of the world, which may always allow for doubts, mistakes, and even gestalt switches. A problem with RI is that it tends to develop (social) scientific pictures games of the world that it treats as if they had the certainty of experience games.

Analyzed using the terms of RI, Mark Blyth suggests that the problem is that RI scholars assume that most phenomena are explainable in terms of "Knightian risk," as part of a directly observable world in which agents can calculate the subjective probability of the likely outcomes of their preferences, such as in the U.S. Congress. But much of the phenomena that RI scholars seek to explain are not directly observable and are much closer to "Knightian uncertainty" because of the impossibility of knowing let alone statistically predicting the effects of all the forces that may have an impact on economic and political realities. For these phenomena, agents are not simply unsure about how to achieve their interests but also unsure of what their interests are, given that the uncertainties are too great, the moment unique, prediction impossible, and agents' interests always structurally underdetermined. Thus, for example, the Great Depression of the 1930s and the economic crisis following the oil shocks of the 1970s were both cases of Knightian uncertainty, as governments, business, and labor at these critical junctures all sought to reconstitute interests through alternative narratives and causal stories about the reasons for the crisis, seeking to produce new political coalitions for collective action, with new ideas about how to replace existing institutions.

Needless to say, the economic crisis that began in 2008 is a similar moment of Knightian uncertainty, when the economists' predictive models of rationalist behavior proved unable to cope not simply because they wrongly predicted but because their use actually altered the market, by acting, in the words of Donald Mackenzie, as an "engine" transforming the environment, not a "camera" recording it. It is important to note, however, that while the predictive failure of economists' picture games contributed to the radical uncertainties of the economic crisis, where bankers went very wrong is when they ignored what they knew with a high degree of certainty from their cumulative experiences of lending and of assessing the reliability of risk, creditworthiness, and the likelihood of repayment over time and turned instead to predictive models that they believed were more certain because they were based on "scientific" methods.

Knightian uncertainty need not always be connected to such dramatic moments, however. DI scholars in the RI tradition have identified numerous cases in which ideas about interests may be in question under more everyday circumstances. For example, actors may not know what their interests are because they are in a new area of activity and thus have to determine which utility to maximize (interests), how to maximize it (strategies), and to what end (goals). Alternatively, long-standing ideas about interests may come into question at a critical juncture, say, when a central figure in a system signals an idea that leads to a shift in belief system. In both of these instances, scholars challenge RI logics only in special circumstances—with new ideas in new areas of activity or when old ideas are questioned. In both cases, however, by limiting the importance of ideas to the period of uncertainty between the end of the old institutional "game" and the beginning of the newly agreed institutional "game," DI scholars risk making it appear that DI is significant only at the critical moment of changing DI ideas, which is preceded and followed by RI-crystallized preferences and frozen institutions. Institutions, however, also change over time as the ideas that infuse them change, as other DI scholars in the RI tradition suggest. This is because institutions themselves are not neutral structures of incentives but, rather, as Bo Rothstein suggests, may be the carriers of ideas or collective memories that make them objects of trust or mistrust and changeable over time as actors' ideas and discourse about them change in tandem with changes in their performance.

DI scholars who engage with the RI tradition, then, like RI scholars, speak the language of interests, incentive structures, and collective action. But they see these as infused with a wide range of ideas and norms rather than narrowly focused on an instrumental rationality of utility maximization, with incentive structures normative rather than neutral, interests subjective rather than objective, and their explanations, where these are RI pictures of the world, much more uncertain than RI scholars recognize.

Endogenizing Change in Historical Institutionalism

HI explores how institutions, understood as sets of regularized practices with rulelike qualities, structure action and outcomes. It emphasizes not just the operation and development of institutions but also the path dependencies and unintended consequences that result from such historical development. The emphasis of HI on macrostructures and path dependence means that it has no agency built into it, making it difficult for it to explain why change may occur other than exogenously. And by focusing on critical junctures, with big bangs followed by path-dependent continuities, HI can be as equilibrium based as RI—which is even more problematic for an approach that purportedly explains "history." HI's inability to explain change from the inside along with its lack of agents has spurred scholars in the HI tradition to seek to endogenize change. And here, whereas for some this meant remaining within HI to theorize incremental change and/or to turn for agency to RI, for others it has meant a turn to SI and, increasingly, to DI.

In their attempts to introduce agency, HI scholars have most often looked to RI for the microfoundations to their macropatterns. But in so doing, they have often simply reinforced the immobility of institutions. One example of this is the varieties of capitalism (VOC) school pioneered by Peter Hall and David Soskice, which explicitly married the two frameworks in its analysis of the binary division of capitalism into liberal and coordinated market economies. VOC is HI in its definition of the historically grounded macro-institutional rules and regularized practices of the two different capitalist varieties, RI in its focus on the rationally based, microfoundational logic of coordination games among firms and other relevant actors. But, however valuable the insight into the rationalist logics of complementarities among components and coordinating mechanisms among corporate actors within different macro-institutional contexts, the result is a very static depiction of capitalism that critics have also found overly functionalist and unable to account for the changing conditions resulting from global and regional economic and institutional forces.

Recent revisionist approaches to HI led by Kathleen Thelen and Wolfgang Streeck, which describe incremental change in institutions through endogenous processes of layering of new elements onto the old, through conversion by means of reinterpretation or redirection, or by drifting through deliberate neglect or exhaustion, do offer a way out of the HI statics of VOC. But they do this at the expense of VOC's theoretical RI logic, since allowing for incremental change by definition makes for unfixed preferences and unstable institutions. Their "soft" RI framework of strategic actors trying to achieve advantage by interpreting or redirecting institutions enables them at best to provide empirical accounts of rationalist behavior. And they still cannot *explain* preference formation or why any given institution was the object of layering or conversion in one or another way, although they can *describe* it. Peter Hall and Kathleen Thelen do more to explain preference formation, with a clearer theoretical picture of the use of RI for HI incremental change, when they cast institutions as the target of rationalist strategic action by economic actors, who use them as resources to achieve their goals, with change depending on deliberative interaction, defection, and reinterpretation. But if actors are engaged in constant deliberation and reinterpretation of their perceived—read subjective—interests, then here too, the use of RI cannot go very far in theoretical terms because preferences are not fixed, are subjective rather than objective, and institutions are not stable enough to theorize as incentives. And once preferences are seen as subjective, with agency consisting of deliberation and reinterpretation, the way is open to taking seriously the role of ideas in altering agents' perceptions of their preferences and of discourse in deliberating and reinterpreting agents' institutions.

The HI analytic framework is generally more open to the turn to ideas than RI. This is because whereas RI has certain ontological and epistemological presuppositions about agency that clash with those of DI, HI has none, since it lacks agency. As a result, whereas RI scholars have largely resisted the turn to ideas, HI scholars have been divided over how far to go with regard to ideas. The question here is where the tipping point is between HI scholars who continue to see institutions as constitutive of ideas and those who might better be called DI scholars within an HI tradition because they see ideas as constitutive of institutions even if shaped by them. Interestingly enough, even foundational books that are purportedly exclusively HI often contain chapters that can be seen as DI, whether because they focus on the role of ideas and knowledge in the making of policy, add to RI explanations of interest calculations a focus on processes of power and persuasion, or mix HI and DI (in the HI or SI tradition). These may involve showing how policy actors may consciously layer new policy ideas onto the old or illustrating how battles over ideas generate new institutional paths of development.

But if HI and DI approaches can be found in the same articles and chapters, then the question needs to be raised about how to reconcile HI and DI. For some DI scholars in the HI tradition, HI and DI can fit easily together, with HI providing structures, DI agency. Often, this is formulated as actors' ideas and discourse set the goals and indicate motivation while the (historical) institutional context provide the constraints for actions that also structure political openings for mobilization and articulation of interests. The problem with this mix is that it risks papering over some very real differences between HI and DI, in particular that HI portrays institutions as constraining structures external to actors whereas DI defines institutions as internal ideational constructs and structures (discussed as follows). Moreover, it leaves open the question of whether there can be a specifically HI approach to agency.

Recent endogenous approaches to agency in HI have tended to borrow from evolutionary biology to explain institutional change in terms of how populations' genetic predispositions, combined with environmental factors, make for the success, replication, proliferation, and genetic feedback of certain preferences. The problem with this approach, from a DI perspective, is that it appears mechanistic, with no sense of the critical thinking of sentient agents (read real people) consciously changing their institutions—for better or for worse—through deliberation and contestation, as well as consensus building around ideas. Sven Steinmo is arguably the only HI scholar who has managed to combine DI with an HI approach to agency through evolutionary biology, when he provides evolutionary narratives of the trajectories of change in states' economic and social systems that show not only how human institutions evolve but also how human agents who are creative, have ideas, and communicate with one another about what they are doing are also a key element in this approach, along with the unanticipated consequences to purposive behavior, and the fact that what they do occurs within evolving institutional context. This, then, is a mix of HI and DI, but one in which the HI tends to predominate.

But how, then, to give each analytic framework its due? Some scholars separate the HI examination of the institutional context of historical rules and regularities, critical junctures, and incremental change from the DI analysis, in which they then use the results of the HI investigation as background information. This helps show how sentient agents may infuse HI rules with contextualized meanings, construct understandings and responses to critical moments, or come up with the ideas that lead to the layering of one institution over another, the reinterpretation of an institution, or the conversion of agents to another institution. Other DI scholars interweave HI and DI together in discussions of evolutionary changes across time, while giving primacy to the ways in which evolving ideas affect changes in institutions.

This said, DI does not purport to explain all change—this would be a big mistake since "stuff happens," events outside of people's control occur all the time, material conditions do change, actions often have unintended consequences, and actors often act without prior ideas and discourse about what it is they will do. As HI scholars remind us, processes of change are often unconscious—as people may act without any clear sense of what they are doing, creating new practices, renewing old rules, or destroying them through drifting or exhaustion. DI, however, shows that much change can and should be explained in terms of sentient agents' ideas about what to change (or continue)—if nothing else, in response to occurrences on the outside—that is, to the stuff that happens.

DI scholars who engage with the HI tradition, then, like HI scholars, also speak the language of institutional rules and regularities, critical moments, and incremental change. It is just that they infuse these structures with agency by focusing on the ideas of real actors that help explain changes in institutions or continuities, at critical moments or incrementally over time.

Endogenizing Change in Sociological Institutionalism

SI focuses on the forms and procedures of organizational life stemming from culturally specific practices, with institutions cast as the norms, cognitive frames, scripts, and meaning systems that guide human action according to a logic of appropriateness. In SI, therefore, one cannot talk about a turn to ideas as such, since ideas have always been at the basis of the approach—as norms, frames, and meaning systems—and constructivism as opposed to RI's positivism as the generally accepted view of the nature of reality. One can, however, nevertheless talk about a split in SI between those whom we could continue to label as SI scholars because they see ideas more as static ideational structures, as norms and identities constituted by culture that frame agents' actions and identities, and those whom we could call DI scholars in the SI tradition, because they see agents' ideas as constituting culture and framing action.

DI scholars who engage with the SI tradition, then, like SI scholars, also speak the language of cultural framing, ideas, and discourse. It is just that they ensure that these are more dynamic and, thereby, better able to explain institutional change (and continuity). Importantly, DI scholars go beyond the SI scholars who put ideas into cultural context to put them into their "meaning" context as well—that is, by treating ideas as empirical subjects to be studied in their own right. And such meaning contexts constitute very different kinds of institutions from those of RI, HI, and SI.

For the three older neo-institutionalisms, institutions are structures external to agents that constitute rules about acting in the world that serve mainly as constraints—whether by way of rationalist incentives that structure action, historical paths that shape action, or cultural norms that frame action. For DI, by contrast, institutions are internal to sentient agents, serving both as structures (of thinking and acting) that constrain action and as constructs (of thinking and acting) created and changed by those actors. This internal capacity to create and maintain institutions derives from what Vivien Schmidt defines as agents' *background ideational abilities*. This is a generic term for what John Searle defines as the *background abilities* that encompass human capacities, dispositions, and know-how related to how the world works and how to cope with it or for what Pierre Bourdieu describes in the *Logic of Practice* as the *habitus* in which humans beings act "following the intuitions of a 'logic of practice.'" But the psychology of cognitive dissonance is also relevant here, which shows that people generally act without thinking and become conscious of the rules that might apply only if they are in contradiction. These background ideational abilities underpin agents' ability to make sense in a given meaning context, that is, to "get it right" in terms of the ideational rules or rationality of a given discursive institutional setting.

But how, then, do we theorize about the process through which sentient agents get it right or, better, manage to bring about change in the ideational rules? Theoretical approaches in DI on how to plot change in ideas remain underdeveloped, despite much empirical analysis on changes in ideas.

Some of the most popular theories of ideational change focus on the notion of paradigm shift, building on Thomas Kuhn's seminal work in the philosophy of science. Peter Hall, who has produced one of the most influential such analyses in terms of paradigms, formalized the process of ideational change by identifying three orders of change in paradigms: minor first-order change of policy instruments, moderate second-order change of policy instruments and objectives, and revolutionary third-order change of instruments, objectives, and core ideas. The first two orders of change suggest evolutionary development within a paradigm through first-order renewal and second-order recasting of ideas, while the third order of change is revolutionary, since it would replace one paradigm with another. This approach takes us a lot farther than HI's critical juncture approach, by looking into the moment of crisis to explain where the ideas came from, who picked them up, and whether or not this produced a major change in ideas. But however evocative the concept of paradigm shift may be as a metaphor for change, the theory itself still has problems similar to the HI critical juncture literature. It does not theorize closely enough the conceptual processes of ideational change, that is, how old ideas fail and new ideas come to the fore; the reasons for ideational change, that is, why certain ideas are taken up rather than others; the agency in ideational change, that is, who is projecting the ideas and how; and the defining moment(s) of transformation, since paradigm theory's emphasis on abrupt shifts in ideas rules out not only evolutionary change but also revolutionary change in ideas that is not abrupt.

One promising way forward is to build on the work of discourse analysts who can be loosely seen as DI scholars in the SI tradition. Discourse analysts theorize the process of ideational continuity and change by showing how different elements may be added to ideas embedded in discourse, thereby bringing about change in ideas incrementally even in times of stability, and not just at critical junctures during paradigm shifts. The theoretical concepts of the various discourse analysis schools—once translated from the sometimes difficultly accessible and internally referential language—can provide added value to the analysis of ideas. For example, discourse analyses that build on Michel Foucault can offer insights into how to investigate the "archeology" of what was acceptable in a given discursive formation over time, from one period's *episteme* to the next, through examination of networks of rules establishing what is meaningful at any given time. Conversely, discourse theories built on the work of Ernesto Laclau and Chantal Mouffe can point to different ways in which concepts may be employed, such as nodal points from which all other ideas take their meanings in an ideological system, for example, how communism in Central and Eastern Europe served to distinguish between "real" (communist) democracy and "bourgeois" democracy.

There is one final problem with this focus on ideas, which is that we have yet to fully explain the dynamics of institutional change through agency. Although concentrating on ideas gets us closer to why institutional changes occur, they still do not explain how such institutional changes occur, that is, how the ideas themselves promote institutional change. For this, however, we need to consider another aspect of DI, which is the interactive side of discourse. How ideas are generated among policy actors and communicated to the public by political actors through discourse is the key to explaining institutional change (and continuity).

Endogenizing Change in Discursive Institutionalism

DI is an umbrella concept for the vast range of works in political science that take account of the substantive content of ideas and the interactive processes by which ideas are conveyed and exchanged through discourse. So far, we have mainly focused on the substantive dimension of ideas and discourse. But even here, we have only touched on the surface of the range of discursive institutionalist approaches. DI scholars consider ideas and discourse at different levels of generality, going from policy ideas to programmatic ideas or paradigms to deeper philosophical ideas. They also consider different types of ideas, including cognitive ideas justified in terms of interest-based logics and necessity and normative ideas legitimated through appeal to values and appropriateness. And they consider different forms of ideas and discourse, including frames, narratives, myths, story lines, collective memories, scripts, argumentative practices, discursive struggles, and more. Many of these approaches tend to refer to agency, but often in a residual manner, through reference to the carriers of ideas. But the interactive dimension of discourse, which focuses on agents who communicate ideas, is equally important to the endogenization of change in DI.

Studies of the interactive dimension of discourse also come in many forms. They may be divided into those focused on what Vivien Schmidt has called the discursive construction of ideas in the "coordinative" policy sphere or the discursive communication of ideas in a "communicative" political sphere. The coordinative discourse encompasses the wide range of policy actors engaged in policy construction who may be organized in epistemic communities of elites with shared ideas, in advocacy coalitions of elites with shared ideas and policy access, and advocacy networks of activists contesting ideas in international politics or who may act as entrepreneurs who serve as catalysts for the ideas of such discursive communities. The communicative discourse encompasses the wide range of political actors who bring the ideas developed in the context of the coordinative discourse to the public for deliberation and legitimation. These actors may include political leaders involved in the top-down mass electoral process of public persuasion, in public debates or in policy forums of informed publics. Or they may be members of civil society engaged in the bottom-up discursive interactions of grassroots organizations, of social movements, or local participatory governance and of citizens whose voices are heard not only in opinion polls but also in votes—where actions speak even more loudly than words.

This interactive dimension is key to the endogenization of change in DI. Without discourse understood as the exchange of ideas, it is very difficult to explain how ideas go from individual thought to collective action. We do not, after all, know what people are thinking or why they act the way they do until they say it. And we do not for the most part engage in collective action or in collective (re) thinking of our actions without the articulation, discussion, deliberation, and legitimization of our ideas about our actions. This is why, in addition to the background ideational abilities that explain the internal processes by which institutions are created and maintained, we need to recognize the importance of what Schmidt has called the *foreground discursive abilities* through which sentient agents may change (or maintain) their institutions following a logic of communication. This is a generic term for what Jürgen Habermas calls *communicative action*, and it is at the basis of theories about deliberative and discursive democracy, about public debate, as well about coordinative discourses of policy construction and communicative discourses of political communication.

These foreground discursive abilities are essential to explaining institutional change because they refer to people's ability to think outside the institutions in which they continue to act, to talk about such institutions in a critical way, to communicate and deliberate about them, to persuade themselves as well as others to change their minds about their institutions, and then to take action to change them, whether by building discursive coalitions for reform against entrenched interests in the coordinative policy sphere or informing and orienting the public in the communicative political sphere. Conveying "good" policy ideas through a persuasive discourse helps political actors win elections and gives policy actors a mandate to implement their ideas.

Scholars in the SI tradition have little difficulty with this approach to discourse, especially since, as we have already seen, discourse analyses of all kinds are loosely seen as part of SI. Moreover, even when the word *discourse* is not used, DI scholars in the SI tradition often elucidate its interactive effects, as in recent work on contentious politics, which weds organizational and social movements theory and offers evidence of how leaders, social movement activists, and the everyday public spur change through ideas that persuade through discourse.

Scholars in the HI tradition also have little difficulty with discourse, since DI can add dynamics to the historical processes of ideational change, by focusing on who talks to whom, where, and when. Differentiating between a coordinative discourse in the policy sphere and a communicative discourse in the political sphere implicitly acknowledges the importance of institutional structures as well as practices. By the same token, however, HI can provide additional structure to DI by describing the formal institutional contexts that shape interactive patterns of discourse.

Scholars in the RI tradition have the greatest difficulty dealing with the interactive process of discourse, or taking the exchange of ideas in public debates seriously, because talk is by definition cheap while instrumental actions are assumed to speak more loudly than words. But can the substance of ideas not matter, as part of the persuasive power of discourse? Margaret Levi, in her presidential address at the American Political Society Association (APSA) in 2006, tacitly acknowledged this when she called for research on leaders' communication because leaders have the power to inspire change as well as the capacity to change constituents' beliefs—although she never engaged with DI work on leadership, discourse, or deliberative democracy.

RI's problems with ideas, discourse, and deliberation follow from its restricted definition of agency and rationality. In RI, agents are rational in an unthinking manner, meaning that they respond to incentive structures in ways that maximize their interests (expected utility), pursuing their goals in accordance with their beliefs about the facts. In DI, agents are rational in a thinking manner: They also pursue their goals in accordance with their beliefs about the facts, but—as already noted—they are not only able to think, say, and act but also to think about their thoughts, reflect on their actions, state their intentions, alter their actions as a result of their thoughts about their actions, say what they are thinking of doing, and change their minds in response to persuasion by others regarding what they are thinking, saying, and doing. Such self-consciousness and self-knowledge along with the ability to express it is summed up in the term *sentient* when used to define agents in DI (scholars also use the term *reflexive*), who may change their minds based on persuasion—by contrast with RI's *rational* agents, for whom interaction is based on manipulation, as agents calculate how they will influence others to serve their own interests. A problem for RI scholars as a result of their definition of interaction as manipulation is that they cannot explain how one overcomes entrenched interests—that is, ones that cannot be coerced, tricked, or bribed into changing their actions.

DI approaches focused on deliberative democracy in particular have elaborated on such insights related to communicative action. Deliberative democracy is seen to occur when parties are reasonable and use evidence-based arguments to reach agreement, where persuasion is the key to creating shared understandings and building consensus, and in which the process itself is based on inclusive, open, trusting, and consensual interaction. Deliberative democracy is considered to be a better form of decision making because open dialogue may unlock untapped knowledge, generate new skills and know-how, produce higher quality reasoning for more legitimate policies, and create new, more collaborative interrelationships among the parties to the deliberation. Deliberation need not be limited to idealized communication situations, however, especially since power and interests cannot easily be eliminated from deliberations, although being aware of these may help minimize the potential effects of domination. But awareness of power and interests or even manipulation is no guarantee of discursive success.

Deliberation on its own, in other words, does not necessarily ensure a more democratic outcome. Power and position do matter. The question is how to define power and position in such a way as to also take account of the power of ideas and discourse. The problem with RI and HI is that they tend to reify questions of power and position by assuming that power is a function of position and that strategic interests derive primarily from agents' power and position. DI holds instead that power cannot be defined by (objective) position alone, since ideas and values infuse the exercise of power and (subjective) perceptions of position. Moreover, actors can gain power from their ideas even where they may lack the power of position—as in the case of social movements or entrepreneurial actors who set the agenda for reform in policy or political spheres. Power itself, moreover, derives not only from position, meaning actors' ability to wield power, but also purpose, since actors' ideas and discourse about how they can and should wield that power (i.e., not just in their own strategic interests but in the general interest) may reinforce or undermine the power they derive from their position, depending on the responses of their audience to their stated purposes. This is the essence of political leadership.

Further support for the view that discourse and deliberation are necessary complements to investigations of power, position, and interests also comes from experimental political psychology, which seeks to probe the nature and limits of (RI defined) human rationality, in particular with regard to framing effects. Framing effects occur when different but logically equivalent phrases cause individuals to alter their preferences *irrationally* (in RI terms), for example, when people reject a policy program when told about its negative effects (e.g., it leads to 5% unemployment) and accept it when told of its positive effects (e.g., it leads to 95% employment). This represents a blow to RI, which assumes total information on the part of rational actors, at the same time that it provides an opening for DI. This is because framing effects are shown to be moderated by contextual forces involving elite competition and rhetoric that result, as James Druckman has shown, in a process of framing and counterframing (DI's communicative discourse), interpersonal conversation in heterogeneous groups among citizens (DI's deliberative democracy), or discussions among homogeneous groups of experts (DI's coordinative discourse). This said, experimental political psychology also demonstrates the limits of deliberative effectiveness and the importance of not idealizing deliberation, given principles of human cognition that point to limited attention spans, cases in which communication may reduce participants' persuasiveness, and the importance of power relationships.

One final illustration of the value of DI approaches to the explanation of change (and continuity) comes from the insights it can lend to the use of the different forms of institutionalism. RI accounts tend to present human responses to given incentive structures as inevitable. This can be seen as part of a normative discursive strategy to get the reader to accept this, or to rebel against it, as in the case of globalization and convergence to a single neoliberal model. HI accounts of path-dependent institutions, in particular where they combine with RI, may add the inexorable to the inevitable. With regard to the globalization of capitalism, it can be seen as part of a normative discursive strategy to suggest that there is no convergence in capitalism since there are two different varieties that will continue into perpetuity. SI accounts of cultural framing may dispute both RI inevitability and HI inexorability by claiming that cultural embeddedness makes all national cultures incomparable. This can in itself be part of a normative discursive strategy to resist attempts to impose any kind of internationalized order on national economies. And what kinds of ideas and normative discourse are embedded in DI, then? That there is nothing inevitable, inexorable, or incomparable in this world, because the future is open to new ideas conveyed by discourse. With regard to capitalism, it would dispute the inevitability of neoliberal convergence, the inexorability of a binary split in capitalism, and the incomparability of culturally embedded forms of capitalism. Instead, DI shows that rationalist logics, historical path dependencies, and cultural frames are conditional on public choices that result not just from the power clash among interests, the prerogatives of position, or the scripts of culture but from the battle of ideas through discourse and deliberation. The global economic meltdown clearly demonstrates the ideational underpinnings of many views of capitalism.

Conclusion

While some scholars have moved from one of the older neo-institutionalisms to DI, others straddle institutionalisms, and yet others remain squarely within one or another institutionalist approach. To get a sense of how all of this fits together in a very general way, Figure 1 situates many of the scholars' works cited above within each of the four institutionalisms while arraying these along a horizontal continuum from interests to culture, with history in between—and along a vertical continuum from statics to dynamics, with interests, history, and culture at the static end, ideas and discourse at the dynamic end. HI sits between RI and SI, mainly because RI and SI are largely incompatible, whereas HI can go to either side when it adds agency. DI comes underneath all three because, although it is distinctive, it can rest on the insights of any one of the three and because scholars often see themselves as continuing to fit into one or another of the traditions even as they cross the line into DI.

This leaves one final question: what is the added value of approaches that take ideas and discourse seriously, by contrast with the other three new institutionalisms? DI endogenizes change, explaining much of how and why public actors bring about institutional change through public action. With regard to the other institutionalisms, moreover, the discursive approach helps explain the actual preferences and strategies of actors in RI and HI, and it helps to explain changes in the normative orientations emphasized by SI. Where DI can go wrong is when it considers ideas and discourse to the exclusion of issues of power (read RI instrumental rationality) and position (read HI institutional structures), when it assumes that DI deliberation necessarily trumps RI manipulation, or when it

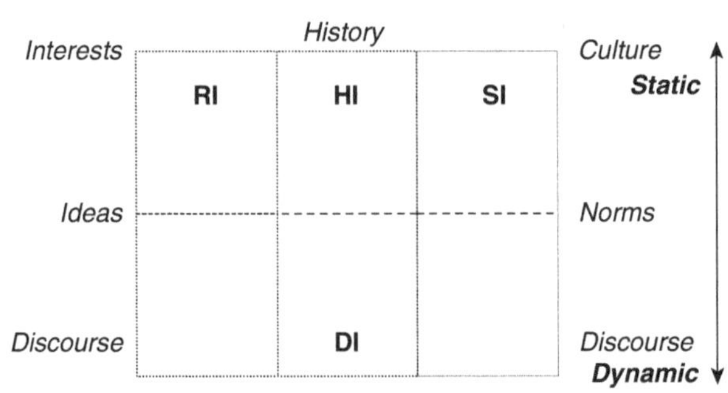

Figure 1 A Visual Map of the Four Institutionalisms

Note: DI = discursive institutionalism; HI = historical institutionalism; RI = rational choice institutionalism; SI = sociological institutionalism.

overdetermines the role of ideas and discourse by forgetting that "stuff happens" or that historical institutions and cultural frames affect the ways in which ideas are expressed and discourse conveyed. We should not forget that ideas and discourse that seek to promote change often have little effect on the crystallized ideas about rationalist interests and cultural norms or on the frozen landscapes of rationalist incentives, historical paths, and cultural frames. The research agenda for political scientists concerned with explaining institutional change endogenously, therefore, should be to use DI to show empirically how, when, where, and why ideas and discourse matter for institutional change, and when they do not, that is, when RI, HI, and SI may be sufficient because change can be explained better exogenously.

Vivien A. Schmidt
Boston University
Boston, Massachusetts, United States

See also Advocacy Coalition Framework; Constructivism; Discourse Analysis; Discursive Institutionalism; Rational Choice

Further Readings

Beland, D., & Cox, R. (Eds.). (2010). *Ideas and politics in social scientific analysis.* Oxford, UK: Oxford University Press.

Blyth, M. (2003). Structures do not come with an instruction sheet: Interests, ideas, and progress in political science. *Perspectives on Politics, 1*(4), 695–706.

Campbell, J. L. (2004). *Institutional change and globalization.* Princeton, NJ: Princeton University Press.

Dryzek, J. (2000). *Deliberative democracy and beyond.* Oxford, UK: Oxford University Press.

Finnemore, M. (1996). Norms, culture, and world politics: Insights from sociology's institutionalism. *International Organization, 50*(2), 325–347.

Gofas, A., & Hay, C. (2009). *The role of ideas in political analysis.* London: Routledge.

Habermas, J. (1996). *Between facts and norms: Contributions to a discourse theory.* London: Polity Press.

Hall, P., & Taylor, R. (1996). Political science and the three new institutionalisms. *Political Studies, 44,* 952–973.

Katznelson, I., & Weingast, B. (Eds.). (2005). *Preferences and situations.* New York: Russell Sage Foundation.

March, J. G., & Olsen, J. P. (1989). *Rediscovering institutions: The organizational basis of politics.* New York: Free Press.

Scharpf, F. W. (1997). *Games real actors play.* Boulder, CO: Westview Press.

Schmidt, V. A. (2008). Discursive institutionalism: The explanatory power of ideas and discourse. *Annual Review of Political Science, 11,* 303–326.

Schmidt, V. A. (2010). Taking ideas *and* discourse seriously: Explaining change through discursive institutionalism as the fourth new institutionalism. *European Political Science Review, 2,* 1–25.

Streeck, W., & Thelen, K. (Eds.). (2005). *Beyond continuity.* Oxford, UK: Oxford University Press.

Thelen, K. (1999). Historical institutionalism in comparative politics. *Annual Review of Political Science, 2,* 369–404.

Institutionalization

Institutionalization is the process by which organizations acquire identity and legitimacy. Institutionalization involves more than building formal structures and processes. For organizations to become institutions, structures need to be, as famously noted by Philip Selznick (1957), "infused with value beyond the technical requirements of the task at hand" (p. 22). This is true for corporations and churches as much as for political parties and government agencies or for entire political systems. Institutionalization means members begin to value the organization for itself; it elicits a normative, value-based commitment or is supported by deeply held cultural beliefs in its mission. The result is a high degree of legitimacy with both members and external stakeholders in the organization's environment. Internally, institutionalization involves achieving a consensus on the organization's mission and goals (identity) beyond the acquisition of necessary resources and skills. Externally, a highly institutionalized organization enjoys a high degree of social acceptability with key constituencies or the public at large (legitimacy). Institutionalization is a process with different stages: Once an organization has developed effective working practices, these are transformed into norms that get accepted and then embedded in organizational life. However, institutionalization is not a linear process. Being, or rather becoming, an institution is a matter of degree. Organizations or political systems for that matter exhibit different degrees of institutionalization. Importantly, over time, institutionalization may move in both directions—that is, increase or erode (deinstitutionalization), or simply stall.

The concept of institutionalization has been developed mainly by organizational sociologists who emphasize that individual action is shaped by, and embedded in, larger social structures. Political scientists have tended to look at institutions as given, fixed frameworks for political behavior but have shown less interest in their emergence, with the exception of constitutional design. The origin of public organizations in particular remains a neglected area of research for which the concept of institutionalization can serve as a useful analytical tool. This entry first reviews different concepts and mechanisms of institutionalization and then presents typical criteria of institutionalization before discussing some constraints and challenges of institutionalization faced by public sector organizations.

Concepts and Mechanisms of Institutionalization

Any discussion of institutionalization needs to be based on an understanding of the term *institution*. At the most general level, we can think of institutions as "patterned behavior," as relatively stable, valued sets of formal and informal rules, norms, and practices that constrain but also enable political behavior. In short, institutions give structure to political life, but they also emerge from actor-based social and political processes. A key question for political scientists then is not only to what extent institutional structures shape or even determine individual political behavior and processes but also to what degree actors can purposefully create, design, or mold institutions to serve their needs or interests. This duality of actor (or agency) and structure lies at the heart of institutionalization research.

There is considerable disagreement among different schools of new institutionalism about the role of institutions and about the drivers and mechanisms of institutionalization. The most important divide runs between rational choice institutionalism and sociological (or organizational or normative) institutionalism. In the rational choice approach, institutions are essentially "rules of the game" that emerge as the result of political choice by self-interested actors, be it to solve collective action problems or to advance specific interests. This suggests that institutional arrangements are rather malleable and open to design. A typical approach in this vein is the principal–agent framework: Political principals create and delegate powers to administrative or international agents to perform certain functions or to entrench their policy preferences. Yet organizational arrangements can be stabilized, or institutionalized, through mechanisms of "lock-in," based on the logic of increasing returns: Actors have an incentive to stay on a path of institutional development once it is chosen not because it is functionally superior but because they are rewarded by positive feedbacks, such as learning and coordination benefits. Historical institutionalism makes a similar argument about the lock-in effect of choices (at critical junctures) in the formative period of institutions ("path dependency"). However, it gives more importance to the role of ideas in sustaining institutional trajectories. This constructivist component brings historical institutionalism closer to sociological institutionalism.

The sociological approach views individual behavior as governed by norms and rules that define appropriate (as opposed to instrumental) behavior according to certain values. The key mechanism of institutionalization is an increase of normative commitment to the organization. In this account, formal structures and processes, which are the center of many rational choice approaches, are only a thin layer; "thick institutionalization" (as Selznick says) occurs when value-based commitment of internal and external stakeholders is solidified, as expressed in unifying ideologies or rituals or in the administrative entrenchment of the organization's mission. A more strongly constructivist strand of the sociological approach holds that culturally determined cognitive beliefs, rather than values, are the main factor in the institutionalization process. Certain organizational practices are "objectified"—that is, they are institutionalized in the sense of being taken for granted as social facts. This is the most powerful form of institutionalization as it does not depend on incentives or shared values any more.

The different institutionalisms shed light on different dimensions and two stages of the institutionalization process. Rational choice approaches take an actor perspective and focus on the initial creation of a formal organization for a specific purpose. This perspective runs the risk of explaining institutional creation by exclusive reference to functional needs and rational calculation. It may overestimate the room for rational design and neglect obstacles to sustained institutionalization. Constructivist schools insist on the overriding importance of the second, more complex step to imbue formal structures with values and beliefs. Conversely, this structural approach leaves open questions as to how the various actors and interests populating the volatile world of politics relate to abstract processes of norm routinization or harmonization (politics of institutionalization).

Criteria of Institutionalization

How can we assess the degree to which an organization has been institutionalized? At a general level, the degree of standardization of organizational procedures and practices is an important indicator. However, routinization of behavior may in practice be disconnected from "value infusion"—that is, from the degree of legitimacy that the organization can command. Samuel Huntington proposed four more specific criteria or attributes: (1) *adaptability* refers to the extent to which organizations have learned to adapt to, and deal with, a dynamic environment, which is largely a function of age and experience; (2) *complexity* (the internal equivalent of adaptability) refers to the capacity of the organization to develop differentiated internal structures (diversification) that create stability and help it thrive in a changing environment; (3) *autonomy* is not only the most interesting criterion from a public organization's perspective but also the most difficult to measure; it seeks to capture the extent to which an organization is independent and able to make its own decisions based on protection from external influence and control over its resources; (4) *coherence* refers to the degree of internal discipline and unity, the level of consensus on institutional purposes and procedures; more coherence results in more effective ways of working.

The profile of a highly institutionalized organization or entity, then, would include the following features: advanced internal differentiation of structures as well as solid consensus and coherence, control over decisions, including resources, and the capacity to manage the boundaries with the organization's environment.

In the case of public sector entities, however, institutionalization, defined as the attempt to maintain some autonomy from the environment through internal differentiation and external boundary management seems particularly difficult to achieve—and not always desirable from a perspective of democratic control. Unless the organization in question occupies a monopoly or a similarly privileged position (National Aeronautics and Space Administration [NASA] is a good example), there are many constraints holding back public sector organizations in their quest to fully institutionalize.

Constraints and Challenges of Institutionalization in the Public Sector

First, public organizations often operate under a rigid mandate that imposes complex and mutually exclusive goals. The use of public authority and associated norms of accountability and predictability demand that public organizations formalize their practices to a higher degree and demonstrate sufficient congruence with the social environment that they are supposed to serve or regulate. Ambitious expectations, set by a political process that has to accommodate various interests, are often not matched by sufficient resources. Politicians may be loath to delegate sufficient powers and discretion. The political process is highly volatile, and especially a start-up organization may not be granted sufficient time by impatient constituencies to prove itself and consolidate. Second, newcomers often face tough competition for turf in a crowded institutional space. Successful institutionalization may even require the dismantling or deinstitutionalization of competing structures or organizations. Third, there is the normative concern in democratic societies about "runaway bureaucracies"—public organizations that abuse autonomy by placing their own interests above the public mission. However, keeping public entities strictly accountable and responsive may curtail their ability to develop their own identity and ambition; there might be a trade-off between internal identity and external legitimacy.

Given all these constraints, how is successful institutionalization at all possible? The public administration literature is indeed replete with accounts of failed institutionalization and pathologies of misguided institutionalization. At the same time, successfully institutionalized public organizations do exist. A functional account that explains the origin of public organizations by the needs they purportedly serve (to cope with new tasks or conditions) is clearly inadequate as it ignores the complex politics of institutionalization that is conditioned by existing institutional orders and power distributions. First, contingent events, such as the occurrence of crises, can be an important factor to explain the success of an institution: It manages to position itself as the adequate, even necessary, response to an urgent situation. Second, some institutional newcomers benefit from fashionable trends in public sector organization, such as the creation of agencies at arm's length from political executives. Start-ups that conform to these "isomorphic pressures" are more likely to overcome obstacles to institutionalization. Third, and finally, the role of leadership deserves further study, as suggested by Arjen Boin and Tom Christensen: leaders not in the sense of charismatic visionaries but leaders as facilitators of process who guide the emerging entity through the different stages of institutionalization, striking the right balance between internal development and external demands.

Burkard Eberlein
York University
Toronto, Ontario, Canada

See also Agencies; Autonomy, Administrative; Bureaucracy; Change, Institutional; Institutional Theory; Institutions and Institutionalism; Organization Theory

Further Readings

Boin, A., & Christensen, T. (2008). The development of public institutions: Reconsidering the role of leadership. *Administration & Society, 40,* 271–297.

Huntington, S. P. (1965). Political development and political decay. *World Politics, 17,* 386–430.

Peters, B. G. (2005). *Institutional theory in political science* (2nd ed.). New York: Continuum.

Peters, B. G. (2008). Institutional theory: Problems and prospects. In J. Pierre, B. G. Peters, & G. Stoker (Eds.), *Debating institutionalism* (pp. 1–21). Manchester, UK: Manchester University Press.

Scott, W. R. (2008). *Institutions and organizations* (3rd ed.). Thousand Oaks, CA: Sage.

Selznick, P. (1957). *Leadership in administration: A sociological interpretation.* New York: Harper & Row.

Institutions and Institutionalism

Most fundamentally, the social sciences have defined institutions as human made. As they were created by men and women, institutions order social, political, economic, and even cultural intercourse. Indeed, institutions constitute the very basis for human interaction. Consequently, institutions bear within them equally the potential danger of the most deep-seated social control as well as the promise of human liberation from both the social bond and the constraints of nature. Institutionalism is the study of the origins, effects, and potential for reform of institutions.

Definitions

The meaning of the term *institution* is wide ranging, from more restricted to more elaborate and also along several dimensions. One dimension is the degree of formalization of an institution. At the most informal pole, it is common to speak of habits, customs, or conventions. A habit is any action whose repetitive nature comes to be recognized by a self-conscious actor and thus is internally represented. A custom is a habit that is shared by members of a collectivity and hence social. A convention is any agreed-on procedure. Language itself is a convention, as both the meanings of words and syntactical structures require social agreement for communication. The same is true for other social "codes" such as myths and rituals that both embody, and thus communicate, social ideas and ideals but yet require some understanding of such collective representations for their decoding. To the extent that a convention is adopted by ever larger numbers of people and comes to be collectively binding, it is eventually described as an institution. This movement from an informal to a formal setup is termed *institutionalization*. As it entails a shift from an individual to a society and from freedom to constraint, it can be viewed as a transition from nature to culture.

The degree to which institutions are collectively binding, however, constitutes a second dimension of variation. A tradition or folkway has been followed over time and by a particular group, such that an individual's cultural identity may incline him or her to adhere to a given custom. The French term *moeurs* and the English *mores*, which correspond to the German *Sitte*, connote slightly more social obligation. A norm, which may be defined as an internalized belief, is more strongly binding, because its transgression is open to moral or social sanction. The Hegelian distinction between *Sittlichkeit* and *Moralität* is based on the isolation of the moral rule from the original moral community (*Gemeinschaft*) and its transfer to the society (*Gesellschaft*), after which, ultimately, it undergoes a synthesis through the state (*Staat*). A law is a collectively binding decision whose interpretation is subject to adjudication only in specialized juridical bodies and by breaking which one is subjected to punishment, again by public institutions with a monopoly on the exertion of legitimate force, as pointed out by Max Weber. Consequently, the workings of some institutions may depend on other institutions or on institutionalized settings. As discussed in classical political theory, the establishment of the state or Leviathan is the decisive shift accomplished by the move from the state of nature to civil society.

In a similar vein, institutions vary with regard to whether they are self-reinforcing or require intervention by some sort of meta-institutions. If a certain rule is adhered to by all relevant actors because it is in their self-interest to conform, the rule is termed to be self-enforcing. However, some perspectives on institutions claim that rules need to be elaborated for actors to be able to understand how to follow them—or indeed to calculate their self-interest—such that cultural and social guidelines as to what is appropriate behavior must flesh out the skeletal "rules of the game." Furthermore, some sets of preferences and rules (such as majority rule) may not necessarily produce stable outcomes. Instead, more elaborate procedures may set limits to the possibility of choosing, such that one may speak of institutional or structure-induced equilibrium, as opposed to a natural or preference-induced equilibrium. This is the subject both of public choice or rational choice theory and of institutional economics. Here, we see that the study of institutions may extend from a narrowly defined set of rules to, first, a more elaborated context necessary for understanding the workings of these institutions and, second, as T. R. Voss emphasizes, to an analysis of the equilibrium outcomes produced by these institutions and institutional contexts.

The term *institution* refers to the action of introducing an institution, to the identity of the actor (*Instituteur*) that introduced the institution, and to the thing that has been introduced. Institutions can be introduced by religious and secular authorities as well as by groups and communities, as in canonical institutions, institutions of inheritance, and social institutions. Institutions are created by divine or mortal beings and, hence, set apart from nature. Institutions may produce a person of high morality, a group, or a regime. Even Charles de Montesquieu defined laws very broadly to include both the institutions of the legislature and the mores and manners of the nation, in general. Thus, institutions include the totality of social forms and structures and may be established by law or custom. Consequently, three types of institutions are especially important: (1) social institutions, such as kinship, marriage, family, and inheritance; (2) constitutions, which are the written or unwritten law governing the exercise of public power and the procedures for making laws themselves; and (3) regimes, which refers to the process of giving something the character of an institution. Social institutions govern relationships among individuals within societies and hence establish a social order. Constitutions regulate the relationships among citizens, political representatives, and the state and hence create a political order. Regimes are often found in the international arena, where, being beyond the reach of the sovereignty of nation-states, international agreements are used to create international regimes or international orders, and international organizations with the legitimacy and normative weight of an institution are active in the implementation of the agreed-on normative order or international norms.

To *institutionalize* something or the *institutionalization* of something may refer to the frequency, permanence, or widespread nature of a habit, a virtue, or even a vice—the granting of an official status as institution to a custom or procedure. *Institution* also refers to the inculcation, indoctrination, or introduction of norms, habits, and knowledge in various forms of instruction, education, or upbringing. In addition, *institution* or *institute* may refer to the corporate body or building from which such instruction is imparted, such as a private institution or institute of scientific study. Institutions meant for instruction or induction (e.g., the military, clerical institutions) form and regulate individuals and hence should (in theory) be reliable. Closed or total institutions are responsible for psychic and physical healing, such as hospitals or psychiatric institutions. Financial institutions and institutional investors hold money in trust for large numbers of individuals and should (again, in theory) be held accountable to their investors. Individuals who have fully imbibed and internalized such instruction and are employees of such institutions are known as professionals. In each of these trust relationships, there is a potential for betrayal of trust, which has been the focus of much social scientific analysis of institutions and professions.

Financial institutions, institutional investors, and the governmental framework for monetary transactions all form markets. Political institutions and constitutions frame public policies. Social institutions help socialize individuals; different psychological stages, pedagogy, and social relations help form the psyche. The study of these institutional effects is known as institutionalism. Unlike institutions that are viewed as arbitrary, institutionalism is by nature a relativistic approach: Institutions that may have been introduced as arbitrary results of contingent events may have unintended consequences for human nature, societies, politics, and markets. Consequently, institutionalists view developments in these spheres as artifacts of institutions, and hence, they are neither natural nor necessarily desirable.

Institutions and Institutionalism Spanning the Social Sciences

The study of institutions and institutional effects spans the social sciences. In the areas of philosophy of knowledge, philosophy of right, and political philosophy, institutions have been viewed both as mental representations and concrete political structures. As cognitive representations, institutions help structure thought, thus constituting perceptual lenses or schema. The origins and legitimacy of social and political institutions has been a perennial problem, being divided into historical or empirical and rational views. The historical view shared by classical authors such as Georg Friedrich Hegel sees traditions, customs, norms, laws, and institutions as inheritances that have achieved legitimacy (if they have indeed achieved it) by standing the test of time. Moreover, their functioning rests on this historical context. The rational view, by contrast, aims to distill the essence of an institution via logical analysis, often through recourse to a hypothetical account of institutional origins or the use of a particular procedure, as in the contract theory of Thomas Hobbes or John Locke. The work of Jean-Jacques Rousseau bridges these extremes by taking a historical, anthropological view of the development of social institutions but a contract view of institutional legitimacy; freedom is defined as living under a rule one makes for oneself. Such procedural legitimacy is further developed by Immanuel Kant, John Rawls, and Jürgen Habermas but has been called into question in the so-called communitarianism debate.

One strand of the sociological and anthropological tradition views institutions as cultural products that substitute for instinct and thus confer an evolutionary advantage for human societies with particular institutions. More generally, institutions create social order both by specific sets of positive and negative sanctions imposed to prevent social deviance and by giving symbolic expression to the social order, for example, through myths and rituals. Indeed, the very categories of thought, such as notions of time and space, are socially contingent and linked to social organization. Thus, the sociological meaning of the term *institution* ranges from concrete social practices or structures to ideas, representations, and even socially contingent interpretations of ideas and categories, as we observe in the social thought of Émile Durkheim.

A central division deals with whether institutions are functional and hence have evolved from universal human needs, even if the exact institutional configurations vary from society to society, or whether institutions are more aptly viewed as historical residues and products of social interpretation. A second problematic concerns the issue of free will versus determinism (also referred to as agency vs. structure): Do institutions *determine* behavior or simply make some courses of action more likely because they appear to be "normal" or "appropriate" and may be sanctioned by punishment or social disapproval if not followed? Talcott Parsons's theory of action proposed that previous patterns of behavior serve as points of orientation for actors, for example, in establishing a repertoire of social roles, but that individuals are free to conform or deviate from these expected patterns.

The lines between sociological, social-psychological, and psychological views on institutions are blurred, as all share a focus on mental representations, of which language and cognitive operations are central. Here, the idea that the meaning of sounds is arbitrary and that meaning arises from the juxtaposition of phonetic oppositions as well as the focus on classificatory systems, binary codes, and cognitive routines from the fields of computer science and artificial intelligence have been quite influential. These representations or routines not only mediate between the individual subject and the external world but are also formed or canalized through these interactions, as in Jean Piaget's theories of developmental stages or Sigmund Freud's focus on early childhood traumas. Given the potentially arbitrary nature of these historic residues, an emancipatory program in social psychology is possible—although its adherents, such as Erich Fromm or Herbert Marcuse, vary in the extent to which they stress social and economic versus purely psychological causes for personality (and societal) deformation.

The institutional tradition in economics stresses the "embeddedness" of economic transactions in social structures and culture. In contrast to Adam Smith's claim that "man" has a "natural" tendency to "truck, barter and exchange," economic institutionalists emphasize the cultural, social, and even normative bases for exchange as well as the ways in which social and cultural motivations and practices—such as striving for social honor—shape and even distort economic behavior. Some examples include Torsten Veblen's "conspicuous consumption" of the leisure class, John Commons's analysis of the impact of historical experience and government policies on the organization of industrial relations, and Max Weber's classic analysis in *The Protestant Ethic and the Spirit of Capitalism*. Even Joseph Schumpeter, who coined the phrase *methodological individualism* and drafted the economic model of democracy, stressed the ways in which historic residues predating the capitalist era buttressed capitalist economic arrangements and argued that as these precapitalist foundations are on a decline, capitalism itself will become unstable. Similarly, the work of Karl Polanyi analyses the economic and political instability resulting from the historically unique effort of capitalism to disembed the market from social arrangements and institutions.

In law and political science, political institutions were long understood in terms of the norms embodied in constitutions. Nevertheless, both the social context for political institutions and the rise of the modern state, as well as the impact of institutional arrangements on the behavior of politicians and voting patterns, were considered by classic political institutionalists, such as Alexis de Tocqueville and Max Weber.

Behavioralism Versus Institutionalism

In the aftermath of World War II, however, a behavioralist revolution swept through the social sciences, pushing institutions and institutionalist analysis into the background. Though more popular in the United States than in Europe and other parts of the world, behavioralism focused on assumed universal regularities of behavior: In psychology, Burrhus Frederic Skinner studied scientific stimulus and response; in sociology, Talcott Parsons proposed structural functionalist requirements and a universal movement from traditional to modern society; in economics, the neoclassical model with its universal uniformities of market behavior rose to undisputed dominance; in political science, pluralists including Robert Dahl and David Truman, among others, focused on the observable behavior of voters and interest groups. By the end of the 1960s, however, limitations of these behavioralist models led to a rediscovery of institutions, which James March and Johan Olsen labeled the *new institutionalism*.

Rational Choice and the New Institutional Economics

Rational choice theorists and new institutionalist economists understand institutions as a response to dilemmas of collective choice and collective action. Assuming human actors to be rational, self-interested utility maximizers, these scholars investigate the irrational or suboptimal consequences of such rational action when outcomes depend on the decisions of more than one actor; that is, they study strategic action.

Rational choice studies of legislative decision making are based on the Condorcet Paradox or Arrow impossibility theorem, which demonstrates that even when individuals possess transitive preference orderings (e.g., preferring Restaurant A to Restaurant B to Restaurant C), group decision making may not result in a stable choice. As a result, majority rule is inherently unstable, and these institutionalists study both the conditions for democratic stability and the ways in which institutional rules, such as the agenda-setting privilege of the political executive or the veto powers of parliamentary chambers or committees, allow stable political choices to be made. Spatial models of preferences serve as an important tool for this type of analysis. Game theory is simply a method of economic analysis based on the payoff functions of the actors (or players) and the rules for their choices (or moves). Such games often result in suboptimal outcomes, as in the famous prisoners' dilemma, in which both prisoners confess to a crime out of fear that their co-conspirator will betray them. Institutional rules or particular strategies may be of some help in improving these outcomes, for example, by turning a noncooperative game, such as the tragedy of the commons, into a cooperative one.

The new institutionalist economics explores the origins of economic institutions and their effects, especially the legal framework for the market, which directly affects the distribution of property rights and the calculation of transaction costs. Some influential models for understanding the development of institutions are transaction cost economics, which postulates that institutions develop to minimize all costs related to economic transactions, including information costs and the dangers of mutual dependence; principal–agent theory, which understands contracts and organizational structures as responses to the need of "principals" to control their "agents," such as owners–managers, governments–bureaucracies, and voters–politicians; and path dependency, which uses the concepts of sunk costs and increasing returns to explain why initial contingent events lead to inefficient but stable paths of economic or political development. Central issues deal with whether or not socialized or disembedded individuals can be taken as the point of departure for these models, whether institutional arrangements can be modeled as if emerging from a state of nature, and whether historically given institutional starting points are necessary.

Sociological Institutionalism and Economic Sociology

As sociology deals with the social order, the entire field can be said to be institutional. Nevertheless, a distinct group of sociologists have built on the behavioral psychology and organization theory to elaborate a view of individual cognition and collective decision making within organizations that they have termed *sociological institutionalism.* Here, cognitive limits on human capacities for gathering and processing information (bounded rationality) result in various coping mechanisms, such as accepting the first more or less acceptable alternative (satisficing) in place of maximizing utility or reliance on standard operating procedures that reduce choice and thereby structure and coordinate action. Routines and scripts may produce patterns of organizational behavior that can be termed *quasi-chaotic*, as in the garbage can model, which posits that choices within organized anarchies are largely random. Newer applications of this perspective have focused on the reliance of myth and ceremony even in modern business organizations, the socialization in time of various managerial cohorts, and the role of organizational isomorphism between political systems and organizations of immigrants to produce particular cultural patterns of postmodern citizenship. Social constructivist approaches have stressed especially the socially contingent development of norms, ideas, and institutions, even in the international arena. Economic sociology also focuses on the social and cultural bases of economic institutions and concepts, such as inheritance or the household, thus adhering to the institutionalist tradition in economics more faithfully than the new institutional economics or new economics of organization.

Historical Institutionalism

The concepts of economic sociology, also found in the corporatism and other varieties of capitalism literature, focus on the historical, social, and organizational conditions for alternate modes of capitalist economic formation. Historical institutionalism, more generally, follows the research program of Max Weber in understanding economy, politics, and society in terms of historically contingent, particular developmental paths, whose meanings depend on the subjective interpretations of human actors. Some historical institutionalists emphasize path dependency, sequences, and temporal orderings. Others argue that the historical approach may give us leverage precisely on questions of human agency and configurational causality. The main problem with this approach is related to the causes of institutional stability and change. Its main methods are process tracing and thick description as well as, in some cases, analytic narratives.

Current Debates

Institution is so fundamental to the social sciences that it is not surprising that the definition of and research on institutions spans an enormously broad range of concepts, methods, and topics. Nevertheless, the study of institutions deals with the formation and impact of stable social arrangements, even if these may range from ideas and normative concepts to actual local, national, and international organizations, associations, and states. The central cleavages within institutionalist analysis help study whether a state of nature can be posited or whether particular culturally and historically grounded starting points must be addressed, whether institutions evolve or are products of conscious human design, and whether institutionalist outcomes are functional or historically contingent, and if so, what normative consequence follows from the artifactuality of institutions and their impact on social life.

Ellen M. Immergut
Humboldt University Berlin
Berlin, Germany

See also Behavioralism; Change, Institutional; Constructivism; Discursive Institutionalism; Institutional Theory; Institutionalization; Logic of Appropriateness; Path Dependence; Process Tracing; Rational Choice; Rousseau, Jean-Jacques; Schema; Script; Veto Player; Weber, Max

Further Readings

Douglas, M. (1986). *How institutions think*. Syracuse, NY: Syracuse University Press.

Hall, P. A., & Soskice, D. (Eds.). (2001). *Varieties of capitalism*. Oxford, UK: Oxford University Press.

Hodgson, G. M. (1994). The return of institutional economics. In N. J. Smelser & R. Swedberg (Eds.), *The handbook of economic sociology* (pp. 58–76). Princeton, NJ: Princeton University Press.

Immergut, E. M. (2005). Paradigms of change in political science: Historical-institutionalism and the problem of change. In A. Wimmer & R. Kößler (Eds.), *Understanding change: Models, methodologies and metaphors* (pp. 237–259). Basingstoke, UK: Palgrave Macmillan.

March, J. G., & Olsen, J. P. (1984). The new institutionalism: Organizational factors in political life. *American Political Science Review, 78,* 734–749.

Pierson, P. (2004). *Politics in time: History, institutions, and social analysis*. Princeton, NJ: Princeton University Press.

Powell, W. W., & DiMaggio, P. J. (Eds.). (1991). *The new institutionalism in organizational analysis*. Chicago: University of Chicago Press.

Steinmo, S., Thelen, K., & Longstreth, F. (Eds.). (1992). *Structuring politics: Historical institutionalism in comparative analysis*. Cambridge, UK: Cambridge University Press.

Streeck, W., & Thelen, K. (Eds.). (2005). *Beyond continuity: Institutional change in advanced political economies*. Oxford, UK: Oxford University Press.

Tsebelis, G. (2002). *Veto players: How political institutions work*. Princeton, NJ: Princeton University Press.

Weingast, B. R. (1996). Political institutions: Rational choice perspectives. In R. E. Goodin & H.-D. Klingemann (Eds.), *A new handbook of political science* (pp. 167–191). Oxford, UK: Oxford University Press.

Williamson, O. E. (2000). The new institutional economics: Taking stock, looking ahead. *Journal of Economic Literature, 38,* 595–613.

Integration

See Political Integration

Intellectuals

The concept of intellectual as a category emerged in the late 19th century and bloomed with the political phenomena of the 20th century. Before that, as in the work of the medieval historian Jacques Le Goff, for example, the term referred to clerics. Intellectuals appeared in France during the Dreyfus Affair of 1894, in which Captain Alfred Dreyfus, a French artillery officer of Jewish descent, was tried and falsely convicted of treason; he was later exonerated and, in 1906, received a full pardon. The term *Dreyfus Affair* was coined by the writer Maurice Barrès in 1898 to designate the writers, scholars, and publicists who were convinced of Dreyfus's innocence. It is thus at the intersection of science and public debate that the intellectual stands. Throughout the 20th century, intellectuals emerged as major players in politics and public affairs. If one speaks in the plural, intellectuals designate a group of scholars and artists whose intervention in public space finds its legitimacy in their expertise and knowledge. Very soon, the figure of the intellectual also appeared in the singular as a symbol of political idealism or commitment in the political struggles of the century. Today, they are represented by writers such as Salman Rushdie, who have been persecuted for their beliefs and writings and have become symbols of freedom of expression. During the last quarter of the 20th century, the growing part played by intellectuals in economic debates on globalization as well as in discussions on issues of redistribution and social justice allowed the emergence of new actors. In this entry, the changing roles of intellectuals and the new challenges facing them are discussed.

Intellectuals and Engagement

The Dreyfus Affair established the legitimacy of intellectuals to intervene in public debate in the name of universal values. From that moment onward they have never left the political scene, announcing or accompanying its principal evolutions. The history of intellectuals during the first half of the 20th century is marked by both fascism and communism. If certain intellectuals such as the philosopher Martin Heidegger, the famous historian of the Middle Ages Ernst Kantorowicz, and the jurist Carl Schmitt appeared favorable to Nazism in its early days, most intellectuals rallied to the camp opposing Hitler. Most, like Stefan Zweig or Walter Benjamin, chose exile. The German novelist and short story writer Thomas Mann and the philosophers Hannah Arendt, Theodor Adorno, and Ernst Cassirer found refuge in the United States. Meanwhile, many intellectuals were attracted by the Soviet system, in which they saw the possibility of the realization of the communist ideal. The interwar period marked a first peak of the membership of intellectuals in communist parties, which was renewed after World War II and the prestige gained by the victory of the Allies. This was then followed by the Cold War, and intellectuals often were regarded as *compagnons de route* in the image of Jean-Paul Sartre in France.

Intellectuals not only participate in political debate, but they also judge political events. They thus played a major role in the interpretation of the Holocaust and in the debates on how to deal with this legacy in public discourses, as in Germany, and also in the interpretation of the Nazi phenomenon and its German roots (see the *Historikerstreit* in 1986 between the historian Ernst Nolte and the philosopher Jürgen Habermas). Intellectuals also have attempted to provide an existential reflection, as in Primo Levi's works. They have been similarly involved not only in the debate against racial discrimination in America in the 1960s (Hannah Arendt and Toni Morrison) and in Third World struggles for independence (Frantz Fanon) but also in the assertion of former colonized cultures—for example, Aimé Césaire and Leopold Sedar Senghor, the spokesmen for Negritude, or more recently, Raphaël Confiant and Patrick Chamoiseau for Creole.

One of the most important influences of intellectuals on political life was the challenging role played by dissidents in the Soviet Union and other communist states. Long persecuted, imprisoned by the Soviet regime, and silenced, they asserted themselves in favor of change in the climate of international relations. The Helsinki Accords of

1975 allowed the appearance of the Charter 77 movement led by Jan Patocka and Vaclav Havel in Czechoslovakia, which placed the defense of human rights at the heart of its approach and appealed to the West, and similar movements in Poland, where intellectuals played a central role in the Solidarnocz movement as also in the round table discussions that allowed the nonviolent transition toward democracy in the late 1980s.

Intellectuals and the End of History

The events of 1989, the year of the fall of the Berlin Wall and the beginning of the collapse of the Soviet empire, would seem to corroborate theories that shook the global intellectual debate since the political scientist Francis Fukuyama in an article, based on a Hegelian reading of history, described the final victory of liberal democracy over totalitarian regimes as "the end of history." By contrast, Samuel Huntington, who propagated the idea of a "clash of civilizations," which the terrorist attacks of September 11, 2001, seemed to confirm, shaped the global debate in a different way.

One of the striking influences that intellectuals have had over the past 20 years concerns the role played by neo-conservatives in the United States. The meeting of a group of students at City College of New York, including Irving Kristol, Daniel Bell, and Irving Howe, led to the birth of neo-conservatism; they combined the anticommunism of the Cold War period and the theories of the philosopher Leo Strauss, who had emigrated to the United States to escape the Nazi regime. Neo-conservatism affirms the equal responsibility of intellectuals and political leaders. Neo-conservatives argue that to combat terrorism, the United States should assert its power internationally to promote the development of democracies. This theory had considerable resonance after the September 11, 2001, attacks. It was on this basis that American forces intervened in Iraq in 2003 to create a new political order.

New Theoretical Objects

Recent years have seen the intellectuals expanding the scope of their study to new objects as well as the emergence of new voices. Following the theories of John Rawls (*A Theory of Justice*, 1971), the Indian economist Amartya Sen, recipient of the Nobel Prize in Economics in 1998, and the Bangladeshi Muhammad Yunus, Nobel Peace Prize laureate in 2006, have played a central role not only in the renewal of economic theory but also in stressing the importance of equality and justice in international relations. This movement signals the new role of today's intellectuals who raise questions of public interest concerning the future of the planet such as the principle of responsibility expounded by philosopher Hans Jonas in the early 1960s about the nuclear threat and now dealing with environmental policies, besides public health and bioethical issues.

Intellectuals are also faced with this question: What is the nature of social change to come? Whether postcolonial thinkers, theorists of the "multitude," representatives of gay theory, or philosophers of recognition, their answers are often combined with a strong critique of democracy. The debate concerns both the nature of power in contemporary societies and the possibility for formerly oppressed groups to express themselves. It allows the renewal of old theories (Marxism, anarchism) at the same time as the emergence of new objects. In recent years, intellectuals dealt with questions of law and justice (Jürgen Habermas, Giorgio Agamben, and Roberto Unger), media and communication (Noam Chomsky), ecology (Vandana Shiva and Peter Singer), or HIV/AIDS. They have especially sought to bring in new players in the line of subaltern studies that developed predominantly in India or Latin America or postcolonial studies (Edward Said, Homi Bhabha, and Paul Gilroy). These theories, postulated by women scholars such as Judith Butler or Gayatri Spivak, were based on the result of gender studies and the formation of identities as ideological constructs. Theorists of recognition (Axel Honneth, Seyla Benhabib, and Nancy Frazer) refer to Charles Taylor's theories of justice as a basis for classifying recognition as a political category.

Politics at the Heart of Intellectuals' Reflection

The current relationship between intellectuals and politics has developed into a more complex form than it had throughout the 20th century. The links between intellectuals and politics assert themselves as more deeply embedded than ever. One could indeed imagine in the early 1970s that the complexity of our societies and the development of globalization heralded the disappearance of intellectuals and their replacement by competent experts and scientists, while new trends such as globalization asserted the primacy of the economy at the expense of politics. Nevertheless, a number of intellectuals today enjoy an international reputation further enhanced by the circulation of ideas, globalization of information, use of the Internet, and mobility of students.

At the international level, the most burning issues remain political. If in Western democratic societies intellectuals agree with the criticism of capitalism, they must nevertheless remember that their existence is linked to the practice of democracy. It is this battle that is waged today by intellectuals in all countries where freedom of expression is restricted. Dissidents under repressive regimes have struggled for historical truth and the recognition of different communities that make up society. The other big question now concerns the dynamics of political and religious radicalization. A number of intellectuals, for example, call for a modernized reading of Islam.

The past decades have discredited the idea of a peaceful unification of the planet and confronted intellectuals with all forms of conflict, from the most global to the most local, bringing out old nationalist confrontations but also religious clashes. "What is most peculiar about our age is the conviction that evil is installed at the core of history and our frenetic rejection of that conviction" (Thérèse Delpech, 2007, p. 175). If they want to meet the challenges of democracy, intellectuals have a long way ahead

Perrine Simon-Nahum
Centre National de la Recherche Scientifique/
École des Hautes Études en Sciences Sociales
Paris, France

See also Agenda Setting; Civil Society; Critical Theory; Globalization; Neoliberalism; Political Philosophy

Further Readings

Aron, R. (1955). *L'Opium des intellectuels*. Paris: Calmann-Lévy. (Translated as *The opium of the intellectuals*, 1977, Westport CT: Greenwood Press)

Delpech, T. (2007). *Savage century: Back to barbarism*. Washington, DC: Carnegie Endowment for International Peace.

Jennings, J., & Kemp-Welch, A. (Ed.). (1997). *Intellectuals in politics: From the Dreyfus Affair to Salman Rushdie*. London: Routledge.

Mannheim, K. (1966). *Ideology and Utopia* (8th ed.). London: Routledge & Kegan.

Walzer, M. (1989). *The company of critics: Social criticism and political commitment in the twentieth century*. London: Peter Halban.

INTELLIGENCE

Intelligence refers to an awareness that leaders hope to have about the threats or opportunities that face their nation, either internally or from abroad. Armed with this information, they may make better decisions about how to protect and advance the national interest. An understanding of threats and opportunities can be reliably acquired only through the careful collection and study of information about domestic and foreign situations, such as plotting by internal subversives or the machinations of external terrorist factions and rival nations. This gathering of information, along with the interpretation of its meaning, lies at the heart of intelligence.

Stated more formally, intelligence is the knowledge and foreknowledge of dangers and opportunities—both domestic and foreign—as a prelude to decision and action by a nation's leaders. Strategic intelligence refers to the objective of achieving a global understanding of dangers and opportunities; tactical intelligence is concerned more with threats and opportunities on specific battlefields or theaters of war.

The academic study of intelligence has progressed by leaps and bounds in recent years. The most important developments in the field are efforts to move beyond spy memoirs and to apply rigorous research standards to the questions of how nations gather and analyze information on world affairs and engage in other intelligence activities. More and more studies are presenting empirical data, testable hypotheses, and theoretical frameworks. Scholars in the field have also been conducting in-depth interviews with practitioners and have benefitted from the extensive number of intelligence documents that have been released in recent decades. In the United States, such documents include the Church Committee reports (1975–1976) as well as reports from government panels examining intelligence such as the Aspin-Brown Commission (1995–1996), the Kean Commission (2004), and the Silberman-Robb Commission (2005).

This entry considers the nature of intelligence, highlighting some key examples involving covert action and counterintelligence activities on the part of the United States. It then examines the results of intelligence activities and notes some distinctive features of intelligence in democratic regimes.

The Nature of Intelligence

Intelligence may be considered a process, a product, a set of organizations, and a set of missions.

Intelligence as a Process

As a process, intelligence is a series of interactive phases whereby government officials plan what information to collect from around the globe, use machines and human agents to gather the information, assign experts ("analysts") to make sense of the information, and finally, distribute the findings to decision makers. This sequence of activities is known as the intelligence cycle.

Intelligence as a Product

As product, intelligence consists of facts and interpretive reports about homeland, world, or battlefield conditions. In the United States, for example, the most prestigious intelligence report is the *President's Daily Brief* (*PDB*), a succinct summary of global events over the past 24 hours, delivered to the president and a few other top policy officials each morning. Important, as well, in the United States, is the National Intelligence Estimate or NIE, which attempts to make more lengthy long-range forecasts about world events and relies on detailed research.

Intelligence as a Set of Organizations

As a set of organizations, a nation's intelligence "community" focuses on a number of responsibilities: code-breaking and electronic-eavesdropping organization, the gathering and interpretation of photography from satellites and reconnaissance aircraft, the interpretation of military information gathered by intelligence units within the uniformed services, and their gathering of tactical information in theaters of combat.

Intelligence as a Set of Missions

Collection and Analysis

As a set of missions, intelligence refers first of all to the range of activities encompassed within the intelligence cycle, known in short as "collection and analysis." This is Mission Number One for a nation's intelligence agencies, that is, the duty to place on the desktops of prominent leaders the best information possible to help illuminate the domestic and foreign security situations they face. In the United States and most other affluent nations, the intelligence agencies have two additional responsibilities: (1) covert action and (2) counterintelligence (CI).

Covert Action

Covert action is a secret activity designed to influence events in other nations in a direction favorable to a nation's best interests, not simply gather information abroad. This mission expanded rapidly in the democracies during the Cold War as a means for combating the aggressive use of intelligence operations by the Soviet Union to spread communism around the world.

Covert action is often grouped into four categories: (1) propaganda, (2) political, (3) economic, and (4) paramilitary activities. Propaganda, sometimes called psychological warfare or simply "psy war," is the most extensively used form of covert action. During the Cold War, for example, the Central Intelligence Agency (CIA) secretly produced a flood of worldwide propaganda disseminated by way of its vast, hidden network of "media assets"—foreign newspaper editors and reporters, television correspondents, magazine editors, and book editors. This source of "perception management" (in the intelligence euphemism) was meant to supplement the normal overt sources of information about the United States distributed through official channels, such as White House press releases and State Department public bulletins.

During the Cold War and till today, political covert action includes secret financial aid to friendly politicians and governmental officials abroad—what British intelligence officers refer to as "King George's cavalry." During the 1960s, the CIA provided covert funding to the Christian Democratic Party in Italy for its behind-the-scenes political battles against the Soviet-sponsored Italian Communist Party. Normally, propaganda and political covert action work together hand in glove.

Covert action in the form of secret economic operations can also be used to undermine adversaries abroad, for example, by encouraging labor unrest (as in Chile during the 1970s) or by sabotaging electrical power lines and mining harbors (approaches used by the United States against Nicaragua during the 1980s). Paramilitary (PM) activities are the most extreme, and controversial, form of covert action. Adopting this approach, a country will enter into warlike operations against an adversary—everything from weapons supplies to one of the sides that is engaged in a foreign civil war to large-scale "secret" (or, at any rate, never officially acknowledged) wars or assassination plots aimed against foreign leaders. Classic illustrations of PM wars are the failed Bay of Pigs operation in Cuba in 1961 and the struggle against communist forces in Laos from 1962 to 1968, with the CIA advising and arming the indigenous anticommunist Hmong tribesmen.

Before assassination as an instrument of U.S. intelligence was prohibited by an executive order signed by President Gerald Ford in 1976, and reaffirmed by every American president since, the White House instructed the CIA to carry out plots to kill Fidel Castro of Cuba and Patrice Lumumba of Congo, among other leaders of small nations caught in the tug-of-war between the United States and the Soviet Union. None of the plots was successful. Despite the executive order against assassinations, a waiver exists in times of authorized war, and as a consequence, the White House ordered CIA plots against the lives of Saddam Hussein of Iraq and Osama bin Laden of the Al Qaeda terrorist organization in the early years of the 21st century. None succeeded. Overt U.S. forces eventually captured Hussein during the Second Persian Gulf War that began in 2003; he was tried and executed by provisional Iraqi authorities. Bin Laden remains at large.

Counterintelligence

The third core intelligence mission is known as counterintelligence (CI). As with covert action, this mission is rarely mentioned in a nation's official documents. Yet CI grew quickly as a mission during the Cold War in the face of the rising confrontation between the Western democracies and the Soviet Union. The purpose of CI (of which counterterrorism is an important subset) is to thwart the hostile activities of foreign intelligence services and terrorist organizations directed against the homeland.

The practice of CI entails both security and counterespionage (CE). Security is the passive or defensive side of CI and relies on static safeguards such as security clearances, polygraphs (lie detection machines), codes, fences, sentries, alarms, badges and passes, curfews, restricted areas, and checkpoints. CE is the aggressive or offensive side of the mission. The ultimate goal is to infiltrate the hostile intelligence service with an agent (or "mole"), a ploy known as a "penetration." With a penetration agent inside the enemy's camp, one can possibly learn what moles the enemy has managed to burrow inside one's own camp. The Soviets successfully used this approach against the United States during the 1980s and 1990s by secretly recruiting Aldrich Ames of the CIA and Robert Hanssen of the FBI, who revealed to their masters in Moscow the names of CIA moles inside Soviet intelligence and other information that undermined the effectiveness of U.S. intelligence operations against the Soviet Union. Other major democracies also experienced Soviet penetrations of their political and intelligence agencies.

Results of Intelligence Actions

In each of these missions—collection and analysis, covert action, and CI—nations have registered successes and failures. In the United States, for example, the CIA successfully tracked the development of Soviet weapons systems by way of surveillance machines and human agents. Yet the agency failed to warn the nation of the Al Qaeda attack of September 11, 2001, against the United States and incorrectly concluded in 2002 that Iraq possessed weapons of mass destruction, thereby helping precipitate the Second Persian Gulf War.

With respect to covert action, the CIA successfully overthrew leaders in Iran (1953) and Guatemala (1954) who were deemed unfriendly to the United States. Yet presidents would soon find out that this secret approach to foreign policy often failed, as with the Bay of Pigs operation during the Kennedy administration. Another failure occurred with the Iran-Contra scandal during the Reagan administration, when—despite an express law that prohibited such activities—the National Security Council staff worked illegally with elements of the CIA to conduct paramilitary operations in Nicaragua (where the anticommunist Contras were at war against a Marxist regime). During the Reagan years, the United States also experienced covert action successes in Afghanistan, when the CIA helped drive the Soviets out of that country. Once more in Afghanistan, this time in the wake of the 9/11 attacks, the second Bush administration enjoyed covert action success when the CIA helped rout the Taliban regime that had provided a haven for the Al Qaeda terrorists who had struck Washington, D.C., and New York City.

Similarly, on the CI front, the United States has caught many spies, including those who stole the secret of the atom bomb and gave it to Moscow; but Washington suffered the failures of Ames, Hanssen, and several other Soviet and Chinese penetrations during the Cold War. In the United Kingdom, Harold "Kim" Philby spied for the Soviet Union at the highest levels during the Cold War. With respect to all three intelligence missions, one can expect ongoing successes and—conducted as they are by mere mortals—inevitable failures, too.

The intelligence agencies of the United States are distinct in some ways from those of other nations. They are large and technically advanced, and they are dispersed in their organization and management far more than is usually the case even in other democracies. The U.S. secret agencies also share common traits with their counterparts abroad, such as an inability to foresee and collect all the information that national leaders may need, a periodic misinterpretation of information by analysts and (sometimes intentionally to further their own political agenda) by decision makers, and from time to time critical failures of CI.

In democratic regimes, another aspect of intelligence has garnered much attention: maintaining accountability over secret agencies as a guard against their abuse of secret power. In the United States, for example, journalists and lawmakers discovered during the 1970s that the CIA and its companion agencies had been misused by politicians to spy against American citizens—chiefly anti–Vietnam War dissenters and civil rights activists. This led to a reform movement and the establishment in Congress of specific intelligence oversight committees with the responsibility of keeping an eye on the secret agencies and rein in any wrongdoing. Compared with the time of benign neglect before the reform movement, the new intelligence accountability has provided a serious check against the abuse of secret power. Critics argue, however, that overseers on Capitol Hill have failed to consistently supervise the intelligence agencies. Moreover, disputes have arisen over whether the second Bush administration misused the agencies once again for spying against American citizens, especially by tapping their telephone conversations without proper warrants. The search continues in the United States and other democracies for the proper balance between efficient intelligence services, on the one hand, and the exercise of proper accountability to preserve liberty, on the other.

Loch K. Johnson
University of Georgia
Athens, Georgia, United States

See also Accountability; Leadership; Liberty; Prediction and Forecasting; Secret Services; Security and Defense Policy; Security Apparatus; Strategic (Security) Studies; Terrorism, International

Further Readings

Betts, R. K. (2007). *Enemies of intelligence.* New York: Columbia.

Johnson, L. K. (Ed.). (2007). *Strategic intelligence* (5 vols.). Westport, CT: Praeger.

Johnson, L. K., & Wirtz, J. J. (Eds.). (2008). *Intelligence and national security.* New York: Oxford University Press.

Lowenthal, M. M. (2008). *Intelligence: From secrets to policy* (4th ed.). Washington, DC: CQ Press.

Turner, A. S. (2005). *Burn before reading.* New York: Hyperion.

Zegart, A. (2007). *Spying blind.* Princeton, NJ: Princeton University Press.

Interaction Effects

Many hypotheses in political science are conditional in nature. Institutional theories typically argue that actors respond differently to similar stimuli when they inhabit different institutional environments. Political culture arguments typically come down to the claim that the ways citizens behave depends on the environment in which they were socialized. Approaches that emphasize strategic interaction identify equilibrium responses that depend on key parameters; when a key parameter is above some critical level, one strategy combination is an equilibrium, while entirely different behavior (as encapsulated in a different comparative static relationship between key variables) is expected when that parameter falls below the critical value. However, many context-conditional claims are tested as if they were unconditional claims. Robert Franzese and Cindy Kam, for example, show that 54% of the articles appearing over a period of 5 years in journals covering three disciplines used statistical methods but only 24% of these used interaction terms in their empirical analysis. The review of the literature by Thomas Brambor, Robert Clark, and Matt Golder is even more discouraging. Examining three leading political science journals over 5 years, they found that more than 90% of the articles that actually specified conditional tests made at least one of the common errors those authors warn about. Some ways to test for interaction effects are presented below.

To get a sense of how multiplicative interaction models allow one to test context-conditional claims, consider the simplest case, where X is hypothesized to be associated with a continuous variable Y in the presence of condition Z but not in its absence. Assume Y and X to be continuous variables and Z is defined such that $Z = 1$ when the factor in question is present and $Z = 0$ otherwise. The multiplicative interaction effect approach to testing such a claim is to estimate using ordinary least squares (OLS) regression as follows:

$$Y = \beta_0 + \beta_1 X + \beta_2 Z + \beta_3 XZ + \varepsilon. \qquad (1)$$

To see how this model can be used to capture a context-conditional claim, examine the case where the condition is absent—that is, when $Z = 0$. Equation 1 would, therefore become

$$Y = \beta_0 + \beta_1 X + \beta_2(0) + \beta_3 X(0) + \varepsilon,$$

which simplifies to

$$Y = \beta_0 + \beta_1 X + \varepsilon.$$

Thus, β_0 and β_1 serve as estimates for the intercept and slope, respectively, in a linear model of the relationship between X and Y in the absence of condition Z. Similarly, Equation 1 allows us to estimate the relationship between these variables when Z is present (i.e., when $Z = 1$). Once again, substituting the value of the modifying variable into Equation 1, we get

$$Y = \beta_0 + \beta_1 X + \beta_2(1) + \beta_3 X(1) + \varepsilon,$$

which simplifies to

$$Y = (\beta_0 + \beta_2) + (\beta_1 + \beta_3)X + \varepsilon,$$

which shows that Equation 1 allows us to estimate the intercept $(\beta_0 + \beta_2)$ and slope $(\beta_1 + \beta_3)$ of the linear relationship between X and Y in the presence of Z. It is the ability to yield estimates of relationship between X and Y for the case where the hypothesized condition is met as well as when the condition is not met—and the ability to *compare* those estimates in a straightforward manner—that makes multiplicative interaction effects models a powerful tool for analyzing context-conditional claims.

The promise offered by interactive models has, more often than not, gone unfulfilled as a result of careless application despite the relative simplicity of the technique. Brambor, Clark, and Golder argue that the most common errors found in the literature related to multiplicative interaction models are (a) the failure to include them when appropriate, (b) omission of the individual terms that make up the interaction, (c) failure to calculate the theoretically relevant quantity of interest, and (d) the standard error of the same.

The previous discussion assumed that the modifying variable, Z, was dichotomous, but it need not be so. In general, we can examine how the relationship between X and Y depends on Z by taking the partial derivative of (1) with respect to X:

$$\frac{\partial Y}{\partial X} = \beta_1 + \beta_3 Z,$$

and we can see that according to (1) the relationship between X and Y is a linear function of Z. This derivative is often referred to as the marginal effect of X on Y at some level of Z. When Z is equal to zero, the effect of X on Y is β_1. But the magnitude and sign of the marginal effect of X on Y can change as Z changes (to the extent that β_3 is nonzero).

This simple setup allows the researcher to test many types of context-conditional claims. For example, the modifying variable, Z, can either *augment* or *inhibit* the relationship between X and Y. Typically, if Z is an augmenting variable, the sign of the coefficient on interaction term (β_3) will have the same sign as the coefficient on the variable being modified (β_1), but if Z is an inhibitor, the sign of the coefficient on the interaction term will have the opposite sign of the coefficient on the variable being modified. If the theory being tested claims that Z either augments or inhibits the effect of X on Y, then it is also useful to check to see if X actually has the hypothesized effect on Y at some levels of Z. To do this, one can calculate the marginal effect of X on Y across the observed range of Z and compare these conditional marginal effects with their associated standard errors to determine if the marginal effect is (a) ever statistically distinguishable from zero, (b) always statistically distinguishable from zero, or (c) is only statistically distinguishable from zero at certain values of Z. If the modifying variable is either dichotomous or ordinal, it is easy to report the effect of X on Y in a simple table of marginal effects and their associated standard errors—a set for each of the values that Z takes on. If Z is a continuous variable, it may be easier to present this information by plotting the line $\beta_1 + \beta_3 Z$ and its associated confidence interval over the full range of Z.

The practical implications are likely to be quite different depending on which of these three situations is the case. For example, if Y is some factor that is considered desirable and one believes that it is brought about by an increase in X but only in the presence of Z, it should be the case that β_3 is greater than zero and $\beta_1 + \beta_3 Z$ is greater than zero when Z is sufficiently high. It is possible that, consistent with its role as an augmenting modifying variable, β_3 is significantly greater than zero but that $\beta_1 + \beta_3 Z$ is not significantly greater than zero over any of the observed ranges of Z. If this is true, then there is no evidence of a relationship between X and Y for Z to modify, and there would be no basis to argue for supplying Z because it encourages the beneficial consequences of X.

In addition to inhibiting or augmenting a relationship between X and Y, the simple model in Equation 1 can be used to capture the case where the modifying variable changes the sign on the marginal effect capturing the relationship between X and Y. It is possible that for some values of Z, X is positively associated with Y, while for other values of Z, it is negatively associated with Y. Evidence of this would be found if $\beta_1 + \beta_3 Z$ is significantly greater than zero for some values of Z and significantly less than zero for other values of Z.

It should be noted that the basic logic of interaction outlined here can be extended to other types of modifying relationships and to estimators other than OLS. For example, the effect of X on Y may depend on the value of X itself (as in quadratic, cubic, and higher order specifications). The effect of X may depend on the value of more than one modifying variable and even the interaction between some or all of those modifying variables. The method is quite flexible and one should, with some creativity, be able to specify a model that with some additional calculation will produce the quantity of interest implied by the theory being evaluated.

William Roberts Clark
University of Michigan
Ann Arbor, Michigan, United States

See also Causality; Regression; Statistics: Overview

Further Readings

Brambor, T., Clark, W. R., & Golder, M. (2006). Understanding interaction models: Improving empirical analysis. *Political Analysis, 14,* 63–82.

Braumoeller, B. (2004). Hypothesis testing and multiplicative interaction terms. *International Organization, 58*(4), 807–820.
Franzese, R. J., & Kam, C. D. (2007). *Modeling and interpreting interactive hypotheses in regression analysis*. Ann Arbor: University of Michigan Press.
Jaccard, J., Turrisi, R., & Wan, C. K. (1990). *Interaction effects in multiple regression.* Newbury Park, CA: Sage.

INTERDEPENDENCE

In political science, *interdependence* refers to independent social actors who wish to preserve their identity but who are structurally affected by one another's behavior, whether they like it or not. The actors are involved in each other's affairs (functional or integrative interdependence), or they are part of the same system (systemic interdependence). These two types of interdependence do not exclude one another: If actors are part of the same system, they are indirectly involved in one another's affairs, and conversely, social systems are based on the involvement of actors with each other. In terms of the structure–agency debate, however, it makes sense to distinguish systemic interdependence from the behavioral, more policy-dependent, types (see Figure 1).

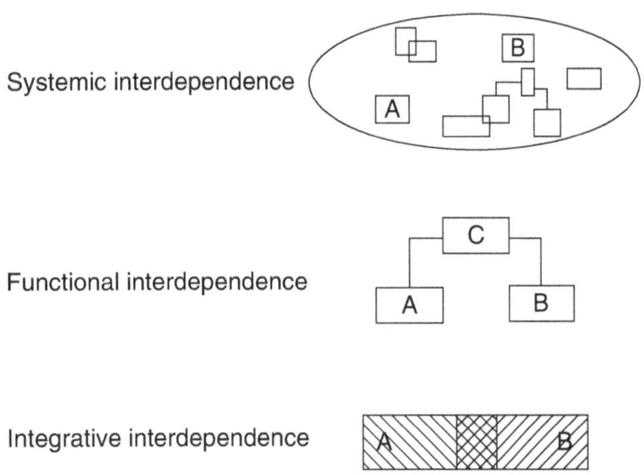

Figure 1 Three Types of Structural Interdependence

Source: de Wilde, J. H. (1991). *Saved from oblivion: Interdependence theory in the first half of the 20th century* (p. 20). Aldershot, UK: Dartmouth.

The structural effect can be operationalized into three qualitative dimensions (see Figure 2). They express how given actors can be mutually affected by one another's behavior. The first dimension concerns the *degree* of mutual involvement. This relates both to the quantitative characteristics of the intertwinement and to the existential value of the relationship for the actors.

The second dimension concerns the *character* of mutual involvement: confrontational versus constructional interdependence. The difference is related to two connotations of the term *dependence*: subordination, and need or want. The more idealist expressions of interdependence rhetoric generally refer to the second connotation: interdependence as the consequence of a mutually perceived necessity of cooperation or interdependence as a symbiosis—two can do more than one. Sometimes this is referred to as positive interdependence. Cooperation creates a surplus value. Especially, economic interdependence is often emphasized in this context. However, interdependence can also be the consequence of a mutually perceived necessity of obstruction or competition. There is a stalemate: Due to the other(s), neither side can reach its goals. Confrontational interdependence is typical for a balance of power. One classical example is the Cold War situation of Mutual Assured Destruction between the United States and the former USSR.

The third dimension concerns the *(a)symmetry* of mutual involvement: the distribution of costs and benefits. Even in the case of a surplus value, there tends to be conflict about the price to be paid. This can relate to the contractual conditions, as is the case in conflicts between employers and labor unions. It can also relate to structural asymmetries in the world economy, as is the case in North–South relations. It can relate to the uneven distribution of costs of preventive measures versus costs of failing measures, as in many environmental issues (e.g., the price for preventing upstream pollution vs. the price of cleaning costs downstream). Additionally, distributional issues are about free-rider dilemmas. It can also relate to issue linkages, for example, the impact of functional and integrative interdependence on the identities of the participating actors. Finally, the existential value of the relationship can be asymmetrical. Robert Keohane and Joseph Nye Jr.

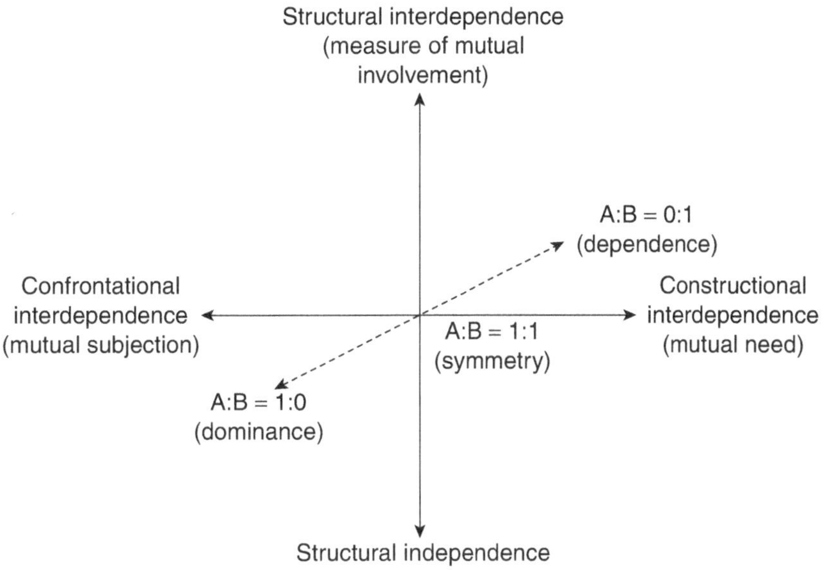

Figure 2 Qualifications of Structural Interdependence

Source: de Wilde, J. H. (1991). *Saved from oblivion: Interdependence theory in the first half of the 20th century* (p. 27). Aldershot, UK: Dartmouth.

(2001) distinguish in this context between sensitivity costs and vulnerability costs. Some actors may be able to develop alternatives for the lost profit, whereas other actors may lack such options.

The concept of interdependence has a long history in political science, but it is seldom defined carefully. Often, it serves rhetorical purposes, emphasizing a need for cooperation, even (or especially) when conflicts are paramount. As such, it can be traced back in the academic literature to the late 19th century, when the first generation of scholars started to talk about globalization and its consequences.

Generally, the rhetoric of interdependence is associated with progressive liberal thought, in which trade relations and social contract are valued as mutually profitable for those involved. Particularly in the work of Sir Norman Angell, this is developed into one of the first interdependence theories. But left-wing syndicalists, such as Francis Delaisi, also expected that economic interdependence would provide a structure that would end political myths about the ideal of the nation-state. In *Les contradictions du monde moderne*, published in 1925, he emphasized the need to manage interdependence by means of permanent international institutions. This comes close to the theory of functionalism as developed by David Mitrany and the pluralist theories of Charles Merriam. A more neutral early attempt to develop interdependence as an analytical concept can be found in *The Interdependent World and Its Problems*, published in 1933 by the historian Ramsay Muir.

All of this literature shares a normative concern about the need to manage globalization: Interdependence means trouble but only when it is neglected. At the same time, the literature has a word of admiration for the achieved levels of globalization. There is a hope for, and a belief in, the possibility of social learning. Therefore, interdependence theories are generally put in the idealist tradition in international relations, even though they are far from utopian.

The contemporary interest in the concept originates in the book *Power and Interdependence*, first published in 1977 by Keohane and Nye. They worked on the same themes as the first generation of theorists: the functional development of international organization in response to (transnational) globalization processes. An important difference is empirical: When Norman Angell, in 1918, argued for the need to create a protective union of democracies, this was a utopian idea, whereas NATO had existed for almost 3 decades when Keohane and Nye reflected on existing international regimes in 1972 and 1977. In addition, they emphasized the consequences of conscious manipulation of interdependencies for purposes of political power. Especially in terms of *soft power*, a term later coined by Nye in 1990, asymmetries in the intertwinement will be contested and can be exploited by the stronger side. The limit of this type of relational power, however, is set by the reciprocity inherent in interdependence: The continued existence of the relationship is a precondition for exploitation of its political power.

Also, in political rhetoric, both the 1970s and the 1990s showed waves of popular use of the term. Politicians, especially those working for international organizations, appeal to interdependence to silence their opposition: Global interests should take precedence over local, ethnocentric interests; or, one step further, the local, ethnocentric interests in the long term require that immediate priority is given to the global interest. In this speech–act capacity, interdependence asks for solidarity where it is lacking (North–South context), for cooperation where it is lacking (East–West context during the Cold War), and for common action where it is lacking (global challenges, e.g., in the environmental realm).

A rather different approach to interdependence has been developed by the sociologist Norbert Elias. His insights are especially relevant for understanding the social impact of the complexity that is typical for situations of complex interdependence, as well as the interdependences created by a division of labor (functional differentiation). In line with Mitrany's findings, Elias emphasizes that increasing interdependence leads simultaneously to increased collectivization and increased individualization.

Isolationism is the first policy response to the discovery of complexity and dependence—an attempt to reduce costs and complexity by neglecting other actors and by pulling out (e.g., U.S. policies toward Europe and Japan after World War I). When this does not work, the second response is imperialism—an attempt to reduce costs and complexity by controlling or conquering other actors (e.g., German and Japanese policies after World War I). Only when this does not work either does a third response emerge: the acceptance of pluralism and a willingness to compromise in face of shared overarching interests (e.g., the creation of the United Nations and the Bretton Woods system after World War II). This tension between the structural dimension of interdependence (i.e., a practical impossibility to achieve aims unilaterally) and the cognitive dimension of interdependence (i.e., the interpretation of the structure by the actors involved) is at the heart of the academic and social-political discourses on interdependence. Overall, the concept of interdependence has discursive functions in trying to show that actors cannot avoid dealing with one another and analytical functions in trying to map out the structure of world politics.

Jaap de Wilde
University of Groningen
Groningen, Netherlands

See also Globalization, Power; Power and International Politics; Sovereignty

Further Readings

Angell, N. (1938). *The great illusion: Now.* Harmondsworth, UK: Penguin.

Barry Jones, R. J., & Willetts, P. (Eds.). (1984). *Interdependence on trial.* New York: St. Martin's Press.

Delaisi, F. (1971). *Political myths and economic realities.* Washington, DC: Kennikat Press. (First published in England in 1925 and in the United States in 1927; Original work published 1925 as *Les contradictions du monde moderne.* Paris: Payot)

De Wilde, J. H. (1991). *Saved from oblivion: Interdependence theory in the first half of the 20th century.* Aldershot, UK: Dartmouth.

Elias, N. (2000). *The civilizing process.* New York: Blackwell. (Original work published 1939 as *Über den Prozess der Zivilisation*)

Jacobson, H. K. (1984). *Networks of interdependence: International organizations and the global political system.* New York: Knopf.

Keohane, R. O., & Nye, J. S. (2001). *Power and interdependence: World politics in transition.* Boston: Little, Brown. (Original work published 1977)

Mitrany, D. (1933). *The progress of international government.* New Haven, CT: Yale University Press.

Muir, R. (1971). *The interdependent world and its problems.* Washington, DC: Kennikat Press. (Original work published 1933)

Rosenau, J. N. (1980). *The study of global interdependence: Essays on the transnationalization of world affairs.* New York: Nichols/Pinter.

Interest Groups

Interest groups are formal organizations, usually based on individual voluntary membership, that seek to influence public policies without assuming government responsibility. The majority of interest groups do not have primarily political goals. They are normally engaged in a disparate range of activities—work, recreational, philanthropic, humanitarian, and cultural—that develop independently in society. Such groups enter the political arena when they require some form of public intervention (financial, administrative, etc.) to support their interests or when they wish to influence the adoption or implementation of government decisions so as to secure some advantage or to protect the interests they represent. The goals of interest groups may be very specific or may be intended to make an impact on the entire political community. The strategies used to influence decision makers involve the combination of a repertoire of tactics, the breadth of which varies in relation to each group's organizational resources. In this entry, the origins and types of such groups and their respective functions in political decision-making processes are discussed. Their role with regard to the quality of democracy is also critically examined.

Since the end of the 19th century, there has been an exponential growth in the number of interest groups, prompted by the changes that have contributed to shaping the contemporary world. Industrialization has played a decisive role in this respect, favoring a specialization of production and services that has in turn given a strong impulse to the establishment of myriad groups with differentiated social interests. The formation and consolidation of nation-states has been equally important. Industrialization and the emergence of nation-states also engendered numerous conflicts of a social, political, and cultural nature that contributed to generating collective movements, interest groups, and parties. The further development of interest groups was encouraged by the extraordinary conditions created by the two world wars, which forced governments to involve the organizations of civil society in managing the emergency created by the wars. The establishment of new groups was also stimulated by the increasingly pervasive role of the state in society in the wake of the development of the welfare state, which created new needs and new interests.

The type of political regime that offers the most opportunities for groups to organize themselves independently and to influence decision makers is liberal democracy. By contrast, in totalitarian or authoritarian regimes, interest groups are established, controlled, or backed by a single party or state and often used exclusively as instruments for mobilizing consensus. This entry deals only with interest groups active in contemporary democracies, as, indeed, does virtually all the literature devoted to these political actors. Particular attention is given to examining the general functions of interest groups in the political system and the obstacles and opportunities they encounter in the various phases of the process involved in influencing public decisions.

Definition

The above definition indicates three distinctive traits of interest groups. First, they are described as formal organizations—in other words, fairly permanent structures governed by clearly defined rules and with an identifiable membership and leadership. These characteristics are absent in informal associations—for example, certain groups of influential citizens, anomic groups, professional elites—which are sometimes included in the family of interest groups. This should, however, be avoided, because the intrinsic difficulties of ascertaining the presence of informal groups would make any reliable census of groups active in different policy arenas impossible, and an analysis of the inner workings of such nebulous associations would be no less problematic.

The second distinctive feature of interest groups is that they are made up of individuals who join on a voluntary basis. Members usually enter freely, participate in the group's activities, and discuss the objectives proposed by the leaders. If they are dissatisfied, they leave the organization. Analysis of the internal functioning of groups clarifies the conditions that favor or discourage participation and collective action. It should also be added that there is a type of interest group where membership is not entirely voluntary. These are *institutional interest groups*, which, as discussed herewith, are not vehicles for democratic participation.

The third qualifying element of interest groups is the particular way in which they try to influence policy making. They do so without seeking government office; indeed, they do not present electoral lists. In this respect, interest groups differ from political parties, for whom it is important to take part in elections in order to be able to exercise political power. As interest groups usually represent fairly circumscribed interests, they cannot hope to win elections and so prefer to convince the elected representatives rather than the voters of the validity of their case. This difference between political parties and interest groups seems to be at least partly contradicted in the real world by the frequent presence of small, single-issue political parties and large interest groups—for instance, trade unions—that have a wide range of concerns. It is also true that political parties appear to be increasingly incapable of representing general concerns, tending instead to turn into vehicles of economic interests. Nevertheless, it is precisely to offset their diminished ability to aggregate political demands that parties tend to increase their delegative powers by occupying public offices, while interest groups limit themselves to supporting, during electoral campaigns, those parties that declare a willingness to respond to their requests; alternatively, they might endorse individual politicians or place some of their representatives in a party's list of candidates.

Types of Interest Groups

The most common typology of interest groups employed in the literature distinguishes between *sectional* or *economic* groups and *promotional* or *cause* groups, which are organized to express particular policy objectives. Economic groups reflect the major "interests" of society and represent people who join the organization mainly because of their occupation. The three main types of economic interest groups are trade unions, business (employers), and professional organizations representing lawyers, doctors, engineers, and so on.

Cause groups consist of organizations that pursue goals not directly related to the material interests of their members. These groups are voluntary organizations formed by people who share some common aspiration unrelated to their jobs. The cause group category can potentially be divided into a multitude of subgroups, because it encompasses all sorts of voluntary organizations. Cause groups include cultural, religious, and recreational associations; organizations for the promotion of human rights and the welfare state; charities; and environmental and peace groups. Many of them are also *public interest groups*—namely, organizations that seek to promote collective goods by securing the approval of policies whose benefits may be shared equally by all people, irrespective of their membership or support of a given group. The development of public interest groups from the 1960s onward was a consequence of more widespread education, the adoption of more sophisticated means of mass communication, social protest, and the introduction of extensive social welfare programs.

Among cause groups, another category that deserves mention are the "not in my backyard" groups, otherwise known as *NIMBYs*, due to their widespread growth in recent years in many countries. NIMBYs are hybrid groups because the motivation of members is basically material and brings immediate benefits for members of that group only. The main goal of NIMBYs is almost always to defend the area in which their membership lives. Typical demands, often accompanied by highly visible forms of protest, are that a nuclear power station or a radioactive waste dump, prison, airport, or main road be built anywhere else rather than "in my backyard." The objectives of NIMBYs may also find support among people outside the "threatened" area, in the name of a wider, shared cause such as environmental conservation or the battle to create alternative energy sources. In this respect, NIMBYs can be related to cause groups and among these, in some cases, to public interest groups.

The distinction between economic and cause groups has led to the formulation of various hypotheses about how they function and their relationship with decision makers. It has been argued, for example, that economic groups are more long lasting because there are material incentives at stake for the membership that cause groups are less likely to be able to offer (see below). It has also been claimed that cause groups, even those with a large following, have a limited impact on policy making because they are barred from the corridors of power, while economic groups, in particular business groups, have easier access. This claim has been contested by Wyn Grant, who distinguishes between *insider* groups, which are consulted regularly by government bodies, and *outsider* groups, which do not want or are unable to establish privileged relationships with policymakers. According to Grant, cause groups may also become insiders, forging special relations with public officials. A further source of debate is the notion that insiders are more influential than outsiders; this too has come in for criticism on the grounds that, in many cases, the latter are also capable of conditioning the political agenda.

Mention must also be made of *institutional interest groups*, which may be either public or private. Institutional public groups are local or regional governments and the various branches of central government, which compete with each other to influence the political process to their own advantage. Institutional private groups are social organizations—industrial and financial companies, universities, churches, and hospitals—which, in certain circumstances, may commit a proportion of their resources to influencing the decision-making process.

As has already been said, the issue of democratic participation is largely extraneous to institutional groups. Unlike economic and cause groups, institutional groups are hierarchical organizations run in a managerial fashion by leaders whose main concern is to ensure the continuity of their institution irrespective of the specific interests of the membership. The decision to enter the political arena is generally taken by leaders without prior consultation of the membership, whether they are blue- or white-collar workers, shareholders, worshippers, or patients. In other words, in contrast to economic and cause groups, institutional groups have less need to obtain the approval of their membership to justify their political engagement or to address their needs and concerns, according to Robert Salisbury (1984). Institutional groups occupy an important position in the branch of literature devoted to the analysis of policy making. This is inevitable, because they have always had a dominant role in U.S. policy making, at both state and federal levels; are always widely present in policy networks active in the European Union; and manage, obviously, to condition the choices of the various national governments.

Levels of Organizational Complexity

Many interest groups have a simple organizational structure. Their political action begins and ends inside the boundaries defined by the local territory in which they operate. For instance, many public interest groups involved in environmental preservation have as their exclusive political targets the city council and/or the regional public authorities. Other groups have a more complex organizational structure with basic units embedded in a national structure. These second-level organizations help shape and unify the disparate demands of first-level organizations, the advantage being that it is possible to supply decision makers with aggregate information and to formulate more effective requests.

Third, there are also "umbrella" organizations called peak associations, which coordinate the activities of various second-level associations from different sectors. For example, in Germany, the main unions of the various categories of workers belong to the Deutsche Gewerkschaftsbund (DGB), which is analogous to the American Federation of Labor and Congress of Industrial Organizations (AFL-CIO) in the United States or the Trade Union Congress in the United Kingdom. In the EU, workers and employers alike are usually represented by second-level associations and by intersectorial peak associations. But many big corporations that represent themselves directly can also be found. There is also an associative level that includes, under a broad umbrella, the peak associations of different member states, giving rise, for example, to the European Trade Union Confederation and the Union of Industrial and Employers' Confederations of Europe.

Second-level and peak organizations are widespread among economic interest groups but are rare among cause groups, perhaps, as Salisbury (1975, p. 187) suggests, because the latter have a shorter lifetime. For this reason, they do not reach the degree of organizational complexity that leads to the formation of second-level and peak associations.

Interest Groups and Public Policy Making: Pluralist and Neo-Corporatist Approaches

The two most important approaches that have been adopted in the literature on interest groups are pluralism and neo-corporatism. Pluralism actually started in Europe at the beginning of the 20th century as a reaction to the monistic theory of the state. However, it was principally developed in the United States as an empirical approach to the analysis of political phenomena, through a series of works on the American political system published between the 1920s and the 1960s. Later adaptations have enabled pluralism to survive the numerous criticisms received in the second half of the century, when the major weaknesses of the approach were highlighted.

According to pluralists, the political process is driven by competition between many interacting groups that tend to self-limit their requests, thereby making the political system more stable. Competition is compatible with democracy because negotiation between many interests favors the dispersion of power, and so, according to David Truman, no one group is able to permanently get the better of the others. Robert Dahl concedes that some groups are stronger than others but argues that the dispersion of political power between the host of government institutions offers the possibility of access to weaker groups, which then have a chance of obtaining a hearing in some crucial phase of the decision-making process. According to pluralists, the competition between groups offers not only stability and democratic compatibility but also the possibility of making a decisive contribution to shaping public policies that have a broad consensus among citizens. Pluralists do not believe in the abstract concept of the general interest because this presupposes that its constituent parts form an indivisible whole, while empirical evidence suggests that many interacting interests influence government decisions, leading the way, but only in a transient fashion, to what is significant for all.

The pluralist approach has been heavily criticized for having presented an erroneous picture of the political system capable of regulating itself exclusively by virtue of the competition and compromises between groups. This view neglects the fact that the relations between groups are not balanced because some exercise a permanent influence while others are marginal or insignificant in the process of decision making. The idea of leaving the adoption of shared policies up to an agreement between partisan interests appears, then, to be both unrealistic and uneven. Their legitimacy would be based on existing power relations between the groups, and their implementation would be to the detriment of the weaker ones. The pluralist illusion of being able to explain the functioning of the political system in terms of the self-regulatory activities of interest groups involves a weakened state authority. In the real world, however, state intervention is indispensable for redressing imbalances in opportunities for access to decision-making arenas. The cogency of these criticisms forced the pluralists to abandon the idea of attributing to interest groups the ability to ensure the governability of the political system. This idea was, however, resumed in Europe by the neo-corporative approach in its reassessment of the role of the state.

Neo-corporatism is the institutionalized participation of interest groups in government activities that favors the elaboration of policies agreed on jointly by major organized groups and decision makers. Some features of neo-corporatist agreements can also be found in the *state corporatism* established in authoritarian regimes, such as in Portugal and Spain between the two world wars. However, neo-corporatism can be distinguished from state corporatism because, according to Philippe Schmitter, the former is a *societal corporatism* that is not imposed from above but arises in a voluntary fashion from within society and is compatible with the system of democratic representation. Instances of a neo-corporatist system were identified in various continental European countries in the 1970s and 1980s, for example, in Scandinavia and Austria. Subsequently, the number of studies based on the neo-corporatist approach diminished considerably, because the changes that have occurred in the international economic system have forced many governments to prefer public policy strategies centered on the market rather than agreements stipulated between groups, which are the most distinctive trait of neo-corporatism.

In a neo-corporatist agreement, the protagonists of tripartite negotiations with a government are the representatives of capital and labor; the policies adopted are economic and relate in particular to the control of prices and salaries. For the neo-corporatists, the state, in contrast to the way in which it is depicted by the pluralists, possesses extensive powers that are used to authorize, regulate, and sanction the activities of organizations to ensure that they respect stipulated agreements and collaborate—sometimes by exercising delegated public functions—to implement agreed policies.

Unions and employers' associations respect commitments undertaken with government because they have a monopoly on representation in their sector and exercise effective control over their members, who are often obliged to lend their support, because respect for various binding norms is a condition of membership. The importance of the control functions assumed by groups over their membership has led neo-corporatists to replace the traditional expression *representation of interests* with of the term *intermediation of interests*.

A favorable condition for trilateral negotiations is the presence of a prolabor party in the government. Unions take part because they feel supported by the left-wing party, which offers, in return for moderate wage claims, measures to boost employment and a commitment to maintaining the welfare state. In turn, employers' associations accept negotiations because they expect the government to maintain a low level of union conflict, thanks to their influence over the unions, and to support investment in industry. The factors that enable trilateral negotiations, according to neo-corporatist scholars, make it possible to produce better and socially more equitable public policies than those implemented by executives operating without the institutionalized collaboration of large, organized interest groups.

Neo-corporatism has greater theoretical ambitions than pluralism, but these have not been achieved because no generally accepted theory has ever been provided regarding the nature of neo-corporative agreements. Are they an extension, within the state machine, of the pluralist representation of interests? Or have they been "captured" by the state, subordinating them to state control? Furthermore, the numerous political and socioeconomic prerequisites necessary for the establishment of a neo-corporatist system have inevitably meant that the empirical cases are limited to the Scandinavian countries, the Netherlands, Austria, Belgium, and, to a more limited degree, Germany. Neo-corporatism cannot, therefore, be viewed as a general theory of the action of interest groups in contemporary democracies. Finally, neo-corporatism lacks a theory of the representation of groups that explains, logically and normatively, the privileged access to decision-making spheres of certain groups (unions and employers' associations) rather than others.

Mobilization

The study of the conditions for collective action is probably the field of interest group research in which there has been the greatest progress. Various contributions have examined the fundamental reasons that lead an individual to join a given organization, the means adopted by leaders to recruit members, and the contextual factors that influence mobilization. The preliminary theoretical basis for this strand of literature was provided by Mancur Olson Jr. in his book *The Logic of Collective Action* (1965). Olson revolutionized previous work on the conditions of collective action and laid the foundations for the development of a coherent body of knowledge. He demonstrated, thereby refuting a pluralist claim, that there is no automatic correspondence between the need of a given social group or category of people to manifest a policy preference and the transformation of that need into organized action. The latter can only occur under certain conditions and with certain resources. Groups that operate in unfavorable conditions and without adequate resources will be penalized in their efforts to influence the shape and outcome of public decisions.

According to Olson, in the most frequently occurring situations, it is not rational for an individual to support an organization that pursues a collective good even if he or she wishes to obtain it. The collective good, for example, the conservation of nature or the improvement of urban transport, is an indivisible good from which everyone can benefit. For this reason, the beneficiaries of collective goods will tend to avoid paying the costs of sustaining the organization (membership fees, participation in meetings and demonstrations, etc.) and act as free riders instead, waiting to reap the benefits of other people's efforts. Furthermore, rational individuals calculate that the contribution of their own effort to the success of a large organization's initiatives will be substantially irrelevant. Moreover, they take advantage of the scale of the organization, concealing their opportunistic behavior behind the anonymity of large numbers.

To overcome the difficulties deriving from the obstructive attitude of free riders, organizations are forced, according to Olson, to come up with selective incentives for its members (insurance policies, legal assistance, etc.) or alternatively to threaten imposing sanctions, a strategy resorted to by many unions in the United States and the UK. Invoking closed-shop legislation, they demand that firms only employ workers who are already union members or willing to become members. Among economic interest groups, Olson adds, it should be easier for smaller organizations to obtain support, because they can offer their membership particularly selective incentives. For example, groups representing farmers or artisans can increase their membership by offering advantageous medical insurance or convenient individual retirement schemes. Olson clarifies that his analysis mainly explains the behavior of economic interest groups, while it applies poorly to associations that do not offer incentives readily translatable into material benefits.

Following the path taken by Olson, James Wilson identified solidarity and purposive incentives in addition to material ones, going on to formulate a theory of collective action applicable to all kinds of interest group organizations. Solidarity incentives offer supporters the gratification that comes from feeling part of a group, while purposive incentives induce the members of an organization to actively promote some good that might also benefit a wider spectrum of nonmembers. Each of the three types of incentives is of varying importance, in relation to the other two, in fuelling individual support for an organization. Individuals join and support organizations for a variety of reasons that are often hard to distinguish from one another. It should, therefore, be taken into account that support for an organization is often the result of a combination of all three types of incentives.

Wilson's theory, with the importance it attributes to solidarity and purposive incentives, gave fresh credit to the widespread conviction that collective action is also motivated by ideals, without any expectation of a material reward. The greatest, and by no means negligible, weakness of this typology is that solidarity and purposive incentives, unlike material ones, are hard to distinguish and measure, making it difficult in turn to assess their specific weight. The subsequent development of the theory of incentives has, however, continued to focus on nonmaterial incentives, without, as a consequence, dispelling doubts stemming from theoretical assumptions that have not been adequately measured and checked.

Olson's theory of selective incentives paved the way for a fuller understanding of the conditions that facilitate or penalize the mobilization of different types of interest groups. Public interest groups such as pacifist, environmental, and child protection organizations are among those that are penalized, making it harder for them to enter the political arena. They have a very wide potential membership, but the incentives are almost exclusively purposive, with little intrinsic value. As the only major investment required is essentially emotional, people join but also abandon such organizations with considerable ease, making them highly unstable. In this respect, they are similar to collective movements. By contrast, economic groups, which have a more limited potential membership and can offer quite considerable material incentives and returns, find it easier to enter the political arena and establish themselves as key interlocutors for public decision makers.

Access

What difficulties and advantages must be taken into account by interest groups when seeking to establish useful contacts with decision makers? An examination of the issue of access does not clarify how groups manage to be influential in the decision-making process but does help ascertain the more or less favorable conditions for exercising influence. In liberal democracies, the possibility of access is conditioned by both variable and permanent factors. Variable factors include the resources available to a group (size of membership, expertise, money, existing contacts with political elites, good reputation, etc.) or the existence or otherwise of a public opinion favorable to the issues interest groups wish to submit to decision makers and the political significance of those issues.

The permanent factors that have a bearing on access include the nature of a country's institutional structure and its policy style. A democracy with a unitary institutional system has fewer access points than a federal democracy, because in the former, power is fairly concentrated, while in the latter, it is distributed among a larger number of independent decision-making bodies. The number of access points in the United States, for instance, is particularly high, due to the nation's federal structure, the division of government between the president and Congress, the powerful congressional committees, and a judicial system with constitutional powers to intervene in legislation. It is also high in the EU, which, like the United States, has an institutional system that separates powers both vertically and horizontally.

The varying degree of accessibility is influenced by the country's prevailing policy style. Every liberal democracy has its own particular policy style, which is perhaps not uniformly discernable in all policy areas but is prevalent in many of them. Policy style is the set of standard procedures generally adopted by institutions to devise and implement public policies, according to Jeremy Richardson, Gunnel Gustafsson, and Grant Jordan (1982). The access of groups to many areas of policy is easier when governments adopt a reactive policy style, because decision-making powers are not concentrated, and public bureaucracies depend in large measure on the technical information supplied by the groups. In these cases, the state usually avoids coercive measures that may discourage the setting up of new groups and reduce the fragmentation of existing ones. Public policies take the form of ad hoc measures uncoordinated with previous decisions and are mostly designed to satisfy the short-term demands of groups with ease of access to public bureaucracies, as noted by Michael Atkinson and William Coleman (1989). The access of groups is more selectively filtered when centralized governments and independent bureaucracies adopt an anticipatory policy style, using intrusive policy methods, without excluding coercion, the aim being to effect significant change in society and the economy.

Governments that adopt an anticipatory policy style may disregard interest groups while pursuing their public policy goals or may involve only broadly representative organizations capable of ensuring that their membership adheres to agreements stipulated by the state. The result, in this case, is greater selectivity in access, which benefits more well-organized groups.

Nowhere in the real world do governments adopt a purely reactive or anticipatory style. Both should therefore be seen as ideal types that represent the opposite extremes of a spectrum of possible combinations, including the various policy styles of the liberal democracies, some closer to the anticipatory model and others to the reactive one.

Lobbying

The main objective of interest groups is to influence governments in order to obtain favorable policy outcomes. However, influence is a continuous and unresolved political process, which by its very nature is unmeasurable. Furthermore, other factors may influence legislators' policy decisions more than interest groups—for instance, other legislators, party leaders, the personal convictions of the legislator, the media, and so on. Faced with the difficulty of measuring influence, scholars have tended to focus on the phenomenon of lobbying, extending the original meaning of the term to encompass the whole set of strategies and tactics used by interest groups to influence policy making.

Lobbying was initially understood in quite specific terms as one or more face-to-face meetings between representatives of an interest group and legislators, sought by the former so as to influence the decisions of the latter in a way that benefits the group's preferences. To be effective, a lobbyist—who may either be a member of the group or an expert hired specifically for the purpose—must establish a relationship of trust with the policymaker, supplying data and information that facilitate the adoption of policies favorable also to the interest group. In its broader reformulation, lobbying involves a much wider range of initiatives, including contacts with bureaucratic bodies, the premier's office, the courts and parliament, the use of the mass media, the preparation of memoranda, the forging of links with individual functionaries, and so forth.

Lobbying has been extensively studied in the United States, where it is widespread. This is due to the multiple points of access offered by the institutional system, the weakness and relative lack of representativity of the political parties, and a dominant political culture that favors pragmatic, nonideological dealings between citizens and legislators. American literature in this field can boast hundreds of case studies devoted to the lobbying activities of pressure groups. However, they have made little contribution to furthering an understanding of the phenomenon because they lack a shared theoretical basis. According to Frank Baumgartner and Beth Leech (1998), scholars tend to use their own method of measuring the impact of lobbying and a generally narrow analytic perspective without adopting a comparative approach or making any attempt to build on previous work.

The results of the large-scale surveys of lobbying in Washington, D.C., and the state capitals in the second half of the 1980s have been more useful. These studies, which are more theoretical, refer to a large number of cases and consider the context; they have shown that the tactic used most widely by lobbyists is to cultivate face-to-face contacts with public bureaucrats, seeking, at the same time, to extend the range of their contacts among public decision makers and those capable of influencing them in order to exchange information, establish cooperative strategies, and anticipate the moves of competitors. Furthermore, the gamut of strategies used varies according to the issue in question and whether it has a moderate or high political saliency or level of conflict. The position occupied by the group in the political process also seems to have considerable bearing on the choice of strategy. Groups operating within the political process adopt *inside strategies* that involve lobbying legislators and bureaucrats, taking legal action, and supporting certain candidates in elections. Marginal groups use *outside strategies* such as public forms of protest and organizing meetings to promote their cause. The media are resorted to in equal measure in both inside and outside strategies.

Lobbying is less developed in Europe than it is in the United States, because the conditions for lobbying are less favorable. In particular, the prevalence of unitary state systems reduces the number of access points and limits the legislative power of parliaments; these are mainly used by representatives of interest groups as a channel for drawing the attention of the media and the government to issues that concern them. Moreover, European scholars have displayed little interest in the theme of lobbying due to the importance attributed in interest group literature to the neo-corporatist approach, which takes it for granted that there is continuing collusion between policymakers and the representatives of economic interests while largely ignoring the lobbying activities of noneconomic groups. Despite these limits, the number of studies of lobbying in different European nations has increased in the past decades. In particular, there has been a steady growth in the amount of research devoted to lobbying in the EU, which has a multilevel institutional structure offering many direct points of access for individual groups and national associations. Both invariably maintain close contacts with national ministers present in Brussels, who often act as intermediaries between interest groups and European institutions.

The majority of interest groups employ one of the many lobbying agencies based in Brussels. At the beginning of the 1990s, it was estimated that more than 10,000 individuals were employed in such agencies, for the most part run by British or American consultants, who generally had more expertise than colleagues from elsewhere in Europe. The result of the lobbying of European institutions is the preponderance of large European industrial groups and their associations in the technical committees set up by the European Commission and the Council of Ministers. Public interest groups are underrepresented or excluded. However, they have greater success with the European Parliament, which is generally more receptive to broader interests. European lobbying seems to be less adversarial and more inclined to favor compromise policy solutions, while in the United States there tends to be just one winner, often the main interest group that has financed the election campaign of the decision makers. Furthermore, in the multilevel system of the EU, lobbying on a certain issue may continue at national, regional, and local levels while the adopted policy is being implemented.

Critical Reappraisals in the Study of Interest Groups

Policy Networks Approach

Since the second half of the 1980s, pluralism and neo-corporatism have come under fire on the grounds that they offer an inaccurate image of the key characteristics of policy making. Critics have noted that in the United States, the prototype of the pluralist political system, a small number of groups adopt collaborative and collusive behaviors in certain areas of policy that are very similar to those described by neo-corporatists. Conversely, in political systems traditionally associated with neo-corporatist agreements, where one would expect cooperation between a small number of groups to be the dominant feature, scholars have identified policy areas corresponding to the pluralist model of a large number of competing groups. To overcome the incongruent features of pluralism and neo-corporatism, European scholars developed the policy network approach. This focuses on the way groups are conditioned by certain characteristics of the state and of policy making. The state has turned into a network of independent administrative apparatuses that forge permanent ties with groups that are recipients of their decisions, while policy making is sectorialized into various different specialized policy areas. As a consequence of this conditioning, the activities of interest groups are channeled into different policy networks, each of which is made up of the public and private actors interested in formulating and implementing given policies.

The task of research is to examine and classify the different types of policy networks that pluralism and neo-corporatism, according to the policy network approach, erroneously reduce to a single typology of policy making. On the contrary, policy making is sectorialized into different areas of policy within which various policy networks may be active. These are differentiated depending on the number of actors, their stability, the degree of rigidity of their boundaries, and various other dimensions. Apart from the differences, the different types of policy networks also have some features in common: The actors cultivate nonhierarchical relations and promote interests that may at times be conflictual but are interdependent, because there is a mutually beneficial exchange of information, expertise, and, with time, trust.

The two most common types of policy networks are *policy communities* and *issue networks*. The former comprise a limited number of groups, are stable over time, have quite rigid boundaries, and are characterized by a consensual decision-making style and a fairly balanced internal distribution of power. By contrast, issue networks are fairly unstable, have uncertain boundaries, are potentially conflictual in terms of interaction, and have an unequal distribution of power.

The limitations of the policy network approach include the absence of shared definitions, the limited operational value of various dimensions used to distinguish the different types of network, the lack of attention devoted to conditions that might lead to the transformation of a network, and the failure to integrate it with any theory of the distribution of power. As regards this final point, however, it should be stressed that the policy network approach seems compatible with pluralism, not only because it admits the existence of an oligopolistic political market dominated by policy communities impenetrable to "unrecognized" groups but also because it emphasizes that policy networks are never entirely closed, that no one interest dominates broad areas of policy, and that policy making takes place within a variety of policy networks characterized by close relations between different interests and different government offices.

The theory of policy networks has the advantage of being a more precise analytic tool than the one proposed by the pluralists and neo-corporatists. What's more, it bridges the gap between studies on interest groups and those on public policies, sharing with the latter an interest in the characteristics of the social and temporal context in which groups operate. The attention to context has enabled the policy network approach to distinguish between issues that provide incentives for participation and those that mobilize a small number of actors. This in turn has made it possible to formulate some useful hypotheses about the differing propensities of groups to participate and the different levels of conflict within networks.

Historical Institutionalism

Historical institutionalism overturns the vision of the relations between interest groups and institutions delineated by pluralism and neo-pluralists who would like to see the state reinforced so as to avoid policy making being dominated by interest groups. Institutionalists hold that the margins for independent initiative on the part of interest groups are actually more limited than neo-pluralists believe, because lobbying must necessarily take place within existing political institutions. The possibility for groups to succeed in influencing public decision makers depends on the structure and functional logic of the institutions that offer highly conditioning restrictions and opportunities. If significant changes take place in institutions, interest groups are obliged to adapt to the new margins of initiative offered by the revamped institutions.

An example of the institutional conditioning of interest group activities is provided by Ellen Immergut in her comparative analysis of health reform policies adopted in three European nations.

Immergut points out that doctors' associations in France, Switzerland, and Sweden tried to prevent the expansion of state control over the medical profession and the establishment of a public health service. The numerous veto points posed by institutions in Switzerland and in France during the Fourth Republic enabled minority, but well-organized, groups to block legislative initiatives in favor of a public service. By contrast, the institutional situation in Sweden and during the Fifth Republic in France favored the formation of governments that were unconditioned by medical associations and their allies and that were thus able to introduce health reforms. Despite the novelty of its proposed analytic criteria, historic institutionalism is not an alternative approach to pluralism and its subsequent reworkings, because the relatively low number of research studies carried out do not provide adequate grounds for empirically justifying its explicative assumptions. Moreover, these do not appear to be entirely incompatible with the basic ideas of pluralism. Rather, they seem to be useful tools that can be used in the crowded field of neo-pluralist studies.

Interest Groups and Democracy

Can interest groups improve the quality of democracy and enhance the development of citizens' representation and good government? Groups promote democracy if they help citizens win better opportunities for representation. And they contribute to good government if they give citizens the possibility of preventing or punishing abuses of power by making governments accountable for their actions toward the political community.

Group Representation in Liberal Democracies

The interest group system favors political equality if it promotes wider representation, so as to prevent governments equipped with partial information about citizens' preferences from favoring the expectations of a minority. However, research conducted in the United States during the 20th century and the early 21st century demonstrates the existence of a permanent imbalance in representation, because business groups and professional associations find it easier to organize themselves than cause groups. They can act more rapidly when they feel threatened, and they represent people with a high social status, income, and education. They are also dominant in areas of policy that have particular strategic significance for the whole political community.

In Europe, a permanent representational imbalance has been detected both within the EU and in individual member states. Large economic groups occupy a preponderant position within European institutions, even though the number of organizations present in Brussels grew continually in the past 2 decades of the 20th century. In member states, permanent representational imbalances were generated by neo-corporatist experiments that benefited business groups and unions and marginalized less organized social categories from policy making. Permanent imbalances have also been detected in policy communities that are dominated by economic interest groups and are inaccessible to citizens.

Therefore, there is a good deal of converging empirical evidence suggesting that interest groups have a limited ability to favor balanced representation in the decision-making process. However, many scholars take a less negative view of the dynamics of representation, stressing that the characteristics of policy making vary in relation to time, area of policy, and the issue at stake. It may be that the relative degree of representational imbalance is more significant in a certain period in a specific area of policy and less so in the same area at a later time. Furthermore, certain decision-making processes prompt the mobilization of just one of the potential parties involved, while others generate disputes in which hundreds of interest groups take part. The variations in the number of actors participating in the decision-making process suggest that the imbalance is probably less uniform and rigid than it has frequently been made out to be and may be susceptible to attenuation.

Pluralists who have advanced such arguments support their case by pointing to the surge in political participation that took place during the collective movements that sprang up in the 1960s and 1970s. The increase in the number of groups also contributed to "opening up" policy communities, which is why the notion of issue networks was developed in the United States to emphasize that the number of actors participating in decision-making processes had grown. More in general, the crowding of the policy-making scene has also made the outcome of decisions more uncertain for business groups. Their omnipresence in the various decision-making arenas is not necessarily proof of their strength but may be the result of a defensive reaction to the wider range of public regulative interventions regarding issues directly affecting their interests. Moreover, the business community is also split by internal divisions that make problematic the formation of unified coalitions for promoting common lobbying strategies.

None of the criticisms leveled at the thesis of representational imbalance denies that it exists. Instead, they stress that this imbalance is an unavoidable result of group competition, and it may be mitigated when competition becomes greater. The debate on representational imbalance suggests that the system of interest groups is relatively open because it enables new actors to enter policy arenas, especially in periods of increased competition and allows many disparate interests to get a hearing from governments. Nevertheless, the group system is characterized by permanent imbalances that penalize citizens and the less organized associations. In this respect, they mirror existing inequalities in society.

Groups and Democratic Accountability

Various factors contribute to defining citizens' political judgment of governments. One of these is the degree of accountability of government action. In the liberal democracies, voters punish abuses of power by voting governments out of office or reelect them if they consider that the government has respected the law and acted in their interests. To monitor the actions of decision makers in the interval between elections, citizens rely on organizations, which are generally better equipped to ascertain when the abuse of power gets the better of responsibility.

The public organizations that monitor government actions are parliament, the judiciary, and various bureaucratic agencies. The most important private ones are the political parties, the media, and interest groups. The latter have an interest in preventing the abuse of power so as to ensure fair competition between all the players in the field and to avoid some groups obtaining an unfair advantage in the decision-making process. Moreover, groups are forced to follow the governmental process very closely because the final decisions on the different issues are highly unpredictable. This explains why researchers have discovered that a large part of group lobbying is devoted to the gathering of information in the face of uncertainty about the intentions of political elites and other players involved in the preparation of ongoing legislation. The need to achieve fair competition and to gather information for reducing their uncertainty about legislators' preferences makes interest groups a sort of watchdog of public officials. In this respect, there is more than a point of convergence among the groups' special interests and those of ordinary citizens for an effective control of decision makers.

But conversely, insofar as they represent particular interests, groups have also the temptation to cultivate confidential relations with governments, and this sometimes leads to collusion. When this happens, the correct functioning of the democratic process is compromised, because it induces decision makers to identify their public mission with the taking of decisions favorable to groups with which they are in collusion. The risk can be reduced when both the groups and governments operate within a system that has effective cross-checks. This works well in liberal democracies if there are strong political parties; a parliament that exercises its powers of control over the executive; an independent judicial system; an efficient, autonomous bureaucracy; and civil society and media that are autonomous from the state. What emerges from the above is that interest group competition enhances the development of open but permanently unbalanced political representation and that the contribution of interest groups to the control of political elites can be effective if carried out in the context of democratic regimes that exhibit high qualitative standards.

As a closing remark, it should be remembered that there are some findings that represent a largely uncontroversial view of interest groups' contribution to democracy. First of all, these judgments emphasize that groups offer significant opportunities for communicating with governments, enabling citizens to influence public decisions more effectively than if they acted individually and limited themselves to exercising their right to vote. In addition, the variety, number, and presence of groups at all levels of the government process guarantees the vitality and capacity for renewal of liberal democracies. Groups contribute by helping produce better citizens and motivating them to participate in elections and engage with issues of public interest. Moreover, the great diversity of views expressed by groups give governments an accurate picture of the worries and concerns of civil society, permitting minorities to voice certain of their key needs on specific issues that distracted majorities resulting from elections might otherwise neglect to represent. Finally, it should not be forgotten that, in collaboration with other political actors—public and private—groups can help create rights and obligations protected by the law and often provide expertise that contributes to improving the quality of policy making.

Liborio Mattina
University of Trieste
Trieste, Italy

See also Accountability; Collective Security; Democracy, Quality; Neo-Corporatism; Parties; Pluralism; Policy Network; Representation

Further Readings

Atkinson, M. M., & Coleman, W. D. (1989). Strong states and weak states: Sectoral policy networks in advanced capitalist economies. *British Journal of Political Science, 19,* 47–67.

Baumgartner, F. R., Berry, J. M., Hojnacki, M., Kimball, D. C., & Leech, B. L. (2009). *Lobbying and policy change: Who wins, who loses, and why.* Chicago: University of Chicago Press.

Baumgartner, F., & Leech, B. L. (1998). *Basic interests: The importance of groups in politics and in political science.* Princeton, NJ: Princeton University Press.

Grant, W. (1989). *Pressure groups, politics and democracy in Britain.* London: Philip Allen.

Heinz, J. P., Laumann, E. O., Nelson, R. L., & Salisbury, R. H. (1993). *The hollow core: Private interests in national policymaking.* Cambridge, MA: Harvard University Press.

Immergut, E. M. (1992). *Health politics: Interests and institutions in Western Europe.* Cambridge, UK: Cambridge University Press.

Lehmbruch, G., & Schmitter, P. C. (Eds.). (1982). *Patterns of corporatist policy-making.* London, Sage.

Lowi, T. J. (1969). *The end of liberalism.* New York: W. W. Norton.

Olson, M. (1965). *The logic of collective action.* New Haven, CT: Yale University Press.

Richardson, J., Gustafsson, G., & Jordan, G. (1982). The concept of policy style. In J. Richardson (Ed.), *Policy styles in Western Europe* (pp. 1–16). London: Allen & Unwin.

Salisbury, R. H. (1975). Interest groups. In F. I. Greenstein & N. W. Polsby (Eds.), *Handbook of political science* (Vol. 4, pp. 171–228). Reading, MA: Addison-Wesley.

Salisbury, R. H. (1984). Interest representation: The dominance of institutions. *The American Political Science Review, 78*(1), 64–76.

Thomas, C. S. (Ed.). (2004). *Research guide to U.S. and international interest groups.* London: Praeger.

Truman, D. B. (1951). *The governmental process.* New York: Knopf.

Wilson, J. Q. (1974). *Political organizations.* Princeton, NJ: Princeton University Press.

Intergovernmentalism

Intergovernmentalism seeks to understand the reasons why states join together and to provide a realistic approach to the analysis of regional integration mechanisms. It tries to overcome the contradiction between Hobbes's vision of a competition among sovereign states and the modern process of regional and global integration. This entry explores how this concept emerged in connection with European integration and has been expanded to analyze forms of political and economic cooperation more generally.

Intergovernmentalism first found expression in the 1960s in the work of Stanley Hoffmann, who took a realistic view of the construction of Europe. Hoffmann, who taught at Harvard and Sciences Po in Paris, attempted to explain why states as nationalistic as France could bring themselves to give up certain sovereign powers in order to promote the common market, while at the same time opposing the strategies of the European Commission (EC). European integration cannot be explained simply in terms of the neo-functionalist spillover effect, according to which successful integration opens the way for new cooperation. Although it is true that Europe developed from an initially common, then enlarged market, the single market was only created when the political decision to set up a single currency was made. Intergovernmentalism thus represented a criticism of both functionalist methods and institutionalist approaches. The former give priority to the process of integration, while the latter stress the significant role of institutions in governing interstate relations.

First, as regards the functionalist theories, it is clear that, as noted by Hoffmann, the interests of political elites do not necessarily coincide with those of the EC bureaucracy and that national elites may use their veto to block any transfer of power affecting their sovereignty; integration cannot be conceived of as a functional process that would be spontaneously built up, as postulated by functionalism. The Empty Chair Crisis, in which President Charles de Gaulle boycotted meetings of the Council of the EC in opposition to the EC's attempt to reduce the scope of application of the veto and increase the EC's own resources, and subsequently the Luxembourg Compromise that ended the crisis in 1966, deciding in favor of France and maintaining unanimity rule, symbolized this resilience of the state. Moreover, again in opposition to functionalism, not all sectors are integrated at the same rate. Some key matters remain within the exclusive domain of intergovernmental cooperation (the second pillar of the Public Environmental Center for Sustainable Development [PECSD], one of the constitutive pillars of the Union—as they were defined by the Treaty of Maastricht, which defied the European "architecture" in 1992—devoted here to defense and security), while others are governed by the simultaneous imperatives of cooperation and integration, as with the fourth pillar (economy and finance) in which the European Central Bank (in charge of integration) coexists with the Economic and Financial Affairs Council (Ecofin Council; in charge of cooperation).

As regards institutionalist approaches, intergovernmentalism suggests that international institutions favor negotiation by reducing transaction costs but that it is more effective in the technical fields of "low politics." In "high-politics" areas of sovereignty, including the most prestigious prerogatives of a sovereign state, states endeavor to protect their powers and thus delegate them with the greatest parsimony. There is, therefore, a major contradiction between technical matters that could be fully integrated and the more political matters in which cooperation requires unanimous agreement and recourse to the veto.

Intergovernmentalism therefore proposes an approach to regional integration through which states accept the principle of cooperation depending on which common interests are at stake. As Morten Kelstrup has shown, the realistic approach becomes compatible with regional integration that allows the sharing of common gains, and thus the external relationships of the states involved are strengthened. Not only do states have an interest in associating, they also remain the chief players in the cooperation or integration policy for this purpose. The successes of the European Union (EU) could thus be explained by the proper functioning of states capable of fostering the opening of civil society and waiving certain attributes of their sovereignty. Intergovernmentalism is therefore more directly concerned with the decision processes used by states in defining and then facing their interests before defining the area of agreement opened up by the relative powers of the parties.

Hence, the integration process must be based first on the awareness that neighboring states have converging interests, a fact that can be attributed to the accelerated maturity of an international anarchy in which sovereign states are in a free competition. In such conditions, interstate cooperation is envisaged as a rational solution to optimize the use of means pooled by the member states. This is why the veto was progressively dropped in favor of a decision-making mechanism via a qualified majority. Sovereignty did not disappear but instead became pooled sovereignty. The European Economic Community was thus envisaged as a multiplier of power for weakened states. The international organizations institutionalized the technique of interstate bargaining. Their decisions became the lowest common denominator on which states could agree. In this ongoing negotiation, the great powers took precedence, but all states were strengthened by their participation in the organization. Contrary to the functionalist or federalist theories, which postulate a metasovereign integration, intergovernmentalism thus suggested that the transfer of power strengthened states internationally and bolstered the political elites with respect to their domestic public opinion.

This initial approach was completed in the 1990s by Andrew Moravcsik, who developed the idea of liberal intergovernmentalism. Like Hoffmann, Moravcsik considered that the decisions of international organizations resulted from bargaining between rational states. The interest of this approach is its liberal aspect, which is revealed by national choices. States always seek to impose their national interests, but these are no longer envisaged purely through the reductionist view of general interest as embodied in a neutral power. On the contrary, the national preferences expressed by government members in regional organizations for cooperation or integration are the result of the demands of social players who have succeeded in imposing their opinions in national administrative and political circles. Liberal intergovernmentalism thus appears to be a method for combining Robert Putnam's internal and external levels and doubly strengthening governmental powers: The external constraints give the executive a means whereby to influence domestic public opinion, and the internal constraints are used to put pressure on the external partners that prefer to reach an agreement rather than face failure. The negotiation that could be complicated by this two-level game is in fact simplified by transparent institutional mechanisms that reduce the transaction costs, fostering trust by guaranteeing mutual respect, and turn out to be effective aids to decision making. Based on Nash's equilibrium, liberal intergovernmentalism explains why and how states manage to come to an agreement by reducing their demands out of fear of marginalization or fear that they will be held liable for failure. The result is that the state, and also the executive, is strengthened by participation in regional organizations of which it controls the agenda, the procedures, the information, and the instruments of legitimation.

Intergovernmentalism is not, however, the only explanation for the construction of Europe. First, it would be an exaggeration to suppose that the integration of the Old World was the sole initiative of the hard core of the EU, constituted by France and Germany. Although these countries played a major role, that should not obscure the fact that horizontal agreements were concluded between the smaller states to oppose this hegemony. Moreover, the United Kingdom balanced things out by backing agreements when it suited its interests. Moreover, while intergovernmentalism provides a good explanation for the role of states in intergovernmental conferences preparing the founding treaties of the EU, it should be noted that the Commission has the power of initiative and that, since the Single Act, which was concluded in 1986 to amend the Rome Treaty and deepen European integration, it is the Commission that has fixed the European agenda. The loss of influence of the Council of General Affairs and External Relations, which for many years was the political hub of Europe, and the rise in importance of the technical councils symbolize the rise of the experts who handle EU business day to day and apply the treaties. Nor is it enough to reduce Europe to the two-level game since, on the contrary, it demonstrates multilevel governance, by which many nonstate players are freed from state interference and develop multiple transnational cooperations that weaken the states. Finally, the overly positivist definition of national preferences taken into account by intergovernmentalism is also criticized by constructivist approaches.

The theory of intergovernmentalism also includes the realist school, which has markedly changed under the influence of these multiple instances of international cooperation. As a result, realism has been modified by four elements. First, the interstate relationship was revisited and appeared as more complex than the traditional jungle, now seen as a mixture of competition, cooperation, and friendship. Second, international anarchy has become the raison d'être of cooperation, since states seek to join forces in a threatening environment. Third, the ongoing bargaining between states provides a satisfactory answer to Joseph Grieco's question as to whether states refuse to conclude agreements from fear that their neighbor might obtain higher relative gains. Finally, intergovernmentalism has become part of a realism that has abandoned the former balance of power in favor of a balance of threat or balance of interests. This neoclassical realism is thus resolutely optimistic since, according to Charles Glazer, cooperation has become the instrument of self-help.

Jean-Jacques Roche
Université Panthéon-Assas
Paris, France

See also Cooperation; European Integration; Institutionalization; Multilevel Analysis; Realism in International Relations; Regionalism; Transaction Costs

Further Readings

Collard-Wesler, S. (2006). Integration under anarchy: Neorealism and the European Union. *European Journal of International Relations, 12*(3), 397–432.

Glazer, C. (1994). Realists as optimists: Cooperation as self-help. *International Security, 19*(3), 50–90.

Grieco, J. (1988). Anarchy and the limits of cooperation: A realist critique of the newest liberal institutionalism. *International Organization, 42,* 485–507.

Hoffmann, S. (1966). Obstinate or obsolete? The fate of the nation-state and the case of Western Europe. *Deadalus, 95,* 862–915.

Keohane, R. O., & Hoffmann, S. (Eds.). (1991). *The new European Community: Decision-making and institutional change.* Boulder, CO: Westview Press.

Moravcsik, A. (1993). Preference and power in the European community: A liberal intergovernmentalism approach. *International Organization, 45,* 19–56.

International Institutions

See International Organizations

International Justice

See International Law

International Law

International law is a system of law that is predominantly created by, and designed to govern the actions of, states. Public international law, the subject of this entry, can be distinguished from private international law, which addresses aspects of private legal relationships that span national borders. International law is a horizontal system of law in which states, at least in legal theory, enjoy sovereign equality. Lacking a legislative body or a law enforcement agency, international law functions very differently than a system of law in a modern liberal democracy. International law has grown enormously in scope and complexity since World War II. The number of states has expanded through decolonization and disintegration, international law has come to address a far wider range of subjects than ever before, and there has been a considerable increase in the number of international courts and tribunals. This entry first looks at how international law is created and enforced, and reviews some of the most significant recent developments in specific fields of international law, before considering competing explanations of the impact of international law on the behavior of states and the attitude toward international law of developing countries, the United States, Europe, and China.

Some scholars consider that the predictable patterns discernible in the interstate relations of the ancient world, including the Greek city-states and Mesopotamia, could be regarded as forerunners to the current system of international law, and systems of international law are also said to have developed in precolonial Africa and South Asia. The modern system of international law is, however, usually dated from the Peace of Westphalia of 1648, and the term *international law* did not come into use until the late 18th century. By the 20th century, international law had evolved into a global system of law. There are contrasting views as to the political significance of the contemporary system. Since the emergence of international relations as a field of study in the early 20th century, the dominant realist paradigm has downplayed the impact of international law on the course of world events. Liberalism assumes an important role for international law as an agent of world peace, but World War II stymied hopes that international law could triumph over military might, especially where accompanied by a political determination to use violence. As international law continues to grow in sophistication, so we are seeing more nuanced theoretical approaches to explicating its impact.

Sources of International Law

There are at least three ways in which the term *source* is used in relation to international law.

Legal Positivism and the Source of Legal Obligation

States have a legal obligation to comply with international law. The theoretical source of this obligation is state consent. Legal positivism, the philosophical foundation of international law since the 19th century, assumes that law is made through human agency as opposed to deriving from the metaphysical or religious realms. States are bound by international law because they have agreed to be bound by that law. Although legal positivism underpins the "real world" of international law, it has plenty of critics in the academy, who regard it as inadequate for the contemporary world. Particularly in the 1990s, much of the scholarship critical of legal positivism and the system of international law founded on legal positivism went under the banners of "critical international legal studies" and "new approaches to international law." This scholarship emphasized the indeterminacy of legal argument and found fault with legal positivism for not taking sufficient account of the role of nonstate actors, the concerns of women, those in postcolonial societies, and indigenous peoples. Heightened awareness of the masculinist bias of international law has given rise to changes in specific fields of international law, including refugee law and international humanitarian law. Liberal scholarship in international law emphasizes the plurality of actors in the international sphere, including transnational networks of judges and government officials.

Formal Sources

The formal sources specify the ways in which international law is made. Article 38 of the Statute of the International Court of Justice, which sets out the sources of international law that the Court is to apply, is usually understood more generally as a statement of the formal sources of international law. Although the statute specifies no hierarchy, the order in which the three sources are listed provides a guide as to the relative practical importance of each source. Listed first are conventions, or treaties, which are legally binding agreements between states and, to a lesser extent, between states and intergovernmental organizations. Second is customary international law. States create custom through their actions, where that practice is accompanied by *opinio juris*, a belief that international law requires the state to behave in that way. The third of the formal sources is general principles of international law. The formal sources of international law permit us to distinguish between rules, principles, and concepts that are, strictly speaking, part of international law and those that are not. Article 38 also specifies two subsidiary means for determining what international law permits or does not permit on a certain subject. These are the writings of distinguished international lawyers and judgments of international courts and tribunals.

Material Sources

If the formal sources elucidate the ways in which international law can be made, the material sources are the specific documents in which a particular point of law is set out—the Charter of the United Nations (UN) or a resolution of the General Assembly, for example. To state that a text constitutes a material source of international law is not to assume that it has legal status as a formal source of international law: The material source may have set out a rule that then becomes binding through another process.

Change Within International Law

The doctrine of sources suggests the processes by which international law evolves. There is no single formal source of international law that serves as the motor of change. International customary law is often codified into treaties. The Third UN Convention on the Law of the Sea, for example, put into written form international law that had already emerged in custom. Usually in such cases, however, the treaty not only codifies custom but also represents the "progressive development" of international law; through this process, international law is updated. Two general principles of law are relevant here: Where the terms of two material sources of international law appear contradictory, the more recent prevails, and where apparently contradicting law can be found both in specific and broadly applicable instruments, the more specific overrides the more general.

Compliance and Enforcement of International Law

Compliance with international law is aided by the fact that, at least in theory, states choose the law to which they wish to be bound. States are not bound by a rule of customary law if they have been persistently objecting to the emergent rule, although, in practice, the crystallization of a rule may be clear only in retrospect. States are bound only by those treaties to which they agree to be bound. Participants in treaty negotiations have an opportunity to help shape the terms of the agreement, although in large-scale negotiations the impact of any one delegation may not be as significant as the theory of state consent might suggest. Compliance with international law is also enhanced by the fact that multilateral treaties commonly permit reservations, which allow states to exclude from their undertakings any provisions with which they disagree. Even those states that have signed a treaty can choose not to proceed to ratify and hence not be bound by the final text of the treaty. The fact that international law is a horizontal system means that one of the most important factors promoting compliance is reciprocity: If one party to a conflict treats the prisoners of war of the other combatant according to international humanitarian law, it is much more likely that its own nationals will in turn be treated appropriately.

There are two alternative approaches to maximizing compliance with international law, and each has its supporters within the academy. One approach takes as its starting point the assumption that states have a propensity to comply and generally only fail to do so when there are financial or bureaucratic impediments. This, the managerial approach, is associated with the writing of Abram Chayes and Antonia Handler Chayes (1995) and emphasizes the continuity of policy choices, to which changes are made only incrementally when perceived as necessary. The second approach is that of enforcement, by which it is assumed that states will only comply where they see a direct benefit from doing so. If a decision to comply is the product of a cost–benefit analysis on the part of national decision makers, rates of compliance should be significantly affected by the presence or absence of enforcement mechanisms. In practice, most fields of international law contain elements of both the "carrot" and the "stick" approach.

There are several methodological problems associated with attempting to determine with precision the rate of compliance with international law—most basically, the fact that there may not be a clear divide between compliance and noncompliance. Many treaty provisions are worded in such a way that it is a matter of interpretation as to whether a particular party has complied with its obligations. It is not difficult to assess whether a state has or has not complied with an obligation to submit a report on its implementation of a human rights treaty, for example, but it may be more difficult to assess on the basis of that report whether the state has implemented the treaty fully, in both letter and spirit.

A notable feature of the system of international law over recent decades has been the growth in the number of international courts and courtlike bodies. Historically, states—or at least their decision-making elite—have been far from keen on the idea of being required to abide by the outcome of a third-party decision in relation to issues with high political stakes. The dispute resolution process within the World Trade Organization stands out because it is compulsory. Any member state that believes that another member has breached an agreement can initiate a case. The dispute is heard by a panel whose report is then adopted by the Dispute Resolution Body unless there is a consensus against adoption. Appeals are heard by an appellate body. Should a member not comply with the outcome of this process, retaliatory trade sanctions may be imposed. Despite the fact that a considerable proportion of trade disputes are settled informally, there is strong scholarly interest in the workings of the dispute resolution process because its establishment in an intergovernmental organization with such large membership is a historically significant development.

The two international courts with the greatest potential impact on world politics are the International Court of Justice (ICJ) and the International Criminal Court (ICC).

The International Court of Justice

The ICJ is one of the principal organs of the UN. The ICJ can hear cases on any subject matter brought to the Court by states, so long as it finds that the states concerned have consented to the jurisdiction of the Court. Expressions of consent may have been open-ended or relate only to the case in question. The Court can issue an order for provisional measures—the equivalent of an interim injunction—which are designed to protect the rights of parties during the period before the Court decides on the case itself. The Court has averaged less than three cases per year but has become increasingly busy in recent years. States have complied with the judgments of the Court in a majority of, though not all, contentious cases, but compliance with provisional measures has not been good. In its 2001 decision in the *LaGrand* Case, the Court confirmed that orders of the Court indicating provisional measures are binding. Should a party to a dispute heard by the Court not comply with the decision of the Court, the other party/parties may request the assistance of the Security Council in obtaining compliance. This would clearly politicize the question and would not be useful if the grievance were against one of the permanent members of the Security Council. The Council has never formally declared that it is acting to enforce a decision of the ICJ.

In addition to hearing contentious cases brought by states, the ICJ can respond to requests by certain bodies within the UN for advisory opinions. These are nonbinding responses to questions of law. Examples include the 1995 opinion on the legality of the threat of use of nuclear weapons and the 2003 opinion on the legal consequences of the construction of a wall in the occupied Palestinian territory.

The International Criminal Court

The establishment of the ICC in 1998 was one of the most momentous international law developments of the late 20th century. The ICC exercises jurisdiction over individuals who commit serious breaches of international law through the crimes of genocide, war crimes, and/or crimes against humanity, and it will have jurisdiction over the crime of aggression once a definition of the crime has been agreed on. A key principle in the statute is that of complementarity; the ICC was not intended to replace national courts but to operate in situations in which states are either unable or unwilling to act. The ICC is set to have significant political impact, in large part because, despite its having jurisdiction over individuals rather than states, this necessarily gives rise to broader political implications. This is particularly evident in the case of aggression. Aggression was included in the Statute of the ICC at the insistence of developing countries, but there was no agreement during the negotiations as to how aggression was to be defined. Historically, aggression has been considered a crime committed by states, but the Nuremburg and Tokyo tribunals after World War II declared that individuals were accountable for crimes against peace. It would be very difficult for the Court to find that an individual had committed the crime of aggression without passing judgment on the actions of the state in question.

The issue is similar in relation to the trigger mechanisms by which a case can be brought before the Court. A situation may be referred to the ICC Prosecutor by a state party or initiated by the prosecutor with the authorization of a pretrial chamber. In both these situations, the state in whose territory the conduct in question occurred or of which the person accused of the crime is a national must have given its consent. A situation can also be referred to the prosecutor by the Security Council, and if brought by this means, the Court will have jurisdiction even if the crime was committed in a nonstate party by a national of a nonstate party and in the absence of consent by the territorial state or the state of nationality of the accused. The United States has not become a party to the statute of the Court, one of its principal objections being that, contrary to the principle of state consent, the Court can hear a case against an individual whose country is not party to the statute. The United States did not, however, veto Security Council Resolution 1593 (2005), which referred the situation in Darfur to the ICC despite Sudan being a nonparty to the statute. The first four situations referred to the Court were all African.

The ICC complements the work of national courts as well as other types of bodies, including criminal courts established on an ad hoc basis and truth and reconciliation commissions. Truth commissions have no prosecutorial powers and are not courts. They attempt to acknowledge and document a history of human rights abuses within a particular country or area—often those that took place under a regime, or during a period of turmoil or civil war—as a step toward healing wounds within that society. They represent a midpoint between a blanket amnesty for perpetrators of human rights and international humanitarian law violations and formal criminal trial. More than 20 truth commissions have been established since 1970, including in Uganda, Nepal, and South Africa. Both a Truth and Reconciliation Commission and a special court established jointly by the Government of Sierra Leone and the UN operated concurrently in Sierra Leone in the wake of its civil war. Other ad hoc tribunals include the International Criminal Tribunal for the former Yugoslavia and the International Criminal Tribunal for Rwanda. Both Timor and Cambodia have hybrid courts in which criminal justice is being pursued through what can be understood as internationalized domestic courts.

The Substantive Content of International Law

International law can be divided into a number of overlapping subfields or regimes. While this is useful as a way of classifying the vast and growing amount of international law, it should be remembered that any single material source may well have relevance to more than one of these fields. Enforcement methods vary between fields and in their mix of carrot and stick approaches.

International Law and the Use of Force

This field of international law specifies the circumstances under which a state may or may not use force against another state. One of the most striking features of the current system of international law is its incorporation of a general prohibition on the threat and use of force in interstate relations. The Covenant of the League of Nations attempted to delay and, if possible, avoid a state resorting to war, but the Charter of the UN goes further and permits states to use force only in self-defense or if authorized to do so by the Security Council. The Charter recognizes the inherent right of a state to self-defense if it is a victim of an armed attack. Having responded in self-defense, the state concerned is expected to report its actions to the Security Council, and it is assumed that the Security Council will then take appropriate action. Although the initial plan was for individual states to make military forces available to the UN, this has not occurred, and in practice, the Council authorizes others to use force on its behalf. What had previously been regarded as the sovereign right of a state to choose to go to war in pursuit of its political objectives was removed by the Charter and in its place was established a system of collective security in which the whole international community is to work together to prevent, and respond to, threats to international peace and security.

The international law of the use of force is not so clear as to how states should respond to acts of violence by nonstate actors, including terrorists. Nor is it well equipped to deal with internal wars. The Charter of the UN upheld sovereignty as a fundamental principle of the international system; according to Article 2(7), the UN is not to interfere in the domestic affairs of states. While a strong affirmation of sovereignty is welcome from the perspective of a developing country being able to strengthen its position against external meddling in its political and economic affairs, it is less useful in safeguarding human rights. This raises the controversial question of the legality of humanitarian intervention. Although the vast majority of international lawyers would agree that humanitarian intervention authorized by the Security Council in response to a threat to international security is legal, only a few believe that contemporary international law permits unilateral acts of humanitarian intervention. Those who do believe that humanitarian intervention is not covered by the general prohibition on the use of force in Article 2(4) of the UN Charter generally seek support for their views in international customary law.

International legal scholarship in this field examines particular instances of the use of force to assess their legality and any likely possible impact on customary international law. In recent years, for example, a focus on the legality of the North Atlantic Treaty Organization's (NATO's) use of force during the Kosovo crisis was followed by debate regarding Operation Enduring Freedom as a response to the terrorist attacks of September 11, 2001, and the scope for a state to justify the use of military force in response to a terrorist attack as a valid act of self-defense. Such debate was then overshadowed by the 2003 Iraq War, which most legal scholars deem to have been illegal. While the United States, the United Kingdom (UK), and Australia claimed to derive authority for their use of force from Security Council Resolution 678 (1990), the vast majority of international lawyers question the assertion that Iraqi noncompliance with Security Council Resolution 687 (1991) could have reactivated the Council's authorization for the First Gulf War. Indeed, both the United States and the UK had written letters to the Council regarding Security Council Resolution 1441 (2002), in which they emphasized that any further Iraqi noncompliance would need to be considered again by the Council.

One of the criticisms most commonly leveled at international law within political science is its apparent inability to enforce rules, particularly those concerning the use of force, against the most powerful. This was a recognized weakness of the UN Charter from its earliest days. Security Council enforcement can ensure compliance on the part of less powerful states and those without an ally among the permanent members of the Council, but international law arguably relies on "carrots" to ensure the compliance of the most powerful. The illegality of the 2003 invasion of Iraq became so clear that, for example, it served to delegitimize and weaken international support for U.S. foreign policy.

International Economic Law

International economic law (IEL) regulates international economic activity. While many aspects of international law have economic implications, IEL is generally understood as incorporating those legal regimes with the most direct economic consequences, such as the international law of trade, investment, currency, and finance. The growth of this field of international law is reflected in the establishment in 2008 of a Society of International Economic Law. International trade law is the most developed branch of IEL. The breakdown of the Doha Round of negotiations in the World Trade Organization and the associated turn to bilateral and regional trade negotiating processes is one of the most significant recent developments in IEL.

For many years, few other than the specialists kept track of what was happening in the periodic negotiating rounds of the General Agreement on Tariffs and Trade and the World Trade Organization. The protests at the 1999 ministerial meeting in Seattle marked a new era. The International Monetary Fund, World Bank, and World Trade Organization have moved to enhance their accountability through increased transparency, and some legal scholars are promoting the need to develop a body of international administrative law to address governance questions in intergovernmental institutions. IEL regulates multinational corporations only indirectly, and developing countries have since at least the 1970s called for more effective regulation of the behavior of multinational corporations, especially in relation to human rights and environmental matters.

International Environmental Law

As a field of international law, international environmental law is relatively recent. Key global treaties include the 1985 Vienna Convention for the Protection of the Ozone Layer and its 1987 Montreal Protocol, the 1992 UN Framework Convention on Climate Change and its 1997 Kyoto Protocol, the 1992 Convention on Biological Diversity, and the 2001 Stockholm Convention on Persistent Organic Pollutants. Climate change is arguably the most significant issue in international environmental law today, with considerable scholarly focus being directed toward the architecture of the post-Kyoto regime and the implications of climate change for other fields of international law, including the international law of human rights and the law of the sea.

There are clear implications of measures taken to protect the environment for international economic relations, and from the perspective of a developing country, this field of law has often been criticized for perpetuating Western colonial dominance. Where an environmental issue—such as ozone depletion—is of a truly global nature, developing countries have, however, found themselves in a stronger negotiating position and able to secure differentiated responsibilities. Types of differentiated responsibilities have included, inter alia, those that distinguish between industrial and developing countries with respect to the central obligations contained in the treaty and those addressing aspects of implementation, such as delayed compliance schedules, and financial and technological assistance.

The Law of the Sea

This is a far older branch of international law and addresses all aspects of ocean use. Historically, customary international law evolved to address navigation and fishing. One of the most fundamental principles in the law of the sea is that of the "freedom of the seas," by which the oceans are a global commons available for use by all. Naval powers—the United States now as with the UK before it—emphasize the importance of this principle. Over time, however, coastal states have increased the extent of their regulatory reach into the oceans adjacent to their territory. The primary material source of international law on the oceans is the 1982 Third UN Convention on the Law of the Sea, which entered into force in 1994 and sets out just who has what sort of rights in which parts of the ocean and seabed. It defines a number of zones, including those of the territorial sea, continental shelf, and exclusive economic zone. The United States has not ratified the Convention but respects most of its provisions, which are also found in customary international law. Topical within the study of the law of the sea in recent years have been questions of maritime boundary determination, protection of fish stocks from overfishing, delimiting the outer edge of the continental shelf, and maritime security. Climate change is raising new questions, including those relating to the melting of polar ice and the future of the maritime zones associated with states that may disappear as sea levels rise.

International Human Rights Law

International human rights law (IHRL) is concerned primarily with the protection of individuals from threats to their human rights stemming from the state. The Universal Declaration of Human Rights, together with the International Covenant on Civil and Political Rights and the International Covenant on Economic and Social Rights together make up what is informally referred to as the International Bill of Rights. There are a considerable number of more specific human rights treaties at a global level, including the 1951 Convention Relating to the Status of Refugees, the 1965 International Convention on the Elimination of all Forms of Racial Discrimination, the 1979 Convention on the Elimination of all Forms of Discrimination against Women, the 1989 Convention on the Rights of the Child, and the 2006 Convention on the Rights of Persons with Disabilities. Global IHRL is complemented by many regional treaties.

Human rights law has traditionally assumed a distinction between public and private spheres of human activity and focused on the first of these to the detriment of those who suffer human rights abuses in the private sphere. Recent years have seen increased recognition within IHRL of the need to increase human rights accountability for corporations, international organizations, multilateral development banks, multinational peacekeeping operations, and individuals. Compliance mechanisms in IHRL often consist of a regularized collection of self-reported data, with review by an international committee. The number of human rights treaties continues to increase, but the focus has shifted to the need to work for better compliance with existing human rights treaties rather than their continued proliferation.

International Humanitarian Law

International humanitarian law (IHL), also known as the international law of armed conflict, addresses human rights in wartime and thus overlaps with IHRL as well as with international criminal law. Traditional means of ensuring compliance with IHL include appeals by the International Committee of the Red Cross, prosecution before international tribunals, training programs in military academies, and condemnation by other states. The war on terror launched by the Bush administration gave extra vigor to debate regarding the relevance of IHL to conflicts involving fighters not representing states and a perceived need to rethink ways of ensuring respect for IHL. The increasing privatization of war has also raised questions regarding the IHL accountability of private security firms.

International Criminal Law

International criminal law (ICL) overlaps both IHRL and IHL as well as other fields such as the law of the sea—consider, for example, the crime of piracy. Transnational offences addressed by international criminal law include drug trafficking, money laundering, and cybercrime. Some actions are specified as international crimes in the relevant treaty. Article 1 of the 1948 Convention on the Prevention and Punishment of the Crime of

Genocide states in that the Contracting Parties "confirm that genocide, whether committed in time of peace or in time of war, is a crime under international law which they undertake to prevent and to punish." Other treaties, including the 1984 Convention Against Torture and Other Cruel, Inhuman, or Degrading Treatment or Punishment, do not explicitly describe the conduct in question as an international crime but require all parties to make the offence a crime in national law and/or to prosecute or extradite the alleged offender.

There is no agreed definition of terrorism in international law, but a number of counterterrorism conventions have been negotiated in response to particular forms and acts of terrorism. These include the 1979 International Convention Against the Taking of Hostages, the 1998 UN Convention for the Suppression of Terrorist Bombings, and the 2000 UN Convention for the Suppression of the Financing of Terrorism. Most counterterrorism conventions define the elements of the offence and incorporate provisions requiring the state in which an alleged offender is found to proceed with extradition or prosecution.

The Impact of International Law on the Behavior of States

Amazing as it may seem to most international lawyers, political scientists are divided over whether international law does or does not influence the way in which states conduct their affairs, particularly as regards the "high-politics" issues of war versus peace and even in relation to "middle-range" political issues in which some degree of national interest is at stake. Fundamental questions concerning state behavior in relation to international law necessarily reflect broader theoretical positions regarding the relationship of international law to world politics. At the time when the discipline of international relations emerged after World War I, liberal internationalists painted a picture of the possibility of a world in which war was not inevitable and promoted international law and institutions as the way to achieve such a world. The idealists shared a moralistic, optimistic outlook on world affairs. The establishment of the League of Nations and the Permanent Court of International Justice could be regarded as embodiments of this idealist perspective. But as the inevitability of world war became apparent in the late 1930s, Edward Hallett Carr spoke out against what by then appeared to be the utopian dreams of the liberal internationalists. In *The Twenty Years' Crisis, 1919–1939*, Carr claimed that it is not that ethics and international law have no place in world politics but that the bottom line is always power.

World War II ushered in an era in which realism dominated the discipline. The United States has functioned as the hegemon of the international relations discipline since World War II, and in the United States, the discipline of international relations is firmly embedded in political science (rather than, e.g., history or philosophy). The leading postwar U.S. realist, Hans Morgenthau, had been disillusioned by the failure of international law to prevent World War II, and the focus of classical realism on power politics and national interest typically leaves little room for international law. Where realists do refer to international law, it is generally to downplay any independent influence of international law on the course of world politics. Realists believe that they deal with the world as it really is rather than as it ought to be.

The seeming mismatch between the hard-line approach of Cold War realism and the reality as lived by government international lawyers encouraged some lawyers to seek to demonstrate that international law did have a real-world impact. One approach was to recount the experiences of foreign policy legal advisers. It appears that there is a wide range of experiences here, from being intimately involved in the decision-making process, as was the case in the United States during the Cuban Missile Crisis, to not even being consulted before a major policy decision with legal ramifications is taken. The role of foreign policy legal advisers can be characterized as generally being that of a neutral professional when first asked for advice on the legality of a proposed course of action, with that role shifting to one of a policy advocate once a policy decision has been taken.

Another approach toward demonstrating the relevance of international law was to speak in terms of the "functions" or "roles" of international law. U.S. scholars tended to focus on crisis situations, at which times international law was shown to be valuable in choosing between and legitimizing policy options and in providing language and institutions through which the parties could communicate with each other. Hedley Bull, associated with the so-called English School of International Relations, believed that despite the anarchical nature of the international system, there is such a thing as international society. According to Bull (1994), international law serves to identify the idea of a society of sovereign states, state the basic rules of coexistence, and help mobilize compliance with the rules of international society. International lawyers, and those international relations scholars with an interest in international law, have generally not needed to justify their respect for international law as much in the UK and Europe as in the United States.

Regime theory flourished in the United States and elsewhere in the 1980s and early 1990s. Regime theory began as an approach to analyzing processes of international cooperation that may or may not incorporate a formal organizational structure of which the particular focus of much research was the General Agreement on Tariffs and Trade. Recognizing that intangibles are integral to processes of formalized and less formal processes of international cooperation, regime theorists referred to norms, principles, rules, and decision-making procedures. The fact that international regimes are generally founded by multilateral treaty opened up possibilities for interdisciplinary cooperation, although there is no single regime theory approach to international law because the regime vehicle has been used by theorists across the spectrum, including those of an essentially realist persuasion.

The primary ongoing use of regime theory is in relation to questions of regime design and effectiveness in the study of environmental cooperation. Even perfect compliance may not mean that a treaty is effective if the provisions it contains are inadequate to meet the objectives for which it was established. It is generally accepted, for example, that even if all parties were to fully comply with their Kyoto commitments, the emissions reduction targets in the treaty were inadequate to make a significant impact on the problem. Names associated with regime theory include Kenneth Abbott, Stephen Krasner, Duncan Snidal, Volker Rittberger, Jørgen Wettestad, and Oran Young.

From the perspective of those who view international law as a largely coherent system of law, much of the international relations literature that does recognize norms—including within a regime framework—remains inadequate because it does not attempt to distinguish a legal norm from any other norm. In 2000, a special issue of the U.S. journal *International Organization* presented a framework within which to analyze "legalization," the increasing amount of law evident in international institutions and process. Current research questions on legalization include those of its causes and consequences and why it is that governments favor legalization in some institutions, issue areas, and regions more than in others. Europe, for example, is much more highly legalized than some other regions of the world.

In recent years, scholarship on the political functioning of international law has been influenced by constructivism. Although, as with realism and liberalism, there are many variants of constructivism, they share a perspective on norms and identity as central to the social and political sphere. Constructivists break down the divide between social structures and agency, regarding structure as being continually recreated by agency, just as norms create identity and expectations. Constructivists acknowledge the interrelationship between international law and world politics. They do not deny the functions of international law as identified by liberals but more consciously point to international law as having a socially constitutive function.

The Global Distribution of Power and Attitudes Toward International Law

Many of the most ardent advocates of international law have been inspired by the ideal of a rule of law functioning in the international sphere to the benefit of all states and people. Given the increasing scope and complexity of international law in the early years of the 21st century, it is thus timely to consider the attitude toward international law of those most and least powerful in the international political system.

Developing Countries and International Law

The rapid process of decolonization resulted in many new states joining the system of international law as political and legal entities in their own right. Acutely aware that their formal legal equality as sovereign states did not equate with economic equality, these states in the 1970s launched a campaign for a New International Economic Order (NIEO). The NIEO agenda included recognition of the right of every country to adopt the economic and social system that it deems most appropriate for its own development, full permanent sovereignty of every state over its natural resources and all economic activities, and the regulation and supervision of the activities of transnational corporations. The campaign failed, although a number of its elements have resurfaced in other contexts. Developing countries are finding new levels of negotiating weight in areas in which their consent and participation are essential to the industrialized world, including in global environmental regimes. Although they have not yet been able to steer the international economic agenda in the direction that they would like it to go, developing countries are now more able to recognize the implications and resist some of the demands of the developed world. It is, nevertheless, necessary to distinguish among developing countries. While the leading developing countries are increasingly becoming active participants in international dispute resolution bodies and in the development of new legal regimes, the least developed simply do not have the legal expertise and financial resources at their disposal to play a full role in international law.

There remains a clear North American and European dominance in international legal scholarship, but there have been a number of influential international lawyers who have voiced a developing world perspective on international law. Most of these scholars prefer to retain the term *Third World*. Some of those who established a strong tradition of Third World scholarship on international law include Georges Abi-Saab, Francisco Garcia-Amador, R. P. Anand, Mohammed Bedjaoui, and Taslim Elias. In recent years, a number of scholars, including Anthony Anghie, B. S. Chimni, Makau Mutua, and B. Rajagopal, have self-identified their work as TWAIL or Third World Approaches to International Law. They have been influenced by postcolonial theory and critical approaches to international law and have contributed to reinvigorated interest in the history of the discipline and its subject matter. TWAIL scholars have emphasized that colonialism was not simply an unfortunate episode in the history of international law but rather constitutive of international law and that international law cannot be separated from its colonial past.

The United States and International Law

The United States played a leading role in establishing most of the key institutions that make up the contemporary international order, including those of the UN, the Nuclear Non-Proliferation regime, and the General Agreement on Tariffs and Trade. From 2001 to 2009, under President George W. Bush, the United States came under considerable criticism for what was seen as an increased tendency toward unilateralism and associated decline in support for international law and institutions. Evidence for this charge included U.S. failure to support the International Criminal Court, the Kyoto Protocol, and the Comprehensive Nuclear Test Ban Treaty. Some practices of the United States for which it came under criticism, such as that of ratifying human rights treaties only to the extent that their provisions corresponded with rights already existing within the U.S. legal system, were not new to the Bush administration. President Barack Obama, elected to office in 2008, recognized that his administration would need to work hard to restore the reputation of the United States so far as its commitment to international law and institutions was concerned. To further this goal, at the time of this writing, the Obama administration was seeking Senate approval for ratification of the Comprehensive Nuclear Test Ban Treaty.

Europe and International Law

Europe was the birthplace of modern international law. During the administration of George W. Bush, some observers contrasted what appeared to be strong European support for international law with the more instrumentalist approach of the United States. The United States was accused of using international law as a tool when it chose to do so, without lending its weight to strengthening universal support for human rights and respect for the international rule of law as something far greater than a U.S. policy tool. The allegedly undesirable U.S. attitude toward international law can be seen reflected in several strands of U.S. scholarship, including recent applications to international law of rational choice and game theory that purport to prove that international law serves as no more than a weak exogenous constraint on state action. And yet, if the U.S. attitude is attributable to its position of hegemony, so could European attitudes be interpreted as a product of relative power. From this perspective, Europe has been determined to shore up its moral and legal weight because it is unable to match the United States in terms of sheer military and economic muscle. Setting aside transatlantic tensions, it cannot be denied that the European Union has a highly effective legal system and the most highly developed system of human rights protection in the world and that Europe remains a bastion of intellectual support for an international law that purports to be of universal value.

China and International Law

With its rising power, China and its attitude toward international law are subjects of increasing interest and speculation. In common with most developing countries, China places greater emphasis on sovereignty than does the rhetoric of Western liberal democracy, but China has nevertheless been supportive of multilateralism and collective security. Some critical commentators see China as drawing on its dual identities of major power and developing country to accept many of the benefits of its increasing economic weight without an associated cost. Cynics also suggest that the apparent commitment of China to multilateralism may be a function of its relative power, a strategy to be pursued until China's position in the international order is such that it can operate unilaterally if it so chooses. And yet, particularly given that nondemocratic countries are generally assumed less likely than democratic countries to uphold international law, China's attitude toward international law and the extent of its integration into the international system have been noteworthy.

Increasing Complexity and Possible Fragmentation of International Law

International law is transforming from a minimalist body of law addressing selected aspects of interstate relations toward a much more dense web of law affecting all aspects and levels of governance and under increasing pressure to tackle issues of normative and institutional hierarchy. Some fields of international law, notably IHRL, do not seek to regulate the external conduct of states but set standards for the internal functioning of states, and international law is thereby permeating domestic legal systems to an increasing degree. The growth in the number of international courts and courtlike bodies is creating the potential for states to "forum shop" as well as for competition between legal regimes. Tensions between, for example, international trade and human rights or the environment may be exacerbated by the degree to which the state's actions in one of the regimes in question—in this case, trade—are subjected to third-party dispute resolution.

One contemporary approach to international law and its place within world politics that is arguably responding to the growing complexity and centrality to world politics of international law is that of international constitutionalism. Writers on international constitutionalism have in common the use of constitutional language derived from the domestic context to interpret the growing complexity of the contemporary system of international law and its constituent regimes. While the language of constitution has long been used within international law—the Third United Nations Law of the Sea Convention has often been referred to as a "constitution for the oceans," for example—the constitutional metaphor is now being employed much more tightly and, in many cases, with a more clearly normative agenda.

Theorists differ as to the extent to which international law is able to function independently of the international distribution of power, but few, if any, would claim that it could disengage completely from fundamental geopolitical shifts in the balance of power. This suggests that with the rise of Asia, including China and India, international law is set to undergo further significant change in the 21st century.

Shirley V. Scott
University of New South Wales
Sydney, New South Wales, Australia

See also Compliance; Constructivism in International Relations; Idealism in International Relations; International Organizations; International Regimes; International Society; Liberalism in International Relations; United Nations

Further Readings

Anghie, A. (2005). *Imperialism, sovereignty and the making of international law.* Cambridge, UK: Cambridge University Press.

Armstrong, D. (Ed.). (2009). *Routledge handbook of international law.* Milton Park, UK: Routledge.

Armstrong, D., Farrell, T., & Lambert, H. (2007). *International law and international relations.* Cambridge, UK: Cambridge University Press.

Barker, J. C. (2000). *International law and international relations.* London: Continuum.

Bull, H. (1994). *The anarchical society: A study of order in world politics* (3rd ed.). New York: Columbia University Press.

Byers, M. (Ed.). (2001). *The role of law in international politics: Essays in international relations and international law.* Oxford, UK: Oxford University Press.

Carr, E. H. (1939). *The twenty years' crisis, 1919–1939: An introduction to the study of international relations.* London: Macmillan.

Chayes, A., & Chayes, A. H. (1995). *The new sovereignty: Compliance with international regulatory agreements.* Cambridge, MA: Harvard University Press.

Goldsmith, J. L., & Posner, E. A. (2005). *The limits of international law.* Oxford, UK: Oxford University Press.

Goldstein, J. L., Kahler, M., Keohane, R. O., & Slaughter, A., (Eds.). (2001). *Legalization and world politics.* Cambridge: MIT Press.

Henkin, L. (1979). *How nations behave: Law and foreign policy.* New York: Columbia University Press.

Kent, A. (2007). *Beyond compliance: China, international organizations, and global security.* Stanford, CA: Stanford University Press.

McCorquodale, R. (2007). An inclusive international legal system. *Leiden Journal of International Law, 17,* 477–504.

Raustiala, K., & Slaughter, A. (2002). International law, international relations and compliance. In W. Carlsnaes, T. Risse, & B. A. Simmons (Eds.), *Handbook of international relations* (pp. 538–558). London: Sage.

Reus-Smit, C. (Ed.). (2004). *The politics of international law.* Cambridge, UK: Cambridge University Press.

Sands, P. (2005). *Lawless world: America and the making and breaking of global rules.* Camberwell, Victoria, Australia: Allen Lane.

Scott, S. V. (2004). *International law in world politics: An introduction.* Boulder, CO: Lynne Rienner.

Slaughter, A. (2004). *A new world order.* Princeton, NJ: Princeton University Press.

United Nations. (1948). *Convention on the prevention and punishment of the crime of genocide.* Retrieved December 15, 2010, from http://www.hrweb.org/legal/genocide.html

Yasuaki, O. (2005). International law in and with international politics: Functions of international law in international society. *European Journal of International Law, 14,* 105–130.

International Monetary Fund (IMF)

The International Monetary Fund (IMF) is a voluntary organization of 187 member countries that operates as a major multilateral institution. Its goals include promoting international monetary cooperation and stability of the exchange rate, thus aiding the expansion of international trade and economic well-being of its member states.

In March 2010, the European Union decided that there might be a need to call the IMF in case one of the members of the eurozone needed financial assistance. In July 2007, less than 3 years before Dominique Strauss-Kahn was appointed managing director of the IMF, the institution had fallen into disrepute and was widely regarded as almost useless; indeed, the primary task of the new managing director seemed to be to cut costs and reduce personnel. There appeared to be no role, in the new world of "great moderation" of the early 21st century, for an institution that had been created in 1944 to police exchange rates and that had progressively become the firefighter and police officer of international financial crises. The global financial crisis that had started as a U.S. banking crisis only weeks before Strauss-Kahn took office radically changed the outlook: Not only was the IMF needed again for emergency lending to countries faced with sudden liquidity shortages, this time mostly in Europe, but its expertise was widely sought in determining the extent of damage in the global banking sector, helping with fiscal consolidation plans in the worst hit economies, and elaborating reform proposals under the mandate of the newly created G20. Just as in the aftermath of each international financial crisis, the IMF is alive and back in business—but in a different business. This entry describes the complex evolution of the IMF, first examining the role of the Washington Consensus and taking into account the 2008–2009 crisis and then investigating the problems that are at stake for the institution.

Structure and Governance

The IMF was created, along with the World Bank, at the Bretton Woods conference in July 1944, only weeks after the landing of allied troops in Normandy. It was initially conceived as the cornerstone of the international monetary system of fixed exchange rates that was to be instituted in the aftermath of World War II. The consensus among the Allied forces at that time was that a fixed exchange rate system was needed to prevent the reappearance of the kind of "competitive devaluation" and other beggar-thy-neighbor policies that had prevailed as reactions to the financial crisis of 1929 and were then widely regarded as having played a major part in the depth and length of the Great Depression of the 1930s. The initial British plan, put forth by John Maynard Keynes, was to institute a world exchange system based on a new world liquidity instrument, the bancor, which would be issued and managed by a genuine world central bank. This plan had been rejected by the U.S. delegation which favored the so-called gold exchange standard: All currencies have to be convertible and have a fixed exchange rate vis-à-vis the U.S. dollar, which by itself is convertible into gold at a fixed parity of $35 (U.S.) per ounce.

In December 1945, when the first Articles of Agreements were signed, the IMF counted 29 member countries. Membership progressively expanded to 187 countries in 2010. Its main governing body is the Board of Governors, which meets once a year, where all member countries are represented by a governor, who is usually the head of the central bank. Most executive tasks are, however, delegated to the executive board, which comprises 24 members. Only large economies have their own representative, the others being distributed in regional groups and electing representatives. In both boards, voting rights are distributed unevenly in broad accordance with relative weights in the world economy (see the last section of this entry). As of August 2010, eight countries had their own representatives in the Executive Board: The percentage of voting rights for the United States of America is 16.74; Japan, 6.01; Germany, 5.87; France, 4.85; the United Kingdom (UK), 4.85; China, 3.65; Saudi Arabia, 3.16; and the Russian Federation, 2.69. The least represented region is sub-Saharan Africa, with only two representatives for 43 countries and a total of 4.35% of voting rights.

From Surveillance to Structural Adjustment

In the original Bretton Woods system, the role of the IMF was essentially one of macroeconomic surveillance: making sure that countries with—partially—convertible currencies (i.e., essentially developed countries of the West and Japan) were managing their economies in a manner broadly in line with the requirements of a fixed exchange rate system—that is, maintaining balance-of-payments disequilibria within reasonable limits in a world of strictly limited and state-controlled international capital movements. In principle, the IMF also had to ensure that enough international liquidity is provided, but in practice, this role was taken over by the United States, which issues the international reserve currency and holds a blocking minority share in the qualified-majority voting mechanism of the Fund. In 1969, the creation of a new reserve instrument, the Special Drawing Rights (SDR), was supposed to give the Fund more leeway. This was initially limited by the U.S. opposition and later became defunct because of the relative abundance and autonomy of international liquidity in the world of global finance in the 1990s. The SDRs were in fact never really used on a significant scale. There were two major allocations of SDRs: In August 2009, a general allocation of 161.2 billion was made to all member countries, and in September, a special allocation was made to members who had joined after 1981 and who had not benefited from the previous allocations. As of August 2010, the total amount of SDRs allocated amounted to 204.1 billion, equivalent to approximately $317 billion (U.S.).

Until the end of the Bretton Woods era (symbolically proclaimed in August 1971 by U.S. President Richard Nixon, who officially suspended the dollar convertibility into gold), the IMF was thus largely confined to making sure that exchange rate adjustments by members would remain infrequent and not too large and that balance-of-payments disequilibria were not excessive, at least outside the United States. It did intervene in a few European countries—most visibly Italy and the UK in 1977—to provide liquidity and assistance in cases of serious difficulties and to gain access to international, private financing. The Jamaica Agreements, in 1976, sealed the end of the Bretton Woods era, by officially admitting the plurality of exchange rate regimes and eliminating gold as a reference in the international monetary system. By the same token, these agreements signaled the weakening of the IMF.

The irresistible rise in international short-term capital flows and international lending, consequent to the generalized floating exchange rate system and to the external-accounts surpluses generated by the first oil shock in Organization of the Petroleum Exporting Countries (OPEC) countries, led to a first wave of sovereign borrowing during the second half of the 1970s, mostly in Latin America, which was then widely regarded as the promised land of economic growth. After the U-turn in U.S. monetary policy in 1979–1981, under Federal Reserve chairman Paul Volcker, to fight two-digit domestic inflation and the second oil shock, Mexico defaulted on its foreign loans in August 1982, thereby signaling the start of a long series of external debt crises. The IMF did not play a major role in the resolution of these crises—the U.S. Treasury acted almost unilaterally to solve a problem that primarily concerned U.S. commercial banks—but emergency lending to distressed sovereign borrowers and technical assistance for adjustment plans became a part and parcel of the IMF's new role in international finance.

The Washington Consensus in Question

One of the major tasks of the IMF was to counsel governments in countries needing structural economic reforms. After the introduction of reforms and the collapse of the Soviet economy, the consequent transition of former centrally planned economies of Central and Eastern Europe provided the Fund's teams with a king-size experiment to elaborate and test ambitious and wide-ranging transformation and adjustment plans that would soon become known as the Washington Consensus: a cocktail of structural reforms usually involving tax reforms, public employment reduction, cuts in social expenditures, privatizations and liberalization of external financial transactions, and standard predicaments for macroeconomic adjustment—fiscal consolidation and tight monetary policy.

The massive privatization movement that ensued in the first half of the 1990s fueled the expansion and globalization of financial markets along with the rise of private borrowing. In parallel, many countries had been moving away from floating exchange rates, which had proved to be a source of instability rather than being the means of national monetary sovereignty. Pegging the exchange rate to a foreign currency became the norm again, not only in Europe but also in Asia and Latin America. This environment led to overconfidence and indeed to excessive reliance on external financing in many countries. The second Mexican crisis in 1994 and the Asian crisis of 1997, soon followed by the Russian and Latin American crises, led the IMF to further increase lending facilities and provided a large-scale experiment for its structural adjustment plans. The social and political costs incurred by national governments, together with the severity of the subsequent recessions, aroused strong criticism of the doctrine on which IMF interventions were based and forced most emerging economies to turn away from external financing. Instead, with policies of pegging their currencies with an undervalued exchange rate, they aimed at external surpluses and foreign exchange reserve accumulation and tried to build regional banks to free themselves from the tutorship of the Fund and rely on a form of "self-insurance."

From Lending to the Poor to Lending to the Rich?

The global crisis of 2008 to 2009 radically changed the outlook. The G20 took over global leadership as of November 2008 and had to rely on existing institutions for expertise and for conducting rescue operations for the worst hit economies. Hence, the Organisation for Economic Co-operation and Development (OECD) and the IMF regained influence, even though their legitimacy could be questioned, not least by the large emerging economies. The IMF became the promoter of coordinated fiscal stimulus plans to prevent generalized deflation and depression; it moved further in the direction of nonorthodox predicaments by advocating a light-handed approach to fiscal consolidation in the aftermath of the crisis, both by pressing governments not to start consolidating too early, which might destroy the fragile recovery, and by suggesting that central banks accept slightly higher inflation targets to ease fiscal adjustment.

In April 2009, at the London Summit of the G20, reforms were announced in diverse areas such as surveillance and monitoring of global financial risks, transparency and the fight against tax havens, and emergency interventions for financially distressed economies, most particularly in Europe. For this purpose, the decision was made to increase the Fund's lending capacity to U.S.$750 billion. Half of this additional funding came from EU countries, and it was soon to be drawn on by other European countries—both from the EU (Hungary, Estonia, and Romania) and from outside the EU (Iceland). Though a few poor countries did get aid from the IMF, it clearly appeared that the larger lending facilities had been designed to help relatively rich countries and incidentally to help the EU Commission and national governments to restore macroeconomic stability and fiscal discipline in economies that had very close links with the core of the EU—that is, the eurozone. In doing so, the IMF also reasserted the structural adjustment plans that had characterized the Washington Consensus, though with apparently greater care for social expenditures. And in March 2010, when the Greek public debt crisis reached a climax, the EU leaders could not agree on a bail-out plan unless the IMF were part of the lending-of-last-resort mechanism, the German government counting on its expertise and the severity of its predicaments to impose discipline on the Greek government or indeed any eurozone member that might, later on, fall victim to speculative attacks on purportedly unsustainable debt.

A New Role in Preventing Financial Instability

Solving the current crisis, which had started in 2008, is only a part of the renewed mandate of the IMF; preventing future ones by reforming international financial governance has also been set high on the G20 agenda, and the IMF is, along with the Basel Committee and the Bank for International Settlements (BIS)—the coordination institutions for major central banks and the major source of the prudential regulation doctrine for commercial banking—a major actor in the new global effort to reduce systemic risk. Thus, the Forum for Financial Stability, a coordination committee within the Fund, has been turned into a full-fledged and permanent Council of Financial Stability, with a mandate to monitor global financial developments and issue early warning signals in case of perceived mounting imbalances and excessive risk accumulation. And the IMF has been entrusted with the mission to study new instruments of banking regulation, including taxation on risk taking, and possible limitations on the free movement of capital, at least for short-term, speculative capital flows. This could clearly yield a radical change in financial globalization. But how far will national governments be willing to go?

Which Legitimacy?

One of the major weaknesses of the IMF lies in its own governance structure and is apparent in its highest ranking officials: Traditionally, while the Chairman of the World Bank is a U.S. citizen, the General Director of the IMF is a European. This dominance of Europe is even reinforced in the current top-ranking management by the fact that, alongside Strauss-Kahn, the chief economist is Olivier Blanchard, a French-born professor of economics at the Massachusetts Institute of Technology. This governance structure itself reflects the distribution of capital and voting rights among member countries. Initially justified by the overwhelming domination of the United States and the European economies in the immediate aftermath of World War II, the country-wise distribution is increasingly being contested, especially by large emerging economies. The latest reform, implemented in 2006, redistributed about 5.4% of voting rights to the benefit of 54 countries; among those who have gained the most are China, Korea, Brazil, and Turkey. However, the United States still possesses nearly 17% of voting rights, which amounts to a veto power, and the EU countries, taken together, have about 32% of voting rights, whereas China has only 3.65%, India 1.89%, and Brazil 1.38%.

At the G20 summit of April 2009, it was decided to reallocate 5% of voting rights. Yet this would not suffice to yield a system of representation more in line with economic and financial weights of countries in the global economy. This very slow change in the IMF governance and practices may well be a major factor in the current acceleration of regional plans, especially in Asia, to organize monetary and financial stability independently of worldwide institutions that appear to be too closely controlled by Western countries. The pending and highly sensitive issue of exchange rates among major international currencies and the evolutions required to facilitate the return to a more balanced international economy still makes the task of the IMF more complex and further weakens the legitimacy of its current governance.

Jacques Le Cacheux
University of Pau and Sciences Po Paris
Paris, France

See also Central Banks; International Political Economy; Multilateralism; World Bank

Further Readings

Aglietta, M., & Moatti, S. (2000). *Le FMI, de l'ordre monétaire aux désordres financiers* [IMF: From monetary order to financial turmoils]. Paris: Economica.

Bretton Woods Project: http://www.brettonwoodsproject.org

International Monetary Fund: http://www.imf.org

Stiglitz, J. E., & Members of a UN Commission of Financial Experts. (2010). *The Stiglitz report: Reforming the international monetary and financial system in the wake of the global crisis.* New York: New Press.

International Organizations

International organizations (IOs) have three defining features: (1) they are constituted by members from more than one state, usually more than two; (2) they are oriented toward the pursuit of common goals, at least initially; and (3) they have a certain level of explicit formal structure, usually established by a treaty or constituent document. IOs are material entities, usually with offices and personnel. In most cases, they have a legal personality, and thus, they can function as actors in national and international politics. In general, organizations exhibit higher levels of goal specificity and formalization than other types of collectivities, such as social movements, informal networks, or more or less diffuse communities.

There are many different types of IOs. The main distinction is between the IOs constituted by states and those that are constituted by other actors. The former are known as intergovernmental organizations (IGOs) and the latter as international nongovernmental organizations (INGOs or sometimes simply NGOs). Some INGOs have individual members, some have a combination of individuals and locally or nationally organized groups as members, and some are umbrella organizations for national nongovernmental organizations.

IGOs have several formal characteristics in common. Since they are established by governments, they have a formal document serving as their "constitution"—usually a formal treaty in line with requisitions in international law. Moreover, they usually have headquarters with permanent staff, regular meetings of representatives of member states, and rules for decision making and other organizational processes. IGOs also differ in important respects, such as competence and membership. Membership is open to all countries or restricted according to geographical, functional, or other criteria. Competence can be wide, covering a broad range of issues, or restricted to a narrow domain.

The category of INGOs is often subdivided into profit- and nonprofit-oriented organizations. Profit-oriented organizations are mostly multinational companies, such as Nike or Shell Oil Company, or various kinds of business organizations representing such companies directly or indirectly, such as the International Chamber of Commerce (ICC). Nonprofit organizations cover wide areas of specific group interests, such as Disabled Peoples' International (DPI), or promote core values, such as peace, human rights (e.g., Amnesty International), and environmental protection (e.g., World Wildlife Federation [WWF]).

This entry, unless otherwise stated, focuses exclusively on IGOs. A final section, though, is devoted to INGOs. In the following two sections, brief overviews of the historical development of IGOs and the study of IGOs are provided. Subsequent sections examine in some depth three aspects of IOs and institutions that have been particularly prominent in international relations (IR) research: Why are IOs established? What do they do? What impact do they have?

The IGO System: Patterns of Development

International cooperation has taken place as long as states have existed, but the first institution that met the conventional defining characteristics of an IGO was the Central Commission for Navigation on the Rhine (CCNR), which was established in 1815. Another 4 decades would pass before the next IGO was established, for the river Donau. The Industrial Revolution and the increase in various forms of communication and transaction across borders led to a more rapid increase from the 1860s. Most of these organizations were established to solve well-defined coordination challenges. Examples include the International Telegraphic Bureau (later International Telegraphic Union), established in 1868; the General Postal Union (later Universal Postal Union), established in 1874; and the International Bureau of Weight and Measures, established in 1875. More than two thirds of the IGOs established before World War I dealt with technical coordination and/or economic activities. Since the end of World War II, growth has been higher for IGOs operating within social and cultural domains. The two world wars reduced the population of the IGOs to some extent, but the first decade or two following the peace settlements saw particularly high growth rates. As the total number of IGOs has increased, the average organization has become more specialized in functional terms and more narrow in terms of its membership base. According to Cheryl Shanks, Harold Jacobson, and Jeffery Kaplan (1996) the involvement in the activities of IGOs differs substantially: "Older" states tend to participate more than "young" ones, rich states more than poor, democracies more than authoritarian and totalitarian regimes, and large countries more than small.

Describing the development of the IGO "population" in numbers is a less straightforward task than one might think. The reason is simply that numbers depend on the precise definition applied. For example, some overviews include only organizations established directly by governments while others also include organizations created by one or more IGOs. The authoritative source is the *Yearbook of International Organizations*, which is published by the Union of International Associations. Table 1 is based on this database and applies this definition.

The total number of IGOs also includes organizations that are created by other IGOs. Shanks et al. (1996) found that these emanations constituted 70% of the total IGO population in the early 1990s, thus bringing the total number up to more than 1,100. The legal status of IGOs that are created by other IGOs is not very clear. New rules were defined in the Vienna Convention on the Law of Treaties Between States and International Organizations or Between International Organizations (VCLTIO), which opened for signature in 1986. At the time of writing, this convention is not yet in force. Questions about their legal status notwithstanding, there can be no doubt that this type of IGO also plays an important role in international relations.

The development of IGOs has been driven partly by changes in the fabric of the international system itself. Two aspects seem particularly important: (1) changes in networks of interdependence and (2) increase in the number of states.

In essence, cooperation is an effort to manage *interdependence*. The more sensitive or vulnerable one actor is to the activities of others, the stronger its incentives to try to influence their behavior. For

Table 1 Number of International Organizations

Year	*1909*	*1956*	*1985*	*1995*	*2005*
IGO	37	132	378	266	246
INGO	176	973	4,676	5,121	7,306

Source: Yearbook of International Organizations, http://www.uia.org. Numbers for 1909 to 1995 are taken from http://www.uia.org/statistics/organizations/ytb299.php (accessed December 1, 2010). Numbers for 2005 are taken from the 2005/2006 yearbook edition, Appendix 3, Table 1, p. 2966.

cooperation to emerge, this interest must be mutual so that both (all) parties see some possibility of improving outcomes by exchanging commitments with prospective partners. Taken together, these observations suggest that the scope and level of cooperation will reflect the strength and configuration of interdependence relationships.

This is a complex hypothesis, and previous research provides only partial tests. In bivariate analysis, conventional measures of interdependence—such as volumes of international trade, investment, and several forms of communication—correlate positively with the number of IGOs. Results are, however, sensitive to the choice of operational definitions of the key variables. The best "fit" is achieved when we link interdependence measured in terms of *absolute* volumes of transactions to the *total* IGO population, including also emanations. However, the basic argument refers to sensitivity and vulnerability, and these are concepts pointing toward *relative* measures of interdependence. Thus, a country's sensitivity to external economic events is primarily a function of the importance of foreign trade to its national income (measured as foreign trade in proportion to gross domestic product [GDP]). When we replace absolute with relative measures, we find that the population of IGOs has grown at a much higher rate than the level of interdependence. Moreover, the argument linking interdependence to organizations puts as much weight on *configurations* of interdependence as on aggregate volumes of transactions. A survey of the case study literature would bring out many observations that support—at least indirectly—the latter proposition. As far as we know, however, no existing database provides the kind of data required for more extensive and refined testing. The upshot of all this is that while we may safely conclude that interdependence is a major factor generating incentives (*demand*) for cooperation, we cannot claim to understand equally well supply-side mechanisms and the interactive dynamics of the demand–supply relationship.

As the first shots were fired in World War I, the number of sovereign states had not yet reached 50. Today, there are about 200 such states. This increase can be expected to lead to more IGOs for at least two reasons. First, as the number of states increases, the average state is left with jurisdiction over a declining share of the world population and world resources. This reduces its capacity to serve its people through purely unilateral measures. Second, as the number of actors increases, so does the number of potential partnerships. This effect is amplified by the fact that states that have recently escaped the rule of their former masters often are particularly eager to engage in cooperative ventures with new partners.

The development of the IGO system also seems to reflect changes in the fabric of national political systems as well. Two features seem particularly important. One is the expansion and upgrading of public policy in relatively "new" domains, such as social security and environmental protection. The other is the tendency for national administrative systems to become increasingly specialized and differentiated. The development of the IGO population, particularly over the second half of the 20th century, reflects both of these changes to a significant degree.

The Study of IGOs

In the first decade or two after World War II, the United Nations (UN) became a special case of IOs as its universal membership and increasing scope of competences made it appear more important than any other IO. Its uniqueness and importance attracted scholars to conduct a number of studies of the internal functions of the UN, such as the voting patterns in the General Assembly and the recruitment of staff to the Secretariat. Pioneers in this field such as Robert Cox and Harold Jacobson studied IOs as bureaucracies with the aim of understanding the decision-making and other political processes taking place within the IOs. This approach provided quite sophisticated classifications of structural and functional aspects and much empirical insight into the work of IOs. It did not to the same degree generate testable propositions linking these taxonomies to variance in performance or impact.

Disillusioned by external developments—the failure of the UN Security Council to deal with pressing issues such as the nuclear arms race and the Vietnam War and occasional setbacks in major regional integration projects—and left with a research program that did not effectively get at the underlying causes of these difficulties, many scholars reoriented their agenda to move away from IGO structures and procedures toward institutions that were defined as sets of rules and norms governing certain activities. The existence of formal organizations was, of course, recognized, but international regimes—defined by Stephen Krasner as the rules, norms, principles, and procedures around which actor expectations converge in a given issue area—emerged as a new and more exciting topic. The interest in international institutions was also driven by a growing critique of the dominant grand theory in the study of international relations: realism. The new emphasis on institutions challenged a core assumption of realism. It did so in part by claiming that states may establish international institutions even if short-term self-interest would be better served by free riding and that these institutions tend to acquire a life of their own by influencing state behavior in their own right. It also did so by suggesting that nonstate actors could significantly influence government policies and outcomes of international processes.

Over the past 10 years or so, there has been a renewed interest in the study of IOs. The constructivist turn of much IR research has inspired some reformulation of the research agenda, highlighting, inter alia, the role of IOs as providers and custodians of norms and rules serving as frames of legitimacy for the behavior of states as well as groups and individuals. It has also led some to revisit "old" questions. For example, Michael Barnett and Martha Finnemore have studied the bureaucratic features of IOs in a somewhat different framework and succeeded in providing new insight into the importance of these features in shaping international politics more broadly.

The split between the study of organization and the study of regimes, though, is by no means total. Many scholars see regimes and organizations as two subgroups of international institutions. Moreover, in real life, organizations and regimes are often intertwined. Starting from the regime tradition, one could say that regimes are often served by organizations; starting from the IO tradition, one could say that organizations often play important roles in developing and managing regimes.

Why and How Do States Establish IOs?

The institutional turn in studies of IOs made the study of international institutions an integral part of the study of international cooperation. International institutions can help states solve common problems through coordinated action. The realist tradition has always pointed to the anarchical structure of the international system as compelling states to be deeply concerned about security and (relative) power. The international system was described as a self-help system where states have to be very cautious about getting involved in cooperative ventures that could benefit others more than themselves. Moreover, they will expect others to free ride as long as they can get away with it. Institutional theory challenges this understanding by, inter alia, pointing to institutional "services" that can reduce uncertainty and help parties negotiate as well as enforce agreements. An IO can, for example, help establish a base of consensual knowledge, facilitate negotiations, and develop operational standards against which performance can be measured and compliance monitored.

Research following this functional approach, first developed by Robert Keohane, has explored how different configurations of preferences can shape outcomes. Much interest has been devoted to the malignant configuration known as the prisoners' dilemma game. If played only once, or a finite number of rounds known in advance, the dominant strategy for each party will be to defect. Evidence from experimental research indicates that individuals playing this game tend to cooperate more than static game theory predicts. Moreover, Robert Axelrod and others have used computational modeling to study the evolution of cooperation in reiterated games and found that certain strategies of conditional cooperation do better than strategies relying more primarily on defection. By acknowledging the political malignancy of certain configurations of interests and at the same time demonstrating how regimes and organizations can inspire and facilitate cooperation, research pursuing the "functional" approach helped bridge the gap between the realist school and the institutionalists. The role of IOs tends, though, to vary with the problem structure. Fortunately, many of the common challenges facing governments generate less malignant configurations than that constituting the prisoners' dilemma game.

The realist tradition claims, in essence, that powerful states will create institutions that serve their interests. IOs that contradict the interests of powerful states will either not be established or, if they are, have little or no impact. The hegemonic stability theory suggests that a "hegemon" is essential for the establishment of strong international institutions and IOs. A dominant actor will have a higher interest in the collective good in question and at the same time possess the capabilities to provide (much of) that good by unilateral action. Now, power defined as the ability to get others to do what they would otherwise not have done can be exercised by various means. In the literature on international institutions, various forms of leadership have been discussed, such as structural leadership, where more general power resources are activated; intellectual leadership, where knowledge is activated in order to facilitate solutions to common problems; or entrepreneurial leadership, where the ability to identify solutions and find compromises is activated. All these various resources or abilities on behalf of individual actors can be important in establishing and maintaining international institutions.

Decision makers as well as students of international cooperation have long recognized that a base of consensual knowledge is a necessary condition for negotiations to succeed. The Intergovernmental Panel for Climate Change (IPCC)—a formal IGO—was established to translate findings from scientific research into usable knowledge for policymakers. The work of the IPCC also illustrates how political conflict can threaten to contaminate such processes and how a combination of organizational design and leadership may provide fairly good protection.

More generally, cooperation often builds on a broadly accepted ideational foundation. IGOs and INGOs often play a role in disseminating causal and normative beliefs that shape the perceptions of international problems. In some cases, they may even contribute to the development of collective identities. Various mechanisms may be at work, but two examples are often in focus. First, an image of a common enemy might increase the actors' perception of common interests and thus strengthen incentives for cooperation. Second, states engaged in cooperation might find themselves to be perceived as a model for others, an effect that might increase the self-confidence of the cooperating parties and lead to further cooperation. Even in the absence of such profound change, ideas can make a significant difference. Particular attention has been given to the role of transnational networks of experts—often referred to as "epistemic communities"—in developing common problem descriptions and diagnoses, combined with ideas about effective "cures."

What Do IOs Do and How Do They Do It?

As pointed out at the beginning, IOs are created for some purpose—usually to achieve goals that their members find it hard to achieve (as effectively) on their own. More specifically, four roles have attracted particular attention.

One is the role of *providing an arena* for exchange of information, negotiation, and related processes. As an arena, an organization establishes a meeting place, specifies the activities to take place under its auspices, and provides rules regulating these activities. As arenas for exchange of information and ideas, IGOs, INGOs, and sometimes even informal networks often facilitate learning and other types of policy diffusion. Although IOs are not the only possible way to establish communication among parties, they have some characteristics that make them efficient in this respect. IOs have some degree of autonomy from the parties involved and can thus be seen as impartial. An IO serves as a place where the parties can meet on neutral ground for negotiations. A prominent example of this is how the secretary-general of the UN is assigned a role where he can offer conflicting parties the use of his "good offices." In general, leaders of secretariats of IOs are often assigned the role of chairing international negotiations. This can imply a more active role than simply providing an arena for negotiations. The assumed impartiality and the expectation that secretariat leaders represent common interests of members make them suited for such assignments. The arena role of IOs makes it possible, at least to some extent, to regulate the access of actors to problems and the access of problems to decision games. And, finally, IOs serve as independent actors in specifying the official purpose as well as the rules, location, and timing of negotiations among the parties.

IOs not only serve as an arena for members to exchange information but also play an active role in providing information themselves. We can distinguish between factual information about the world in general and about characteristics of the member countries, information about actors' behavior, and information that elucidate causal connections—that is, the potential effects of the IO's decisions. Many IOs serve as providers of all these kinds of information in their respective field. The importance of information is connected with the consequences of uncertainty in the relationship between states. Rational actors are assumed to behave purposively on the basis of the information available to them. Thus, the information actors possess about other actors' interests can be a critical determinant of their own behavior. The more information the IOs provide, the less likely it is that there will be misperception and misunderstanding among the member states.

The second aspect is the role of the IOs in creating decision-making rules that affect the subsequent outcome of the interaction of members or other actors. The formation of actors' interests is influenced by various constraints, which will be dealt with in the subsection on framing of decisions below. Here, the focus is on how actors' behaviors that enable them to realize given interests are influenced by constraints caused by decision rules. The decision rule is an important determinant of the capacity of the IO to aggregate divergent preferences. Other things being equal, aggregation capacity reaches its maximum in strictly hierarchical structures and is at its minimum in systems requiring agreement (unanimity). Decision rules in IGOs are affected by the anarchic structure of the international system and accompanying principle of the sovereignty of states. Since there is no formal authority that can enforce decisions, states are only committed to decisions they agree to. Thus, compared with lawmaking in national political systems, the role of international law in general is weak. Consensus is the most common decision-making rule in actual use in IGOs. It is also a very demanding decision rule, leaving the burden of proof with those who want new measures taken and giving a veto to any significant party that is opposed. The majority-voting rule produces more ambitious decisions, but it does so at the risk of more defection in the implementation stage.

In most IGOs, formal decision rules tend to favor small member states. This is most evident where unanimity or consensus is required and also where decisions are made by voting based on the principle of one state, one vote (e.g., the UN General Assembly). Even where votes are weighted, the small will most often be overrepresented. In the EU Council, for example, votes are distributed so that 1 citizen of Luxembourg balances about 24 citizens of Germany. Now, Germany's voting power still trumps that of Luxembourg by a wide margin (29 to 4), and Germany leads by an even larger margin when it comes to power in basic games such as trade and investment. Moreover, if we look at the total population of IGOs, we will find that rich countries participate more than poor, large more than small, democratic states more than authoritarian, and old states more than young. In this respect, the IGO system reflects the social stratification of world society. Although originally made in a different context, Stein Rokkan's well-known observation that "votes count but resources decide" carries an important lesson about IGO politics as well.

The decision rule also influences the relationship between the IO and major powers. Unanimity is likely to produce compliance at a low cost, since the decisions will be self-enforcing compared with a situation where major powers would have to enforce the decision made in the IO. Although the formal decision rule is unanimity, the actual decision making in several IOs is of course influenced by the distribution of power among the members outside the IO. For instance, in the case of the Organization of the Petroleum Exporting Countries (OPEC), large producers such as Saudi Arabia can easily undermine most production decisions of the organization by unilateral market behavior. Subsequently, Saudi Arabia enjoys a stronger influence on OPEC decision than what follows from the one country one vote rule.

IOs are essential for creating rules and regulations for states' behavior in the international system. Sovereign states would be very reluctant to submit themselves to behavior rules if nobody else made similar commitments. When treaties or conventions are negotiated, they are normally subject to subsequent ratification by member states. When a certain number of states have ratified the treaty, it enters into force. This system ensures that the individual state that signs the treaty is only committed when a number of others join. IOs provide an efficient way to promote such conditional cooperation among states in an anarchical system.

The third aspect is the role of IOs in establishing a common perception of problems and solutions. Decision making through negotiations among parties is heavily influenced by the way in which the actors think about their problem. The variation among parties in their perception of the situation, beliefs about their own and others' interests, and cognition of the world in general makes it harder to reach common solutions. In the short run, self-interested actors are influenced by constraints imposed on policy choices by agreed-on rules. In the long run, conceptions of self-interest may be reshaped as a result, in part, of practices engaged in over a period of time. An IO can influence the actors' perceptions of the situation surrounding their decisions; in other words, the organization can frame member states' decisions. International institutions can also play a role in the formation of interests and collective identity among members. An important premise for this aspect is the assumption that states' interests are not exogenously given but are endogenous to interaction among states.

Increased cooperative behavior might come about as a result of several different processes of identity formation performed by the IOs. First, there can be various intersubjective systemic structures consisting of shared understandings, expectations, and social knowledge embedded in international institutions, in terms of which states define their identities and interests. Second, there are systemic processes in the external context of state action that lead to increased interdependence and also imply both an increase in the "dynamic density" of interactions and the emergence of a "common Other." This reduces states' ability to act unilaterally and increases the extent to which actors share a common fate and, thus, their willingness to form international institutions. Third, strategic behavioral practice has two effects on identities and interests: Through interaction, actors form identities by learning, which makes them see themselves as others do, and by engaging in cooperative behavior, an actor gradually changes its own beliefs about what it is, thus helping internalize the new identity.

The fourth aspect is the role of IOs in performing politics on behalf of its members. Volker Rittberger and Berhard Zangl identify five types of IO operations: First, norms and rules usually require further specification and codification to be implemented in practice. This is often done by the member states that have the potential for various interpretations of the practical consequences of the rules and regulations. In several cases, the IO takes responsibility for specifying the rules agreed to by the members. In the EU, this is a task often handled by the EU Commission, and in the World Bank, detailed plans for conditionality of various funds are left in the hands of the World Bank bureaucracy. Second, in a number of areas, the implementation of IO decisions is simply carried out by the IO itself. Several special agencies of the UN are entirely devoted to this kind of operative tasks, particularly in the field of economics and sociology, such as humanitarian relief and development aid, but also in security affairs, when the UN deploys peacekeeping forces. Third, when members themselves implement decisions, the need for independent monitoring arises, particularly to verify accusations of members' defection. Only with a reliable system of monitoring the other parties will the individual members implement their own commitments. This also has a positive feedback on their willingness to make credible commitments in the first place. In case of disagreement among members regarding their compliance, the IO can also perform a role in adjudication. Fourth, if monitoring and adjudication do not make members abide by the rules, sanctions will have to be imposed. These can take the form of verbal or written condemnation, economic sanctions, or the use of force. In many cases, it is the member states that have to exercise the sanctions, but in some cases, the IOs themselves can perform some of the sanctioning acts.

Measuring and Explaining Effects

The importance of IGOs has long been a matter of some controversy in the study of international relations. Realists have consistently argued that IGOs reflect rather than shape configurations of state interests and power and therefore merit attention primarily as tools rather than actors. The fortune of an organization—and ultimately its survival—depends on the extent to which powerful members see it as serving their interests. A somewhat similar argument has been made by scholars inspired by Marxist notions of class conflict. Others, adopting what is often referred to as a sociological approach, have argued that IOs and regimes can best be understood as embedded in, and in important respects also constituted by, normative "deep structures" of international society. A common denominator for all these lines of reasoning is the proposition that IOs grow out of, and therefore also reflect, some more fundamental and important structure of the international political system or international society. In the aggregate, and over the long haul, they may modify or reinforce the structures in which they are embedded, but overall, IGOs can best be understood as "intervening" variables, reflecting at least as much as shaping the international system. Some organizations will be actively involved in international political processes, but few will, by their own weight, leave a distinct and significant imprint on important outcomes.

This pessimistic conclusion has been challenged by scholars working within an institutionalist framework. Grossly simplified, the essence of their arguments may be summarized as follows. First, for an IGO to serve as a useful tool ("agent"), it will need some amount of independence from its "principals." Rational principals understand this and will therefore grant that much autonomy. Second, even without the approval of its principals, an agent—for example, an international secretariat—will often succeed in obtaining some "slack." This slack is likely to be largest for secretariats that work for a politically homogeneous group of members and that have been able to build up substantial expertise or possess other relevant resources. Moreover, an agent is likely to develop its own interpretation of its mission and base its behavior on that interpretation as long as it is not explicitly overruled. Third, over time, most organizations and regimes establish rules and develop practices into which participants—also representatives of member countries—will to some degree be enmeshed and socialized. As these structures and practices mature, they often acquire the status of default options or standard operating procedures.

Despite occasional skirmishes, a fairly broad consensus has emerged that there is at least some merit in all these propositions. A closer scrutiny will show that they, to some extent, refer to different dependent variables, different policy domains, or different causal mechanisms. The realist argument focuses on individual IGOs as actors in "high politics" and measures importance mainly in terms of the extent to which they influence state interests, the distribution of power, or the basic ordering principle of the international political system (anarchy). By this standard, the vast majority of IGOs do indeed obtain a low score, particularly when compared with the great powers that occupy center stage in (neo)realist theory. The so-called functionalist theory focuses on the role of IGOs in managing networks of international interdependence. Growing interdependence is seen as involving increasing sensitivity and vulnerability, which generates new demands for coordination and collaboration—first within "low-politics" domains such as trade and investment, transport and communication, labor market regulations, and health and environment. The IGOs are established and designed to supply coordination services and facilitate collaboration. To the extent that they perform these functions effectively, organizations contribute to further development of interdependence networks, which in turn may generate new demands for IGO services—in part, by changing domestic configurations of interests and influence.

Early functionalist theory sent an upbeat message that this dynamic interaction of demand and supply would eventually lead to the build-up of supranational systems of governance. Empirical evidence and refinement of causal models soon showed that there is nothing compelling about that trajectory; in fact, interactive feedback loops similar to those that generate momentum can also lead to cascading collapse. This does not imply that the basic mechanisms highlighted by (neo-)functionalist theory are not at work; rather, the main lesson seems to be that we are dealing with more complex systems, involving nonlinear relationships, conditional effects, and interplay. Finally, the sociological approach calls attention to IGOs and INGOs as arenas for, and facilitators of, socialization and transnational diffusion of ideas and norms. Most studies examine the role of particular organizations in legitimizing or spreading a more or less well-defined set of ideas, but some take on the demanding challenge of determining the aggregate effect of the universe of organizations on complex macrolevel variables, such as world culture.

The best way to make sense of such diversity is to sort answers and propositions by the questions to which they refer. With a wide range of research interests, this exercise will generate a fairly complex matrix. All we can offer here is a selective and brief overview, focusing on some of the effects that have been subject to extensive study. Although not explicitly used in much of the empirical literature, the distinction introduced earlier between organizations as arenas and organizations as actors may serve as a crude organizing device.

As pointed out in the previous section, IOs can serve as arenas for exchange of information and ideas between member states. Several studies indicate that organizations often enhance policy convergence even in the absence of formal agreement by exposing members to new information and ideas that lead to unilateral adjustments. Others find that individuals who participate actively in the work of an organization over an extended period of time tend to develop a stronger identification with the organization itself and its mission, norms, and values. The strength of this socialization function seems, though, to be moderate. A recent study found that even in a relatively powerful and prestigious bureaucracy (the European Commission), 39% of the staff members interviewed saw themselves as "very attached" to their own nation, while only 25% said the same about Europe. Moreover, socialization seems to leave the greatest impact on staff members recruited to the organization at an early and formative stage of their career before some other identity has been firmly established.

Research aimed at determining the importance of IGOs as actors has pursued two main strategies. One has focused on the capacity to act. Capacity has been defined in somewhat different terms, but most definitions point to at least two components—autonomy and resources. The interest in autonomy is premised on the assumption that independence from member states and other actors is a necessary, though not sufficient, condition for influence. Autonomy is sometimes measured in terms of organizational properties such as decision-making procedures, the existence of a supranational bureaucracy, and the existence of some binding dispute settlement mechanism. One study combines these indicators in a 7-point ordinal scale and applies this index to a sample of 30 regional integration "arrangements." Of their cases, 67% fall within the lower range (0–2) and only 17% within the upper range (4–6). Consistent with functionalist logic, economic interdependence has a positive and significant effect on the autonomy of IGOs. Consistent with institutionalist arguments, IGOs tend to become more independent as they mature over time. Other studies measure autonomy in behavioral terms, in most cases by studying the role(s) played by specific bodies, in particular the secretariat. The most comprehensive study of international environmental regimes found that secretariats have little or no independence in 41% of the cases included. Another study reported that secretariats are confined to functions of office keeping, and information gathering and dissemination in nearly 60% of the cases included in their database. The main conclusion seems to be that a large majority of IGOs obtain a low or, at best, moderate score on structural as well as behavioral indicators of autonomy.

A survey of the resources of IGOs would show a very wide range of variance; the European Union (EU) and the International Whaling Commission clearly play in very different "leagues." And they do so by resource endowments as well as constitutional design.

The other approach is more direct, trying to determine the actual influence of one or more IGOs on particular processes or outcomes. Much of this literature focuses on one or a few cases, most often one of the large and presumably important organizations (such as the UN, the EU, North Atlantic Treaty Organization [NATO], or World Trade Organization [WTO]). A survey of this literature will first of all confirm that IGOs vary substantially in terms of what they achieve as well as how they operate. It will, however, also indicate certain patterns; for example, influence seems to vary with constitutional provisions, resource endowments, and "positive" interdependence among member states. It also provides interesting insights into the roles played by specific bodies or individual leaders. For example, secretariats can exert influence by performing quite different functions—ranging from contributions to the development of a base of consensual knowledge to high-profile political initiatives. The former do not make headlines but may over the long haul be as important. Even a "technical bureaucracy" can make a nontrivial difference by facilitating negotiations or monitoring performance.

The case study literature is rich in interesting observations and important insights, but most refer to one or a few specific organizations or issues. Over the past 2 decades, an increasing number of studies have used large databases that provide a more solid basis for general conclusions. Many of these studies have examined the role of IGOs in managing conflict and fostering or maintaining peace. Findings sometimes diverge, but one may at least conclude that IGOs sometimes contribute significantly. Thus, one study, relying on data covering the period 1946 to 2000, found IGOs to be more successful than any other type of third party in mediating negotiated settlement of military disputes. While this study and several others concentrate on specific functions (such as mediation), others take a broader view and try to determine the overall contribution of IGOs to building or maintaining peace. Much of this research is inspired by Immanuel Kant's vision of "eternal peace," which identified three pillars, today often referred to as democracy, interdependence, and international law and organization. Overall, the findings from previous research support the propositions that democracy and interdependence are positively associated with peace, but results for IGOs vary—some are, in fact, negative. This has led some scholars to suggest that only certain types of IGOs enhance peace—notably, those that are composed largely of democratic states. A study published in 2006 finds robust support for this revised hypothesis. This finding points to a more conditional and less independent role for IGOs in fostering and maintaining peace; the main mechanism at work seems to be one of interplay in which "densely democratic" IGOs serve to amplify the positive impact of member state democracy.

Other studies indicate that there are more mechanisms at work linking IGOs to democratic political systems. States in transition to democracy tend to join IGOs at higher rates than any other group of states. Moreover, democratizing states show a strong preference for IGOs in which most other members are established democracies. Third, it seems that membership and active participation in such organizations tend to reduce the risk of backsliding. All this suggests that IGOs composed largely of established democracies can play a significant role in helping consolidate new and fragile democratic systems. And since relations among democracies are the most peaceful, contributions to consolidating new democratic systems can have a positive, albeit marginal, and indirect effect on world peace. The EU is probably the most well-known example, but the basic proposition is supported also by large-*N* studies, indicating that there is a more general effect.

The research literature is less sanguine about the effect on established democracies of active involvement in the activities of IGOs. Several studies indicate that IGOs sometimes operate in ways that tend to enhance the influence of the executive branch, privilege technical and, in some cases, "scientific" expertise, and in other ways remove decision-making processes from arenas where the ordinary citizen can play an active role. Other studies have found that these effects are at least to some extent offset by other democracy-enhancing features, such as constraints on the power of domestic special interest groups and protection of individual rights. The latter effects seem to be most evident for countries that do not (yet) achieve top scores on democracy scales.

International Nongovernmental Organizations

This entry has so far focused on IGOs. Much of the cooperation that takes place across borders is, however, initiated and conducted by individuals, voluntary associations, or other nongovernmental actors. Civil society seems as involved as governments in cooperative projects with partners in other countries. To develop and manage such areas of cooperation, they often establish international nongovernmental organizations (INGOs), or transnational organizations (TNOs). The UN Economic and Social Council (UNECOSOC) considers all organizations that are not established through formal agreement between or among governments as nongovernmental. Most of the research literature has adopted a more narrow definition requiring that a majority of the members be private parties. Today, INGOs outnumber IGOs by a wide margin, and the growth rate is higher in the nongovernmental sphere. To be sure, most INGOs have small budgets, limited staff, and little or no political influence. But others are impressive organizational complexes. The Catholic Church counts more than a billion "members." Several humanitarian organizations have billion-euro budgets and thousands of employees. Taken together, the 200 largest transnational companies account for about one fourth of the world production of commercial goods and services. In multiple ways, TNOs can indeed be important actors.

In international relations research, INGOs have been studied particularly in their performance of three different functions. One is that of managing activities that most governments do not consider public policy domains. For example, while governments accept overall responsibility for law and order, few, if any, see this responsibility as involving a duty to establish and enforce internal rules for particular sports or proclaim and interpret principles of religious faith. Within the arena of the Organisation for Economic Co-operation and Development (OECD), most governments would see the production and distribution of private goods as activities to be undertaken mainly by the private sector (albeit subject to public regulation). Another function performed by many INGOs is that of advocacy, including activities ranging from high-publicity campaigns to confidential lobbying. Third, some INGOs engage in activities for which most governments accept at least some responsibility. Most important is the area of humanitarian assistance, but INGOs are involved also in what might be called private regulation—most often in the form of standard setting, "enforced" by mobilizing the market power of concerned customers or through public naming-and-shaming campaigns.

Although often studied as different from IGOs, important propositions from research focusing on IGOs apply also to INGOs. Both merit attention as arenas as well as actors. Patterns of growth are strongly correlated (about .80, depending on the exact specification of the model). So are patterns of participation; in fact, INGOs tend to be even more dominated by wealthy and liberal democracies. For both types of organizations, autonomy, resources, and leadership are important determinants of influence. And although INGOs often make headlines by criticizing or opposing governments, relationships are often friendly and supportive. Thus, for many humanitarian organizations, grants from governments and IGOs constitute important sources of income. And in many campaigns, INGOs, governments, and IGOs work side by side—for as well as against a particular cause.

Social science research often portrays (I)NGOs rooted in civil society as, overall, a positive transformative force. At least three more specific propositions to that effect can be found in the research literature. One suggests that TNOs by and large tend to have more democratic internal structures and procedures than their IGO counterparts, providing individual members better opportunities for active participation and real influence. This observation is no doubt true for a number of INGOs, though not for all. The aggregate effect will, however, depend also on who exactly are empowered through these organizations. Even an organization with a perfectly democratic internal structure may speak for only a small fragment of civil society. And as far as it can be determined, the social stratification of world society is reflected as clearly in the nongovernmental sphere as within the IGO system. A second proposition sees transnational cooperation as a worldwide mobilization of concerned citizens in defense of universal values (such as basic human rights) or profoundly important collective goods (such as nature's life support systems). Again, it is easy to identify a number of INGOs that fit this description well. Yet if one looks at aggregate figures, one will also find that the largest group of TNOs consists of those that are established to serve interests related to economic activities. Finally, some scholars, notably John Boli and George Thomas, have suggested that organized transnational cooperation serves, in the aggregate, as a transformative force shaping a new world culture characterized by more inclusive identities ("world citizen") and widespread acceptance of reason and voluntarism as fundamental pillars of authority. This is a bold and interesting hypothesis, but at this point, it seems prudent to postpone judgment until more comprehensive and solid evidence becomes available.

Dag Harald Claes and Arild Underdal
University of Oslo
Oslo, Norway

See also Constructivism in International Relations; Cooperation; Governance, Global; International Law; International Regimes; International Relations, Theory; Neoliberal Institutionalism; Nongovernmental Organizations (NGOs); Realism in International Relations

Further Readings

Axelrod, R. (1984). *The evolution of cooperation.* New York: Basic Books.

Barnett, M., & Finnemore, M. (2004). *Rules for the world: International organizations in global politics.* Ithaca, NY: Cornell University Press.

Boli, J., & Thomas, G. M. (Eds.). (1999). *Constructing world culture: International nongovernmental organizations since 1875.* Stanford, CA: Stanford University Press.

Cox, R., & Jacobson, H. K. (1973). *The anatomy of influence.* New Haven, CT: Yale University Press.

Jacobson, H. K. (1984). *Networks of interdependence: International organizations and the global political system.* New York: McGraw-Hill.

Karns, M. P., & Mingst, K. A. (2004). *International organization: The politics and processes of global governance.* Boulder, CO: Lynne Rienner.

Keohane, R. (1984). *After hegemony: Cooperation and discord in the world political economy.* Princeton, NJ: Princeton University Press.

Krasner, S. D. (Ed.). (1983). *International regimes.* Ithaca, NY: Cornell University Press.

Reinalda, B., & Verbeek, B. (Eds.). (2004). *Decision making within international organizations.* London: Routledge.

Rittberger, V., & Zangl, B. (2006). *International organization: Polity, politics and policies.* Basingstoke, UK: Palgrave Macmillan.

Shanks, C., Jacobson, H. K., & Kaplan, J. H. (1996). Inertia and change in the constellation of international governmental organizations, 1981–1992. *International Organization, 50*(4), 593–628.

International Political Economy

The field of international political economy (IPE) requires two definitions since it is both a subject, a field *of* study, and an object, a thing *to* study. Defining IPE as a thing to study, as an object, is quite straightforward. It refers to the global or international distribution of power, wealth, and prestige among state and nonstate actors. IPE as a field of study, as a subject, in contrast, has at least two different histories and as such requires a more complex explication.

This entry traces the evolution of these twin histories of IPE. The first history pertains to the so-called American school of IPE that emerged during the early to mid-1970s in the context of the oil crises and breakdown of the Bretton Woods system. The second history pertains to the contrasting British school of IPE that has altogether different origins. Rather than forming one body of knowledge, these two schools have developed distinct research trajectories, agendas, and methodological orientations. IPE as a field of study is therefore plural.

In brief, the American school has, over time, become an increasingly analytically coherent and methodologically homogeneous body of scholarship. It emerged during the mid-1970s to analyze a purported crisis of U.S. hegemony and then evolved into a particular set of arguments concerning the importance of institutions, credibility, contracts, and commitment in IPE. The British school has, in contrast, blossomed into a multidisciplinary exercise that is both methodologically plural and decidedly lacking in defined boundaries. The British school began long before the 1970s and has drawn on the contributions of historians, economists, journalists, and geographers. Recently, both schools have had to accommodate still other bodies of scholarship with a claim to be IPE. Contemporary IPE is at the very least, plural.

The Development of American IPE

The Cold War and Political Science Foundations of American IPE

What makes the contrast between the American and British schools of IPE salient is the relationship of American IPE to its parent discipline of political science and the politics of the Cold War, a relationship that does not exist in the UK or elsewhere. American political science has only relatively recently come to embrace political economy as a distinct approach concerned with the core question of distribution. After World War II, American political science was behavioralist and functionalist in its orientation. Its behavioralism developed as a result of the focus of political science after pre–World War II on the formal institutions of society—constitutions and the like. Since this focus failed to anticipate the collapse of interwar democracy in Germany and the emergence of fascism, the lesson learned was to focus on actor behavior, not constitutional form. Second, the United States emerged from World War II as a superpower intimately concerned with the relationship between knowledge and national security—hence the focus of early postwar American political science on policy-relevant scientific knowledge.

While behavioralism dominated the study of American politics, the study of the societies outside the Western core demanded a different analysis. The thrust of these "modernization" arguments was to extend the teleological logic of Talcott Parsons's functionalism to the developmental trajectories of the non-Western world, which was expected to develop in a sequence like that already undergone by the West, especially the United States.

American political science in its moment of refounding the Cold War developed a fourfold division of the field where American politics analyzed the putative end of history for all developing states—the American present; comparative politics analyzed current real-world deviations from that trend and thus how far other countries had to travel to get to that end; international relations situated these processes in the bipolar structure of the Cold War; and political theory, the fourth subfield, kept the Marxists out and the liberals in.

As a consequence, in the early years of the Cold War, the structure of political science in America left very little room for political economy, international or not. In part, because it smacked of Marxism, but also because the move toward ever greater formalism in its sister discipline of economics in this period that depoliticized the subject in another way, IPE as "a way of thinking" had to wait for events to make room for (international) political economy to come back to political science.

That moment arrived in the 1970s when the developed world underwent its first major recession while the experience of the United States in Vietnam tempered belief in its ability to command the world. Stagflation, oil shocks, unemployment, and low growth, coming on the heels of civil right rebellions at home and revolutions abroad, shook the self-confidence of American political science. In this moment of crisis, a few American political scientists began to argue that the separation of politics and markets, especially the sidelining of questions of distribution in international relations and economics, was perhaps part of the problem. It was in this context that the American school of IPE emerged. Where economics retreated, political scientists began to ask a series of questions that would define what IPE (as a subject) was and what it should investigate (as an object) for the next decade and a half; a distinct IPE then began to take shape.

Orienting Issues and Questions of American IPE

The first concern of these theorists was the notion that the United States was in decline. With the U.S. growth rate slowing, its industrial base shrinking, and its deficits rising, Europe and Japan seemed to be in the ascendance, while the United States was falling by the wayside. Yet if the United States was in decline, how could global order be provided in an environment of multiple players, all with different interests? Moreover, if the United States no longer set the terms for the other players in the system, which states would prosper and which would fail in this new world?

Taking up these concerns were scholars such as Robert Keohane and Joseph Nye, whose idea of "complex interdependence" challenged traditional realist notions of state interests and state action. Keohane and Nye argued that as the problems faced by states became more complex and less amenable to unilateral solutions, so the focus of scholars had to be shifted outward from the traditional "high politics" of international relations (qua security politics) to the political economy politics of, for example, trade protectionism and economic development. Such a stance argued for attention to the complexity of ties that bind states and a focus on how markets are important predicates of, as well as arenas for, state action. Such a stance was not without its realist critics to be sure, but this intervention made possible a broader opening of the agenda of American political science to questions of economic governance and distribution; it made room for IPE in the United States.

When complex interdependence was juxtaposed with the question of the decline of the United States, the result was a set of theories called hegemonic stability theory (HST). What animated this scholarship was, in large part, a particular reading of the monetary history of the 20th century inspired by the work of Charles Kindleberger.

Kindleberger's key idea was that a single stabilizer was needed to stabilize the world economy. Drawing this conclusion from a study of the monetary relations of the interwar period, he developed a theory of hegemonic transition that spoke directly to U.S. declinist fears.

From Hegemonic Stability to Regimes

The basic story of HST was that following World War I, the United Kingdom (UK)—once the world's biggest market, banker, and power—emerged severely weakened. While willing to assume the burdens of leadership—that is, act as a lender of last resort, provide a market for distressed goods, and lend countercyclically to promote stability—the UK was simply unable to do so given its diminished capabilities. The United States on the other hand was able to do the same by the 1920s, but it was, because of its domestic politics, unwilling to do so. Lacking such leadership, trade collapsed, nationalism followed, and the turmoil of the 1930s and 1940s ensued. Could the same thing happen again now that the United States was in decline—especially when, unlike the last time, there was no obvious candidate to replace it?

The theoretical lesson drawn from Kindleberger's analysis rested on a classic public goods undersupply argument: a single, large hegemonic state being the only type of state able and willing to take on the cost of providing the public good of financial order because the majority of benefits flowed to itself. Smaller states may benefit from such order, but they have an incentive to free ride in terms of its provision. As such, "no hegemon, no order, big problem" became the lesson American IPE drew from Kindleberger, but it could have been worse. Taking their cue from the same scholarship, but framing it with a realist analysis, scholars such as Stephen Krasner and Robert Gilpin paid attention to the costs and benefits of being the hegemon and suggested that when costs rise and benefits fall in the hegemonic state, with more nimble "challenger states" rising more quickly and seeking to change the distribution of benefits in the system, the result was usually a hegemonic war. The future then, according to this emergent school of American IPE, was bleak if the United States really was in decline.

So how does one save the system from itself in the absence of a hegemon? American IPE scholars, seeking this answer, began to investigate how system governance could be provided in the absence of a hegemon. One solution quickly became dominant: the provision of global public goods either by a limited number of key actors or through the "demand" for "regimes" that could act as functional fillers for systemic governance. This body of work, which became known as regime theory, and later as the turn to the study of international institutions, was a direct consequence of the attempt to puzzle a way through the predicaments of HST.

From Regimes to Institutions and Compliance

For much of IPE, given the purported centrality of a hegemon for stability, cooperation in the face of free riding became a core problem to be explained. Regime theory seemingly offered a way out. The basic idea behind regime theory was that where unilateral state action fails, coordinated action through issue-specific regimes—principles, norms, rules, and decision-making procedures to promote the convergence of expectations—might work. By giving a focal point to such expectations and by reducing uncertainty and transaction costs, cooperation between states (in terms of mutual policy adjustment) may become easier by acting through regimes. As such, regimes were seen as issue-specific informational networks that intervened between interests and outcomes, providing stability in the face of hegemonic decline.

Where regimes came from was, however, another issue. The very public goods undersupply argument that drove HST also haunted regime theory. One could appeal to state interests to supply regimes to be sure, but by the logic of HST, such supply should decline over time as hegemonic state capabilities waned. Moreover, why should states comply with regime dictates?

One set of theories that "solved" this puzzle by virtue of the rationalist logic it employed was the literature that developed out of regime theory in the early 1990s and that went on to become the mainstay of contemporary American IPE research: the literature on international institutions. Following a game-theoretic logic, these theorists argued that self-interested states would comply with regimes to the extent that doing so lengthened the "shadow of the future" for cooperation, thus lessening the present discounted pay-off to free riding in the present.

As such, cooperation via institutions becomes a Nash equilibrium (self-reinforcing) strategy.

Building on this insight, American scholars working in this tradition have highlighted how uncertainty about the future forms a barrier to cooperation. Consequently, what international institutions (G20 meetings, the Basel Agreements, etc.) do is reduce the opacity of the system through the provision of information, which lowers uncertainty and increases the possibility of cooperation and the density of ties, thus making side payments and monitoring possible, thus furthering cooperation still more. Rules thereby act not as limits to state action that states would resist but as resources that allow states to credibly commit to each other, thus lengthening the shadow of the future further.

This move beyond the impasse of regime theory and HST defines the main thrust of American IPE scholarship today. A focus on rules (legalization) and how they are related to bargaining positions, enforcement costs, and credibility have become the touchstones of contemporary analysis across a huge number of issue areas. From questions of institutional design to a generalized use of open-economy macroeconomics as the basic framework for contemporary work harnessed to microeconomic logics and statistical techniques, American IPE has narrowed in its methodological orientation, developing a preference for analytic rigor and theoretical coherence over traditional "big questions" such as America's decline or, contemporaneously, the rise of China. It remains, however, at least in the opinion of its protagonists, the very definition of what IPE is. Regardless of what other practitioners in other places happen to think they are doing, the rationalist study of institutions, bargaining, and commitment is IPE, "American style."

The Other American School(s)

Yet not all American IPE scholars fit so easily into this particular representation of IPE. Realist analyses have hardly given up the field. Work by David Andrews and Jonathan Kirshner on the relationship between power and money in IPE stresses realism's continuing relevance. Similarly, as Rawi Abdelal, Mark Blyth, and Craig Parsons contend, there is also a rich vein of constructivist scholarship within American IPE that deals with issues that are seemingly "off the radar" of mainstream rationalist work. For example, how nationalist and neoliberal ideologies affect state behavior, choice of currency regimes, and even the behavior of international organizations has become grist to this constructivist mill.

Most important in generating this other strand of American IPE has been the existence of the *Cornell Series in Political Economy* as a publication outlet and the pioneering work of Peter Katzenstein, the editor of this series. If scholars such as Keohane and Krasner were instrumental in giving voice to the mainstream of American IPE, Katzenstein's contribution was critical in opening up space for this "other" American scholarship.

Katzenstein's work has always evidenced a strong concern with the interaction of domestic structures and IPE. However, rather than reducing these factors to a study of legislatures, coalitions, and bargaining, as do most mainstream American IPE scholars, Katzenstein developed an understanding of the role of states in IPE that drew on more historical institutionalist understandings of politics. This different approach to what IPE is, in combination with the focus of the *Cornell Series* on cognitive and ideational factors as explanatory variables, opened the door for American scholars who do not sit so easily in the mainstream of U.S. IPE research. In sum, while it is often lambasted as narrow and insular, American IPE contains within it more diversity than its protagonists often admit.

The Development of British IPE

Origins of British IPE

Britain may have also fought the Cold War, but the Cold War did not define its scholarship as it did in the United States. Moreover, skepticism regarding the scientific pretentions of the study of politics runs deep in the UK—hence, in part, its innate methodological pluralism and analytic eclecticism. But what is of critical significance here in understanding British IPE's different orientations are two factors: (1) the failure of British political science to replicate the "four-field" structure of American political science and (2) the very different history of economic and political decline in the UK.

First of all, according to Ben Clift and Ben Rosamond, while the events of the 1970s may have provided the intellectual opening for American IPE, this moment does not mark the critical opening for

IPE scholars in the UK, since British IPE has a far longer lineage than can be ascribed to the economic dislocations of the early 1970s. Second, there never has been a "parent discipline" for British IPE; it has always been a multidisciplinary exercise. British political science neither saw itself as the end of the developmental telos nor sought to "keep the Marxists out." Nor was there any necessary connection to international relations theory in political science.

These differences are themselves explained by the four "drivers" of the British school of IPE. First, there is a long tradition of scholarship that deals with the political economy of British imperialism, which has given much of British social science a particular historicist cast. Second, there is the postwar literature on decolonization and the global role of sterling in that period, which is IPE in all but overt self-identification. Third, there is the enormous literature on the UK's own economic decline, especially the international determinants thereof, which makes the boundary cast in the United States between IPE and comparative political economy much more permeable in the UK. Fourth, there has been a continuing concern with the centrality of the state in both domestic and international economic relations.

As a result of these very different lineages of scholarship, for Rosamond and Clift, the main question has less to do with problems such as the domestic preference formation of states rather than the degree to which the historical resolution of social and economic struggles have become inscribed on the state and predispose it to certain types of action. This view of British IPE gives us an understanding of not just how but why British IPE differs from its American namesake.

In short, lacking the concerns that animated American scholarship and grappling with its own particulars, British IPE has become more historically focused and more open to a variety of perspectives than its American counterpart. It has as its point of departure a basic skepticism of the worldviews that underlie American IPE and the models of cognition and causation that they enshrine. It has never been a subfield of political science, nor is it particularly beholden to political science as a field. IPE in the UK exists in departments of politics, sociology, geography, and anthropology. If American IPE is a subfield of political science, British IPE can (almost) lay claim to being a field of the social sciences in its own right, or at least a reinvention thereof focused on questions of global distribution and power.

The Other Transatlantic Bridge

As well as different material drivers, British IPE has a different set of intellectual progenitors that go beyond the confines of Britain itself but do not include the United States. As Randell Germain has argued, the legacy of the Canadian scholar Robert Cox looms large in this regard. The difference that Cox made was that due to his influence, while historical materialist approaches were marginalized in the United States, in Canada, such "critical" perspectives were constitutive of a very different type of mainstream of research. As such, there was a transatlantic bridge for IPE, but it ran from Canada to the UK and bypassed the United States.

In the UK itself, Benjamin Cohen highlights the influence of Susan Strange as the main protagonist for the development of a British version of IPE. Rather than simply focus on the power structure, as American realists are wont to do, or focus on the informational environment, as American neoliberals are fond of doing, Strange developed a more nuanced conception of power that operated through global knowledge and production as well as military and financial structures. This view of power was relational as well as material, and it paid close attention to the ideological. Strange also stressed the importance of finance for understanding IPE and competition between different global authorities, including private authorities, as key aspects of global governance. She took seriously the notion of IPE as an "open range" where a plethora of approaches should coexist, and in doing so, she anticipated much of what British IPE scholars were to produce over the next 2 decades.

Taken together then, Cox, Strange, and the very different political and institutional legacies of British development and decline gave rise to a distinct and different British school of IPE. This school was not simply a reaction to, or a rejection of, American IPE. Rather, it was a school of thought that had set up its own stall and carried on as if the Americans didn't really exist. The result has been a research community animated by an entirely different set of concerns. This is demonstrated by comparing the publication themes of the two schools in their respective American and British journals.

Comparing American and British IPE

Taking the U.S.-based journal *International Studies Quarterly* (*ISQ*) as representative of American IPE beyond the rationalist mainstream and the British journal *New Political Economy* (*NPE*) as representative of British IPE yields the following comparisons. Of the 372 articles published in *ISQ* over the period 1997 to 2008, 31% were identifiable as "liberal approaches," 17% were "realist," 9% were "mixed," and the rest were scattered across the categories of constructivism, feminism, poststructuralism, and neo-Marxism, which hardly suggests a disciplinary monotheism. Since American IPE exists as a part of political science, it is not really surprising when the biggest single category that emerges from the *ISQ* sample is "questions directly related to existing debates in IR theory," while the second is "security studies," Cohen's (2008) twin cores of U.S. international relations (IR) theory.

Repeating this exercise for *NPE* gives quite different results. Few, if any, of the contributions to *NPE* speak of the core issues of IR theory. Instead, they cluster around three topic areas: (1) the evolution of advanced capitalist states (17%), (2) development (17%), and (3) globalization (14%). The remainder are similarly scattered among various topic areas. Many of *NPE*'s articles would sit well in journals such as *Comparative Studies in International Development*. Given this, what do British scholars publish and research under these rubrics that is so different from the work of American scholars? Several areas stand out in contemporary British IPE that are largely absent in American IPE: a concern with ontology and philosophical foundations, a focus on normative concerns and ethics, critiques of finance capitalism and globalization, and historical materialist, Gramscian poststructuralist, feminist, and "everyday" IPE.

The "Critical" Concerns of British IPE

Angus Cameron and Ronen Palan put it well when they argue that the differences between American and British IPE can be summed up in the quip that in the American school "data and observation are so unproblematic we can accept them as real," while in the British school "data and observation are so problematic that we can dispense with them altogether" (2009, p. 123). However, for the British school, data derive from methods, and prior to methodological choices lie ontological, epistemological, and general philosophical concerns.

Lacking the scientism of their American peers and embracing Cox's injunction that the point of theory is critique, British IPE views the role of IPE as taking the measure of the world rather than simply measuring it: to judge and to evaluate, to be a "critical" body of theory. Doing so necessarily breaks the distinction between positive and normative theory that American IPE relies on and instead opens up British IPE to questions of legitimacy and ethics.

For example, although American IPE scholars have certainly been active in the area of understanding international finance, British scholars have been far more critical in their examination of international finance. From Strange's *Mad Money* (1998) to Paul Langley's concern with the construction of the "ethical investor," British writing on finance has developed a far more critical view of finance in IPE.

Pushing this critical edge still further are the various Marxist scholars who form an important part of British IPE—a species almost extinct in the United States. Building on the legacy of Robert Cox, a new generation of British historical materialists has sought to engage IPE from their own particular intellectual angle. In the hands of these scholars, the notion of hegemony radically departs from its American meaning of simple "dominance" by a state toward its original Gramscian meaning of "intellectual leadership and subordination" by transnational class forces and historic blocs.

Finally, there are scholars within British IPE who try to transcend the very notion of IPE itself. Feminist scholars form one such community within British IPE. Their focus on social reproduction—that is, how the division of labor in capitalism rests on a prior division of labor of the household and how such gendered structures are replicated through the practices of IPE—forms the core of this enterprise.

In a similar manner, the so-called everyday IPE scholars contest the notion of a state-centric IPE. For most IPE scholars, the answer to the question of "who governs?" in IPE is usually "some sort of set of *elite* actors." In contrast, for "everyday" scholars such as Leonard Seabrooke, non-elite actors, the masses, not the elites, their patterns of consumption and production, and crucially their ability to confer legitimacy on or withhold it from elite actions, all come to the fore as explanatory factors in the world economy. Scholarship in this vein has engaged issues as diverse as pension reform, the relationship between housing finance and global financial power, and the ability of microstate tax havens to persist despite OECD efforts to shut them down from this interdisciplinary "bottom-up" rather than "top-down" perspective.

In sum, British IPE is quite a different species from American IPE. It has different origins, orientations, logics, philosophical concerns, targets, agendas, and even views of causation and matter. It is not simply a variation on a theme, it is quite a different beast; hence the claim that IPE is plural. But it may be worse than that, for beyond the United States and the UK, there lie many claims to IPE that can just as easily be recognized as such, even if the authors use different labels.

Asian IPE

The United States and Britain (or more correctly Britain and Canada) are not the only places that have made a contribution to IPE scholarship. As Walden Bello has argued, the distinctive contribution that scholarship "in and about" East Asia has added to IPE is the literature on the developmental state. That is, a literature developed in and about East Asia that focuses on the state as an active agent in economic development. Moreover, there was, argues Bello, a strong normative edge to such scholarship that argued "for" states in development against the neoliberal inclination of American scholarship. From its inception, these models were set up as a challenge to scholarship that sees universalist processes as stemming from the Western experience.

The distinctive focus of this literature on the state-as-actor enables it to open up issues that Western, especially American, IPE approaches miss due to their relegation of such processes to "domestic politics." As such, the economically positive "legacy-effects" of colonialism, the role of labor repression (and the lack of democracy) in state-led industrialization efforts, the importance of equalitarian land reform, and how the politics of firm–state relations changed over time, all come into focus. By tying the actual developmental history of the East Asian states into the story of the evolution of East Asian/developmental state scholarship, Bello argues convincingly that this literature is itself an important contribution to contemporary IPE—a contribution that belongs to neither the United States nor the UK.

Underdevelopment and IPE: France and Latin America

IPE is then not only constituted by what its U.S. and British partisans think it is. There are Asian contributions, and there are also telling absences. Turning first to the lack of IPE in continental Europe, particularly France, Nicolas Jabko highlights three main reasons why IPE remains "underdeveloped" in France. First, in France, heterodox economists, rather than political scientists, tend to be the political economists in France. Particularly important here is the work of the economists of the French "regulation school," who tend to concentrate on the internal dynamics of capitalist economies. As such, both politics and the notion of the "international" as a distinct sphere of action are underplayed. Second, there is a strong bias against importing U.S. scholarship. Third is the relationship to Marxism. While both the UK and France have long-standing legacies of Marxist scholarship, there was, in the postwar period in France, a general flight from Marxism in economics and political science rather than the embrace of it as in the British case. As such, IPE in France, and in Europe, in general, remains, as Jabko puts it, "underdeveloped."

A similar story exists in Latin America, where a strong indigenous theory of IPE—dependency theory—offered a powerful alternative theory of international political and economic processes. Dependency theory argued that capitalism is a system of unequal exchange that locked peripheral economies into exploitative relationships with the core states of the rich North. Rather than stimulate the development of the whole economy and generate broad-based growth, international economic relations retarded the growth of peripheral economies while promoting export enclaves. This in turn produced a politics of inequality domestically that could only be held in check by repressive forces. Jose Gabriel Palma argues that these once popular IPE literatures turned pathological when, over time, the fit between the facts generated by the world economy and the theory diverged so much that the goal of dependency theorists became saving the theory at the expense of reality. As such, the theory lost its relevance, and a genuine Latin American contribution to IPE disappeared and left the field to other approaches.

IPE in All but Name? Sociologists and Economic Historians

One consequence of not being able to "bind" IPE is that one is bound to run into other academics who are doing essentially the same thing, but do not call what they do IPE. So the question becomes to what extent there is any IPE beyond self-described IPE scholars. John Campbell, for example, argues that international political sociologists have for many years been IPE scholars. Such sociologists have studied topics such as the diffusion of norms on an international level, how neoliberalism has been transmitted around the world, how the international division of labor is structured, and how the comparative economic performance of different states is explainable by regime type: literatures that are "IPE in all but name." Michael Oliver provides a second example of "IPE in all but name" in the work of economic historians. Oliver notes that economic historians tend to differ from IPE scholars in two ways. First of all, most economic historians seek neither empirical laws nor narrow methodological perspectives. Yet, despite this difference in approach, there exists a strong similarity between economic history and IPE. In short, some of the biggest names in IPE are economic historians in the broadest sense of the term, in that they use historical sources and construct historical narratives, so there is a natural overlap.

Is the Future of IPE Fractured?

IPE as an object can be reasonably well defined; IPE as a subject, as a way of knowing practiced by a community of scholars sharing a common branch of scholarship, is far more fractured. There is a distinctive American school, based in political science, that is becoming more distinctive over time with its common focus on "open-economy politics," allied to statistical and formal methods centering on questions of institutional design, compliance, and credibility. Yet within this supposed monolith is a thriving IPE scholarship of a different stripe.

There is also a distinctive British school. Its origins and concerns are quite different from those of the American school, and rather than the methodological narrowing we see in the American school, British IPE threatens to become not just an "interdiscipline" but the veritable reinvention of the social sciences. Beyond America and Britain (plus Canada), there are claims to be made for an Asian IPE based on the literature on the developmental state and for the importation of work by sociologists and economic historians. In one sense then, the future of IPE is bright. Monocultures get wiped out by rare events, but hybridized systems do not, and IPE seen globally is certainly hybrid. But in another sense, there are dangers on the horizon.

Although diversified on a global level, local pockets of IPE, especially the American school, are extremely homologous and badly hedged. They constitute a local monoculture that seemed to be on a high for several years, but the recent financial crisis has thrown their methods (the utility of time-series analysis) and insights (the ubiquity of transparency and information as stabilizing technologies) into question in some quarters. Moreover, if the orientation of the project overall is to "become more like economics," then the school risks redundancy, since many scholars do this already and do it better. They are called economists.

The British school, while well diversified, faces a different type of redundancy. If the many different research communities of British IPE "let a thousand flowers bloom," in doing such important work, techniques and technologies established in other fields become rather pointlessly rehashed and reinvented. There is a very real risk that British IPE ethicists skim the philosophy enough to be thinly informed, that everyday British IPE scholars reinvent a weak-kneed sociology of practice, and that British Marxists haul out Louis Althusser and Antonio Gramsci once again without making any actual progress.

In sum, if the boundaries of IPE are not drawn narrowly, it becomes increasingly difficult to say what IPE is, and what it is not. If other fields such as sociology and economic history (and geography) are included, then it has to be defined as an interdisciplinary field in its own right. But doing so has its own costs in terms of coherence and stability, as in any field of knowledge. On the other hand, drawing boundaries too tightly puts at risk its very existence as a field of knowledge.

In many ways, the British school has less at stake. If the orientation of the field is toward "a thousand flowers," then cross-pollination and what Strange calls "open range" are virtues. British IPE will persist no matter what form it takes because its precise form is less important than its (hybridized) content. In contrast, the American school has much more at stake, but this stake rests on a series of rather narrow technologies and theories that may not be as transcendentally appropriate as many of its protagonists think. By either measure, IPE is (at least) a plural field of study with an interesting future.

Mark Blyth
Brown University
Providence, Rhode Island, United States

See also Economic Policy; Hegemony; Liberalism; Power; Realism in International Relations

Further Readings

Abdelal, R., Blyth, M., & Parsons, C. (2010). *Constructing the international economy.* Ithaca, NY: Cornell University Press.

Andrews, D. M. (Ed.). (2006). *International monetary power.* Ithaca, NY: Cornell University Press.

Bello, W. (2009). State and markets, states versus markets: The developmental state debate as the distinctive East Asian contribution to IPE. In M. Blyth (Ed.), *The Routledge handbook of international political economy: IPE as a global conversation* (pp. 180–201). New York: Routledge.

Blyth, M. (Ed.). (2009). *The Routledge handbook of international political economy: IPE as a global conversation.* New York: Routledge.

Blyth, M. (2009). Torn between two lovers: Caught in the middle of British and American IPE. *New Political Economy, 14*(3), 329–336.

Cameron, A., & Palen, R. (2009). Empiricism and objectivity: Reflexive theory construction in a complex world. In M. Blyth (Ed.), *The Routledge handbook of international political economy: IPE as a global conversation* (pp. 112–125). New York: Routledge.

Campbell, J. (2009). What do sociologists bring to international political economy? In M. Blyth (Ed.), *The Routledge handbook of international political economy: IPE as a global conversation* (pp. 266–280). New York: Routledge.

Clift, B., & Rosamond, B. (2009). Lineages of a British international political economy. In M. Blyth (Ed.), *The Routledge handbook of international political economy: IPE as a global conversation* (pp. 77–93). New York: Routledge.

Cohen, B. J. (2008). *International political economy: An intellectual history.* Princeton, NJ: Princeton University Press.

Cohen, B. J. (2009). The multiple traditions of American IPE. In M. Blyth (Ed.), *The Routledge handbook of international political economy: IPE as a global conversation* (pp. 23–36). New York: Routledge.

Cox, R. W. (1981). Social forces, states and world orders: Beyond international relations theory. *Millennium, 10*(2), 126–155.

Germain, R. (2009). Of margins, traditions, and engagements: A brief disciplinary history of IPE in Canada. In M. Blyth (Ed.), *The Routledge handbook of international political economy: IPE as a global conversation* (pp. 77–93). New York: Routledge.

Gilpin, R. (1981). *War and change in world politics.* Cambridge, UK: Cambridge University Press.

Hoskyns, C., & Rai, S. (2007). Recasting the global political economy: Counting women's unpaid work. *New Political Economy, 12*(3), 297–317.

Jabko, N. (2009). Why IPE is underdeveloped in continental Europe: A case study of France. In M. Blyth (Ed.), *The Routledge handbook of international political economy: IPE as a global conversation* (pp. 231–243). New York: Routledge.

Katzenstein, P. J. (1985). *Small states in world markets.* Ithaca, NY: Cornell University Press.

Katzenstein, P. J. (2005). *A world of regions: Asia and Europe in the American imperium.* Ithaca, NY: Cornell University Press.

Keohane, R. O. (1984). *After hegemony: Cooperation and discord in the world political economy.* Princeton, NJ: Princeton University Press.

Keohane, R. O., & Nye, J. S., Jr. (Eds.). (1977). *Power and interdependence: World politics in transition.* Boston: Little, Brown.

Kindleberger, C. P. (1973). *The world in depression 1929–1939*, London: Allen Lane.

Krasner, S. D. (Ed.). (1983). *International regimes.* Ithaca, NY: Cornell University Press.

Morton, A. D. (2007). *Unraveling Gramsci: Hegemony and passive revolution in the global political economy.* London: Pluto Press.

Oliver, M. (2009). Economic history and the IPE. In M. Blyth (Ed.), *The Routledge handbook of international political economy: IPE as a global conversation* (pp. 290–307). New York: Routledge.

Palma, G. (2009). Why did the Latin American critical tradition in the social sciences become practically extinct? In M. Blyth (Ed.), *The Routledge handbook of international political economy: IPE as a global conversation* (pp. 243–266). New York: Routledge.
Seabrooke, L. (2006). *The social sources of financial power: Domestic legitimacy and international financial orders.* Ithaca, NY: Cornell University Press.
Sharman, J. C. (2006). *Havens in a storm: The struggle for global tax regulation.* Ithaca, NY: Cornell University Press.
Strange, S. (1988). *States and markets.* London: Pinter.
Strange, S. (1998). *Mad money.* Manchester, UK: Manchester University Press.

International Public Opinion

Three points structure this consideration of international public opinion. First, international public opinion research relies on statistical methods used in domestic marketing and polling research. Second, public diplomacy is closely related to consideration of public opinion dynamics in international affairs. Finally, international public opinion research has rested on a particular understanding of the organization of the international system. As information technologies change the nature of community and individual identity formation, we should expect concomitant changes in the organization and analysis of public opinion.

The utility of opinion metrics, both in business and politics, is found in the ability to reveal projected variation in cognitive and affective responses to variation in product design, price points (when relevant), or other changes in key stimulus features, regardless of whether they are commercial or political in nature. Do changes in some sort of stimuli produce changes in attitudes about the object of matter at hand? Whether we are considering a "new and improved" product or a new campaign slogan, precise public opinion metrics offer an important means of evaluating variation in design, availability, and product presentation.

With respect to *international* public opinion, the analytical specificity that undergirds market research (target marketing of micropopulations facilitated by data mining and computer analysis) and public opinion polling in political and policy domains (often with the same level of specificity found in consumer marketing) is often lost. In domestic spheres in advanced market economies in Europe, North America, and elsewhere in the world, consumer data and survey data are used to populate statistical programs that create groupings or clusters of consumers (or voters or any other germane activity). Niche media markets are then used (and often created) to reach precisely constructed market niches. The reader can see evidence of this phenomenon by visiting a local magazine distributor and noting the numerous and often esoteric variety of magazines catering to every taste, hobby, or habit. Magazines devoted to sailing, for example, aggregate consumers who share this interest, and in doing so, they provide a platform for advertisers to efficiently reach that precise audience. Similarly, users of online booksellers will be met by an opening web page that is populated by book suggestions that are uniquely tailored to that person according to his or her past purchases.

As we move away from the specification of niche populations according to complex mathematical analyses of demographic data concerning the minutiae of economic behavior, lifestyles, and political life, we usually lose this degree of specificity. Instead, we tend to see aggregations involving more general features of entire nation-states and regions. Analyses are less nuanced. The degree of specification changes, in part, owing to the enormous costs associated with multinational data collection and analysis. It is also limited by challenges associated with variations in language, culture, and economic systems, all of which put strains on both the internal and the external reliability of statistical analyses. External validity, for example, concerns the extent to which one might safely generalize the causal inference—first, from the sample studied to the defined target population and, second, to other populations that exist across time and space. Put in less technical terms, serious questions arise as to whether we can, with any confidence, speak of public attitudes about culturally specified concepts such as freedom, democracy, and rights in large-scale multinational studies.

There are, however, several noteworthy studies that have attempted to do serious transnational comparative survey work. One of the more important efforts at overcoming these limitations is the Pew

Research Center's *Global Attitudes Project*. As of 2009, Pew has conducted more than 175,000 interviews in 55 countries. Another example is found in WorldPublicOpinion.org, a consortium of domestic polling organizations from around the world that was organized and managed by the Program on International Policy Attitudes at the University of Maryland. At the time of this writing, the consortium includes research centers in more than 25 countries across all the major continents. A number of associations and academic organizations are also involved in the analysis of international public opinion. One of the oldest is the World Association for Public Opinion Research, founded in 1947.

Noteworthy efforts such as these aside, the scale of international public opinion measurement tends to limit the practical application of metrics. Publics in international public opinion are most often defined by the commonality of manageable geographical space, usually defined in terms of the nation-state and its subdivisions in provinces, states, or districts. That is, statistically and demographically specified subgroups, as found in commercial or domestic political marketing, are not found in most publicly available analyses of international public opinion. Instead, pollsters, policymakers, scholars, and politicians speak of larger aggregations, such as American, Japanese, Russian, or other nationally defined collective of common identity.

Besides its broader nature, international public opinion is also more likely to be concerned with the dynamics of international public standing of nation-states and closely related questions about the effectiveness of various public diplomacy programs intended to affect those standings. Clarifying this idea requires a brief detour into public diplomacy.

Whereas traditional diplomacy involves negotiations, démarches, and other forms of official communication between representatives of nation-states, public diplomacy by contrast focuses on the ways in which a government of one country communicates with and therefore influences (or so it is assumed) publics in another country or region. The term *public diplomacy* was first used in 1965 by Edmund Gullion, then dean of Fletcher School of Law and Diplomacy at Tufts University. He defined it as

> the influence of public attitudes on the formation and execution of foreign policies. It encompasses dimensions of international relations beyond traditional diplomacy . . . [including] the cultivation by governments of public opinion in other countries; the interaction of private groups and interests in one country with those of another . . . (and) the transnational flow of information and ideas. (From an early brochure of the Edward R. Murrow Center of Public Diplomacy, Fletcher School, Tufts University)

There is, however, no generally accepted or broadly shared definition of public diplomacy. For example, it isn't clear whether it involves only international broadcasting (and today Internet outreach) or if it also properly includes educational and cultural exchange programs, disaster relief and aid programs, and other forms of international communication of cultural, political, and policy intent. Nor is there a well-specified social science theory or set of theories that serve to ground the expectations some observers have concerning what public diplomacy can realistically achieve by affecting international public opinion. Therefore, those responsible for public diplomacy may lay out ambitious goals such as improving international opinion toward the United States, when in fact there are major methodological challenges associated with measuring the extent of such change. It is not clear how one might go about finding communication stimuli capable of producing a measurable cognitive effect in a generally specified foreign audience over the short term. As Robert Entman has made clear, political communication and social psychological research findings do not support such an optimistic expectation.

In sum, international public opinion is often contextualized by an undertheorized discussion about international public opinion concerning broad aggregations, such as the standing of the United States in world opinion. Unlike the analysis of domestic public opinion in politics and economics, methodological, logistical, and theoretical encumbrances limit the sorts of data collected and questions asked. Generally, international public opinion analysis tends to follow the contours of geopolitically drawn maps: We are presented with aggregate statistics about opinion profiles according to national identity.

Target marketing strategies that rely on rich streams of demographic and lifestyles data point to forms of aggregating "publics" that do not necessarily rest in geopolitically determined identities. Put differently, an underlying premise in international public opinion research is that publics, by nature, can be understood or conceived of only in terms of the coincidental sharing of geographical space. Where one is born is, along with socialization, a fundamental element to public opinion. International public opinion is therefore analyzed according to a particular understanding of the nature of the international system itself. Comparative opinion profiles according to national boundaries are most often understood as defining the parameters of the concept itself. We can speak of how a given nation-state is held in good (or low) regard by the citizens of an array of other nation-states.

But as Benedict Anderson has taught us, aggregations of this sort, as natural as they may seem, are synthetic and, relatively speaking, quite new to human history. Anderson (1991) defines a nation as "an imagined political community [that is] imagined as both inherently limited and sovereign" (p. 7). An imagined community is different from an actual community because it is not (and cannot be) based on everyday face-to-face interaction between its members. Such a thing is possible only in communities rooted in a shared and small geographical space. Instead, in a nation-state, members hold in their minds a mental image of their affinity. We are "Americans," "Germans," or "Russians" not because we know all of our kinsmen but rather because of a mental state that defines the contours of a mapped affinity group—the nation.

The formation of such an imagined affinity group became feasible only with the rise of print capitalism. Anderson (1991) notes that the basic structure of two forms of imagining that first flowered in Europe in the 18th century were the novel and the newspaper. "For these forms provided the technical means for 're-presenting' the kind of imagined community that is the nation." (p. 25). The nature of possible imagined communities is associated with the nature of communication systems.

The information environment of the first decade of the 21st century, where communities and individuals across the globe are knitted together by high-speed and low-cost computer and telecommunication links, opens the door to new forms of imagined communities constituted by aggregations rooted in cyber rather than physical space. As with imagined communities qua nation-states, the basis of collective affinity is a sense of communicated and shared values and norms. But whereas newspapers and, to a lesser degree, books were confined to a fixed geographical space, communication today is uprooted from both space and time. Communication appears everywhere in real time.

James Rosenau's work, especially *Along the Domestic-Foreign Frontier* and *Distant Proximities*, has led the way in helping us think about the international system in this new way. An alternative model to the geocentric understandings of the public and public opinion is therefore found in the consideration of affinity groups consisting of individuals working collaboratively according to shared norms and values, though not necessarily in shared physical space. In this way, one might even say that we move away from international—where the nation is still the central organizing principle—public opinion to global public opinion.

One expression of global public opinion, understood in this way, can be found in nongovernmental organizations (NGOs), or what Ann Florini calls a third force in the international system. Between 1973 and 1983, the number of transnational human rights organizations doubled from 41 to 89. In the next decade, the number doubled again. Between 1973 and 2000, the number of NGOs working for women's rights increased by 300%, a figure that probably underestimates the larger number of organizations that work for women's rights but not exclusively. There is little doubt that NGOs of all types—working for human rights, environmental issues, nuclear nonproliferation, economic development, and many other causes and concerns—are a growing factor in international affairs. The point here is that transnational advocacy organizations and social movements constitute an expression of a nongeographically rooted public created by a set of values and norms that are shared across the globe through new media. Supporters and constituent elements of transnational NGOs are members of a community of shared beliefs and values—publics—without necessarily being members of a shared geographically defined community. They constitute a new type of international public opinion.

But their importance is perhaps found not in the growth of their individual numbers but rather in the growth of their coordination and cooperation. In domestic politics, it is often said that public opinion exerts pressure to create particular outcomes. In international affairs, communities of like-minded individuals and organizations may achieve something similar. Margaret E. Keck and Kathryn Sikkink (1998) define transnational advocacy networks (TANs) as "characterized by voluntary, reciprocal, and horizontal patterns of communication and exchange" (p. 8). Networks are "communicative structures." Communication structures create new forms of imagined communities, as Anderson argued. This opens up fascinating new ways to conceptualize and study international public opinion.

This entry has reviewed international public opinion in the context of the more precise domestic analysis of opinion research. It has also noted the close relationship between international public opinion and public diplomacy. Finally, this entry has reviewed recent thinking among international affairs scholars with regard to the changing nature of the organization of the international system. New information technologies open up the possibility of imagined communities that are not rooted in geographical space but rather in cyberspace. In short, we may now consider the public opinion measurement of communities consisting of those who share similar values and norms and organize themselves into communities accordingly but who do not share common physical space.

Steven Livingston
The George Washington University
Washington, D.C., United States

See also International Solidarity; Political Communication; Public Opinion

Further Readings

Anderson, B. (1991). *Imagined communities*. London: Verso.

Anholt, S., & Hildreth, J. (2009). *Brand America: The mother of all brands*. London: Cyan Books.

Bimber, B. (2003). *Information and American democracy: Technology in the evolution of political power*. New York: Cambridge University Press.

Castells, M. (2003). *Rise of the network society*. New York: Wiley.

Entman, R. (2008). Theorizing mediated public diplomacy: A case study. *International Journal of Press/Politics, 13*(2), 87–102.

Florini, A. (Ed.). (2000). *The third force: The rise of transnational civil society*. Washington, DC: Carnegie Endowment for International Peace.

Keck, M., & Sikkink, K. (1998). *Activists beyond borders: Advocacy networks in international politics*. Ithaca, NY: Cornell University Press.

Tan, P., Steinback, M., & Kumar, V. (2006). *Introduction to data mining*. Boston: Pearson Addison-Wesley.

Turow, J. (1997). *Breaking up America: Advertisers and the new media world*. Chicago: University of Chicago Press.

International Regimes

Unlike many concepts in international relations, there is broad agreement on the definition of international regimes. Stephen Krasner (1983) provided the standard definition, according to which international regimes are "principles, norms, rules, and decision-making procedures around which actor expectations converge in a given issue-area" (p. 1). Regime theorists generally try to explain the emergence, persistence, change, and decline of these relatively stable patterns of international collaboration and coordination. International regimes are to be distinguished from national regimes, which describe the formal and informal structure of political power in a country.

All major theoretical schools of international relations are represented in the study of regimes. The first articulations of the realist theory of hegemonic stability and of (neo)liberal institutionalism appeared in the early 1970s. Arguably, the first coherent expressions of constructivism in international relations also appeared in this period and treated the diffusion and use of knowledge in relation to technology transfer. The study of international regimes experienced its golden age from the early 1980s to the late 1990s, but the remarkable productivity of the research program has since shifted the focus of inquiry to the related normative questions of global governance and toward disaggregating regime theory to include the influence of domestic interests on the international delegation of authority and sovereignty.

Realists' Regimes

Many realists see in international regimes an extension of the power politics that suffuse all international political life and apply economic rationality to explain the creation and demise of regimes. According to the hegemonic stability theory of international regimes, only powerful states can supply regimes as public goods, and they will do so only when they expect a net gain in their relative power positions as a result. Other states are then able to act as free riders by benefitting from the regime without contributing to its provision, or they can be caught as forced consumers if they do not desire the regime but cannot escape its scope. Though the hegemonic stability theory of international regimes can explain the demand for and supply of regimes, it has been criticized with the observation that many regimes are not strictly public goods because they are excludable and potentially rivals. Moreover, a group of states might be able to supply the regime jointly in the absence of a hegemon, as is the case with the small minority of states that provides the vast majority of the United Nations' (UN's) budget.

Some scholars have modified this realist account by positing that states are not uniformly sensitive to gains reaped by others. A given state is less likely to measure its own gains relative to those of an ally or a small and distant state than to those of a rival or powerful neighbor. Weighing relative gains implies that all states, rather than a lone hegemon, will seek to create and maintain regimes as long as they assess their own benefit to be greater than the benefit accrued by other relevant states. The resurgence of classical realism, which is less reliant on an economic concept of rationality, also provides a modified institutionalist explanation according to which dominant states will establish regimes with rules congenial to themselves in order to create an institution whose normative and regulatory inertia will benefit them even after their power begins to wane. That the five great power victors of World War II have the only seats on the UN Security Council endowed with permanence, veto power, and a UN-sanctioned right to possess nuclear weapons serves as an example. Other variables, such as whether a state is revisionist or satisfied with the status quo as well as the polarity of the international system, can also be integrated into such analyses.

Neoliberals' Regimes

Neoliberal theories also heavily incorporate microeconomic analogies. Liberal theories of international regimes that focus on domestic preference aggregation and upward causality also exist, but they tend to be less well developed than the neoliberal theories. The core theses of the neoliberal account are that regimes would be unnecessary were it not for the "market failures" of an anarchical system, that international regimes are not mere epiphenomena of power, and that many states are interdependent, such that the advantage to the one depends on the success of the others. Specifically, market failures include the lack of an authoritative international legal framework, imperfect information, and transaction costs, all of which inhibit states from having confidence in contracts. Regimes alleviate this problem by providing states with more and better information about others' activities, reducing transaction costs by providing a single standard for all rather than many bilateral standards, and extending the shadow of the future so that defectors can be punished.

The neoliberal literature relevant to international regimes is vast, but there are several common elements. Among these are the analytical assumption of states as unitary, utility-maximizing actors and the use of game-theoretic analogies to formalize the collective action problems that give rise to regimes. Briefly, there are assurance games in which all parties prefer the same outcome and for which no regime is required, coordination games in which there are multiple outcomes that the parties find acceptable and that will often require a mere convention, and collaboration games in which the parties must forgo their maximum strategies to achieve the optimal outcome. Examples of these would include food safety (where there is little or no incentive to cheat), a common language for international flight personnel (where several coordination points are effectively equivalent), and the nuclear nonproliferation regime (where there are strong incentives to cheat), respectively.

The microeconomic logic used in neoliberal regime analysis provides a parsimonious framework, but it naturally assumes knowledge of actors' interests, which are in turn a function of their preferences. However, this framework provides no insight about the sources or form of these preferences, and the neoliberal approach has been criticized for imposing definitions of utility on actors rather than discovering them. The assumption of a single, definitive preference ranking for each actor and a neglect of the normative consequences of regimes are further sources of criticism.

Constructivists' Regimes

Whereas the realist and neoliberal approaches assume unitary actors with clear and singular preference structures, the constructivist approach problematizes these and seeks to ascertain actor preferences rather than assign them. Instead of assuming that actors follow a logic of consequences, which is based on their assessments of the costs and benefits of different courses of action, constructivists would argue that decision makers follow a logic of appropriateness, in which they choose a course of action based on their perception of the situation and of their roles in it. Accordingly, the way in which an issue is framed and the inputs of the domestic and international political processes are important determinants of the final regime outcome.

One source of input that can operate at domestic and international levels is epistemic communities. These are networks of professional experts with technical knowledge about the problem a regime could solve. For example, the Bretton Woods institutions would have been anathema to both the protectionist and liberal Ricardian ideas that had dominated before World War II, but institutional innovation was clearly required to rebuild the world economy in its wake. As Keynesian liberal interventionism gained currency among economic experts, however, the victors were able to agree on institutions that would allow both free trade and an active industrial policy, though such institutions had been previously unthinkable. Without changing the physical nature of the problem or the constitution of the actors, new knowledge can substantially recast actors' understanding of a problem and their likely courses of action.

Many constructivists would argue that cooperation in the context of regimes presumes a preexisting repertoire of shared normative concepts and communicative deeds. Taking this line of argument further, some constructivists problematize the normative structures and social institutions that, they would argue, provide the conditions of possibility for concepts such as rationality, legitimacy, and cooperation in the first place. Hypothesizing such malleability in international institutions has led many critical theorists to question whether the current configuration of international regimes could not be recast to become more just by making them less reflective of the prevailing power and distributional structures. The constructivist approach has been criticized for lacking some elements that would support a cumulative research agenda, such as a falsifiable corpus of theory and hypothesis-generating research questions.

Empirical Analysis and Open Questions

In the empirical study of regimes, qualitative methods dominate because though there are some regime characteristics that most studies seek to explain, such as effectiveness, robustness, and change over time, the issue areas and characteristics of particular regimes differ too much for the construction of data sets and quantitative methods to be practical. Where theoretically applicable, researchers often devise a formal model, such as a game-theoretic matrix; derive hypotheses from the model; and try to show the similarities between the model and the case in question. Where comparison between regimes is sensible, comparative case studies are also widely used. One recent project has produced the International Regimes Database, which includes data pertaining to 23 regimes and 172 regime elements. The researchers involved hope that this will allow others to analyze certain dimensions of regimes across cases and to develop broadly valid hypotheses and generalizations. Because comparison between regimes is often not sensible, it has also been suggested that counterfactuals could be an appropriate tool to isolate the independent effects of regimes. In fact, a proposal has even been made to study international nonregimes—that is, issue areas in which the conditions indicate that a regime would be likely to occur but none is present.

Despite these innovative proposals, scholarly interest has somewhat migrated away from the study of international regimes as such. This change shows that regime theory is partially a victim of its own success. The research program has served to move the debate beyond the crude conceptions of international anarchy that had previously dominated it, but attention has now broadly shifted to the normative consequences of different forms of international and global governance and the closer examination of mechanisms within and below regimes. Specifically, much research in the rationalist framework has begun to examine how authority is delegated from various domestic structures and processes to international and supranational decision-making fora. Constructivist research is now primarily concerned with the legitimacy of the authority thus delegated and how to make the resulting decisions and policies more representative of interest groups at all levels. Recent studies have also begun to consider the transnational aspects of international regimes more closely by investigating when and how private entities, such as firms and cartels, have developed regulatory regimes among themselves. This trend is also visible in the research treating the governance implications of public–private partnerships, in which governments and private firms contract to perform some function.

Ben Kamis and Andreas Hasenclever
Universität Tübingen
Tübingen, Germany

See also Anarchy; Constructivism in International Relations; Cooperation; Delegation; Governance, Global; International Organizations; International Political Economy; International System; Market Failure; Neoliberal Institutionalism; Public Goods; Realism in International Relations

Further Readings

Hasenclever, A., Mayer, P., & Rittberger, V. (1997). *Theories of international regimes*. Cambridge, UK: Cambridge University Press.

Krasner, S. D. (Ed.). (1983). *International regimes*. Ithaca, NY: Cornell University Press.

March, J., & Olsen, J. (1998). The institutional dynamics of international political orders. *International Organization, 52,* 943–969.

Young, O., & Zürn, M. (2006). The international regimes database: Designing and using a sophisticated tool for institutional analysis. *Global Environmental Politics, 6,* 121–143.

International Relations, History

The academic field of international relations (IR) is barely a century old. Its roots, however, go much further back. This entry exposes some of these historical roots before it describes the emergence of academic IR—with its university departments, specialized courses, and plethora of journals and books devoted to the causes of war and the preconditions for a lasting peace.

The entry pays much attention to the evolution of IR in the aftermath of World War I and the emergence of its distinctive issues and approaches. Then, it follows the growth of IR as a more mature, multiparadigmatic social science in the wake of World War II. The final sections of the entry emphasize the tempestuous discussions that have marked scholarly IR after the end of the Cold War.

Philosophical Forebears

When did the science of IR emerge? According to the popular foundation myth formulated by Edward Hallett Carr in the late 1930s, it emerged from World War I, driven by a wish to create a peaceful world. Myths are not wrong, but they are not historical descriptions either. The science of IR has a more complicated birth than this. Its subject matter has been adumbrated by scholars, statesmen, and soldiers for centuries.

What is the subject matter of IR? At its core lie discussions of war and peace—not only from the standpoint of single states but also as properties of a larger society or system of states. Thus defined, foreshadowings of IR are found already in antiquity—in the West, most famously in Thucydides' *The Peloponnesian Wars* (ca. 550 BCE) and in the East, in Kautilya's *Arthaśāstra* (ca. 300 BCE). However, as antique state structures unraveled or were swallowed up by empires, discussions of interstate relations disappeared; early-medieval authors like Cassiodorus, Procopius, and al-Shaybānī discussed both war and diplomacy, but relations among states were not in their purview.

Discussions of interstate relations reappeared, however, in the postimperial age. The rise of city-states in Italy and the rediscovery of classical authors like Thucydides were attended by probing discussions of war and peace and relations among states. In Florence, for example, authors like Niccolò Machiavelli and Francisco Guicciardini reintroduced antique themes of power and princely leadership and applied them to the affairs of their own times.

Renaissance discussions tended to concern philosophical issues such as the nature of the good society and the qualities of political leadership. In the wake of the Reformation, the scholarly discussions grew more descriptive and practical, partly because of the advent of more effective state structures ruled by powerful dynasties who concentrated political power, religious authority, and military command in royal hands and partly because of the emergence of new concepts and secular theories.

Sovereignty, Contract, and Perpetual Peace

The important concept of sovereignty emerges in the late Renaissance. It received its classic formulation by Jean Bodin. The social and political implications of the concept were explored by the Dutch jurist Hugo Grotius, who wrote a learned treatise titled *Law of War and Peace* (1625), which discussed IR in light of natural law and human gregariousness. The English social philosopher Thomas Hobbes presented a different view. He argued in his *Leviathan* (1651) that rational individuals safeguard their interests by agreeing to establish a powerful state that will establish laws and protect them all. No such arrangement exists among states, however; states exist in a lawless "state of nature."

Such discussions evolved hand in hand with the 16th- and 17th-century evolution of the modern state—by the development of fiscal and military structures, by the concentration of power in the hands of powerful monarchs, and by growth in international trade. New political concepts and theories emerged, many of them grafted on to the theories of social contract expressed by Hobbes during the English civil wars and, later, by John Locke during the Glorious Revolution of 1688.

Hobbes and Locke based their political philosophies on the same thought experiment: They imagined what relations among sovereign human actors might have looked like in the absence of any overarching state authority. The resulting vision—the imaginary "state of nature"—opened up a new way of conceptualizing relations among sovereign political units, on the individual as well as the collective level. Subsequent authors applied this vision to relations among sovereign states. The Dutch philosopher Benedict de Spinoza evolved from Hobbes's argument a bleak description of interstate relations in terms of jealous sovereign actors that pursued their interests in ruthlessly egotistical ways. Christian Wolff and Émeric Vatell pursued the vision of Locke and developed a more harmonious view of rational actors that pursued their individual goals yet also understood the role played by common interests and cooperation.

These two attitudes to the world—the Hobbesian and the Lockean—evolved and interwove in subsequent years. A new step in the history of IR began during the Enlightenment, when the early notions of conflict and cooperation gave way to a more widely shared systemic perspective on the interrelations among sovereign actors.

This perspective was first expressed in two discourses that emerged in the 18th century: one orbiting the concept of balance of power and the other concerning plans for a perpetual peace. The notion of political balance is old—it was noted by Thucydides and invoked by Renaissance scholars like Francesco Guicciardini. These early authors, however, tended to apply the notion to the policy of single states (later called "containment") or to relations between pairs of states (later called "counterpoise"). But a new notion appeared during the wars of Louis XIV, when authors like Francois Fénelon noted that the order of all of Europe was maintained by a principle of balance. In 1713, the diplomats who wrote the Treaty of Utrecht noted that their aim was to establish "a durable balance" in Europe. These examples suggest a new understanding of the balance of power as a mechanism that would bring order to Europe's state relations. They indicate that Europe's macropolitical scene is seen as a unity composed of several sovereign states.

This portrayal of Europe as a system of states evolved in subsequent decades. It reached its mature form in the work of William Robertson, who set out to explain both the origins of balance-of-power policies and the mechanisms of its operation. Robertson's explanation was very influential. On the basis of it, Edward Gibbon argued that balance-of-power dynamics have prevented the multistate system of Europe from sliding back into empire. Gibbon, thus, drew an analytical distinction between a balance-of-power system of sovereign states and an empire.

The notion of a perpetual peace, too, has long forbears—its roots can be traced back to religious thinkers like Augustine, Aquinas, Dante, and Erasmus. During the Enlightenment, however, secular scenarios for a new and peaceful world order were expressed by thinkers who relied on appeals to human reason, natural rights of freedom, the reality of historical progress, and an implied notion of Europe as a system of sovereign states. Duc de Sully was among the first thinkers to propose a way of establishing peaceful relations among the sovereign states of Europe. Abbé de St. Pierre was another important contributor.

When major Enlightenment philosophers began to wrestle with the question of peace and cultivated new cosmopolitan ideals, the theoretical trickle became a flood: The cosmopolitan approach held that human beings are rational and peaceful and that conflict and war are the result of dysfunctional regime types. This attitude was expressed most famously by Prussian philosopher Immanuel Kant in his essay *Perpetual Peace: A Philosophical Sketch* (1795).

The Turn-of-the-Century Breakthrough

Balance-of-power theories and perpetual-peace plans were products of the early Enlightenment and were infused with the optimism of the age. Both theories invoked the use of reason in the service of a better world. By the 19th century, their themes and concepts were applied by soldiers, statesmen, and scholars in various fields—in history, in law, and in the new social sciences (geography, economics, sociology, and political science). Two developments helped pave the way for a more mature notion of IR.

First, there emerged a clearer notion of Europe as a system of states. The German historian Leopold von Ranke contributed to this by introducing the concept of "the Great Powers." It simplified the discussion because it reduced the Western system of states to a few formative states—*die grossen Mächte*—that drove the process and imposed their rules of conduct on the system at large.

Second, historians began to explore the interstate affairs of the very recent past and, even, current events. In England, John Seeley and Edward Freeman made the case for "contemporary history" as a worthy object of study. In Germany, Heinrich von Treitschke examined the nature and evolution of states. In his extremely popular lecture series on politics, Treitschke included some thoughts on the contemporary relations among states, during which he noted that there existed two basic approaches to the subject: The first was the "moralizing doctrine" of the British advocates of free trade; the other was the "naturalistic" approach, anchored in social philosophers like Machiavelli and Hobbes. Treitschke ridiculed the first and condoned the second.

Geographers began, in the wake of the Franco-Prussian War, to view the state in light of biological theories—Friedrich Ratzel and Johan Rudolf Kjellén saw states as organisms and interstate relations as competition for scarce resources and living space. Economists observed novel relations in international trade. French writers were quick to observe these new relations. The economist Paul Leroy-Beaulieu wrote an influential book on colonialism, *De la colonialisation chez des peoples modernes* (Of Colonization Among Modern Nations, 1874); the sociologist Jacques Novicow sought to capture interstate relations in social science terms in his *Politique internationale* (International Politics, 1886). International questions were discussed in magazines—first in the many monthlies and quarterlies that emerged in the final decades of the century (*The North American Review*, *The Review of Reviews*, *Journal des deux mondes* [Review of the Two Worlds], and many others) and then in professional social science journals (*Political Science Quarterly*, *American Political Science Review*, and *Journal of Race Development*).

A most significant contributor to the evolution of IR theory was a new movement in international law. It was explicitly cosmopolitan and sponsored by an international network of legal activists. They founded a journal, *Revue de droit international et legislation compareé* (*RDI*; *Journal of International and Comparative Law*), as well as the Institute of International Law in Ghent. They were wedded to the idea that international conflict could be avoided by the elaboration of international law—indeed, they believed that conflicts could be solved by the establishment of international institutions devoted to adjudication and arbitration.

One of them, the Scottish scholar James Lorimer, wrote an essay that reduced centuries of scholarly speculation to a few basic points. In an essay for the *RDI* in 1871, titled "Final Problem in International Law," Lorimer explained that international politics is played out in a community of states whose members are sovereign and that it, as a result, lacks a central body of legislation. It is, thus, a lawless society—an "anarchy," as Lorimer dubbed it. Lawlessness is, however, not the same as orderlessness, continued Lorimer. Order is imposed on this anarchical society by two mechanisms: (1) the political principle of balance of power and (2) the economic principle of interdependence. Since neither result in a stable order, it will be necessary to add a third ordering principle—namely, a centralized legislature and mechanisms that can enforce its laws.

In the liberal states of the West, other activists entertained similar views. A growing number of people joined organizations that opposed war and promoted peace. Members of national assemblies established the Inter-Parliamentary Union (1889) designed to solve conflicts and ease international tensions. Such efforts contributed greatly to the Peace Conference in Hague in 1899, which, in turn, established the Permanent Court of Arbitration. This Hague conference was attended by nearly all the sovereign states in the world. And it was eagerly supported by more than 400 peace organizations.

This optimistic atmosphere waned during the final years of the century by the new and darker mood of *Realpolitik*. The German historian Heinrich von Treitschke expressed this new sentiment with his portrayal of politics as a competition among territorial states for power and influence. This change was noted by the American historian and diplomat Paul Reinsch in *World Politics* (1900). The "age of reason" was in his opinion replaced by an "age of force." The change was, according to Reinsch, hastened by the Franco-Prussian War (1871), which led to the unification of Germany and to the alteration of Europe's established political relations. It was also hastened by the growth of industrialism and nationalism.

The new zeitgeist was well represented by the advent of social Darwinism and by the new imperialism, which Reinsch held to be one of the most influential ideas of the age. Other ideas also emerged in the wake of the Franco-Prussian War and affected scholarly discussions of war and peace. Among them were liberal and radical ideas that protested the new militarism and warned against new wars on the continent. Critical voices were carried by members of the evolving social sciences: geography, economics, sociology, and political science all made their imprint on the systematic study of war, peace, and IR. Norman Angell's *Great Illusion* (1910), for example, drew on liberal theories of finance and trade to warn against war in the industrial age and to condemn statesmen who foolishly still imagined that wars could be won. Weapons systems are now so destructive and industrial nations are so tightly tied together in webs of interdependence that war among them would bring disaster on them all.

World War I and After

The debate about IR has a long prehistory. World War I converted this debate into a field of scholarly study. It happened quickly, as a sudden burst when the war deteriorated, counter to all military opinions, into a stalemate of deadly trench warfare. Between 1914 and 1917, the vast armies of Europe's industrial states shelled each other senseless at the average cost of 100,000 young soldiers' lives per week. How could this meaningless slaughter happen? How could it be brought to an end? What could be done to prevent a similar catastrophe in the future? Statesmen and scholars struggled to answer these questions. And the scholarly study of IR emerged as one of the results.

Similar questions had long been discussed by historians, lawyers, and antiwar activists. Two additional groups added their voices and helped boost the scholarly study of IR. The first group consisted of wealthy industrialists who had sponsored research on war and education for peace before World War I—men like Alfred Nobel,

Andrew Carnegie, and Richard Garton. The second group consisted of political operatives—men like James Bryce and Philip Noël Baker in England and Woodrow Wilson in the United States. For with the senseless destruction of World War I, civil servants, diplomats, statesmen, and their advisers also grew increasingly concerned with issues of war and peace.

War as a Catalyst

The outbreak of war in 1914 spurred a flurry of attempts to explain its causes and identify the conditions for a lasting postwar peace. G. Lowes Dickinson, a classics scholar at Cambridge University, argued that although Prussian militarism was an immediate cause of the war, the deeper cause was the lawless or "anarchic" state of affairs among sovereign states. He justified his claim in a slim 1916 book, *The European Anarchy*.

Other authors and activists, too, designed proposals for such ordering organizations. In the United States, Yale mathematician Irving Fisher presented an idea for a "league of peace." A most influential scheme was presented by Leonard Woolf, a British civil servant turned author and publisher. His *International Government* (1916) deeply influenced diplomats and statesmen like Robert Cecil, Jan Smuts, and Woodrow Wilson. At the Peace Conference in Paris (1919), President Wilson relied on Woolf's argument to push for a League of Nations.

Wilson's initiative transformed international politics. His arguments at the Paris Peace Conference challenged the views of old statesmen. His vision of a League of Nations appealed greatly to the broad public. It formulated, among other things, a need for research and education in international affairs.

While Wilson met with other statesmen in Paris to convince them of his vision for a postwar League, legal experts and scholarly advisers met to discuss postwar collaboration in international research and education. The world's first Department of International Politics was established at the University of Wales, Aberystwyth, in 1919—financed by a generous endowment from the wealthy industrialist David Davies. Institutes of International Affairs were founded in Britain and the United States in 1920. The London School of Economics and Political Science (LSE) established a department of IR (1924). In the United States, comparable departments were established at Georgetown University (Edmund A. Walsh School of Foreign Service, 1919), University of Southern California (School of International Relations, 1924), and University of Chicago (The Committee on International Relations, 1928), to mention but a few. The impression left by this development is that the scholarly study of IR emerged during the 1920s as an English-language discipline—in spite of the fact that Switzerland established the first school entirely devoted to IR (Geneva's Graduate Institute of International Studies, 1927).

Early IR continued the perpetual peace tradition. Kant's famous essay *Perpetual Peace* was a central text in many early reading lists that were steeped in a liberal faith in free trade, popular democracy, and collective security. Contemporary popular textbooks were written by Ernest Satow, David P. Heatley, S. H. Allen, and P. Potter. They tended to discuss the causes of war and the preconditions for peace—and commonly saw the causes of war as irrationality or ill will and the preconditions for peace in rational diplomacy with an eye toward establishing norms, rules, and international institutions.

Idealism and the First Great Debate

These first years of scholarly IR were conducted in President Wilson's shadow. This is easy to understand: In the wake of a shockingly destructive war, the tired populations of the West cleaved to Wilson and his League as their one great hope (he was awarded the Nobel Peace Prize in 1919 and was generally hailed as a worthy recipient). Also, the League was in its earliest years an active and apparently effective organization. The foreign ministers of the Great Powers attended League meetings and used the League machinery to improve relations and settle their differences.

Not all observers, however, shared this general confidence in human reason, trade, and international law. Some still saw world events through prisms of competition and power. Their case was strengthened as world events were marked by deepening economic crises and interstate competition, and the League met with declining success. The League could not prevent the Chaco War, Japan's occupation of Manchuria, Italy's invasion of Abyssinia, or Germany's rearmament. The changing relations among the Great Powers, combined with the advent of insistent rhetoric drawn from strong political ideologies, altered the political climate. And the study of IR altered with it.

There emerged authors who, invoking the apparent ineffectiveness of the League, criticized its cosmopolitan advocates and called them "idealist" or "utopian." In the name of "realism," they rejected the idea that international organizations such as the League could prevent war. Authors like Frederick L. Schuman, Frank H. Simonds, and James T. Shotwell rejected the assumption that undergirded liberal internationalism—that human beings are inherently pacific and, if left to their own devices, would establish peaceful relations with one another. Many authors held that humans are basically self-interested and that, although they pursue their egotistical goals in rational ways, they will inevitably enter into conflicts with one another. Others argued that humans are not fully rational. Still others claimed that evil and sinful impulses have corrupted human reason and behavior.

The American theologian Reinhold Niebuhr drew on all these arguments. In *Moral Man and Immoral Society* (1932), Niebuhr argued that individual humans may be both well-meaning and rational but that these qualities do not apply to human collectivities—such as states—whose behaviors tend to be both amoral and irrational. He also argued that the Idealist and the Romantic fail to understand the brutal character of the behavior of all human collectives and the power of self-interest and collective egoism in all intergroup relations.

Such bleak assumptions were commonly held by refugees from Europe's illiberal states. Among them were Jewish scholars who fled Nazi Germany in the 1930s and settled in Britain or the United States. Some of them—for example, John Herz and Hans Morgenthau—found teaching jobs at U.S. universities. Arnold Wolfers, who taught at Yale in the late 1930s, argued that the discipline of IR was suspended between two poles or traditions—a liberal tradition rooted in Locke and Vatell and a realist tradition informed by Machiavelli and Hobbes.

This idea of two traditions received a particularly influential formulation by Carr. He taught IR at the University of Wales in the late 1930s and divided the evolution of the scientific study of IR into two phases: first a utopian, League-focused phase that emerged in the wake of World War I and then a second, realist phase that emerged in the 1930s after a critical Great Debate. Carr expressed his two-phased account in *The Twenty Years' Crisis* (1939). The book was immensely influential and his thesis of considerable didactical value.

The French philosopher Alexandre Kojève presented an alternative account. And if Carr influenced a generation of English IR scholars, then Kojève influenced a generation of French social philosophers. Kojève was, like Carr, a Hegelian and argued that ideological strife ended with the French Revolution and that after Napoleon, the Enlightenment ideals of reason, rights, and equal recognition were universally accepted in the West. History was, in his view, at an end. His opponents begged to differ. They argued that world events were, in fact, deeply affected by ideological strife between liberalism, communism, and fascism. This clash was all the more serious, they argued, as each ideology had a Great Power behind it to back it up.

This late-interwar discussion included a broad range of perspectives. Liberal internationalism was beleaguered. On its left were socialist and communist parties and labor unions whose discussions about war and peace were informed by an alternative internationalism. Socialists and communists drew on Marxist political economy, elaborated in the shadow of Nikolai Bukharin's and Vladimir Lenin's theories of imperialism. On the far right were nationalist and fascist arguments, often informed by a social Darwinism that saw IR as a perpetual struggle among countries and races for power and living space. The fascist movement was largely anti-intellectual and poor on theory; however, there were exceptions—the antiliberal arguments of the German lawyer Carl Schmitt being a notable case.

World War II and After

By the end of the 1930s, liberal internationalism had lost its luster, squeezed between realism and radical approaches—both of which saw international politics as a struggle for power.

The war also added geopolitical dimensions to IR theorizing. Whereas World War I had largely been a European civil war, World War II was a global struggle. Also, World War II was fast paced: If the fighting paused in one theatre, it flared up in another region. Adolf Hitler and Joseph Stalin fought the war with maps of Europe in hand; Winston Churchill and Franklin Roosevelt consulted globes in their offices.

The United States emerged as the preeminent Great Power during the course of the war. President Roosevelt had two wartime aims: (1) to bring Germany and Japan to unconditional surrender and (2) to build a strong antifascist alliance of states—the United Nations (UN)—which would last beyond the war and provide the stable basis for a postwar world order. Roosevelt worked hard to achieve both goals. Like Wilson before him, Roosevelt established a worldwide political organization based on the principle of collective security, the United Nations Organization (UNO). In addition, he worked to establish economic organizations to coordinate the world's commercial relations. In 1944, delegates from the UN alliance met in the New Hampshire town of Bretton Woods and established the International Monetary Fund (IMF), the World Bank, and a liberal set of trade rules (GATT). This Bretton Woods system was meant to secure a postwar world of open, democratic states in free pursuit of commercial ventures. Roosevelt's scheme was, in other words, informed by a liberal vision of order and peace.

Just as American politicians emerged as leaders of the liberal world in the wake of World War II, so also did American scholars emerge as leading practitioners of scholarly IR. Quincy Wright was one of them. In 1941, he published *The Study of War*—an encyclopedic tome of more than 1,000 pages. Bernhard Brodie of Yale University was another of these leading scholars. Soon after the war, Brodie published *The Absolute Weapon* (1946), a book that discussed the destruction of Hiroshima and Nagasaki and assessed the impact of atomic weapons on IR. Its message was that atomic power will change the way we think about strategy and diplomacy, and war and peace. Would atomic weapons destroy the world, or would they inaugurate an era of stable world peace, wondered Brodie, echoing Kant's question of 150 years before.

Realism and the Second Debate

The realist approach was entrenched when relations between the United States and the former USSR descended into enmity and competition in the wake of World War II. The U.S. diplomat George Kennan relied on traditional *Realpolitik* when he reassessed the U.S.–Soviet relationship in 1946 and recommended that President Harry Truman adopt a foreign policy stance based on a doctrine of unwavering containment.

Morgenthau, too, advocated a realist approach. His *Politics Among Nations* (1947) quickly became a basic textbook in IR. It exercised an immense influence in the United States and elsewhere. Realism was also embraced by other influential scholars, like Georg Schwartzenberger in Great Britain and Raymond Aron in France. All saw IR as a high-stakes game played out in a system of sovereign, self-interested states who all seek to maximize power, security, and chances of survival.

Although realism dominated postwar scholarship, it was not the only approach. Realism was well suited to capture the deteriorating postwar relations between the United States and the former USSR, but it was hard to view other state relations through those very same realist lenses. It was difficult to grasp the development issues of non-Western states—their efforts to achieve political independence, economic growth, and peaceful interrelations did not suit the realist vocabulary well. It was also hard to capture some Western issues. Relations between North and South America were a case in point; communication or discussion in this context was often phrased in radical—sometimes even Marxist—terms of exploitation and repression. Relations among the United States and Western Europe were also hard to grasp in realist terms; they were commonly discussed in terms of liberal internationalism instead. Postwar relations among the states of Western Europe were also marked by a degree of cooperation and coordination insufficiently captured by the old realist concepts of "alliance" and "league." Politicians like Jean Monnet and academics like Ernest Haas used terms such as integration and federation to describe new, tighter, and more peaceful forms of interstate relations.

Also, realism showed signs of deteriorating. It provided a convenient discourse for warning against Soviet expansionism, but leading realist scholars (like Niebuhr, Morgenthau, and Kennan) cautioned against the uncritical use of terms such as balance and containment to justify ideological crusades against communism. Another movement emerged in the United States whose members criticized the realists for their excessive reliance on "wisdom" and on the anecdotal use of historical "interpretation." They argued that IR should be studied through more scientific approaches with an eye to establishing patterns or regularities in interstate behavior. They compiled data sets on conflicts and wars and used statistics to identify regularities and patterns in them. This, it was argued, would enable IR to establish general propositions about interstate behavior and escape the old "interpretive" approaches.

Wright had paved the way: His painstakingly compiled data of centuries of past wars and his statistical analyses provided the basis for his encyclopedic *Study of War* (1941)—this substantial tome was equipped with figures, charts, and foldout tables. The advocacy of quantitative methods triggered a new "great debate" in the IR community. This debate was part of a larger "behaviorist" orientation in the social sciences and related to the development of computer technologies and the hope of subjecting vast data sets to statistical analyses.

New Schools and Approaches

This Second Great Debate found its classic representation in an exchange between J. David Singer and Hedley Bull. Singer was a behavioralist from the University of Michigan and an early compiler of data on conflicts and war—such as the important Correlates of War Project. Bull was an influential traditionalist scholar from the LSE and Oxford and a member of the British Committee on International Relations, the members of which had developed an alternative approach that stressed cooperation over confrontation—an English School that had Grotius and his notions of law and society as major sources of inspiration.

The debate between the two was largely a discussion of methodology. Other issues were soon pulled into its wake, however. One such issue concerned the value of IR as a field of knowledge; the other its proper object of study.

Kenneth Waltz touched on all these issues in his book *Man, the State, and War* (1959). Waltz sought to identify and map the main arguments that philosophers and statesmen had applied to the study of IR through the ages. He isolated their theoretical cores and categorized them according to three "images"—that is, whether they were located at the individual, the social, or the systemic level of analysis.

Waltz' book anchored IR theory in history and defined the scholarly field as part of a rich tradition of political ideas. LSE professor Martin Wight did much of the same thing. He too identified three schools of thought in IR and called them realism, rationalism, and revolutionism. Each school represented a distinct ontology, argued Wight—a distinct view of the world. Realism sees the world in terms of states, state interests, and power; rationalism perceives the world as inhabited by rational humans driven toward cooperation; and revolutionism observes the world through the lenses of right and wrong and dreams of a peaceful and unified world. Each approach constituted a distinct school of thought, sustained by a distinct tradition, argued Wight. He demonstrated how philosophers like Hobbes, Grotius, Kant, and others had contributed to these schools in various ways.

As the 1950s evolved into the 1960s, new controversies were added to the scholarly debate. For a time, the influential schemes of Waltz and Wight helped keep a certain order on the debate. But controversies soon emerged that defied easy categorization. Within the scientist camp, for example, there emerged a political dividing line. On one side were scientists who were concerned with issues of security. These scientists collaborated with the U.S. government and established a new field of security studies; among them were scholars like Albert Wohlstetter and Thomas Schelling, who were associated with the RAND Corporation, a private research center that was largely funded by the U.S. Air Force. On the other side were social scientists who were concerned with justice and peace; among them were the economist Kenneth Boulding and the sociologist Johan Galtung. These scholars updated the old banner of the peace movement to include opposition against atomic weapons and claimed a new field of peace research.

These two scientific communities contributed importantly to IR over subsequent decades. They were very similar in methodological orientation, but they disagreed strongly on epistemological and ontological issues. They were matching bookends, enclosing the social-scientific approaches to issues of war and peace but from opposite sides, disagreeing strongly on the ultimate nature of politics and the reasons for studying it.

Systems and Structures

Political discussions intensified as the Cold War entered a new phase. In the wake of World War II, colonies in Africa and Asia had demanded self-government. As the old imperial powers were reluctant to grant such independence, the locals organized liberation movements to fight for sovereignty and self-rule. The 1960s saw a growing number of armed struggles directed against French and British rule.

Soviet Premier Nikita Khrushchev observed that armed rebels challenged the imperialist powers of the capitalist West and began to support them. The Americans responded, predictably, by trying to contain what they saw as Soviet expansionism. This quickly involved U.S. forces in conflicts around the world, and American statesmen and scholars were confronted with a horrible dilemma.

The U.S. containment of anticolonial movements in the Third World led the United States to side with the old colonial powers of Europe and seriously undermined America's liberal advocacy of free trade and anticolonialism. This became painfully obvious as the United States increased its support for the French war effort against anticolonial rebels in Indochina. In 1954, the French pulled out, and the United States continued the war in Vietnam on its own.

The escalation of the Vietnam War changed the world's perception of the United States and fueled criticism of U.S. policies. Members of the profession engaged in the general debate on colonial independence, sovereignty, development, and the reasons behind U.S. engagements in foreign wars. Professors and students drew on increasingly radical perspectives that portrayed U.S. behavior as driven by the internal needs of the capitalist system and portrayed the United States as a prowling, neo-imperialist Great Power. Some added, invoking the Marxist notion of false consciousness, that the capitalists legitimized their expansion through the production of false ideology and presented it as universal truth. Such radical arguments were also voiced by non-Western political leaders—Mao Zedong, Fidel Castro, "Che" Guevara, and Ho Chi Minh. They gained adherents among radical IR scholars.

One effect of this development was to boost what Wight had called the revolutionary approach to IR and elevate it on par with the two established traditions of realism and rationalism. By 1970, IR was commonly presented as having three rivaling approaches or schools or—invoking Thomas Kuhn's fashionable term—three "paradigms," each with its own distinct ontology.

Another effect was to challenge the traditional concept of power—one of the key concepts of IR. The traditional definition viewed power in terms of specific resources—as the outcome of a systematic application of force, wealth, or propaganda. Discussions about colonialism and conflict, and wars and wealth in the Third World pulled alternative definitions of power in its wake. Power could, for example, be seen in terms of social relationships—a state possesses power by virtue of its position in a social structure or its ability to define the main rules of interaction. By this view, the Great Powers of the West derived their superior resources and privileges from their ability to maintain an international world economy that enriched them while they exploited, impoverished, and repressed everyone else.

A third effect of this was to direct attention toward what Waltz had called the systemic level of analysis. Revolutionist theorists included sweeping discussions of the inherent needs of the capitalist system. They developed new theories of imperialism. André Gunder Frank portrayed the United States as a metropole and other countries as satellites and identified the mechanisms that enriched the first but impoverished the second. Immanuel Wallerstein's *Modern World System* (1974) presented 500 years of world history in terms of interactions between a powerful and wealthy world core and a poor periphery. This analysis of the modern world economy had a deep and long-lasting influence on IR scholarship.

Realist authors, too, developed systemic approaches. Waltz defined the interstate system in terms of the distribution of capabilities among major power centers or "poles." His *Theory of International Politics* (1979) presented a reformulation of the old balance-of-power theory, anchoring it in sociological theory and in microeconomic reasoning. Robert Gilpin presented a similar argument in his *War and Change* (1981). He argued that Great Powers always sought to impose their own rules on international games in an effort to bring about a world order that suited their own interests. He then portrayed the history of the modern world as a system in which Great Powers had regularly risen to and fallen from hegemonic status, igniting major "hegemonic wars" in the process, with each new hegemon imposing its own order on the post-war world. George Modelski and William Thompson followed up this idea and developed a theory of long cycles or waves of hegemonic leadership.

Authors from the rationalist tradition followed suit. Robert Keohane presented a systemic alternative to Waltz and Gilpin's neorealism. The fall of a Great Power is not necessarily attended by war and followed by a new world order, he argued. If U.S. hegemony were to unravel, the system that the United States established after World War II is so rational and serves everyone so well that it will not be essentially changed by America's demise, argued Keohane in *After Hegemony* (1984). The demise of the United States will, in other words, not necessarily cause strife and conflict.

By the mid-1980s, then, the scholarly field of IR was dominated by three main approaches, each with grand, systemic theories at its core. These theories were all affected by economic reasoning: the radical approach most directly, as it relied on concepts and arguments from classical political economy, and the realist and rationalist approaches more subtly. Waltz drew on theories of neoclassical oligopolistic competition, while Keohane drew on neo-institutionalist economics. Both incorporated game theory. Scholars who explored these two traditions further found so much similar ground that they began to transcend the ancient rivalry of realism and rationalism and merged into a so-called neo-neosynthesis.

The End of the Cold War and the Ideational Turn

Systemic theories met with much skepticism. Realists claimed that such theories were static and could not easily account for change. Rationalists argued that they were abstract and excluded human elements. International politics involve people who make decisions and shape events, they argued. States do not balance; statesmen do. And when statesmen decide to balance, they do not heedlessly react to abstract concepts such as "capabilities"; they balance against what they perceive as concrete and tangible threats.

Some scholars retorted that statesmen may well act on perceptions, but such perceptions are in turn part of larger systems—of "epistemological communities"—that socialize statesmen into the collective norms of distinct societies and thus condition their perceptions of the world.

This was the vantage point of Richard Ashley whose "Poverty of Neorealism" (1984) amounted to a sweeping condemnation of Waltz. Neorealist theory is a distinct epistemic system, argued Ashley; it is totalizing and repressive and invokes the authority of "science" to justify its claim for objective knowledge where no such claim could exist, he argued. Other writers added their voices to this critical charge. Neither neorealism nor any other IR theory offer objective knowledge of the world. They are all mere reflections of distinct epistemic communities and contingent on particular conditions in time and space. This was the message of the scholars who contributed to James Der Derian's book *International/Intertextual Relations* (1989). They portrayed IR as resting on a flimsy foundation of subjective assumptions that belonged to a narrow group of privileged, largely White, middle-class males who forced their articulations on more marginalized others, whose voices were consequently silenced by the imposition.

This criticism was not new. But whereas earlier criticism had flowed from materialist social science theories (e.g., from the Marxist false-ideology thesis), the critical claims of the 1980s hinged on ideational philosophies—on, for example, semiotics, linguistics, or symbolic interactionism (often inspired by Parisian postmodernists). These philosophies became a springboard of the poststructuralist turn that affected the social sciences in the 1990s.

Globalization and Change

Several long-term trends conspired to enhance the force of this poststructural turn in IR. Two of them are indicated by the terms *communication revolution* and *globalization*. The means and modes of international transport were changed by new technologies. Goods, money, text, and images were brought faster and cheaper around the world, fueling a steady expansion of commerce and credit. Easier travel encouraged increased migration, and whereas earlier waves of migration had brought Europeans out into the world, a new wave brought non-Europeans in. Such trends were long studied in terms of the old IR concept of interdependence. During the 1980s, however, when the introduction of relatively inexpensive personal computers represented a quantum leap in worldwide interconnectedness, new concepts and theories were applied—such as textual interrelationships, symbolic interaction, and multiple identities.

The liberal democracies of the West adapted to globalization. They did not always do it peacefully—national groups with traditional truth claims and monocultural assumptions clashed with immigrant demands for tolerance and understanding. Communist dictatorships, however, did not adapt well. Around 1990, the Soviet Union collapsed—for a variety of reasons; the refusal to adapt to the communication revolution for fear of losing political control was, perhaps, the most important one.

The Soviet collapse altered world politics. When Russia, the former USSR's crisis-ridden and noncommunist successor, was in no shape to assume the role of America's superpower rival, the Cold War ended. The collapse also altered the perception of world politics. On the one hand, it reduced the relevance of neorealism and revolutionism—the fall of the former USSR weakened neorealism by striking at its assumption of a bipolar balance; revelations of the cruelties and the deep illegitimacy of the Soviet system weakened the ideological appeal of revolutionism. On the other hand, the Soviet collapse enhanced the relevance of ideational approaches. For it was not only the material capabilities of the old USSR that collapsed around 1991, it was also the Stalinist system, and it was the exhaustion of the old communist outlook that altered the international climate and ended the Cold War. Many observers concluded that ideas shape policy and that power capabilities may be the foreign policy tools of states but that ideas define the uses to which the tools are put. Alexander Wendt made this point in a much discussed 1992 article, "Anarchy Is What States Make of It."

Finally, the Soviet collapse embarrassed the more formal or scientific approaches to IR. It came as a total surprise to scholars who had long argued that the scientific method could produce general explanations of the past as well as predictions for the future. Their failure to predict the Soviet collapse embarrassed them and made their scientific approach vulnerable to criticism. A new Great Debate ensued. It was all the more heated as IR's entire philosophy of science was suddenly questioned.

Fragmentation, Realignment, and Ideational Approaches

The conceptual toolbox of IR became richer and more diverse during the 1990s. It was filled with new approaches imported from other disciplines—neo-institutionalism, gender theory, culture studies, postcolonial analysis, and literary criticism among them. The substantial foci of IR, however, changed less. One of the established issues, the relationship of the Great Powers, reemerged in the wake of the Cold War: With the dissolution of the USSR, the world was no longer a bipolar system, but what kind of system was it? The United States emerged from the Cold War as the only remaining superpower, but what kind of power did it have?

Joseph Nye adumbrated an answer in *Bound to Lead* (1990): namely, that the United States led a unipolar system by virtue of its ideas, ideals, and example—that is, by its "soft power." Other authors made similar points. Samuel Huntington argued in *The Clash of Civilizations* (1993) that the Soviet collapse would be followed by an age deeply affected by conflicts of faith and civilizational ideas and ideals. Robert Kaplan wrote influential reports from regions of conflict—*Soldiers of God* (1990), *Balkans Ghosts* (1993), and *The Ends of the Earth* (1996)—and described these conflicts as driven by religious faith and ethnic identities.

Such claims stirred much debate. Francis Fukuyama protested the notion that future wars would be civilizational in nature. He argued instead that war would steadily diminish in the post–Cold War world and that there was now only one sustainable route to modernity: the liberal-democratic path. With communism on the ropes, liberal democracy had emerged dominant. Liberal definitions of reason, rights, and equal recognition were striking roots everywhere, pushing religion, nationalism, and other philosophical relics into the dustbin of history. The age of the great ideational struggles was over, argued Fukuyama. Not only is the Cold War at an end, history itself is at an end, he concluded in *The End of History and the Last Man* (1992)—with a nod to Friedrich Hegel and Alexandre Kojève. Bruce Russett formulated a similar argument but from a scientist's perspective—and with a nod to Kant. In *Grasping the Democratic Peace* (1993), he argued that democratic states trade with one another, evolve interdependencies, and common interests. Democracies do not go to war with each other. By this logic, the spread of democracy was practical peace work.

Fukuyama and Russett were right about one thing: The number of interstate wars dropped after the Cold War. But Huntington and Kaplan, too, had a valid point: There were regions in the world that did not conform to the worldwide trend of growing order and peace. Conflict and war still marked an area between the eastern Mediterranean and the Indian Ocean—a vast region from the Balkans via the Middle East, along the Caucasus and the Hindu Kush, to the Bay of Bengal. Some of its conflicts were related to the retreat of the former USSR and some to the expansion of the United States. Most of them involved national and religious identities.

This was worrisome. For this vast and varied region of sustained conflict also contained the world's richest stores of oil; Western statesmen feared that conflict would disrupt its extraction and smooth transport. This region was also predominantly Muslim; Western analysts feared that conflict might produce new and radical mutations of political Islam as well as proliferation of nuclear arms and other weapons of mass destruction (WMDs)—especially if crisis-ridden Russia lost control of its old Soviet WMD stockpiles.

Such fears soared to new heights on September 11, 2001, when Islamist terrorists crashed hijacked passenger jets into the Pentagon near Washington, D.C., and into Manhattan's World Trade Center. The newly elected president George W. Bush responded by striking out against Afghanistan, ousting its Islamist government, and installing a friendly regime in its stead. In the fall of 2003, President Bush ordered an invasion of Iraq. Amid loud protests and shrill warnings, he declared a "war on terror," arguing that Iraq's dictatorial regime had stockpiles of WMDs and nursed terrorist connections.

No WMDs were found in Iraq. No terrorist connections were convincingly established. Many in the world, including IR scholars, argued that the Bush administration had invaded Iraq either as the result of panic or confusion, or as a calculated effort to secure access to the region's oil reserves. Regardless of reason, the faraway and costly wars in Iraq and Afghanistan wasted America's soft power and weakened its standing in the world—partly by its ongoing costly military exploits and by its policy of cutting taxes while increasing spending. In the first years of the new millennium, America's role in the post–Cold War world was increasingly described in terms of empire rather than hegemon: The United States was more commonly seen as an imperialist than as a democratizing force.

Turmoil and wars in the Middle East and Central Asia sparked new energy debates. The Great Powers of the world—with the significant exception of Russia—were deeply reliant on foreign oil, and their dependence presented a serious security risk for each of them. Also, the continued consumption of fossil fuels represented a security risk for them all: Many scientists claim that the burning of oil released such large amounts of carbon gases that it altered the composition of the earth's atmosphere and changed the global climate—and thus created a security risk of another kind. By the end of Bush's second term, the United States was still the world's most powerful country, but it was deeply distrusted. When the American economy entered a deep economic crisis, its image as a leading world power was on the rocks. Fareed Zakaria spoke on behalf of many observers when, in *The Post-American World* (2007), he portrayed the international system as increasingly multipolar, where countries such as Brazil, Russia, India, and China might represent new centers of power alongside an enfeebled and distrusted United States.

Conclusion

The contours of scholarly IR that emerged in the wake of the Franco-Prussian War (1871) grew more defined during the subsequent years of imperialist expansion. It came into its own as a scholarly field during World War I, emerging as a branch of the social sciences in the wake of that Great War. It was then preoccupied with the causes of war and the preconditions for a stable peace.

IR has since added other concerns to its scholarly ambit and evolved as a more varied scholarly field. It has become too varied, according to some observers—especially as IR scholars have engaged in abstract philosophy-of-science theorizing. True, IR may no longer have a sharp and single focus. However, its core concerns are still apparent as a set of overlapping issues, such as war and peace, wealth, and power. And these are maintained by the disciplinary history that marks IR as a scholarly field.

Also, the theoretical foundation of IR has remained fairly constant over time. IR scholars still hang on to their old notion of a pluralist field composed of opposing approaches. The two classic approaches—the Hobbes-based realism and the Locke-derived rationalism—are still dominating the scholarly debate (although both have adapted to the changing world). A third approach has drifted in and out of the field, advocating change and revolution—now in world affairs, now in scholarly approaches, but it has always sought to introduce critical, collectivist, and, one is tempted to add, romantic perspectives to the field. At the beginning of the 21st century, the basic approaches of IR, then, still conform to the three perspectives described by James Lorimer at the end of the 19th century.

Torbjørn L. Knutsen
Norwegian University of Science and Technology (NTNU)
Trondheim, Norway

See also Balance of Power; International Law; Liberalism; Realism in International Relations; War and Peace; Westphalian Ideal State

Further Readings

Armstrong, D. (1993). *Revolution and world order.* Oxford, UK: Clarendon Press.

Bauer, H., & Brighi, E. (Eds.). (2003). *International relations at the LSE: A history of 75 years.* London: Millennium.

Baylis, J., Smith, S., & Owens, P. (Eds.). (2008). *The globalization of world politics: An introduction to international relations.* Oxford, UK: Oxford University Press.

Burleigh, M. (2009). *Blood and rage: A cultural history of terrorism.* London: HarperCollins.

Calleo, D. (2001). *Rethinking Europe's future.* Princeton, NJ: Princeton University Press.

Frieden, J. A. (2006). *Global capitalism: Its fall and rise in the twentieth century.* New York: W. W. Norton.

Gat, A. (2001). *A history of military thought.* Oxford, UK: Oxford University Press.

Goldstein, S. J. (2007). *International relations.* London: Longman.

Knutsen, T. L. (1997). *A history of international relations theory.* Manchester, UK: Manchester University Press.

Long, D., & Wilson, P. (Eds.). (1995). *Thinkers of the twenty years' crisis: Inter-war idealism reassessed.* Oxford, UK: Clarendon Press.

Luard, E. (Ed.). (1992). *Basic texts in international relations: The evolution of ideas about international society.* New York: St. Martin's.

Olson, W. C., & Groom, A. J. R. (1991). *International relations then and now: Origins and trends in interpretation.* London: Routledge.

International Relations, Theory

International relations (IR) theory is an area of social theory that seeks to account for international or world political events, patterns, relations, and interactions. Traditionally, as the concept implies, the focus of IR theory has been on the study of interstate relations and interactions: mainly on why states go to war with each other and why, under certain conditions, they may refrain from doing so. Yet it is important to note that in recent decades, the meaning, scope, and the interests driving IR theorists have expanded significantly beyond traditional interstate concerns. This expansion has been driven by the increased awareness of challenging new issues in international politics, such as globalization, human rights, global poverty, environmental threats, and global gender hierarchies. Interest in these issue areas has not only stimulated developments within traditional IR-theoretical approaches, such as realism and liberalism, but it has also seen a significant pluralization within the field to include a host of new perspectives.

When considering the history of IR theory, a subject that first emerged in the aftermath of

World War I and became consolidated in the post–World War II environment, it is notable that the meaning of the notion "IR theory" has developed in two distinct senses over the years: in terms of the perceptions scholars have of the scope of "IR" and, simultaneously, in terms of the meanings attached to the notion "theory."

Having been a part and parcel of historical, economic, philosophical, or political inquiry during earlier centuries, in the 20th century, IR theory came gradually to form a disciplinary field distinct from other subfields of political science, such as political theory, or a base for theorizing in other social science disciplines, such as sociology, history, or economics. IR theory, as conceived by many commentators in the mid-20th century, focused primarily on state interactions on the level of the international system (not within the state) and in reference, by and large, to political relations (not economic or social relations). However, driven by the increasingly transnational and crosscutting nature of global problems, the boundaries between IR theory and other social sciences have been progressively reconceived by IR theorists during the past few decades. Many IR theorists now analyze phenomena beyond interstate relations and often use concepts and theoretical premises usually characteristic of other fields, whether it be economic analysis, the study of domestic social relations, or ethical or philosophical inquiry. Hence, it is not surprising that the nature of IR theory as a discrete academic subfield has been under some debate recently.

It should also be noted that while the scope of IR has expanded, the meaning of what counts as theory has at the same time shifted within the field. A number of so-called postpositivist scholars have in recent decades turned away from explanatory science, traditionally IR theorists' main focus, in favor of understanding meanings and ideas in international politics. Thus, different views have arisen of the very meaning of theory. While for some it entails explanatory theory aimed at trying to establish the causes of world political developments, for others it is concerned with interpretive theory, seeking an understanding of why specific ideas or discursive systems of meaning have come to proliferate. In addition, some scholars make the argument that IR theory should primarily be viewed as normative theory (i.e., dealing with questions of "ought" and not just "is"), while others argue that it should function as critical theory (i.e., challenging existing systems of power and oppression in world politics).

Given the contestation over the scope of the subject matter of IR theory and the meaning and purpose of theorizing itself, there is thus no singular conception of IR theory that we can turn to but rather a number of contested visions of it. In view of this, it is important to understand the plurality of ways of framing IR theorizing today. Whereas 40 years ago, three theories of IR were commonly referred to as exhausting the field—realism, liberalism, and either the English School or Marxism—today, a number of critical and postpositivist traditions of thought have entered this field, such as constructivism, critical theory, normative theory, poststructuralism, postcolonialism, feminism, and green theory.

This entry first discusses, in historical perspective, how theoretical arguments have developed around the idea of IR. Second, it discusses the distinct theoretical schools of thought, or isms, commonly conceived to be characteristic of IR theory today, highlighting key issues and themes on which theorists agree and disagree. This discussion is followed, finally, by a brief assessment of key developments in IR theory, with a view to deciphering where future interests and fault lines of IR theorizing might lie.

IR Theory in Historical Perspective

The idea that there should be such a thing as IR theory at all is of a relatively recent origin, being in many ways a 20th-century invention. IR theory is a term that arose in the early and mid-20th century with the attempt by a specific set of, mostly Anglo-American, academics to develop systematic theoretical thought to serve as the basis for a newly emerging (sub)field of the social sciences—IR or international politics. While initially conceived as a subject matter for historians, lawyers, or political theorists, the professionalization and institutionalization of academic disciplines during this period also led scholars interested in the empirical domain of IR to establish a discipline of their own, including a set of specific theoretical assumptions and concepts appropriate to its study.

These concepts did not arise from nowhere, however. In fact, many 20th-century IR theorists have taken their cue from much earlier thinkers. It could be argued that IR theory—that is, the attempt to systematically understand why states or political units go to war with each other or engage in other international forms of social interaction—was first developed in ancient Greece by Thucydides in his account of the Peloponnesian wars. IR was also clearly theorized in the medieval and early-modern periods in various scholastic and republican tracts, perhaps most notably in Niccolò Machiavelli's writings and in the treatises of those interested in the ethics and legality of war, such as Francisco de Vitoria and Hugo Grotius. From these early writings on IR arise not only many of the patterns of thought that continue to characterize IR today, such as the view of IR as power politics, but also many concepts used in current theory, such as the notions of sovereignty or just war. Yet these texts were not explicitly IR-theoretical: They were seen as part and parcel of wider historical, legal, political, or ethical reasoning.

The theorization of IR as we tend to understand it today arose in the 20th century. It is closely tied to the rise of the discipline of IR, which arose also in a very specific context, since it was "invented" to address the problem of war in the aftermath of World Wars I and II. After World War I, an impetus arose to address, urgently and systematically, the question of why states ended up engaging in destructive wars. To study this subject, the first Chair of International Politics was established at the University of Wales, Aberystwyth, in 1919, and in the 1920s and 1930s at a few other universities. The focus of postwar IR specialists was thus on developing a systematic understanding of why wars occurred, specifically with the aim of allowing the international society to avoid them in the future. A number of commentators, such as Alfred Zimmern and Leonard Woolf, developed and argued for notions of collective security capable of averting the kind of disaster that World War I had been.

However, the most famous IR theory text that was to arise in the first part of the 20th century came in reply to the interwar commentators. It was written by Edward Carr, the Chair in International Politics at Aberystwyth at this time, and was called the *Twenty Years' Crisis*. Carr was one of the early key scholars seeking specifically to establish a theoretical understanding of IR. In so doing, he drew attention to the failings of the interwar commentators. He argued that they had been far too "idealistic," prioritizing normative and utopian ideals instead of recognizing the "realities" of power politics. Carr dismissed these idealists in favor of the development of "realist" theorizing, which took seriously the sources of conflict between states, the role of national interest in shaping states' actions, and the role of power politics in IR more widely.

Carr played a key role in setting out the theoretical parameters of what became known as realist IR theory, and it is also fair to say that he was instrumental in establishing realism in the post–World War II context. Realist thinking was also strengthened by the onset of the Cold War, which seemed to prove the importance of power politics, as well as by the influence that Hans Morgenthau came to have during this period. In *Politics Amongst Nations*, he argued that international politics is shaped by objective laws based on human nature and, crucially, that the key to understanding IR lies in the idea of interest defined in terms of power. Unlike liberal idealists, he claimed that the actions of states should not be judged in terms of universal moral standards but with reference to the specific interests that states hold and by the need for prudential action on the part of their leaders. Power politics may be necessary in international politics in defense of the national interest.

It is the centrality of power in these early realist analyses that initiated a whole set of fascinating work on the core dilemmas in international politics, notably on the idea of security dilemma, explored initially, for example, by John Herz: How can states cooperate when the attempts of some to gain security inevitably create insecurity in other states?

Although realism became the core strand of thought in Anglo-American IR theory during these years, it was substantially modified as a theoretical system by Kenneth Waltz, who in 1979 made a radical break with the classical realist tradition by modeling the international system in accordance with the methods of positivist science. He characterized this system as one of anarchy, within which all states are conceived as "like units," interested ultimately in nothing but their own survival. This structural, or neorealist, argument set a new standard in IR. Not only did it reshape realist thought, but it also influenced the work of the new brand of liberal internationalists in the 1970s, such as Robert Keohane—even though Keohane believed that the self-help logic could be mitigated in international politics through the development of international institutions. In its more classical forms, realism also strongly influenced the so-called English School developed in the United Kingdom (UK); for while the focus here was on the idea of an international society, the realist prioritization of state relations still formed the core of this school.

It is important to note that realists, many liberals, and many English School thinkers share certain important assumptions about what IR theory is and should consist of. Paradoxically, the best statement of this notion of IR theory is provided in Martin Wight's essay "Why is there no international theory?" Wight was skeptical of the possibility of international theory because of the perception of war as recurrent and inevitable by many and because of the attractions among political scientists of political theory conceived in terms of the "good life"—patterns of thought that, in his view, seemed far removed from the realities of international politics. Yet Wight gave a very clear account of what IR theory should be: It should be concerned exclusively with international and not domestic politics, and it should be able to deal with, although possibly also look beyond, the endless recurrence of war. This was precisely the sort of theory that Edward Carr, Hans Morgenthau, Hedley Bull, Kenneth Waltz, and others developed for the discipline. Despite some methodological disagreements between scholars (the so-called second debate) throughout the 1950s and 1960s, there was substantial agreement on the meaning of the focal point of IR theory, at least in terms of its object of study—state behavior and the explanation of the causes of war and conditions for cooperation. This consensus on the theory of IR broke down, however, in the 1970s and 1980s with the rise of the interparadigm debate and, subsequently, the fourth debate.

The interparadigm debate in the 1970s challenged the classical understandings of IR theory in terms of what the field should focus on. In light of both the oil and the financial crises in the 1970s, two new perspectives gained currency: complex interdependence theory and Marxism. These paradigms were conceived to challenge the realist focus in two respects: First, while accepting the state as a key actor, both refused to reduce all international politics to the pursuit of national interests, instead looking beyond the state to the role of economic factors and nonstate actors; second, they challenged the negative conclusions of the realists, arguing instead that forms of cooperation beyond mere constant struggle for survival was possible. This entailed a challenge to both the dominance of realism and the realist theoretical obsession with survival and brute (military) power; there was now a need also to explain why states cooperated and, for Marxists, why certain patterns of inequality outside mere military relations continued to persist and structure IR.

These echoes critical of realism were picked up and developed even further in the 1980s when a variety of so-called postpositivist theorists started to criticize realism, not just on the basis of its theoretical assumptions about the state but also because of its philosophical, normative, and political leanings. Philosophically, realist theory was accused of positivism in its attempt to establish laws and regularities in international politics as well as objective scientific knowledge of human affairs—goals that were viewed as unfeasible and inappropriate within the social sciences. In addition, realism was condemned normatively and politically for constituting a conservative bulwark for statists and Great Power apologists; it was seen to be reproducing a negative and cynical vision of the world and one that unfairly prioritized the interests of great powers over other parts of the world. Critical theorists extended this criticism to include many liberals as well—those who had accepted some central assumptions of realism, notably with a focus on the self-interested state.

Critical theorists emphasized the need to go beyond problem-solving theory (perceived as central for realists, liberals, and even some Marxists), by unraveling the ways in which theories of IR reproduced particular ideological interests and power relations in the world.

The postpositivist criticism led to the proliferation of a whole new set of IR theories—feminism, constructivism, poststructuralism, and critical theory—and caused the onset of a more theoretically pluralist way of approaching IR theory. Indeed, whereas in the 1970s and mid-1980s many IR theory textbooks highlighted just three traditions of IR theory (realism, liberalism, and either the

English School or Marxism as a third option), today IR theory textbooks cover anywhere between 8 and 14 different theoretical approaches (see Scott Burchill et al., 2005; Timothy Dunne, Milja Kurki, & Steve Smith, 2007).

IR Theories

Given the plurality of approaches that exists today in IR theory, we must, to understand contemporary IR theory, engage with the theoretical pluralism in the field. With this in mind, this section examines some of the core isms in IR theory today and the issues and debates that divide them.

The Isms

To characterize any field in terms of a set of "isms" is hugely problematic, although often also attractive for cognitive reasons. While this approach is used here, because such a terminology is seen to have distinct advantages in clarifying some of the key divisions of thought on IR theory, this usage also has important problems that need to be kept in mind.

First, it must be remembered that it can be historically misleading to characterize the thought of specific individuals as belonging to unified isms. Thus, for example, as historians of the discipline have noted, idealists in the interwar period were not necessarily unified in their frameworks of thought constituting an ism, and nor were they necessarily idealists. Indeed, the use of the *ism* label can be a useful way of rhetorically dismissing or sidelining thinkers, and Carr's attack on idealism can be seen as one such rhetorical attack. Second, it is important to note that isms may be identified on very different grounds in analyses. Thus, in IR theory, some isms may be strictly IR-theoretical isms, such as realism, but others may have much wider meanings alongside their meanings in IR (e.g., constructivism in philosophy and social theory, liberalism in political theory and economic science) or meanings entirely beyond IR (e.g., critical realism in philosophy). Third, and perhaps most crucially, the isms approach to any subject creates the problem of specifying which isms "count." Talking in terms of isms is one way of justifying and legitimizing some approaches over others and simultaneously of excluding some of them. Now, the approach adopted here to IR theories is expansive, yet it by no means includes within it all the approaches that could be considered IR-theoretical. For example, anarchism is not treated here as a distinct IR-theoretical school, although grounds exist for saying that it might constitute one. It should also be noted that within the approaches adopted here, there are various subdivisions and also that not all authors have consistently throughout their career sought to serve a single and unified idea of an ism.

With all the above caveats in mind, the isms that are discussed here are realism, liberalism, the English School, Marxism, critical theory, feminism, constructivism, poststructuralism, postcolonialism, green theory, and normative theory. These constitute the core theoretical strands of thought currently commonly referred to and developed in IR, although they are not isms in the same sense (normative theory, e.g., may be conceived as a subfield of study and poststructuralism as an ethos rather than a theory).

Realism

As pointed out earlier, realism provides the core reference point for much of IR theory. This is not because realism is necessarily correct but because it has played a significant role in the rise of the idea of IR theory and because the very idea of IR conceptually remains tied to key realist assumptions. The core realist assumptions can be defined as threefold. Realist IR theory argues (a) that the state is the core unit of international politics, (b) that the national interests of the state play a crucial role in defining the shape of international politics, and (c) that because of the emphasis of states on survival and self-interest, cooperation between states is difficult to maintain, and war between states is always a danger and likely to be recurrent. While these constitute core assumptions that most realists would agree on, there are important subdivisions within realist thought that need to be considered.

Neorealism is a term coined to refer to those realists who follow Waltz's reformulation of realism—that is, a theory that bases its analysis on the postulation of a structural impediment to state cooperation, the structure of anarchy in the international system. Given the structural constraint of anarchy, states are predisposed toward self-help behavior. Classical realists, whom Waltz criticized, explain the causes of war in terms of individualistic or state-based levels or, like Ned Lebow, have turned to the language and theoretical explanations of classical Greeks rather than modern social science to generate explanations of current affairs. Offensive and defensive realisms are strands of thought that both often follow a neorealist or structural-realist theoretical framework, yet they disagree on how states are likely to act in the pursuit of their interests. Defensive realists emphasize that self-help states can satisfy their security by pursuing defensive postures by seeking to balance against rising powers. Offensive realists, drawing on John Mearsheimer's work, argue that states in a self-help system always strive to maximize their power and to dominate the system and, thus, are inherently offensive in their posture.

Liberalism

Liberalism is another core IR theory school. Its basic principles arise from liberal political theory but are extended to the international realm, albeit as with realism, in a variety of different forms. Classical liberals tend to advocate a form of liberal internationalism, believing that the expansion of liberal principles, when more universally embraced, result in more peaceful international interactions. One core doctrine that has arisen from classical liberalism is democratic peace theory, which—drawing on Immanuel Kant's thought—argues that democratic states are unlikely to wage war with other democratic states.

There are also, however, other strands of liberal IR theorizing. Complex interdependence is a concept launched by Robert Keohane and Joseph Nye in the 1970s. They argued that states by this time had become so interdependent with one another in nonmilitary issue areas, such as the economy and the environment, that this entailed that the typical hierarchization of national security and military capabilities was not necessarily any longer regarded as a top priority on the part of states or that cooperation between states in the other areas was impossible. *Neoliberal institutionalism*, developed by Keohane and others in the mid-1980s, was, on the other hand, based on the claim that even if one accepts the neorealists' prioritization of self-interest and anarchy as a given structural condition, it does not necessarily lead to the conclusion that states will not cooperate with one another. This is in large part because states often prioritize absolute gains over relative gains and hence can be persuaded to pursue cooperative endeavors in ways that contravene the realist logic. In the case of the European Union, for example, the neoliberals argue that a preference for absolute gains and mutual cooperation has overridden the relative gains logic of the realists.

The English School

The English School is a tradition of thought associated with a number of English or U.K.-based scholars who have shared a certain set of methodological and conceptual starting points in the analysis of IR. Key figures here include Martin Wight, Hedley Bull, and John Vincent, and more recently Barry Buzan, Robert Jackson, Nicholas Wheeler, and Tim Dunne. The English School thinkers share a historical and interpretivist approach to IR; that is, they do not tend to apply quantitative methods to the study of IR as many realists and liberals do, but rather, they emphasize the interpretation of the motives, norms, and understandings of actors.

Crucially, they focus conceptually on the theme of international society: The English School conceives of international politics in terms of a rule-bound society of states, which forms an international society in which a set of rules, norms, and institutions are mutually agreed on. English School thinkers are not necessarily cosmopolitans or postrealists, however. In fact, the English School is subdivided into *solidarist* and *pluralist* strands. While the solidarists accept the idea of human rights and humanitarian intervention as increasingly important, with mutually accepted rules defining the nature of international society, pluralists continue to maintain a belief in nonintervention and sovereignty as the key principles of international society.

Marxism and Historical Materialism

Although Marxism has its roots in the 19th-century writings of Karl Marx, within IR theory, it made a somewhat belated appearance compared with the other social sciences. Although some realists had an interest in Marxism early on (notably

Carr), Marxism entered IR theory debates only in the late 1970s. At that time, it came to be associated in particular with the so-called world systems theory developed by Immanuel Wallerstein. Contra the realists, he argued that the driving dynamics of world politics was economic in nature: The structure of the capitalist mode of production globally is what positioned states within international politics and influenced their interactions. Wallerstein divided the world into the core (West), the semiperiphery (East Asia), and the periphery (the developing world), each zone possessing distinct functions in the global capitalist system of production and hence also in the state system.

World systems theory was heavily criticized for what many perceived to be its overly structural and economistic focus. Yet Marxist ideas have also been developed by others, notably the so-called neo-Gramscian school drawing on Robert Cox and other historical materialists, such as Justin Rosenberg and Mark Rupert. The neo-Gramscian strand of thought is most famous in extending the politico-economic understanding of IR to the analysis of hegemony—that is, the way in which ideological consensus is created and reproduced in IR and how this is tied to specific class or economic interests.

Critical Theory

Critical theory is a multifaceted set of ideas associated with the idea of emancipation and one with origins in the so-called Frankfurt School theory of Max Horkheimer, Theodor Adorno, and Jürgen Habermas. Critical theorists in IR have tended to emphasize the idea of critical theory as distinct from problem-solving theory. Cox famously argued that problem-solving theory fails in being unable to transcend existing social reality by narrowing its focus merely to solving specific technical problems within the parameters of otherwise unquestioned social conditions, whether it be the capitalist system of production, patriarchal gender relations, or narrowly electoral systems of democracy. Contrary to such traditional theorizing, critical theorizing has the aim of challenging and rethinking the ideological premises that exist for the dominant perceptions of reality that make societies function as they do and that blind us to many forms of oppression that we live with on an everyday basis. Critical theory thus aims to go deeper in its critique of societal underpinnings: It seeks the emancipation of people from societal and structural systems of oppression that often go unnoticed in realist and liberal problem-solving theorization. In IR theory, these themes have been developed most notably by Andrew Linklater.

Constructivism

Constructivism starts from the premise that social reality, rather than being fixed and natural, is premised on and depends on the thinking and intersubjective agreement of human actors. This means that social reality, including international political social reality, is socially constructed.

In IR theory, there have been numerous extensions and applications of constructivist theoretical ideas. Wendt's argument that international anarchy is socially constructed has been one important development of constructivism. Wendt argued that we cannot assume, as the realists do, that the lack of international government necessitates a self-help system. Instead, anarchy is what "states make of it": That is, those states that have developed relations of trust and shared norms between them are likely to interact in "friendly" ways with each other, even if other states have been socialized into distrust and hence to realist politics of self-help. Others, such as Jeffrey Checkel and Friedrich Kratochwil, have applied constructivism to explain developments such as the end of the Cold War, whereas Martha Finnemore has used it in understanding the expansion of human rights norms. In the post–Cold War setting, constructivism has provided a fruitful way of developing dynamic interpretations of change in world politics.

Yet it is important to note that constructivist ideas can be developed and applied in very different ways. While Wendt's constructivism is explicitly moderate and seeks to build bridges with the positivist realist and liberal IR scholars, other constructivists, such as Friedrich Kratochwil and Karin Fierke, argue for more extensive interpretive and linguistic forms of constructivism, where the idea of social construction is recognized as a deep-running aspect not just of social forms "out there" but also of our explanatory categories themselves. Constructivism, we must recognize then, is no united theoretical camp, and indeed, various subdivisions have been recognized to exist within this broad school (moderate or "thin" constructivism vs. radical or "thick" constructivism; American vs. continental constructivism).

Feminism

Feminism emerged in IR in the late 1980s but has been a rather contested addition to the field. This is because feminism tends not to study IR as classically conceived. Cynthia Enloe famously argued that feminists are concerned not only with the international but also with the way in which the international is penetrated and constituted by the personal. International power relations for feminists are built on a whole set of global and domestic interpersonal power relations. Thus, relations between husband and wife in a diplomatic family or between Western consumer women and women working in the "feminized" garment industry in Indonesia are global relations of power too and important for making the world of international politics go around as it does.

Feminists argue that if social actors are really socially constructed, as many constructivists and others have argued, then IR theorists must also recognize that social actors and social relations are also constructed in gendered ways. Indeed, IR, feminists argue, has been constructed as a field of masculine actors pursuing masculine aims. Not only have women been silent in the discipline and practice of diplomacy, but they have also been an uninteresting area of study and simply do not seem to matter for IR theory as traditionally conceived. However, if theory and IR are conceptualized differently—as analysis interpersonally constituted in the form of global (rather than merely international) relations of power—then perhaps there is much more to IR and many more layers of power than traditional IR theory recognizes. This is what the feminists, through various interesting studies of war, tourism, the sex industry, and peace building, have tried to demonstrate.

Poststructuralism

Poststructuralism has been an influential force in the field since the 1980s, especially in Europe. Yet this is a difficult approach to label, in that many of its advocates reject any *ism* label as a valid description of their approach. Nevertheless, scholars such as James Der Derian, Jenny Edkins, David Campbell, and R. B. J. Walker do seem to share certain assumptions that distinguish them from other IR theorists and that could be termed poststructuralist in nature. Their key contribution is that they take the epistemological critique of positivist knowledge to its fullest conclusion: They highlight that instead of an analysis of international politics "out there" (the ontology of international politics), we should study the discourses that make particular realities (or ontologies) seem natural. In short, for them, international politics is what it is because people accept particular discursive ways of understanding what IR consists of. This is why IR theorists should be aware of how international political actors and IR theorists themselves, by working with particular theoretical notions, come to reproduce or bring into existence particular "realities." This insight has been applied in fruitful ways: Poststructuralists have studied, for example, how discourses of "othering" create enemies in IR or how discourses of nationalism and ethnicity construct wars and civil strife.

Another key aspect of this theoretical stance is its refusal to advocate a specific set of political or policy convictions; positive, "truth-bound" ethical and political positions characteristic of realist, liberal, and Marxist and critical theory schools of thought are seen as dangerous in world politics. Instead, they advocate an attitude of critique and inquiry over assertive statements of truth, knowledge, and action. Thus, as Campbell has argued, poststructuralism is not a specific theoretical or political account of what world politics should look like but rather a critical ethos of approaching the analysis of IR, which places emphasis on deconstructing existing schools of thought (see Campbell in Dunne et al., 2007).

Postcolonialism

Postcolonialism is a line of thought that in many ways shares in the poststructuralist skepticism of "true" and "objective" knowledge claims. Knowledge claims, they argue, have tended to exclude and marginalize many parts of the world as "uncivilized," "barbaric," and hence legitimately "governed," with significant consequences for the colonized or the developing states and populations. Postcolonialism has as its building block the realization that knowledge is always produced from somewhere, from particular social and political conditions, and that knowledge makers can often be unaware of the way in which their knowledge creates the "self" and the "other"—that is, how it constructs visions of ourselves and how it might exclude or silence "the others." Edward Said famously argued that in Western knowledge of the Middle East, for example, an Oriental subject was considered as a particular kind of inferior, barbaric individual, while the West was idealized as civilized, peaceful, and educated. The key aim of postcolonialism is to challenge such biased readings, whether it be in international law, democratization, or gender relations/analysis.

Green Theory

Green theory provides another important, and for many a timely, corrective to the way in which IR theorists have framed and thought about the nature of world politics. Green theorists challenge the assumption that the "high politics" of international politics concerns matters of interstate war, highlighting instead the inherent and deeply challenging nature of environmental risks as a crucial aspect of contemporary world politics. Green theorists also challenge the ecology-blind or ecology-unfriendly frameworks of theoretical thought that have dominated the discipline. They seek to direct us to consider the ways in which anthropocentric assumptions about humans and nature have informed IR theorizing to the exclusion of values of interconnectivity with nature. There are various strands of green thought and theorizing, extending from more limited engagements with environmental thinking to "deep ecological" frameworks.

Normative Theory

Normative theory is a subfield of IR theorizing (rather than a specific school of thought as such) that specializes in understanding the different normative and ethical underpinnings that are given for actions or interpretations in IR. Normative theory was ignored in the discipline by the realists and neoliberals, who conceived of the study of international politics in purely explanatory and value-neutral terms. Normative theorists have been at pains to point out that normative assumptions about what is desirable or good are constantly made by IR scholars—even when theorists are incognizant of such normative assumptions. Thus, normative theorists have pointed out, for example, that realists argue not just for a particular explanatory account of the causes of war but also implicitly in so doing for a communitarian ethic, which sees the state as a key moral community in international politics. Normative theory scholarship sometimes also goes under the title *international political theory* or *international ethics*, terms that, while not interchangeable with the idea of normative theory, also indicate the considerations and intersections of normative thought with political theory and international law as well as ethics. One of the key issues in international political theory and in international ethics has been the question of just war: that is, what constitutes just behavior in conditions of war and in justifications for war. Other key questions concern global poverty and the duties of redistribution of wealth globally, as well as an engagement with the normative implications of dealing with climate change.

Themes That Divide IR Theorists

As seen above, there are a number of and diverging approaches that one can take in theorizing about IR. This section briefly highlights the core differences between these on certain key issues.

The Scope of the Field

As previously mentioned, a key line of division in IR theory during the past few decades has concerned the scope of the study of IR. The classical thinkers, realists, liberals, and the English School thinkers had a clear sense of the scope of the discipline: It focused exclusively on the question—the core focus of IR—of why states go to war or why they decide to cooperate. Yet in the 1980s, a plurality of challenges to the state centrism of IR theorizing emerged. Critics, from feminists, to poststructuralists, to postcolonialists, have argued that IR encompasses not just interstate relations but also the transnational politics of trade, the ideological construction of states, the nature of policies and polities, and interpersonal global relations of power.

With this development, there has also been a strong tendency in recent years to import into IR theory assumptions, knowledge, data, and models from other social sciences. This is evident both from the increased popularity of positivist approaches, within which rational choice theorizing, an interdisciplinary movement in the social sciences, has played an important role, and from the emergence of feminist, Marxist, and poststructuralist forms of thought. There has been an expansion within all these theoretical schools in cross- and interdisciplinary research, although some doubts still remain as to just how much IR theorists are listened to in other fields.

These interdisciplinary moves have generally been welcomed within IR, but they have also led to discussions about the boundaries of IR. Indeed, what is IR theory today as opposed to economic, sociological, or political theory? There is no fixed answer among IR theorists at present, which has given IR theory as a discipline something of a brittle basis. Indeed, some have argued that IR theory as a project has failed and that we would be better off doing away with the idea of IR theory as a separate body of thought and to engage in general social theorizing instead. Alternatively, many argue, we should rename the field and its theories by using the terms *world politics* or *global sociology*. So displeased have some scholars become with the parochial insistence of some IR theorists on the discreteness of the field that they have abandoned the discipline to engage theoretically with sociologists, economists, lawyers, or historians instead.

Yet the social structure of IR persists. As Ole Wæver has suggested, IR theory is not just an abstract academic exercise but also a social structure within academia. IR labels, approaches, and positions continue to structure the research of academic scholarship, arguments, and careers, as well as teaching. Indeed, given the deep entrenchment of IR and IR-theoretical "identities" in academia as well the intellectual benefits of teaching IR in terms of a set of discreet theoretical perspectives, IR theory still exists and continues to be framed as by and large distinct if linked to other social-scientific perspectives.

Philosophy of Science, Methods, and Epistemology

Another clear line of division in IR theory has revolved around the idea of positivism—that is, around the claim that IR can and should be studied by means of scientific methods aimed at finding regular patterns of behavior and interaction and that IR scholarship can and ought to be objective and value-neutral. The methods of knowledge construction in IR have always been a subject of debate in IR, and positivism has not always been influential. Carr and Morgenthau, for example, were strong advocates of a historical and interpretivist approach and adverse to positivist attempts to systematize IR into a study of regular patterns and variables. It was only by the 1960s and 1970s that a positivist (or behavioralist) worldview obtained a strong foothold in American IR, and as a result, there has been a distinct turn within it toward systematization and the observational testing of theories.

Despite the central position of positivism within IR, the postpositivist movement of recent decades has posed a strong challenge to this philosophy of science. Indeed, the third and fourth debates in IR were brought on by the head-on collision between mainstream American IR scholars' advocacy of positivist language and methods, on the one hand, and the claim by many critical theorists (many of them outside the United States), on the other, that this view of science was blind to many important theoretical developments and unfairly delegitimized approaches that did not conform to its research agenda.

The sharp dichotomization on how to generate knowledge in IR (a question that involves differences in philosophy of science, epistemology, and methodology) was given both an explanation and in some senses a justification by Martin Hollis and Steve Smith's famous *Explaining and Understanding International Relations*, which argued that there is a fundamental philosophical dualism at work in the social sciences, including IR, which makes it impossible to reach an agreement on whether the aim of IR should be generalization (positivism) or interpretive understanding (postpositivism). Both approaches, Hollis and Smith argued, have their strengths and their weaknesses, but they remain mutually exclusive. Hollis and Smith's "two-stories account" has had a strong impact during the past few decades, especially in Europe. Nevertheless, it has been challenged, notably in the form of the so-called critical-realist movement, which seeks to transcend the polarization of positivist and postpositivist scholarship by advancing a new philosophy of science that is critical of both the objectivism of positivism and the relativist excesses of some forms of postpositivism.

Theory Versus Practice

There has also been a deep disagreement among IR theorists about the aims of IR theorizing. Notably, there is a division in the discipline between those that see a strong policy-making role for IR theory and those who would like to refrain from excessive interaction with policymakers and their particular interests.

A famous exchange between William Wallace, Ken Booth, and Steve Smith during 1996 to 1997 brought out the dynamics of the theory-versus-practice debate very well. While for Wallace IR as a discipline had become too abstractly theoretical, with many (especially critical) theorists retreating to their ivory towers and disengaging from policy making, for Booth and Smith the problem was that (a) not all academics, from all theoretical schools of thought, would be freely invited to engage with policymakers because of the inherent biases and interests that drive decision making and (b) the practice of teaching and creating alternative views of knowledge could itself be seen as a form of political practice, potentially being more influential than entering into the halls of power.

There seems to be no solution to the theory–practice dilemma in contemporary IR theory, but the accusation that IR theory is too abstract to be useful continues to be made by some scholars and policymakers. At the same time, some theorists complain of policymakers' lack of interest in alternative ways of framing and understanding problems. The picture is in other words mixed: While some IR theorists are closely engaged in policy making, others have decided not to engage with, or are pushed out from, policy-making circles.

Trends in IR Theory

As emphasized and exemplified above, IR theory is strongly characterized by theoretical pluralism. But what are the key debates in IR theory at present and what are they likely to be in the future? This is a difficult question, for it depends on whom one asks and where one looks.

Interestingly, it seems that there are distinct geographical differences in what kinds of IR theory are seen as preponderant or promising. In the United States, it is fair to say that realism and liberalism in their neo-forms, as well as increasingly in their more classical forms (neoclassical realism and Kantian liberalism), play a key role. Realism and liberalism are arguably dominant also in debates on IR in China and Russia. In addition, constructivist analysis is increasingly being taken seriously in the mainstream American context. Indeed, it seems that currently these three theoretical schools—realism, liberalism, and constructivism—usefully cross-fertilize each other.

Yet, curiously, while this triumvirate of theoretical approaches dominates and frames debates in key journals such as *International Organization* and *International Studies Quarterly*, it could also be argued that increasingly, theoretical debates are currently being conducted largely *within* and not just between these theoretical schools. Indeed, much of realist debate at present concentrates on arguments between offensive and defensive realists, and neoliberals have also turned inward to discuss different ways of understanding institutional logics. Thus, there is a curious fragmentation of debates in IR, as Wæver has pointed out (see his chapter in Dunne et al., 2007).

Different perspectives tend to dominate in Europe. First, it is notable that constructivism is very popular in Europe, especially in Germany but also within the UK. Yet in both the UK and on the Continent the scene is also more varied. Realists tend to be few, while critical theorists of various persuasions have a strong position in the field. In the UK, for example, Marxism and Gramscian thought still play key roles in debates, as does critical theory, both in its classical and poststructuralist formulations.

IR theory, albeit sometimes in fragmented forms, continues to be developed and reconfigured. However, it seems to develop in different ways in different geographical contexts. This is partly because IR theory does not develop in a vacuum: Like any social theory, it is tied to specific social and political contexts and interests. With this in mind, it is important to note that IR theory continues to be mainly an Anglo-American discipline and that theoretical voices from Latin America, Africa, or Asia are rarely listened to, and they certainly do not structure the field (but often seek to fit in it).

In any case, and despite its many failings and silences, IR theory is by no means on its deathbed. As Alexander Wendt and Duncan Snidal, the editors of the new *International Theory* journal, have argued, in many ways international theorizing is at its liveliest at the present juncture: There is a great deal of work being done in different traditions, and different theoretical tools are used by the scholars involved. Moreover, IR theory continues to be firmly embedded in the social and institutional structures of academia. In other words, it continues in being a placeholder—even if a contested one—for many scholars trying to grapple with international and world political trends as well as with the plurality of approaches being used by their colleagues to explain these.

Milja Kurki
Aberystwyth University
Aberystwyth, United Kingdom

See also Anarchy; Constructivism in International Relations; Critical Theory in International Relations; Feminist Theory in International Relations; Idealism in International Relations; International Relations, History; International Relations as a Field of Study; Liberalism in International Relations; Positivism; Realism in International Relations; War and Peace

Further Readings

Ashley, R. (1988). Untying the sovereign state: A double reading of the anarchy problematique. *Millennium: Journal of International Studies, 17*(2), 227–262.

Booth, K. (1997). Discussion: A reply to Wallace. *Review of International Studies, 23*(2), 371–377.

Brown, C. (1992). *International relations: New normative approaches.* Basingstoke, UK: Macmillan.

Burchill, S., Linklater, A., Devetak, R., Donnelly, J., Patterson, M., Reus-Smit, C., et al. (Eds.). (2005). *Theories of international relations* (3rd ed.). London: Palgrave.

Carr, E. H. (1946). *Twenty years' crisis, 1919–1939: An introduction to the study of international relations* (2nd ed.). London: Macmillan. (Original work published 1939)

Chowdhury, G., & Nair, S. (Eds.). (2002). *Power, postcolonialism and international relations: Reading race, gender and class.* London: Routledge.

Cox, R. (1981). Social forces, states and world orders: Beyond international relations theory. *Millennium: Journal of International Studies, 10*(2), 126–155.

Dunne, T., Kurki, M., & Smith, S. (Eds.). (2007). *International relations theories: Discipline and diversity.* Oxford, UK: Oxford University Press.

Enloe, C. (1990). *Bananas, beaches and bases: Making feminist sense of international politics.* Berkeley: University of California Press.

Hollis, M., & Smith, S. (1990). *Explaining and understanding international relations.* Oxford, UK: Clarendon Press.

Keohane, R. O. (2005). *After hegemony: Co-operation and discord in the world political economy.* Princeton, NJ: Princeton University Press.

Smith, S. (1997). Power and truth: A reply to William Wallace. *Review of International Studies, 23*(4), 507–516.

Wallace, W. (1996). Truth and power, monks and technocrats: Theory and practice in international relations. *Review of International Studies, 22*(3), 301–321.

Wallerstein, I. (1982). *The modern world system: Volumes I and II.* New York: Academic Press. (Original work published 1974)

Waltz, K. (1979). *Theory of international politics.* London: McGraw-Hill.

Wendt, A. (1999). *Social theory of international politics.* Cambridge, UK: Cambridge University Press.

Wight, M. (1966). Why is there no international theory? In H. Butterfield & M. Wight (Eds.), *Diplomatic investigations* (pp. 89–131). London: Allen & Unwin.

International Relations as a Field of Study

The field of international relations (commonly abbreviated IR) focuses on a variety of subjects. The many connotations that are usually associated with the term *relations* (one of the most under-specified terms in the field itself) and the aesthetic quality that accompanies relating the name of the field (IR) to a broad set of subjects subsumed under the same term in lowercase letters, "international

Note: Due to limitations of space, the number of references had to be restricted. A fully referenced version of this article is available at http://www.soz.uni-frankfurt.de/hellmann/mat/IPSA.pdf.

relations," help explain why both *IR* and *international relations* are still widely accepted. Of course, this is not to say that there is consensus. Both the name of the field and the description of its subject matter(s) have always been contested. Different observers have argued that *international* ought to be replaced by *interstate*, *transnational*, or *global*—to name just a few. Others would like to see *relations* replaced by *studies* or *politics*. A brief look at some of these alternative combinations—for example, "interstate relations," "transnational politics," or "global studies"—would give any reader a quick idea as far as different emphases are concerned, even if he or she is not familiar with the normative and theoretical underpinnings that inform these alternative descriptions of the field of study and its subject matter(s). For this reason, conceptual contestation is unsurprising; it is already an expression of the inevitable and recurring ascertainment of the borders of a field of study by the community of scholars belonging to it and claiming it as their own.

In the case of IR, contestation extends well beyond the question of how a rather loosely defined field of study—or "fragmented 'nonfield'" (James Rosenau, 1993)—is to be properly named. Especially in the English-speaking world, IR is sometimes defined in terms of an academic discipline of its own, separate from political science, or as a multidisciplinary field of study. On a global scale, however, this is not normally the case. Here, it is usually considered to be one of the major subfields (or subdisciplines) of political science. Even if the term *discipline* may sometimes be used interchangeably with *field of study*, it is meant in the sense of a more loosely defined field that keeps the outer borderlines both fairly fluid and permeable while, at the same time, emphasizing that its core is more clearly demarcated and in some ways also more stable. Of course, any such characterization of the field is in itself contestable. More specifically, two caveats need to be kept in mind with regard to any exercise in "mapping" a field of study. First, as Hilary Putnam put it, any such overview necessarily involves a particular "view from somewhere" that is shaped by specific individual and cultural formative experiences. Even if this view of IR is shaped by an environment that allows for pluralism with regard to normative commitments, theoretical orientations, and methodological preferences, it is inevitably limited by what IR scholarship is actually accessible via particular languages and academic infrastructures. The academic infrastructure of IR is lacking in crucial respects when measured against the ideal of a global discipline that is living up to the spread, reach, and interconnections of its subject matter. Second, there is also an inevitable temporal dimension of contestation. Any overview of IR as a field of study necessarily resembles a snapshot of the field at a particular point in time and will, almost inevitably, be the view of how the discipline used to operate in the past. This notion of IR as an evolving and historically situated field becomes strikingly clear when one compares similar overviews of the field in approximately 10-year intervals from the early 1920s onward. Not only do descriptions of the subject matter change. Rather, change is ubiquitous with regard to the borderlines drawn to other (sub)fields and the names used to denote and demarcate the field's most prominent theories. Therefore, this overview ought to be seen as a "disciplining" exercise in the dual sense of the word. It is supposed to provide a perspective on the structure of the discipline and familiarize the reader with some of the prominent conventions, theories, and practices of the field of IR as they are currently viewed in the field in terms of a history of the present. At the same time, it ought to be kept in mind that the very concept of scholarship points at moving beyond these conventions, theories, and practices. By de-emphasizing disciplinary stability in favor of an evolutionary perspective, this way of proceeding does not deny that a structural view of the discipline may be useful. As a matter of fact, it is—and such a structural perspective will be applied in the first section of this overview. However, looking at the discipline with a bird's-eye perspective necessarily emphasizes the big picture and will thus almost inevitably appear fairly static. The second, shorter section of this entry therefore applies a more historical and dynamic perspective depicting the field as an expanding one along many frontiers simultaneously.

The Structure of Global International Relations

What a field is made up of in terms of intellectual substance—that is, its conceptualization of the subject matter, its theories, and its understandings of appropriate procedures in producing knowledge—is not dictated by the subject matter itself. Rather, it results from the interplay of specific social structures (such as institutional arrangements along disciplinary lines within universities or structures of communication in the form of journals, etc.) and intellectual structures (i.e., what counts as knowledge and how different bodies of knowledge connect to make up a discipline). Both are closely interconnected. As far as the social structure of IR is concerned, Ole Wæver (2007) has argued that it is best viewed as "a mix of a U.S./global system and national/regional ones with varying degrees of independence" (p. 296). Thus, two elements are characteristic of IR in terms of its global structure. First, IR in the United States is predominantly *North American* IR and *global* IR. Second, other IR communities show a great variety in terms of size and intellectual traditions. However, what is most noticeable from a global perspective is the extent to which they relate to IR in the United States. This is another way of saying that Stanley Hoffmann's (1977) famous line about IR being "an American social science" reverberates until today. Yet although the dominance of American IR remains clearly visible, a broad-brush global perspective on disciplinary developments would stress the distinction between the West and the non-West rather than the United States versus the rest. One of the distinguishing marks of the current developmental stage of IR from a global and evolutionary perspective may well be its post-Western and its post-Westphalian character. However, from a bird's-eye view of the structures of the discipline, the West seems very well entrenched.

Size and Power

Admittedly, the IR community in the United States still plays in a league of its own. Just in terms of sheer size, it easily outdistances that of any other country by multiples. A 2009 survey by Richard Jordan, Daniel Maliniak, Amy Oakes, Susan Peterson, and Michael Tierney counted more than 4,100 IR scholars in the United States with an active affiliation with a university, college, or professional school. (As of early 2009, the American Political Science Association listed close to 4,700 members who had identified IR as their "general field.") Although similarly detailed figures are not available for many countries, a very rough estimate based on a variety of sources would probably put the U.S. share of IR scholars around the world at approximately 25% to 30%. Another 15% to 25% could probably be added for Canada, Europe, Israel, and Australasia, putting the Western share of global IR production capacity at 40% to 55% overall.

Although the size of academic communities is an important structural feature, in and of itself it says little about the global structure of IR in terms of institutional, structural, and productive power. Yet even if one adds such a perspective, it is fairly clear that the United States occupies the most influential position at the center, with European IR communities plus Israel and Australasia forming an appendix to the core that tries to establish a somewhat more independent profile (and has partly succeeded in doing so). Three observations are noteworthy in this context. First, the institutional and structural power of U.S. IR is reflected in how IR scholars in other parts relate to it. For IR scholars in Western Europe, Israel, and South Asia, and to a lesser degree in East-Central Europe and some parts of Latin America, gaining recognition in the United States (i.e., in U.S.–based IR journals in particular) continues to be a crucial element for professional advancement compared with IR scholars elsewhere. Since the editors of key journals are drawn largely from the IR community in the United States, scholars aiming at being published in these journals have to address the concerns of this community. Yet as many studies have shown, the theoretical debates in the United States are largely driven by American foreign policy concerns, not broader global concerns. A 2009 survey by Tom Biersteker of the assigned or required readings for PhD candidates specializing in IR in the 10 leading U.S. departments of political science showed that, on average, 94% of the assigned readings were written by scholars who have spent most or all of their careers in the United States. As a result, the segment of global IR scholarship that aims at the most prestigious journals in the field will inevitably face editors whose academic careers have been largely shaped by U.S. concerns. Non-American Western IR scholars are more likely to be able to meet the expectations of these editors, and to the extent that their work is actually being published, it is therefore also more likely to speak to an agenda shared by Western societies and states. The same applies vice versa for the increasing number of U.S. scholars being published in European peer-reviewed journals such as *European Journal of International Relations* and *Journal of International Relations and Development.* Although the differences between the United States, on the one hand, and Europe and Australasia, on the other, are noteworthy and have often been described, these differences fade away against the many similarities if one contrasts IR research practices and priorities in the West as a whole with those in the non-West.

The second observation extends the emphasis on disciplinary autonomy within largely national borders from the United States to the global level. Although the orientation toward the United States and its standards of IR scholarship in a fairly small (though influential) set of countries reinforces American dominance, it is by far not a universal phenomenon. A global structure dominated by Western standards of science and thematic agendas coexists with significant degrees of local autonomy in IR communities around the world, according to Arlene Tickner and Ole Wæver. For a field focusing on phenomena that by their very nature transcend national boundaries, it is noteworthy how parochial (or detached from a truly global discourse) *all* IR communities are around the world. This is amply visible in an almost universal preoccupation with the foreign policy agendas of the respective countries. In the context of the United States and intellectually linked IR communities such as Europe, this concern is embedded in or dominated by an explicit theoretical framing of specific problems. In many other countries where the intellectual structure of the discipline is less dominated by the imperatives of theory production, these foreign policy agendas often translate quite directly into research agendas. Therefore, a certain parochialism seems to be an almost inevitable and universal characteristic of IR globally. In part, this is also due to the fact that the social structures of the academy have their own life and in many ways follow national patterns. Sometimes national IR communities may be clustered into regional groups with distinct characteristics, such as an "Anglo-American" way of doing IR or a "Continental" one. However, national profiles often remain clearly visible. For instance, even a quick look at the social and intellectual structure of IR in Italy, France, Germany, and the Netherlands immediately reveals remarkable differences as well as similarities in the relatively narrow space of the European continent. In a longer historical perspective, however, the patterns of academic institutionalization and professionalization of IR during the 20th century have also converged, often following the American model of treating IR as a more or less integral part or subdiscipline of political science.

Third, it certainly matters whether one pursues (more or less parochial) IR concerns in the United States, Britain, Denmark, China, Thailand, Nigeria, or Brazil, to name just a few sites. Although this entry is not the place for a detailed analysis of the global social structure of IR (on this, see Tickner & Wæver, 2009), three layers of IR communities can be distinguished in terms of power, international connectedness, and international visibility.

International Relations as a Three-Tiered Discipline

The Dominance of U.S.–American IR

As mentioned before, first, the IR community in the United States stands out in terms of size and power. In the United States, whether or not an IR scholar engages with or is knowledgeable about IR elsewhere has little influence with regard to professional advancement, and thus, U.S. scholars may neglect the rest of the IR world. Second, to the extent that other IR communities relate to U.S. discourses, many largely emulate or implicitly follow the U.S. model and the theories propagated there. This can be taken by some IR scholars as evidence of the institutional and productive power exercised by American IR or even as evidence that the American way of doing IR is the "right" way. Third, to the extent that IR communities in other countries are essentially decoupled from U.S. (and thus globally dominant) discourses, this is mostly due to the fact that local political concerns dominate research agendas and that theory (as defined in the U.S.-dominated discourse) is largely irrelevant. Therefore, IR scholars from the United States may find little incentive to investigate IR in such states. Against this background, it is worth emphasizing that the International Studies Association (ISA)—the most important professional organization of

IR/international studies around the globe that originated in the United States and still largely comprises U.S. scholars as members—has been quite supportive of efforts to build up professional structures of academic communication beyond it. Yet despite these efforts, ISA conventions—one of the premier sites of intellectual exchange about IR on the global stage—have largely remained intra-Western scholarly exchanges. Whereas a systematic analysis of attendance patterns at the ISA conventions in Toronto (1997), Portland (2003), and New York (2009), based on the institutional origin of the respective scholars attending, shows a noteworthy increase of European Union–European scholars (16% in 1997, 15% in 2003, and 25% in 2009) relative to North American scholars (United States plus Canada: 76% in 1997, 74% in 2003, and 62% in 2009), there was essentially no change if one compared attendance along a Western versus non-Western distinction (see Figure 1).

The Second Tier of Semivisible IR Communities

Compared with U.S. insularity, the situation is quite different if one looks at IR from a global perspective with regard to a second category of IR communities, such as Britain, China, Denmark, or Canada. As different as these IR communities are in terms of university systems, professional incentive structures, and national traditions and as much as the American dominance may be resented in some quarters there, many of the influential IR scholars in these countries do (have to) relate to American IR in one way or another, if only by distancing themselves as to the way IR is done in the United States. Therefore, what distinguishes these communities from the U.S. IR community, on the one hand, and a third category of peripheral IR communities, on the other, is a medium level of international visibility. International visibility (defined in terms of a certain amount of recognition by other scholars around the world) may result from very different sources, such as the natural advantage of communicating in the lingua franca (as in the case of British IR) and/or the recognition by significant others that the work published in these communities matters, be it for purely academic reasons or due to other considerations.

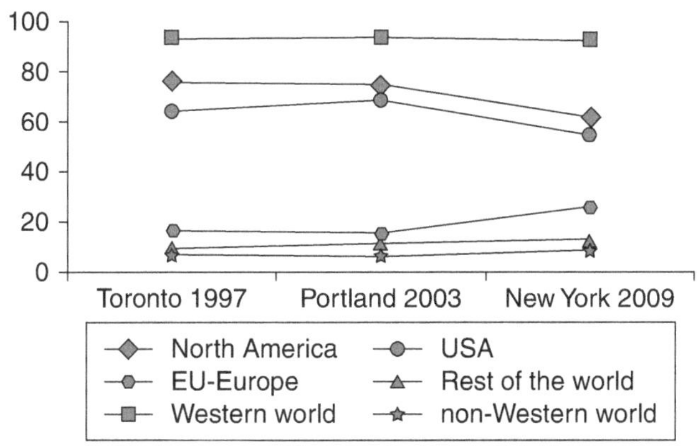

Figure 1 Origin of Scholars Attending International Studies Association (ISA) Conferences

Source: Author's analysis based on the convention programs as they were made available via the ISA website: http://www.isanet.org/conventions/2007/04/previous_isa_an.html. Scholars were grouped according to the state of their institutional affiliation, not their nationality.

Note: "Western world" comprises OECD (Organisation for Economic Co-operation and Development) member countries (including Israel but excluding Japan and Turkey).

a. Among the latter, one can single out the phenomenon of national "schools" of IR, which provide for a specific variant of this second type of IR communities with a medium level of international visibility. The so-called English School, for instance, represents a conscious effort on the part of scholars in the United Kingdom (UK) to establish the idea of an international "society of states" as a distinct theoretical concept synthesizing elements that have been assigned in American IR to competing (realist and liberal) schools of thought. In contrast to American IR, the English School scholarship exhibits a deep-seated skepticism vis-à-vis the "scientific" study of international relations and accordingly pays much more attention to historical processes. These substantive differences notwithstanding, insiders have argued that the English School essentially marks "a delayed response to Britain's loss of Empire and world status" (Richard Little, 2008, pp. 685–686). In forming such a school, however, Britain's IR community has not only tried to come to terms with the changed international role of the UK. It has also left a mark of distinction vis-à-vis the quasi-hegemonic U.S. discourse, thereby establishing a widely recognized corporate IR identity globally. IR communities in other countries that are habitually ranked among the "great powers" (e.g., Russia, Japan, and China) are increasingly engaged in debates whether or not to establish national schools similar to the English School (even South Korea is contemplating such a strategic move). China is the most obvious and most noteworthy case, both because of the size of the country and due to the Eastern tradition. Influential Chinese scholars nowadays openly advocate the establishment of a "Chinese School of IR Theory" as an "inevitable" step in the maturation of Chinese IR (Yaquing Qin, 2007). Yet as in the case of the English School, the emphasis on building such a distinct Chinese school on a set of core assumptions about the "material world" and the "speculative world," distinct from dominant IR theories in the West in general and the United States in particular, only reinforces the picture of the global preeminence of a particular U.S.-led type of theorizing centered on realist theory and its competitors as well as on rationalist and constructivist approaches to doing IR from an epistemological and/or methodological point of view. It is against this background that scholars from non-Western IR communities feel at least uncomfortable if not offended if they are asked why they have not yet come up with some IR theory of their own. A special issue of the journal *International Relations of the Asia-Pacific* carried the question "Why is there no non-Western IR theory?" quite prominently in the title (Amitav Acharya & Barren Buzan, 2007). To be sure, the whole thrust of the project was based on the intention to stimulate a debate about and the development of non-Western IR theory in Asia. Yet the way the question was framed already carried a specific understanding as to what good IR is all about—that is, that it ought to put a premium on theory, that it is fairly obvious what distinguishes theory from nontheory, and that IR communities in states such as China are not (yet) doing enough good theory. Judging from recent trends, some segments in countries such as China appear willing to take up this challenge. In part, this is due to a spreading realization among IR scholars that IR theories (broadly defined) do not only structure our view of the world in a very basic sense but that they are also tools for governing the world. In this analysis, both the world and IR often appear as if governed by the United States. Empirical analyses by Chinese scholars show that this power of disciplinary socialization via Western, especially U.S., theory discourses works even in a country such as China with a large IR community and a very distinct and old tradition of its own. For instance, with the exception of one book, all of the 86 IR books translated into Chinese by five leading publishers since 1990 were originally written in English, and the overwhelming majority of these books had American IR scholars as authors. Thus, even if a Chinese school of IR drawing heavily on distinctly Chinese traditions emerges eventually, it will have been mediated via theory as practiced in the English-speaking, mostly U.S.-dominated, Western world of IR.

b. A similar mixture of orientation toward American IR while tying IR scholarship back to local concerns and intellectual traditions is observable in a second variant of internationally more visible IR communities. Some IR communities in Western and East-Central Europe and in Israel belong to this group. What unites them in terms of institutional, structural, and productive power is that they can only draw in rather limited ways on the advantages that the British or the Chinese IR communities enjoy. While IR scholars in significant numbers in these communities publish in English, this is certainly not the case for all of them (as is the case in the UK). Also, in contrast to China, none of these states are expected to play a crucial role politically in the years to come in order to pay special attention to their possibly unique ways of doing IR research. Moreover, in contrast to the UK or China, most of these IR communities neither have the size nor the ambition to establish distinct national schools of IR. Still, in some countries, substantive research programs, such as the Copenhagen School of security studies, have gained international recognition as distinct approaches well beyond the regional context. In the case of the Copenhagen School's "securitization" research program, distinction was achieved with a more focused approach (in terms of both the theoretical scope and the substantive ground covered as far as the subject matter was concerned) than what is usually subsumed under the much broader label of a "paradigm" in the U.S. context. Debates in such communities are similar to those in the United States in putting a premium on theoretical work. However, even though theory debates in the

United States are at least taken note of in most of these, they are not (or no longer) simply replicated. Rather, an increasing amount of IR in Europe, Australia, New Zealand, or Canada is by now often inspired by philosophical and/or social science traditions and research practices distinct from those present in IR debates in the United States. Here, they are increasingly dominated by rational choice and formal modeling. Since these are not easily exportable, dominant U.S. theory preferences entail a "de-Americanization of IR elsewhere" (Wæver, 1998). Another way to put this is to point to an ever-present, often largely ignored and now rediscovered, cultural specificity (e.g., in French IR); an intra–Anglo-Saxon divide between "post-Imperial 'crimson' locales," on the one hand (made up essentially of Britain, Canada, Ireland, Australia, and New Zealand), and the United States, on the other; and, more generally, the newfound "autonomy" in Europe of a specific "Continental" brand of Western IR or at least a claim of an "intrafamilial emancipation" (e.g., in Germany). To the extent that this type of work gains international recognition, this is seldom due to the size of the respective IR community, the respective country's global political significance, or other such factors pointed to by science studies. Rather, genuine intellectual appeal and/or resonance appears to be more closely associated with quantitative as well as qualitative output resulting from comparative advantages in terms of sheer resources available and devoted to the task (as in the field of European studies) and the fact that some of the original theory products travel fairly easily to other regions (as in the case of securitization theory). Moreover, in the European context, in particular, the international visibility of European studies and distinct approaches such as the Copenhagen School has been enhanced by the establishment of several new journals (many of which are published in English). Some of these, such as the *European Journal of International Relations*, have quickly established themselves among the leading journals in the field globally. These successes and differences between the United States and other Western IR communities notwithstanding, it needs to be emphasized that the non-U.S. West offers a broad variety of intellectual profiles, not all of which are as much interested in connecting via English-language publications internationally as are, for instance, IR scholars in the English-speaking world, Scandinavia, the Netherlands, or Germany. As a matter of fact, sizable communities with original theoretical work, such as the French, are quite detached from the rest of the West and have fairly little impact globally. Thus, geographical location is not necessarily a good indicator of whether an IR community may achieve international visibility.

In any case, from a power perspective, few non-Western IR communities can be counted to the semiperiphery of the second tier. Even Japan, with its sizable IR community and conscious institutional efforts at increasing its visibility globally—recently by establishing the peer-reviewed English-language journal *International Relations of the Asia-Pacific*—neither has much of an impact globally nor has succeeded in establishing a distinct Japanese IR profile, according to Takashi Inoguchi. China currently seems to be the only serious candidate for such a rise to the semiperiphery, or to put it less pejoratively, only China appears able in the medium to long term to engage in competition with the West for productive power in actually "constructing the world" in a language and in theories that are distinctly Chinese. Yet even sympathetic observers remain somewhat skeptical about whether a distinct and globally visible Chinese school of IR might indeed be established.

The Third Tier: Sizable and (Self-)Marginalized

The third group of IR communities is both the largest (in terms of the number of national IR communities belonging to it) and the most isolated and marginalized (in terms of international visibility and power). As a matter of fact, one of the expressions of its marginalization is that much less "is known" about these IR communities compared with the two other groups. In part, this is because scholars from the other two groups, who are usually instrumental in producing such international visibility due to disciplinary power structures, normally pay little attention to the research conducted there. Indeed, one could easily turn the complaint (sometimes heard in the non-U.S. West) that American IR treats research originating in Europe, Canada, or Australasia with indifference against the plaintiffs themselves since the same pattern of ignorance may be observed in their relationship to most IR communities in Asia, Africa, and Latin America (many of which have, of course, suffered through European colonization). In part, however, marginalization also results from the self-conscious separation or self-reliance of IR communities in Asia, Africa, and Latin America or from these countries simply refraining from engaging in IR research. Some of the IR communities in this third group (such as the Indian or Brazilian) are fairly sizable, though not necessarily tightly organized professionally, as their counterparts are in the United States or Europe. Many others are tiny, with no professional organization whatsoever. In quite a few third-tier countries, IR as an academic (sub)discipline is not even present at universities or—to the extent that it actually is present—is largely characterized by the dominance of research questions that reflect the respective countries' foreign policy agenda. As a matter of fact, there is often a very close connection between the foreign policy establishments and official state institutions in these countries, on the one hand, and IR departments, on the other, since the latter often exist primarily because they are expected to supply future diplomats for the respective foreign services. Theory-oriented research as practiced and cherished in the West does not play much of a role here. Theory—conceived of in very general terms as a necessary precondition for reality-constituting observation—is ever present. Yet it transpires largely *implicitly* in empirical analyses. The prime research objective is seldom theorizing as such. Moreover, against the foil of Western theory discourses, this implicit form of theory application carries more realist than nonrealist themes. A similar observation can be made with regard to the role of methods. Where the role models of Western IR scholarship call for methodological reflection at a minimum (and often excel in offering highly sophisticated methods that are understood and applied by very small communities of scholars), the requirements for methodological rigor and metareflection in third-tier countries are much less stringent. Typically, academic publications display a combination of some form of institutional and/or historical analysis without engaging in a justificatory argument as to why a particular method or form of presentation has been chosen or rejected.

From a structural perspective, there is fairly little intellectual exchange both among third-tier communities and between them and IR communities from the first and second tiers. Moreover, some of the interaction that can be observed is stimulated by foundations located in the West that (often unintentionally) tend to reproduce existing uneven global structures of knowledge production. For instance, as the volume by Tickner and Wæver (2009) has shown, the funding provided by Western foundations (such as Ford) in countries such as India, East-Central Europe, Latin America, or South Africa has often been very influential in developing local IR communities. One key reason was simply that state funding was limited. Yet since the type of research that was funded primarily addressed questions of more immediate local policy relevance, the overall effect was to reinforce the global intellectual division of labor whereby theory is "produced in the center and consumed and applied in and by the periphery" (p. 332). These effects are particularly surprising for countries (e.g., India) that have both a comparatively old and large IR community and a philosophical tradition of their own. As a matter of fact, the Indian political philosopher Chanakya (ca. 350–283 BCE), who is usually know in the West by the name Kautilya and who is sometimes claimed among Western scholars as one of the founders of realism, is apparently not even taught in any principal IR theory course in India itself, according to Navnita Behera (2007). Similar patterns of forgetfulness and/or neglect of homegrown traditions can be observed in Japan and recently also in China. From a postcolonial point of view, this devaluation of homegrown traditions is just one (often unreflected) expression of a "colonized" mind-set that stems from a discipline of IR that is at its very core an "expression of the Western theory of progress" (David Blaney & Naeem Inayatullah, 2008, p. 672). This postcolonial message starts to resonate even among scholars from third-tier countries who have been socialized into Western IR thinking.

The Social Structure of the Discipline

The overall picture that emerges by looking at the social structure of IR from a global perspective is much more one of intellectual segmentation and stratification than one of intellectual integration, which one might think the subject matter itself to be suggesting. This impression of a three-tiered system is reinforced if one examines another dimension of the social structure of the discipline—that is, its publication system in general and its hierarchy of journals in particular. If access limitations (as measured in terms of journal acceptance rates) are accepted as a measure of reputation, clearly the most competitive journals of the discipline are published in the United States and Europe. In the United States and several European countries, getting published in these top journals is of central importance to climb the academic career ladder. Most of the highest ranking journals are still published in the United States and/or controlled by American IR scholars. As a matter of fact, a recent survey in the IR communities of 10 English-speaking countries found that at least four tiers can be distinguished when IR scholars from these countries are called on to list those journals "that publish articles with the greatest influence on the way IR scholars think about international relations" (Jordan et al., 2009, p. 49): (1) *International Organization* is in a league of its own and is mentioned by 73% of the scholars questioned; (2) the second group is made up of *International Security* (45%) and *International Studies Quarterly* (44%); (3) *American Political Science Review*, *World Politics*, and *Foreign Affairs*, mentioned by 28%, form the third group; and (4) *European Journal of International Relations* and *Review of International Studies* are the only non-American journals mentioned alongside *Journal of Conflict Resolution* with a mere 14% (for *European Journal of International Relations* in particular, the ranking is much better if one follows the Social Science Citation Index). Thus, interdependence structures are still quite asymmetrical within the West, with U.S. journals clearly outdistancing the top European journals.

In other parts of the world (including some parts of the West), publishing in internationally recognized

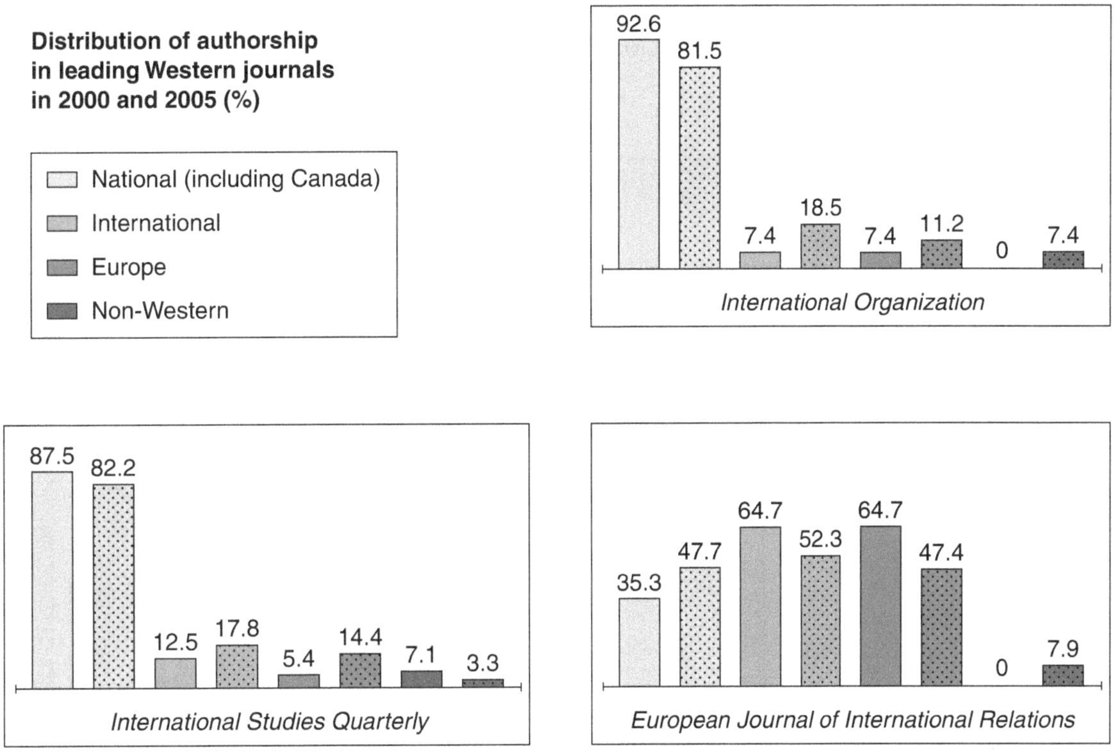

Figure 2 Authorship in Western International Relations Journals

Source: Friedrichs, J., & Wæver, O. (2009). Western Europe: Structure and strategy at the national and regional levels. In A. B. Tickner & O. Wæver (Eds.), *International relations scholarship around the world* (pp. 260–285). London: Routledge.

Note: Solid bar is 2000; dotted bar is 2005.

journals is not as central for recruitment practices and academic success. At the same time, the "international" profile of non-Western IR journals is much more pronounced than in the West, as a survey of selected non-Western journals shows, in contrast to a similar survey conducted for Western journals. For instance, more than 80% of the articles published in *International Organization* or *International Studies Quarterly* in 2000 and 2005 have been published by authors located in the United States or Canada (see Figure 2).

For the Turkish IR journal *Alternatives*, the *South African Journal of International Relations,* and the journal *International Relations of the Asia-Pacific*, the number of national authors has often been lower than the number of international authors, even decreasing between 2000 and 2005 (see Figure 3). Also, the number of non-Western authors (including national authors) being published in these journals has been increasing in most of these journals recently. This is in stark contrast to Western IR journals, which largely remain outlets for scholarship from Western IR scholars in general and scholars from the United States in particular. In other words, whereas the West remains fairly closed off from the rest of the world, there is much more of a balance between national and international authorship in non-Western IR journals.

The Intellectual Structure of the Discipline

Another characteristic of the publication system of Western IR is the distinct profile of mixing theory and empirical analysis. All of the IR journals ranked among the top 20 of all political science journals in the Social Science Citation Index distinguish themselves as theory-oriented journals in this sense. As Kjell Goldmann (1996) pointed out in a comparison of Western IR journals from the early 1970s and early 1990s, as far as "methodological approaches" are concerned, ever more articles published in the 1990s combined some form of theorizing with empirical observation. If anything, this trend has been reinforced during the past decade. Again, the contrast with non-Western IR journals is noticeable: With the possible exception of the Japanese journal *International Relations of the Asia-Pacific*, all of these journals primarily publish articles that eschew explicit theoretical discussion (see Figure 4).

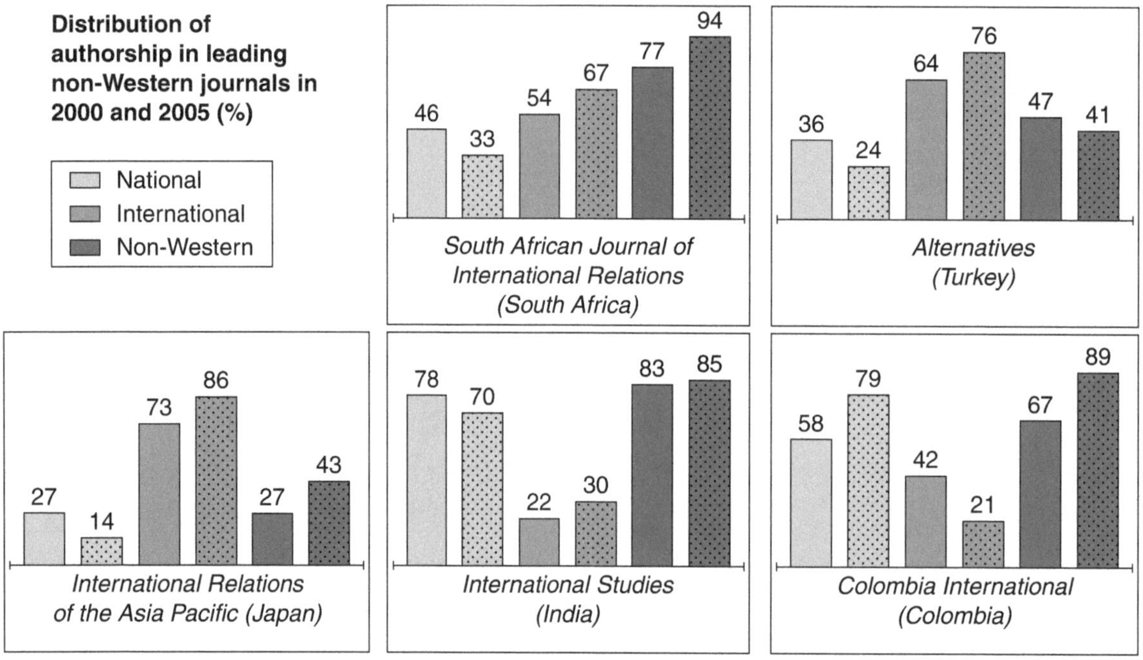

Figure 3 Authorship in Non-Western International Relations Journals

Note: Solid bar is 2000; dotted bar is 2005.

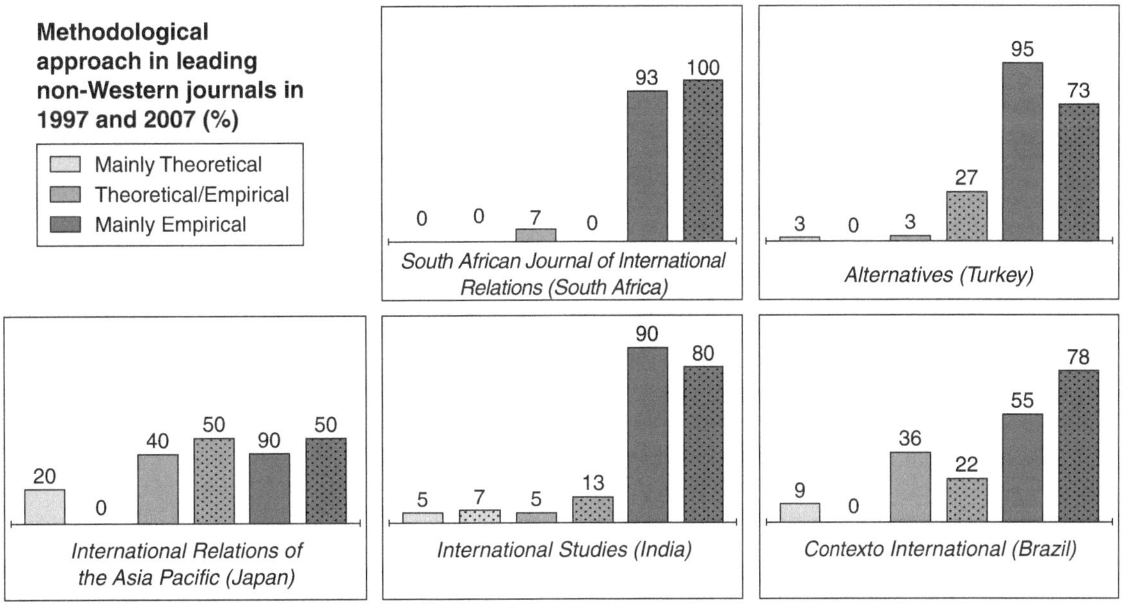

Figure 4 Methodological Approaches of Non-Western International Relations Journals

Note: Solid bar is 1997; dotted bar is 2007.

Paradigmatism and Great Debates

One of the oldest features of the intellectual structure of the discipline is paradigmatism. In IR, it has come to be understood as a disciplinary preoccupation with and segregation into separate "metascientific constructs" with distinct ontologies, epistemologies, and methodologies (Yosef Lapid, 1989). Although the allusion to Thomas Kuhn's paradigmatic view of the evolutionary development of scientific disciplines only spread in IR in the 1970s, the phenomenon as such has been a core feature of the discipline's intellectual structure (at least in its Western segment) since the mid-20th century. Realism, idealism, rationalism, and constructivism are usually mentioned as examples of such paradigms. Surpassed only by questions of epistemology and methodology, such "paradigmatic" differentiation continues to generate the most division among Western IR scholars (Jordan et al., 2009). What is more, IR scholars in 10 English-speaking countries, surveyed by Jordan and colleagues (2009), estimate that almost 90% of all IR literature is devoted to some form of paradigmatist analysis. Yet although one out of four considers his or her own work to be falling outside any paradigmatist frame, more than three quarters of the time is devoted to IR paradigms in IR introductory courses taught by these scholars. In other words, the intellectual structure of discipline continues to be reproduced along paradigmatist lines even though many IR scholars do not believe that such a focus is particularly useful in their own research.

This gap in (Western) IR between the prominence of paradigmatism in teaching and that in individual research reflects on what sociologists call "task uncertainty"—that is, the extent to which scholars in a discipline agree on what rules are to be followed and what work techniques are acceptable in producing knowledge (Wæver, 2007). In IR, the level of task uncertainty is quite high since there is fairly little agreement as to what the overarching disciplinary questions are or how one should go about tackling them. The TRIP survey found that two thirds of IR scholars questioned believe that methods and epistemology generate the most division in the discipline. Yet despite this diversity, there has at least been a widespread (if sometimes only implicit) understanding that paradigms *as such* are a key instrument for organizing the discipline, especially as far as IR's recurring great debates are concerned. This not only shows in how the discipline's history is usually told or how IR is taught but is also evident in textbooks and handbooks—that is, in works that are supposed to introduce novices to the field or that provide summaries and syntheses of what is normally claimed to be disciplinary knowledge. Two recent examples are illustrative. As the subtitle of *International Relations Theory: Discipline and Diversity* (Tim Dunne, Milja Kurki, & Steve Smith, 2007) indicates, the editors are keen to emphasize both the necessity of a certain disciplinary coherence and its diversity. Yet the organization of the book around nine "distinct theories of International relations—realism/structural realism, liberalism/neoliberalism, the English School, constructivism, Marxism and critical theory, feminism, poststructuralism, green theory, postcolonialism" (p. 3) shows that diversity is expressed not in the form of theoretical controversies over core substantive questions of international relations (e.g., what causes war, what causes poverty) or methods but through paradigms. The same understanding is reflected in a 2008 handbook by Christian Reus-Smit and Duncan Snidal, where the presentation of a somewhat different set of nine "major theoretical perspectives" takes up almost half the space of the volume (the theories discussed here include (1) realism, (2) Marxism, (3) neoliberal institutionalism, (4) the new liberalism, (5) the English School, (6) constructivism, (7) critical theory, (8) postmodernism, and (9) feminism). In other words, whereas IR scholars may disagree sharply as to the particular value of different paradigms, there at least seems to be widespread agreement that it is useful to conceive of the discipline in terms of paradigmatic differentiation and great debates.

However, from a longer historical perspective, the period during which paradigmatism and great debates were widely acknowledged as dominant features of the discipline's intellectual structure may come to an end. Recent self-reflective observations of the historiography of the discipline have convincingly shown that even in Western IR, the focus on great debates may have been as much a reflection of the perceived need of a novel academic field to identify a disciplinary core as a reflection of a common tendency in the social sciences to delimit the number of basic rival positions to a low number of macrolevel theories. As a matter of fact, the invocation of great debates as a typical characterization of overarching disciplinary divides did not begin until Hans Morgenthau introduced the term in the early 1950s to depict what soon came to be known as the debate between realism and idealism. Moreover, it reached its pinnacle with the announcement of a second great debate in the 1960s pitting traditionalists against behavioralists (or scientists) in a clash over what methods IR scholars ought to use in studying international phenomena. It was in this context that Kuhn's concept of a paradigm was first combined with the focus on great debates, most explicitly (if somewhat misleadingly) in an article by Arendt Lijphardt (1974) in which he identified the second great debate as "a dichotomous one between two opposing paradigms" (p. 18). Yet the third debate marked the end of agreement over how to describe what it was supposedly all about. Alternatively, it was framed as a debate between realism and globalism; between realism, pluralism, and structuralism; between positivists and post-positivists; or between "a broad body of interdisciplinary literature commonly (and often indiscriminately) labeled 'critical theory,' 'post positivism,' 'discourse analysis,' or 'post-structuralism,'" on the one hand, and "the intellectual imperialism of the modern, post-Cartesian 'scientific' approach to knowledge and society," on the other (Jim George, 1989, p. 270). Others suggested that the latter two descriptions marked the fourth debate, which in itself could be subdivided into two subdebates between reflectivists and rationalists, on the one hand, and between neorealists and neoliberal institutionalists, on the other. Thus, not only the intervals between debates have become longer since the first debate was invented, but after the second debate, there has also been ever more contention as to whether a third and/or fourth great debate actually took place and, if so, what it was all about. In any case, no fifth debate currently appears to be forthcoming.

Even if great debates were indeed a thing of the past, paradigmatism appears to be more resilient. In Andrew Abbott's reading of "generational paradigms," the emphasis on the economizing strategies of informational overload suggests a certain disciplinary immaturity in coming up with more sophisticated and adequate coping strategies. More critical readings—such as Niklas Luhmann's related lamentation about "multiple paradigmatasis" in sociology—in contrast highlight the unforced ignorance vis-à-vis large segments of knowledge that necessarily accompanies paradigmatic self-restriction. This latter perspective has recently won more recognition. Two prominent representatives of rationalism and constructivism, for instance, have joined voices in rejecting the implicit offer to conduct another "battle of analytical paradigms," since any such battle would "at the very least . . . encourage scholars to be method-driven rather than problem-driven in their research" (James Fearon & Alexander Wendt, 2002, p. 52). Rather than looking at the relationship between rationalism and constructivism in terms of a "debate," they pleaded for looking at it in terms of a "conversation" between two approaches that, "when understood pragmatically, [are] largely either complementary or overlapping" (Fearon & Wendt, 2002, p. 68). Similarly, the recent *Oxford Handbook of International Relations* prominently positioned the chapter "Eclectic Theorizing in the Study and Practice of International Relations" at the very beginning of the section that presented the nine "major theoretical perspectives" referred to above (Peter Katzenstein & Rudra Sil, 2008). In it, the authors advocate analytic eclecticism, an approach to research in IR that replaces paradigm-driven research with a strategy drawing widely on seemingly divergent research traditions built on distinct concepts, methods, analytics, and empirics.

Thus, although the intellectual structure of the discipline continues to be shaped by distinctions drawn in terms of paradigms (or the equivalent major theoretical perspectives, etc.), paradigmatism as such has been losing some of its grip. To the extent that there is an inherent tension between method-driven approaches or paradigmatism, on the one hand, and a focus on a problem-driven approach, on the other, the shift toward the latter can be seen as a sign of maturation. To be sure, a loss of disciplinary coherence may loom as a downside if IR loses its traditional paradigmatic signposts, according to Wæver (2007). Yet the same development can also be interpreted as an advance toward a more self-confident academic profession that need no longer engage in stylized battles to distinguish itself from adjacent (and presumably more reputable) disciplines such as history, law, economics, or sociology. Moreover, such a move can also be justified epistemologically since the earlier rationalization for paradigmatic separation—the usual reference to the idea of "incommensurability" in Kuhn's theoretical vocabulary—has hence been problematized in the philosophy of science. For a long time, Kuhn's term of incommensurability was understood to mean that the theoretical vocabularies of separate paradigms were not intertranslatable. Yet as Richard Rorty (1991), among others, has argued, "untranslatability does not entail unlearnability" and "learnability is all that is required to make discussability possible" (p. 48). Paradigmatic separation, therefore, is a disciplinary convention, not an epistemological necessity. Recently, this approach to "interparadigm" debates has been spreading in IR at least subliminally, if not explicitly, according to Colin Wight. Irrespective of whether one welcomes or criticizes such a development, it is yet another sign of a much broader development in the discipline: its expansion along many dimensions.

The Expansion of International Relations

Thus far, the discipline has been examined largely in terms of its social and intellectual structures. This inevitably entails a rather static view that does not sufficiently acknowledge the tremendous dynamism of IR. Yet the dynamic development of the field is perhaps the most striking feature of the discipline. Ever since the early days of modern IR in the early 20th century, the discipline has been expanding. Although this intellectual expansion may resemble earlier colonial practices of the West in some respects (and may therefore also be described in diverse vocabularies), the phenomenon as such appears to be largely uncontroversial. Four dimensions of intellectual expansion can be distinguished:

1. territorial expansion (or spread) from a largely Western core to other countries;
2. disciplinary expansion within political science as measured in terms of chairs designated with denominations that are normally considered to be IR;

3. substantive expansion as measured in research problems being taken up by scholars identifying themselves as doing IR and in interaction with the latter; and
4. theoretical and methodological expansion.

Of course, none of these expanding moves ought to be imagined as linear or unidirectional. When knowledge travels, it always intermingles and, thereby, transforms. John Agnew notes refers to the image of a marketplace where Western IR is "exported" to non-Western regions and countries or where IR "imports" from other disciplines such as philosophy or where economics misconstrues knowledge as a commodity changing hands without being affected by the very transaction. If we take this transformational dimension into account, however, the metaphor of expansion quite cogently describes a phenomenon that is as familiar as a subject matter to the IR scholar as it is ubiquitous if one looks at the dynamic development of the discipline.

Given the limits of space and the earlier discussion of the global structure of IR, the territorial and disciplinary expansion can be kept short. As mentioned earlier, territorial expansion was for a long time characterized (and in many ways still is characterized) by the discipline's failure to engage with the non-Western world. To the extent that such engagement did take place, it often followed general patterns of colonial interaction. Western IR presented its way of practicing the craft as exemplary, while scholars in non-Western regions would either emulate Western IR practices (thereby, perhaps, gaining some recognition from abroad) or keep to whatever local forms of scholarship were deemed suitable to study things "international" (and remain largely marginalized). In the late 20th century and early 21st century, there has been quite a bit of change with respect to the quantitative enlargement of IR communities outside the West and a much more self-conscious redefinition of what it may mean to conduct IR in places such as China, India, Kenya, or Mexico. This expansion has been aided by global shifts in power as well as theoretical innovation (e.g., postcolonialism). The World International Studies Committee (WISC), an organization of national International Studies associations that has been active since the turn of the century, has certainly helped as well. Measured in terms of chairs in IR, the discipline even seems to be expanding much more rapidly in non-Western regions, Latin America, and Asia in particular (see the 2009 special issue of *International Relations of the Asia-Pacific*). Nevertheless, even though almost no comparative data are available on the number of chairs in IR around the globe or relative to other disciplines in political science, Hans-Dieter Klingemann notes that IR appears to be growing numerically even in Europe and North America, if only at the expense of other subdisciplines.

The Expansion of the IR Research Agenda

By most accounts (Western) IR is essentially an invention of the 20th century (for a contrasting perspective, see William Olson & John Groom, 1991). Even if some of its origins may have been romanticized in one way or another, it is widely accepted as common knowledge among IR scholars that the primary subjects of study in the first half of the 20th century were almost exclusively related to governmental activities crossing national boundaries. Against the background of the two World Wars, the question of war and peace loomed large. Accordingly, early (Western) IR framed its research agenda mainly in the vocabulary of international law and diplomatic history. The methods and approaches associated with these disciplines were thought to offer the best hope for "the problem of international governmental reorganization and practice" (Pitman Potter, 1923, p. 391), without necessarily succumbing to the sort of "idealist internationalism" for which the discipline was later chastised by realists in particular (Olson & Groom, 1991). In the middle of the 20th century, the agenda was broadened to include international economics and all those aspects of international relations that could be "described in terms of decision-making by identifiable individuals or groups of individuals" (Frederick Dunn, 1948, p. 145). More important, ever more scholars seemed ready to subscribe to the view that international politics rather than international organization constituted the core of a slowly maturing discipline. While the latter was said to have been approached predominantly with a constitutional frame, the image of an international system made up of states that were interacting "almost like

Leibnizian monads" (Morton Kaplan, 1961) and the accompanying clash of national interests and power were considered to be more properly dealt with in a political framework (William Fox, 1949). The first great debate was an expression of this shift.

The war experience (which had involved all those countries crucial for the discipline's development in the 1950s and 1960s) and the spreading realization that the advent of the nuclear age would not only revolutionize warfare but also affect the very survival of humankind pushed the expanding research agenda of IR scholarship into the field of strategic studies with its focus on state practices such as deterrence thinking and arms control negotiations. While essentially remaining in the classical IR domain of state-based international politics, the novel process of European integration at least offered a paradigmatic alternative to the traditional focus on great-power competition. It not only inspired a series of similar political projects in other parts of the world but also helped stimulate a new and vibrant field of study focused on comparative regional integration. In addition, the process of decolonization laid the foundation for expanding both the territorial reach of IR research beyond the confines of the Western world as well as the disciplinary focus on politics by intensifying the link with economics. Paradigmatically, though, the two major alternatives of the emerging development studies, modernization theory and dependency theory, continued to draw almost exclusively on the Western tradition. (Neo-)Marxist-inspired analyses of capitalism's contribution to the "underdevelopment" of non-Western regions by scholars such as André Gunder Frank, a University of Chicago–trained economist, helped pave the way for international political economy to fully establish itself as one of the major subfields of IR, starting in the 1970s. On a parallel track, the study of foreign policy, which had been one of the major sections in any North American IR/political science curriculum, continued to thrive as an ever more "scientific," increasingly separate and differentiating field. Foreign policy analysis (or FPA) was the prime subfield of IR, expanding into those neighboring disciplines (such as psychology and sociology) that were deemed useful in coming up with theoretical and methodological tools for making sense of group decision-making processes under routine bureaucratic or crisis situations.

With the advent of the East–West détente and the 1973 oil crisis, the disciplinary horizon broadened further. Although the classical focus on "high-politics" security issues kept its prominent place, other issues gained in importance or were added anew to the IR research agenda. First, the introduction of the concept of "transnational politics" at the end of the 1960s contained an unveiled critique of the state centrism of classical IR. It also foreshadowed the broadening of the more narrowly circumscribed foreign policy perspective during the 1970s and 1980s by also looking at nonstate actors and their activities and interactions at the systemic level. Second, the Club of Rome's "The Limits to Growth" report of 1972, the first United Nations Conference on the Human Environment in the same year, and the oil crisis in the following year set the stage for environmental issues to be added to the IR research agenda. Third, transnational relations and environmental politics both fitted in neatly with perhaps the most prominent new theme in IR since the 1970s: the spreading interest in the phenomenon of interdependence and globalization. This image of an increasingly globalizing world that affected every corner of the globe and reached across all issue areas in turn helped push a final expansion of the research agenda: the inclusion of an ever-larger group of nonstate actors, to use the mainstream IR vocabulary. Alternatively, critical, postmodern, feminist, and/or postcolonial theories identified a huge, highly diverse, and often indiscernible group that they called the marginalized: victims of war, poverty, or colonialism; women; or, more generally, all human beings who had become mere objects of structures and practices of power rather than being political subjects. At the beginning of the 21st century, there are, thus, few phenomena that cannot be framed in one way or another as legitimate objects of study under the heading of IR. Indeed, some even argue that the discipline has to rename itself in order to do justice to the causal and constitutive connections that link so many levels of political action in global society.

It is hardly surprising, therefore, that both the structure of the most influential professional organization in the field of international studies, the International Studies Association, and the most recent comprehensive survey of the major topics of the field appear to cover essentially any phenomenon of politically relevant social action transcending state borders. The book version of the ISA "compendium" encompasses 12 volumes and more than 8,000 pages of text (Robert Denemark, 2010). The open-ended online compendium is even more voluminous. The same applies as far as the structure of the ISA is concerned. The 24 sections are impressive not only for their breadth but also for the fact that paradigmatism is much less visible at this level of organization. Section themes include professional and pedagogical concerns (as in the sections "Women's Caucus" and "Active Learning in IS") and epistemological and methodological concerns (as in the sections "Comparative Interdisciplinary Studies" and "Scientific Study of International Processes"), but most often, they cover a broad range of substantive issues (e.g., "Diplomatic Studies"; "Environmental Studies"; "Ethnicity, Nationalism, and Migration Studies"; "Feminist Theory and Gender Studies"; "Foreign Policy Analysis"; "Global Development Studies"; "Human Rights; "Intelligence Studies"; "International Communication"; "International Education"; "International Ethics"; "International Law"; "International Organization"; "International Political Economy"; "International Political Sociology"; "International Security Studies"; "Peace Studies"; "Political Demography"; and "Post Communist States in International Relations"). The only exception as far as a paradigmatic orientation is concerned relates to the section "English School."

Theoretical and Methodological Expansion

Theoretical and methodological sophistication is almost universally accepted as a key criterion for judging the quality and status of a scholarly discipline. In both respects, IR has seen tremendous, sometimes even exponential, growth. If we concentrate on the 20th century, the formative period of IR up to the 1950s was largely marked by an understanding of theory and method common among the (usually much older) disciplines from which IR was drawing its new talents: (diplomatic) history, (international) law, economics, what is nowadays called area studies, and the study of (domestic) politics. Many of these were considered to be part of the humanities rather than the (social) sciences. Accordingly, the distinction between the empirical and the normative, drawn in a particularly strong fashion in the course of the "behavioral revolution," was mostly not deemed appropriate then. To be sure, "science" was already cherished among IR novices. Yet it was not yet as strongly associated with a notion of the natural sciences as was the case in the 1960s and 1970s.

The revolutionary shift to the new mantra of "applying scientific methods" was perhaps best captured in the transition from the 1st edition (published in 1961) to the 2nd edition of *International Politics and Foreign Policy*, a textbook edited by Rosenau (1969), who, perhaps along with Hayward Alker, is himself an exemplar of the shifting epistemological, theoretical, and methodological currents of the discipline over the past 50 years. In introducing the 57 chapters of the 2nd edition, Rosenau apologized for including "only 9 percent of the original selections" even though he himself had stated in 1961 that "articles were included 'only if they seemed likely to be useful in twenty years.'" Yet rather than taking this to be a "cause for embarrassment," he saw "cause for satisfaction" due to the "remarkable growth in the scope and pace of the theoretical enterprise" and the "increasingly sophisticated penetration of the mysteries of international life" (Rosenau, 1969, p. xvii). The book contained 25 articles on 14 different types of "theories and approaches" as well as 17 articles on different "research techniques and orientations." For many older IR scholars, this was a misguided fixation on an ideal of science that was wholly inadequate for the subject matter of international politics. Yet Rosenau's candid assessment and selections illustrate the predominant mood and trends in the 1960s and 1970s quite well. Although "classical" approaches and methods continued to have their followers—and actually benefitted themselves from the behavioral revolution—the wave of the future seemed to be an understanding of "science" that required "an articulated secondary language that permits reasonable precision and replicability" (Kaplan, 1966, p. 4) as well as sophisticated techniques for gathering and processing data.

Mere listing of all the new methods and techniques that were invented and/or imported in IR during that phase could spread out over a couple of pages. Suffice it to say that such a list would include almost the whole range of tools applied in other academic disciplines—ranging all the way from some of the humanities to other social sciences and the natural sciences. Nevertheless, even some of its initial adherents later granted that "the promises of behavioralism were not fulfilled" (Rosenau, 1993, p. 459). Against this background, among others, the third (or fourth) debate in particular represented a move beyond methodology by digging deeper to address the underlying epistemological and ontological questions. Yet rather than shrinking the space, this debate enlarged it further through reinvigorating reflection on the reach and uses of qualitative methods and by problematizing the very basis of theory formation. In many ways, the qualitative label reinforced an encroaching dualistic conception of methodology—with a quantitative pole on the other side. Of course, some influential theories and/or methods (e.g., rational choice and other formal methods) that actually thrived during the 1980s and 1990s in American IR could not easily be subsumed under such a dualistic conception. However, influential publications that reached far beyond IR (e.g., Gary King, Robert Keohane, & Sydney Verba, 1994) actually tried to ease the tension by arguing that there is a unified logic of scientific inference across a large spectrum of different methodologies. While this proposition was hardly acceptable to everyone, it did mirror a widespread understanding of scientific analysis among IR scholars according to which the essence of scholarship lay in "linking theory to evidence." In the 2002 *Handbook of International Relations*, this is the title of the single explicitly methodological chapter covering the whole spectrum from rationalist to constructivist theories, the latter even including critical theory. One set of methods that thrived in IR since the 1980s, the so-called case study methods—which were actually put at the center of qualitative methods by some more "scientifically" inclined scholars—actually expressed this understanding most clearly and, for many IR scholars, convincingly.

While it certainly mirrored "mainstream" understandings, the fixation on somehow linking theory and evidence with the help of certain methods had its critics—and increasingly so. As a matter of fact, since the early 1980s, an ever-larger number of scholars subscribed to a variety of postpositivist approaches that all posited the mutual impregnation of theory, reality, and descriptions thereof (evidence). Most important, from a methodological point of view, theories such as feminism, postmodernism, poststructuralism, critical theory, pragmatism, and postcolonialism all questioned whether "social facts" could indeed be treated like "natural facts," as implicitly assumed by the mainstream approaches (Friedrich Kratochwil, 2008). The answer was an outright "No." Since nature did not "speak," concepts and even whole vocabularies had to be invented in order to relate to "the world out there" when one wanted to describe and explain how even small parts of it (not to mention everything) actually hang together. In this view, the issue was not whether (and if so, how) one would come up with the "correct" description to work within the actual business of explanation. Rather, one of the key questions was how we came to describe the world in a particular vocabulary in the first place and what this description did to our being in and relating to the world.

This amounted to a radical critique of the whole enterprise of how the "science" of international relations was practiced by positivists. In a sense, the weight of the charge was equivalent to the one that scientists had leveled against traditionalists during the second debate: the charge of actually misconstruing what scholarship about the international was all about. Methods, however, were not relegated to the dustbin as charges about "anything goes" seemed to indicate. Indeed, if anything, the third (or fourth) debate helped further broaden the theoretical and methodological horizon of the discipline by opening it for a rediscovery of earlier roots in international law and normative theory and by more explicitly incorporating sociological perspectives (as illustrated by the founding of the journal *International Political Sociology* in 2007). To be sure, few of its adherents would claim that a switch to a postpositivist stance would be rewarded with any of the earlier promises of "cumulation of knowledge" or "progress" (the latter is at least kept as an option in a Lakatosian assessment of different IR research agendas). Yet leaving behind the straitjacket of "method-drivenness"—which has even become a dirty word for the self-proclaimed positivists (Fearon & Wendt, 2002)—seems to be enough in terms of gratification for them. In sum, even if the discipline may not have advanced much on the path of cumulation and progress, it seems to have progressed steadily on the path of theoretical and methodological sophistication.

Conclusion

The story of the field of international relations could be told in an analogous fashion to the story of "the expansion of international society." It may well be that a casual reader of this entry 20 or 50 years from now might actually have precisely that impression—with all the critical undertones that a postcolonial perspective would want to add. Yet this probably is how "the state of the art" appears to a big group of practitioners of IR scholarship today. As has been discussed above, the discipline is in many ways not up to the task (yet?) of tackling, not to mention overcoming, its many awkward parochialisms. These are all the more glaring given the almost universal expression of an ever more globalizing world—irrespective of how one may define the phenomenon of globalization—and the fact that the discipline itself lays claim to actually analyzing these processes and features within its purview.

Gunther Hellmann
Goethe-University Frankfurt/Main
Frankfurt am Main, Germany

See also International Law; International Political Economy; International Relations, History; International Relations, Theory; Normative Theory in International Relations

Further Readings

Abbott, A. (2001). *Chaos of the disciplines*. Chicago: University of Chicago Press.

Acharya, A., & Buzan, B. (2007). Why is there no non-Western international relations theory? An introduction. *International Relations of the Asia-Pacific, 7,* 287–312.

Behera, N. C. (2007). Re-imagining IR in India. *International Relations of the Asia-Pacific, 7,* 341–368.

Biersteker, T. (2009). The parochialism of hegemony: Challenges for "American" international relations. In O. Wæver & A. B. Tickner (Eds.), *International relations scholarship around the world* (pp. 307–326). London: Routledge.

Blaney, D. L., & Inayatullah, N. (2008). International relations from below. In C. Reus-Smit & D. Snidal (Eds.), *The Oxford handbook of international relations* (pp. 663–674). Oxford, UK: Oxford University Press.

Denemark, R. A. (Ed.). (2010). *The international studies encyclopedia* (12 vols.). Chichester, UK: Wiley-Blackwell.

Dunn, F. S. (1948). The scope of international relations. *World Politics, 1,* 142–146.

Dunne, T., Kurki, M., & Smith, S. (Eds.). (2007). *International relations theories: Discipline and diversity*. Oxford, UK: Oxford University Press.

Fearon, J., & Wendt, A. (2002). Rationalism v. constructivism: A skeptical view. In W. Carlsnaes, T. Risse, & B. Simmons (Eds.), *Handbook of international relations* (pp. 52–72). Thousand Oaks, CA: Sage.

Fox, W. T. R. (1949). Interwar international relations research: The American experience. *World Politics, 2,* 67–79.

George, J. (1989). International relations and the search for thinking space: Another view of the third debate. *International Studies Quarterly, 33,* 269–279.

Goldmann, K. (1996). International relations: An overview. In R. E. Goodin & H. D. Klingemann (Eds.), *A new handbook of political science* (pp. 401–427). Oxford, UK: Oxford University Press.

Hoffmann, S. (1977). An American social science: International relations. *Daedalus, 106,* 41–60.

Inoguchi, T. (2007). Are there any theories of international relations in Japan? *International Relations of the Asia-Pacific, 7,* 369–390.

Jordan, R., Maliniak, D., Oakes, A., Peterson, S., & Tierney, M. (2009). One discipline or many? In *TRIP Survey of International Relations Faculty in Ten Countries*. Williamsburg, VA: Institute for the Theory and Practices of International Relations, College of William and Mary. Retrieved May 19, 2009, from http://irtheoryandpractice.wm.edu/projects/trip/Final_Trip_Report_2009.pdf

Kaplan, M. A. (1961). Is international relations a discipline? *Journal of Politics, 23,* 462–476.

Kaplan, M. A. (1966). The new great debate: Traditionalism vs. science in international relations. *World Politics, 19,* 1–20.

Katzenstein, P., & Sil, R. (2008). Eclectic theorizing in the study and practice of international relations. In C. Reus-Smit & D. Snidal (Eds.), *The Oxford handbook of international relations* (pp. 109–130). Oxford, UK: Oxford University Press.

King, G., Keohane, R. O., & Verba, S. (1994). *Designing social inquiry*. Princeton, NJ: Princeton University Press.

Kratochwil, F. (2008). Sociological approaches. In C. Reus-Smit & D. Snidal (Eds.), *The Oxford handbook of international relations* (pp. 444–461). Oxford, UK: Oxford University Press.

Lapid, Y. (1989). The third debate: On the prospects of international theory in a post-positivist era. *International Studies Quarterly, 33,* 235–254.

Lijphardt, A. (1974). International relations theory: Great debates and lesser debates. *International Social Science Journal, 26,* 11–21.

Little, R. (2008). International relations theory from a former hegemon. In C. Reus-Smit & D. Snidal (Eds.), *The Oxford handbook of international relations* (pp. 675–687). Oxford, UK: Oxford University Press.

Olson, W. C., & Groom, A. J. R. (1991). *International relations then and now: Origins and trends in interpretation.* London: HarperCollins.

Potter, P. B. (1923). Political science in the international field. *American Political Science Review, 17,* 381–391.

Qin, Y. (2007). Why is there no Chinese international relations theory? *International Relations of the Asia-Pacific, 7,* 313–340.

Reus-Smit, C., & Snidal, D. (Eds.). (2008). *The Oxford handbook of international relations.* Oxford, UK: Oxford University Press.

Rorty, R. (1991). Objectivity, relativism, and truth. In *Philosophical papers* (Vol. 1). Cambridge, UK: Cambridge University Press.

Rosenau, J. N. (1969). *International politics and foreign policy: A reader in research and theory* (2nd ed.). New York: Free Press.

Rosenau, J. N. (1993). International relations. In J. Krieger (Ed.), *The Oxford companion to politics of the world* (pp. 455–460). New York, Oxford, UK: Oxford University Press.

Tickner, A. B., & Wæver, O. (Eds.). (2009). *International relations scholarship around the world.* London: Routledge.

Wæver, O. (1998). The sociology of a not so international discipline: American and European developments in international relations. *International Organization, 52,* 687–727.

Wæver, O. (2007). Still a discipline after all these debates? In T. Dunne, & M. Kurki, & S. Smith (Eds.), *International relations theories: Discipline and diversity* (pp. 288–308). Oxford, UK: Oxford University Press.

International Society

The concept of "international society" was first elaborated as a key concept for international relations analysis in Charles Manning's book *The Nature of International Society* (1962). Manning's younger colleague at the London School of Economics and Political Science, Martin Wight, produced a series of works that largely remained unpublished during his lifetime; in these, he elaborated on what he called a society of states, which he juxtaposed with a system of states. Besides Manning, with whom he remained at intellectual loggerheads, Wight was indebted to the deliberations of the British Committee on the Theory of International Politics, of which he was a founder member since 1958, for his ideas. These ideas found further fertile ground in the mind of Hedley Bull (1977), who juxtaposed Wight's two key concepts in a double definition, whereby "a system of states is formed when two or more states have sufficient contact between them and have sufficient impact on one another's decisions to behave at least in some measure—as parts of a whole" (pp. 9–10). "A society of states (or international society)," on the other hand,

> exists when a group of states, conscious of certain common interests and common values, form a society in the sense that they conceive themselves to be bound by a common set of rules in their relations with one another, and share in the working of common institutions. (p. 13)

These foundational definitions, along with a number of others, are to be found in what remains the major text on international society—namely, *The Anarchical Society.*

Indeed, Bull's concept of international society has since been given so much attention, particularly in Britain, Australia, and South Africa, but also in Scandinavia and Italy, that there has evolved a self-conscious tradition or school of thought that refers to itself as the English School of international relations or indeed the international society approach. The English School forms a separate section within the International Studies Association and has its own website. The question of who is in and who is out of this school has been discussed at narcissistic length. For an overview of this matter, the reader is referred to Chapter 2 of Andrew Linklater and Hidemi Suganami's book the *English School of International Relations* (2006), a book that is also an excellent introduction. Timothy Dunne and Brunello Vigezzi are the school's own principal historians.

There has been extensive debate within the English School about whether the concept of international society may best be understood as a stylization of historical sequences or as a functional construct. James Mayall (1990) sees it as basically historical, Alan James would see it as basically theoretical, whereas Barry Buzan once saw it as a hybridization, arguing that the emergence of international society may be understood as an ideational process turning on a meaning that is inextricably tied up with the functional emergence of an international system. In a later work, however, Buzan (2004) did away with the distinction altogether. There is a strong case for doing so. As Max Weber had already pointed out, the most instrumental action is still imbued with meaning, and the most symbolic action also has some instrumentality. Furthermore, it is difficult to imagine that two polities would be aware of one another, let alone communicate, without a modicum of shared meaning and some regularity in the quality of interaction. Ontically, the difference between international system and international society seems unsustainable. As demonstrated by the output of the school, however, it has proven itself to be a nice analytical tool, which means that we may recognize it as an analytical concept on pragmatic grounds.

Bull was very interested in discussing different existing and possible world orders. Building on Wight's (1977) historical work, the school has evolved a body of work on the comparative sociology of status systems that includes a hypothesis that world history oscillates between periods of empire and periods of state systems, a study of interaction between different polities over a period of 60,000 years, and a study of how European international society expanded to the world at large (Bull & Watson, 1984).

If an international society exists when states are conscious of common interests and values and share in the working of common institutions, then the places to look for it are surely in people's thinking about international relations as well as in the patterned practices of states as they exist in specific fields. Note that international society should, therefore, seemingly be understood as a kind of structure that may only be studied through its effects and that is, by the same token, constituted by those effects. Dunne called his history of the school's origins *Inventing International Society* to underline precisely this imagined nature of international society as well as the constitutive, and hence political, role played in its invention of imagination by those working within the confines of the school. The two following sections of this entry look at the institutions and the thinking that are said to be constitutive of international society. A final section discusses the significance of the school.

The Institutions

To some scholars, it is clear that international society has the philosophical status of a structure. One of the characteristic traits of the English School, however, is its unwillingness to deal with the philosophy of science (see section on significance below). It is, therefore, far from clear what kind of status the several members of the school seem to give to the various phenomena that they discuss. To Wight, who offered a number of different lists detailing what kinds of institutions international relations were made of, institutions seem to be social practices, and so constitutive. Wight also insisted that diplomacy, understood as the system and the art of communication between powers, was the master institution of international relations. To Bull, who refined Wight's taxonomy and concentrated on five institutions—the balance of power, international law, diplomacy, war, and great power (concert)—these institutions do not seem to be constitutive of international society but reflective of it. In his view, what constitutes order are the primary goals of states—security, the sanctity of agreements (*pacta sunt servanda*), and territorial property rights—and international society is no more than the form a particular order happens to take. In this way, diplomacy and international society are framed simply as ideational and reflective of international order and begin to take on an epiphenomenal hue.

There exist book-length studies of four of the five institutions postulated by Bull that are variously informed by the international society perspective. Richard Little traced the emergence of the concept of the balance of power and discussed its centrality for international society. His is the treatment that sticks closest to the concept of international society. Buzan's (2004) treatment of great powers focuses on the present time, giving pride of place to the United States. James Der Derian's study of diplomacy breaks with previous work of the school by drawing extensively on continental social theory, arguing that the emergence of the institution of diplomacy may be alternatively understood as humankind's negotiation of alienation. Evan Luard's discussion of war in international society is more of a preliminary study that may serve as a platform for an international society–inspired analysis. Adam Roberts and others have conducted a number of international society–based shorter studies of how law constitutes international society.

The Thinking and the Thinkers

It is another characteristic of the school that it is more concerned with the thinkers of international society than with the thinking of international society. Whether we should think of this as a consequence of methodological individualism is a moot question in the school's own terms, for on this point, as elsewhere, the school does not dwell on the status of the phenomena it discusses. In Bull and Watson's coedited *Expansion of International Society* (1984), Bull fruitfully uses the concept of an international political culture to discuss the diffusion of ideas and practices and in his evaluation of the extent to which "The Revolt Against the West" challenged world order at large. There exist important studies of how specific themes have been thought up against international society: for example, *Nationalism and International Society* (Mayall, 1990), which argues that mainstream liberal thinking over the past 200 years or so was both statist and nationalist, and *Revolution and World Order: The Revolutionary State in International Society* (David Armstrong, 1993), which generalizes that revolutionary regimes will initially break with the idea of an international society, only to come back at some later point. John Vincent mapped the historical case for nonintervention, leaving Nick Wheeler to set out the case for humanitarian intervention.

These remain exceptions, however. The school has mainly preoccupied itself with how specific philosophers and statesmen have conceptualized global politics, particularly the degree to which and the way in which they have dwelled on the existence of a possible international society. Rather than following the lead of Manning, who looked at patterns of thought, the school has followed Wight, whose interest was what he called traditions of thought. Wight (1966) contrasted political theory with what he refers to as international theory. Whereas the former consists of a succession of classics from Jean Bodin to John Mill, there is no succession of first-rate books about the states system and diplomacy. As pointed out by Suganami, inasmuch as "politics" concerns the working of the *polis*—that is, the working of a social collective that strives to maintain its boundaries toward the outside, there can be no such thing as international politics. As a response to this situation, Wight fastened on the concept of "diplomatics" as a more accurate and more technically correct way of referring to his preferred object of study than "the international" of everyday speech. Everything that is not politics, then, is diplomatics, but by the same token, everything that has nothing to do with the internal life of the state and with the specific relations between states is ruled out as an object of study.

In a standard lecture course that has served as a template for many a later school lecturer, Wight (1991) postulated three traditions of diplomatics for all international intercourse, its purposes and objects, in times of peace. These were the Machiavellian (or, to Bull, Hobbesian), the Grotian, and the Kantian. As is evident from the use of the names of specific philosophers, these traditions were conceptualized as chains of specific philosophers and statesmen who shared an affinity for conceptualizing international in one of three ways. Sometimes a fourth is added to make room for the principle that he traced back to Guiseppe Mazzini—namely, that the world may be divided into national states. Since this is definitely a prescriptive idea of how global politics should be ordered, nationalism does in this sense give rise to an international doctrine—namely, that the subjects of global politics should be nation-states.

The school's three traditions—with Hobbesians arguing that covenants without the sword are but words, Grotians arguing that *pacta sunt servanda* (treaties should be observed), and Kantians arguing in favor of cosmopolitanism—clearly have heuristic value. Given the way discourse about the international realm is still set up, they also have a certain predictive value, since one may readily expect that debates about any problem that arises (say, a humanitarian intervention or the setting up of a new international organization [IO]) will include voices growing out of these three broad representations of which duties, if any, transcend borders. As Wight himself acknowledged, however, it is also the great weakness of the scheme that it cannot be a proper categorization in terms of covering all possibilities. Specific dates will, by necessity, come with their own specific colorations. One may add that Wight's historiosophy, which saw what happened in the international realm as endless repetition, precluded him from thinking about more basic change.

International society is conceived as an anarchical society. As Émile Durkheim pointed out, however, societies are despotic, in the sense that they lay down what should count as normal behavior and so may be seen as a structure of power (systems are arrangements through which values are authoritatively allocated for a society, as David Easton would have it). The tension between anarchy, on the one hand, and society, on the other, is the constitutive tension of the school. By dint of an internal logic, then, the Grotian tradition seems to be the broad home for the school itself. According to the school, it comes in two variants: pluralist and solidarist. Pluralists celebrate the cultural pluralism displayed throughout international society, giving pride of place to the importance of systems maintenance. One recognizes an affinity to the prudence of the Hobbesian tradition. Solidarists, on the other hand, concentrate on how international society should be strengthened by forging ever new ties between its members, giving rise to new institutions and conventions that warrant the forging of minimum standards binding on all. Here, one recognizes an affinity to Kantian cosmopolitanism.

Note that these are self-reflective normative concerns; the school is tied together by the celebration of a real-existing international society and divided by debates about how far this celebration should be taken. Solidarist tendencies usually come with an interest in how international society, conceptualized as a society of states, is related to world society, conceptualized as a society of sundry agents. While maintaining that states make up the dominant system of units, the school has sought to incorporate the further complication of nonstate actors more fully within its theoretical schema—an aim it shares with the existing global polity theory. Just as states make up a system, nonstate actors are theorized increasingly to make up a nonstate system of their own (although this, it is maintained, depends ultimately on the state system). This system is embedded in a nonstate set of norms, rules, values, and conventions—that is, a "world system" of nonstate actors is embedded in a "world society" of nonstate values, rules, institutions, and so on (Buzan, 2004).

Significance

Much like the body of literature on geopolitics, the major significance of the literature on international society is to allow a wide-ranging investigation of some deeply pertinent questions that are key to the discipline of international relations at large. Again, like geopolitics, the claims that emerge from these investigations tend to be rather sweeping. Unlike geopolitics, however, the style is historical and empirical, and the methodology is implicit and commonsensical. The English School is English not least in its empiricism. Some scholars believe that Dunne is right in stressing that the invention of an interpretative approach to the history of ideas about international relations is a constitutive as well as a crowning achievement of the school. However, when compared with other and parallel attempts to invent such approaches in the social sciences, some think that the school comes up a bit short. In Germany, there emerged concurrently with the first English School writings, in the early 1960s, a tradition of conceptual history led by Reinhart Koselleck. This work has resulted in multivolume treatments of the German and French political languages. Meanwhile, in France, Michel Foucault initiated a number of studies where the history of ideas is paired to social history in a different but comparable manner. Finally, in the very same university where the British Committee met, at the same time, and out of the same broadly empirical Anglo-American tradition to which the English School itself belongs, there emerged an undertaking spearheaded by Cambridge historians such as Quentin Skinner to write the history of the past in terms of the ideas that animated it. This undertaking has resulted in a number of meticulously researched monographs as well as methodological essays. Alexander Wendt's work, where the school's concept of the three traditions of thinking about international relations is modified and applied in his theorizing of how international society may mature, demonstrates how this body of work may be paired up with wider theorizing to produce new insights.

Nowhere is the historical bent of the international society tradition more on display than in a book with the telling title *The Expansion of International Society* (Bull & Watson, 1984). Suganami noted in his contribution on Japan's entry into international society how Admiral Perry used deliberate mistranslation of a key treaty to secure the United States permanent representation in Japan. Expansion is a power-laden process. This fact is not adequately on display in works on international society.

Expansion is also a process that is imagined as spreading outward from a center. Although there may be setbacks and even reversions, the conception is of a process where one party imposes its order on the other, with little or no residue and without being itself changed by the experience. It is of course true that European international society has expanded to cover the entire globe, so in terms of teleology, this perspective on history is not unwarranted. The problem is, however, that it is not relational. It does not invite scrutiny of the relations that went into producing the result of European expansion. This is scientifically problematic, for we want to know what kinds of tensions and conflicts gave rise to the consequences of European expansion. It is also politically problematic, for it invites a reading where an "us" expands at "their" expense rather than demonstrating the power asymmetries and hybridizations that marked the process.

Manning criticized Wight for not empathizing with his aim of establishing international relations as a social science. Similar critiques have accompanied the school at every turn since then. The school would have come off on an even better footing if it had followed Manning's aspiration to write works that were both studies of international relations *and* contributions that were explicitly dialogical in their relation to the (rest of the) literature on social phenomena. The school has followed Wight's lead and styled its work as a series of comments on the general flow of history, instead of Manning's competing vision of doing something more in the vein of the sociology of knowledge of international relations. What the English School seems to need at the present juncture is to complement in many ways the unique historical and taxonomic work already carried out by sustained, theory-led studies that may bring the school closer to the general style of work in the social sciences.

Iver B. Neumann
Norwegian Institute of International Affairs (NUPI)
Oslo, Norway

See also Balance of Power; International Relations, Theory; State

Further Readings

Armstrong, D. (1993). *Revolution and world order: The revolutionary state in international society.* Oxford, UK: Oxford University Press.

Bull, H. (1977). *The anarchical society: A study of order in world politics.* London: Macmillan.

Bull, H., & Watson, A. (Eds.). (1984). *The expansion of international society.* Oxford, UK: Clarendon.

Buzan, B. (2004). *From international to world society: English School theory and the social structure of globalization.* Cambridge, UK: Cambridge University Press.

English School of International Relations Theory: http://www.polis.leeds.ac.uk/research/international-relations-security/english-school

Linklater, A., & Suganami, H. (2006). *The English School of international relations.* Cambridge, UK: Cambridge University Press.

Manning, C. A. W. (1962). *The nature of international society.* London: G. Bell & Sons for London School of Economics and Political Science.

Mayall, J. (1990). *Nationalism and international society.* New York: Cambridge University Press.

Vincent, J. (1974). *Nonintervention and international order.* Princeton, NJ: Princeton University Press.

Watson, A. (1991). *The evolution of international society.* London: Routledge.

Wight, M. (1977). *Systems of states* (H. Bull, Ed.). Leicester, UK: Leicester University Press.

Wight, M. (1991). *International theory: The three traditions* (G. Wight & B. Porter, Eds.). Leicester, UK: Leicester University Press.

Wight, M., & Butterfield, H. (Eds.). (1966). *Diplomatic investigations: Essays in the theory of international politics.* London: Unwin.

Index

Entry titles and their page numbers are in **bold.**